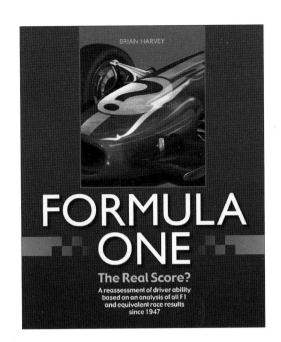

BRIAN HARVEY

FORMULA ONE

ONE

The Real Score?

A reassessment of driver ability
based on an analysis of all F1
and equivalent race results
since 1947

www.veloce.co.uk

First published in September 2017 by Veloce Publishing Limited, Veloce House, Parkway Farm Business Park, Middle Farm Way, Poundbury, Dorchester DT1 3AR, England. Fax 01305 250479 / e-mail info@veloce.co.uk / web www.veloce.co.uk or www.velocebooks.com. ISBN 978-1-787110-27-4 / UPC 6-36847-01027-0

BRIAN HARVEY

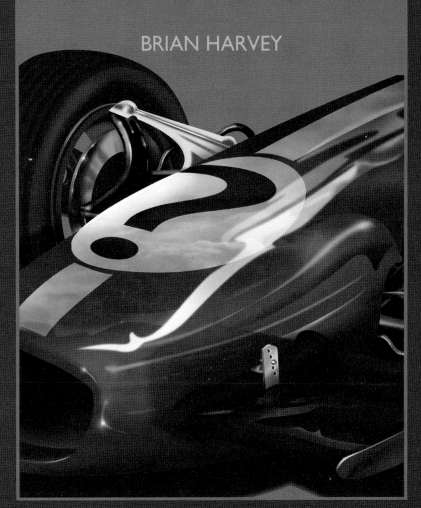

FORMULA ONE

The Real Score?

A reassessment of driver ability
based on an analysis of all F1
and equivalent race results
since 1947

Contents

Introduction

I well remember my elder brother returning from the Easter motorcycle races at Oulton Park in 1957, and me begging my father to take us to the next Bank Holiday races there a few weeks later. The sights and sounds were instantly addictive, and the skill and bravery of the competitors were clear. I was particularly intrigued by the 2-, 3- and 4-wheel action at the October meeting there that year; a very rare combination. The real attraction for me was the appearance of John Surtees, with the screaming 'fire-engine' 500cc MV Agusta, who promptly won with ease. He also won the 350cc 'Junior' race on one of the many Manx Nortons, proving that he didn't need an 'unfair advantage' as he had perhaps had in the 500cc race. Both lap records were duly shattered. Those events took place before lunchtime, and, for me, the main event was now over. I regarded the afternoon's 'International Gold Cup' race for Formula Two cars as a supporting event ... until I saw it. It was won by someone called Jack Brabham (I'd never heard of him, nor of the expected stars of the meeting Tony Brooks and Roy Salvadori).

The four cars on the front row of the grid were covered by just one fifth of a second, and were four seconds faster than John Surtees' new motorcycle lap record ... and these were only F2 cars! From that day, my enthusiasm for motor racing would equal that for the bikes, and, after a few years, become my prime passion.

The following May, at Silverstone, I got to see my first Formula One race with the big stars. It was the tenth running of the *Daily Express* International Trophy, begun in 1949, a year before the World Driver's Championship began – the first British GP having been held there a year earlier in 1948.

I'll never forget the journey there on the back of a friend's BSA. I had 'mugged up' on the route from Stafford and decided that following the A34 south through Birmingham was the right direction. At about 6am we arrived in the town of Southam, whereupon my knowledge ran out. There was no-one about until I spotted a large gentleman with his back to me filling up his car – a Jaguar saloon I believe. I cagily approached him from behind and, not wishing to surprise him, softly said "Excuse me, sir." The surprise was then all mine – indeed, it was a huge 'wakey-wakey' moment, to quote his catchphrase, when I was presented with the large round face of Billy Cotton, the legendary bandleader and megastar of the then music and television world. I immediately became a gibbering idiot, and spluttered something like "Erm ... erm, I don't suppose you know the way to Silverstone, do you, sir?" He was most helpful, and if I'd known what I now know – that he'd raced in the British GP in 1949 – maybe I would have begged a lift (joking). Thanks entirely to him, we arrived just as the first race started, and missed nothing.

The crowd was absolutely immense, and the atmosphere electric. Somehow, having to watch the cars whizz past between the heads of the people in front seemed to add to it. Every crowd creates its own tension and anticipation, and this crowd was every bit as large as the one that attended July's British Grand Prix there. The Trophy race was won by Peter Collins' Ferrari at a speed sufficient to win the Grand Prix in July – which he did at just 0.23mph faster. A new track record was set by Collins' Ferrari and Jean Behra's BRM, and wasn't beaten in July – or the year after!

But what is the status of that event?
The feeling I got was that Formula One is Formula One, Championship or not. The International Trophy meeting was NOT a minor event. Is it fair for a victory like that of Peter

Collins to be ignored by the Grand Prix record? *The Oxford English Dictionary* defines the term 'Grand Prix' as:

(a) A race forming part of the World Championship for racing cars or motorcycles
(b) A very important competitive event

Since the term literally translates as 'Big Prize,' and the winner at both Silverstone F1 events received identical prizes – £750 for both the *Daily Express* Trophy and the Grand Prix – clearly the latter definition applies to both races, as, of course, it did for many races before the World Championship began.

By inference, the title 'Grand Prix' is not necessary either. According to Shakespeare, "A rose by any other name would smell as sweet." A Formula One 'Grand Prix' by any other name would be just as great, and, in times past, 'smell as sweet.' (Oh! If only they still used Castrol R racing oil!)

So, races acquired their status by virtue of history rather than their title – as at Silverstone. I suggest that if, for any reason, the Vettels and Hamiltons of today and their teams took part in an extra F1 race without Championship points, it would be just as compelling to watch (maybe even more, as the winner would take all). That is the status that many of those unfairly ignored races had to any motor racing fan ... I know because I was there, with over 100,000 others. Oh, and it was on FA Cup Final day, one of the most famous international sporting events on earth then. *More people were at Silverstone!*

P.S. It has come to light just before this book went to print that, with reference above to a non-points race between the Vettels and Hamiltons of this world, **the new 'F1 boss' Ross Brawn has suggested that exact idea**.

Brian Harvey

VISIT VELOCE ON THE WEB – WWW.VELOCE.CO.UK
All current books • New book news • Special offers • Gift vouchers • Forum

7

Preface &
Acknowledgements

'Formula One' – 'World Championship'
The term 'Formula One' was coined to describe the cars – not the race – so any competition between them was, unarguably, a Formula One race. The term 'World Championship' describes the race – not the cars – which, as shown later, was not always for Formula One anyway. When a modern driver's Formula One wins are said to have matched those of a historic figure (Moss – 16, Fangio – 24) a modern complete career is being compared with a selective partial one, because only Championship figures are ever quoted. This is only fair between careers which began after 1979. I don't believe that Formula One fans of today realise how much serious F1 activity is ignored by the records due to this apparent modern view that 'a non-Championship race was a non-event'; a statement which I intend to show is an aberration born, perhaps, of historical ignorance.

At the outset of the World Championship, it was but a small part of a thriving Formula One scene, the governing body deciding that just a single race from each active country was necessary to be representative, despite the existence of many other established races at that time. Perhaps because of this, the Championship was far from enthusiastically received, as it introduced an artificial differential from the other races, which were well established, and matched the selected races in nearly all cases. Grids did vary – as they did in Championship races (Argentina 1958; Italy 1960; USA 2005) – but that wasn't an indicator of the quality of race in prospect. I intend to show that the vast majority of these extra races should be recognised as being of 'Championship quality'. The 'Championship only' attitude has created ignorance of more than half of all the Formula One races run prior to 1980. I have no criticism of Championship monopoly, but, if it's correct now, then surely it should have been so all along.

Another disadvantage for those drivers was the car reliability factor. It is now rarely less than 90 per cent, whereas it used to be mostly under 50 per cent – and the career survival rate somewhere in between. To eradicate this, I have introduced a new, but significant, factor: identification of all race leads undeservedly lost to the driver, which were much more prevalent in the last century, and indicate a driver's 'strike capability.' These are included right up to the present time. With all these starts, wins and losses of every 'Championship quality' race since the beginning of Formula One, I can attempt to redress the balance and reveal what I offer as the ... 'REAL SCORE of Formula One.'

There's more!
A significant theme of this book is 'Wherever the Great and Good Met,' so the history of their racing activity extends to other series they entered, in Formula One or with equivalent machinery. These began with the South American Temporada series of 1949 and 1950, run in advance of the European season. Ten years later came the 'down-under' racing from 1959 to 1969 which spawned the Tasman Championship series. In 1961 came the Inter-Continental Formula series, challenging the new F1 by giving extra life to 1960 F1 cars. This, and some down-under series, involved more powerful cars than contemporary F1. This reveals almost 700 Formula One and equivalent races, prior to the monopoly years, of which only 317 appear in the F1 record ... until now.

And even more!
The 'great and good' also met frequently in Formula Two races from 1948 to 1973. A European Championship was introduced in 1967, and a grading system identified the

most successful F1 drivers who, whilst allowed to race, were excluded from that Championship. As they were for secondary formula cars, inclusion in this book would perhaps be too much – maybe a theme for another book – but it shows how much racing top racers did to realise their earnings potential. The dates are included, however, in the annual diaries to prove how busy Formula One drivers were then.

Acknowledgements

My first and most sincere thanks must go to Rod Grainger of Veloce Publishing for having the faith to invest in me, a novice author, and in my first book. I have purchased many Veloce books over the years and to have my name included in his author listing makes me very proud. Thanks also go to Tim Wright, Zoe Schafer and the researchers of LAT for access to their amazing archive, from which all photos in this book are taken. After meeting Roger Smith, author of *All the Races* at Goodwood I was able to assist a little in his second edition, for which he gave me a kind appreciation. In return, I am most grateful for contacts he gave me and his guidance on finding a publisher, which helped me to the destination I have found. I am grateful to Richard Page of the Formula 1 Register for the contact and information exchange we have had: the 10 volumes of *A Record of Grand Prix and Voiturette Racing* by Paul Sheldon, Duncan Rabagliati and Richard have proved invaluable to my research. In the same vein I thank the *MotorSport* magazine proprietors for offering to the public the series of Archive Discs giving limitless access to the whole of its output since 1924: these were a very important source. Thanks also are due to Ian Dussek of the Michael Sedgwick Trust for, although this book was outside the remit of the trust, his publishing contacts were most helpful. Sincere thanks also to author Graham Gauld for his willingness to help a novice and search his archives.

The original impetus was the gift some years ago of 1950s *Autosport* magazines and race programmes which made me realise how much racing had become ignored over time. For this I am hugely indebted to my fellow villager and friend Donald Carr, and also to his wife Sylvia for her help in searching for (and finding), textual errors; a task which might have been onerous. If it was she never said so, and accepted with her usual good grace. Having just celebrated their Diamond Wedding, I doubt they ever imagined that, after all these years, they would be involved in something like this.

Acceptances and apologies

A work of this size has involved many sources which sometimes were not in agreement on every aspect. Reports 'on-the-spot' and submitted, no doubt, against time schedules have occasionally been different from later accounts. I have made my best judgement as to resolving these instances. However, I accept that any errors in this book are my responsibility entirely.

The scope of this book has uncovered over ONE HUNDRED AND FORTY different venues. I have taken the decision that to include circuit diagrams would stretch the work considerably and effectively require a second volume. There are already books and online sources covering nearly all of these which I hope you'll take advantage of – some listed in the bibliography. I hope I have not disappointed anyone in this regard.

Dedication

To my late wife Margaret, for the support she gave, through 46 years of marriage, to my passion for motor sport, and for help, encouragement and patience at the outset of this project.

VISIT VELOCE ON THE WEB – WWW.VELOCE.CO.UK
All current books • New book news • Special offers • Gift vouchers • Forum

9

Chapter 1

All races count

Every Formula One driver's record should include ALL of his races

The terms 'sport' and 'sporting' are related (or used to be), and no-one voluntarily demonstrated that better than the 1958 double Silverstone F1 winner, Peter Collins, at Monza 1956 – see the race report. In Collins' and others' interests I feel we should be sporting, and credit ALL 'Championship quality' Formula One wins to a winner's record, so that sensible comparisons can take place. I have no doubt that many will question my assertion, but please bear with me, and see if the rationale given convinces you of the fairness of my view.

The only exceptions I have are the Indianapolis 500 races of the '50s, which were given Championship status, I believe, as an honorary gesture, as they are very different disciplines of racing for both designer and driver. No interaction between the two took place but for the attempt by Ferrari with Alberto Ascari in 1952. I assert that they were NOT Formula One races.

Look how much Grand Prix careers have changed! The Championship has increased from six rounds in 1950 to 21 in 2016, yet there were twenty-four F1 races in 1950, and over sixty before that! The retirement rate is now a fraction of that before the modern era (55 per cent in 1950, 15 per cent in 2015), and now points are scored down to 10th place instead of 5th, despite fields being no larger than before. A top Formula One driver today may well have a career double the length of drivers of those early years (thankfully). Combining these factors means that the opportunity to accumulate scores on the Championship record has increased by 600 per cent – and winning by 250 per cent. So, year-on-year, early careers are slowly being submerged by the 'totting-up wins' culture being made

exclusive to World Championship rounds, irrespective of race starts or, sadly, truncated careers.

Pre-Championship races

These cannot be called 'non-Championship races' as no Championship existed to exclude them from. Dozens of true Formula One races took place before the World Championship began, so how should racing history treat these pre-Championship races? They cannot be regarded as lesser events as they provided the exact scene in which the Championship was set. Of the first 'RAC Grand Prix' at Silverstone in 1948, respected motor racing journalist Gerard 'Jabby' Crombac wrote: "This was the first important event in England since the war, while on the Continent we had already had a dozen proper Grands Prix." They were the very trigger for the World Championship. Consider that no change to Formula One or Two took place at all until the Championship had been running for four years. So why should those drivers, whose careers were under way or over by the time of the inaugural World Championship race at Silverstone, have their results effectively wiped from the Formula One record?

An overlooked fact is that Fangio is credited with 24 Grand Prix wins, but these are only his Championship victories, and do not include his amazing five GP wins in 1949. Having raced both Maserati and Simca-Gordini in Argentina against European aces, he began his racing campaign in Europe as a virtual unknown, and beat all the regulars on circuits he had never seen before. He promptly returned home in August when his funds – from the Argentine government – dried up. No Championship had been available to cement that record into the modern archive. In fact, the absence of the dominant Alfa Romeo team that year may be regarded as having created, for drivers, a more level playing field. This incredible achievement is long overdue for recognition.

Perhaps even worse: Jean-Pierre Wimille was already winning races and, more to the point, dominating his teammates before 1947, driving the all-conquering Alfa Romeo 158. It was around this car and its chief challengers that the basis of Formula One was formed. His winning continued throughout 1947/8, but his tragic death early in 1949, when swerving to avoid persons on the track, means that he never took part in a World Championship Formula One race, and, therefore, gets no mention in many so-called 'Formula One encyclopaedias.' Sadly, he never got to race against Fangio. Let's remember him and give him his place within the pantheon of Formula One.

Extra races for World Championship cars

Almost 400 races fall into this category!

I hate the term 'non-Championship race,' which nowadays pejoratively implies 'non-event' – which the majority certainly were not. I prefer 'Extra-to-Championship' or perhaps just 'Extra' race. Of course, I accept that event standards varied, as did a few Championship rounds, and so categorisation is necessary. I explain my method of dealing with this in the next chapter.

Evidence shows that the World Championship series was not created by cherry-picking the principal races of the time, as many circuits had a Grand Prix race series running long before the Championship, or even Formula One, was inaugurated. Instead, they lost out because of the chosen method of 'one-round-per-nation.' Of course, they continued to run their important series: the Pau, San Remo and Albi Grands Prix are typical. It is worth noting that Alfa Romeo did not restrict its 1950 return solely to the Championship rounds, but completed an almost full season. Countries with more than one major race each year sometimes changed the nominated circuit, yet the un-nominated track would still run the same event. Those race entries often consisted principally of the same drivers and cars as those of 'The Championship,' and were often run over similar distances. The French F2 Championship of 1952 actually presaged modern practice whereby teams signed up for the series – one of which was the French round of the World Championship – and each one of three hours' duration! The World Championship was run for those very cars that year and in 1953. So they were neither F1 nor World Championship, but undoubtedly matched Championship quality.

I have titled this section using the description 'World Championship Cars' because the world title was fought out in 1952 and 1953 with Formula Two cars, due to the dearth of F1 cars of the day. Extra races during those years for F2 cars, therefore, fall within that description, being *per se* the

premier competition between drivers of those years. Formula One regained its supremacy with the start of the new 2.5-litre rule in 1954, with an engine capacity only slightly larger than those F2 cars. Formula Two was, therefore, effectively a precursor to the new Formula One. A handful of F1 races were actually run in 1952/3, so those must be included also.

I've already said that although the quality of these events varied, a significant majority were of a standard similar to some World Championship events. But what is/was that standard? The presence of the majority of the main contenders was not required. Consider that quite a few World Championship Grands Prix which had significant absentees were included without hesitation. No Ferraris or BRMs took part in the inaugural World Championship Grand Prix event at Silverstone in May, leaving Alfa Romeo completely unchallenged, yet were present (sadly, the BRM only at the drop of the flag) at the same venue the following August in the International Trophy. Which race was technically and competitively the best or most important? Which would you sooner have attended? During the 1950s and 1960s Ferrari developed a reputation for occasional non-appearance, such as the 1959 British and 1961 American GPs, but neither event lost Championship status, and rightly so.

In the Italian Grand Prix of 1960, all principal teams but Ferrari boycotted the event because of the combined use of the road circuit with the notoriously bumpy banked track. The demands of running on a high banking with the suspension under both heavy compression and side-load was not deemed suitable for the new breed of rear-engined lightweight cars designed for road circuits. So it was Works front-engined Ferraris versus back-of-the-field also-rans and F2 cars. Its use was perceived by some as a ploy to make the Ferrari 256, by then obsolete, competitive in its home race. The event's Championship status was retained despite the absence of the leading contenders. The most infamous of these incomplete fields occurred in modern times at the notorious United States Grand Prix of 2005, with only six cars 'competing.' The Ferrari team had no effective opposition at all after the withdrawal of the Michelin-shod cars, which had comprised 70 per cent of the field. All Michelin-shod cars were obliged, for safety's sake, to withdraw after the formation lap due to the tyre failures in qualifying on the Indianapolis banking, thus leaving the Ferrari team unopposed by the 'back-of-the-grid' teams – a repeat of Italy 1960. Ferrari team leader Michael Schumacher could even be sure that his teammate would, I believe contractually, offer no challenge. The result was a demonstration event, yet it still stood as a Championship win; lucky Michael Schumacher! The 1980 Spanish and 1981 South African Grands Prix, however, were lost to the Championship due to the FISA/FOCA wars, but were still run with 75 per cent of the regular contestants. The 'manufacturer' teams of Ferrari, Alfa Romeo and Renault withdrew to avoid risking their competition status with the governing body since they raced to sell their road cars. These were far better races than Italy 1960 or USA 2005.

The 1959 German GP on the Avus banking was run as a two-part aggregate time race, so I also see no reason why two-part 'extra' races shouldn't be included. F1 races a bit shorter than Championship distance should also be included, since results of red-flagged Championship Grands Prix are allowed to stand, even when the race has run only a few laps; as in Australia 1991. Is a 100 metre athletic event a lesser contest than 5000 metres?

Try this ... The inaugural 2010 Korean Grand Prix 'began' behind the safety car due to atrocious track conditions, and remained that way for three laps when the field was halted and held on the grid under a red flag. I was amazed to learn later that, had the race then been abandoned without the cars being released, the rules dictated that half points would have been awarded and a race victory notched up for the lucky pole position driver, even though no competitive racing activity had taken place at all, because: "The race had been deemed to have started!" What? Would they allow the World Championship leader to lose the title in the final round in that manner? I think not. So, considering all this, I conclude that: there is no minimum standard for a World Championship race.

A great advantage of the extra races was the opportunity to compete on many of the world's great tracks. Isn't it unthinkable that F1 would never have visited places like Goodwood, a special challenge where, sadly, Stirling Moss'

career ended, and Oulton Park – a true driver's circuit on which Moss was never beaten in a racing car. Other great tracks visited included Solitude in Germany (a mini-Nürburgring); Pau in France – not *that* dissimilar to Monaco, and Siracuse in Sicily – a testing road circuit where, in 1955, history was made. Formula One would have been much poorer without these venues, and others too numerous to mention.

To sum up. The idea that races involving the same drivers in the same cars, competing on often the same tracks with the same intensity and risk, should be separated on the grounds that 'competition levels in Championship races were always superior' is an aberration. So, let's bring these past extra races in from the cold and complete the full Formula One record.

A small apology. I had intended to include circuit diagrams in this book, but realised that there are so many involved that a separate book would be needed, and some exist already. All details are available online now, through sites such as Wikipedia, and one dedicated site (theracingline.net/racing circuits), so I thought it best for you to discover what you wish to know through these means. To include them would have increased the book price and these sites are free. I hope that's okay.

Furthermore, many additional photos of events listed are available for viewing via the internet, but, due to copyright law and associated costs, I cannot include them here. These begin with the very first event in Marseille '46. Happy hunting.

VISIT VELOCE ON THE WEB – WWW.VELOCE.CO.UK
All current books • New book news • Special offers • Gift vouchers • Forum

12

Chapter 2

Race assessment & grading

Obviously event quality varied, so I have created a system of five levels, the top four being graded, based principally on the strength of driver entry. The sole criterion is this: Did a race with this level of competition ever take place within the World Championship? If the answer is yes, then it has a top three grading. Not all World Championship race entries were of top standard. Take the German Grand Prix of 1958, for example. It had only 12 F1 cars, with just eight Works entries, and with the field bolstered by F2 cars – a grade 'B' event. The 1958 Argentine Grand Prix had a field of only ten cars, with Ferrari being the only Works team entered, and Fangio in a private Maserati – a grade 'C' event. Despite that, the result was very historically significant. Other races fell below that minimum Championship quality, but are worth grading due to particular interest, and so have been allocated grade 'D.' This leaves about 50 races unworthy of grading, and these are listed, with winner, in Appendix A. Neither these, nor grade 'D' events, are included in 'The Real Score.'

Grading is indicated with the race title highlighted as follows:

'A': Entry of good Championship quality – ✱✱✱ prefix.
'B': Equal or better than the 1958 German GP – ✱✱ prefix.
'C': Equal or better than the 1958 Argentine GP – ✱ prefix.

Results of above grades give podium finishers and are included in the 'Real Score' figures.

'D': Short of top drivers or distance, but of historical interest – no-star prefix.

Results of this grade are limited to winner and runner-up. Only races with both star prefixes and boxed results are included in 'The Real Score,' as all others were not run to FIA formulae; which applies to Tasman and some other races.

All graded races are given in chronological order to give the context in which the extra F1 races occurred. Championship races are included, for reasons of space, only to the end of 1972, as, from that date the intention to phase out extra races was clear. Championship rounds grew from 88 per cent of races in 1973 to an intended 100 per cent in 1980 and thereafter – but the FOCA/FISA wars delayed things a bit.

Notes on results

Where elimination heats took place, the figures given are for the final. However, the fastest lap quoted is that achieved in the whole event.

Event distance quoted is for heat plus final, ie total distance covered by the winning car.

Races run in more than one part show the result of aggregate speeds and times.

Front row grid positions are given. Times are additional to the pole time. No indication is implied as to which side of the grid pole position was placed.

Speeds are in miles per hour in the right hand column – conversion miles to kilometres is 1.6093.

Deficits to the winner's time are also given in the right hand column.

Speed or distance conversion			
mph	**kph**	**mph**	**kph**
50	80.47	55	88.51
60	96.56	65	104.60
70	112.65	75	120.70
80	128.74	85	136.79
90	144.84	95	152.88
100	160.93	105	168.98
110	177.02	115	185.07
120	193.12	125	201.16
130	209.21	135	217.26
140	225.30	145	233.35
150	241.40	155	249.44

VISIT VELOCE ON THE WEB – WWW.VELOCE.CO.UK
All current books • New book news • Special offers • Gift vouchers • Forum

14

Chapter 3

Do speed figures matter?

Notes on race and lap lengths and quoted speeds

Does speed matter? Well, the most tangible element of a race result is the race speed. It most reflects the nature of an event, and its possible risk, and is surely of interest to circuit operators. 'The first driver to break the xxx mph barrier' is an accolade many would like to have. But how can we be sure that it's true? From the early days speed was always quoted to a supposed accuracy of two decimal places, which, for 100.00mph, means an accuracy of 1 part in 10,000. Track measurement has rarely ever matched that accuracy, and elapsed times have been measured to that degree only since the '70s. In my research I have often found sources to have time/speed figures for race and lap not producing, on calculation, the quoted lap length and/or race distance. I have, therefore, used the best matched figures from such an event and adjusted the others to fit: hence the differences to speeds quoted in other publications. However, at least all figures for every event in this book tally. Some tracks, particularly street circuits, seemed to have frequently varying lengths quoted. I have made best informed decisions as to whether the track actually did change by the often minor difference quoted or whether the length had more likely been misquoted; in which case I have kept to the previously quoted length, for sake of continuity and comparison. The Pau Grand Prix is a case in point.

Also of interest is Goodwood. The official circuit length from its inaugural meeting in 1948 was given as 2.4 miles, and is used to the present day. But official figures for the last race of 1951 give time/speed figures converting to a length of 2.38 miles. Only this single meeting ever used that circuit length. The track was due to have a chicane added for 1952, so clearly the circuit was re-measured then and the discrepancy discovered. With the 2.4 figure being used

thereafter, the 2.38 figure must have been the true length prior to 1952. I have, therefore, used it for that period. A small difference maybe (0.83 per cent) but this means 90.00mph is corrected to 89.25mph.

Of greater interest are Brands Hatch and Oulton Park, purchased by MotorSport Vision (MSV) in 2004, the circuit lengths of which have since been re-measured and independently verified. Very significant differences from the previous familiar lengths are now quoted. On researching the reason for this, I was very grateful to have received by email the following reply in respect of Brands Hatch, and which had also been carried out at Oulton Park:

"The official length is found by measuring the outside and inside lengths of the tarmac and taking the average. This has been carried out by MSV staff and external licensing bodies with the same result. Despite some minor circuit alterations *we cannot explain the difference in length or past administrations' reasons for quoting them.*" (My italics)

We must accept the validity of these results as, unlike earlier figures, we have an explanation of how the measurement took place, and must conclude that earlier figures were incorrect. For Oulton Park this has produced a reduction in quoted length from 2.775 miles (after back straight deviations in the '90s) to 2.692 miles. Applying the reduction to the original 2.761 gives a corrected 2.678 miles: a contraction of exactly 3.00 per cent. For Brands Hatch a far greater error was found. Track alterations up to 1976 changed the original 2.65 quoted length to 2.614 miles, and, in 1999, it increased to 2.6228. Overnight, this now became 2.433. Applying this correction of 0.1898 to the original 2.65 gives a corrected figure of 2.460miles: 7.2 per cent down! So the

1976 figure should have been 2.424 miles. I have used these figures to recalculate retrospectively all race distances and speeds at these venues. This means that the first man to lap Oulton Park at 100mph would be the person to lap in 1m 36.4s: not Jim Clark in 1963 but Jack Brabham in April 1967 when he shattered it by four seconds. At Brands, the correct target was 1m 28.5s: achieved by Jochen Rindt in the 'Race of Champions' 1969 with 1m 26.8s, and not Clark's lap of 1m 35.4s in 1965. Sorry on both counts, Jim.

What instrument would give such massive errors yet be accepted? Surely it's the odometer. I have noticed that distances recorded on cars I have owned over identical routes have varied by up to 9 per cent (new Ford Sierras) and my last two Citroëns by 4 per cent. My belief is that they used a reset trip meter on the start line, drove the middle of the track, stopped at the nearest whole increment and measured to the start line. Thus was preserved any error of the odometer, whilst providing a figure supposedly accurate to three decimal places. Did this happen at any other circuit? – Who knows? But at Brands Hatch and Oulton Park we have a good result thanks to MotorSport Vision.

Chapter 4

The route to Formula One

Let's dispense with a common misconception: Formula One did NOT begin with the World Championship in 1950.

Since 1914, Grand Prix cars were subject to regulations of maximum engine size and minimum weight to provide for competitive racing and to control speeds. These were dictated by the ruling body, the AIACR, and had changed every few years. When speeds increased to over 150mph, it was felt that power could be reined-in by limiting maximum vehicle weight to 750kg; the reasoning being that more power needs more weight, so no maximum engine size was needed. How wrong! This idea was introduced in 1934, and begat the fabulous cars from Mercedes and Auto Union. The power of those cars, up to 646bhp from 5.6-litre supercharged engines, wasn't exceeded in Grand Prix racing for over 45 years, and straight line speeds in 1937 reached 200mph! This ruling was supported by the introduction of a secondary class, called 'Voiturettes,' totally dominated by Maseratis which were available for privateers (that was until the brilliant Alfa Romeo 158 – Works only – arrived in August 1938 and won first time out in the Coppa Ciano race at Livorno). Having realised its mistake, the governing body changed the Grand Prix formula for 1938 to 3000cc maximum supercharged, and 4500cc unsupercharged. Still the Germans dominated, so, in 1939, the Italians decided to run their important Tripoli GP for Voiturettes, thus ensuring a win for Italy – Libya being an Italian colony then. Astonishingly, within a few months, Mercedes secretly produced a 240bhp 1500cc s/c car, the type W165, and destroyed the Italian hopes, with Lang beating the Alfa Romeo 158s by over 7 minutes in 2 hours of racing! In September that year the war stopped all racing.

Following the end of the war the two formulae were reinstated, but the Germans were banned from international competition. So dominant had been the German cars that no other country had offered any credible challenge, and those Grand Prix formula cars that were available were hardly any quicker than the pre-war Alfa Romeo 158 Voiturette cars. As soon as Alfa-Romeo returned to the tracks, these 158 'Alfettas,' as they were known, were clearly the fastest race cars of all, irrespective of engine size.

The Grand Prix scene was back in business by 1946, and, on 28th February, a new premier formula was established by the new ruling body, the FIA. Effective from 1948, this recognised that Tripoli 1939 proved that engines of only 1500cc were capable of beating unblown 4500cc cars. Originally called 'Formula A,' it soon became known as 'Formula One,' and clearly predates the Driver's World Championship by some years.

The identity of the first Formula One race is, I believe, open to some interpretation, due to matters of logic, officialdom, and the 'spirit of the rules.' The intended inauguration may have been 1948, but sufficient cars already existed, and no new ones were likely before 1948, so why wait? Once the formula was known, other cars were effectively made obsolete, so conforming cars became virtually de rigueur. The Gran Premio del Valentino race at Turin on 1st September 1946 was actually the first specifically run by any organiser to the new formula; all subsequent Grand Prix races following suit. Machinery remained virtually unaltered into 1948, so 1947 is clearly the first full operative year. The Marseille Grand Prix in May 1946, however, was typical in style and technical content of the new formula, so this race demonstrated 'the spirit of the rules.' Officialdom tacitly acquiesced to a 'force majeure,' so perhaps the first Formula One race has to be the bizarre event in February 1947 at Rommehed in Sweden, in which only three pre-war ERAs and an ancient Bugatti started. All the 'serious' continental competitors were on an ice-bound vessel in Gothenburg harbour, and so, when freed from the ice, a consolation event was held near Stockholm on a track over three miles long on a frozen lake! So, was that the first decent Formula One race? The next race was in April at Pau – a 'normal' race.

Officialdom may say 1948 saw the first F1 race, and you're welcome to take your pick, but I've opted for Marseille, 13th of May 1946 for the first true 'men and machine' battle: exactly four years to the day before that inaugural World Championship round at Silverstone in 1950. As for Sweden, it was off the Formula One map for a long time.

The term 'Formula One' doesn't seem to have been widely promoted, as the term 'Grand Prix' was in the public mind and a new name would only have caused confusion. When Formula Two arrived in 1948, for 2-litre unsupercharged cars, the term 'Formula One' had some comparative purpose, and so 'Formula One' and 'Grand Prix' came to denote the same events.

VISIT VELOCE ON THE WEB – WWW.VELOCE.CO.UK
All current books • New book news • Special offers • Gift vouchers • Forum

18

Chapter 5

1945/46
Prepare for take-off

Only a few weeks after World War Two ended, a race meeting to celebrate was run on 9th September in the Bois de Boulogne in Paris. Three races were run, and the main race for single-seaters, wonderfully titled 'Coupe des Prisonniers', was won by Jean-Pierre Wimille in a 4700cc Bugatti type 59/50B, from Raymond Sommer's Talbot 26. There were, of course, no new cars available, but, while the Bugatti's win was sadly the swansong of the renowned marque, and could not feature in the future Formula One, the 4500cc us/c Talbot 26 would be useful for quite a few years yet. Most racing marques had been produced for sale in the pre-war years, but Alfa Romeo did not offer its supreme 158 model to others for sale or loan. In the pre-war Voiturette class the 158s had dominated, despite a horde of Maseratis providing all the opposition, and it was feared that when they reappeared they would continue where they had left off. The best available now were those Maseratis, the 4CL and the older 6CM, with 1500cc s/c units of about 220bhp. Then came the Talbot 26, and the best of the rest was the 3300cc Delahaye 135S, but both of these were really stripped-down sports cars which, in good hands, put in some surprising performances thanks to their fuel economy, compared to the thirsty 1500cc s/c thoroughbred racers.

Back in 1936, France, not wishing to feed the German ego by losing to the 'Silver Arrows' in Grand Prix racing, had decided to concentrate its efforts on 'sports cars' designed for serious competition. This encouraged Talbot, Delage and Delahaye to produce models with large unsupercharged engines, which, shorn of all things unnecessary for the race track, could compete reasonably in single-seat categories, and now fulfil the 4500cc unsupercharged element of the proposed 'Formula One,' the other element being 1500cc supercharged. In that category, sooner or later, the Maseratis would meet those Alfa Romeo 158s again, which were much more developed, and had almost 300bhp (but what state had they been kept in during the war?). So, by 1946, the two recognised stars, Wimille and Sommer, had already shone, but the undisputed greatest pre-war driver of all, Tazio Nuvolari, hadn't appeared in Paris, it having been an all-French affair (because of Italy's role in the war, perhaps?).

It would be the Grand Prix de Marseille the following May that, I believe, first represented a typical future F1 race. The drivers were all from France, Italy or Switzerland, and Maseratis were now there in quantity; no fewer than 17 of them being entered. The same was nearly true of the GP de Nice a few weeks earlier, but Raymond Sommer drove an Alfa Romeo 308 which had a 3000cc s/c engine, so was not a 'future F1' car, so I believe the 'spirit of F1' began at Marseille where all serious competition involved 'future F1' cars. Races producing this scenario are all included in this list, whatever the engine limit specified for the race. The only car threatening the 'future Formula One' cars had been the occasional Alfa Romeo 308, in the hands of either Sommer or Wimille, so, as the cars and drivers already existed, the organisers of the Gran Premio del Valentino at Turin on 1st September 1946 decided not to wait, and specified the incoming Formula One as their race rule. So, from an organisational and technical viewpoint, **this was the first designated Formula One race**. The organisers of the next two events followed suit, despite these three events not being sanctioned by the FIA.

The spirit of Formula One is born
✷✷ 1er Grand Prix de Marseille
15 lap heats +35 lap final of 2.23 miles = 111.5 total miles.
36 entries – 11 started/heat – 7 finished final.
Poles: Heat one – R Mazaud (Maserati 4CL) – 2m-11.0s

(61.26mph); Heat two – M Balsa (Bugatti 51) – 2m-13.7s (60.05mph).

13-MAY: 'The spirit of F1.' So is this the first F1 race? Basically a coast road and a feeder road in T formation, involving three hairpins turning cars down the opposite side of each straight, with a just rudimentary barrier between! Mazaud and Sommer won the heats, but valve trouble stole Tazio Nuvolari's victory on the last lap of heat two. Sommer romped away in the final, and chaser Mazaud hit the chicane. The drivers soon became household names – Tazio Nuvolari already being world renowned. The few 'non-future Formula One' cars played no part in the result. Sommer took Nuvolari (who shared the controls) on his lap of honour. Next to Balsa in heat two was a name that would be winning in F1 sixteen years later: a true survivor – Maurice Trintignant.

1st	R Sommer (SM)	Maserati 4CL-s/c in 1h-20m-37.7s	58.06
2nd	E. Platé	Maserati 4CL-s/c	1 lap
3rd	G Grignard	Delahaye 135S	1 lap
F lap	T Nuvolari (SM)	Maserati 4CL-s/c (heat 2) in 2m-06.7s	63.34

✷✷ 1er Coupé René la Begue (St Cloud – Paris)

30 laps of 3.728 miles = 111.8 miles.
28 entries – 22 started – 11 finished.

Front row: R Sommer (Maserati 4CL) – 2m-59.2s (74.90mph); J-P Wimille (Alfa Romeo 158) 2.5s.

9-JUN: The fabulous prewar Alfa Romeo 158s now arrived on the scene, driven by Wimille and Farina. In the wet, Sommer was first away, but Wimille passed on the first lap. Sommer managed to split the Alfas, both of which retired with clutch trouble: Farina from third behind Sommer on lap 16, and Wimille from the lead on lap 19. So, Sommer's amazing pole position earned its just reward. This race sealed his credentials as a supremo – no-one else challenged the Alfa Romeo 158s, which would then not lose another race for five whole years. It would take a new marque to do so.

1st	R Sommer (SM)	Maserati 4CL-s/c in 1h-38m-42.0s	67.99
2nd	L Chiron (W)	Talbot-Lago T26	17.6s
3rd	R Mazaud (EFA)	Maserati 4CL-s/c	1 lap
F lap	G Farina (W)	Alfa Romeo 158-s/c in 3m-08.4s	71.24

✷✷ VIII Grand Prix d'Albi

2 x 16 laps of 5.527 miles = 176.0 miles.
19 entries – 14 started – 7 finished.

Front row: R Parnell (Maserati 4CL) – 3m-42.3s (89.51mph); 'Raph' (Maserati 4CL) 3.4s.

14-JUL: Nuvolari wins a Formula One race! Yes, but not until Raymond Sommer and England's best, Reg Parnell, had retired from the first heat, and Villoresi had non-started. Nuvolari had won the first part by no less than 3m-22s – almost a lap. This was enough for him to pit for plugs in heat two and retain his overall lead. Villoresi had won the second part from Nuvolari by 1m-09s. It should also be remembered that Nuvolari was 53 and in poor health, collapsing at the end due to inhalation of fumes. It was an amazing victory! Tazio Nuvolari is still rightly regarded as one of the greatest drivers in motor racing history.

1st	T Nuvolari (SM)	Maserati 4CL-s/c in 1h-55m-44.6s	91.67
2nd	H Louveau (SM)	Maserati 4CL-s/c	1 lap
3rd	'Raph' (ENC)	Maserati 4CL-s/c	1 lap
F lap	L Villoresi (SM)	Maserati 4CL-s/c in 3m-22.3s	98.36

✷✷✷ 1er Grand Prix des Nations (Geneva)

32 lap heat + 44 lap final of 1.856 miles = 141.1 miles.
26 entries – 23 started – 8 finished.

Poles: Heat one – J-P Wimille – 1m-37.5s (68.53mph); Heat two – G Farina – 1m-38.3s (67.97mph).

21-JUL: Every major team entered this race, Alfa Romeo sending four cars, as two entries at St Cloud had proved vulnerable. Sommer had finished only sixth in heat one, so started the final at the back of the grid. After a lap he was already fourth behind Wimille, Farina and Varzi, and ahead of Trossi's Alfa! After teammate Achille Varzi pitted, Farina and Wimille battled until implored from the pits to ease up. Nuvolari tangled when being lapped by Wimille, then spun, stalled and restarted in third thanks to stopping on a downhill section. The black flag was shown to Nuvolari who … er … failed to notice it, so they put it away! Ah well! Varzi's pit stop dropped him to seventh, so all Alfas finished. Wimille had the only single-stage blown Alfa – the others were twin-stage. 'Naughty' Nuvolari led the 'non-Alfa brigade' in fourth, ahead of deGraffenried's Maserati and Bira's ERA.

1st	G Farina (W)	Alfa Romeo 158-s/c in 1h-15m-49.4s	64.62
2nd	Count C Trossi (W)	Alfa Romeo 158-s/c	71s
3rd	J-P Wimille (W)	Alfa Romeo 158-s/c	1 lap
F lap	J-P Wimille	Alfa Romeo 158-s/c in 1m-36.4s	69.30

✳✳✳ III Gran Premio del Valentino (Torino)

60 laps of 2.795 miles = 167.7 miles.
35 entries – 20 started – 9 finished.

Front row: G Farina; J-P Wimille; Count C Trossi; A Varzi (all Alfa Romeo 158). Times unknown.

1-SEP: Did it all start here? The organisers ran this race as conforming to the 1947 Formula One. Five Alfa Romeo entries (Consalvo Sanesi the new recruit – at the insistence of the trade union) meant there should be competition for victory. Farina's Alfa broke its axle at the start, so the order was: Varzi, Wimille, then Nuvolari's Maserati, Trossi and Sanesi. Nuvolari lost a wheel on lap 15, so Sommer now led the Alfa-chasers. Only three Alfas finished as Sanesi retired on lap eight. After Wimille and Varzi swapped the lead a few times Wimille obeyed orders so Varzi took the win. Trossi's Alfa fell to sixth with gear problems.

1st	A Varzi (W)	Alfa Romeo 158-s/c in 2h-35m-45.8s	64.62
2nd	J-P Wimille (W)	Alfa Romeo 158-s/c	0.8s
3rd	R Sommer (SM)	Maserati 4CL-s/c	2 laps
F lap	J-P Wimille (W)	Alfa Romeo 158-s/c in 2m-22.4s	70.68

✳✳ III Circuito di Milano (Sempione)

20 lap heats + 30 lap final of 1.74 miles = 87 miles.
22 entries – 20 started – 6 finished.

Poles: Heat one – Count C Trossi; Heat two – G Farina. Times unknown.

30-SEP: Another F1 race. No Wimille here, but the four Alfas still had things their own way. In the final Nuvolari was fourth when he retired, ahead of Farina's Alfa. This left Villoresi and Sommer battling to be best of the rest, and ahead of Farina who had spun and then withdrew. Villoresi won this Maserati 4CL battle, beating Sommer by 0.2 secs. Trossi had led at first, but dropped to third before storming through to regain a lead he never lost. Nuvolari was in ill-health – his retirement a relief.

1st	Count C Trossi (W)	Alfa Romeo 158-s/c in 56m-6.0s	55.82
2nd	A Varzi (W)	Alfa Romeo 158-s/c	18s
3rd	C Sanesi (W)	Alfa Romeo 158-s/c	36s
F lap	A Varzi /G Farina	Alfa Romeo 158-s/c in 1m-50.4s	56.73

✳✳ II Grand Prix du Salon (Bois de Boulogne)

80 laps of 1.984 miles = 158.7 miles.

26 entries – 16 starters – 8 finished.

Front row: H Louveau (Maserati 4CL) – 1m-37.6s (73.19mph); 'Levegh' 3.8s; R Sommer 4.2s.

06-OCT: This race also ran to the nascent Formula One. No Alfas present should have meant a field day for Raymond Sommer, but Henri Louveau in his Maserati 4CL-s/c easily took pole position. However, it was Sommer and Chiron, from near the back of the grid, who battled for the lead, leaving the rest well back. Chiron hit a dog and lost much time in repairs, which left Sommer far ahead but still driving in his usual entertaining manner, and he won in style. Henri Louveau dropped to fourth.

1st	R Sommer	Maserati 4CL-s/c in 2h-12-39.7s	71.78
2nd	'Raph' (ENC)	Maserati 4CL-s/c	3 laps
3rd	'Levegh'	Talbot-Lago T150C	3 laps
F lap	R Sommer	Maserati 4CL-s/c in 1m-35.4s	74.88

Winners of the seven best pre-F1 races of 1946 – quantity & quality of success

3 wins	R Sommer (3B)	4 wins	Maserati (4B)
1 win	G Farina (A) A Varzi (A) T Nuvolari (B) C Trossi (B)	3 wins	Alfa Romeo (2A, B)

So, top class racing was now under way, and a full season was being established. If there had been a World Championship in 1946 then Raymond Sommer would have won it with his three wins and a third from the seven races shown. Alfa Romeo had, in truth, shared the spoils between its Italian drivers, but Jean-Pierre Wimille was generally reckoned to be the fastest of the team – yielding to Varzi at Turin must have absolutely rankled with him. Would he have done that if a Championship was at stake? I doubt it.

Non-Works teams were formed, some of which seemed to be private entrants under a business name running a single car. I regard those as private rather than team entries. Multi-car teams achieving a podium finish are indicated in the results as follows:

Ecurie Franco-Americaine (EFA). Run by Lucy O'Reilly Schell, an American married to Frenchman Laury Schell and runner of Delahayes pre-war. Mother of later famous driver and well liked 'hell-raiser' Harry Schell.

Ecurie Naphtra Course (ENC). Founded by 'Raph' (Count Raphael Bethenod de las Casas) to run Maserati 4CLs for

himself and a second driver. Even Wimille drove for it.
Scuderia Milan (SM). This was thought of as a quasi-Works Maserati outfit.
Works teams are shown (W) irrespective of their actual team name.

Private entrants are without designation.
Pseudonyms : 'Raph' is given above, and 'Levegh' is Pierre Eugêne Alfred Bouillon.

VISIT VELOCE ON THE WEB – WWW.VELOCE.CO.UK
All current books • New book news • Special offers • Gift vouchers • Forum

22

Chapter 6

1947
Now it's official ... surely?

Originally called 'Formula A', it soon became known by its present title – though there seems to be no date for an official change in nomenclature. The 'new' formula was bound to reflect the technology of the existing cars, as few had funds for new machinery in the early post-war years. The Monkhouse/King Farlow book *Grand Prix Racing* gives 1948 as the start, but that would have been the first year by which the new name was settled. But 'what's in a name?' as Shakespeare said. Surely 1947 is when it was *meant* to start, and the formula remained unchanged until 1954. Three full-scale 'rehearsals' had already been run, so the field was ready and waiting. Alfa Romeo was intending to race only four times, as in 1946, so it was up to the others to 'make hay' before the Alfas arrived. Starting in Sweden seems an oddity, as are the venues there. France was the dominant country for venues, as using public roads for racing made creating circuits easy; and some were already familiar. This was denied to the British by the law forbidding the use of public roads for racing. So, Jersey in the Channel Isles and the Isle of Man stepped in to open up racing to British-based racers. They included 'B Bira', the racing pseudonym of Eton-educated Prince Birabongse Bhanudej Bhanubandh of Siam (Thailand) – a very useful truncation.

The Grand Prix driver's diary of single-seater racing for 1947

9th February	KAK Vinter Grand Prix at Rommehed (Sw) – 64.3 miles
23rd February	Stockholm Grand Prix at Lake Vallentuna (Sw) – 77.8 miles
7th April	Grand Prix de Pau (F) – 188.7 miles
27th April	Grand Prix de Rousillon at Perpignan (F) – 91.5 miles
8th May	Jersey Road Race (UK) – 160.0 miles
18th May	Grand Prix de Marseille (F) – 188.6 miles
1st June	Grand Prix de Nimes (F) – 226.3 miles
8th June	Grosse Preis der Schweiz at Bremgarten (S) – 227.5 miles
29th June	Grand Prix de Belgique at Spa Francorchamps (B) – 315.1 miles
6th July	Grand Prix de Reims at Reims-Gueux (F) – 247.7 miles
13th July	Grand Prix d'Albi (F) – 220.6 miles
13th July	Grand Prix de Bari (I) – 165.9 miles*
20th July	Grand Prix de Nice (F) – 199.7 miles
3rd August	Grand Prix d'Alsace at Strasbourg (F) – 191.6 miles
9th August	Ulster Trophy at Ballyclare (UK) – 149.1 miles*
10th August	Grand Prix de Comminges at St Gaudens (F) – 205.1 miles
21st August	British Empire Trophy at Douglas (IoM) – 155.0 miles*
7th September	Gran Premio d'Italia at Sempione, Milano (I) – 214.0 miles
21st September	Grand Prix de l'ACF at Lyon (F) – 317.0 miles
5th October	Grand Prix de Lausanne (F) – 181.8miles
16th November	Grand Prix du Salon (Montlhéry) – 187.4 miles

21 events of total race mileage = 3975 miles

* See Appendix A for these ungraded race results

KAK Vinter Grand Prix (Rommehed)
20 laps of 3.217 miles = 64.34 miles.
15 entries – 4 started – 3 finished.

No grid positions available.

09-FEB: Did Formula One officially start in Sweden on packed snow with added hot gravel? It seems so. Three Brits (Reg Parnell, George Abecassis and Leslie Brooke) arrived with their 10+ year-old ERAs, plus Gustaf Nobellus, a local with an even older Bugatti 35! The problem was that all the other entrants – nine of them – were stuck on an ice-bound ship in Gothenburg harbour! Who was on the front row? Well, they all were – like a motorcycle speedway race. Reg Parnell led the whole way, with Brooke close but unable to pass. Nobellus did four laps. That was it! Was this the great Formula One? Or a rather bizarre false start ... ?

1st	R Parnell	ERA 'R1A'-s/c in 59m-02.2s	65.39
2nd	L Brooke	ERA 'R7B'-s/c	0.6s
F lap	L Brooke	ERA 'R7B'-s/c in 2m-51.8s	67.41

∗ Stockholm Grand Prix (Lake Vallentuna)
25 laps of 3.11 miles = 77.8 miles.
11 entered and started – 6 finished.
No grid positions available.

23-FEB: Now that the others had been freed, an extra race was added and took place on a frozen lake! No grid seems to have been available. Chiron led at first but was soon passed by Sommer, Parnell and Abecassis. Reg Parnell led when Sommer spun (he recovered, but a second spin then finished his race). Abecassis slowed and Chiron's Talbot succumbed to a puncture, gifting Parnell an easy win. He was the only one to use twin rear wheels, á la British Speed-Hill-Climb practise. Chaboud was third, ahead of a clutch of Delahayes. Perhaps the Rommehed race was good practice for the Brits. A crowd of 30,000 watched!

1st	R Parnell	ERA 'R1A'-s/c in 1h-08m-18.8s	68.23
2nd	G Abecassis	ERA R2A' -s/c	1m-01s
3rd	E Chaboud (EF)	Delahaye 135S	1m-30s
F lap	R Sommer	Maserati 4CM-s/c in 2m-26.2s	76.51

∗∗ VIII Grand Prix de Pau
110 laps of 1.715 miles = 188.7 miles.
15 entries – 14 started – 7 finished.
Front row: R Sommer – 1m-49.2s (56.54mph); E Chaboud 3.4s. Row two: 'B Bira' 4.4s; 'Levegh' 6.3s.

07-APR: The Pau race was now established as a classic. There were no Alfas, but Wimille gave the new Simca-Gordini its

first outing. Sommer tore off, chased by Bira (ERA), Chaboud (Talbot), Pagani and Wimille, whose little car was well suited to the tight street circuit. Chaboud went out on lap five, and a bad pit stop, magneto trouble, and a spin resulting in a collision with a tree did for Sommer. A few spectators were hurt but Sommer wasn't seriously injured. Bira's engine blew up, and Wimille retired (clutch), so 'Nello' Pagani won his third F1 start! In 1949 he would be World 125cc Motorcycle Champion ... a versatile man.

1st	N Pagani (SM)	Maserati 4CL-s/c in 3h-38m-31.2s	51.78
2nd	'Levegh' (EG)	Deláge 3000	2 laps
3rd	H Louveau (SM)	Maserati 4CL-s/c	2 laps
F lap	R Sommer	Maserati 4CM/4CL-s/c in 1m-49.1s	56.59

∗∗ II Grand Prix de Rousillon (Perpignan)
58 laps of 1.577 miles = 91.5 miles.
15 entries – 12 started – 7 finished.
Front row: R Sommer – 1m-34.8s (59.89mph); J-P Wimille.
Row two: E Chaboud; H Louveau.

27-APR: Scuderia Milan withdrew its Maseratis because of start money, so no Nello Pagani or Enrico Platé. Sommer had the only Maserati in the race, and duly led off, soon breaking the track record. Wimille's Gordini and Chaboud's Talbot held the next two places on lap eight when a multiple crash followed a spin by George Grignard's Delahaye. Most got away again, though. Wimille overheated and Sommer's gearbox broke, handing victory to Chaboud. Henri Louveau and Yves Girard-Cabantous put on a good show for second place, finishing a second apart a lap down. The Talbot-Lago was a large car for a street circuit.

1st	E Chaboud (EF)	Talbot-Lago T26 in 1h-35m-06.3s	57.71
2nd	H Louveau (EF)	Deláge 3000	1 lap
3rd	Y Giraud-Cabantous (EF)	Delahaye 135S	1 lap
F lap	R Sommer	Maserati 4CM-s/c in 1m-34.2s	60.28r

∗∗ 1st JCC Jersey Road Race
50 laps of 3.2 miles = 160 miles.
28 entries – 25 started – 11 finished.
Front row: B Bira – 2m-06.4s (91.13mph); R Parnell (2.6s);
N Pagani (3.8s); R Sommer (3.8s).

08-MAY: This was the first post-war meeting for the 'Junior Car Club' and, with Brooklands and Donington no longer available, it chose to go to Jersey as racing was not allowed on public roads in England. This was fast for a street venue. No fewer than 20 Maseratis and ERAs were entered. British-based drivers were out in force, and, surprisingly, a few came from nearby France, but they were top quality men. Bira and Sommer shared the lead at first, but both hit trouble – tyres for Bira and engine for Sommer – and handed the lead to Parnell. After Parnell's fuel stop, Chiron's team thought Chiron was leading and slowed him down when he was actually a lap behind! Their lack of a lap chart thwarting any chase, despite more oil stops for Parnell.

1st	R Parnell	Maserati 4CL-s/c in 1h-53m-33.0s	84.52
2nd	L Chiron (SM)	Maserati 4CL-s/c	1 lap
3rd	R Mays	ERA 'R4D'-s/c	2 laps
F lap	R Sommer (SM)	Maserati 4CL-s/c in 2m-06.2s	91.28

✳✳ VI Grand Prix de Marseille
69 laps of 2.734 miles = 188.6 miles.
24 entries – 22 started – 9 finished.
Front row: R Sommer – 2m-14.7s (73.06mph); L Villoresi (1.1s). Row two: E Chaboud (7.5s); L Chiron (9.3s).
18-MAY: Back to Marseille where (I think) it had all started. Villoresi accelerated away at the start, leaving even Sommer trailing. But he paid the price with engine failure, and, soon after, so did Sommer, now suffering his fourth successive retirement from pole position. Was Chaboud very surprised to inherit a lead after being so outpaced? Maybe not, as the 4.5-litre unsupercharged Talbots were economical, not needing to refuel. He was well in charge by half distance. Did this pressure the Maseratis to risk pressing on too hard? Perhaps so, as only Enrico Platé's finished out of seven that started.

1st	E Chaboud (EF)	Talbot-Lago T26 in 2h-50m-23.6s	66.42
2nd	E Platé	Maserati 4CL-s/c	1 lap
3rd	H Louveau (EG)	Deláge 3000	2 laps
F lap	Villoresi (SA)/ Sommer (SM)	Maserati 4CL-s/c in 2m-17.2s	71.74

✳✳ III Grand Prix de Nimes
70 laps of 3.233 miles = 226.3 miles.
29 entries – 26 started – 12 finished.
Front row: L Villoresi on pole – time unknown – no other info.
01-JUN: The Works Simca-Gordinis led by Wimille disappointingly failed to arrive. Villoresi led Chiron, while Sommer lost a minute at the start. He stormed through to

sixth by lap six, the crowd on their feet, willing an end to his extraordinary run of bad luck. Chiron's Talbot duly took the lead at Villoresi's overlong pit stop, but his lead was then wasted when he glanced a wall, having to change a wheel, and handing the lead back to Villoresi. Amazingly, Sommer had joined the leaders before halfway, but was robbed by engine failure yet again, on lap 46, leaving Villoresi on his own.

1st	L Villoresi (SA)	Maserati 4CL-s/c in 3h-38m-39.4s	62.10
2nd	L Chiron (EF)	Talbot-Lago T26	2m-37s
3rd	R Parnell	Maserati 4CL-s/c	1 lap
F lap	L Villoresi	Maserati 4CL-s/c in 3m-00.4s	64.51

✳✳✳ VII Grosser Preis der Schweiz (Bremgarten Berne)
20 lap heat + 30 lap final of 4.55 miles = 227.5 miles.
32 entries – 27 started – 17 finished.
Pole position heat one: Count C Trossi – 2m-49.2s (100.53mph). Pole position heat two: J-P Wimille – 2m-47.9s (97.54mph).
08-JUN: This was the first visit by Formula One to a major classic circuit, and the Alfa Romeos were back. So which of the four would win? Tragically, lack of control over the crowd resulted in three fatalities when spectators ventured onto the track. The drivers drove cautiously after that. Sommer's Maserati 4CL, as usual, gave the greatest challenge to Wimille and Varzi, but had to refuel while they didn't. He lost a minute, yet still finished fourth, ahead of the Alfa Romeo of Sanesi. The two-stage supercharged Maserati was still no real match for Alfa Romeo. The crowd invaded the track again after the race, but, luckily, the drivers were expecting it.

1st	J-P Wimille (W)	Alfa Romeo 158-s/c in 1h.25m-09.1s	96.16
2nd	A Varzi (W)	Alfa Romeo 158-s/c	44.7s
3rd	Count CF Trossi (W)	Alfa Romeo 158-s/c	77s
F lap	J-P Wimille	Alfa Romeo 158-s/c in 2m-47.0s	98.06

✳✳✳ X Grand Prix de Belgique (Spa Francorchamps)
35 laps of 9.004 miles = 315.1 miles.
22 entries – 18 started – 7 finished.
Front row: J-P Wimille – 5m-12.5s (103.73mph); A Varzi; L Chiron.
29-JUN: Another classic venue was back on the calender, so Alfa Romeo made an appearance. Amazingly, Chiron's

Talbot 26 got among them on the grid! Sommer's Maserati mixed it with the Alfas, being second behind Varzi after a lap, but by lap six Wimille and Sanesi had passed Sommer. The only trouble for any Alfa was when Trossi was hit in the face by a stone, and manager Guidotti deputised for a couple of laps while he was being treated. Sommer re-passed Sanesi's Alfa, but chassis failure put him out after an amazing display against the odds. Wimille ignored Alfa's wish that Varzi win this race, and sped away. Sanesi had trouble with a lap to go, but stopped at his pit. He should have waited at the finish line and rolled over to be classified as a finisher – the start line and pits at Spa were on a slope. Bob Gerard and Cuth Harrison shared the fourth place ERA, three laps down.

1st	J-P Wimille (W)	Alfa Romeo 158-s/c in 3h-18m-28.6s	95.27
2nd	A Varzi (W)	Alfa Romeo 158-s/c	1 lap
3rd	CFTrossi/Guidotti (W)	Alfa Romeo 158-s/c	2 laps
F lap	J-P Wimille	Alfa Romeo 158-s/c in 5m-18.0s	101.94

✳✳ XVI Grand Prix de Reims (Reims-Gueux)
51 laps of 4.856 miles = 247.7 miles.
24 entries – 20 started – 7 finished.
Front row: C Kautz – 2m-51.1s (102.17mph); H Louveau +8.5s; R Sommer 9.4s.

06-JUL: Another classic venue, but there were no Alfa Romeos this time. It was just a week after Spa, and Alfa entered only when its cars had fully recovered from previous outings and were race-prepared. Others had to race to survive, so sometimes chance was perhaps an element. The Swiss Christian Kautz led from pole, with Villoresi, Sommer and a certain Alberto Ascari (his first Grand Prix) chasing closely. It appeared as if it would be an Maserati affair: Villoresi twice took the lead only to lose it with engine trouble. Ascari's car also suffered engine trouble, and Sommer's transmission failed on lap 38, so the Maserati party was over. A race of attrition saw only seven finishers – even Louis Chiron was out of fuel as he finished. The Gerard/Harrison duo again benefitted. Debutant Ascari had the new lower Maserati 4CLT, but his mentor and teammate, the experienced Villoresi, didn't, so clearly Ascari was highly rated already!

1st	C Kautz (EP)	Maserati 4CL-s/c in 2h-34m-50.0s	95.97
2nd	L Chiron (EF)	Talbot-Lago-T26	2m-39s
3rd	R Gerard/C. Harrison	ERA 'R14B'-s/c	3 laps
F lap	L Villoresi (SA)	Maserati 4CL-s/c in 2m-58.2s	98.10

✳ IX Grand Prix d'Albi
40 laps of 5.516 miles = 220.6 miles.
31 entries – 25 started – 7 finished.
Front row: H Louveau – 3m-38.6s (90.90mph); J-P Wimille (5.9s); E Mouche (7.1s).

13-JUL: Alfa Romeo was at a very minor event at Bari on the same day unopposed, its unworthy 'victory' not worth recalling in this list. Half the entry was from the proposed Formula Two (2000cc us/c), including Wimille and Sommer in works Gordinis. Leader Villoresi mistimed a fuel stop and ran dry, losing a likely win. Wimille had amazingly been second on the grid but lasted only seven laps. Rosier and Chaboud (Delahaye) took over when others stopped for fuel, but Chaboud crashed unhurt on the last lap, to Sommer's benefit. Today, Chaboud would have retained third place. Again, Talbots benefitted by their fuel economy.

1st	L Rosier	Talbot 150SS-us/c in 2h-29m-40.8s	88.41
2nd	R Sommer (W)	Simca-Gordini T11 (F2)	2m-02s
3rd	C Pozzi	Delahaye 135S	1 lap
F lap	L Villoresi (SA)	Maserati 4CL-s/c in 3m-26.4s	96.25

✳✳✳ VI Grand Prix de Nice
100 laps of 1.997 miles = 199.7 miles.
21 entries – 19 started – 8 finished.
Front row: L Villoresi – 1m-43.3s (59.60mph): R Sommer 1.3s; A Ascari 2.6s.

20-JUL: This was the fifth major race in as many weekends, and still a good entry was received – even Chaboud who had crashed into a ditch the previous week! Sommer was fast away, with Villoresi's and protégé Ascari's Maseratis chasing, but, for Sommer, a fire soon after a pit stop put an end to his race. Chiron's Talbot was now in third place, but engine trouble handed the old ERA of Parnell the spot. Parnell's long pit stop then allowed Wimille into third in the little Gordini. Misfiring saw Ascari drop from second to fourth at the end, thus promoting the little Gordini into second place, and the ERA back into third. Only Wimille's mastery could produce this result.

1st	L Villoresi (SA)	Maserati 4CL-s/c in 3h-07m-07.1s	64.04
2nd	J-P Wimille (W)	Simca-Gordini T15 (F2)	2 laps
3rd	F Ashmore/ R Parnell	ERA 'R1A'-s/c	2 laps
F lap	R Sommer	Maserati 4CL-s/c in 1m-44.0s	69.13

✳✳ II Grand Prix d'Alsace (Strasbourg)

85 laps of 2.254 miles = 191.6 miles.

18 entries – 16 started – 9 finished.

Front row: L Villoresi – 1m-49.5s (74.10mph); A Ascari 0.3s.
Row two: L Chiron 0.7s.

03-AUG: Sommer's Maserati was still hors-de-combat, but almost all the other stars came. The track was so narrow it only allowed for a 2-1-2-1 grid formation. Villoresi led from pole and pulled away. Ascari's Maserati was overhauled by Chiron's Talbot for second, who then reeled in Villoresi and deservedly led when the leader pitted for plugs. No luck for Chiron, though, as a broken gear lever soon intervened. Ascari suffered a bent valve, so Villoresi won easily. Even Girard-Cabantous lapped Rosier three times.

1st	L Villoresi (SA)	Maserati 4CL-s/c in 2h-45m-41.9s	69.37
2nd	Y Girard-Cabantous (EF)	Talbot-Lago T26SS	1m-14s
3rd	L Rosier	Talbot 150SS	3 laps
F lap	L Villoresi	Maserati 4CL-s/c in 1m-47.2s	75.69

✳✳ XIII Grand Prix du Comminges (St Gaudens)

30 laps of 6.836 miles = 205.1 miles.

42 entries – 34 started – 17 finished.

Front row: L Villoresi on pole – time unknown – no other info.

10-AUG: A vast entry! Perhaps the lack of Alfas attracted them. Villoresi led a Maserati trio with Ascari and Serafini (the latter succumbing to a broken steering column). The subsequent collision with a tree caused him very serious injuries, taking him out of racing for a long time. Ascari had ignition trouble which cost him over a lap. Heavy rain fell as Villoresi refuelled, and he promptly spun off, as did others. Chiron looked all set for victory, but a terrific chase by fellow veteran Girard-Cabantous (both racers since the 1920s) very nearly succeeded. If Maseratis had been as reliable as the Talbot-Lagos, the results could have been very different.

1st	L Chiron (EF)	Talbot-Lago T26 in 2h-35m-37.4s	79.06
2nd	Y Girard-Cabantous (EF)	Talbot-Lago T26SS	0.5s
3rd	E Chaboud	Talbot-Lago T150C	1m-36s
F lap	D Serafini (SM)	Maserati 4CL-s/c in 4m-15.5s	96.31

✳✳✳ XVII Gran Premio d'Italia (Parco Sempione – Milano)

100 laps of 2.14 miles = 214 miles.

28 entries – 22 started – 9 finished.

Front row: C Sanesi – 1m-44.0s (74.16mph); Ct CF Trossi +0.8s; L Villoresi +1.4s.

07-SEP: The Alfas were back, but Monza was still war-damaged so it was off to Sempione Park in nearby Milan. Villoresi led the chaotic start, but was soon swallowed up by three of the four Alfas. Trossi soon began to swap the lead with Varzi while pulling away from Sanesi. The workforce had persuaded the management to allow mechanic Gaboardi a drive, and he replaced Wimille. Maserati-powered Ascari was clearly the best non-Alfa, challenging Sanesi and well ahead of Gaboardi, but a stop to fix the fuel tank strap and bodywork dropped him six laps back; yet he finished fifth! Already he was proving that a new name had arrived. The crowd called him 'ciccio' (chubby), and, of course, knew that he had a famous racing pedigree from his father Antonio. Trossi deliberately allowed Varzi to catch up, and the pair almost staged a dead-heat, which was unpopular with the crowd.

1st	Count CF Trossi (W)	Alfa Romeo 158-s/c in 3h-02m-52.0s	70.29
2nd	A Varzi (W)	Alfa Romeo 158-s/c	0.1s
3rd	C Sanesi (W)	Alfa Romeo 158-s/c	1 lap
F lap	Count C F Trossi	Alfa Romeo 158-s/c in 1m-44.0s	74.16

✳✳ XXXIV Grand Prix de l'ACF (Lyon)

70 laps of 4.53 miles = 317.1 miles.

22 entries – 18 started – 8 finished.

Front row: H Louveau – 3m-17.9s (82.75mph); L Chiron +0.4s; E Chaboud +5.5s.

21-SEP: The title shown here denotes the premier race in France, the ACF being the principal French authority for motor sport (like the RAC in England). The title 'French Grand Prix' was sometimes used by lesser events. This being so, it was strange that Alfa Romeo withdrew its entries, but Wimille found himself a drive in a Talbot. The Maseratis arrived late, as usual, and started from the back. However, Villoresi took just three laps to gain the lead from Louveau, and just one more for his motor to go 'bang.' deGraffenried led, then Chiron, and, when deGraffenried retired Chiron pulled well away. A leaky head gasket forced him to ease up, though. He 'soft-pedalled' past the pits, cutting the engine sound, hopefully avoiding alerting the opposition. It worked, as Louveau's pits failed to notice. If only they'd known they might well have won. Sadly, Sommer's CTA-Arsenal, in its race debut, broke a driveshaft on the line, á la BRM in 1950 (and that would be with the same driver).

1st	L Chiron (EF)	Talbot-Lago T26 in 4h-03m-40.7s	78.09
2nd	H Louveau (EP)	Maserati 4CL-s/c	1m-38s
3rd	E Chaboud	Talbot-Lago T150C	1 lap
F lap	Ascari/Villoresi (SA)	Maserati 4CLT-s/c in 3m-17.5s	82.58

✲✲✲ 1er Grand Prix de Lausanne
90 laps of 2.02 miles = 181.8 miles.
18 entries – 16 started – 8 finished.
Front row: Pole – A Ascari; R Sommer; P Taruffi. Times unknown.
05-OCT: Wimille's Gordini had a 1220cc motor, but was competing against 1500cc cars! Ascari led at the start, and pulled away until lap 14, when a split brake pipe put him out. Villoresi now led from Sommer's Maserati, Wimille's Simca-Gordini, and Chiron's Talbot. After the fuel stops Sommer's car failed due to a variety of troubles. Wimille unlapped himself and, amazingly, finished second, just 64 seconds adrift, in a small car and after nearly three hours of racing! Chiron's difficulties saw him drop to fourth.

1st	L Villoresi (SA)	Maserati 4CL-s/c in 2h-49m-30.4s	64.37
2nd	J-P Wimille (W)	Simca-Gordini T15 1.2	1m-04s
3rd	E deGraffenried (SP)	Maserati 4CL-s/c	4 laps
F lap	A Ascari (SA)	Maserati 4CL-s/c in 1m-46.5s	68.31

✲ III Grand Prix du Salon (Montlhéry)
48 laps of 3.905 miles = 187.4 miles.
27 entries – 13 started – 9 finished.
Front row: L Chiron – 2m-36.0s (90.12mph); Y Giraud-Cabantous 0.8s; E Chaboud 1.5s; C Pozzi 2.4s.
16-NOV: Although many had retired for the winter, there were enough cars and good drivers around for a decent race. Sommer missed the start as his engine wouldn't fire up. Chiron's Talbot 26 led at first from Giraud-Cabantous, Chaboud and Louveau. Lap five and Giraud-Cabantous now led with Sommer already fifth! By lap ten Sommer was third and catching Chiron, helped by Chaboud stopping to fix his loose bonnet. Sommer shattered the track record at will, but sadly both he and Chiron dropped out, so Yves Giraud-Cabantous won at a canter thanks to Chaboud's stop.

1st	Y Giraud-Cabantous (EF)	Talbot-Lago T26 in 2h-06m-28.2s	88.93
2nd	E Chaboud	Talbot-Lago T26SS	3 laps
3rd	C Pozzi	Delahaye 135S	3 laps
F lap	R Sommer	Maserati 4CL-s/c in 2m-29.4s	94.07

Jumping the start – Always a temptation
The stars of the immediate post-war period were now established. Jean-Pierre Wimille shone in and out of an Alfa Romeo 158-s/c. Raymond Sommer regularly gave the Alfas their biggest threat, and, like Wimille, performed wonders with the small Gordini. Luigi Villoresi was always to be reckoned with, and his protegé Alberto Ascari soon gave indication of what he was to become. Louis Chiron and Achille Varzi hadn't lost their touch either. Alfa Romeo did choose events carefully, and its cars were reliable, fast, well prepared and only factory-entered, unlike the many blown Maserati 4CLs and unblown Talbot-Lagos which raced so frequently that preparation often suffered. But decent racing would not have been possible without opposition to the Alfas, and the seemingly lumbering Talbots found a way of winning with fewer pit stops; and winning's what counts. There were no less than 17 decent F1 races in 1947 – ignoring the Swedish 'false start' – but Formula One was still Europe-bound.

This first year showed that Formula One was already in a reasonably healthy state. For those 17 races a total of 407 entries were received, of which 338 started and 158 finished. This gives a reasonable 17 per cent of non-starters and an average grid size of very close to 20 cars – very satisfactory. A finish rate of 46.8 per cent was only just higher than the infamous 1980s turbo era, and, while not great, it would undoubtedly improve as outfits became more efficient and experienced. The exception to those figures was Eugêne Chaboud, who drove Talbot and Delahaye cars, and started all but two of the races. He won twice and retired just twice – a finish rate of 86.7 per cent – amazing! The most prolific driver was Henri Louveau, who drove Maserati and Delage cars, and only missed a single race, achieved four podium finishes, but retired six times and was disqualified once (at Reims for outside assistance). The 'prize' for worst finish rate went to one of the best drivers of all – Raymond Sommer, driving Maserati, Gordini and the CTA-Arsenal. He started 15 times – four times from pole – yet finished just twice.

More non-Works teams were formed, the most successful being:

• SFACS Ecurie France (EF) which ran Talbot and Delahaye cars

• Ecurie Gersac (EG) which ran Delage 3000s
• Scuderia Platé (SP); formed by Enrico Platé for himself and others to run Maseratis
• Scuderia Ambrosiana (SA); formed before the war by Luigi Villoresi and others, and revived in 1947 to run Maseratis, principally for Villoresi and Alberto Ascari but was open to others, mostly from Britain. Members supplied the cars, and the Scuderia provided organisation of entries and finance. This solved exchange control regulations in Italy and Great Britain, and made international racing possible in the circumstances.

Some drivers switched teams and cars, the exception being Alfa Romeo, of whose five drivers only Jean-Pierre Wimille drove for another team when not required (Simca-Gordini, which also only entered Works cars).

A retro World Champion?
The 1950 World Driver's Championship had only six rounds. A look at the six best supported events of 1947 shows that Jean-Pierre Wimille won two, and was second twice. A Championship would have yielded him the title.

Winners of the 18 graded F1 races of 1947 – quantity & quality of success

4 wins	L Villoresi (2A, 2B)	7 wins	Maserati (2A, 5B)
3 wins	R Parnell (B, C, D)	6 wins	Talbot-Lago (4B, 2C)
2 wins	J-P Wimille (2A) L Chiron (2B) E Chaboud (2B)	3 wins	Alfa Romeo (3A)
1 win	C Trossi (A) C Kautz (B) N Pagani (B) L Rosier (C) Y G-Cabantous (C)	2 wins	ERA (C, D)

VISIT VELOCE ON THE WEB – WWW.VELOCE.CO.UK
All current books • New book news • Special offers • Gift vouchers • Forum

29

Chapter 7

1948
Formula One is now established

There were 17 decent Formula One races this year, often only a week apart. And total race time was almost *44* hours! This is 19 more than from the same number of Grands Prix of 2012. They didn't corner at 4g, or have nearly so many corners, but clearly stamina and nerve in the face of constant danger was at a premium on those narrow unguarded circuits, and much stamina was needed to 'hang on' (no billiard table surfaces then, or power steering). While to modern eyes the race speeds seem rather slow, it should be recalled that many of these races were run on tight 'round the houses' circuits, such as Monaco, and were utterly unforgiving. The attitude was that everyone was glad to be racing – and racing anywhere. No-one questioned circuit safety. The reasoning being that it's an elemental sport – a battle against the elements, as mountain climbing defeats the mountain, so racing defeats the road ... It's road racing, and it's always been dangerous: If you don't like it, don't do it.

Developments in F1 car design since then have vastly outstripped any expected speed increase ... impossible to survive today. There was rarely any possibility of introducing the run-off areas now necessary. The speed of Formula One cars has been matched by amazing safety improvements, and drivers now routinely walk away from total wrecks. In that drivers now see their careers through, that aspect of racing is way better nowadays, but the challenge is not the same if your survival is not a factor to be taken into account. Twenty-first century racers leap from their cars seemingly as fresh as when they got in them. Personally, I'd rather they looked a bit more tired (perhaps they would after three hours). And with full-face helmets they keep their youthful looks – no weather-beaten faces anymore. Perhaps it was more of a 'hard man's game' then ...

The Grand Prix driver's diary of single-seater racing for 1948

29th March	F1 – Grand Prix de Pau (F) – 188.7 miles
15th April	F2 – Grand Prix de Rousillon (F) – 106 miles
29th April	F1 – Jersey Road Race (UK) – 176.0 miles
2nd May	F1 – Grand Prix des Nations at Geneva (S) – 147.7 miles
16th May	F1 – Grand Prix de Monaco (M) – 197.6 miles
25th May	F1 – Britsh Empire Trophy at Douglas (IoM) – 139.6 miles
25th May	F2 – Grand Prix de Rousillon (F) – 105.7 miles
30th May	F1 Grand Prix de Paris at Montlhéry (F) – 194.7 miles
30th May	F2- Gran Premio di Bari (I) – 194 miles
30th May	F2 – Stockholm Grand Prix (Sw) – 125 miles
13th June	F2 – Coppa Giorgio e Alberto Nuvolari at Mantova (I) – 56 miles
27th June	F1 – Gran Premio di San Remo (I) – 178.4 miles
4th July	F1 -Grosse Preis d'Europe at Bremgarten (S) – 180.6 miles
18th July	F1- Grand Prix de l'ACF at Reims-Gueux (F) – 310.8 miles
1st August	F1 – Grand Prix de Comminges (F) – 205.1 miles
7th August	F1- Grote Prijs van Nederland at Zandvoort (N) – 166.7 miles
29th August	F1 – Grand Prix d'Albi (F) – 187.3 miles
5th September	F1- Gran Premio d'Italia at Torino (I) – 233.7 miles
18th September	F1 – Goodwood Trophy at Goodwood

	(UK) – 11.9 miles*	
19th September	F2 – Gran Premio di Napoli at Posillipo (I) – 153 miles	
26th September	F2 – Circuito di Firenze (I) – 157 miles	
2nd October	F1- British Grand Prix at Silverstone (UK) – 238.6 miles	
10th October	F1 – Grand Prix du Salon at Montlhéry (F) – 187.4 miles	
17th October	F1- Gran Premio dell'Autodromo di Monza (I) – 313.2 miles	
24th October	F1 – Circuito del Garda (I) – 183.1 miles*	
31th October	F1- Gran Premio do Peña Rhin at Barcelona (E) – 193.9 miles	

26 events of total race mileage = 4532 miles, 4107 max (simultaneous events)

*See Appendix A for these ungraded race results

✳✳✳ IX Grand Prix du Pau

110 laps of 1.715 miles = 188.7 miles.
16 entered and started – 7 finished.

Front row: J-P Wimille – 1m-49.7s (56.28mph); R Sommer (Maserati 4CM) +0.4s; Y Giraud-Cabantous +2.2s.

29-MAR: Like 1947, Wimille amazed by putting the Simca-Gordini on pole position ahead of Sommer's Maserati 4CM. They duly swapped the lead a couple of times until Wimille pulled ahead, but then, on lap 37, a pit stop disaster cost him five laps. Sommer and Pagani fought it out when Chiron retired, but Sommer pitted for water. He charged back but hit a kerb near the end, bent a wheel, and, amazingly, retook the lead! Not surprisingly, though, it gave way on the last lap. Unlike today, he wasn't classified as second finisher, despite covering a greater distance than Yves Giraud-Cabantous. In those days one had to cross the finish line to be classified, even if it meant pushing the car over!

1st	N Pagani (SP)	Maserati 4CL-s/c in 3h-33m-30.3s	53.02
2nd	Y Giraud-Cabantous (EF)	Lago-Talbot T26	2 laps
3rd	C Pozzi (EL)	Lago-Talbot T26	2 laps
F lap	J-P Wimille (W)	Simca-Gordini T15 1.43 in 1m-49.8s	56.23

✳ II JCC Jersey Road Race

55 laps of 3.2 miles = 176 miles.
29 entries – 22 started – 11 finished.

Front row: B Bira – 2m-01.4s(94.90mph); L Villoresi 0.8s; R Gerard +7.2s; R Parnell +8.0s.

29-APR: Disappointingly, there were no French entries here despite the water crossing required being much shorter than that of the British. So, many thanks to Luigi Villoresi and Scuderia Ambrosiana (see SA in Appendix B). Bira and Villoresi's Maseratis led off, but Villoresi soon retired, giving second to Reg Parnell. Lap 20 saw Bira lose a tyre tread, and fourth was the best he could finish after a number of pit stops. Long-range tanks allowed Bob Gerard to overtake Parnell, who had to refuel, and his gamble paid off so he cruised to victory. So, Gerard, his ERA, and his strategy still had the ability to win in the presence of well-driven Maseratis.

1st	R Gerard	ERA R14B-s/c in 2h-00m-56.2s	87.32
2nd	G Abecassis	Maserati 6CM-s/c	1 lap
3rd	R Parnell	Maserati 4CL-s/c	1 lap
F lap	R Gerard	ERA R14B-s/c in 2m-07.4s	90.43

✳✳✳ II Grand Prix des Nations (Geneva)

80 laps of 1.846 miles = 147.7 miles.
20 entries – 17 started – 6 finished.

Front row: Pole – G Farina; E deGraffenried; L Chiron. No times available.

02-MAY: Sadly, Ascari was not present, but Farina was added to the teams from Pau. He led from the start, with Bira, the sole British-based entry, chasing, but losing 30 seconds in ten laps. Bira was followed by deGraffenried and Villoresi (Maserati 4CL), who spun wildly and retired soon after. Bira had stopped earlier, so deGraffenried and Sommer were left to follow Farina – who pitted for fuel, losing three minutes – and repassed deGraffenried. Chiron's Talbot was out after just two laps. Finishing just one lap down in an F2 car was a terrific result for Sommer.

1st	G Farina	Maserati 4CLT-s/c in 2m-23s 58.2s	61.55
2nd	E deGraffenried (SP)	Maserati 4CL-s/c	1m-48s
3rd	R Sommer (EI)	Ferrari 166 (F2)	1 lap
F lap	G Farina	Maserati 4CLT-s/c in 1m-44.1s	63.86

✳✳✳ X Grand Prix de Monaco

100 laps of 1.976 miles = 197.6 miles.
21 entries – 19 started – 8 finished.

Front row: G Farina – 1m-53.8s (62.51mph); J-P Wimille (Gordini 11) +3.4s; L Villoresi (Maserati 4CLT) +0.5s.

16-MAY: Alfa Romeo didn't enter, regarding this race as not important enough, so Wimille was free to drive for Simca-Gordini. Wimille, Farina, then Villoresi led the first lap.

However, an amazing 12-second lead for Villoresi evaporated due to gear trouble on lap four. Farina then pulled away from Wimille, who dropped back as Chiron took second place. Though lapped by lap 48, Chiron unlapped himself when Farina refuelled, and was only 35 seconds adrift after over three hours of racing. deGraffenried was challenged hard for third by Maurice Trintignant, who was very good in the Simca-Gordinis.

1st	G Farina	Maserati 4CLT-s/c in 3h-18m-26.9s	59.74
2nd	L Chiron (EF)	Talbot-Lago T26	35.2s
3rd	E deGraffenried (SP)	Maserati 4CL-s/c	2 laps
F lap	G Farina	Maserati 4CLT-s/c in 1m-53.9s	62.45

✳ X British Empire Trophy (Douglas)
36 laps of 3.879 miles = 139.7 miles.
28 entries – 21 started – 8 finished.
Front row: R Gerard (ERA) – 3m-10s (73.49mph); R Parnell (+3s); A Rolt (Alfa Romeo 8C-3400) (+5s).

25-MAY: Travelling twice over the water to the Isle of Man didn't appeal to continental drivers, or maybe it was the title, so this 'International' was just a British affair. Parnell led from Tony Rolt, but was soon passed by Bob Gerard and Bob Ansell. Brooke was third after Gerard's departure, ahead of Geoff Ansell and David Hampshire. Bob Ansell passed Parnell, and held him off for seven laps, but fell away to retire with a broken conrod. Parnell's win surely. No – he ran out of fuel on the last lap – a nice present for Geoff Ansell. As was the rule of those times, Parnell wasn't a classified finisher, having failed to cross the finish line after the race winner, so Cuth Harrison was fourth, a lap down. Leslie Johnson's 'E' type ERA was fifth; a rare finish.

1st	G Ansell	ERA R9B-s/c in 2h-03m-45s	67.69
2nd	D Hampshire	ERA R1A s/c	43s
3rd	L Brooke	ERA R7B-s/c	1m-34s
F lap	R Parnell	Maserati 4CL-s/c in 3m-13s	72.35

✳ II Grand Prix de Paris (Montlhéry)
50 laps of 3.915 miles = 195.8 miles.
28 entries – 23 started – 12 finished.
No grid positions available.

30-MAY: Only French entries here, just as the previous race had been all British. Yves Giraud-Cabantous in the new Talbot T26C led all the way, originally from Chiron and

Louis Rosier. Brake problems delayed Chiron, and Rosier soon dropped out, promoting French champion Eugêne Chaboud to second. Chiron recovered second spot with his newly-adjusted brakes, and the race ran out in procession. A 43 year old beat a 48 year old. Not a young man's game then?

1st	Y Giraud-Gabantous (EF)	Talbot-Lago T26 in 2h-08m-52.2s	91.14
2nd	L Chiron (EF)	Talbot-Lago T26	2m-0s
3rd	E Chaboud (EL)	Delahaye 135S	3 laps
F lap	Y Giraud-Cabantous	Talbot-Lago T26 in 2m-28.8s	94.10

✳✳ III Gran Premio di San Remo (Ospedaletti)
85 laps of 2.10 miles = 178.5 miles.
23 entries – 16 started – 10 finished.
Front row: L Villoresi – 2m-07.4s (59.34mph); A Ascari (+2.2s); G Farina (+2.4s).

27-JUN: Handy for both French and Italian racers, this race introduced a much-revised and lower Maserati, the 4CLT/48, to be driven by the Scuderia Ambrosiana duo of Villoresi, who took pole position easily, and Ascari. It was Ascari, Villoresi and Farina, in an older 4CLT, for some time, until Villoresi's pit stops ended his chase of Ascari. Farina retired and thus gave third to Sommer (F2 Ferrari) who dropped back, handed it to Bira (Maserati 4CL) who, out of fuel at the end, handed it to Bucci.

1st	A Ascari (SA)	Maserati 4CLT/48-s/c in 3h-03m-34s	58.36
2nd	L Villoresi (SA)	Maserati 4CLT/48-s/c	1 lap
3rd	C Bucci (SM)	Maserati 4CL-s/c	2 laps
F lap	L Villoresi	Maserati 4CLT/48-s/c in 2m-02.8s	61.58

✳✳✳ IX Grand Prix d'Europe (Bremgarten Berne)
40 laps of 4.515 miles = 180.6 miles.
28 entries – 20 started – 9 finished.
Front row: J-P Wimille – 2m-42.5s (100.02mph); G Farina (+n/a); L Villoresi (+14.2s).

04-JUL: Alfa Romeo was back for the 'classic' races, so the playing field wasn't so level. Would the new 'San Remo' Maserati provide a challenge? Tragically, pre-war ace Achille Varzi, still a force to be reckoned with, was killed in his Alfa Romeo during practice on a wet track. Wimille led off, with the Maseratis of Farina and Villoresi leading fourth-placed Trossi but, by lap 13, it was Alfas first and second. Tragedy struck again, on lap three, when Kautz died after crashing with deGraffenried and Fagioli. Farina's engine failed on lap 28 to Villoresi's benefit. After the refuelling stops, Wimille had to stop again for water, handing the lead to Trossi, and his chase back very nearly succeeded. Villoresi, however, had defeated fourth-placed Sanesi's Alfa. A major race lasting less than two hours was considered rather short for the time. What a doubly tragic event this had been.

1st	CF Trossi (W)	Alfa Romeo 158-s/c in 1h-59m-17.3s	90.84
2nd	J-P Wimille (W)	Alfa Romeo 158-s/c	0.2s
3rd	L Villoresi (SA)	Maserati 4CLT/48-s/c	2m-37s
F lap	J-P Wimille	Alfa Romeo 158-s/c in 2m-51.0s	95.05

✱✱✱ XXXV Grand Prix de l'ACF (Reims-Gueux)

64 laps of 4.856 miles = 310.8 miles.
25 entries – 19 started – 10 finished.
Front row: J-P Wimille – 2m-35.2s (112.64mph); A Ascari (+9.5s); C Sanesi (+16.0s).
18-JUL: Ascari was loaned to 'the opposition' Alfa team here, replacing an unwell Trossi. A number of pit stops for Wimille for water and tyres gave Ascari the lead on a couple of occasions. Villoresi's brave challenge in his Maserati, third on lap one, went unrewarded, as the pressure caused several pit stops, during one of which Nuvolari took over, and they finished seventh. The Alfas romped home as usual. Ascari slowed significantly, dropping to third behind Sanesi (team orders, probably). Comotti's Talbot was fourth, two laps down, and Wimille won despite his five pit stops! It should be mentioned that Alfa Romeo was the only team entering Works cars at this time – not even Maserati was doing so! Comotti, in fourth, led a trio of Talbots, two laps down. In 11th place on the grid had been an Argentinian in a Simca-Gordini. He retired, unnoticed, after 41 laps.

1st	J-P Wimille (W)	Alfa Romeo 158-s/c in 3h-01m-07.5s	102.95
2nd	C Sanesi (W)	Alfa Romeo 158-s/c	24.5s
3rd	A Ascari (W)	Alfa Romeo 158-s/c	25.0s
F lap	J-P Wimille	Alfa Romeo 158-s/c in 2m-41.2s	108.44s

✱✱ XIV Grand Prix de Comminges

30 laps of 6.838 miles = 205.1 miles.
26 entries – 20 started – 7 finished.
Front row: L Villoresi – 4m-02.3s (101.60mph); 'Raph' (+17.8s); Y Giraud-Cabantous (Talbot 26) (+19.3s).
01-AUG: Disappointing withdrawals, including Farina, Sommer, and Bira, meant a virtual walkover for Luigi

Villoresi, particularly as teammate Ascari (back with Scuderia Ambrosiana), didn't arrive. Many early drop-outs on a wet track included Giraud-Cabantous' Talbot. Rosier, in a new Talbot T26C, plodded his way to fourth, a lap down. Retirements seemed to have been the only source of place changes, in a dull, attritional event. No-one noticed the absence of that Argentinian who had retired at Reims, and who was down to drive a Maserati 4CL. There would probably have been a race if he'd come. His initials: JM F …

1st	L Villoresi (SA)	Maserati 4CLT/48-s/c in 2h-11m-45.5s	93.42
2nd	'Raph' (EMC)	Talbot-Lago T26	4m-30s
3rd	L Chiron (EF)	Talbot-Lago T26	1 lap
F lap	L Villoresi	Maserati 4CLT/48-s/c in 4m-12.8s	97.38

Grote Prijs van Zandvoort

24 lap heats +40 lap final of 2.605 miles = 166.7 total miles.
21 entries – 19 started – 12 finished.
Poles: Heat one – C Harrison (ERA) 2m-03.8s (75.75mph); Heat two – B Bira 2m-00.2s (78.03mph).
07-AUG: Should I include this race? The opening meeting of Zandvoort was British run, and for British licence holders only. Reg Parnell and Bira won the heats, but in the final, Major Tony Rolt, a former Colditz prisoner-of-war, led away, but was soon relegated when Bira overtook first Parnell and then Rolt, and held the lead to the end. Rolt gave great chase, however, and recovered to within a whisker.

Hang on! British drivers only? Well, Bira was a Siamese Prince, but was Eton-educated and had lived in England since 1927 … so there was a slight international touch, then.

1st	B Bira	Maserati 4CL-s/c in 1h-25m-22.2s	73.24
2nd	A Rolt	Alfa Romeo 3.4 litre (de-supercharged)	0.1s
F lap	B Bira	Maserati 4CL-s/c (heat 2) in 1m-53.6s	82.56

✱ X Grand Prix d'Albi

2 x 17 laps of 5.516 miles = 187.3 miles.
25 entries – 23 started – 11 finished.
Front row: L Villoresi 3m-14.2s (102.29mph); P Etancelin (+6.0s); L Brooke (Maserati 4CLT/48) (+7.1s).
29-AUG: No Wimille, Sommer or Ascari, unfortunately. The Albi event was always run as a two-part race, won on aggregate time. These could produce an odd result. Villoresi was the main star and on pole position by six seconds. His Maserati teammate this time being Briton Leslie Brooke. Villoresi duly won both heats. In the first he had plug

problems, though, which meant he had to fight back to retake the lead from Bira. He did this in just eight laps, from tenth place, and won by 30 seconds from Comotti's Talbot and Brooke. The second heat was won by 27 seconds from Chiron's Talbot and Etancelin. 'Phi-phi' Etancelin was fourth and third, yet was second overall. But two sixth places was enough for Rosier to finish third on aggregate! At least the right man won.

1st	L Villoresi (SA)	Maserati 4CLT/48-s/c in 1h-52m-57.9s	99.65
2nd	P Etancelin	Talbot-Lago T26	1m -43s
3rd	L Rosier	Talbot-Lago T26	1 lap
F lap	L Villoresi	Maserati 4CLT/48-s/c in 3m-10.1s	104.45r

✱✱✱ XVIII Gran Premio d'Italia (Torino)
75 laps of 2.983 miles = 223.7 miles.
35 entries – 20 started – 11 finished.
Front row: J-P Wimille – 2m-16.6s (78.61mph); Count Trossi (+1.8s); L Villoresi (+3.4s); R Sommer (+3.8s).

05-SEP: Ferrari enters Formula One. Raymond Sommer, Giuseppe Farina and B Bira drove the first ever F1 team entry. Sommer was on the front row of the grid and even led the Alfas off the line on a very wet track! Wimille soon powered away with Sommer and Villoresi fighting for second place. This battle lasted all race, but Sommer was caught by Wimille and lapped twice, crossing the line 0.6 seconds behind the winner, with Villoresi nearly being caught by Wimille for the second time. Ascari's Maserati had tyre trouble, but he recovered to finish fourth ahead of Parnell's Maserati. Farina had been fourth when he crashed due to a brake grabbing, and Bira was out with transmission failure on lap 66 when well up. Only one of the three Alfas finished (Sanesi crashed and Trossi became unwell). What a great start for Ferrari: a marque only a year old and already threatening Alfa Romeo!

1st	J-P Wimille (W)	Alfa Romeo 158-s/c in 3h-10m-42.4s	70.38
2nd	L Villoresi (SA)	Maserati 4CLT/48-s/c	1 lap
3rd	R Sommer (W)	Ferrari 125 V12 1.5 litre-s/c	2 laps
F lap	J-P Wimille	Alfa Romeo 158-s/c (lap 4) in 2m-22.4s	75.41

✱✱ III British Grand Prix (Silverstone)
65 laps of 3.67 miles = 238.6 miles.
31 entries – 25 started – 12 finished.
Front row: L Chiron – 2m-56.0s (75.07mph); deGraffenried (+1.0s); Etancelin (+2.0s); Gerard (+2.2s); Johnson (+2.6s).

02-OCT: Britain was in business. The Alfas wanted £2500 to race (no deal), but the best of the rest arrived. The grid was 5-4-5-4, so no fewer than nine cars had a clear way ahead at the start! Chiron's Talbot led from pole position, while Ascari and Villoresi started from the back due to late arrival; a Maserati habit! Just three laps later, though, they were one/two! Johnson's 'E' type ERA started from the outside of the front row, but hit a marker barrel, breaking a driveshaft and splitting the fuel tank. Villoresi was faster on track and in the pits, but let Ascari close towards the end. Chiron retired with gearbox trouble. Gerard's ERA passed Rosier's Talbot on lap 55 despite losing over a minute at pit stops. His being just two minutes behind after over three hours was amazing. Was there ever a better ERA pilot than Bob Gerard when at one with his car?

1st	L Villoresi (SA)	Maserati 4CLT/48-s/c in 3h-18m-03.0s	72.28
2nd	A Ascari (SA)	Maserati 4CLT/48-s/c	4.0s
3rd	R Gerard	ERA R14B	2m-03s
F lap	L Villoresi	Maserati 4CLT/48-s/c in 2m-52.0s	76.81

✱ IV Grand Prix du Salon (Montlhéry)
48 laps of 3.905 miles = 187.4 miles.
35 entries – 25 started – 10 finished.
Front row: L Johnson (ERA); L Rosier;'Levegh'; Bira no times available.

10-OCT: Jean-Pierre Wimille wanted to enter this race but Alfa Romeo didn't, so, being without Sommer as well, this race lost some importance. Louis Rosier realised his chances were better because of this, and drove more determinedly than usual. This paid off with a flag-to-flag win. Bira's early challenge in his new Maserati faded due to tyre failure, and Reg Parnell's similar new 'San Remo' Maserati never featured, coming home eighth – six laps down. Leslie Johnson's new 'E' type ERA (on pole) stopped on lap three with its fuel tank split again – a legacy of Silverstone? After Bira's demise, Rosier was never threatened.

1st	L Rosier	Talbot-Lago T26C in 2h-03m-52.9s	90.76
2nd	'Levegh'	Talbot-Lago T26C	1m-16s
3rd	Y Giraud-Cabantous	Talbot-Lago T26	2 laps
F lap	B Bira	Maserati 4CLT/48-s/c in 2m-25.9s	96.34r

✱✱✱ 1mo Gran Premio dell'Autodromo di Monza
80 laps of 3.915 miles = 313.2 miles.
30 entries – 20 started – 11 finished.

Front row: J-P Wimille – 1m-59.6s (117.83mph); P Taruffi (+4.0s); Trossi (+4.0s); Sanesi (+4.0s).

17-OCT: The Italian GP had already been run but Monza was back in action so the thinking was 'we'd better have a Grand Prix to celebrate.' All teams were out in force, with Piero Taruffi added to the Alfa Romeo squad. The four-car front row for Alfa looked ominous, but Sommer's Ferrari chased Wimille from the start. Sadly, though, after only seven laps an asthma attack forced him out! After fuel stops Villoresi (Maserati) and Farina (Ferrari) led Taruffi's Alfa for fourth place, but were eliminated on laps 48 and 53 respectively, both with transmission trouble. So again Wimille dominated his teammates in an Alfa Romeo 'full-house' finish.

1st	J-P Wimille (W)	Alfa Romeo 158-s/c in 2h-50m-44.4s	110.05
2nd	CF Trossi (W)	Alfa Romeo 158-s/c	42.6s
3rd	C Sanesi (W)	Alfa Romeo 158-s/c	1m-40s
F lap	C Sanesi	Alfa Romeo 158-s/c in 2m-00.4s	117.05

✳✳ IX Gran Premio do Peňa Rhin (Montjuic Parc)

70 laps of 2.77 miles = 193.9 miles.
29 entries – 22 started – 10 finished.

Front row: L Villoresi; B Bira (Ferrari 125GP); G Farina (Ferrari 125GP); A Ascari (Maserati 4CLT/48).

31-OCT: No Alfa Romeos meant a level playing field, but all the others were there. Scuderia Ferrari had Bira to accompany Farina this time*. A great scrap involved Villoresi and the Ferraris of Bira and Farina, and Bira led on lap 12. So, this was the first time a Ferrari had led a designated F1 race* and the driver was B Bira. How's that for a quiz question? Parnell was pretty close behind, though. This order continued after the fuel stops until both Farina and, ten laps later, Bira retired. So Parnell claimed a worthy second. A tremendous race, proving that Alfas were not essential for racing excitement.

* Farina's Ferrari 125GP had won at Garda a week earlier, but it was not an F1 race, and had mostly F2 and sports cars to beat.

1st	L Villoresi (SA)	Maserati 4CLT/48-s/c in 2h-10m-12s	89.44
2nd	R Parnell	Maserati 4CLT/48-s/c	28s
3rd	L Chiron (EF)	Talbot-Lago T26C	3m-14s
F lap	L Villoresi	Maserati 4CLT/48-s/c in 1m-46s	94.16

A look back at 1948

Ferrari had arrived on the scene with a V12 supercharged car, and was a force to be reckoned with from day one. Maserati produced the 4CLT/48 model, which became known as the 'San Remo' mid-season, but, despite quality pilots, neither Ferrari nor Maserati could provide a concerted challenge to the supreme Alfa Romeo 158-s/c ... when they turned up, that is (this they did only four times, possibly due to financial pressures). The 4.5-litre Lago-Talbot T26C had the crumbs left by the supercharged cars – sometimes a lot of them. Ferrari named his cars according to the size of their cylinders – hence the 125 V12 would be 1500cc. All his cars were V12s until 1952. He continued this nomenclature until the mid-1950s.

Alberto Ascari had joined the 'big names' in a very short time, with a little help from his friend and mentor Luigi Villoresi. Drivers at that time would also race in F2 and sports-car races, sometimes on the same race card as the F1 race – and sometimes for weeks in a row. Do modern Grand Prix drivers seem like part-timers? Well they weren't encumbered then with the modern arduous task of corporate appearances, and I've no doubt the twenty-first century driver would rather race than be just a 'professional smiler.'

Teams new to finishing on the podium during 1948 were:
Ecurie Lutetia (EL), a stable formed by Charles Pozzi and Eugene Chaboud
Ecurie Inter, which seems to have run F2 Ferraris
Ecurie Mundia-Course (EMC), a name change of Ecurie Naphtra Course

Winners of the 17 graded F1 races of 1948 – quantity & quality of success

4 wins	L Villoresi (3B, 1C)	9 wins	Maserati (3A, 4B, C, D)
3 wins	J-P Wimille (3A)	4 wins:	Alfa Romeo (4A)
2 wins	G Farina (2A)	2 wins	ERA (2C)
1 win	C Trossi (A) N Pagani (A) A Ascari (B) B Gerard (C) L Rosier (C) G Ansell (C) Y G-Cabantous (C) B Bira (D)		Talbot-Lago (2C)

A retro champion?

The 1950 World Drivers' Championship had only six rounds, and a look at the six best supported events of 1948 shows that Jean-Pierre Wimille won three and was second once. A 1950-style Championship would almost certainly have yielded him the title.

Chapter 8

1949
A level playing field now?

Alfa Romeo was in a very unfortunate situation in that it had lost two of its main drivers: Achille Varzi at Bremgarten the previous year; and Trossi through cancer. The announcement, late in 1948, that Alfa Romeo would not be competing the following season was perhaps not surprising, as it had nothing to prove, but it was still greeted with disappointment: the great sights and sounds were lost, as was the benchmark for performance. How would anyone know whether the cars of 1949 were capable of, at last, challenging or even beating the 158s?

Ferrari had appeared late in 1948 with the '125', a 12-cylinder supercharged car; would this be the new benchmark? A new marque, but Enzo Ferrari was hugely respected when it came to running a racing team, and he wouldn't be there just to make up the numbers. Talbot-Lago T26Cs could perhaps challenge now that refuelling was essential for the others, and some Maseratis would be using two-stage supercharging – not frugal in the fuel department. However, Alfa's supreme driver Jean-Pierre Wimille would now be competing on a more level field, although he had already proved that he could win in cars other than Alfa Romeos, so the personal challenge to beat him would still be great. That was the view at the end of 1948, anticipating a good 1949.

Then, catastrophically, Wimille died during practice for his first race of 1949, in the Argentine Temporada. So, with the top driver gone the doors were open for fresh talent to shine. Would new talent emerge as Ascari had done in 1948? If anyone was to take over the role of supremo vacated by Wimille's sad death the results suggested it would surely be Raymond Sommer, with Alberto Ascari an outsider. A couple of drivers (Benedicto Campos and Juan-Manuel Fangio) had arrived from Argentina with government support, having performed well in the 'Temporada.' They were new

to Europe, though, so little was expected of them on these unfamiliar circuits ...

The Grand Prix driver's diary of single-seater racing for 1949

30th January	F1 – Gran Premio del Gen Perón y Buenos Aires (Ag) – 105.7 miles
6th February	F1 – Gran Premio de Eva Duarte Perón at Buenos Aires (Ag) – 90.6 miles
13th February	F1 – Copa Accion de San Lorenzo at Rosario (Ag) – 87.4 miles
27th February	F1 – Gran Premio del Gen Martin at Mar del Plata (Ag) – 82.7 miles
20th March	F1 – Gran Premio de Interlagos at São Paulo (Bz) – 74.2 miles
27th March	F1 – Gran Premio da Rio de Janeiro at Gavea (Bz) – 101 miles
3rd April	F1 – Gran Premio di San Remo (I) – 189 miles
18th April	F1 – Grand Prix de Pau (F) – 188.7 miles
18th April	F1 – Richmond Trophy at Goodwood (UK) – 23.8 miles*
24th April	F1 – Grand Prix de Paris at Montlhéry (F) – 194.7 miles
28th April	F1 – Jersey Road Race (UK) – 176 miles
7th May	F1 – Grand Prix de Rousillon (F) – 157.6 miles
14th May	F1 – British Grand Prix at Silverstone (UK) – 300 miles
22nd May	F1 – Grand Prix de Marseille (F) – 123 miles
26th May	F1 – British Empire Trophy at Douglas (IoM) – 139.6 miles

2nd June	F2 – Gran Premio di Roma (I) – 160 miles
5th June	F1 – Grand Prix des Frontiéres at Chimay (B) – 108.1 miles
12th June	F2 – Gran Premio di Bari (I) – 265 miles
19th June	F1 – Grand Prix de Belgique at Spa Francorchamps (B) – 315.2 miles
26th June	F2 – Gran Premio dell Autodromo di Monza (I) – 313 miles
3rd July	F1 – Grosse Preis der Schweiz at Bremgarten (S) – 180.6 miles
10th July	F1 – Grand Prix d'Albi (F) – 215.1 miles
10th July	F2 – Circuito di Garda (I) – 183 miles
17th July	F1 – Grand Prix de France at Reims-Gueux (F) – 310.8 miles
17th July	F2 – Coupe de Petites Cylindrees at Reims-Gueux (F) – 126 miles
31st July	F1 – Grote Prijs van Nederland at Zandvoort (N) – 169.3 miles
20th August	F1 – *Daily Express* International Trophy at Silverstone (UK) – 150 miles
27th August	F1 – Grand Prix de Lausanne (F) – 181.3 miles
11th September	F1 – Gran Premio d'Italia at Monza (I) – 313.2 miles
17th September	F1 – Goodwood Trophy at Goodwood (UK) – 238 miles*
25th September	F1 – Grand Prix de Czechoslovakia at Brno (C) – 221.3 miles
9th October	F1 – Grand Prix du Salon at Montlhéry (F) – 249.9 miles

32 events of total race mileage = 5520 miles – 5213 max due to simultaneous races.

All the F2 races listed involved F1 stars.

*See Appendix A for these ungraded race results.

An early start – The Argentine 'Temporada'

Just before Christmas 1948, a ship containing ten of the latest F1 cars, to be driven by the cream of European racers and the best that South America could muster, left Italy for Argentina. The races were nominally Formule Libre, but the Europeans all took F1 cars, though Farina's car had a 2-litre engine. Considering the F1 representation that was there, and in the interest of recording as far as possible all races between the best F1 drivers in F1 cars, I have decided to include this series in the F1 pre-championship list, and include the results in the drivers' 'Real Score' records.

✳✳ Gran Premio del General Juan Perón y de la Ciudad Buenos Aires

35 laps of 3.02 miles = 105.7 miles.
25 entries – 20 started – 8 finished.

Front row: A Ascari – 2m-36.8s (69.36mph); L Villoresi +0.5s; J-M Fangio +1.0s. All Maserati 4CLTs.

30-JAN: What a title! Run in Parco Palermo, a huge blow was dealt to motor racing in practice with the death of Jean-Pierre Wimille in his Works Simca-Gordini. The cause seems uncertain, but swerving to avoid a spectator was well reported and resulted in his hitting a tree. Juan-Manuel Fangio, who would eventually take up the mantle of 'The greatest of his time,' was alongside Ascari and Villoresi on the grid. Ascari dominated from the start, while Fangio challenged Villoresi for second, but a tyre change dropped him to fourth overall behind Galvez in his Formule Libre 3.8s/c Alfa-Romeo.

1st	A Ascari (W)	Maserati 4CLT/48-1.5s/c in 1h-30m-23.1s	70.23
2nd	L Villoresi (W)	Maserati 4CLT/48-1.5s/c	41.0s
3rd	O Galvez	Alfa Romeo 308 3.8s/c	2m-32s
F lap	Ascari/Villoresi	Maserati 4CLT/48-1.5s/c in 2m-32.4s	71.36

✳✳ Gran Premio de Eva Duarte Perón

30 laps of 3.02 miles = 90.6 miles.
10 started – 5 finished.

Front row: L Villoresi – 2m-30.2s (72.45mph); J-M Fangio (+2.8s); A Ascari (+3.1s); B Bira. All Maserati 4CLTs.

06-FEB: The race was also dedicated to Wimille. This second race was run on the same track as the previous week, but in bad weather and shortened from 35 laps. Villoresi led away but retired on lap 11, and Farina crashed the Works Ferrari. Ascari took the lead, but, on lap 25, a broken exhaust threatened to cause a fire so he stopped. Fangio now led but side-swiped a tree (resulting in only paint damage to the car) but the delay gave the race to Galvez. Despite that, it seems Fangio had been at least two laps ahead of the other F1 runners. He was still unheard of in Europe, but now this new star had shown his potential. Was this his first Formula One win? I think so.

1st o/all	O Galvez	Alfa Romeo 308 3.8s/c in 1h-31m-04s	59.75
1st (F1)	J-M Fangio	Maserati 4CLT/48-1.5s/c	2 laps
2nd (F1)	E Cantoni	Maserati 4CL-1.5s/c	3 laps
3rd (F1)	A Malusardi	Maserati 4CLT	3 laps
F lap	L Villoresi (W)	Maserati 4CLT/48-1.5s/c in 2m-50.7s	63.75

✳✳ Copa Accion de San Lorenzo (Rosario)

50 laps of 1.748 miles = 87.4 miles. 12 started – 7 finished.

Front row: L Villoresi – 1m-42s (61.6 mph); G Farina; A Ascari.
13-FEB: Farina's Works Ferrari was repaired. Villoresi was clearly the master of qualifying, though the term was not used then. This was another very wet race, so Reg Parnell must have felt at home, and his result reflects that. Villoresi managed only fourth place here, a lap down. Fangio was driving a works Simca-Gordini, which, perhaps, better suited the tight track. However, a first lap crash put him out. Galvez was seventh behind Campos (Ag) and Cantoni (Uruguay).

1st	G Farina (W)	Ferrari 125F1-2.0s/c in 1h-48m-18.8s	48.34
2nd	R Parnell	Maserati 4CLT/48-1.5s/c	31.4s
3rd	A Ascari (W)	Maserati 4CLT/48-1.5s/c	1m-51s
F lap	L Villoresi (W)	Maserati 4CLT/48-1.5s/c in 2m-02s	51.60

✳ Gran Premio del Generale Martin (Mar del Plata)
35 laps – 2.514 miles = 82.7 miles.
11 started – 7 finished.
Front row: L Villoresi – 2m-07.2s (71.14 mph); J-M Fangio +3.2s; G Farina (Ferrari 125) +3.3s.
27-FEB: Villoresi, Fangio, Farina, Ascari was the order on the front row. Fangio, unknown outside South America, was now amongst the cream of European racers. Race progress has proved very difficult to find but we do know that Farina retired on lap eight (oil pump), Villoresi on lap 25 (bearings), and Ascari soon after on lap 27 (engine). Reg Parnell retired with fuel problems. So here begins a famous winning streak.

1st	J-M Fangio	Maserati 4CLT/48-1.5s/c in 1h-16m-31.3s	68.67
2nd	B Bira	Maserati 4CLT/48-1.5s/c	1 lap
3rd	O Galvez	Alfa Romeo 308 3.8s/c	1 lap
F lap	L Villoresi (W)	Maserati 4CLT/48-1.5s/c in 2m-05.1s	72.33

✳ Gran Premio de Interlagos (São Paulo)
15 laps of 4.948 miles = 74.2 miles.
5 finished. No grid positions available.
20-MAR: Three weeks had passed and the Europeans had repaired their cars. Farina, driving a Ferrari 125C, crashed on lap three, but Villoresi beat the locals on the twisty, cobbled street circuit. Ascari finished fourth. So the visitors did better than at Mar del Plata, but still reliability was a problem. Francisco Marques was the discovery in Brazil, replacing the threat from Fangio who remained in Argentina.

1st	L Villoresi	Maserati 4CLT/48-1.5s/c in 1h-20m-30.9s	54.24
2nd	F Marques	Maserati 4CL-1.5s/c	2m-20s
3rd	A Fernandez	Maserati 4CLT/48-1.5s/c	2m-21s

✳ Gran Premio da Ciudad de Rio de Janeiro (Gavea)
15 laps of 6.73 miles = 101 miles.
14 entries – 10 started – 6 finished. No grid positions available.
27-MAR: Ascari was forced off the road by a local driver on lap three. He ended up in a field, hit a tree, flew out of the car and broke a collar bone and some ribs. He returned home late and missed the start of the European season. Francisco (Chico) Landi set fastest lap on lap seven before crashing, so would he also have made his mark with the visitors? They would find out later when he went to Europe.

1st	L Villoresi (W)	Maserati 4CLT/48-1.5s/c in 1h-57m-07.6s	51.45
2nd	G Farina (W)	Ferrari 125F1-2.0s/c	42.0s
3rd	F Marques	Maserati 4CL-1.5s/c	6m 1s
F lap	F Landi	Maserati 4CLT/48-1.5s/c	

Local driver Oscar Galvez drove the only non-F1 based car to finish amongst the F1 brigade, but his performances must be excluded from F1 records as his supercharged car used a 3800cc engine – more than double the F1 limit. However, it dated from 1938, so we must appreciate that the result does reflect Galvez's likely ability. The Alfa Romeo Works hadn't entered, and now, with the loss of superstar Jean-Pierre Wimille at Buenos Aires, and Achille Varzi the previous year, as well as Count Trossi being terminally ill, Alfa decide to give 1949 a miss. This series showed that Argentina possessed a secret weapon that would soon be unleashed on the Europeans with devastating effect. So very sad that he never raced against Wimille.

✳✳✳ IV Gran Premio di San Remo (Ospedaletti)
2 x 45 laps of 2.100 miles = 189 miles.
27 entries – 22 started – 9 finished.
Front row: B Bira – 2m-00.6s (62.69mph); J-M Fangio +0.2s; R Sommer (Ferrari 125) +0.6s.
03-APR: Who is this guy Fangio? Apparently he'd done well in the Temporada series in his homeland a few months earlier, when some of the best Europeans had gone there. Unknown in Europe, here he was on the front row of the grid between Sommer and Bira. The entry was first class, but Fangio led off, pulling away steadily, with Bira over 30 seconds behind at the end of the first half of the race. The second half was a repeat. Race average almost matched pole speed. However, Bira had set the fastest lap over four seconds better than pole,

and a 59-second deficit in a race of over three hours is not a massive margin – just half of one per cent. Bira was reckoned to be quite a cautious driver who knew his limits, so could he have challenged stronger? Well Fangio's maxim of 'win at the slowest possible speed' may have been in action here. His legend began here ... not in 1950.

1st	J-M Fangio (ACA)	Maserati 4CLT/48-s/c in 3h-01m-28.6s	62.49
2nd	B Bira (SA)	Maserati 4CLT/48-s/c	59s
3rd	E deGraffenried (SP)	Maserati 4CLT/48-s/c	1 lap
F lap	B Bira	Maserati 4CLT/48-s/c in 1m-56.0s	65.18r

✳✳ X Grand Prix de Pau
110 laps of 1.715 miles = 188.7 miles.
15 entries and starters – 7 finished.
Front row: J-M Fangio – 1m-47.5s (57.43mph);
E deGraffenried +1.1s; B Campos +1.8s.

18-APR: Now Fangio was on pole position by over a second against opposition almost as good as at San Remo. His compatriot Benedicto Campos was also at the front, with deGraffenried between them. After two laps the order was Fangio, deGraffenried, Chiron, Pagani and Campos. By lap ten three Talbots and Chaboud's Maserati had failed. The first fuel stops saw Fangio behind deGraffenried for a couple of laps and at the same time Rosier handed over his Talbot to Chaboud. His feet were being burned in the cockpit (had he told Chaboud?). Fangio drew well ahead and took a second precautionary fuel stop, confident of soon recovering his lead. deGraffenried promptly took the lead 20 laps from the end and Fangio promptly took it back again. Pagani's Maserati retired on lap 46 and gave Campos third. These Argentinians were to be taken seriously. Fangio was almost 38 – surely at his peak? The Rosier/Chaboud Talbot retired from a very good fourth, very near the end and only a lap down. A question: Has anyone else ever changed marque during a Formula One race as Chaboud had? Friendlier days ...

1st	J-M Fangio (ACA)	Maserati 4CLT/48-s/c in 3h-36m-11.9s	52.35
2nd	E deGraffenried (SP)	Maserati 4CLT/48-s/c	16.8s
3rd	B Campos (ACA)	Maserati 4CLT/48-s/c	1 lap
F lap	J-M Fangio	Maserati 4CLT/48-s/c in 1m-49.0s	56.64r

✳ III Grand Prix de Paris (Montlhéry)
50 laps of 3.914 miles = 195.7 miles.

19 entries – 14 started – 6 finished. No grid positions available.

24-APR: There was an almost entirely French entry for this race, with the addition of Britons Roy Salvadori and Lance Macklin in elderly Maseratis. The shortage of star Maserati drivers gave a golden opportunity for the, now sorted, Talbot-Lagos to 'make hay.' At first Guy Mairesse led from Etancelin, Rosier, Grignard and 'Levegh' – all Talbots – but Etancelin led from lap two to the end. Pierre 'Levegh' (Talbot-Lago), looked like getting second place until engine problems dropped him back, and then Rosier stopped on lap 15. The Simca-Gordinis, unfortunately, disappointed, with Trintignant out by lap six and Manzon on lap 18. These guys were getting on a bit – Etancelin 52 and the 'two Gs' both mid-40s. At 32, Johnny Claes was the youngster.

1st	P Etancelin	Talbot-Lago T26C in 2h-05m-31.8s	93.55
2nd	Grignard/Girard-Cabous	Talbot-Lago T26C	2m-07s
3rd	J Claes (ENB)	Talbot-Lago T26C	4 laps
F lap	L Rosier	Talbot-Lago T26C in 2m-24.8s	97.33r

✳✳ III JCC Jersey Road Race
55 laps of 3.20 miles = 176 miles.
28 entries – 19 started – 12 finished.
Front row: L Villoresi – 2m-00.0s (96.00mph); B Bira +2.4s;
L Chiron (Talbot 26C) +3.6s.

28-APR: Surprisingly, only Chiron, Villoresi and deGraffenried represented Europe. Bira (Maserati 4CLT/48) led after one lap of this wet race but Villoresi was soon past. He pitted for plugs on lap seven but ignition problems meant he finished only sixth. Bira led easily now but even in the rain he was guzzling fuel, and a long fuel stop dropped him to third, which he then lost to Mays. The charging Gerard and deGraffenried were grateful. A great wet drive by Bob Gerard! This race was an ERA/Maserati battle won by the older British car – and by some margin. Gerard and the R14B was a formidable racing partnership.

1st	R Gerard	ERA 'R14B'-s/c in 2h-16m-58.6s	77.10
2nd	E deGraffenried	Maserati 4CLT/48-s/c	1m-40s
3rd	R Mays	ERA 'R4D'-s/c	2m-27s
F lap	L Villoresi (SA)	Maserati 4CLT/48-s/c in 2m-08.1s	89.93

✳✳✳ IV Grand Prix de Roussillon
2 x 50 laps of 1.576 miles = 157.6 miles.
12 entries – 11 started – 9 finished.
Front row: B Bira – 1m-27.9s (64.55mph); J-M Fangio +1.3s.

Row two: L Villoresi +1.6s; B Campos n/a.

07-MAY: A small but top quality entry for this two-part race. In the first heat Fangio took off from second grid slot, and was soon joined in battle by Villoresi. Bira gave chase when Villoresi had problems but was 25 seconds behind at the end, with Campos third. In the second heat Bira took off like a bat out of hell, and he and Fangio had a terrific scrap. Fangio got past on lap 12, but Bira was in rare aggressive mood and led again two laps later. Fangio didn't need to win this part, though, and possibly risk retirement, so followed Bira home. Villoresi was third, but beaten by Campos on aggregate time. Fangio now had three starts and three wins.

1st	J-M Fangio (ACA)	Maserati 4CLT/48-s/c in 2h-33m-16.7s	61.69
2nd	B Bira	Maserati 4CLT/48-s/c	24.6s
3rd	B Campos (ACA)	Maserati 4CLT/48-s/c	2 laps
F lap	J-M Fangio	Maserati 4CLT/48-s/c in 1m-27.9s	64.55r

✲✲ IV British Grand Prix (Silverstone)
100 laps of 3.00 miles = 300 miles.
29 entries – 25 started – 11 finished.
Front row: L Villoresi – 2m-09.8s (83.20mph); Bira +0.4s; Walker (ERA) +3.4s; deGraffenried +3.8s; Gerard +4.6s.

14-MAY: This time the track used the perimeter road with a very slow chicane at Club Corner into the mouth of a runway. This was now an important race, with good European entries. Gerard was fast away, but Villoresi's Maserati led after two laps. A long fuel stop, then oil shortage put him out. Bira was now marching ahead, till a slide meant fouling of a marker barrel and the end of his race. Reg Parnell's new lead was halted by axle trouble. deGraffenried's victory proved that adage: 'to finish first, first you must finish.' Taking fourth sharing David Hampshire's ERA, just a lap down, was bandleader Billy Cotton – hugely famous in showbiz. This race, at almost four hours (in the dry), was the longest non-stop F1 race ever ... wet or dry!

1st	E deGraffenried	Maserati 4CLT/48-s/c in 3h-52m-50.2s	77.31
2nd	R Gerard	ERA 'R14B'-s/c	1m-05s
3rd	L Rosier	Talbot-Lago T26C	1 lap
F lap	B Bira	Maserati 4CLT/48-s/c in 2m-10.4s	82.82

✲ III Grand Prix de Marseille
25 laps + 50-lap final of 1.64 miles = 123 miles.
32 entries – 28 started – 8 finished.
Poles – Heat one: J-M Fangio – 1m-35.1s (62.10mph). Heat two: M Trintignant – 1m-35.1s (62.10mph).

22-MAY: Should this race be included, as it was for unsupercharged cars only (meaning only F1 Talbots and Delahayes v F2 cars)? I believe that the driver entry justifies inclusion. Fangio unveiled a wraparound screen on race day, to the surprise of the others. This helped him to beat the 4.5-litre Talbot-Lagos in a 1430cc de-supercharged F1 Gordini (therefore an F2 car). He finished second in the first heat, 1.5 seconds behind Etancelin. The second heat was won by compatriot Benedicto Campos in his Gordini, by a whisker from Trintignant. In the final, Fangio pulled away to win easily. His fastest lap was much quicker than pole. This was now an astonishing four wins from four starts. No-one had ever started a season like that before.

1st	J-M Fangio (SAV)	Simca-Gordini T15 (F2) in 1h-18m-33.0s	62.65
2nd	P Etancelin	Talbot-Lago T26C	18.6s
3rd	M Trintignant (W)	Simca-Gordini T15	35.5s
F lap	J-M Fangio	Simca-Gordini T15 in 1m-32.2s	64.05

✲ XI British Empire Trophy (Douglas-Isle of Man)
36 laps of 3.88 miles = 139.7 miles.
25 entries – 16 started – 13 finished.
Front row: R Parnell – 3m-06s (75.10mph); P Walker +3s.
Row two: R Gerard +8s; St J Horsfall +9s.

26-MAY: Of the foreign entries, which included Villoresi, only Claes' Talbot arrived, and only a few good F1 cars were there. However, the best drivers now all had strong international reputations. Parnell flew at the start with a lead of six seconds after one lap, and doubled it on lap two. Was it all over? No, he was out after two more laps with a broken supercharger – and right by a pub! Maserati unreliability was almost legendary now, so maybe Parnell should have borne this in mind. Ashmore took over, ahead of Gerard and Walker's ERA, but a stop for fuel and oil gave the lead to the shrewd Bob Gerard. Ashmore hit a kerb in his chase of Gerard, and stopped for a new wheel, putting him in third place, behind St John Horsfall, but ahead of Peter Walker who'd dropped back. His spirited chase to recover second place only just failed. Gerard's fastest lap against the rather-more-recent (by ten years) Maseratis of Parnell and Ashmore says everything about this British 'unsung hero.'

1st	R Gerard	ERA 'R14B'-s/c in 1h-57m-56s	71.06
2nd	St J Horsfall	ERA 'R5B'-s/c	1m-27s
3rd	F Ashmore (SA)	Maserati 4CLT/48-s/c	1m-31s
F lap	R Gerard	ERA 'R14B'-s/c in 3m-09s	73.90r

XIX Grand Prix des Frontiéres (Chimay)
15 laps of 6.754 miles = 108.1 miles.
15 entries – 8 started – 5 finished.
Front row: G Mairesse; C Pozzi. Row two: P Meyrat; J Claes (all Talbot-Lago).
05-JUN: An established event yet a poor entry and few starters makes this an unworthy event to stand comparison with others. Only Macklin came across The Channel. Mairesse won easily, but behind him Claes was chasing, after an appalling start, and passed Macklin on the penultimate lap. He then overshot the first corner and fell back to fourth. Pierre Meyrat thought Johnny Claes was out and eased up. Bad judgement, as he was beaten to third on the line by 0.4 seconds. Pozzi's Talbot lasted just six laps.

1st	G Mairesse (EF)	Talbot-Lago T26C in 1h-10m-10.0s	86.63
2nd	L Macklin	Maserati 4CM-s/c	3m-27s
F lap	G Mairesse	Talbot-Lago T26C in 4m-32.0s	89.39

✱✱✱ XI Grand Prix de Belgique (Spa)
35 laps of 9.006 miles = 315.2 miles.
14 entries and starters – 7 finished.
Front row: L Villoresi (Ferrari 125); J-M Fangio (Maserati); P Etancelin (Talbot 26C). No times available.
19-JUN: This classic was an invitation-only event, and at last Ascari returned to the fray, having recovered from his injuries in Brazil, so he and Fangio finally met. Fangio's Maserati engine failed on the second lap, leaving Farina and Villoresi swapping the lead. Farina went off at La Source on lap seven, giving second place to Ascari. Ferraris led 1-2, but they needed new tyres (and fuel), Ascari losing a lot more time than Villoresi. So, Etancelin now led until Villoresi passed on lap 14, but then the Talbot retired with gearbox trouble. Ferrari refuelling stops then handed an easy victory to the non-stopping Louis Rosier. This race was a real pointer to the future, and Ferrari took note! Ferrari was surely better than Talbot at un-supercharged engine technology ...

1st	L Rosier (W)	Talbot-Lago T26C in 3h-15m-17.7s	96.95
2nd	L Villoresi (W)	Ferrari 125-s/c	49.1s
3rd	A Ascari (W)	Ferrari 125-s/c	4m-11s
F lap	G Farina	Maserati 4CLT/48-s/c in 5m-19.0s	101.64

✱✱✱ Grosser Preis der Schweiz (Bremgarten Berne)
40 laps of 4.515 miles = 180.6 miles.

25 entries – 20 started – 17 finished.
Front row: G Farina – 2m-50.4s (95.40mph); B Bira (Maserati) +2.8s; A Ascari +4.3s.
03-JUL: Finances made Fangio miss this race. It was Ascari, Bira, Villoresi and Farina at first, but Farina was challenging Ascari by lap seven, but soon Farina's oil loss left him and his car fuming. The Ferraris then took command, Ascari heading Villoresi's long-range-tanked Ferrari and Bira's Maserati. Ascari re-caught Villoresi after refuelling, with some plainly superior driving, but Villoresi still had to stop on lap 34 despite his big tanks. Bira's fuel stop dropped him to fifth, where he finished. The non-stopping Talbot-Lagos nearly made second and fourth (Etancelin). More fuel for the un-supercharged, less-fuel cause?

1st	A Ascari (W)	Ferrari 125-s/c in 1h-59m-24.6s	90.76
2nd	L Villoresi (W)	Ferrari 125-s/c	56.6s
3rd	R Sommer	Talbot-Lago T26C	1m-07s
F lap	G Farina	Maserati 4CLT/48-s/c in 2m-52,2s	94.39

✱✱ XI Grand Prix d'Albi
5-lap heat +34 lap final of 5.516 miles = 215.1 total miles.
22 entries – 16 started – 9 finished.
Front row: J-M Fangio – 3m-11.9s (103.30mph); B Bira +4.4s; G Farina (Maserati) +5.4s.
10-JUL: Ferrari entries for Ascari and Villoresi were withdrawn, sadly, reducing the status of the event. A single five-lap qualifying heat decided the grid for the final, and Fangio blitzed everyone so pole position was his. Bira had retired in the short heat, but Fangio loaned him a manifold to allow him to start from the back, though they were in different teams (Ah, what different times!). There was no real opposition for Fangio once Farina's car failed to start after its refuelling stop. Bira swiped a straw bale near the end, but restarted without losing his second place – from starting at the back! This time, the non-stopping Talbot-Lagos were unable to challenge. Fangio's Argentinian team had funds left for just one more race.

1st	J-M Fangio (ACA)	Maserati 4CLT/48-s/c in 1h-54m-30.6s	98.27
2nd	B Bira (SP)	Maserati 4CLT/48-s/c	2m-47s
3rd	L Rosier	Talbot-Lago T26C	1 lap
F lap	J-M Fangio	Maserati 4CLT/48-s/c in 3m-14.4s	102.17

✱✱✱ V Grand Prix de France (Reims-Gueux)
64 laps of 4.856 miles – 310.8 miles.

20 entries – 17 started – 6 finished.
Front row: L Villoresi (Ferrari 125) – 2m-42.0s (107.91mph);
J-M.Fangio (Maserati); L Rosier (Talbot 26C).

17-JUL: The senior annual F1 race in France was usually titled 'GP de l'ACF' but the Auto Club de France had used this for a sports car race this year, so the 'lesser' title was given here. After regrinding a valve seat himself overnight Fangio took his place in the centre of the front row. Villoresi's lone Works Ferrari soon passed Campos to lead Fangio who, with compatriot Campos, then soon relegated the Ferrari to third. A seized brake soon put Villoresi out, so Fangio and Campos led from Bira. Both Argentinians shared the lead, but by halfway had retired so Bira now led from Chiron and Whitehead, but, unlike Talbot-Lagos, the Maseratis and Ferrari's had to refuel. On lap 56 Whitehead passed Chiron to lead, but his gearbox stuck in fourth so the newcomer failed to win a just victory. The Argentinians went home – Fangio having won 5 out of 7 races!

1st	L Chiron (EF)	Talbot-Lago T26C in 3h-06m-33.7s	99.96
2nd	B Bira (SP)	Maserati 4CLT/48-s/c	17.6s
3rd	P Whitehead	Ferrari 125-s/c	48.5s
F lap	P Whitehead	Ferrari 125-s/c in 2m-46.2s	105.18

✱✱✱ II Grote Prijs van Zandvoort

25-lap heat + 40-lap final of 2.605 miles = 169.3 total miles. 20 entries – 16 started – 10 finished.
Poles: Heat one: G Farina (Maserati) – 1m-51.8s (81.70mph).
Heat two: A Ascari (Ferrari 125) – 1m-55.0s (81.55mph).

31-JUL: Fangio had left for home, so this was Britain versus Europe in the driver stakes. Villoresi and Ascari drove Works Ferraris. Villoresi and Parnell won the eight-car heats. All heat finishers started in the final. Farina and Parnell jumped the start – penalty 1min – which spoilt the race somewhat. Villoresi and Ascari Ferraris overtook the impatient Maseratis soon, allowing themselves the luxury of swapping the lead in a Ferrari 1-2 until six laps from home when Ascari's car shed a front wheel – fortunately without injury. Bira then lost third on the road to deGraffenried with a failing engine, but this became second when Farina's penalty dropped him from second to fourth. Parnell's penalty took him from fourth to sixth.

1st	L Villoresi (W)	Ferrari 125-s/c in 1h-21m-06.9s	77.08
2nd	E deGraffenried (SP)	Maserati 4CLT/48-s/c	30.3s
3rd	B Bira (SP)	Maserati 4CLT/48-s/c	41.9s
F lap	R Parnell (SA)	Maserati 4CLT/48-s/c in 1m-57.8s	79.62

Modern Silverstone really began at this next meeting: the circuit was now devoid of the unpopular chicane; took on a favoured higher speed aspect; and remained virtually unchanged till 1975 when the slight deviation was installed into Woodcote Corner. It was, at the time, regarded as a medium-speed circuit, becoming seen as 'high-speed' when Spa and other circuits were slowed by chicanes or realigned, which became necessary for safety. The book *Design and Behaviour of the Racing Car* by Laurence Pomeroy and Stirling Moss of 1963 has a graph extrapolating Silverstone lap speeds for the '60s. They said 117 mph, but it was 130+ and rising fast. A suggestion of lapping at 161mph by 1985 would have been thought ridiculous then, I think.

✱✱✱ 1st *Daily Express* International Trophy (Silverstone)

20 heats + 30 lap final of 2.889 miles = 144.45 total miles.
38 entries – 36 started – 20 finished.
Poles: Heat one: A Ascari – 1m-56.0s (89.67mph). Heat two: E deGraffenried – 1m-55.0s (90.44mph).

20-AUG: A crowd well in excess of 100,000 arrived (with, amazingly for 1949, over 14,000 cars, plus coaches). A tremendous entry, better than the British GP, gave 18 starters in each heat. The first was won by Bira from Ascari by less than a second at 88.88mph, and the second by Farina from Villoresi by five seconds at 87.24mph. Ascari led the final, with Villoresi passing Bira and Parnell to take second place. Parnell dropped out and Farina fought back from a bad start to take second from Villoresi. He caught Ascari and even led for a few seconds, but Ferraris had more power. Farina fought fiercely but swiped a straw bale at Stowe Corner losing ten seconds. A great fightback followed, but Ascari was kept informed and held on. Peter Walker took fourth in the 'E' type ERA, its best ever showing. This had been a great event of true Grand Prix quality – a clean contest without pit stops to interrupt it. Tragically, the well respected St John Horsfall died when his ERA overturned at Stowe.

1st	A Ascari (W)	Ferrari 125-s/c in 59m-42.6s	87.09
2nd	G Farina	Maserati 4CLT/48-s/c	1.8s
3rd	L Villoresi (W)	Ferrari 125-s/c	36.4s
F lap	A Ascari/B Bira	Ferrari 125-s/c/Maserati 4CLT in 1m-54.6s	90.75

✱✱✱ II Grand Prix de Lausanne

90 laps of 2.014 miles = 181.3 miles.
19 entries – 16 started – 10 finished.
Front row: G Farina – 1m-42.4s (70.72mph); A Ascari +0.6s;

L Villoresi (Ferrari 125) +0.8s.

27-AUG: Ferrari confidence was shaken when Farina's Maserati took pole position, but the Ferraris of the inseparable duo Ascari and Villoresi held the first two places after the start, with Farina in their slipstream. Bira, deGraffenried and Etancelin followed. However, Farina led by lap nine, and even retained his lead when he stopped for fuel before Ascari. Everyone but Ascari had been lapped by lap 50. Bira retired whilst in fourth place, and problems for Villoresi dropped him to sixth. A steady drive by deGraffenried awarded him with third, but at this time Farina was the 'Maestro di Maserati.'

1st	G Farina	Maserati 4CLT/48-s/c in 2h-44m-37.3s	66.08
2nd	A Ascari (W)	Ferrari 125-s/c	1m-20s
3rd	E deGraffenried (SP)	Maserati 4CLT/48-s/c	3 laps
F lap	A Ascari	Ferrari 125-s/c in 1m-42.8s	70.54r

✱✱✱ XIX Gran Premio d'Italia (Monza)
80 laps of 3.915 miles = 313.2 miles.
29 entries – 24 started – 9 finished.

Front row: A Ascari – 2m-05.0s (112.75mph); Villoresi +0.4s; G Farina +2.8s; R Sommer (+4.8s).

11-SEP: The Italian Grand Prix came back to its spiritual home with the added grandiose title of GP d'Europa. An honorary title passed around the major events as recognition of their history. The Ferraris of Ascari, Villoresi and Sommer were now two-stage supercharged, and were clearly the fastest cars. Thus, Ferrari had no trouble securing pole position and dominating the race from start to finish. Teammate Villoresi's gear lever broke, and Farina's Maserati retired on lap 17, so Etancelin's usual Talbot drive, forceful yet careful, made second place, only one lap down out of 80. But Ferrari had to do better as it was still seconds seconds down on Alfa's 1948 times, so an Alfa return would likely restore the status quo from the previous year.

1st	A Ascari (W)	Ferrari 125C-s/c in 2h-58m-53.6s	105.04
2nd	P.Etancelin	Talbot-Lago T26C.	1 lap
3rd	'B Bira' (SP)	Maserati 4CLT/48-s/c	3 laps
F lap	A Ascari	Ferrari 125C-s/c in 2m-06.8s	111.15

✱✱ VIII Grand Prix of Czechoslovakia (Brno)
20 laps of 11.07 miles = 221.3 miles.
25 entries – 24 started – 11 finished.

Front row: B Bira; G Farina. Row two: E deGraffenried (all Maseratis) no times available.

25-SEP: The best British drivers entered but Works Ferraris were absent, leaving everything in Peter Whitehead's hands. The grid was a rare 2-1-2-1 arrangement, so narrow was the track. Bira took the lead, and it looked good for him when both Farina (second) and Parnell (fourth) crashed at the same spot on the next lap. Then Bira joined them a lap later! deGraffenried then led, but pitted for plugs, whereupon Chiron took over, but he, too, was out on lap 13! Whitehead refuelled then easily caught Etancelin to win.

1st	P Whitehead	Ferrari 125-s/c in 2h-48m-41.0s	78.72
2nd	P Etancelin	Talbot-Lago T26C	35.6s
3rd	F Cortese	Ferrari 166 F2	4m-49s
F lap	Bira/deGraffenried (SP)	Maserati 4CLT/48-s/c in 8m-03s	82.48

✱ IV Grand Prix du Salon (Montlhéry)
64 laps of 3.904 miles = 249.9 miles.
25 entries – 18 started – 9 finished.

Front row: G Grignard – 2m-25.1s (96.87mph); Y Girard-Cabantous +0.2s; 'Levegh'; G Mairesse – (all Talbot-LagoT26C).

09-OCT: Named after the Paris Salon Motor Show, there were no San Remo Maseratis or Works Ferraris here. Sommer was only on the third row of the grid! He led from the off, helped when Whitehead, 'Levegh' and Giraud-Cab' had a get together, all retiring. Also involved was motorcycle champion Jean Behra, new to car racing, who restarted. Lap 12 saw tyre problems and a long pit stop put Sommer back to eighth place, Harry Schell now leading. From two minutes behind Sommer stormed back and was second by lap 25 and leading ten laps later. People thought he'd overstressed his engine and it would fail – not so.

1st	R Sommer	Talbot-Lago T26C in 2h-42m-16s	92.38
2nd	H Schell (EF)	Talbot-Lago T26SS	2m-10s
3rd	P.Meyrat (EL)	Talbot-Lago T26C	4 laps
F lap	R Sommer	Talbot-Lago T26C in 2m-23.8s	97.75r

A look back at 1949
Juan-Manuel Fangio was the undeniable sensation of this season, with nationally sponsored funds for seven F1 races. All these tracks except Reims were new to him, yet he won five and retired from the lead at Reims. Oh, I forgot to

mention ... within two years he would be 40 years old! Rising star Alberto Ascari had been injured in South America, and didn't return to racing until the Belgian GP in June. Unfortunately, this meant that, with Fangio and Campos funded for only seven races, the two only clashed once in Formula One in Europe; a pity.

Fortunately, however, they met twice in Formula Two this year, and these meetings are worth a mention. A poor race in Rome in June, using a converted sports Maserati instead of the Gordini, caused Fangio to ask his sponsors to purchase a Ferrari 166. Considering his successes already that year, one was bought for the 'Gran Premio dell' Autodromo di Monza' on 26th June. A Monza slipstreamer developed involving Fangio, Ascari, Villoresi, Bonetto, Landi and Stuck. At half distance (it was a 313-mile F2 race!) it was Ascari, Fangio and Bonetto. Pit stops separated them, and Fangio had to fight back from 19 seconds down. He pulled back to five seconds, but Ascari reacted and pulled away again, only to get stuck in third gear. So it was Fangio, Bonetto and Ascari, now one lap back, at the finish, but the Works had been beaten. Fangio was then drafted into the Works team for the 'Coupe des Petites Cylindreés' at Reims on 17th July which supported the F1 Grand Prix. After 14 laps, Fangio led Ascari by 23 seconds, but gearbox failure put him out, Ascari going on to win this 126 miler.

Six finishes in ten races was good, then, but this was six wins and nearly seven in his F1 and F2 outings! His return home was a cause of national celebration in Argentina. The World Championship had yet to be conceived, but it may be argued that this was his greatest season of all! His win rate in his Championship career is a still unbeaten 47 per cent, yet in 1949 he achieved 71 per cent in F1!

Teams achieving a first podium finish during 1949 were:
Automovil Club Argentina (ACA) – the national sponsor for Fangio and Campos
Scuderia Achille Varzi (SAV) – the name used by the Argentinians for F2 car entries and F1 in 1950

Ecurie Belge (ENB) – as name implies, a Belgian team, principally assisting Johnny Claes

Winners of the 25 graded F1 races of 1949 (including Temporada) – quantity & quality of success

7 wins	J-M Fangio (2A, 3B, 2C)	11 wins	Maserati (3A, 5B, 3C)
4 wins	A Ascari (3A, B)	6 wins	Ferrari (4A, 2B)
3 wins	L Villoresi (A, 2C)	4 wins	Talbot-Lago (2A, 2C, D)
2 wins	G Farina (A, B) B Gerard (B, C)	2 wins	ERA (B, C)
1 win	L Rosier (A) E deGraffenried (B) L Chiron (A) P Whitehead (B) P Etancelin (C) R Sommer (C) G Mairesse (D)	1 win	Simca-Gordini (C)

A retro champion?

The 1951 World Driver's Championship had only seven rounds, chosen from 19 decent races; a look at the seven best-supported events of 1949 shows that Ascari and Fangio won three each, but Ascari had a second place. A 1951-style Championship would have almost certainly yielded Alberto Ascari the title (30 points) – but would Fangio (26 points) have gone home so early with a title on offer? No way! Argentine money would have been found. As it was, Ascari missed half the season recovering from injuries received in Argentina, and Fangio left halfway, so perhaps the hypothesis is reasonable. Take your pick, but, for me, this season deserves a 'Champion Emeritus' for 'rookie' Juan-Manuel Fangio. More than any other year, this one shows how skewed modern records are.

VISIT VELOCE ON THE WEB – WWW.VELOCE.CO.UK
All current books • New book news • Special offers • Gift vouchers • Forum

44

Chapter 9

1950

A World Championship is installed

Formula One was already into its third year in 1949 when Italian delegate Count Brivio proposed to the FIA that it should instigate an annual 'World Championship of Drivers,' starting the following year. It was accepted and, though no less than 18 F1 races per year was normal, a list of just six was chosen, on a national basis, to produce the season's champion. A points system of 8, 6, 4, 3, 2 and 1 for fastest lap was introduced so it was no longer 'winner takes all.' Was Count Brivio influenced perhaps by the two-wheeled brigade who had started their championships that year in 1949 and was likely to produce an Italian champion in two of the four capacity classes? Or was the catalyst Fangio's 1949 season (he had won five of the seven F1 races he started)? If so, then surely he deserves to be awarded a retro world title.

Was this a watershed change in culture and attitude? No career could rest on such a small list of events. The hugely respected Gerard 'Jabby' Crombac wrote in *MotorSport* magazine in 1998 that "It was rightly perceived as a manoeuvre from the Italian Federation within the FIA to create a Championship which, at this period, could only crown a driver of an Italian car." The Italians would have presumed, I think, that the driver would also be Italian, since it was 'The World Championship of Drivers.' For 1950 it was right (only just), but after 1953, it would be frustrated – and is still waiting. It is now, at the time of writing, sixty-two years since an Italian won the title. Italy is now in the situation that Britain was in with Wimbledon before 2013, and needs to find a Formula One version of 'Andy Murray.'

Alfa Romeo had retired from racing in 1949, and must have felt that a World Champion should be driving the best car: its. Alfa knew that Maserati and Ferrari hadn't produced anything new, so, I believe, it returned to racing to correct what it would have regarded as an anomaly. The team driver

line-up was: Giuseppe Farina; veteran Luigi Fagioli, who had raced the legendary Mercedes-Benz and Auto-Union 'Silver Arrow' cars before the war, with some success; and new star Jean-Manuel Fangio who, after 1949, simply couldn't be ignored. Others would be drafted in from race to race, as, sometimes, four cars were entered. One such driver was Reg Parnell, Britain's best post-war driver, who was given a place in the British Grand Prix.

Ferrari provided the only likely opposition, with the talents of Alberto Ascari, Luigi Villoresi, Raymond Sommer, and a now recovered Dorino Serafini. The only non-Works car was driven by Briton Peter Whitehead. A note about Ferrari engine size might be helpful to avoid confusion. Prior to 1956, all racing models were designated by the size of each cylinder. Multiply by number of cylinders and you have the engine size. For example, the 125 was a V12 of 1500cc s/c. Later, the 375 V12 had 4500cc us/c.

Maserati would have Louis Chiron and Franco Rol, plus various customer teams and privateers, but still it was the 4CLT/48 that would have to do.

The only other constructor with regular Works drivers was Simca-Gordini, which had Robert Manzon, Maurice Trintignant and André Simon to drive the diminutive six-cylinder 1500cc cars.

Talbot-Lago would use various people when the Works itself entered, but mostly its cars were privately-entered. It was alone in using a 4500cc us/c car – economy being its forte.

BRM (British Racing Motors) was effectively the 'British National Team,' having involved many of the best British companies in providing parts and expertise for its high-revving V16, with, uniquely, a centrifugal supercharger capable of high boost. Over two years work had gone into it now, and this was the year this complex car, from equally complex creators, would come to fruition. However, it had yet to race, so couldn't be said to have a regular driver line-up.

The Grand Prix driver's diary of single-seater racing for 1950

18th Dec 1949	F1 – Gran Premio del Gen Perón y Buenos Aires (Ag) – 151 miles
8th January	F1 – Gran Premio de Eva Duarte Perón at Buenos Aires (Ag) – 90.6 miles
15th Jauuary	F1 – Gran Premio del Gen. Martin at Mar del Plata (Ag) – 93.0 miles
22nd January	F1 – Copa Accion de San Lorenzo at Rosario (Ag) – 87.4 miles
19th March	F2 – Grand Prix de Marseille (F) – 121.2 miles
10th April	F1 – Richmond Trophy at Goodwood (UK) – 26.2 miles
10th April	F1 – Grand Prix de Pau (F) – 193.7 miles
16th April	F1 – Gran Premio di San Remo (I) – 189.0 miles
30th April	F1 – Grand Prix de Paris at Montlhéry (F) – 195.2 miles
7th May	F2 – Preis von Ostschweiz at Erlen (S) – 69.6 miles
7th May	F2 – Gran Premio di Modena (I) – 188.9 miles
7th May	F2 – Grand Prix de Cinquantenaire at Roubaix (F) – 186.5 miles
13th May	F1 – **British Grand Prix** at Silverstone (UK) – 202.2 miles
14th May	F2 – Grand Prix de Mons (B) – 189.6 miles
21st May	F1 – **Monaco Grand Prix** (M) – 197.6 miles
28th May	F2 – Gran Premio dell Autodromo di Monza (I) – 187.9 miles
28th May	F2 – Circuit du Lac at Aix-les-Bains (F) – 105.7 miles
4th June	F1 – **Grosse Preis der Schweiz** at Bremgarten (S) – 190.0 miles
4th June	F2 – Prix de Berne at Bremgarten (S) – 95.0 miles
11th June	F2 – Gran Premio di Roma (I) – 149.6 miles
11th June	F2 – Circuit de Remparts at Angulême(F) – 104 miles
15th June.	F1 – British Empire Trophy at Douglas (IoM) – 139.6 miles
18th June	F1 – **Grand Prix de Belgique** at Spa Francorchamps (B) – 307.1 miles
2nd July	F1 – **Grand Prix de l'ACF** at Reims-Gueux (F) – 310.8 miles
2nd July	F2 – Coupe des Petites Cylindrees at

	Reims-Gueux (F) – 126.3 miles
9th July	F1 – Gran Premio di Bari (I) – 198.4 miles
13th July	F1 – Jersey Road Race (UK) – 176.0 miles
16th July	F1 – Grand Prix d'Albi (F) – 188.1 miles
23rd July	F1 – Grote Prijs van Nederland at Zandvoort (N) – 234.5 miles
30th Jul	F1 – Grand Prix des Nations at Geneva (S) – 169.0 miles
30th July	F2 – Prix de Genêve (S) – 111.8 miles
15th August.	F1 – Circuito di Pescara (I) – 256.5 miles
20th August	F2 – Grosser Preis von Deutschland (D) – 226.7 miles
26th August	F1 – *Daily Express* International Trophy at Silverstone (UK) – 144.4 miles
3rd September	F1 – **Gran Premio d'Italia at Monza** (I) – 313.2 miles
10th September	F2 – Grandee Tropheé Entre Sambre et Meuse at Mettet (B) – 230 miles
15th October	F2 – Circuito del Garda (I) – 183.4 miles
30th September	F1 – Goodwood Trophy at Goodwood (UK) – 28.6 miles
29th October	F1 – Gran Premio do Peña Rhin at Pedralbes (E) – 194.2 miles

24 F1+15 F2 events of total race mileage = 6553 – 6061 max due to simultaneous races.

F2 dates are events with F1 driver participation.

Races in bold type are World Championship rounds – just 25 per cent of F1 races run.

An earlier start even than '49 – The Argentine 'Temporada'

As per the previous year, a packed ship left Italy for Argentina, with the 'Temporada' now a major draw for Europeans. The whole F1 'circus' decamped there – Raymond Sommer being the only absentee. Shorter races, but I find it impossible to view them in a lesser light, since the driver presence exceeded that at most rounds of the new 'World Championship of Drivers.' It may technically have been Formule Libre, but it was every bit the equal of F1. The decision to take Formula Two Ferraris for this series on twisty tracks was vindicated in no uncertain terms as they won every race. Fangio states in his autobiography *My Twenty Years of Racing* that his car was unsupercharged (therefore a true F2 car), but some other sources doubt this. I'm taking his word for it. A 'free-for-all' maybe, with some Maseratis slightly oversize, but it was all F1/F2 based – and great!

✳✳✳ Gran Premio del General Juan Perón y de la Ciudad Buenos Aires

15+35 laps of 3.02 miles = 151 total miles.

24 started – 11 finished.

Heat result gave grid front row: L Villoresi; A Ascari; G Farina.

18-DEC-1949: The 15-lap heat decided the grid places so Villoresi, Ascari's Ferraris and Farina's Maserati lined up ahead of Fangio's and Campos' Ferraris. It was the latter who led at first, but Ascari soon took over, pulling away as Fangio lost second to Villoresi. Despite his car firing on just 11 of its 12 cylinders, Villoresi held off Fangio until Ascari was well away. Fangio closed but a spin on oil destroyed his challenge for the lead. Farina retired half way, having been unable to pose an effective challenge.

1st	A Ascari (W)	Ferrari 166C-2.0 in 1h-29m-00.2s	71.26
2nd	J-M Fangio	Ferrari 166C-2.0	29.4s
3rd	L Villoresi (W)	Ferrari 166C-2.0	1m-38s
F lap	J-M Fangio	Ferrari 166C-2.0 in 2m-29.2s	72.87

✳✳✳ Gran Premio Extraordinario de Eva Duarte Perón

30 laps of 3.02 miles = 90.6 miles.
23 started – 12 finished.

Front row: J-M Fangio (Ferrari 166C) – 2m-29.9s (72.53mph); A Ascari (Ferrari 166C) +0.5s; L Villoresi +1.5s.

08-JAN: Returning to the same track as the previous week, now Fangio led from Ascari, but this didn't last long as Ascari struck straw bales and punctured the radiator. Villoresi was now in hot pursuit, and a 'battle royale' developed until a spin dropped him back by ten seconds. The race was Fangio's – or was it? He copied Ascari and touched the bales, pitting and dropping to fourth. How rare for the two top stars of the era to make similar mistakes in the same race. Shows how important every race was then.

1st	L Villoresi	Ferrari 166C-2.0 in 1h-18m-20.8s	69.38
2nd	D Serafini	Ferrari 125	25.0s
3rd	C Bucci	Alfa Romeo 12C (4.6s/c)	27.2s
F lap	L Villoresi	Ferrari 166C-2.0 in 2m-28.4s	73.26

✳✳✳ Gran Premio del Generale Martin (Mar del Plata)

37 laps – 2.514 miles = 93.0 miles.
12 started – 21 finished.

Front row: A Ascari – 2m-03.7s (73.16mph); L Villoresi (0.5); J-M Fangio (0.8s).

15-JAN: Ascari's turn for pole now, but Fangio took the lead, with Ascari and Villoresi joined by Farina in a three-pronged attack. Farina dropped out and, soon after, Villoresi made a desperate dive inside Fangio as he lined up for a corner. Villoresi lost it and collected Fangio. This was a slow corner so only the cars were damaged. Fangio was yet to win, having led twice.

1st	A Ascari	Ferrari 166C-2.0 in 1h-20m-45.3s	69.11
2nd	G Farina	Maserati 4CLT/48-1.7s/c	19.5s
3rd	P Taruffi	Maserati 4CLT/48-1.7s/c	23.8s
F lap	L Villoresi	Ferrari 166C-2.0 in 2m-04.7s	72.58

✳✳✳ Copa Accion de San Lorenzo (Rosario)

50 laps of 1.748 miles = 87.4 miles.
21 started – 10 finished.

Front row: J-M Fangio – 1m-43.1s (61.04mph); A Ascari (Ferrari 166C) +0.9s; G Farina +2.0s.

22-JAN: The same foursome took charge of the last race in this small but fascinating season. Fangio led Ascari again, but a stray newspaper stuck to Ascari's radiator and the car (and he, no doubt) overheated and retired. Now 'local' Froilán González led the chase from Villoresi and Farina. Surely Fangio's good lead would hold. But no, only Villoresi had a trouble-free run.

1st	L Villoresi (W)	Ferrari 166C-2.0 in 1h-30m-51.6s	57.72
2nd	B Campos	Ferrari 166C-2.0	22.9s
3rd	G Farina	Maserati 4CLT/48-s/c	1 lap
F lap	J-M Fangio	Ferrari 166C-2.0 in 1m-43.6s	60.74

✳✳✳ XI Grand Prix de Pau

110 laps of 1.761 miles = 193.7 miles.
14 entries – 13 started – 8 finished.

Front row: J-M Fangio – 1m-43.1s (61.49mph); L Villoresi +0.3s; R Sommer (Ferrari 125) +1.4s.

10-APR: Two F1 Works Ferraris were entered for Sommer and Villoresi, and an F2 car for Ascari. However, with no Alfa Romeo presence, Fangio was free to drive the same Maserati as last season. Sommer's Ferrari led while Villoresi fought with Fangio, but Fangio took over the lead on lap 15, and, despite all Villoresi's efforts, held it to the end. Fuel stops were the key here as Villoresi's took 30 seconds less than Fangio's, and allowed him to get within three seconds, but Fangio pulled away again. Sommer's stop was chaotic, dropping him well behind Rosier in his non-stop Talbot, and he was lapped with 12 laps to go. Rosier put in a great performance to be just

62 seconds adrift of Fangio in over three hours. He was 2.9s slower than Fangio in practice, yet just 0.56s slower per lap over the race, which shows how much time he recovered by not stopping. Fangio's race and lap speeds eclipsed even the pre-war Mercedes figures, and this in a non-Works car not reckoned to be the equal of the Works Ferrari.

1st	J-M Fangio (SAV)	Maserati 4CLT/48-s/c in 3h-14m-20s	59.80
2nd	L Villoresi (W)	Ferrari 125-s/c	30.5s
3rd	L Rosier	Talbot-Lago T26C	1m-2s
F lap	J-M Fangio	Maserati 4CLT/48-s/c in 1m-42.8s	61.67r

Richmond Trophy (Goodwood)
11 laps of 2.38 miles = 26.18 miles.
15 entries – 11 started – 9 finished.
Front row (ballot): C Harrison (ERA) – 1m-44.4s;
P Whitehead – time n/a; R Parnell 1m-40.4 (86.06mph).
10-APR: The Goodwood races were now getting a little longer – by a lap. A little international element was now present in the Enrico Platé Maseratis of Bira and deGraffenried. Parnell was fastest in practice in 1m-40.4s, just 0.4s ahead of deGraffenried, but the ballot system placed Harrison on pole, four whole seconds slower than Parnell! It was Bira who made a great start in torrential rain from near the back and led deGraffenried, Parnell and Shawe-Taylor. Soon Bira lay third, but stopped when visibility worsened. Parnell shot away from lap seven – a true 'regenmeister' – leaving deGraffenried to just fend off Shawe-Taylor. Few stars were there, but then the race length suggests that Goodwood had few international aspirations then.

1st	R Parnell (SA)	Maserati 4CLT/48 s/c in 20m-14.4s	77.61
2nd	E deGraffenried (SP)	Maserati 4CLT/48 s/c	46.0s
F lap	R Parnell	Maserati 4CLT/48 s/c in 1m-46.0s	80.83

✳✳✳ V Gran Premio di San Remo (Ospedaletti)
90 laps of 2.10 miles = 189 miles.
21 started – 6 finished.
Front row: A Ascari 1m-52.2s (67.32mph); J-M Fangio +0.2s;
L Villoresi +0.4s.
16-APR: This was the debut of Alfa's 1950 car, and, with Farina injured, Fangio was selected to drive it. Ferrari realised his 1949 form was at risk so entered six Works cars, plus that of Whitehead. A dozen Maseratis and a Talbot filled the grid. On a very wet track, Ascari, Villoresi and Sommer's Ferraris led

Fangio at first. By lap ten, however, Fangio was second, and led as Ascari spun under pressure on lap 13. Ascari closed the gap but spun again, hitting a wall. Only Villoresi's Ferrari finished as they overheated, and perhaps the ensuing power loss caused Ascari to try too hard! So a single Alfa was enough!

1st	J-M Fangio (SAV)	Alfa Romeo 158-s/c in 3h-10m-8.4s	59.59
2nd	L Villoresi (W)	Ferrari 125-s/c	1m-1s
3rd	A Pian (SAV)	Maserati 4CLT/48-s/c	2 laps
F lap	L Villoresi	Ferrari 125-s/c in 2m-01.2s	62.32

IV Grand Prix de Paris (Montlhéry)
50 laps of 3.904 miles = 195.2 miles.
16 entries – 11 started – 3 finish.
No grid positions available.
30-APR: This was really a French-only event, except for the two HWM F2 cars of Stirling Moss and George Abecassis. Five Talbots, a Maserati, and three Delages made up the starters. The Talbots of Sommer, Rosier and Grignard led, with Moss sixth. The lead changed twice, but, on lap ten, Rosier fell back with overheating problems, retiring on lap 21. Sommer's engine failed on lap 33 from a strong position – he never took it easy – nor did Moss, who had passed Gerard's Delage for third so he would have been second. What an attritional race with just three finishers! The fewest of any race in this book.

1st	G Grignard	Talbot-Lago T26C in 2h-05s-38.8s	93.23
2nd	L Gerard	Delage 3000	4 laps
F lap	R Sommer	Talbot-Lago T26C in 2m-20.3s	100.19r

The FIA 'World Championship of Drivers' arrives
What febrile anticipation was there for this Royally attended 'watershed' event in May 1950 at Silverstone? It was already the third major Formula One event of the year, and, while naturally a huge crowd attended, I note that the long established and highly respected magazine *MotorSport* in its race coverage shows that, for it, the Championship merited no mention at all. Was that a petulant British attitude to disguise the absence on the grid of the long awaited British BRM – it only demonstrated a few laps – or did it think it irrelevant?

✳✳✳ (WC1) V British Grand Prix (Silverstone)
70 laps of 2.889 miles = 202.2 miles.
23 entries – 21 started – 11 finished.
Front row: G Farina – 1m-50.8s (93.85mph); L Fagioli +0.2s;

J-M Fangio +0.2s; R Parnell +1.4s all Alfa-Romeo.

13-MAY: The first World Championship event was given the honoured title of Grand Prix d'Europe. No Ferraris were entered, presumably because if they couldn't beat Fangio in a Maserati they had no hope with him in the Alfa Romeo 158 team. The long-awaited British hope, BRM, only demonstrated prior to the main race – how frustrating! So an Alfa Romeo walkover was a certainty. However, the inclusion in the team of Britain's number one, Reg Parnell, gave real interest to the home crowd. The 'three Fs' were covered by just 0.2s on the grid, with Parnell a second adrift and Bira's Maserati 0.4s from him. Farina led nearly all the way, swapping places early on for the crowd and at the half-way fuel stops. If this was meant to be Farina's race, Fangio hadn't read the script and closed to within 0.6s of him, but struck a straw bale. The subsequent oil loss took its toll, stopping him on lap 62; a great finish spoilt. Bira was the closest challenger, but dropped from fifth on lap 32, retiring on lap 49. Old man Yves Giraud-Cabantous beat fellow Talbot pilot Rosier to fourth, two laps down. Enzo Ferrari's absence showed that he wasn't interested in points for fifth place (though it would have been fourth, of course). The culture of 'racing for points' hadn't been discovered then. It's a pity it ever was, as is the ambivalent attitude to an auspicious occasion.

1st	G Farina (W)	Alfa Romeo 158 s/c in 2h-13m-23.6s	90.95
2nd	L Fagioli (W)	Alfa Romeo 158 s/c	2.6s
3rd	R Parnell (W)	Alfa Romeo 158 s/c	52.0s
F lap	G Farina	Alfa Romeo 158 s/c in 1m-50.6s	94.02

✳✳✳ (WC2) X Grand Prix de Monaco
100 laps of 1.976 miles = 197.6 miles.
26 entries –19 started – 7 finished.
Front row: J-M Fangio – 1m-50.2s (64.53mph); G Farina +2.6s; F González (Maserati 4CLT/48) +3.5s.

21-MAY: Ferrari obviously fancied its chances at a slow circuit, but it was Fangio's compatriot Froilán González who split the Alfas in third grid place. Even Etancelin's Talbot-Lago was fourth, ahead of Fagioli's Alfa. A wave had crashed over the sea wall at Tabac and caught out Farina in second place on lap one. The ensuing debacle eliminated nine cars, including Fagioli's, leaving Fangio an easy victory in the sole remaining Alfa Romeo – races were not stopped then, even though the track was almost completely blocked. González suffered burns when his damaged car caught fire soon after leaving the scene. Ascari and teammate Villoresi scrapped for second until lap 63 when Villoresi retired. Sommer's Ferrari had been second on lap two, but was only fourth at the end.

1st	J-M Fangio (W)	Alfa Romeo 158 s/c in 3h-13m-18.7s	61.33
2nd	A Ascari (W)	Ferrari 125 V12 s/c	1 lap
3rd	L Chiron (W)	Maserati 4CLT/48 s/c	2 laps
F lap	J-M Fangio	Alfa Romeo 158 s/c in 1m-51.0s	64.09r

Championship positions:
Farina and Fangio 9; Fagioli and Ascari 6.

✳✳✳ (WC3) X Grosser Preis der Schweiz (Bremgarten-Berne)
42 laps of 4.524 miles = 190 miles.
22 entries –18 started – 11 finished.
Front row: J-M Fangio – 2m-42.1s (100.45mph); G Farina +0.7s; Fagioli +3.1s.

04-JUN: This track was faster than Silverstone, yet Ferrari was here. Ascari had put his car between Fangio and Farina as they left the grid – was there a challenge to Alfa after all? He lasted just two laps, though, and teammate Villoresi just six more. Fangio's lead was taken by Farina after a few laps. As at Silverstone with a few laps to go, a potential lead battle disappeared as Fangio retired with engine trouble. Farina eased and Fagioli dutifully followed him in a demonstration finish. These losses would actually cost Fangio the inaugural title. Third spot went to a Talbot, again proving the value of fuel economy. It now had about 280bhp, but surely Ferrari or Maserati could produce more than that from 4500cc unsupercharged, if they were interested.

1st	G Farina (W)	Alfa Romeo 158 s/c in 2h-02m-53.7s	92.76
2nd	L Fagioli (W)	Alfa Romeo 158 s/c	0.4s
3rd	L Rosier (W)	Talbot-Lago T26C	1 lap
F lap	G Farina	Alfa Romeo 158 s/c in 2m-41.6s	100.78r

Championship positions:
Farina 18; Fagioli 12; Fangio 9.

✳ XII British Empire Trophy (Douglas)
36 laps of 3.879 miles = 139.64 miles.
18 entries – 13 started – 7 finished.
Front row: C Harrison – 3m-10s (73.50mph); A Rolt (Delage 15S8) +2s; R Gerard +3s.

15-JUN: A British entry, plus deGraffenried (an Anglophile?) saw Parnell lead Gerard whenever his slipping clutch allowed; the slipping eventually dropped him back. Bira, starting at the back, was coming through when he was involved in a three-car crash. So the two top places were settled. deGraffenried took third place from Shawe-Taylor on the last lap, but still followed the old ERAs. Parnell's clutch improved and he got fastest lap near the end, but was relegated to sixth by then.

1st	R Gerard	ERA 'R14B'-s/c in 1h-59m-36.8s	70.07
2nd	C Harrison	ERA 'R8B'-s/c	1m-32s
3rd	E deGraffenried (SP)	Maserati 4CLT/48-s/c	2m-48s
F lap	R Parnell (SA)	Maserati 4CLT/48-s/c in 3m-08s	74.28r

** (WC4) XII Grand Prix de Belgique (Spa Francorchamps)

35 laps of 8 774miles = 307.1 miles.
14 entries and starters – 8 finished.
Front row: G Farina – 4m-37s (114.03mph); J-M Fangio +0s; Fagioli +4s.

18-JUN: No works Maseratis were entered – they'd had a poor showing so far – but Ferrari had woken to the message given by the Talbot's performances and entered Ascari's car with a 3300cc unsupercharged engine. Sommer's Talbot was a place ahead on the grid, but Ascari passed him soon, taking fifth behind the three leading Alfas and Villoresi's supercharged Ferrari 125. Ascari was then passed by a trio of Talbots headed by Sommer, driving so well that he took the lead as the Alfas refuelled ... at Spa! Sadly, though, his engine cried enough on lap 20 when in third and still leading Fagioli. Rosier was now in the leading Talbot, ahead of Ascari whose car as yet couldn't match the Talbot's frugality, despite being over a litre smaller, so he refuelled. Villoresi's Ferrari had dropped behind them. On lap 20 Fangio took the lead from Farina, who dropped to fourth with transmission trouble.

1st	J-M Fangio (W)	Alfa Romeo 158 s/c in 2h-47m-26s	110.05
2nd	L Fagioli (W)	Alfa Romeo 158 s/c	2.6s
3rd	L Rosier (W)	Talbot-Lago T26C	2m-19s
F lap	G Farina (W)	Alfa Romeo 158 s/c in 4m-34.1s	115.23

Championship positions:
Farina 22; Fagioli 18; Fangio 17.

** WC5) XXXVII Grand Prix de l'ACF (Reims-Gueux)

64 laps of 4.856 miles = 310.8 miles.
22 entries – 18 starters – 6 finished.
Front row: J-M Fangio – 2m-30.6s (116.10mph); G Farina

+1.9s; L Fagioli +4.1s.

02-JUL: Now both Ferrari Works entries had 3.3-litre engines, but were withdrawn, leaving a field unable to provide any challenge to the Alfa-Romeo 158s. No challenge to Alfa could happen until Ferrari got its act together, while Alfa Romeo had no reason to change anything. Farina led until fuel starvation dropped him way back, whereupon Fangio took over. Farina recovered to third place but stopped with ten laps to go with more fuel trouble. Ferrari must have been pleased it had sold a car to Peter Whitehead who made a podium finish from the back of the grid. The long straights of this circuit gave the Talbots and Maseratis no chance here at all. The surprise was a fourth place for Manzon's Works Simca-Gordini on the same lap as Whitehead.

1st	J-M Fangio (W)	Alfa Romeo 158 s/c in 2h-57m-52.8s	104.28
2nd	L Fagioli (W)	Alfa Romeo 158 s/c	25.7s
3rd	P Whitehead	Ferrari 125s/c	3 laps
F lap	G Farina (W)	Alfa Romeo 158 s/c in 2m-35.6s	112.36r

Championship positions:
Fangio 26; Fagioli 24; Farina 22.

** IV Gran Premio di Bari

60 laps of 3.307 miles = 198.4 miles.
19 entries – 15 started – 9 finished.
Front row: G Farina – no other information.

09-JUL: This race was just a week after the French Grand Prix, and the Works Maseratis were not repaired so withdrew. Ferrari changed its entries to F2 cars, as its latest F1 cars were still faulty, but at least Ferrari was here with Ascari and Villoresi. It was as if it had skipped Reims to better prepare for Bari. If so, it proves that the Championship wasn't as important to Ferrari then. Farina led Fangio for ten laps, followed him for the next three, then took over until the finish. Fangio had to do a last lap 'splash and dash'. Ascari's F2 Ferrari retired early and he took over Villoresi's to battle with Moss' offset HWM. Moss won the 'class' as both Ferraris' rear axles failed. So HWM (or was it mostly Moss?) beat Ferrari! This was a driver's circuit.

1st	G Farina (W)	Alfa Romeo 158-s/c in 2h-34m-29.6s	77.07
2nd	J-M Fangio (W)	Alfa Romeo 158-s/c	46.4s
3rd	S Moss (W)	HWM-Alta	2 laps
F lap	J-M Fangio	Alfa Romeo 158-s/c in 2m-26.5s	81.54

1st	L Rosier	Talbot-Lago T26C in 1h-53m-08.6s	99.73
2nd	F González (SAV)	Maserati 4CLT/48-s/c	27.3s
3rd	M Trintignant (W)	Simca-Gordini T15 s/c	1 lap
F lap	J-M Fangio (SAV)	Maserati 4CLT/50-s/c in 3m-06.7s	106.65r

✳ IV JCC Jersey Road Race
55 laps of 3.2 miles = 176 miles.
23 entries – 19 started – 12 finished.
Front row: D Hampshire – 2m-02.4s (94.12mph);
P Whitehead +0.8s; R Gerard (ERA) +2.0s; C Harrison
(ERA) +2.4s.

13-JUL: The Works Maseratis were still not repaired from
their Reims engine failures and ready to challenge Peter
Whitehead's sole Ferrari 125 so withdrew, but private entries
compensated well. It was Whitehead all the way, easing up
at the end and lapped the field after a fast and faultless drive.
At first it was Parnell, Bira, deGraffenried and Hampshire
who gave chase, but Bira stopped after six laps, and soon
after Hampshire pitted with engine trouble. He restarted and
stormed back to fourth only to retire on lap 22. deGraffenried
took second from Parnell on lap 16 until lap 45 but then
needed to pit twice for oil ... the usual Maserati failing.
Hampshire's engine was off colour and stopped on lap 22.
Had he over-revved it in practice?

1st	P Whitehead	Ferrari 125s/c in 1h-56m-02.6s	91.00
2nd	R Parnell (SA)	Maserati 4CLT/48-s/c	1 lap
3rd	E deGraffenried (SP)	Maserati 4CLT/48-s/c	1 lap
F lap	D Hampshire (SA)	Maserati 4CLT/48-s/c in 2m-02.0s	94.43r

✳✳✳ XII Grand Prix d'Albi
2 x 17 laps of 5.531 miles = 188.1 miles.
18 entries – 16 started – 10 finished.
Front row: J-M Fangio – 3m-06.7s (106.65mph); F González
+1.9s; R Sommer (Talbot-Lago) +3.3s.

16-JUL: Alfa Romeo didn't enter, so Fangio was available
to the Argentinian team (named after the late Achille
Varzi). In the first heat he looked a certainty, when a
Maserati fault (oil leak) intervened and set his car on
fire. Sommer passed him on the last bend but ran wide,
collecting a straw bale (and its onboard photographer!),
crossing the line a second ahead of Fangio who fought to
the line in his flame-ridden car – battling then to stop it
and extinguish his trousers! Did the photographer win the
first heat then? Sommer and Fangio were hors de combat
for heat two. Rosier held a 47-second lead over González
from heat one so it was all over really and he eased up,
content to finish 20 seconds adrift in the second heat.
Farina's Maserati had faltered in heat one and was 14th,
three laps down and, though third in heat two, was out of
it. Trintignant was fifth in each part yet got third.

✳✳✳ Grote Prijs van Nederland (Zandvoort)
90 laps of 2.605 miles = 234.5 miles.
14 entered and started – 7 finished
Front row: R Sommer 1m-51.8s (83.89mph); J-M Fangio
(Maserati) +1.2s; F González (Maserati) +2.9s

23-JUL: A small but select field was chosen by the organisers
hoping to achieve Championship status next year, but Alfa
Romeo declined and Farina and his private Maserati were also
absent. Fangio was Maserati-equipped again, as was teammate
González, but Sommer overtook them both on lap six ... a Talbot
passing a Maserati driven by Fangio! It seems that Fangio had
suspension problems, though, and he retired on lap 24 after
losing ground. Sadly, Sommer's storming drive came to naught
when he retired on lap 37 with terminal clutch trouble. Rosier
now led, helped by a long fuel stop for second-placed González,
which involved putting out a fire, and so careful Rosier led to
the end. Brilliant Ascari's F2 Ferrari lapped Whitehead's steadily
driven F1 machine in fourth place! Surely Villoresi and Ascari
must have arranged a staged finish in their works F1 and F2 cars.

1st	L Rosier (W)	Talbot-Lago T26C in 3h-03m-35.3s	76.62
2nd	L Villoresi (W)	Ferrari 125-s/c	1m-13.0s
3rd	A Ascari (W)	Ferrari 166 F2	1m-13.4s
F lap	R Sommer (W)	Talbot-Lago T26C in 1m-52.1s	83.67r

✳✳✳ III Grand Prix des Nations (Geneva)
68 laps of 2.486 miles = 169.0 miles.
22 entries – 20 started – 8 finished.
Front row: J-M Fangio 1m-46.7s (83.86mph); A Ascari
(Ferrari 125) +2.0s; L Villoresi (Ferrari 125) +2.0s.

30-JUL: A very interesting event. Alfa Romeo took this,
rather grandiosely titled, race seriously, so entered four cars.
Ferrari had a surprise for Alfa, though, as both its type 125
cars were now unsupercharged. Ascari's 4.1-litre was second
on the grid, and Villoresi's 3.3-litre third, ahead of the Alfas of
Farina, Taruffi and deGraffenried – the latter having his debut
in these great cars. Fangio pulled away at the start, but Ascari
couldn't hold on to him and was 50 seconds adrift by lap 30.
After Fangio's inevitable fuel stop, Ascari harried the Alfa
Romeo until retiring with just six laps to go, so the game was

changing at last with a serious challenge from Ferrari! Before that Villoresi spun on oil, crashed into straw bales, overturned and seriously injured himself but, much worse, his car had vaulted into the crowd and killed three spectators. Farina in third place spun to avoid the meleé but crashed. Today Ascari would have been classified fourth, but in those days only cars running at the finish were classified. The Giraud-Canbantous Talbot was classified fourth, but did only 62 laps, so had not passed Ascari, as he had achieved that distance much earlier. The dispassionate way that spectator deaths were reported in the motoring press then (for example, in *The Autocar*) seems shocking to us today, but that's just how it was.

1st	J-M Fangio (W)	Alfa Romeo 158s/c in 2h-07m-55.0s	79.28
2nd	E deGraffenried (W)	Alfa Romeo 158s/c	2 laps
3rd	P Taruffi (W)	Alfa Romeo 158s/c	2 laps
F lap	P Taruffi	Alfa Romeo 158s/c in 1m-45.1s	85.14

✳✳✳ XIX Circuito di Pescara

16 laps of 16.03 miles = 256.5 miles.
21 entries – 15 started – 6 finished.

Front row: J-M Fangio – 10m-37.6s (90.52mph); L Fagioli +20.4s; L Rosier +48.4s.

15-AUG: This was the longest circuit ever used for Formula One, a triangle of approximately equal sides with Adriatic coastal town Pesacara at the southern corner. There, the road set off twisting through villages and up into the mountains. Then came a long straight back to sea level, and another back to Pescara where a chicane slowed the cars; a circuit for the brave.

Neither Works Ferraris nor Chiron's Works Maserati appeared, so the two Alfas should run away with the race; and so it proved, with Luigi Fagioli scheduled to win this one. However, with six miles to go, a front suspension unit collapsed. Fangio saw the damage, but persuaded him to continue with the wheel touching the body, and followed with his eye on his mirrors. Then, on the long final straight, Rosier was seen closing on them, so Fangio zoomed off to the finish. Rosier got second with just over 100 metres to go. A prize for fastest speed along the timed kilometre was won by Fangio ... with 192.5mph average!

1st	J-M Fangio (W)	Alfa Romeo 158s/c in 3h-02m-51.4s	84.16
2nd	L Rosier	Talbot-Lago T26C	17.6s
3rd	L Fagioli (W)	Alfa Romeo 158s/c	23.6s
F lap	J-M Fangio	Alfa Romeo 158s/c in 10m-37.6s	90.52

✳✳✳ II *Daily Express* International Trophy (Silverstone)

15 lap heat + 35-lap final of 2.889 miles = 144.4 total miles.
32 entries – 27 started – 14 finished.

Poles: Heat one – G Farina – 1m-52.s (92.86mph); Heat two – J Claes (Talbot-Lago) – 1m-52.s (92.86mph).

26-AUG: As in 1949, the International Trophy outdid the British GP for entries. The BRDC in its wisdom decided to record lap times in whole second increments! How can they quote speeds to two decimal places, when one increment equates to almost a whole 1mph? It could also make grid positions something of a lottery – who really was the fastest of two (or more) identical times? The time credited to Claes did raise a few eyebrows I think. In the 1954 British GP it would deservedly haunt them. The long awaited BRM V16, in the experienced hands of Raymond Sommer at last broke cover for racing, and, shamefully, also its drive shafts on the start line in heat two, to much ridicule. It was reckoned to have moved about a foot. Had no-one ever tried a racing start with it before? If so ... what an aberration! Alfas won both heats, but in heat two Ascari, in Vandervell's Ferrari 125 'Thinwall,' challenged Fangio, but was overcome by fumes and spun off in the wet. So the final was an Alfa benefit, with Fangio and Farina sharing the lead and winning as they pleased without approaching the times of the British GP. Cuth Harrison's ERA lost out to Peter Whitehead for third by 0.6 seconds. Also amazing was Moss' sixth place in an F2 HWM; lapped only once – and only by the Alfas!

1st	G Farina (W)	Alfa Romeo 158s in 1h-07m-17.0s	90.17
2nd	J-M Fangio (W)	Alfa Romeo 158s/c	0.4s
3rd	P Whitehead	Ferrari 125s/c	1m-4s
F lap	Fangio/Farina	Alfa Romeo 158s/c in 1m-52s	92.86

✳✳✳ (WC6) XX Gran Premio d'Italia (Monza)

80 laps of 3.915 miles = 313.2 miles.
32 entries – starters – 7 finished.

3-SEP: See championship summary for race report.

Front row: J-M Fangio – 1m-58.6s (118.83mph); A Ascari +0.2s; G Farina +1.6s; C Sanesi +1.8s.

1st	G Farina (W)	Alfa Romeo 158s/c in 2h-51m-17.4s	109.63
2nd	Serafini/Ascari (W)	Ferrari 375	1m-18.6s
3rd	L Fagioli (W)	Alfa Romeo 158s/c	1m-35.6s
F lap	J-M Fangio	Alfa Romeo 158s/c in 2m-00.8s	117.44r

Final Championship positions:
Farina (WC) 30; Fangio 27; Fagioli 24.

Only now came the acknowledgement from the 'establishment of British motor racing' – in the premier magazine of the sport *MotorSport* – that a World Champion has been crowned. Yet Giuseppe Farina was acknowledged by only in a minor article in its magazine – the Dundrod TT race being seen as much more important.

Goodwood Trophy (Goodwood)
12 laps of 2.38 miles = 28.6 miles.
17 entries – 14 started – 9 finished.
Front row (ballot): J Claes (Talbot-Lago); G Whitehead (ERA); J Ashmore (ERA); G Watson (Alta).
30-SEP: Another short race at Goodwood, which meant that the F1 race, despite a decent entry, is just a footnote in Formula One records. Reg Parnell's gentle start in the rain (no Silverstone repeat) still allowed him to lead away. Bira gave chase to no avail. Gerard stole third from deGraffenried near the finish. BRM had won something, but not trust ... yet.

1st	R Parnell (W)	BRM V16 s/c in 20m-58.4s	81.70
2nd	B Bira (SP)	Maserati 4CLT/48s/c	12.4s
F lap	R Parnell	BRM V16 s/c in 1m-41.8s	84.16

✶✶ X Gran Premio do Peňa Rhin (Pedralbes)
50 laps of 3.884 miles = 194.2 miles.
24 entries – 22 started – 9 finished.
Front row: A Ascari – 2m-23.8s (97.24mph); D Serafini; P Taruffi; R Parnell (BRM V16).
29-OCT: Alfa Romeo was absent, having raced 11 times this year to the four of 1949, but Ferrari was out in force, and BRM arrived in Europe. The much revised track now had a straight of 1.72 miles, on which Parnell did a timed kilometre at 186mph! What was his maximum then? His BRM joined the Ferraris on the front row, but five seconds slower. The track had exposed the BRM's aggressive power delivery, and consequent difficulty in getting power down on exiting the three slow corners. Ascari led from flag-to-flag. He dominated to the extent that, when easing up, he let Serafini unlap himself twice! The Parnell BRM failed after just two laps, while Walker's retired from fourth after lap 33. The new Ferrari had shown potential, and BRM its outright speed. Another accident with two spectator deaths but an uninjured driver suggests that spectators simply accepted it. Crazy times.

1st	A Ascari (W)	Ferrari 375 in 2h-05m-14.8s	93.02
2nd	D Serafini (W)	Ferrari 375	1m-41s
3rd	P Taruffi (W)	Ferrari 125/340	2 laps
F lap	A Ascari	Ferrari 375 in 2m-24.2s	96.95

Winners of the 24 graded F1 races of 1950 – quantity & quality of success

7 wins	J-M Fangio (7A)	11 wins	Alfa Romeo (10A, B)
5 wins	G Farina (4A, B)	6 wins	Ferrari (4A, B, C)
3 wins	A Ascari (2A, B)	3 wins	Talbot-Lago (2A, D)
2 wins	L Rosier (2A) L Villoresi (2A) R Parnell (2D)	2 wins	Maserati (A, D)
1 win	P Whitehead (C) B Gerard (C) G Grignard (D)	1 win	ERA (C) BRM (D)

Summary of 1950 – the overall picture
Many other races matched the Championship rounds for quality of entries, so it cannot be said that the new Championship was a completely dominating feature of the season, with just six rounds selected from over 17 races. Alfa Romeo raced only a few times in the years 1946-49, yet entered no less than 11 times this season, so clearly saw the non-Championship races as worthy events, and remained completely undefeated despite a slight scare at Monza. Ferrari eventually produced a very promising car in the Ferrari 375 V12, and took over the 4.5-litre unsupercharged aspect of the Formula, leaving Talbot-Lago, who had shown the way, well in its wake. Maserati, however, was now out of the main hunt: the 4CLT/48 being now three years old, and the updated 4CLT/50 being no better. 1951 could be very interesting, though, if Ferrari promise was fulfilled. I haven't mentioned BRM ... perhaps better not ...

Fangio was beaten for the World Title, but was the most successful driver overall in 1950, with seven wins and two second places, all in good quality races. Since he first arrived to race seriously in Europe the previous year, he had yet to finish outside the top two places! Including the previous year's Formula Two races, he'd won 13 times, finished second twice, and retired nine times. No one else could claim a score sheet anywhere near that.

The World Championship
By the opening round at Silverstone, Juan-Manuel Fangio had already won the major Grands Prix of Pau and San

Remo, in a Maserati and an Alfa Romeo respectively, so, together with his 1949 performances, already had a fine reputation and was favourite for the title. However, teammate Farina had yet to race against him that year, and it was he who took the initial honours, while Fangio retired from second place with engine trouble with ten per cent of the race remaining; perhaps influenced by swiping a straw bale a few laps earlier. The Ferrari team wasn't present, so the Alfa team was, realistically, unopposed. Fangio won at Monaco while Farina crashed on lap one when a wave crashed onto the track at the Tabac corner and caused a pile-up, so the scores were level. It was Farina again in the Swiss GP (Fangio retiring), and Fangio at Belgium with Farina fourth, retaining the championship lead by four points. This was lost to Fangio in the next GP at Reims as Farina retired from third.

So, to the finale at Monza: Fangio on 26 points with Farina on 22, but Alfa Romeo's third driver, Fagioli, had split them on 24 points by virtue of four second places, so could spoil the whole party with a first win and fastest lap if the main protagonists retired: unlikely, but possible. Farina had to at least get second place to stand a chance, and in the event he led for the first 13 laps to be overtaken by none other than Ascari's Ferrari – giving the Alfas their first real fright – but led again after two laps and held on to the end. A second place for Fangio would have sealed the crown for him, but near half distance he retired from this invaluable place having only got the single point for fastest lap. So Farina and Fangio had won three races each, but Farina was the first World Champion by three points; this being his fourth place in Belgium – strangely the only finish outside a win for either of the duo. It has to be recalled that Fangio had lost three second place finishes, any of which would have made him Champion. Awkward question: What would have happened if Fagioli, clearly a support driver, had won the title? I bet

there were a few sighs of relief as its credibility would have been seriously in doubt. Surely, winning the title by winning races had to be the purpose of it all.

A week after the Italian Grand Prix came the awful news of the death of the very fine Raymond Sommer. He had accepted an invitation to race at Cadours in a minor Formula Two race as a crowd-puller. Driving an 1100cc V-twin Cooper-JAP; he is believed to have suffered a seized wheel bearing and he crashed, somersaulted into a tree and, wearing his usual linen helmet, a great driver was now gone. It was a catastrophe for France, having lost Wimille the year before, and it would be so many years before France produced someone of the status of a Sommer or Wimille ... and that would be ... Alain Prost.

Some overlooked Championship facts

Non-scorer Luigi Villoresi retired twice from third place with car trouble. These would have yielded him sixth place that year, and well reflected his contribution to the competition, but a glance at the points table fails to find him. His prime years being perhaps the pre-Championship ones.
Dorino Serafini only ever competed in one Championship Grand Prix, the 1950 Italian, and was in third place (4 points) when his car was taken over by Ascari (allowable then) at his routine pit stop for tyres. He advanced it to second place (6 points), but shared drives also shared the points, so each driver got 3. I wonder if Serafini would have preferred the 4 points for a lone drive to third place. That extra point would have elevated him from equal tenth to equal seventh place ... and from a single drive. Good, don't you think?
Odd fact : Not one of the first round point-scorers also scored in the second!

VISIT VELOCE ON THE WEB – WWW.VELOCE.CO.UK
All current books • New book news • Special offers • Gift vouchers • Forum

54

Chapter 10

1951
What will Alfa do now?

At last a challenger to Alfa Romeo had emerged, in the form of the Ferrari 375 V12. This car had possessed the technical brilliance to lead and then split the Alfas at the finish in the Italian Grand Prix the previous year, in the hands of Alberto Ascari. He had won at Barcelona, admittedly in the absence of Alfa, so reliability seemed to be there also. They say that it only takes two to make a fight, and there were only two marques that could be relied upon to turn up. Thankfully, the two-cars-per-team rule of modern times hadn't been thought of, and, at Monza, between them, the Italian giants would enter no fewer than ten cars.

On the horizon was the British BRM which, after the debacle at Silverstone, had won a meaningless race at Goodwood, but, at least, was up and running. Would it go as well as it sounded? People dared to hope. It was so immensely full of sound and fury that it must signify something (to borrow from the Bard). The BRM couldn't come soon enough, and, if it did, a great year was in prospect.

Maserati had nothing new to offer for 1951, the old 4CLT/48 being just a grid-filler. The company seemed more interested in sports cars; F1 being a lost cause requiring too many funds to compete with any hope of success. Talbot-Lago Works had no funds to update its obsolete car, and retired from racing, leaving the private owners to do their best, which was to fill the grids and provide mid-field scraps for scraps ...

Most teams were using the same line-up as the previous year, but Alfa Romeo added Consalvo Sanesi. It had responded to the Ferrari danger by finding more power from increased engine speed – up from around 8500 to about 9500, with a resultant power increase from 370 to over 400 – some sources quoting 425bhp. Greater thirst – 1.6mpg – meant larger tanks and extra weight. It's worth recalling that a good fuel crew might add 75 gallons (340 litres) in

little over 30 seconds, gravity fed – that's not far short of the rate (12 litres/sec) used in recent F1! Rear suspension was modified, and the new cars designated were '159,' but didn't appear until Silverstone.

Scuderia Ferrari had a very useful addition to the squad in the name of Froilán González – fame awaited him – and, occasionally, Piero Taruffi. Ferrari had produced 380bhp from the 4.5-litre engine, so Alfa should worry, as the Ferrari wouldn't be much slower than the 159 on the track, and could be more economical. Tony Vandervell had purchased a Ferrari 375 to fit his thin shell bearings into, replacing the standard roller type. Known as the 'Thinwall Special,' a variety of top people would drive it.

BRM was now operational, after a fashion, and would use Reg Parnell and Peter Walker. Power figures of over 500bhp had been seen, apparently, but reliability was, sadly, still a dream at this point.

Simca-Gordini was the only other Works team, with Robert Manzon, Maurice Trintignant and André Simon trying their best in a hopeless task.

No serious opposition would come from any other quarter, as Maserati 4CLTs and Talbot-Lagos were well outdated.

The Grand Prix driver's diary of single-seater racing for 1951

11th March	F1 – Gran Premio di Siracusa (I) – 268.4 miles
26th March	F1 – Richmond Trophy at Goodwood (UK) – 286 miles
26th March	F1 – Grand Prix de Pau (F) – 193.7 miles
8th April	F2 – Grand Prix du Marseille (F) – 149.3 miles
22nd April	F1 – Gran Premio di San Remo at

	Ospedaletti (I) – 186.5 miles	
29th April	F1 – Grand Prix de Bordeaux (F) – 187.8 miles	
5th May	F1 – *Daily Express* International Trophy at Silverstone (UK) – 144.4 miles	
13th May	F2 – Gran Premio dell' Autodromo di Monza – 195.8 miles	
14th May	F1 – Festival of Britain Trophy at Goodwood (UK) – 524 miles	
20th May	F1 – Grand Prix de Paris at Bois de Boulogne (F) – 194.4 miles	
20th May	F2 – Gran Premio del V Centenario Colombiano at Genova (I) – 179.4 miles	
27th May	F1 – **Grosse Preis der Schweiz** at Bremgarten (S) – 190 miles	
2nd June	F1 – Ulster Trophy at Dundrod (UK) – 200.1 miles	
3rd June	F2 – Circuit du Lac at Aix-les-Bains (F) – 105.7 miles	
17th June	F1 – **Grand Prix de Belgique** at Spa Francorchamps (B) – 315.9 miles	
24th June	F2 – Gran Premio di Napoli at Posillipo (I) – 152.8 miles	
1st July	F1 – **Grand Prix de l'ACF** at Reims-Gueux (F) – 373 miles	
14th July	F1 – **British Grand Prix** at Silverstone (UK) – 259.9 miles	
22nd July	F1 – Grote Prijs van Nederland at Zandvoort (N) – 234.5 miles	
29th July	F1 – **Grosse Preis von Deutschland** at Nürburgring (D) – 283.2 miles	
5th August	F1 – Grand Prix d'Albi (F) – 189.2 miles	
15th August	F1 – Circuito di Pescara (I) – 192.6 miles	
2nd September	F1 – Gran Premio di Bari (I) – 223.7 miles	
16th September	F1 – **Gran Premio d'Italia at Monza** (I) – 313.2 miles	
23rd September	F2 – Gran Premio di Modena (I) – 155.8 miles	
29th September	F1 – Goodwood Trophy at Goodwood (UK) – 357 miles	
28th October	F1 – **Gran Premio d'España** at Pedralbes (E) – 274.8 miles	

27 events of total race mileage = 5281 miles – 5073 max due to simultaneous races.

Events in bold are seven World Championship rounds – 33.3 per cent of the 21 F1 races run.

✴✴ 1mo Gran Premio di Siracusa
80 laps of 3.355 miles = 268.4 miles.
13 entries – 12 started – 5 finished.

Front row: A Ascari; G Farina. Row two: L Villoresi; D Serafini. No times available.

11-MAR: Two of the Ferrari entries were for 2.54-litre V12 cars (prototypes for 1954 F1?). Released by Alfa, Farina carried Maserati's hopes, and placed himself on the front row alongside Ascari on the 2 x 2 grid. He then chased the lead-swapping Ascari and Villoresi for 47 laps, but then retired. Ascari led from lap 38 until engine failure with 11 laps to go. So, the small-engined Ferraris beat the two old Talbots despite being three laps back, while Bira's and Harry Schell's Maseratis joined Farina's in failure.

1st	L Villoresi (W)	Ferrari 375 in 2h-52m-31.6s	90.72
2nd	D Serafini (W)	Ferrari 212 2.54lt	3 laps
3rd	R Fischer (EE)	Ferrari 212 2.54lt	3 laps
F lap	A Ascari (W)	Ferrari 375 in 2m-06.1s	95.79

✴✴ XII Grand Prix de Pau
110 laps of 1.761 miles = 193.7 miles.
16 entries – 15 started – 6 finished.

Front row: A Ascari – 1m-40.8s (62.89mph); L Villoresi 1.3s; D Serafini (Ferrari 212) 3.6s.

26-MAR: Easter Monday meant the classic Pau race clashing with Goodwood. Nimble Gordinis joined the Siracuse cars. Ascari led from Villoresi and they swapped places a couple of times then Ascari led from lap 11 until retiring on lap 46 with transmission failure – a second race lost. deGraffenried's Maserati held third until refuelling, and had recovered third when Ascari stopped. He was behind Rosier then and retired handing the place to Farina, who had dropped to last on lap three when stopping for new plugs. Rosier had driven unusually hard and was rewarded for his effort as the only unlapped finisher.

1st	L Villoresi (W)	Ferrari 375 in 3h-17m-39.9s	58.80
2nd	L Rosier	Talbot-Lago T26C	1m-36s
3rd	G Farina (SM)	Maserati 4CLT/48 s/c	3 laps
F lap	A Ascari (W)	Ferrari 375 in 1m-41.7s	62.34r

Richmond Trophy (Goodwood)
12 laps of 2.38 miles = 28.6 miles.
17 entries – 10 started – 7 finished.

Front row: R Parnell (Maserati); B Bira (Maserati?); G Whitehead (ERA). No times available.

26-MAR: By this time Goodwood had 'stretched' its F1 race to 12 laps. Were people slowly realising that such short events didn't do justice to Formula One racing? If so, they were very slow. Talbot-Lagos were present, but loved long races so fuel economy didn't help them. Parnell led away, but Bira beat him out of Madgwick Corner. Parnell went off when replying, recovered his place, but then his chase broke the engine. Bira's 4.5 OSCA engine car set a new record. A first defeat for Parnell at Goodwood.

1st	B Bira (SP)	Maserati-4CLT-OSCA in 19m-44.0s	86.84
2nd	B Shawe-Taylor	ERA B type	17.2s
F lap	B Bira	Maserati 4CLT/48-OSCA in 1m-35.4s	89.81r

✳✳ VI Gran Premio di San Remo (Ospedaletti)
90 laps of 2.073 miles = 186.5 miles.
20 entries – 17 started – 7 finished.
Front row: A Ascari – 1m-52.0s (66.63mph); L Villoresi (Ferrari 375) 0.4s; E deGraffenried (Maserati) 3.2s.
22-APR: Farina didn't arrive, so there was no stopping more domination and place swapping by Ascari and Villoresi, but this time Villoresi crashed on lap 62 and crawled back to the pits. Serafini and Fischer then held their podium places to the finish. deGraffenried repeated his Pau race, this time losing fourth at the pits to Fischer and then retiring on lap 60 to the benefit of Harry Schell. A fine performance by Stirling Moss in his now central-seat F2 HWM saw him finish fifth ahead of the lumbering Talbot-Lagos. Claes' Talbot had crashed in practice due to a fracture brake pipe, and had killed a few people. From a modern perspective it's impossible to understand how spectator deaths like this could be accepted, but that's how it was. This was racing on public roads, obviously not designed for spectators, and there was no pressure for purpose-built circuits.

1st	A Ascari (W)	Ferrari 375 in 2h-57m-08.2s	63.19
2nd	D Serafini (W)	Ferrari 375	1m-25s
3rd	R Fischer	Ferrari 212	2 laps
F lap	A Ascari	Ferrari 375 in 1m-53.8s	65.57
Pole	A Ascari	Ferrari 375 in 1m-52.0s	66.63

✳ Grand Prix de Bordeaux
123 laps of 1.527 miles = 187.8 miles.
16 entries – 15 started – 7 finished.
Front row: L Rosier; M Trintignant (Simca-Gordini 15); H Schell (Maserati 4CLT/48). No times available.
29-APR: No Works Ferraris, but Fischer's 2.5-litre car and Whitehead's old 1.5-litre s/c represented 'The Prancing Horse'. World Champion Farina had his Maserati, but was tenth on the grid, and retired with blower failure. Fischer scorched ahead of Rosier but, after only 14 laps, brake fade meant that Rosier now led. Whitehead's steady pace netted third. Bira's OSCA-engined Maserati was fourth, four laps down after four stops, each of

which probably cost him the best part of a lap! The Works Simca-Gordinis were poor on a suitable tight circuit, and the British F2 HWMs got seventh, with Chiron, and Macklin retired.

1st	L Rosier	Talbot-Lago T26C in 3h-07m-11.3s	60.21
2nd	R Fischer	Ferrari 212	1m-9s
3rd	P Whitehead	Ferrari 125 s/c	2 laps
F lap	L Rosier	Talbot-Lago T26C in 1m-28.1s	62.41

✳✳✳ III *Daily Express* International Trophy (Silverstone)
15-lap heat + 35-lap final of 2.888 miles = 144.4 miles.
34 entries – 30 started – 17 finished.
Poles: Heat one: F Bonetto – 1m-46s (98.08mph); Heat two: C Sanesi (Alfa Romeo) – 1m-52s (92.83mph).
05-MAY: Alfa brought four of the new 159s, but, sadly, Ferrari withdrew its entries for Ascari and Villoresi. Tony Vandervell had bought a Ferrari 375, and fitted his renowned thin shell bearings – this car being known as the 'Thinwall Special.' Shamefully, no BRMs were entered. Fangio and Bonetto swapped cars for heat one, putting Bonetto on pole with Fangio's time! In that heat Parnell, from the third row, split the Alfas, having caused Fangio to receive a 'speed up' sign! Farina's and Sanesi's Alfas had the second heat from Bira's 4.5-litre Maserati-OSCA. Then came the final – a hailstorm monsoon exploded at the start, with which only Parnell's car coped. Speeds were down by over a third, and the race was abandoned after six of the 35 laps. So, was this the first Alfa defeat after all? Perhaps not. However, Parnell had shown what the Ferrari could do.

1st	R Parnell (GAV)	Ferrari 375 'Thinwall' in 16m-48s	61.89
2nd	D Hamilton	Talbot-Lago T26C	22s
3rd	J-M Fangio (W)	Alfa Romeo 159s/c	1m-10s
F lap	G Farina (W) (heat 2)	Alfa Romeo 159s/c in 1m-47s	97.17r

✳ Festival of Britain Trophy (Goodwood)
7 lap heats +15-lap final of 2.38 miles = 52.4 miles.
20 started.
Poles: Heat one: R Parnell – 1m-32.0s (93.12mph). Heat two: B Bira (Maserati/OSCA) 1m-36.0s (89.25mph).
14-MAY: Listed as Formule Libre but all the serious racing done by F1 cars – so it's an F1 competition. To celebrate the London 'Festival of Britain' the World Champion Farina was invited. Heats were won by Parnell and Bira ahead of Farina, and promised a good final. Parnell led off and appeared to be

in command but Farina closed with a track record. Parnell realised the danger and pulled away exploding the new lap record. Sadly, Bira's OSCA-engined Maserati had failed at the start so we will never know how much he might have got involved. deGraffenried was only 0.6 seconds clear of Shawe-Taylor's ERA.

1st	R Parnell (GAV)	Ferrari 375 'Thinwall' in 23m-34.2s	90.88
2nd	G Farina	Maserati 4CLT/48s/c	10.8s
3rd	E deGraffenried	Maserati 4CLT/48s/c	43.6s
F lap	R Parnell	Ferrari 125/375 'Thinwall' in 1m- 31.4s	93.75r

✷✷ V Grand Prix de Paris (Bois de Boulogne)
125 laps of 1.555 miles = 194.4 miles.
16 entries – 14 started – 8 finished.
Front row: E deGraffenried (Maserati) 1m-19.2s (70.69mph); G Farina (Maserati); P Etancelin (Talbot-Lago).
20-MAY: Too close to the Swiss GP for Ferrari and Alfa to enter, but Fangio, Farina and González found drives – Fangio for the Gordini Works – which recovers the status of this race. Manzon's Works Simca-Gordini took off like a rocket, but Farina led after ten laps as Manzon's clutch played up and put him out after 20 laps. Fangio soon took his little Gordini past Farina to lead a few laps, but then cylinder head trouble delayed him a lot. Then the problem was fixed he obliterated the lap record, only to retire on lap 49. González, new to a Talbot-Lago and 13th on the grid, actually led for 30 laps after Farina pitted, but dropped back after losing the lead. Quiz question: What was the most laps of any F1 race? Here's the answer you've always wanted to know.

1st	G Farina (SM)	Maserati 4CLT/48-s/c in 2h-53m-12.5s	67.33
2nd	F González	Talbot-Lago T26C	39.6s
3rd	L Rosier	Talbot-Lago T26C	1 lap
F lap	J-M Fangio (W)	Simca-Gordini T15-s/c in 1m-18.7s	71.14

✷✷✷ (WC1) XI Grosser Preis der Schweiz (Bremgarten-Berne)
42 laps of 4.524 miles = 190 miles.
26 entries –21 started – 12 finished.
Front row: J-M Fangio – 2m-35.9s (104.46mph); G Farina 1.9s; L Villoresi (Ferrari 375) 3.4s.
27-MAY: The four Alfa 159s faced three Ferrari 375s, but no BRMs arrived, just the usual. Fangio, Farina and Villoresi made up the front row, with deGraffenried's Alfa (drafted in on his home ground) next to Sanesi on row two. Ascari was

centre of row three, recovering from burns received a week earlier in an F2 race. A brilliant victory by Fangio ensued, in appalling conditions. He briefly lost the lead to Farina as he exited the pits after his fuel stop, but was soon back in front of Farina's Alfa, which, incidentally, had enlarged fuel tanks to obviate a fuel stop. This, though, didn't stop him being caught rapidly by Taruffi's Ferrari at the end, and losing second with just a lap to go. The non-stopping strategy hadn't worked for Alfa, probably because the weight of the fuel must have handicapped Farina. Consalvo Sanesi's Alfa was fourth, a lap down. Villoresi retired from third on lap 12, while off-form Ascari started and finished sixth. He was passed on lap five by Taruffi who stormed into third by lap 14 and held it all the way until catching Farina. Of the seven key players only Villoresi's Ferrari retired while Alfa was still in charge.

1st	J-M Fangio (W)	Alfa Romeo 159 s/c in 2h-07m-53.6s	89.13
2nd	P Taruffi (W)	Ferrari 375	55.2s
3rd	G Farina (W)	Alfa Romeo 159 s/c	1m-19s
F lap	J-M Fangio	Alfa Romeo 159 s/c in 2m-51.1s	95.18

✷ V Ulster Trophy (Dundrod)
27 laps of 7.416 miles = 200.2 miles.
24 entries – 19 started – 12 finished
Front row: G Farina – 4m-51.8s (91.51mph); R Parnell 5.4s; B.Shawe-Taylor (ERA) 25.0s
02-JUN: Another Alfa (Farina) and Ferrari (Thinwall Special) duel was in prospect on Britain's best road circuit, and of Grand Prix length, too. It would be a simple head-to-head as next on the grid was Shawe-Taylor's uncompetitive ERA; over eight per cent slower! This time Farina drew well ahead, but his necessary fuel stop took 43 seconds, which gave Parnell the lead. Two laps later Farina was ahead again, pulling away and achieving 160mph on the straight on the narrow road. A terrific ERA scrap saw Shawe-Taylor beat Bob Gerard by the smallest margin, and beating the Talbot-Lago of Giraud-Cabantous into fifth place.

1st	G Farina	Alfa Romeo 159s/c in 2h-11m-21.8s	91.46
2nd	R Parnell	Ferrari 375 'Thinwall'	1m-12s
3rd	B Shawe-Taylor	ERA 'R9B s/c	1 lap
F lap	G Farina (W)	Alfa Romeo 159s/c in 4m-44.0s	94.01

✷✷✷ (WC2) XIII Grand Prix de Belgique (Spa)
36 laps of 8.774 miles = 315.9 miles.
17 entries –13 started – 9 finished.

Front row: J-M Fangio – 4m-25s (119.19mph); G Farina 3s; L Villoresi 4s.

17-JUN: This time it was three apiece for the 'big boys,' as the Vandervell Thinwall Ferrari 375 for Parnell didn't arrive. Seven Talbot-Lagos completed the grid, and would at least give spectators something to look at as they waited for the real competitors to reappear. Villoresi had been just a second adrift of Farina in third grid spot, and it was he who led at first. Farina passed him on lap three, though, followed by Ascari (fit and well, having recovered from his burns), then Fangio, who soon took second place. Taruffi's Ferrari retired after eight laps, and Sanesi's Alfa soon after. Fangio's pit stop was an unmitigated disaster: 14 minutes to replace a wheel due to a spoke jamming the hub splines. No force would shift it, so a new hub and drum had to be found! Ascari passed Villoresi on lap 20, and the podium positions were now settled. A 120mph lap was a new landmark – the Alfas achieving over 190mph down the Masta straight. My God, I wish I'd seen that! Fangio was last finisher in ninth.

1st	G Farina (W)	Alfa Romeo 159 s/c in 2h-45m-46.2s	114.32
2nd	A Ascari (W)	Ferrari 375	2m-51s
3rd	L Villoresi (W)	Ferrari 375	4m-22s
F lap	J-M Fangio	Alfa Romeo 159 s/c in 4m-22.1s	120.51r

Championship positions:
Farina 12; Fangio 10; Taruffi 6.

✷✷✷ (WC3) XXXVIII Grand Prix de l'ACF (Reims-Gueux)
77 laps of 4.856 miles = 373.0 miles.
25 entries –23 started – 9 finished.

Front row: J-M Fangio – 2m-25.7s (119.99mph); G Farina (Alfa Romeo) 1.7s; A Ascari 2.4s.

01-JUL: The longest Championship race distance ever! It was now Ascari's Ferrari alongside the Alfas on the grid, but still in third spot. It was Ascari, Fangio, Villoresi, Sanesi, González and Farina for three laps. So that was Ferrari, Alfa, Ferrari, Alfa, Ferrari, Alfa – WOW! What could be better? Was the denouement of this three-act play at hand, or were there more to come? There is no script any more. Ascari led until retiring on lap nine – a relief for Alfa. Fangio had magneto trouble on the next lap and pitted, so Farina, sixth on lap one, now led from Villoresi and González. Fangio soon retired, and he and Ascari took over their teammates' cars at the fuel and tyre stops. This left Farina well away but he also had magneto trouble on lap 44 and dropped back to fifth. Fangio pitted, but Ascari didn't need to so led, until brake fade gave back the lead to Fangio from lap 51 to the finish. After practice Reims thought it was faster than Spa; not so. A lucky escape for Alfa; now for the next act.

1st	Fagioli/Fangio (W)	Alfa Romeo 159 s/c in 3h-22m-11.0s	110.97
2nd	González/Ascari (W)	Ferrari 375	58.2s
3rd	L Villoresi (W)	Ferrari 375	3 laps
F lap	J-M Fangio	Alfa Romeo 159 s/c in 2m-27.8s	118.29r

Championship positions:
Fangio 15; Farina 14; Ascari 9.

––––––––––

Clearly only the car was required to complete the whole race distance, a replacement driver having probably spent a little time waiting to take over. It is beyond dispute that it was almost always the right thing to do to get the car to the finish in the best position, and the main credit will go to the man who improves the position. But, looking back, it seems strange that a Driver's World Championship had been created rather a constructors' title.

Having said that, since the car carries the race number, lap scoring the drivers would have been impossible.

––––––––––

✷✷✷ (WC4) VI British Grand Prix (Silverstone)
90 laps of 2.888 miles = 259.9 miles.
25 entries –23 started – 9 finished.

Front row: F González – 1m-43.4s (100.57mph); J-M Fangio 1.0s; G Farina 1.6s; A Ascari 2.0s.

14-JUL: The two 'armies' had four 'tanks' each here, Bonetto replacing Fagioli for Alfa, and Peter Whitehead in the Thinwall Ferrari supplementing the three Works regulars. Alfa must have worried with González taking Ferrari's first pole, with Ascari on the outer flank. The BRMs arrived at last, but too late to practise, so they started at the back (frustratingly). Strangely, it was Bonetto at the lead for a lap, but he was soon put in his place by the rest. González had led for nine laps when Fangio overtook, but González held Fangio in his sights and, amazingly, retook the master on lap 39. Ascari, to his credit, later refused the offer of the car at a pit stop – he was team leader – and little-known González sailed on to a famous, fully-deserved victory. The BRMs lasted, and were fifth and seventh, five laps down. Trouble was that the noise they made demanded a result to shout about.

However, the shouting was about Ferrari! It had been on the cards for a while, but now we have the variety that is the spice of life – and the lifeblood of sport. An unbroken reign of five years was brought to a close.

1st	F González (W)	Ferrari 375 in 2h-42m-18.2s	96.11
2nd	J-M Fangio (W)	Alfa Romeo 159 s/c	51.0s
3rd	L Villoresi (W)	Ferrari 375	2 laps
F lap	G Farina (W)	Alfa Romeo 159 s/c in 1m-44.0s	99.99r

Championship positions:
Fangio 21; Farina 15; Villoresi 12.

✳ II Grote Prijs van Nederland (Zandvoort)
90 laps of 2.605 miles = 234.5 miles.
15 entries – 12 started – 8 finished.
Front row: G Farina – 1m-52.9s (83.06mph); L Chiron (Talbot-Lago) 1.2s; A Pilette 1.3s.
22-JUL: Alfa and Ferrari concentrated on the German GP. Farina and González entered Maseratis, but González didn't arrive. Farina duly led, with Pilette in second, but he lost that place to Etancelin on lap five. Farina's joy ended in Maserati fashion with oil shortage on lap 19 and a fresh supply didn't cure things. Rosier now led, having been tenth on lap one, and pulled away to a clear victory. Moss climbed from tenth on lap three to fourth on lap 29. Fischer and Etancelin both punctured, giving Moss second on lap 75. Pilette relieved Etancelin of third place on lap 80, but five laps later he slid off on the sandy circuit (a natural Zandvoort hazard), and a wheel broke throwing him out as the car rolled, but not seriously injuring him. Moss pitted with misfiring with two laps left, and, with Etancelin fast approaching, Moss was pushed back into the race minus bonnet, but it was too late.

1st	L Rosier	Talbot-Lago T26C in 2h-19m-19.4s	78.45
2nd	P Etancelin	Talbot-Lago T26C	1 lap
3rd	S Moss (W)	HWM-Alta (F2)	1 lap
F lap	A.Pilette (ENB)	Talbot-Lago T26C in 1m-54.0s	82.26

✳✳✳ (WC5) XVI Grosser Preis von Deutschland (N Nürburgring)
20 laps of 14.16 miles = 283.2 miles.
27 entries – 22 started – 11 finished.
Front row: A Ascari – 9m-55.8s (85.64mph); F González 1.7s; J-M Fangio 3.2s; G Farina 5.2s.
29-JUL: It happened again! Germany was now back on the racing calendar, and Fangio's Alfa was only third on the grid! However, he led until lap five when Ascari took over. Fangio made the first of his two stops on the next lap, and led again when the Ferraris had their single stop. But the Alfas were

in trouble with overheating, and Farina lasted just eight laps. Fangio was unable to make enough ground to overcome his second fuel stop and Ascari swept past. An unexpected late tyre stop still left Ascari and Ferrari triumphant. González and Villoresi followed, so Fangio had averted a Ferrari podium whitewash. Over the last three Championship rounds Ferrari's campaign against Alfa had been unstoppable. The former status quo was now on its head.

1st	A Ascari (W)	Ferrari 375 in 3h-23m-03.3s	83.76
2nd	J-M Fangio (W)	Alfa Romeo 159 s/c	30.5s
3rd	F González (W)	Ferrari 375	4m-39s
F lap	J-M Fangio (W)	Alfa Romeo 159 s/c in 9m-55.8s	85.64

Championship positions:
Fangio 27; Ascari 17; González/Farina/Villoresi 15.

✳ XIII Grand Prix de Albi
34 laps of 5.564 miles = 189.2 miles.
16 entries – 14 started – 8 finished.
Front row: M Trintignant – 3m-08.8s (106.09mph); L Rosier 0.7s; A.Simon 1.6s.
05-AUG: Seven Talbot-Lagos and four Works Simca-Gordinis, plus a few F2 cars, but a good race took place. Andre Simon and Maurice Trintignant in Simca-Gordinis swapped the lead many times until two laps from home when Simon retired – as Gordinis were expected to. Manzon's Gordini had done likewise early in the race, which at least allowed the supposed favourites to get second and third. Trintignant's car survived and produced the first win for a supercharged Simca-Gordini.

1st	M Trintignant (W)	Simca-Gordini T15-s/c in 1h-51m-23.1s	101.87
2nd	L Rosier (ER)	Talbot-Lago T26C	2m-26s
3rd	L Chiron (ER)	Talbot-Lago T26C	1 lap
F lap	M Trintignant	Simca-Gordini T15-s/c in 3m-11.6s	104.54

✳✳ XX Circuito di Pescara
12 laps of 16.05 miles = 192.6 miles.
15 entries and starters – 8 finished.
Front row: A Ascari 10m-43.6s (89.79mph); L Villoresi 5.6s; L Chiron 39.9s.
15-AUG: Ferrari entered but not Alfa Romeo – both or neither was best for a good race. González, new to this very long circuit, was behind Chiron's Talbot who took the outside of the front row – a brilliant effort. Ascari retired with

overheating after only a minute, and it was Villoresi from González on lap one, with Chiron and Rosier well back in a race of their own. Ascari took over Villoresi's car at its tyre stop after only four laps. So keen was he that he tried to start with the car still jacked up! Transmission failure stopped him within a lap. González now led easily, and two tyre stops were accommodated. Chiron's third place but brakeless Talbot hit the final chicane and finished fourth, disguised as a tractor delivering straw.

1st	F González (W)	Ferrari 375 in 2h-14m-59.8s	85.61
2nd	L Rosier	Talbot-Lago T26C	7m-20s
3rd	P Etancelin	Talbot-Lago T26C	9m-10s
F lap	F González	Ferrari 375 in 10m-44.8s	89.62

✳✳✳ V Gran Premio di Bari
65 laps of 3.441 miles = 223.7 miles.
21 entries – 19 started – 8 started
Front row: J-M Fangio – 2m-20.2s (88.36mph); A Ascari 1.0s; F González 1.4s.

02-SEP: Both big teams entered here in strength, making this a major event. Stirling Moss arrived to drive a promised Ferrari but found the new 2.5-litre engined F2 car given to Taruffi. A snub never forgotten after such a long trek. Fangio led from Ascari, Villoresi and Farina, who retired on lap eight when in second, having passed the two Ferraris. Ascari stopped ten laps later when in second. At Fangio's pit stop Villoresi took the lead, but he had been clouted at the back by another car, and a lap later the damaged oil system lost him his oil. González had dropped to the back at the start, but by lap ten was in fifth place, having benefitted from the retirements. So had third-placed 'old man' Taruffi, from 11th grid spot. Where would Moss have finished?

1st	J-M Fangio (W)	Alfa Romeo 159-s/c in 2h-39m-58.3s	83.89
2nd	F González (W)	Ferrari 375	1m-12s
3rd	P Taruffi (W)	Ferrari 500/625	3 laps
F lap	J-M Fangio	Alfa Romeo 159-s/c in 2m-20.6s	88.11

✳✳✳ (WC6) XXI Gran Premio d'Italia (Monza)
80 laps of 3.915 miles = 313.2 miles.
25 entries – 22 started – 8 finished.
Front row: J-M Fangio – 1m-53.2s (124.49mph); G Farina 0.7s; A Ascari 1.9s; F González 2.7s.

16-SEP: Four Alfas and five Ferraris started, but sadly no BRMs. Fangio and Farina were over a second ahead of the Ferraris on the grid, so it looked as though the rot had been addressed. Fangio led Ascari at first, lost the lead, retook it. but then had to pit for tyres on lap 14. He dropped to fifth, recoverd to third, but his engine failed on lap 39. deGraffenried's Alfa had lasted only one lap, and Farina's only six. Farina took over Bonetto's car, but his pursuit was fruitless as he had to refuel. The speed advantage over the Ferrari was now too small for Alfa Romeo to overcome its thirst handicap. Fangio's title now looked very shaky.

A hat-trick now for Ferrari. Alfa Romeo would have dismissed such a thought as impossible at the season's start.

In the battle for 'fastest track' status between Spa, Reims and Monza the latter was now clear, but car 'updates' had helped.

The BRM saga – The cars had arrived for Parnell and test-driver Ken Richardson. However, after a spin in practice the RAC refused to recognise Richardson as qualified to race. Parnell was eighth on the grid in 2m-02.2s, and Hans Stuck had replaced Richardson, but after a few laps a serious gearbox problem reared its head, perhaps due to the high speed circuit. Designer Perter Berthon saw potential seizure as dangerous and withdrew the cars. This was disaster for F1 as a whole.

1st	A Ascari (W)	Ferrari 375 in 2h-42m-39.3s	115.52
2nd	F González (W)	Ferrari 375	35.6s
3rd	Bonetto/Farina (W)	Alfa Romeo 159M s/c	1 lap
F lap	G Farina (W)	Alfa Romeo 159M s/c in 1m-56.5s	120.97r

Championship positions:
Fangio 27; Ascari 25; González 21.

IV Goodwood Trophy (Goodwood)
15 laps of 2.38 miles = 35.7 miles.
21 entries – 16 started – 9 finished.
Front row: G Farina; R Parnell; B Shawe-Taylor; A Rolt no times available.

29-SEP: Another mouth-watering Parnell/Farina duel was in prospect, with Farina in the latest Alfa. Parnell was away first, but Farina passed on the second lap and held Parnell off. He pulverised the lap record to do it, though. As his winning margin was only 5.6 seconds, so did Parnell, and the average was well up on the previous lap record! Tony Rolt with a famous Delage, of originally 1927 vintage and ERA-powered, was amazing with third, one lap down and beating all the ERAs.

1st	G Farina (W)	Alfa Romeo 159M-s/c in 22m-31.2s	95.11
2nd	R Parnell (GAV)	Ferrari 375 'Thinwall Special'	5.6s
F lap	G Farina	Alfa Romeo 159-s/c in 1m-28.0s	97.36r

✷✷✷ (WC7) XI Gran Premio d'España (Pedralbes)

70 laps of 3.925 miles = 274.8 miles.
25 entries – 19 started – 9 finished.
Front row: A Ascari – 2m-10.59s (108.19mph); J-M Fangio 1.68s; F González 3.42s; G Farina 4.35s.

28-OCT: Only the best four Championship results counted, and Fangio and Ascari had already scored four times, but still, whoever won would be Champion – not forgetting González who could trump both of them if he won and they failed to score. It was Ascari, Farina and Fangio for two laps when Fangio took the lead on lap four to the flag. Ascari's challenge had been scuppered when Ferrari decided to use smaller 16in wheels on all its cars, and the faster spinning tyres threw treads. Ascari pitted on only lap eight, but González lasted until lap 15 when 17in wheels were fitted, which solved the problem. He salvaged second for Ferrari. Ascari made his third stop on lap 28 when, by now, the solution had been found, and he received 17in wheels. He was by now out of contention, though, but made fourth. A classic case of 'If it ain't broke, don't fix it?' What if … ?

1st	J-M Fangio (W)	Alfa Romeo 159 s/c in 2h-46s-51.1s	98.76
2nd	F González (W)	Ferrari 375	54.28s
3rd	G Farina (W)	Alfa Romeo 159 s/c	1m-46s
F lap	JMFangio (W)	Alfa Romeo 159 s/c in 2m-16.93s	103.18

Final Championship positions:
Fangio 31; Ascari 25; González 24.

Summary of 1951

Nineteen decent races were run, all within Europe, yet only seven counted for the World Championship.

The most prolific was privateer Louis Rosier who competed in 18 and finished all but one of his starts. Seventeen finishes out of 18 starts is outstanding in any era, but when the finish rate is less than half that's just phenomenal. He won twice and was six times in the podium positions. They called him a plodder, but I wonder how many were a little jealous of him at the end. Farina was next most prolific with 16 starts and four victories.

Winners of the 21 graded F1 races of 1951 – quantity & quality of success

4 wins	J-M Fangio (4A) G Farina (A, B, C, D)	9 wins	Ferrari (4A, 4B, C)
		7 wins	Alfa Romeo (5A, C, D)
3 wins	A Ascari (2A, B)	2 wins	Talbot-Lago (2C) Maserati (B, D)
2 wins	F González (A, B) R Parnell (A, C) L Villoresi (2B) L Rosier (2C)	1 win	Simca-Gordini (C)
1 win	M Trintignant (C) B Bira (D)		

The World Championship

Although the title race again went to the final race, no other driver could claim that ill-fortune alone had robbed him of the title. This title campaign was a narrow victory for Juan-Manuel Fangio. After an early challenge by Fangio's teammate, the inaugural World Champion 'Nino' Farina, his challenge faded and he was out of the running before the final.

Going into that final round at Pedralbes both Alfa Romeo and Ferrari had scored three victories, shared between four drivers, three of whom could still take the crown, so the contest was wide open. However, the title was only truly settled when Fangio crossed the line, as his retirement could have presented the top prize to González if he'd got the fastest lap point. They would both have had two wins, but Fangio had shared one of his, so González would have been crowned. No-one remembers how close he came to that, and few mention him in that vein. Ascari had to win to increase his points total, but was soon out of the running with tyre trouble.

It looks strange that Fangio had to drop points for the win at Reims in favour of a second place score, but that victory was shared and therefore worth four points increased to five with the fastest lap point. This is still less than the six points gained for an unshared second place. Not many people appreciate these days how near Ascari and particular González came to the world title in 1951. Though it wasn't the 'be-all-and-end-all' it is now.

Interestingly, had there been a manufacturer's title, then the supposedly unbeatable Alfa Romeos would have lost out to Ferrari. But the whole show was still an Italian affair as far as manufacturers were concerned. This was the last year that forced-induction cars would race in the Championship until 1977, when Renault brought turbocharging into Formula One.

The Alfa Romeo stranglehold on Formula One races had been shown in 1950 to be perhaps not impossible to challenge, but I don't think anyone expected such a great contest for the

World Championship as the two giant teams produced. This was, of course, due to Ferrari having seen the light shown by the Talbot-Lago 26C a few years before. Even though Ferrari was a recent addition to the top marques in F1, it was Ferrari, not Talbot, that had the finance and technical skills to exploit the possibility it had seen. The Ferrari 375 used less than half the fuel of the latest Alfa Romeo 159, whose extra power over the 158 was at the expense of worse economy and reliability. So the seeds of this great battle were sown, with the best talent shared by the teams.

The chances of a repeat battle for 1952 exploded when Alfa Romeo announced its withdrawal from racing. Its 158/159 models were developments of a pre-war design, and the company was unable to fund a completely new car,

the creation of which was now necessary to be competitive. The only hope was for a miracle at BRM. So, following this great season, after just two years the credibility of the World Championship must have seemed in jeopardy – a very worrying thought.

New teams of 1951

GA Vandervell (GAV): The team that would become Vanwall, run by the bearing tycoon. This was the very beginning of an historic British team, which would ultimately show the way for British success in Formula One.

Ecurie Rosier (ER): Louis Rosier expanded to enter others as well as himself.

VISIT VELOCE ON THE WEB – WWW.VELOCE.CO.UK
All current books • New book news • Special offers • Gift vouchers • Forum

63

Chapter 11

1952

What now?

1951 had shown that it takes just two good teams to make a battle worthy of the title 'World Champion.' But now there is just one: Ferrari. The old guard had not only been beaten, but had' thrown in the towel' and run off. For over three years the British had been waiting for its 'national' team of BRM to join the fray, having produced a fantastically sounding car with a radical centrifugally supercharged engine offering very high boost and potentially huge power. It was extremely unreliable, however, and, for the drivers, its massive power surge made it very difficult in corners and spun its wheels on the straights – a 'point and squirt' car which Stirling Moss considered the worst he ever drove. Trouble was that this side of the Formula One equation was now seen to be of dubious value against the big-engined Ferrari. It was too late to change course now, and anyway, a new Formula had been announced the previous year to replace this one in 1954, just two years away. So a new 4.5-litre car would likely be a total waste of money; time would be better spent on a car for 1954.

To sum up: Formula One was in utter turmoil. No Alfa Romeo. Where oh where was BRM? There was Ferrari who had, with its 4.5-litre unblown 375 model, beaten Alfa's 159. Then there were ... er ... a few also-rans.

No challengers = no contest = no public interest = no worthy champion.

Formula Two, on the other hand, couldn't have been in better health. Ferrari, Gordini (now separated from Simca), HWM, Cooper-Bristol, and soon Maserati, all had Works teams representing three different countries. The cars were cheaper to build and operate and, in the case of Ferrari, Maserati and Cooper, were built in numbers for sale. Also, Enrico Platé ran a team of much-modified Maserati 4CLT/48 based cars. Two

years hence, F1 would be for 2500cc cars and F2 was for 2000cc, so the formula could be a useful proving ground.

The final chance for F1 was at Valentino Park, Turin in April, and confirmed the worst diagnosis when BRM didn't arrive. Game over for F1.

At that time, the purpose of the Championship was to discover 'The World Champion Driver,' not car, and the top Championship contenders had competed in this formula also. Championship credibility now demanded that the formula that provided the best possible competition between the best drivers must be used for the Championship, and this was clearly Formula Two.

So Formula Two is the saviour of the Championship
The choice of 'extra' races (see page 11) in this book now extends to suitably graded Formula Two races. They were neither F1 nor Championship races, but were for 'World Championship Cars,' often with their regular drivers, so were serious events. Those of the French Formula Two Championship offered a million francs per race (c £1350) more than most World Championship Grands Prix; and a set three hours' duration ... serious stuff. Teams were required to sign up in advance just as they are today. One of these races was the French round of the World Championship, so the others would indeed be of similar quality. This has produced a large increase in events to cover.

Ferrari had produced for Formula Two a smart, simple-looking 4-cylinder car, the '500' – it had 500cc cylinders and c180bhp. The driver squad consisted of the brilliant Alberto Ascari, Giuseppe Farina, and Luigi Villoresi.

Maserati would without doubt be Ferrari's chief opposition, with its new car, the A6GCM straight 6, driven by Juan-Manuel Fangio, Froilán González and Felice Bonetto and having similar power to the Ferraris.

Maserati-Platé was a different marque created by Enrico Platé using modified ex-F1 Maserati 4CLT/48 cars with engines de-supercharged and bored out. The cars were lightened, but 150bhp wasn't enough. Count Emanuel deGraffenried and Harry Schell were the main pilots.

Gordini was now separate from Simca and had a 6-cylinder full-size engine of 155bhp and the use of Robert Manzon, Jean Behra and B Bira.

Britain was represented in F2 primarily by HWM and Cooper-Bristol. The former ran Works cars with Stirling Moss and Lance Macklin amongst their drivers, while the latter was used by Mike Hawthorn to make his name. Alta and Connaught were also on offer for privateers to buy. None had more than circa 145bhp.

The Grand Prix driver's diary of single-seater racing for 1952

16th March	F2 – Gran Premio di Siracusa (I) – 201.3 miles
6th April	F1 – Gran Premio del Valentino at Torino (I) – 156.4 miles
14th April	F1/2 – Richmond Trophy at Goodwood (UK) – 288 miles
14th April	F2 – Lavant Cup at Goodwood (UK) – 144 miles*
14th April	F2 – Grand Prix de Pau (F) – 169.8 miles
19th April	F2 – Formula Two race at Ibsley (UK) – 32 miles*
27th April	F2 – Grand Prix de Marseille (F) – 222.3 miles
10th May	F2 – *Daily Express* International Trophy at Silverstone (UK) – 146.4 miles
11th May	F2 – Gran Premio di Napoli at Posillipo (I) – 152.9 miles
18th May	F2 – **Grosse Preis der Schweiz** at Bremgarten (S) – 280.5 miles
25st May	F2 – Eifelrennen at Nurburgring (D) – 99.1 miles
25th May	F2 – Grand Prix de Paris at Montlhéry (F) – 288.9 miles
1st June	F1 – Grand Prix d'Albi (F) – 189.1 miles
1st June	F1 – Grand Prix des Frontieres at Chimay (B) – 148 miles*
7th June	F1 – Ulster Trophy at Dundrod (UK) – 252.1 miles
8th June	F2 – Gran Premio del Autodromo di Monza (I) – 274.1 miles
8th June	F2 – Circuit du Lac at Aix les Bains (F) – 122.1 miles
21st June	F2 – West Essex F2 Race at Boreham (UK) – 30 miles*
22nd June	F2 – **Grand Prix de Belgique** at Spa Francorchamps (B) – 315.9 miles
29th June	F2 – Grand Prix de Marne at Reims (F) – 317.5 miles
6th July	F2 – **Grand Prix de l'ACF** at Rouen les Essarts (F) – 240.8 miles
13th July	F2 – Grand Prix de Sables d'Olonne (F) – 198.6 miles
19th July	F2 – **British Grand Prix** at Silverstone (UK) – 248.8 miles
19th July	F1 – *Daily Express* Trophy at Silverstone (UK) – 102.5 miles
27th July	F2 – Grand Prix de Caen (F) – 188.3 miles
2nd August	F1 – *Daily Mail* Trophy at Boreham (UK) – 201.0 miles
3rd August	F2 – **Grosse Preis von Deutschland** at Nürburgring (D) – 255.1 miles
10th August	F2 – Grand Prix de Comminges at St Gaudens (F) – 259.1 miles
17th August	F2 – **Grote Prijs van Nederland** at Zandvoort (N) – 234.5 miles
23rd August	F1 – Scottish National Trophy at Turnberry (UK) – 35 miles
23rd August	F2 – National Trophy at Turnberry (UK) – 26 miles*
24th August	F2 – Grand Prix de La Baule (F) – 231.5 miles
31st August	F2 – Genzlandring-Rennen (D) – 67 miles*
7th September	F2 – **Gran Premio d'Italia at Monza** (I) – 313.2 miles
14th September	F2 – Gran Premio di Modena (I) – 143.3 miles
14th September	F2 – Circuit de Cadours (F) – 112.3 miles
27th September	F1/2 – *Daily Graphic* Trophy at Goodwood (UK) – 36 miles
27th September	F2 – Madgwick Cup at Goodwood (UK) – 16.8 miles*
28th September	F2 – International Avusrennen at Berlin (D) – 129.1 miles*
4th October	F2 – Joe Fry Memorial Trophy at Castle Combe (UK) – 36.8 miles*
11th October	F1/2 – *Daily Record* Int Trophy at Charterhall (UK) – 80 miles
11th October	F12 – *Newcastle Journal* Trophy at Charterhall (UK) – 80 miles*

42 events of total race mileage = 6686 miles – 6126 maximum due to simultaneous races.

Events in bold are World Championship rounds – 22.6 per cent of F2 races run.

* See appendix 'A' for these ungraded race results.

✷✷ II Gran Premio di Siracusa

60 laps of 3.355 miles = 201.3 miles. 17 entries – 15 started – 7 finished.

Front row: A Ascari – 2m-16.0s (88.82mph); L Villoresi 0.8s; G Farina 1.0s.

16-MAR: Four Works Ferraris arrived but there were none from Maserati. Ascari, Villoresi and Farina had the front row, and the first non-Ferrari was deGraffenried's Maserati-Platé 4CLT on row four in tenth spot! Ascari glanced the straw bales at the first bend but took the lead from Rudi Fischer's private Ferrari 500 on the second lap and that was that. Taruffi and Farina were soon second and third, but Farina passed Taruffi, who then disobeyed orders at the end to snatch second. An angry Farina then cruised home. A Ferrari clean sweep as the Maserati-Platés failed. Villoresi's fuel problems cost him seven laps. Twelve of the starters were Ferraris – the new 500 4-cylinder or the old 166 V12. Ferrari, it would seem, was the saviour of single-seat racing.

1st	A Ascari (W)	Ferrari 500 in 2h-16m-24.6s	88.55
2nd	P Taruffi (W)	Ferrari 500	58.6s
3rd	G Farina (W)	Ferrari 500	1m-26s
F lap	L Villoresi (W)	Ferrari 500 in 2m-13.0s	90.82

✷✷ (F1) VI Gran Premio del Valentino

60 laps of 2.607 miles = 156.4 miles.
20 entries – 13 started – 6 finished.

Front row: G Farina; A Ascari: L Villoresi; P Taruffi no times available.

06-APR: This was F1's final chance and it blew it when only Ferrari brought recent cars. BRM entered cars for Fangio, Moss and Wharton, but withdrawn, although, in truth, BRM boss Raymond Mays had arranged for Fangio to try the cars back at base that day. Ascari and Villoresi's F1 Ferrari 375s swapped the lead until Ascari secured it for good ... well, until his fuel tank split and he stopped four laps short. Farina suffered gearbox trouble at the start and his record breaking pursuit was a highlight of the race, but he crashed on lap 31. Old man Taruffi's F2 car was just 69 seconds down in second place after over two hours of racing. The sport's governing body, the FIA, had had enough – bye bye F1 – we're off to F2 for the Championship.

1st	L Villoresi (W)	Ferrari 375 in 2h-06m-25.3s	74.25
2nd	P Taruffi (W)	Ferrari 500 (F2)	1m-09s
3rd	R Fischer (W)	Ferrari 500 (F2)	2 laps
F lap	G Farina (W)	Ferrari 375 in 2m-01.2s	77.45

(F1) Richmond Trophy (Goodwood)

12 laps of 2.4 miles = 28.8 miles.
18 entries – 14 started – 12 finished.

Front row: F González; G Abecassis (HWM); A Rolt (Delage15S8); G Whitehead (ERA) no times available.

14-APR: Goodwood was in its own world of sprint races again – very nice in its way – so another short F1 race was offered. There were no BRMs, though, even in their own country! González had the Ferrari Thinwall Special and no opposition. Mike Hawthorn's average speed of 86.33mph was way faster than his F2 win earlier. He had started seventh on the grid; clearly a special talent. Goodwood was now 'chicaned,' and the length increased from 2.38 to 2.4 miles, so new records were set.

1st	F González (GAV)	Ferrari 375 'Thinwall' in 19m-35.0s	88.23
2nd	M Hawthorn	Cooper-Bristol (F2)	26.0s
F lap	F González	Ferrari 375 Thinwall (F1) in 1m-36.0s	90.00

✷✷✷ XIII Grand Prix de Pau

3 hours on a circuit of 1.715 miles.
18 entries – 17 started – 7 finished.

Front row: A Ascari – 1m-43.3s (59.77mph): L Villoresi (Ferrari 500) 0.7s; L Macklin (HWM) 3.1s.

14-APR: The French F2 Championship began here. Macklin's HWM was alongside two Works Ferraris on the grid, with deGraffenried's Maserati fourth. Macklin was second at the start, which must have been music to British ears, with these cars seeming to be World Championship contenders now. Villoresi soon passed him, though, and followed Ascari until a slide damaged a wheel on lap 78. Macklin's HWM split a brake pipe, losing many laps. Jean Behra took his first podium finish.

1st	A Ascari (W)	Ferrari 500 99 laps in 3h-0m-53.5s	56.33
2nd	L Rosier (ER)	Ferrari 500	3 laps
3rd	J Behra (W)	Simca-Gordini T15	5 laps
F lap	A Ascari	Ferrari 500 in 1m-44.4s	59.14

✷✷✷ X Grand Prix de Marseille

3 hours, on a circuit of 1.659 miles.
18 entries and starters – 5 finished.

Front row: A Ascari – 1m-17.8s (76.77mph): R Manzon 1.2s; L Villoresi (Ferrari 500) 1.9s.

27-APR: The second round of the French F2 Series saw Manzon's new Gordini 16 sitting front and centre of the grid, but 1.2 seconds adrift of Ascari. This was good for Formula

Two, as a Ferrari lockout of the top spots wasn't the best for sport. However, there were many more cars than F1 could find. Ascari and Farina led, swapping on laps 22 and 26. Ascari needed tyres on lap 109, so Farina led, but, two laps later, he crashed. Manzon retired from third on lap 25, handing the position to Macklin who lasted another 35 laps. Manzon took over Bira's car to good effect, but nowhere near able to compete with the Ferraris. New boy Peter Collins (HWM) was fifth at one point, from 12th grid spot, but rear axle trouble cost much time. Surely one to watch.

1st	A Ascari (W)	Ferrari 500 134 laps in 2h-59m-12s	74.43
2nd	Bira/Manzon (W)	Simca-Gordini T15	5 laps
3rd	J Claes (ENB)	Simca-Gordini T15	7 laps
F lap	G Farina (W)	Ferrari 500 in 1m-15.4s	79.21

✷✷ IV *Daily Express* International Trophy (Silverstone)
15+35 laps of 2.927 miles = 146.4 miles.
42 entries – 31 started – 17 finished.
Poles: Heat one – M Hawthorn (Cooper-Bristol) – 2m-00s (87.81mph); Heat two – R Manzon (Gordini 16) 2m-01s (87.08mph).

10-MAY: The pits and start/finish line were now after Woodcote Corner, and the slight re-profiling of some corners produced an increase of circuit length to 2.927 miles, which would remain until 1975. Ferrari Works entries withdrew, but happily two privately-entered Ferrari 500s, as used by the Works, arrived – one for Rudi Fischer. Yet it was HWM's day. Hawthorn, Behra (Gordini) and Fischer headed the field, but Hawthorn's gear lever and Behra's final drive soon gave the English HWMs a one-two position, which it was never to lose. Both had passed Rudi Fischer's more powerful Ferrari on lap four so Macklin, who was fifth at the start, now led. deGraffenried overtook Fischer with four laps left, pulling away by eight seconds. A great result for the unsung heroes of British racing, who knew, unlike BRM, that to advance, one had to turn up.

1st	L Macklin (W)	HWM-Alta in 1h-11m-58s	85.41
2nd	A Rolt (W)	HWM-Alta	10s
3rd	E deGraffenried (SP)	Maserati-Platé	25s
F lap	R Fischer (EE)	Ferrari 500 in 1m-58s	89.30

V Gran Premio di Napoli (Posillipo)
60 laps of 2.548 miles = 152.9 miles.
13 started – 5 finished.

Front row: G Farina; P Taruffi; A Simon. No times available.
11-MAY: Looking back, it seems that, given a chance, Ferrari was only too happy to perform unopposed. Instead of two cars proving themselves against a good field at Silverstone, three cars proved nothing at all at Naples. Ascari was at Indianapolis, and Villoresi was unwell, so Farina and Taruffi led the whole race, with Farina putting on a show. Teammate Simon, who had been third all along, crashed on lap 34. Comotti was third, but lapped five times, one less than fourth man Rossi in a Stanguellini.

1st	G Farina (W)	Ferrari 500 in 2h-19m-44.0s	65.57
2nd	P Taruffi (W)	Ferrari 500	1m-49s
F lap	G Farina	Ferrari 500 in 2m-15.1s	67.89

✷✷✷ (WC1) XII Grosser Preis der Schweiz (Bremgarten-Berne)
62 laps of 4.524 miles = 280.5 miles.
25 entries – 20 started – 8 finished.
Front row: G Farina – 2m-47.5s (97.23mph); P Taruffi 2.6s; R Manzon (Gordini 16) 4.6s.

18-MAY: Ascari was still at Indianapolis with an adapted F1 Ferrari, and Villoresi was recovering from a road crash, so the team was the same as at Naples. Farina was expected to star in Ascari's absence, and, sure enough, he headed the grid and led till retiring on lap 16, and Taruffi took over till the end. Stirling Moss soon put his British HWM into third place ahead of the Works Ferrari of Simon on lap two from ninth on the grid, but then pitted on the next lap for plugs. He dropped to the back and fought back to seventh on lap 20, whereupon HWM withdrew its cars, following two rear stub axle breakages, one losing a wheel. A great shame as Moss' class was clearly showing now. Farina took over Simon's car, but retired. Jean Behra had been second from lap 22 to 35, but was passed by Simon and Fischer's Ferraris, which was to be expected, but third place marked him out.

1st	P Taruffi (W)	Ferrari 500 in 3h-01m-46.1s	92.59
2nd	R Fischer (EE)	Ferrari 500	2m-37s
3rd	J Behra (W)	Gordini 16	1 lap
F lap	G Farina (W)	Ferrari 500 in 2m-49.1s	96.31

✷ XVI International ADAC Eifelrennen (N Nürburgring)
7 laps of 14.17 miles = 99.2 miles.
19 entries – 16 started – 5 finished.
Front row: R Fischer; S Moss; D Hamilton; K Wharton (Frazer-Nash). No times available.

25-MAY: International racing returned to Germany, but it was Fischer who made pole position, with a British trio alongside. Stirling Moss soon took the lead from Willi Heeks (AFM), but Fischer's Ferrari had a top speed advantage, and he used it on lap three to lead and pull away easily. Moss coped with his extinguisher going off in the cockpit without losing a place! Heeks lost a wheel when third, so Hamilton was fourth despite a broken seat. All the Brits finished this race of attrition.

1st	R Fischer (EE)	Ferrari 500 in 1h-16m-58.3s	77.25
2nd	S Moss (W)	HWM-Alta	41.2s
3rd	K Wharton (W)	Frazer-Nash FN48	2m21s
F lap	R Fischer	Ferrari 500 in 10m-51s	78.37

✱✱✱ VI GP de Paris (Montlhéry)
3 hours on 3.904 mile circuit.
19 entries – 18 started – 3 finished.
Front row: R Manzon – 2m-21.5s (99.34mph); P Taruffi 1.2s; L Villoresi 1.3s.

25-MAY: French F2 series – Round 3. Ascari was at Indianapolis and Robert Manzon's new Gordini T16 beat the Ferraris to pole, so there were interesting race prospects. Manzon's and Behra's Gordinis led Villoresi and Taruffi (Ferrari) and fought strongly for 19 laps before Behra retired with rear axle failure. Farina handed an ailing car to Simon and took over an unwell Villoresi's car, which had gained then lost the lead to Manzon. Farina sadly retired from a seemingly secure lead on lap 59 (another axle). Taruffi stormed past leader Farina who promptly spun off into a drain, used help, and was disqualified. So Farina lost a shared second place with Villoresi only to finish in ... er ... a shared second place with Simon. Funny old times then?

1st	P Taruffi (W)	Ferrari 500 74 laps in 3h-01m-55s	95.28
2nd	G Farina/A Simon (W)	Ferrari 500	3 laps
3rd	L Rosier (ER)	Ferrari 500	4 laps
F lap	P Taruffi	Ferrari 500 in 2m-21.2s	99.54

✱ (F1) XIV Grand Prix d'Albi
34 laps of 5.563 miles = 189.1 miles.
19 entries – 18 started – 9 finished.
Front row: J-M Fangio (BRM V16) – 2m-55.1s (114.37mph); F González (BRM V16) 7.3s; L Rosier 10.1s.

01-JUN: An all Formula One race, and the BRMs finally performed. They provided their own fanfare with the unforgettable sound of 11,000rpm plus supercharger wail,

but proved fragile. The opposition was week, with no Works Ferraris entered as Ferrari favoured the following week's non-Championship F2 race at Monza over this F1 bash. Fangio had clearly mastered this car and stormed off the line, with González slow away but second after two laps. The glory soon ended when González retired on lap five after setting fastest lap with an almost full fuel load but ten seconds down on pole. Fangio could take it easy, but retired on lap 15 with engine trouble, so Ferraris now had a 1-2. Rosier and 'Chico' Landi made a fight of it for a while, but Rosier pulled clear. Jean Behra lay third now in his F2 Gordini, but the rear axle failed. So, 47 year old Giraud-Cabantous had fourth, two minutes ahead of Albert Crespo in his Talbot. Reports say that Crespo was the most exciting driver to watch cornering, " ... every way except backwards." The BRM was clearly not wanting for speed, but its unreliability (it could be relied on – to fail) had ruined the status of F1.

1st	L Rosier (EF)	Ferrari 375 in 1h-50m-39.0s	102.56
2nd	F Landi	Ferrari 375	17.6s
3rd	Y Girard-Cabantous (ER)	Talbot-Lago T26C	1m-12s
F lap	F González (W)	BRM V16-s/c in 3m-06.0s	107.67

✱ (F1) VI Ulster Trophy (Dundrod)
34 laps of 7.415 miles = 252.1 miles.
19 entries – 13 started – 6 finished.
Front row: P Taruffi – 5m-06s (87.26mph); M.Hawthorn 3s; L Rosier 10s.

07-JUN: Six days later and the BRMs were on the grid again, but at the back due to late arrival. Stirling Moss joined Fangio this time. Glory this time was due to Mike Hawthorn for leading eight laps in his F2 car in the wet, ahead of Taruffi in the much more powerful Ferrari Thinwall Special. Taruffi's fuel stop gave Hawthorn the lead, but not for long. Fangio got to third on lap 25, then retired with engine failure again. Moss never really got going at all, retiring on lap three with ... engine trouble. Hawthorn's little Cooper had a slipping clutch later, but he held on to second after a magnificent drive, of which Ferrari would take note.

1st	P Taruffi (GAV)	Ferrari 375 (F1) in 3h-05m-47.0s	81.43
2nd	M Hawthorn	Cooper T20-Bristol (F2)	3m-26s
3rd	J Kelly	Alta GP3 (F2)	6m-55s
F lap	P Taruffi	Ferrari 375 (F1) in 4m-53.0s	91.12

Fangio had 22 hours to get to his next race at Monza. He flew to Paris, but bad weather stopped flights to Milan. He set off late evening for Monza 500 miles away in a car loaned by Louis Rosier, crossing the Alps and arriving with less than two hours to go. His autobiography confirms that tiredness after such a drive caused the outcome.

✴✴✴ V Gran Premio dell'Autodromo di Monza
2 x 35 laps of 3.915 miles = 274.1 miles.
29 started – 16 finished.

Front row: A Ascari; G Farina; F González; L Villoresi. No times available.

08-JUN: Fangio started from the back, with Maserati teammate González looking promising amongst the Ferraris on the front row. On lap two, already having stormed to seventh place and passed 22 cars, Fangio was slow to correct a slide and crashed heavily at Curva di Seraglio, breaking his neck and ending his season. González and teammate Bonetto mixed it with Ascari and Farina at first, but González retired. Ascari won by a minute. The second heat saw Ascari, Farina, Simon and Bonetto scrapping at first. An Ascari-Farina scrap ended when Ascari retired and Farina then romped home. Bonetto retired from third place near the end, but Maserati had shown potential to challenge Ferrari. If the weather hadn't prevented flights to Milan – what then? If ... if ...

1st	G Farina (W)	Ferrari 500 in 2h-31m-15.0s	108.70
2nd	A Simon (W)	Ferrari 500	1 lap
3rd	R Fischer (EE)	Ferrari 500	4 laps
F lap	G Farina	Ferrari 500 in 2m-06.2s	111.67

✴ IV Circuit du Lac (Aix les Bains)
2 x 40 laps of 1.526 miles = 122.1 miles.
12 started – 9 finished.

Front row: J Behra; M Trintignant; H Schell (Maserati). No times available.

08-JUN: On the same day as Monza, with Works entries from Gordini and HWM – the latter supported both events! Two works Ferraris were withdrawn a week before the race. Trintignant's Ecurie Rosier-entered Ferrari 500 led from the off, but lost it to Behra who held him off for 20 laps, but retired when leading with magneto trouble. So Behra and Manzon won heat one for Gordini. The Gordini duo led heat two until Manzon retired. deGraffenried's gearbox spoiled a good second place fight. The small British HWM team led by Lance Macklin wasn't far off the pace of the Gordinis. If Moss had been at the wheel, though ... who knows?

1st	J Behra (W)	Gordini T16 in 2h-10m-42.1s	56.04
2nd	L Macklin (W)	HWM-Alta	44.2s
3rd	E deGraffenried (SP)	Maserati-Platé	1m-26s
F lap	J Behra	Gordini T16 in 1m-35.2s	57.70

✴✴✴ (WC2) XIV Grand Prix de Belgique (Spa)
36 laps of 8.774 miles = 315.9 miles.
22 entries and starters – 15 finished.

Front row: A Ascari – 4m-37s (114.03mph); G Farina 3s; P Taruffi 9s – all works Ferrari 500s.

22-JUN: Ascari's pole lap was only just over four per cent slower than the mighty Alfa Romeo of the year before on this very high speed circuit! Maserati, strangely, declared itself unfit for this race – or did Fangio's incapacity decide it? Ascari and Farina led away on a damp track, but wasn't fast enough to hold off the amazing Gordini of Jean Behra who led at the end of lap one. However, on the next lap the expected order was resumed. Taruffi's Ferrari took 13 laps to catch and pass Behra, then spun and sadly collected Behra following close behind. Ascari and Farina cruised home. Hawthorn was fourth in his Cooper-Bristol, a lap down.

1st	A Ascari (W)	Ferrari 500 in 3h-03m-46.8s	103.12
2nd	G Farina (W)	Ferrari 500	1m-55s
3rd	R Manzon (W)	Gordini 16	4m-28s
F lap	A Ascari	Ferrari 500 in 4m-54.0.s	107.07

Championship positions:
Ascari and Taruffi 9; Fischer and Farina 6.

✴✴✴ XX GP de Marne (Reims)
3 hours on a 4.472-mile circuit.
23 entries – 22 started – 11 finished.

Front row: A Ascari – 2m-26.2s (110.12mph); G Farina 1.8s; R Manzon (Gordini 16) 2.1s.

29-JUN: The fourth round of the French series took place on a shorter Reims circuit, cutting out Gueux village, and an historic race took place. Still no Maseratis, though, so the grid was led by two Ferraris and two Gordinis, ahead of Villoresi's Ferrari. Trintignant joined Gordini as the expected Ferrari for Rosier's team didn't arrive. Alan Brown's Cooper-Bristol had brief glory alongside Ascari at the start, but it was the Gordini of Behra which led the first lap, with Ascari on his exhaust pipe. Behra held him off, even pulling away a little, then Ascari pitted for plugs on about lap 12, and handed over to Villoresi whose car had failed after just four laps. Farina couldn't challenge Behra, and Manzon closed on him but retired on lap 49 having been hurt in a supporting sports car race. It was near the end when their Ferrari passed Bira's Gordini for third. Behra's Gordini beating Ferrari by a lap on such a fast track was momentous indeed. Perhaps it was easy on transmissions (Gordini's Achilles Heel).

1st	J Behra (W)	Gordini T16 71 laps in 3h-0m-27s	105.57
2nd	G Farina (W)	Ferrari 500	1 lap
3rd	A Ascari/L Villoresi (W)	Ferrari 500	1 lap
F lap	A Ascari	Ferrari 500 in 2m-28.2s	108.63

✳✳✳ (WC3) XXXIX Grand Prix de l'ACF (Rouen-Les-Essarts)
3 hours on a 3.169-mile circuit.
22 entries – 20 starters – 12 finished.
Front row: A Ascari – 2m-14.8s (84.63mph); G Farina 1.4s; P Taruffi 2.3s.

06-JUL: This race was also the fifth round of the French series, and Ferrari produced more powerful engines here to counter the Gordini threat of the previous week. Works Maseratis were still absent, but one of its latest cars was entered by Escuderia Bandiarantes for Etancelin! Ascari and Farina took off together, with Manzon third after a lap. Behra also chased, but the Gordinis were soon in trouble; Behra crashing and being helped out of a ditch by patriotic fans. Damage repairs dropped him to the back, but he recovered to finished seventh. Manzon was still suffering from the previous week's accident, and slowed, letting Taruffi past, whereon the Ferraris held station. Manzon finished fourth – very creditable. Trintignant's Gordini battled with Collins' HWM for fifth all race, except when Hawthorn's Cooper passed them before a misfire set in. The Reims race had been better.

1st	A Ascari (W)	Ferrari 500 76 laps in 3h-00m-20.3s	80.13
2nd	G Farina (W)	Ferrari 500	44.4s
3rd	P Taruffi (W)	Ferrari 500	1 lap
F lap	A Ascari	Ferrari 500 in2m-17.3s	83.09

Championship positions:
Ascari 18; Taruffi 13; Farina 12.

✳✳✳ II Grand Prix de Sable d'Olonne
3 hours on a 1.46-mile circuit.
17 entries – 14 started – 4 finished.
Front row: A Ascari – 1m-12.9s (72.11mph); G Farina 0.1s; R Manzon 1.7s.

13-JUL: The sixth French series round and the fourth race in four weeks, but still no Works Maseratis. Sadly, Behra crashed in practise and was out with a broken scapula. The early order was Ascari, Farina, Manzon, Villoresi, and Macklin, putting in a good show for HWM but he later had to pit. Trintignant in a Works Gordini recovered from a very poor start, but passed Bira and Schell. Bira pitted, and Manzon took over the car, having handed over his own to Trintignant earlier. Schell's Maserati-Platé seized and spun just as Ascari came to lap him. The ensuing melee eliminated Ascari, Farina, Trintignant, and Cantoni in the latest Maserati. Now it was Villoresi, with the HWMs of Macklin and Giraud-Cabantous, who retired late on. The sole Ferrari survived and won, and Peter Collins salvaged some glory for the British team In a race ruined by the melee.

1st	L Villoresi (W)	Ferrari 500 136 laps in 3h-00m-06s	66.15
2nd	P Collins (W)	HWM-Alta	3 laps
3rd	J Claes (ENB)	Simca-Gordini T15	5 laps
F lap	L Villoresi	Ferrari 500 in 1m-12.3s	72.71

✳✳✳ (WC4) VII British Grand Prix (Silverstone)
85 laps of 2.927 mile circuit – 248.8 miles.
34 entries – 31 started – 22 finished.
Front row: G Farina – 1m50s (95.79mph); A Ascari 0s; P Taruffi 3s; R.Manzon 5s.

19-JUL: Five weeks – five races – still no Works Maseratis. Ascari and Farina tied for pole (likely when using whole seconds) but the first to do it was Farina. They led away but it was Ascari's flag-to-flag race. Farina dropped to seventh on lap 26 for plugs and never recovered. British Connaughts, HWM and Cooper-Bristols had almost filled the second and third grid rows, and Connaughts were third, fourth and fifth on lap two but needed a fuel pit stop later. Taruffi came through from a slow start as expected, but was no challenge to Ascari. The Connaught pit stops gave Hawthorn third place, the first podium finish for a British car in a Championship race, followed by Denis Poore's Connaught in fourth place. A very promising British showing.

1st	A Ascari (W)	Ferrari 500 in 2h-44m-11s	90.92
2nd	P Taruffi (W)	Ferrari 500	1 lap
3rd	M Hawthorn	Cooper T20-Bristol	2 laps
F lap	A Ascari	Ferrari 500 in1m-52s	94.08r

Championship positions:
Ascari 27; Taruffi 19; Farina 12.

Daily Express Trophy (Silverstone)
35 laps of a 2.927-mile circuit – 102.5 miles.
25 entries – 22 started – 13 finished.
Front row: F González (BRM V16) 1m-47s (98.48mph); L Villoresi 2s; K.Wharton (BRM V16) 5s; P Taruffi 6s.

19-JUL: Supporting the British GP, this was a Formule Libre event, which, as usual for these races, was actually fought between regular F1/F2 cars. BRMs for González and Wharton fought against four Ferraris: Villoresi's Works car; Taruffi's Thinwall; and others for Louis Rosier and 'Chico' Landi. Yes there was the odd sports car, but they did the honours and kept out of the way. Taruffi jumped the start and got a 30 second penalty, so González actually led Villoresi, Wharton, Landi then Taruffi. González lost the BRM at Stowe, pitted and took over Wharton's car to challenge Villoresi, but gearbox trouble stopped him with a lap left. Taruffi, meanwhile, overcame Villoresi and his penalty to win easily. Here we have a distinct comparison between the best of F2 and F1 on the same circuit, day, and conditions, and the difference was seen to be just 3 seconds per lap.

1st	P Taruffi (GAV)	Ferrari 375 Thinwall 1h-06m-02.8s	93.07
2nd	L Villoresi (W)	Ferrari 375	14.2s
F lap	Taruffi/González	Ferrari/BRM in 1m-49s	96.67

1er Grand Prix de Caen
75 laps of 2.510 miles = 188.3 miles.
16 entries and starters – 8 finishers.
Front row: M Trintignant; L Rosier; Y Giraud-Cabantous. No times available.

27-JUL: This was not a qualifying round of the French Championship. Only Gordini and HWM sent Works cars to this event but neither ran their number one drivers. Harry Schell was on the Gordini strength this time. The HWM's were for Frenchmen Andre Simon and Yves Giraud-Cabantous. The three main stars set off in the order in which they finished. Giraud-Cab' and Schell almost challenged, but retired. The entry was devoid of the biggest stars but just qualifies for inclusion.

1st	M Trintignant (W)	Gordini T16 in 2h-15m-34.4s	83.32
2nd	J Behra (W)	Gordini T16	36.6s
3rd	L Rosier (ER)	Ferrari 500	2m-23s

✷✷ (F1) II *Daily Mail* Trophy (Boreham)
67 laps of 3 miles = 201 miles.
38 entries – 35 starters – 22 finished.
Front row: L Villoresi – 1m-44.4s (103.45mph); F González

1.8s; C Landi 4.6s; K Wharton 5.9s; L Rosier 7.8s.

02-AUG: Three Ferraris, two BRMs, Talbot-Lagos and many F2 cars filled the grid, but there was no Thinwall Special because of start money issues. González' BRM was second to Villoresi on the grid, which, on this airfield circuit, was so wide it had five cars aligned. The second row was aligned with the front row gaps, so no fewer than nine cars had a clear road ahead as they awaited the start! Rain arrived just before the starter's flag, and Villoresi led the three Ferraris, then González' BRM, and Hawthorn's F2 Cooper was, amazingly, fifth. González soon passed Rosier's Ferrari 375 for third, but he then spun the difficult car. The conditions favoured a nimble car without an excess of power. Hawthorn took the lead on lap 30 and stretched it to 40 seconds by lap 42; extraordinary! The track dried and his lead was lost ten laps later to Villoresi, and soon after Landi took second as Hawthorn's Cooper was ailing near the end. He had now really arrived! Wharton's BRM retired with gearbox woes.

1st	L Villoresi (W)	Ferrari 375 (F1) in 2h-25m-26.0s	82.92
2nd	C.Landi (Eba)	Ferrari 375 (F1)	36.6s
3rd	M Hawthorn	Cooper T20-Bristol (F2)	2m-23s
F lap	L Villoresi	Ferrari 375 in 1m-59.8s	90.15

✷✷✷ (WC5) XVI Grosser Preis von Deutschland (Nürburgring)
18 laps of a 14.17-mile circuit = 255.1 miles.
36 entries – 30 started – 10 finished.
Front row: A Ascari – 10m-04.4s (84.42mph); G Farina 2.9s; M Trintignant 14.7s; R Manzon 20.9s.

03-AUG: One Works Maserati appeared for Felice Bonetto – at last! As at Silverstone, many 'local' entries filled the large grid, BMW powered – mostly AFM or Veritas. Another flag-to-flag drive for Ascari looked to be a routine, but he pitted for oil two laps from the end, and Farina passed him but thought it was Taruffi so maintained pace. A bad decision, as Ascari repassed at the end of the lap. Trintignant's Gordini failed after a lap, while Manzon's held fourth till losing a wheel on lap nine. Taruffi lost third on the last lap to Fischer with DeDion tube failure. Fischer was good, so maybe his deficit was due to privateer caution. Due to the system of only counting the best four scores from each driver, Alberto Ascari was now uncatchable as World Champion.

1st	A Ascari (W)	Ferrari 500 in 3h-06m-13.3s	82.20
2nd	G Farina (W)	Ferrari 500	14.1s
3rd	R Fischer (EE)	Ferrari 500	7m-10s
F lap	A Ascari	Ferrari 500 in10m-05.1s	84.32

Championship positions:
Ascari (WC) 36; Taruffi 22; Farina 18.

✱✱✱ XVI Grand Prix de Comminges

3 hours on a 2.727-mile circuit.
20 entries – 19 started – 6 finished.
Front row: A Ascari – 1m-53.3s (88.28mph); M Trintignant 2.9s; R Manzon 3.1s.

10-AUG: Ascari took pole, but Manzon, Ascari, Trintignant was the first lap order. Then, from his Gordini sandwich position, Ascari pitted with steering problems and took over Simon's car. Manzon's engine expired and Ascari's twelfth place amazingly became first on lap 21. Behra refused instructions to hand over to Manzon and the result justifies that – he'd beaten the Ferraris at Reims. Trintignant's axle failed on lap 67 handing third to Behra. The latest Maserati A6GCMs were still in a private team led by 'Chico' Landi, but retired near to halfway. The HWMs disappointed with magneto trouble.

1st	A Simon/A Ascari (W)	Ferrari 500 95 laps in 3h-00m-38s	86.05
2nd	G Farina (W)	Ferrari 500	1 lap
3rd	J Behra (W)	Gordini T16	6 laps
F lap	A Ascari	Ferrari 500 in 1m-51.2s	88.36

✱✱✱ (WC6) III Grote Prijs van Nederland (Zandvoort)

90 laps of 2.605 miles = 234.5 miles.
18 entries and starters – 9 finished.
Front row: A Ascari – 1m-46.5s (88.07mph); G Farina 2.1s; M Hawthorn 5.1s.

17-AUG: In only three years the Zandvoort race had achieved World Championship status. Mike Hawthorn in a Cooper-Bristol augmented his growing stature by making the front grid row ahead of Villoresi, and then following Ascari into the first bend. He soon had to settle for fourth, though, as the Ferraris had about 25 per cent more power. He was able to maintain this position to the end, finishing two laps down on the Ferraris but a lap ahead of the Works Gordinis, which were now even slower than before. Ascari's pole and fastest lap had been much faster than Formula One cars had ever gone here. F2 was not slow!

1st	A Ascari (W)	Ferrari 500 in 2h-53m-28.5s	81.09
2nd	G Farina (W)	Ferrari 500	40.1s
3rd	L Villoresi (W)	Ferrari 500	1m-34s
F lap	A Ascari	Ferrari 500 in 1m-49.8s	85.42r

Championship positions:
Ascari 36 (WC); Farina 24; Taruffi 22.

(F1) Scottish National Trophy (Turnberry)

20 laps of 1.76 miles = 35.2 miles.
21 entries – 14 started – 8 finished.
Front row: M Hawthorn – 1m-16s (83.37mph); R Parnell (BRM) 1.0s; K Wharton (BRM); R Flockhart (ERA).

23-AUG: A BRM/Ferrari Thinwall battle again. Repairs to a fuel line on Parnell's BRM took place on the grid as Hawthorn had told them "Take your time, they can't start without us". (Thanks to the Formula One Register for that quote). Both BRMs and Hawthorn were slow away, with Barber's Cooper-Bristol leading initially. Parnell led after a few laps, but Hawthorn retired with gearbox trouble and Wharton's BRM with broken steering. Gaze amazed in his (technically, Formule Libre) old Maserati.

1st	R Parnell (W)	BRM P15 V16 s/c in 26m-33s	79.55
2nd	A Gaze	Maserati 8CM	10s
F lap	M Hawthorn	Ferrari 375 Thinwall in 1m-16s	83.37

✱✱✱ VI Grand Prix de la Baule

3 hours on a 2.661-mile circuit.
19 entries and starters – 9 finished.
Front row: A Ascari – 1m-57.5s (81.52mph); R Manzon (1.0s). Row two: G Farina 1.4s; L Villoresi 2.0s.

24-AUG: This was the final round of the French series. Manzon led off the staggered 2 x 2 grid, but Ascari led after one lap. Farina ran into and over Manzon's back on the second lap, and both were out – rather spoiling any lead battle. Ascari went on his way from Villoresi, Trintignant and lapping fourth place Behra on lap 19. Trintignant retired on lap 36, and soon third was handed to new-boy Peter Collins (HWM) as Behra briefly pitted. Behra recovered third but retired, and Rosier deprived Collins of third.

1st	A Ascari (W)	Ferrari 500 87 laps in 3h-01m-00.7s	76.73
2nd	L Villoresi (W)	Ferrari 500	1 lap
3rd	L Rosier (ER)	Ferrari 500	4 laps
F lap	L Villoresi	Ferrari 500 in 2m-01.1s	79.10

✱✱✱ (WC7) XXII Gran Premio d'Italia (Monza)

80 laps of 3.915 miles – 313.2 miles.
35 entries – 24 starters – 15 finished.
Front row: A Ascari – 2m-05.7s (112.11mph); L Villoresi 0.9s; G Farina 1.3s; M Trintignant 1.5s.

07-SEP: The start was restricted to 24 cars for safety reasons – not often a major factor in Italy. González' alcohol-fuelled car stormed away from the second row, leaving the Ferrari team behind. He planned to refuel at halfway, but his poor stop let Ascari and Villoresi get well ahead. Trintignant's Gordini had been on the front row, but dropped out from third after just three laps; but teammate Manzon scrapped for fourth place with Farina and Bonetto, but pitted on lap 37 to drop right back. González recovered second from Villoresi on lap 62, with Farina fourth and Bonetto's Maserati fifth, so, at last, the famous marque rivalry was fully engaged. However, Farina had things in hand and finished only seven seconds behind Villoresi. The HWM team had failed to qualify; the leading British team being Connaught – for whom Moss retired after reaching seventh at one point, and Wharton ninth.

1st	A Ascari (W)	Ferrari 500 in 2h-50m-45.6s	110.04
2nd	F González (W)	Maserati A6GCM	1m-02s
3rd	L Villoresi (W)	Ferrari 500	2m-04s
F lap	A Ascari/F González	Ferrari/Maserati in 2m-06.1s	111.76

Final Championship positions:
Ascari 36 (WC); Farina 24; Taruffi 22.

✱✱✱ III Gran Premio di Modena

100 laps of 1.434 miles = 143.4 miles.
17 entries – 16 started – 10 finished.
Front row: A Ascari – 1m-04.4s (80.17mph); L Villoresi 0.8s.
Row two: G Farina 1.0s; F González 2.0s.
14-SEP: Hawthorn had been offered a trial here for Ferrari, but crashed his Cooper when attempting to brake at the same point as he'd done with the Ferrari. No problem for either party – he signed for Ferrari from his hospital bed and Sighinolfi took the drive. A superb entry for this race, a Ferrari/Maserati showdown on their home ground. Ascari, Villoresi, González and Farina was the early order. González pitted to clear his radiator and then Ascari retired and took over Sighinolfi's car. González took the lead with nine laps to go. Then, on lap 98, on lapping Carini (HWM) yet again, the ex-Ferrari pilot chopped him so badly that Villoresi's 1.5-second deficit was overcome and he passed into the lead. A near dead heat resulted. Did Carini help Ferrari?

1st	L Villoresi (W)	Ferrari 500 in 1h-51m-21.0s	77.27
2nd	F González (W)	Maserati A6GCM	0.0s
3rd	Sighinolfi/Ascari (W)	Ferrari 500	28.6s
F lap	Villoresi and González	Ferrari / Maserati in 1m-05.0s	79.40

IV Circuit de Cadours

15-lap heat +30 lap final of 2.495 miles = 112.3 miles.
21 entries – 18 started – 6 finished.
Poles: Heat one – L Rosier 1m-58s (76.12mph). Heat two – H Schell 2m-01s (74.23mph).
14-SEP: The short Modena track limited its entries, so the remainder came here. Despite a reasonable length track, only nine starters per grid were allowed due to width. Heat one saw Collins (HWM) finish a close second to Rosier, but his engine was failing. Harry Schell took the second heat from deGraffenried's Maserati 4CLT/Platé. In the final, Schell took the lead from Rosier on lap three. He built a lead of 17 seconds by lap 15, only for valve trouble to slow him. Rosier accepted the lead from him on lap 25.

1st	L Rosier (ER)	Ferrari 500 in 1h-01m-42s	72.81
2nd	H Schell (W)	Gordini T16	45s
F lap	H Schell	Gordini T16 in 2m-00s	74.86

Daily Graphic Trophy (Goodwood)

15 laps of 2.4 miles = 36 miles.
13+ starters.
Front row: F González; K Wharton; G Farina; R Parnell. No times available.
27-SEP: Formule Libre in title, but, in reality, it was F1 BRMs vs F2 as, sadly, Farina's Ferrari Thinwall non-started. Alan Brown's F2 Cooper-Bristol, amazingly, lay third behind González and Parnell for a lap, whereupon Wharton passed and made it a BRM 1-2-3, though the last two BRMs were ailing by the finish. Behind them an F2 scrap saw Poore's Connaught pass Brown for fourth place. Brown dropped out, and Moss, in an ERA Type G, was fifth, ahead of Salvadori's Ferrari 500. The new lap record beat that set by González' Ferrari Thinwall setup in April. The fact that three BRMs started and all finished is worth noting. Did the crowd have ear defenders then?

1st	F González (W)	BRM T15 V16-s/c in 24m-30.6s	88.13
2nd	R Parnell (W)	BRM T15 V16-s/c	7.6s
3rd	K Wharton (W)	BRM T15 V16-s/c	18.2s
F lap	R Parnell	BRM T15 V16-s/c in 1m-35.6s	90.38r

✱ *Daily Record* International Trophy (Charterhall)

40 laps of 2.0 miles = 80.0 miles.
10+ starters.
Front row: G Farina – 1m-23.0s (86.75mph). No other information.

11-OCT: I break a rule for this race. The Formule Libre tag could so easily keep a good race or memorable performance from the Grand Prix record, for what to me is a trivial reason. Here is a case in point. This time, a supercharged car of over the F1 limit of 1.5 litres competed and won. This was Bob Gerard's 2-litre ERA R4A – no way as powerful as the F1 cars present, and of some 17 years vintage – so let's be generous. The season-long BRM/Thinwall Ferrari dispute had polarised some fans who had formed supporters clubs, each with appropriate badges. The battle would be between them, surely. Hwever, in front of 50,000 fans, Bob Gerard's old ERA fled at the start and led for four laps, ahead of Farina. Wharton flew past both to lead and promptly spun, returning to third place. Farina then led but retired with axle failure, so Gerard led again. Wharton fought his way back, took the lead, lost it, regained it, but spun again! Parnell's BRM faded from fifth place. Gerard's win was his best ever. Astonishing! The script had gone out of the window. Rarely has any driver been so 'at one' with an individual machine as Bob Gerard with his own ERA. The BRMs needed long straights to overcome their traction problem exiting corners, exploited to the full by Bob Gerard's pressure. A David and Goliath story worth recalling, I think you'll agree.

1st	R Gerard	ERA R4A 2.0 s/c in 58m-17.2s	82.35
2nd	K Wharton (W)	BRM T15 V16-s/c	5.4s
3rd	L Rosier (ER)	Ferrari 375	1 lap
F lap	G Farina (GAV)	Ferrari 375 'Thinwall' in 1m-24.7s	85.00

The 1952 seasonal review

Only four dedicated Formula One races were run all year, while Formula Two simply had a ball. With both French and World Championships running concurrently, this was the only place to showcase talent.

The withdrawal of Maserati Works cars after the June Monza race was a real disappointment, leaving Ferrari with only Gordini to worry about, and not a big worry at that. Mike Hawthorn was the find of the year, and had been duly rewarded with a Ferrari contract for 1953: his combination of determination and calmness surely suitable for the big occasion. He seemed to outperform his humble Cooper-Bristol (with just 140bhp from its push-rod engine compared to 175 for Ferrari's thoroughbred racing unit and about 160 from Gordini). His two fourth places in the Belgian and Dutch Grands Prix netted him fifth in the World Championship. Cooper-Bristols run by private teams, together with Works HWM-Altas, appeared across Europe, but the other British team, Connaught, rarely left British soil

until late in the season. There were now six manufacturers, which was a healthy state of affairs.

Alberto Ascari competed in 16 high quality races this year (not including Indianapolis) and won 11. This total of wins was not broken for 11 years, until Jim Clark's 12 in 1963. Michael Schumacher's achievement of 11 wins from 17 races in 2002 only equalled this. Choosing to miss the opening round of the World Championship must say something about the perceived importance (or lack of it) to Ascari. Had the French Championship races told him all he needed to know? However, Indianapolis gave Ferrari something to do with its slightly moribund F1 car, and, of course, help sell Ferraris in the USA.

Winners of the 32 graded F1 and F2 races of 1952 – quantity & quality of success

11 wins	A Ascari (10A, B)	24 wins	Ferrari (15A + 3B + 2C + 4D)
4 wins	L Villoresi (2A, 2B) P Taruffi (2A, C, D)	3 wins	Gordini (A + C + D)
2 wins	J Behra (A, C) G Farina (A, D) L Rosier (C, D) F González (2D)	2 wins	BRM (2D), HWM (B + C)
1 win	L Macklin (B); R Fischer (C) M Trintignant (D) B Gerard (C) R Parnell (D)	1 win	ERA (C)

World Championship review

Alberto Ascari won every World Championship race he entered – a feat still unique – despite an average race finishing rate of only 49.4 per cent. Only González sharing fastest lap in the final race at Monza prevented Ascari from an absolute maximum score of 54 points from six wins each accompanied by the fastest lap point! It has to be noted, though, that Fangio was not competing since he was recovering from his Monza accident. Would he have dethroned Ascari? See 1953 where both used updated versions of the same machinery they had used in 1952. The winner of the first race, Piero Taruffi, was no strong challenger once Ascari had opened his score. His win, however meant that Ferrari had won every round this year. Another feat never since repeated. Let's not forget that the Ferrari team included 1950 World Champion 'Nino' Farina, who is still remembered as a very forceful driver, and who would have given no quarter to young upstart Alberto Ascari.

Odd fact: Yet again, none of the points scorers in the first round scored in the second as in 1950! Perhaps this time

Ascari's absence from the first race (he was at Indianapolis) had a little to do with it.

Another surprise: So far no-one had retired from the lead of any of the twenty World Championship races run since it was inaugurated, despite a finishing rate of just over 50 per cent!

A thought: Juan-Manuel Fangio didn't lose the 1952 World Championship, because he never took part. Maserati wasn't ready for the first round, and he had narrowly survived breaking his neck before the second round. This does not suggest that he would have beaten Ascari, as, in the following season, Ascari still won.

Chapter 12

1953
More of the same?
– Yes, please

1952 had seen a huge increase in the popularity of motor racing, both on track and at trackside, despite Formula One, the so-called major category, having been sidelined and become a rare event. There were only two international F1 races scheduled, both in France, and these needed F2 cars to bolster the entries. A few races were run in Britain, designated Formule Libre as was common there, but they were, in fact, F1/F2. I have included these here to fill-out the F1 record. The new 'major' formula had, like in 1952, over twenty decent races, but only eight were World Championship rounds: not nearly enough to sustain a professional racing career.

For the first time the World Championship expanded outside Europe to Argentina. This, rightly, recognised the large contribution made by that country to the collective driver skills demonstrated in what was otherwise an entirely European activity.

Both Ferrari and Maserati had improved their cars, and were now claiming 190bhp – Maserati a little more. Its car was now designated A6SSG, having been redesigned by ex-Alfa Romeo designer Gioacchino Colombo. There was little point in developing these cars for this formula alone, as this would be the last season they would hold sway over the now defunct Formula One. Any progress would be geared to the new Formula One coming the following year, which, while only 500cc larger, would require new cars from the major marques. This 2000cc Formula Two would be unlikely to have any significant life beyond being used as a way into the new Formula One for private owners.

Fangio was now in full health, so a great battle was expected wherever he and Ascari met. The Ferrari driver strength consisted of Italians Alberto Ascari, Giuseppe Farina and Luigi Villoresi, plus Englishman Mike Hawthorn,

while Maserati had Argentinians Juan-Manuel Fangio, Froilán González and Onofre Marimón, plus Italian Felice Bonetto. Gordini main drivers were Robert Manzon, Maurice Trintignant, Jean Behra and Harry Schell – all French (well, Schell had American parentage, but was born and raised in France).

BRM, now under the control of Sir Alfred Owen's Rubery Owen manufacturing empire, continued to improve the V16 which, no doubt, was responsible for the slow progress of the new F1 car for next year. A head-to-head battle of sprint races was in prospect in Britain between the improved BRMs and the Ferrari 375s, of which Tony Vandervell's was the Thinwall Special due to its use of his famous bearings. This was the main racing interest in Britain, and pulled in the crowds. Technically Formule Libre, I regard them as F1/F2 events since that's where the competition would come. The sound of a BRM V16 on song at 12,000rpm – its blower running at four times engine speed – was something that was never forgotten to this day, believe me. A few years ago I missed a rehearsal of the classical choir I sang with explaining that I had tickets to hear 'The Sixteen' – a famous classical choral ensemble. The choirmaster asked what they were performing and I informed him it was actually a 16-piece pipe band. I didn't tell him it was an exhaust-pipe band. The venue was, of course, Goodwood, and its wonderful Revival Meeting. So, though Formula One was defunct internationally, in Britain it still lived a little, and in the hands of the maestros Fangio, González and Farina amongst others.

The Grand Prix driver's diary of single-seater racing for 1953

18th January   F2 – **Gran Premio do Argentina** at Buenos Aires (Ag) – 235.8 miles

22nd March	F2 – Gran Premio di Siracusa (I) – 268.4 miles
6th April	F2 – Grand Prix de Pau (F) – 181.8 miles
6th April	F1/2 – Glover Trophy at Goodwood (UK) – 36 miles
6th April	F2 – Lavant Cup at Goodwood (UK) – 16.8 miles*
18th April	F2 – AMOC F2 Race at Snetterton (UK) – 27.1 miles*
3rd May	F2 – Grand Prix de Bordeaux (F) – 187.8 miles
9th May	F2 – *Daily Express* International Trophy at Silverstone (UK) – 146.4 miles
10th May	F2 – Gran Premio di Napoli at Posillipo (I) – 152.9 miles
16th May	F2 – Ulster Trophy at Dundrod (UK) – 180 miles
23th May	F2 – Winfield JC F2 Race at Charterhall (UK) – 40 miles*
24th May	F2 – Grand Prix des Frontiéres at Chimay (B) – 134.5 miles
25th May	F2 – Coronation Trophy at Crystal Palace (UK) – 13.9 miles*
30th May	F2 – Coronation Trophy at Snetterton (UK) – 27.1 miles*
31st May	F2 – Eifelrennen at Nurburgring (D) – 99.1 miles
31st May	F1/2 – Grand Prix d'Albi (F) – 155.9 miles
7th June	F2 – **Grote Prijs van Nederland** at Zandvoort (N) – 234.5 miles
21st June	F2 – **Grand Prix de Belgique** at Spa Francorchamps (B) – 315.9 miles
28th June	F1/2 – Grand Prix de Rouen-les-Essarts (F) – 190.1 miles
5th July	F2 – **Grand Prix de l'ACF** at Reims (F) – 311.2 miles
11th July	F2 – Crystal Palace Trophy (UK) – 20.9 miles*
12th July	F2 – International Avusrennen at Berlin (D) – 128.9 miles*
18th July	F2 – **British Grand Prix** at Silverstone (UK) – 263.4 miles
18th July	F1/2 – *Daily Express* Trophy at Silverstone (UK) – 49.8 miles
25th July	F2 – USAF Trophy at Snetterton (UK) – 40.7 miles*
26th July	F2 – Circuit du Lac at Aix les Bains (F) – 131.3 miles
2nd August	F2 – **Grosse Preis von Deutschland** at Nürburgring (D) – 255.1 miles
8th August	F2 – Mid-Cheshire MC F2 Race at Oulton Park (UK) – 49.6 miles*
9th August	F2 – Grand Prix de Sables d'Olonne (F) – 164.9 miles
15th August	F1/2 – *Daily Record* Trophy at Charterhall (UK) – 100 miles
23rd August	F2 – **Grosse Preis der Schweiz** at Bremgarten (S) – 294.1 miles
30th August	F2 – Circuit de Cadours (F) – 112.3 miles
6th September	F2 – Sachsenringrennen (GDR) – 65.1 miles*
13th September	F2 – **Gran Premio d'Italia at Monza** (I) – 313.2 miles
19th September	F2 – London Trophy at Crystal Palace (UK) – 28 miles*
20th September	F2 – Gran Premio di Modena (I) – 143.3 miles
26th September	F1/2 – Goodwood Trophy (UK) – 36 miles
26th September	F2 – Madgwick Cup at Goodwood (UK) – 16.8 miles*
3rd October	F2 – Joe Fry Mem Trophy at Castle Combe (UK) – 36.8 miles*
17th October	F2 – Curtis Trophy at Snetterton (UK) – 40.7 miles*

40 events of total race mileage = 5246 miles – 5147 max due to simultaneous races.

Events in bold are World Championship rounds – 23.5 per cent of F2 races run.

* See Appendix 'A' for these ungraded race results.

✱✱✱ (WC1) VII Gran Premio de la Republica Argentina (Buenos Aires No 2)

3 hours on a 2.431-mile circuit.

17 entries – 16 started – 9 finished.

Front row: A Ascari – 1m-55.4s (75.83mph); J-M Fangio (Maserati) 0.7s; L Villoresi 1.1s; G Farina.

18-JAN: A field entirely of Works cars – like modern times: Four Maseratis; four Ferraris; five Gordinis and three Cooper-Bristols. Maserati had a car for local hero Oscar Galvez, Gordini two for Carlos Menditeguy and Pablo Birger, and Cooper used Adolfo Cruz. An introduction to Argentine 'organisation' was when President Perón opened the gates to "all his children" and half a million crammed round the small circuit – a recipe for disaster. The National Anthem was played, the police stood to attention while the barriers were broken down. Fangio was within a second of Ascari in practise but it was business as usual – a flag-to-flag victory. A boy ran across the track, and poor Farina, in third place on lap 32, instinctively swerved into the crowd to avoid him, causing many fatalities. No race stoppage, of course, as a riot would have occurred. If Farina had run down the boy many lives would have been saved but maybe not his own! A crowd mentality was common in South America then. Fangio was second on lap 37 when a shaft failed. Hawthorn, on his Ferrari debut, dropped from sixth to 13th on lap one, but recovered to third by half distance. González passed him and Villoresi for second, but Villoresi retook the place. Best 'local' was Galvez in fifth.

1st	A Ascari (W)	Ferrari 500 97 laps in 3h-01m-04.6s	78.13
2nd	L Villoresi (W)	Ferrari 500	1 lap
3rd	F González (W)	Maserati A6SSG	1 lap

Championship positions:
Ascari 9; Villoresi 6; González 4.

✶✶ III Gran Premio di Siracusa

80 laps of 3.355 miles = 268.4 miles.
15 entries – 14 started – 5 finished.
Front row: A Ascari; G Farina; L Villoresi no times available.

22-MAR: Four Works Ferraris would surely dominate this race, as Maserati sent only one car for Sergio Mantovani. So Ascari, Farina, Villoresi and new boy Hawthorn led from deGraffenreid in the Platé team entry. Villoresi retired on lap four, and Ascari pitted with a broken wheel, so now Farina led. The Cooper-Bristol of Tom Cole crashed, and Mantovani struck it and was out. Ascari retired on lap 37 and took over Hawthorn's car, but it, and Farina's, had retired by three-quarter distance. So that was it for Ferrari and one-up to Maserati thanks entirely to its one customer, who had always led the Works car in the Ferrari chase.

1st	E deGraffenried	Maserati A6GCM in 2h-57m-31s	90.72
2nd	L Chiron	OSCA 20	3 laps
3rd	R Nuckey	Cooper T23-Bristol	6 laps
F lap	A Ascari (W)	Ferrari 500 in 2m-05.0s	96.62r

✶✶✶ XIV Grand Prix de Pau

3 hours of a 1.715-mile circuit.
16 entries – 14 started – 8 finished.
Front row: A Ascari – 1m-39.2s (62.24mph); G Farina 0.1s; M Hawthorn 1.0s.

06-APR: No deGraffenried and no Works Maseratis, so only 'Nello' Pagani's car represented the marque. Villoresi wasn't here, but the other Ferraris had the front row and duly led at the start, chased hard by Behra (Gordini). After seven laps, however, Behra crashed and was injured. The Ferraris swapped the lead until Farina spun after 33 laps and failed to restart on the uphill section. Ascari then drew out a 60-second lead over Hawthorn within 30 laps. Schell passed

Chiron (OSCA 20) to finish third. No Ferrari valve trouble this time, and no real challenge from anyone after Behra's departure. He recovered well.

1st	A Ascari (W)	Ferrari 500 106 laps in 3h-00m-33.6s	60.42
2nd	M Hawthorn (W)	Ferrari 500	1 lap
3rd	H Schell (W)	Gordini T16	4 laps
F lap	A Ascari	Ferrari 500 in 1m-38.9s	62.42r

Glover Trophy (Goodwood)

15 laps of 2.4 miles = 36 miles.
23 entries – 11 started – 7 finished.
Front row: K Wharton – 1m-35.0s (90.95mph); R Salvadori (Connaught A) 0.4s; deGraffenried; R Parnell.

06-APR: F1/2 masquerading as Formule Libre. An earlier sprint race caused many non-starters. Ken Wharton made this race his own, leading the whole way. His race speed was faster than the lap record held by Parnell, regarded by many as the better of the two! Parnell's BRM lasted only four laps, then deGraffenried's F2 Maserati ran second, but was soon passed by Taruffi, who finished 16.8 seconds ahead of him. Wharton was too far ahead for Taruffi to get close, partly because he was cautious out of the chicane.

1st	K Wharton (W)	BRM T15 V16 s/c in 23m-52.6s	90.47
2nd	P Taruffi (GAV)	Ferrari 375 'Thinwall'	6.0s
F lap	K Wharton (W)	BRM T15 V16 s/c in 1m-33.8s	92.11r

✶✶✶ III Grand Prix de Bordeaux

123 laps of 1.527 miles = 187.8 miles.
16 entries and starters – 8 finished.
Front row: L Villoresi – 1m-23.6s (65.77mph); A Ascari 0.1s; M Trintignant 0.6s.

03-MAY: Works cars from Ferrari (Ascari, Farina, Villoresi), Gordini (Trintignant, Fangio, Schell, Mieres) and HWM (Bira, Macklin, Giraud-Cabantous). Trintignant couldn't keep up with the Ferraris after the flag fell. The two leaders swapped places every so often during the first half. Farina retired on lap 60, followed shortly by Trintignant. This left Fangio in third, a lap down and nursing his engine, with Schell fourth. Near the end, both their Gordinis developed trouble and slowed badly yet kept their places. Elie Bayol's OSCA got to third at one point, but a wheel change dropped him back to fifth. Claes' Connaught was sixth, eight laps down.

1st	A Ascari (W)	Ferrari 500 in 2h-58m-59.5s	62.97
2nd	L Villoresi (W)	Ferrari 500	49.5s
3rd	J-M Fangio (W)	Gordini T16	4 laps
F lap	G Farina (W)	Ferrari 500 in 1m-24.6s	64.99r

✷✷ V *Daily Express* International Trophy (Silverstone)

15 + 35 laps of 2.927 = 146.4 miles.
46 entries – 36 started – 21 finished.
Poles: Heat one – deGraffenried (Maserati) 1m-51s (94.93mph); Heat two – K Wharton (Cooper-Bristol) 1m-52s (94.08mph).

09-MAY: As usual in Britain, a huge entry, but where were the Works Ferraris or Maseratis at this prestige event? DeGraff won heat one at 90.89mph by 5 secsonds from Moss (Cooper-Alta). Hawthorn took heat two at 92.81mph by 1 second from Wharton (Cooper-Bristol). The final saw deGraffenried anticipate the start, stop, and then get swamped by the front row. However, he led the first lap and, on lap 16, learned that he had a 1 minute penalty and withdrew in disgust ... yet it was a 35 lap race! Hawthorn then eased away. Trintignant lost a wheel and third place, and Moss fell way back from fourth. Wharton then held third, but fell to fifth with a misfire. From then Salvadori, Rolt and Bira (Maserati A6GCM) held position ahead of Wharton, but everyone was spread out. HWM was well beaten by Connaught, as at Bordeaux, for best British team, but none could match Ferrari.

1st	M Hawthorn (W)	Ferrari 500 in 1h-06m-36s	92.29
2nd	R Salvadori (W)	Connaught A type	12s
3rd	A Rolt (RW)	Connaught A type	42s
F lap	Hawthorn/deGraffenried	Ferrari/Maserati in 1m-51s	94.93r

✷✷ VI Gran Premio di Napoli (Posillipo)

60 laps of 2.548 miles = 152.9 miles.
8 entries and starters – 6 finished.
First row: G Farina : A Ascari; J-M Fangio. No times available.

10-MAY: So, the missing Works Ferraris (3) and Maseratis (2) were here instead of on the previous day at Silverstone. Has there ever been such a small but select field? Were other Italians deterred by the 'big five' presence (the other entries were just three sports cars)? The term 'starting money' comes to mind. Ascari led at first but pitted with a broken throttle pedal and lost four laps. Then Fangio led, but Farina soon passed in a do-or-die manoeuvre, both cars sliding, and

pulled away. Villoresi finished a lap down and Ascari five. All the five stars finished, but Maserati still had to improve.

1st	G Farina (W)	Ferrari 500 in 2h-12m-17.1s	69.33
2nd	J-M Fangio (W)	Maserati A6SSG	18.7s
3rd	F González (W)	Maserati A6SSG	1m-22s
F lap	G Farina	Ferrari 500 in 2m-07.7s	71.81r

✷ VII Ulster Trophy (Dundrod)

10-lap heats + 14-lap final of 7.416 miles = 180 total miles.
38 entries – 29 started – 14 finished.
Poles: Heat one – S Moss (Connaught) 4m-59s (89.29mph); Heat two – M Hawthorn 4m-51s (91.74mph).

16-MAY: One Works Ferrari for Hawthorn was all the team needed, as Gordini withdrew its entries. Heat and final were won with ease. Moss led heat one in a Connaught, but had only two gears after two laps. He pitted to no avail, but managed to recover to within nine seconds of leader Duncan Hamilton (HWM). Moss would have won the final but wasn't able to start. Wharton and Baird battled for second place nearly all race. Baird faded but was well ahead of Peter Whitehead's Cooper.

1st	M Hawthorn (W)	Ferrari 500 in 1h-12m-01.6s	86.49
2nd	K Wharton	Cooper T23-Bristol	1m-13s
3rd	B Baird	Ferrari 500	1m-46s
F lap	M Hawthorn	Ferrari 500 in 4m-54s	90.81

XXIII Grand Prix des Frontiéres (Chimay)

20 laps of 6.727 miles = 134.5 miles.
23 entries – 19 starters – 5 finished.
Front row: M Trintignant – 4m-11.0s (96.48mph); J Claes (Connaught) 4.0s. Row two: B Bira 5s; R Laurent 5s.

24-MAY: Only Trintignant in a Works Gordini and Bira's private Maserati A6GCM had any postwar reputation. Perhaps many avoided this long, fast, dangerous course which offered little reward. Trintignant duly led from the start, followed by Bira, who crashed when lapping a backmarker on only lap three! Johnny Claes fought with Laurent, but failed to out-brake him on lap 18 and they collided, with Claes' Connaught injuring spectators. Fred Wacker's Gordini was third, well back.

1st	M Trintignant (W)	Gordini T16 in 1h-25m-59.5s	93.86
2nd	R Laurent	Ferrari 500	1m-11s
F lap	M Trintignant	Gordini T16 in 4m-11.0s	96.48r

✳ XVII ADAC Eifelrennen (N Nürburgring)

7 laps of 14.16 miles = 99.1 miles.

35 entries – 28 started – 12 finished. No grid positions available.

31-MAY: A stronger international content to the annual German event this year. deGraffenried took the lead from the sole Ferrari 500 of Kurt Adolff, whose modest cornering but good straight-line speed held up Moss and the rest to the extent of 15 seconds after just one lap. Second place Moss' HWM had trouble on lap two, so Collins and Frére passed Adolff, and Frére chased and almost caught an unaware deGraffenried. Collins spun when his extinguisher came loose, but finished third.

1st	E deGraffenried (EP)	Maserati A6GCM in 1h-24m-32s	70.36
2nd	P Frére (W)	HWM-Alta	1.7s
3rd	P Collins (W)	HWM-Alta	16.3s
F lap	E deGraffenried	Maserati A6GCM in 11m-24.3s	74.47

✳✳✳ (F1) XV Grand Prix d'Albi

10-lap heats + 18-lap final of 5.563 miles = 155.8 total miles.

21 entries – 19 started – 7 finished.

Front row (F1): J-M Fangio – 2m-52.5s (116.10mph); A Ascari (Ferrari 375) 2.9s; F González 6.4s.

31-MAY: A real F1 race at last. Three BRMs were there ... and fast! Now could they beat the Works Ferrari 375s of Ascari and Farina. One heat was for F2 (nine starters), and another for F1 (ten starters). Rosier was in both, and won the first heat in his Ferrari 500 at 98.29mph. Fangio's pole was 2.9 seconds faster than Ascari's Works Ferrari – but two years too late. If only ... if only ... Rosier finished third in the F1 heat behind two BRMs; Ascari's gearbox and Farina's engine had failed! All was set for BRM to finish flying high after four years of woes. And it nearly was, as the opposition had vanished. However, the now fabulous cars shredded their tyres; all pitting – Fangio to retire with rubber in the brakes. Wharton's car was destroyed in a 130mph smash, hitting a building. Amazingly, he survived almost unscathed, and González couldn't recover all the time lost. So BRM snatched defeat from the welcoming arms of victory. Ah well! – thanks for all the noise. From now on the V16 was almost a novelty act. This was the last serious race to the 1.5s/c / 4.5 us/c F1 rules which started in 1947.

1st	L Rosier	Ferrari 375 (F1) in 56m-38.6s	106.06
2nd	F González	BRM 15 V16-s/c (F1)	31.0s
3rd	M Trintignant	Gordini T16 (F2)	1m-54s
F lap	J-M Fangio (heat two)	BRM 15 V16 (F1) in 2m-52.2s	116.30r

✳✳✳ (WC2) IV Grote Prijs van Nederland (Zandvoort)

90 laps of 2.605 miles = 234.5 miles.

20 entries – 19 started – 9 finished.

Front row: A Ascari – 1m-51.1s (84.41mph); J-M Fangio 1.6s; G Farina 1.9s.

07-JUN: At last the World Championship was under way again, after a wait of almost five months. A lead battle never happened, though, as Ascari led flag-to-flag. Villoresi and Farina swapped second place a few times, Farina taking hold on lap 47, Villoresi retiring 20 laps later. Fangio's Maserati retired from fourth on lap 36. González' start was dreadful – 14th on lap one but fifth on lap 16. His car failed at a point just behind the pits, so he was soon able to take over Bonetto's car. He chased and caught Mike Hawthorn then pulled away preventing a 1-2-3 for Ferrari. So, no real battle yet between the main protagonists. It must happen soon surely.

1st	A Ascari (W)	Ferrari 500 in 2h-53m-35.8s	81.03
2nd	G Farina (W)	Ferrari 500	10.4s
3rd	Bonetto/González (W)	Maserati A6SSG	1 lap
F lap	L Villoresi (W)	Ferrari 500 in 1m-52.8s	83.14

Championship positions:
Ascari 17; Villoresi 7; Farina 6.

✳✳✳ (WC3) XV Grand Prix de Belgique (Spa)

36 laps of 8.774 miles = 315.9 miles.

22 entries – 20 started – 12 finished.

Front row: J-M Fangio – 4m-30s (116.98mph); A Ascari 2s; F González 2s.

21-JUN: At last the World Championship status quo was challenged by Maserati as its cars sandwiched Ascari's Ferrari on the grid. It was González who led Fangio and they easily left Ascari well behind until lap 11 when González' accelerator pedal broke! Next lap Fangio's engine failed, and he took over Johnny Claes' car. So, Ascari luckily led from Farina who soon retired. Hawthorn was now second, but a split fuel pipe spoilt his race. Fangio battled back to third on the last lap, whereupon his steering failed after Stavelot, and he was lucky to avoid serious injury. Today he would have kept his place, as he hadn't been lapped. Ascari's nine successive Championship wins remains unbeaten, and was only equalled by Sebastian Vettel sixty years later!

1st	A Ascari (W)	Ferrari 500 in 2h-48m-30.3s	112.47
2nd	L Villoresi (W)	Ferrari 500	2m-48s
3rd	O Marimón (W)	Maserati A6SSG	1 lap
F lap	F González (W)	Maserati A6SSG in 4m-34.0ss	115.28

Championship positions:
Ascari 25; Villoresi 13; González 7.

✳ (F1) III Grand Prix de Rouen

60 laps of 3.169 miles = 190.1 miles.
17 entries – 15 started – 10 finished.
Front row: G Farina – 2m-12.2s (86.30mph): M Hawthorn 1.1s; M Trintignant 1.3s.
28-JUN: No BRMs were here, and Ferrari used the race to test its 1954 engines in its F2 cars, as did Gordini with Trintignant. The Ferrari 500/625s easily outpaced Rosier's 'full size' Ferrari 375 (but he was never very fast) and the outdated Talbots. Hawthorn led for four laps, then Farina overtook in desperate fashion! Hawthorn challenged but was told to hold place. Trintignant and Rosier retired, so Schell's F2 Gordini and Etancelin's F1 Talbot battled for third – settled at Schell's stop for plugs. Local man 'Phi-Phi' Etancelin (57 years old!) ended his career to huge cheers after the usual spirited drive in his old machine – his name for ever associated with these cars. This was the last major race for the expiring 1.5s/c / 4.5us/c Formula One after seven years.

1st	G Farina (W)	Ferrari 500/625 (F1) in 2h-15m-05.8s	84.45
2nd	M Hawthorn (W)	Ferrari 500/625 (F1)	1.2s
3rd	P Etancelin	Talbot-Lago T26C (F1)	3 laps
F lap	M Hawthorn	Ferrari 500/625 (F1) in 2m-12.8s	85.91r

✳✳✳ (WC4) XL Grand Prix de l'ACF (Reims)

60 laps of 5.187 miles = 311.2 miles.
25 entries starters – 14 finished.
Front row: A Ascari – 2m-41.2s (115.83mph); F Bonetto 0.3s; L Villoresi 0.7s.
05-JUL: On the extended course, which now crossed the road from Gueux to join the RN31 at the sharp Muizon bend, one of the greatest races ever took place. Ten Ferraris and Maseratis occupied the front four grid rows – no-one else was getting a look in. González was low-fuelled, so led for 29 laps, emerging from his pit in sixth place, the plan having just failed. He joined five scrapping cars, but it was Fangio and Hawthorn who shared the lead, swapping no less than 11 times, and that was just at the start/finish line – there was plenty more elsewhere. Ascari fought with González to the end, just five

seconds covering the first four. So, Ascari's winning streak was ended, having never led the race. It was Hawthorn who did it, but Ferrari's winning streak was continuing.

1st	M Hawthorn (W)	Ferrari 500 in 2h-44m-18.6s	113.64
2nd	J-M Fangio (W)	Maserati A6SSG	1.0s
3rd	F González (W)	Maserati A6SSG	1.4s
F lap	Ascari/Fangio	Ferrari 500/Maserati in 2m-41.1s	115.90

Championship positions:
Ascari 28.5; Hawthorn 14; Villoresi 13.

✳✳✳ (WC5) VIII British Grand Prix (Silverstone)

90 laps of 2.927 miles = 263.4 miles.
30 entries – 28 started – 10 finished.
Front row: A Ascari – 1m-48s (97.57mph); F González 1s; M Hawthorn 1s; J-M Fangio 2s.
18-JUL: Ascari retook command of the Championship with an almost flag-to-flag run – only beaten into the first bend by Fangio, from the outside of the front row, who slid wide on exit. González passed Fangio on the next lap, while Reims hero Hawthorn spun out of fifth place right to the back of the field; trying too hard too soon. A black flag for oil on lap 16 probably cost González third as Fangio and Villoresi passed as he pitted, but emerged without losing any more places. Then the top four places remained unaltered for 50 laps. Villoresi retired on lap 65 with rear axle trouble. González took third then, only to lose it to Farina. Hawthorn recovered to fifth at that time, and the race ran out unchanged. Bonetto took sixth after Marimón and Rolt retired, and Jimmy Stewart (Jackie's brother) crashed during a heavy shower. No points for sixth, then.

1st	A Ascari (W)	Ferrari 500 in 2h-50-00s	92.97
2nd	J-M Fangio (W)	Maserati A6SSG	1m-00s
3rd	G Farina (W)	Ferrari 500	2 laps
F lap	Ascari/González	Ferrari 500/Maserati in 1m-50s	95.79r

Championship positions:
Ascari 33.5; Hawthorn 16; González 13.5.

✳ (F1) *Daily Express* Trophy (Silverstone)

17 laps of 2.927 miles = 49.8 miles.
19 entries – 16 starters – 10 finished.
Front row: J-M Fangio – 1m-46s (99.41mph); G Farina 1s; K Wharton 2s; M Hawthorn 4s.
18-JUL: Supporting the British GP – a shorter F1 race. BRMs

on the front row – a home win? Mike Hawthorn's Works Ferrari 500/625 led off the line, but was soon passed by Farina and Fangio. Hawthorn's engine expired after only four laps, so Ken Wharton was now third. Farina became the first man to lap a British circuit at over 100mph. If Fangio couldn't win from pole in the BRM, then no-one could. The truth was that even Silverstone was too twisty for the BRM, it wanted longer straights.

1st	G Farina (GAV)	Ferrari 375 Thinwall in 30m-50.8s	96.79
2nd	J-M Fangio (W)	BRM T15 V16 s/c	11.2s
3rd	K Wharton (W)	BRM T15 V16 s/c	43.2s
F lap	G Farina	Ferrari 375 Thinwall in 1m-45.2s	100.16r

✻ V Circuit du Lac (Aix les Bains)
2 x 50 laps of 1.497 miles = 149.7 miles.
12 entries – 11 started – 5 finished.
Front row: H Schell – 1m-20.0s (67.37mph); O Marimón 0.3s; M Trintignant.
26-JUL: HWM and Gordini had three-car teams, and Maserati one Works entry for Marimón. He led heat one, but soon Schell's Gordini passed, only for Marimón to make contact with his tail. A Marimón/Trintignant battle ended with a spin and a dropped valve respectively. Behra won from Bayol. The second heat saw Bayol lead from Behra and Rosier. Behra's 23 seconds in hand from the first heat vanished due to axle failure. So this was a first win for an OSCA, a company formed by the Maserati brothers.

1st	E Bayol	OSCA 20 in 2h-22m-45.4s	62.92
2nd	L Rosier	Ferrari 500	2m-03s
3rd	L Macklin (W)	HWM-Alta	4 laps
F lap	J Behra (W)	Gordini T16 in 1m-20.0s	67.37

✻✻✻ (WC6) XVI Grosser Preis von Deutschland (N Nürburgring)
18 laps of 14.17 miles = 255.1 miles.
40 entries – 34 started – 16 finished.
Front row: A Ascari – 9m-59.8s (85.07mph); J-M Fangio 3.9s; G Farina 4.3s; M Hawthorn 12.8s.
02-AUG: An entry bolstered with 16 from Germany, mostly Veritas- and BMW-powered. No HWMs, though, due to poor starting money – disgraceful. Thankfully that aspect is long gone. Ascari soon passed Fangio to lead and easily pull away. At four laps he was 40 seconds ahead of Hawthorn! Then disaster – a wheel came off, and he crawled all the way back losing four minutes. Hawthorn's lead lasted two

laps when Farina and Fangio overtook. Ascari and Villoresi exchanged cars so Ascari stopped at the end of his ninth lap and Villoresi his tenth. Ascari never did a tenth lap, and Villoresi did two. The car carries the race number not the driver – still strange as it was a Drivers' Championship not a Constuctors'. The Villoresi/Ascari car was closing on Hawthorn when its engine expired. Ascari's fastest lap was only 0.2 seconds off his record of 1951 ... with half the power!

1st	G Farina (W)	Ferrari 500 in 3h-22m-25.0s	83.91
2nd	J-M Fangio (W)	Maserati A6SSG	1m-04s
3rd	M Hawthorn (W)	Ferrari 500	1m-44s
F lap	A Ascari (W)	Ferrari 500 in 9m-56.0s	85.61

Championship positions:
Ascari 33.5; Farina 20; Fangio 18.5.

✻ III Grand Prix de Sables d'Olonne
2 x 45 laps of 1.832 miles = 164.9 miles. 12 entries & starters – 6 finished.
Front row: H Schell; M Trintignant; J Behra. No times available.
09-AUG: Entry very similar to 'Circuit du Lac,' with Stirling Moss in Cooper-Alta added. Works Gordini driver Behra won heat one – his teammate Trintignant retiring. All was set for Behra to win again, but he spun and crashed, somewhat inexplicably, damaging the rear axle, so Trintignant won the heat. Chiron and Rosier had a second and third each with total times favouring Rosier. Moss had gearbox trouble in each heat, yet fourth and fifth places gave him third overall. Without that trouble he could well have won. So, a Ferrari had lost twice to a Gordini, yet won! Gordini entered in Germany and here – pity Ferrari or Maserati didn't.

1st	L Rosier	Ferrari 500 in 2h-12m-56.1s	74.42
2nd	L Chiron	OSCA 20	28.2s
3rd	S Moss	Cooper T24-Alta	3 laps

✻ *Daily Record* International Trophy (Charterhall)
50 laps of 2 miles = 100 miles.
13+ starters.
Front row: G Farina – 1m-21.8s (88.02mph); K Wharton 2.6s; R Flockhart 3.6s.
15-AUG: Listed as Formule Libre but in reality F1 and F2 – a Ferrari Thinwall/BRM scrap. Parnell's BRM crashed in practice and non-started. Lap one and Farina's Thinwall, Moss (F2 Cooper-Alta), Wharton and Rolt held the front

places. Moss was passed by Wharton and, four laps later, by Rolt. Farina drew away from Wharton but, on lap 14, his race was run. John Coombs (Connaught) deprived Moss of third place, and soon Moss was out with trouble in the fuel injection system. Roy Salvadori had taken over Fairman's car, and Coombs lost third place to him before retiring.

1st	K Wharton (W)	BRM T15 V16 s/c in 1h-12m-33s	82.70
2nd	A Rolt	Connaught A type (F2)	1 lap
3rd	J Fairman/R Salvadori	Connaught A type (F2)	1 lap
F lap	K Wharton	BRM T15 V16 s/c in 1m-24.0s	85.71r

✱✱✱ (WC7) XIII Grosse Preis der Schweiz (Bremgarten Berne)
65 laps of 4.524 miles = 294.1 miles.
23 entries – 20 started – 7 finished.
Front row: J-M Fangio – 2m-40.1s (101.72mph); A Ascari 0.6s; G Farina 2.5s.

23-AUG: The two best drivers of the era were, unsurprisingly, well ahead of anyone else on this dangerous, drivers' circuit. Ascari appeared to have destroyed the last Championship hopes of Farina and Fangio until he pitted on lap 40 for plugs and carburettor work. This dropped him to fourth behind Farina, Marimón and Hawthorn, but ahead of Fangio. Marimón soon retired, and, on lap 54, Ascari was ahead again having ignored signals to hold station. He was World Champion again. Fangio had led off the line but was dispatched by Ascari – the Ferrari had superior handling – essential on this fast, dangerous circuit with hardly any straights and many fast sweeps. At quarter distance Fangio swapped with Bonetto but later retired. However Bonetto made fourth place so they shared the three points. What would Fangio have done if he had continued in this car? Could he have kept ahead of Ascari? He must have known that sharing a car (and points) had put himself out of the Championship contest. This shows that winning was more important to him than points. And the Alfa 158 lap record had gone.

1st	A Ascari (W)	Ferrari 500 in 3h-01m-34.4s	97.12
2nd	G Farina (W)	Ferrari 500	1m-13s
3rd	M Hawthorn (W)	Ferrari 500	1m-36s
F lap	A Ascari (W)	Ferrari 500 in 2m-41.3s	100.96r

Championship positions:
Ascari (WC) 34.5; Farina 24; Fangio 20.

✱ V Grand Prix de Cadours
15-lap heats + 30-lap final of 2.495 miles = 112.3 total miles.
20 entries – 16 started – 7 finished.
Poles: Heat one – M Trintignant – 1m-57s (76.77mph); Heat two – L Rosier – 2m-00s (74.85mph).

30-AUG: The Gordini were challenged mainly by the Ferrari 500 of Rosier, deGraffenried's Maserati and Bayol's OSCA. Heat winners Trintignant and Schell dominated the ten car final, easing up to allow an off-form Behra to join them. Rosier had fuel feed trouble yet finished 48 seconds behind Behra. Could he have spoilt Gordini's party? Bayol retired early on, and the HWMs retired or crashed with Giraud-Cabantous suffering a sudden tyre deflation on the last lap when sixth.

1st	M Trintignant (W)	Gordini T16 in 1h-00m-52s	73.78
2nd	H Schell (W)	Gordini T16	4s
3rd	J Behra (W)	Gordini T16	5s
F lap	M Trintignant	Gordini T16 in 1m-56s	77.43r

✱✱✱ (WC8) XXIII Gran Premio d'Italia (Monza)
80 laps of 3.915 miles = 313.2 miles.
30 entries and starters – 20 finished.
Front row: A Ascari – 2m-02.7s (114.86mph); J-M Fangio 0.5s; G Farina 1.2s.

13-SEP: The final Championship race looked a real showdown, with six cars from Ferrari – two were prototypes for 1954, and four from Maserati. Gordini, HWM and Connaught sent three cars each. Moss had a Works Cooper-Alta using nitro-methane fuel! First lap order was Ascari, Marimón, Farina, Fangio and Moss(!). As usual with a Monza slipstreamer race, lap charts would vary at differing points on the track. Who knows which of the main four led and when? Trintignant's Gordini was the first non-Italian car, in sixth place most of the time. Lap 46 and Marimón pitted, lost four laps, and rejoined the scrapping trio leading. And so to the last corner. Ascari led, threw his car past a slower car but spun on oil, Marimón rammed him, Farina touched Marimón, and Fangio thought 'thanks I'll have this one,' so he did. Ascari was already champion, but still he was desperate to win, saying it was almost his duty to try even in the face of danger particularly in front of his home crowd. Like Fangio in the Swiss race he felt that the race itself was everything – it's what people pay to see.

1st	J-M Fangio (W)	Maserati A6SSG in 2h-49m-45.9s	110.68
2nd	G Farina (W)	Ferrari 500	1.4s
3rd	L Villoresi (W)	Ferrari 500	1 lap
F lap	J-M Fangio (W)	Ferrari 500 in 2m-04.5s	113.19

Championship position:
Ascari (WC) 34.5; Fangio 27.5; Farina 26.

** IV Gran Premio di Modena

100 laps of 1.433 miles = 143.3 miles. 14 entries – 13 started – 5 finished.

Front row: J-M Fangio – 1m-06.2s (77.96mph): O Marimón 0.2s; E deGraffenried 0.4s.

20-SEP: After the previous week's Italian GP, Enzo Ferrari had grumpily threatened to quit Grand Prix racing, so he would have lost face if he'd entered here. Sadly, a non-Works Ferrari overturned in practice, killing driver Baron de Tornaco. The four works Maseratis feared little from the works Gordinis and Connaughts, though Salvadori's Connaught was just 0.4 seconds from them on the grid. From the rolling start Fangio and protegé Marimón circulated together, Marimón sometimes leading, but his engine ran rough toward the end. Bonetto's works Maserati retired, so teammate deGraffenried was third. Salvadori retired and Trintignant's Gordini was fourth.

1st	J-M Fangio (W)	Maserati A6SSG in 1h-52m-08.9s	76.67
2nd	O Marimón (W)	Maserati A6SSG	39.1s
3rd	E deGraffenried (W)	Maserati A6SSG	2 laps
F lap	J-M Fangio	Maserati A6SSG in 1m-05.4s	78.91

Goodwood Trophy (Goodwood)

15 laps of 2.4 miles = 36 miles.
16 entries – 12 started – 9 finished.

Front row: J-M Fangio – 1m-34.0s (90.91mph); M Hawthorn 1.0s; R Salvadori 1.0s; K Wharton 1.2s.

26-SEP: Another BRM/Ferrari Thinwall Special duel which drew big crowds – the duellists of the French Grand Prix were here. This time, the Ferrari had the legs of the BRMs even with Fangio driving one, and Hawthorn was now acclaimed as Britain's best. Wharton took two laps to pass Salvadori's brilliantly driven F2 Connaught, which then spun as Salvadori was trying to keep up. Fangio spun on lap eight, handing second place to Wharton, and then retired on lap 11 with gearbox trouble. Bob Gerard's Cooper-Bristol was third a lap down. Hawthorn had blown the lap record apart. But for its short length, this would have been a higher grade event.

1st	M Hawthorn	Ferrari 375 Thinwall in 23m-17.8s	92.70
2nd	K Wharton (W)	BRM T15 V16 s/c	23.0s
F lap	M Hawthorn	Ferrari 375 Thinwall in 1m-31.4s	94.53r

1953 seasonal review

Only a single decent Formula One race took place this year, at Albi, where BRM threw away a chance to shine (at long last), with a 1, 2, 3 result. Although the Works Ferraris had unexpectedly failed in the heats, the BRMs' tyres weren't up to the job of delivering the massive horsepower surge from the unforgettably noisy cars. The Rouen F1 race was devoid of any of the serious cars, so it was left to the Formule Libre races to present the other F1 Ferrari/BRM duels. All serious single-seat racing cars belonged to either of the major formulae so the nomenclature 'Formule Libre' only really served to allow in slower sports cars. That's why I have regarded them as de facto Formula One races. Only the British Grand Prix support race at Silverstone was over 50 miles long, which is a criteria for a grade three event.

Formula Two continued in the great manner of 1952, and it was hoped that the standard would be maintained into the 1954 season of new Formula One rules. Maserati had not challenged Ferrari nearly as strongly as hoped for, coming on strong late in the year at Monza, its only Championship win. Gordini was, as ever, short of funds to develop the cars, though they occasionally showed potential in the hands of Trintignant. Connaught and Cooper had now taken over as the most promising of the F2 teams.

Twenty top three graded F2 races were run, of which Alberto Ascari won five Championship and two non-Championship races, clearly still the master despite Fangio's presence. If Fangio's 1952 season hadn't been curtailed, there seemed little doubt that Ascari's amazing 1952 full-house would have been unaffected. His nine successive World Championship wins has only been equalled by Sebastien Vettel in 2013, after sixty years!

Winners of the 26 Premier Formulae races of 1953 – quantity & quality of success

7 wins	A Ascari (7A)	17 wins	Ferrari (10A, 2B, 4C, D)
4 wins	G Farina (A, B, 2C) M Hawthorn (A, B, C, D)	4 wins	Maserati (A, 2B, C)
2 wins	J-M Fangio (A, B) L Rosier (A, C) E deGraffenried (B, C) M Trintignant (C, D) K Wharton (C, D)	2 wins	Gordini (C, D); BRM (C, D)
1 win	E Bayol (C)	1 win	OSCA (C)

1953 World Championship review

Another runaway year for Alberto Ascari, who retained the

world title with a race to spare. He clearly had the edge on Farina, and perhaps Hawthorn was the number two now. It was unfortunate that after three rounds Ascari had 25 points from three wins and Fangio had yet to score. The system of only retaining the best five results from the eight rounds meant that Fangio could get back into the chase if Maserati reliability was improved – it had scared Ferrari a bit in Belgium. The fact that he finished second at year's end is testimony to his genius – not forgetting a little help from the last lap fracas at Monza. Two fifth places (the lowest scoring place) for Trintignant is all that was scored by non-Italian cars. It should be noted, though, that if sixth place had scored a point, as it did after 1959, then Stirling Moss would have been on the score sheets earlier than was the actual case for him. Ferrari had also collected **14 successive World Championship wins**. This is also unbeaten to this day and, conceivably, never will be! The nearest to Ferraris 1952/3 campaigns which yielded 14 wins from 15 races would be the 1988 season of McLaren with 15 wins from 16 rounds shared by Senna and Prost.

VISIT VELOCE ON THE WEB – WWW.VELOCE.CO.UK
All current books • New book news • Special offers • Gift vouchers • Forum
•

85

Chapter 13

1954

Formula One back in charge

The new Formula One was eagerly anticipated, being a replacement for both F1 and F2. The original 1947 Formula One created a level playing field for the majority of existing pre-war cars of varying quality. Now, in 1954, there would be a more exciting situation, with all cars of contemporary design – as had actually been the case with Formula Two. Ferrari had produced a 4-cylinder, 2.5-litre engine, installed it in his F2 car, and raced it in a few F1 races in 1953. The F1 car itself would now be known as the 625, but he had entered, purely as support, a totally new car, the 553, in the Italian Grand Prix the previous year. Would this be developed? Maserati produced the now revered 250F model, which it would sell to privateers – a very useful decision for all concerned, and no doubt helping to finance its own racing team. Poorly financed Gordini simply expanded its engine in the previous year's cars. So now we have the existing teams with their principal drivers as follows:

Scuderia Ferrari with Giuseppe Farina, Froilán González, Mike Hawthorn, and soon Maurice Trintignant.
Officine Alfieri Maserati with Fangio (pre-Mercedes), Alberto Ascari and Luigi Villoresi (pre-Lancia), Onofre Marimón, Luigi Musso, and a private (but Works-supported) car for Stirling Moss.
Gordini had Jean Behra and Elie Bayol, and a lot of hope.

Excitingly, it was known that Mercedes-Benz had been working for some time on a new radical straight-eight car, and would surely be formidable, particularly as it had signed Juan-Manuel Fangio to join two of the best German drivers: Karl Kling and Hans Hermann. Mercedes was, however, returning only for the World Championship rounds, selling road cars being its preoccupation. Mercedes wasn't a 'racer-

from-birth,' though, unlike Ferrari, who always said that he sold road cars to pay for the racing. Fortunately, Mercedes allowed its drivers to race other cars when not required, so the quality of driver participation was carried over to extra races beyond the Championship, which were lucrative and plentiful. If the other manufacturers had done as Mercedes did, then it's difficult to see how Formula One would have flourished with only nine events instead of more than double that. Thank heavens for these extra races which were the very life-blood for all F1 entrants.

There was no sign of Alfa Romeo returning, but another eagerly anticipated Italian 'newcomer' was Lancia, who had surprisingly signed the inseparable Alberto Ascari and Luigi Villoresi from under the nose of Ferrari. Lancia was working on a V8 engine – the first time this configuration entered F1 – and was also radical in having the fuel tanks between the wheels. It would join the fray a little later – the sooner the better, with Ascari largely sidelined.

The British were an unknown quantity in this F1. Industrial tycoon Tony Vandervell, the creator of the Ferrari Thinwall Special, seen in F1 races in 1951 to '53, was going it alone, having despaired of BRM, and produced a car with its four cylinders based on the successful Manx Norton racing motorcycle engine. Would the Vanwall be as good as the bike? Peter Collins would be the main pilot.

Connaught enlarged the Alta engine in the previous year's car, but the Bristol engine in the Coopers wasn't suitable for expansion, and Coopers faded from the scene for a few years. BRM had been sidetracked by the V16, trying to save face, and was very slow off the mark again for this formula. HWM had been the first British team to make a mark in post-war single-seater racing, but never tackled the new Formula One, making just a few appearances with enlarged engines.

Overall it was a very encouraging situation, and intriguing with the radical new teams having secured the services of the two very best drivers of the day. Unlike today, teams were not limited to two cars, so often a team would be augmented. Full grids dominated by Works machinery should now be the norm, and couldn't be more different to the hopeless situation of Formula One in 1952.

But what might have been if the British weren't so trusting? The Coventry Climax engine company had been working during 1953 on a new V8 racing engine (called 'Godiva') to supply to British marques, and had produced 260bhp with it, but Ferrari and Maserati were claiming up to 280bhp. Their claims were dubious, though, as 240 was much nearer the truth; it was pure gamesmanship. Strange, really, as one would have thought that understatement might have been a better tactic to entice others into complacency. It worked, however, and Coventry Climax swallowed the bait and abandoned its engine, leaving Britain trailing for a few years. With unfortunate irony, when it did power the British to success after a few years, it did so with less horsepower than the 'Godiva' unit.

The Grand Prix driver's diary of single-seater racing for 1954

17th January	**Gran Premio do Argentina** at Buenos Aires (No 2) (Ag) – 211.5 miles
31st January	Gran Premio di Buenos Aires (No 4 layout) (Ag) – 190 miles
11th April	Gran Premio di Siracusa (I) – 273.4 miles
19th April	Grand Prix de Pau (F) – 186.9 miles
19th April	Lavant Cup at Goodwood (UK) – 16.8 miles*
9th May	Grand Prix de Bordeaux (F) – 187.8 miles
15th May	*Daily Express* International Trophy at Silverstone (UK) – 146.4 miles
23rd May	Gran Premio di Bari (I) – 206.5 miles
5th June	Curtis Trophy at Snetterton (UK) – 27.1 miles*
6th June	Gran Premio di Roma at Castel Fusano (I) – 245.7 miles
6th June	Grand Prix des Frontiéres at Chimay (B) – 134.5 miles*
7th June	BARC F1 Race at Goodwood (UK) – 12 miles*
7th June	Cornwall MRC F1 Race at Davidstow (UK) – 37 miles*
19th June	Crystal Palace Trophy (UK) – 13.9 miles*
20th June	**Grand Prix de Belgique** at Spa Francorchamps (B) – 315.9 miles
4th July	**Grand Prix de l'ACF** at Reims (F) – 314.7 miles
11th July	Grand Prix de Rouen-les-Essarts (F) – 302.8 miles

17th July	**British Grand Prix** at Silverstone (UK) – 263.4 miles
25th July	Grand Prix de Caen (F) – 131.3 miles
1st August	**Grosse Preis von Deutschland** at Nürburgring (D) – 311.7 miles
2nd August	August Trophy at Crystal Palace (UK) – 27.8 miles*
7th August	International Gold Cup at Oulton Park (UK) – 96.4 miles
14th August	Redex Trophy at Snetterton (UK) – 108.4 miles*
15th August	Circuito di Pescara (I) – 254.1 miles
22nd August	**Grosse Preis der Schweiz** at Bremgarten (S) – 240.3 miles
28th August	Joe Fry Mem Trophy at Castle Combe (UK) – 27.6 miles*
5th September	**Gran Premio d'Italia at Monza** (I) – 313.2 miles
12th September	Circuit de Cadours (F) – 112.3 miles
19th September	Grosse Preis von Berlin at Avus (D) – 309.4 miles
25th September	Goodwood Trophy (UK) – 50.4 miles
2nd October	*Daily Telegraph* Trophy at Aintree (UK) – 51 miles
24th October	**Gran Premio d'Espagna** at Pedralbes (E) – 313.2 miles

32 events of total race mileage = 5030 miles – 5001 max due to simultaneous races.
Events in bold are World Championship rounds – 25 per cent of F1 races run.
* See appendix 'A' for these ungraded race results.

✳✳✳ (WC1) VIII Gran Premio de la Republica Argentina (Buenos Aires No 2)

3 hours on a 2.431-mile circuit.
18 entries – 16 started – 9 finished.
Front row: G Farina – 1m-44.8s (83.60mph); F González 0.1s; J-M Fangio 0.7s; M Hawthorn 2.2s.

17-JAN: Ferrari, Maserati and Gordini sent Works teams, with Maglioli added to Ferrari's squad here. They were 'assisted' by the blue Equipe Rosier team with Trintignant. The Maseratis works had Fangio, Marimón and Bira (Ascari and Villoresi absent), and were supplemented by re-engined 1953 cars in the hands of privateers. Gordini entered Behra, Bayol and Loyer. Farina led at first from Fangio, Hawthorn and González, but by lap 15 González had passed them all. A downpour occurred on lap 30, and González spun, while Farina pitted for a visor, so now Hawthorn led. The rain eased and the Ferraris led again – until it rained again – then Fangio led again. Hawthorn spun twice, had outside assistance and was disqualified. Fangio pitted for 'rain cut' tyres but Ferrari manager Ugolini claimed that more than three had worked on the car. He slowed his drivers believing his claim would hold up– it didn't – this was Argentina after all. So Fangio retook the lead and pulled easily away.

1st	J-M Fangio (W)	Maserati 250F 87 laps in 3h-00m-55.5s	70.13
2nd	G Farina (W)	Ferrari 625	1m-18s
3rd	F González (W)	Ferrari 625	2m-01s
F lap	F González	Ferrari 625 in 1m-48.2s	80.88r

✱✱✱ IX Gran Premio de Buenos Aires (Buenos Aires No 4)

65 laps of 2.924 miles = 190.0 miles.
22 entries – 21 started – 10 finished.
Front row: G Farina; F González; M Hawthorn; M Trintignant all Ferrari 625s. Times not known.

31-JAN: The Argentine GP was repeated here on a different layout and with a few 'locals' added. Maglioli, Farina and Hawthorn led, but, from lap four, Hawthorn pulled well away. Maglioli hit trouble and Farina stopped on lap 11, taking over González' car. Behra's Gordini had been well up, and he finished fourth on the lead lap despite spinning more than once. Then, on the very last bend, Hawthorn's engine blew and he spun. Privateers were first and second. Farina was followed home by Schell (Maserati), Behra, and Hawthorn. Fangio retired with transmission breakage. Tragedy occurred when Daponte's Maserati suffered a locked differential when entering his pit. The car slewed and fatally injured Enrico Platé – the popular private team entrant.

1st	M Trintignant (ER)	Ferrari 625 in 2h-38m-35.0s	71.55
2nd	R Mieres	Maserati A6GCM/250F	29.4s
3rd	González/Farina (W)	Ferrari 625	37.6s
F lap	G Farina	Ferrari 625 in 2m-22.4s	73.96

✱ IV Gran Premio di Siracusa

80 laps of 3.417 miles = 273.4 miles.
13 entries – 8 started – 6 finished.
Front row: O Marimón – 2m-02.6s (100.35mph); F González 0.0; G Farina 0.4s.

11-APR: The withdrawals of four private Maseratis and Fangio's Works car, left a meagre field, but of quality drivers. Marimón was third behind Hawthorn and González at first, but, on lap four, he overtook both to lead. Then he side-swiped straw bales creating a dust storm, and causing Hawthorn, unsighted, to hit a wall. He leapt out of the burning car, rolling over to put himself out. González

stopped, thinking Hawthorn was in trouble, but his car rolled into Hawthorn's, becoming engulfed also. Farina took the lead from Marimón, and positions remained unchanged till lap 71 when Marimón crashed due to a clutch fault.

1st	G Farina (W)	Ferrari 625 in 2h-51m-57.2s	95.40
2nd	M Trintignant (W)	Ferrari 625	2 laps
3rd	L Mantovani (W)	Maserati 250F	5 laps
F lap	O Marimón (W)	Maserati 250F in 2m-03.8s	99.38r

✱✱ XV Grand Prix de Pau

3 hours on a 1.715-mile circuit.
12 entries and starters – 7 finished.
Front row: G Farina – 1m-36.3s (64.11mph); M Trintignant 1.0s. Row two: F González 1.7s; O Marimón 1.8s.

19-APR: Ferrari, Maserati and Gordini teams, and Rosier's customer Ferraris all made for a good race. Farina fluffed his start and then immediately hit Marimón, putting him out, so Trintignant led González and Behra. Farina pitted to repair suspension. González' engine blew up and he spun on lap two, Martin (Gordini) crashing in near-avoidance. Trintignant had a lead of 30 seconds by lap 50, but Behra pulled this back, took the lead on lap 100, and won a terrific scrap! So Behra and Gordini beat the Ferrari and Maserati giants fair and square, taking almost four seconds off the lap record! This proves that history is unfair to them both, as neither won a World Championship race, but were indeed Formula One winners ... the records have deceived us.

1st	J Behra (W)	Gordini T16 109 laps in 3h-00m-02.2s	62.31
2nd	M Trintignant (W)	Ferrari 625	0.2s
3rd	R Mieres (W)	Maserati A6GCM/250F	3 laps
F lap	J Behra (W)	Gordini T16 in 1m-35.2s	64.85r

✱✱ III Grand Prix de Bordeaux

123 laps of 1.527 miles = 187.8 miles.
13 entries – 12 started – 7 finished.
Front row: M Trintignant – 1m-21.8s (67.21mph); F González 0.3s; J Behra 0.8s.

09-MAY: With Farina and Hawthorn being hors de combat, González and Trintignant drove the Works cars and led in that order until passed on lap six by Behra's Gordini. González retook the lead and a duel ensued until Behra needed new plugs, as did Trintignant on lap 25, who had dropped back. Rain began to fall but everyone coped. Much to the crowd's chagrin, Behra retired on lap 34 and Bayol was told to hand his car to Behra but ignored the instruction, subsequently being sacked from the team. Trintignant then lost second gear, and was hampered by oil on his pedals. Stirling Moss struggled in the conditions but pitted to exchange the Dunlops for Pirellis – a deal struck by his legendary mechanic Alf Francis during the race! This improved things no end, and Moss recovered over two laps to finish fourth in his first Maserati 250F drive, two laps down on González. If he'd been on Pirellis from the start … He was the marque's only finisher of three starters – Bira and Schell retiring their converted F2 cars of the previous year. Why should Italian tyres have been better in the rain than British – doesn't seem logical does it?

1st	F González (W)	Ferrari 625 in 3h-05m-55.1s	60.62
2nd	R Manzon (ER)	Ferrari 625	44.5s
3rd	M Trintignant (W)	Ferrari 625	1m-3s
F lap	F González	Ferrari 625 in 1m-22.7s	66.48

✱✱✱ VI *Daily Express* International Trophy (Silverstone)
15 lap heat + 35 lap final of 2.927 miles = 146.4 miles.
31 entered – 28 started – 15 finished.
Poles: Heat one – F González – 1m-48s (97.57mph); Heat two – M Trintignant – 1m-52s (94.08mph).
15-MAY: Ferrari sent a new 553 model (known as the 'Squalo') and among the opposition was a Vanwall driven by Alan Brown. González took pole for heat one no less than three seconds ahead of Behra, and won easily in very wet conditions. The leading British car was the Vanwall in sixth place. Teammate Trintignant won the second heat on a drying track, after passing Parnell's older car on lap 11. González' engine had seized, so he started the final in Trintignant's car and Trintignant in Maglioli's – tough on him as he'd finished fourth in his heat. It was the non-Works Ferrari's that led off the line with Parnell and Manzon, but González and Moss' Works-entered Maserati led after a lap, and Manzon and Parnell were out within five laps. Lap six saw Behra in his Gordini pass Moss who struck back on lap 15 only for his de Dion axle to break ten laps later. Bira's Maserati retired from fourth on lap 12. On lap 16, when in fifth place, Alan Brown retired the Vanwall – a very encouraging debut. It was a good result for 'poor' Gordini – well ahead of the Works Maserati of Roberto Mieres.

1st	F González (W)	Ferrari 625 in 1h-06m-15s	92.78
2nd	J Behra (W)	Gordini T16	36s
3rd	A Simon (W)	Gordini T16	1 lap
F lap	F González	Ferrari 625 in 1m-50s	95.79

✱✱ VII Gran Premio di Bari
60 laps of 3.442 miles = 206.5 miles.
12 started – 7 finished.
Front row: F González; M Trintignant; J Behra. No times available.
23-MAY: Three-car teams from Ferrari and Maserati, and two from Gordini, but the only Italian drivers were Umberto Maglioli and Sergio Mantovani – neither major F1 stars. Trintignant took the lead, but, on lap three, González overtook to hold a steady lead thereafter. Marimón was third from row two, but lost it to Behra on lap 17. A spin by Behra and a record lap saw Marimón retake third but then lost it again at water and fuel stops. A hat-trick for Ferrari who seemed all set to challenge Mercedes and Lancias when they appeared. The season was now well under way without them.

1st	F González (W)	Ferrari 625 in 2h-21m-08.4s	87.80
2nd	M Trintignant (W)	Ferrari 625	6.9s
3rd	J Behra (W)	Gordini T16	1m 01s
F lap	O Marimón (W)	Maserati 250F in 2m-16.5s	90.77

✱✱ XII Gran Premio di Roma (Castel Fusano)
60 laps of 4.095 miles = 245.7 miles.
21 entered – 14 started – 6 finished.
Front row: O Marimón – 2m-15.4s (108.87mph); R Manzon 1.8s; S Moss 1.9s; J Behra 2.6s.
06-JUN: At last Ascari in a Lancia D50 and Fangio in a Works Maserati were entered, as were three Works Ferraris. Great entries but none arrived. Marimón was way fastest in practice, but Behra led off the line. Marimón passed on lap one and led unchallenged all the way. Mieres came through from seventh on lap one to third on lap nine but soon the engine failed. On lap 15 Behra had a front stub-axle break and the wheel broke loose at 100mph. Great skill was required to avoid disaster. Moss' private Maserati was now second from fifth at the start. Simon (Gordini) was third but fell back, so Behra was installed in the car to finish fourth. Moss' transmission failed on lap 52 when just under a minute behind Marimón. This was Onofre Marimón's first F1 win, and marked him out as a potential big star, being in the same type of car as Stirling Moss.

1st	O Marimón (W)	Maserati 250F in 2h-18m-48.6s	106.20
2nd	H Schell	Maserati A6GCM	2 laps
3rd	S Mantovani (W)	Maserati 250F	2 laps
F lap	O Marimón	Maserati 250F in 2m-15.7s	108.63

✳✳✳ (WC2) XVI Grand Prix de Belgique (Spa)

36 laps of 8.774 miles = 315.9 miles.

16 entries – 15 starters – 7 finished.

Front row: J-M Fangio – 4m-22.1s (120.51mph); F González 1.5s; G Farina 3.9s.

20-JUN: After a five month gap, the Championship got under way again, but Ascari, his Lancia, and the Mercedes team were still missing, so Fangio was still with Maserati. His pole lap with a 250bhp car equalled the record set with a 400bhp Alfa Romeo in 1951. But it was González who shot off at the start, with Fangio eighth. At the end of lap one it was Farina, Hawthorn and Fangio, with González out. Two laps later and Fangio led. Farina challenged and led laps 11 to 13, whereupon his engine failed. From then it was Fangio all the way. Trintignant passed Hawthorn, who slowed due to inhaling exhaust fumes, and handed over to González. This let Moss through, in his private Maserati. There was drama at the end as Fangio's car had suspension failure, but he nursed it to the finish, with Trintignant closing. Pilette was fifth for Gordini. Only Maseratis, Ferraris and Gordinis took part.

1st	J-M Fangio (W)	Maserati 250F in 2h-44m-42.4s	115.06
2nd	M Trintignant (W)	Ferrari 625	24.2s
3rd	S Moss	Maserati 250F	1 lap
F lap	J-M Fangio (W)	Maserati 250F in 4m-25.5s	118.97

Championship positions:
Fangio 17; Trintignant 9; González 6.5.

✳✳✳ (WC3) XLI Grand Prix de l'ACF (Reims)

61 laps of 5.159 miles = 314.7 miles.

25 entries – 21 starters – 6 finished.

Front row: J-M Fangio – 2m-29.4s (124.30mph); K Kling 1.0s; A Ascari 1.1s.

04-JUL: The Reims track had been extended to Muizon corner creating the hugely fast back straight. Mercedes had arrived, so Ascari replaced Fangio at Maserati. At last the main protagonists were to meet. The Mercedes astonished everyone with their streamlined bodywork – open-wheeled

aspect not compulsory until 1960. German efficiency replaced Italian enthusiasm as the way to win. Farina was injured in a Monza accident. A Mercedes demonstration followed, with Fangio and Kling swapping places no less than eight times. Villoresi was the sole survivor in fifth place from the whole Ferrari and Maserati Works squads: engine failures all-round. They weren't alone, though, as Herrmann's Mercedes also expired with engine problems.

1st	J-M Fangio (W)	Mercedes W196 in 2h-42m-47.9s	115.98
2nd	K Kling (W)	Mercedes W196	0.1s
3rd	R Manzon (ER)	Ferrari 625	1 lap
F lap	H Herrmann (W)	Mercedes W196 in 2m-32.9s	121.46r

Championship positions:
Fangio 25; Trintignant 9; González 6.5.

✳✳ VI Grand Prix de Rouen-les-Essarts

95 laps of 3.187 miles = 302.8 miles. 17 entries – 14 started – 8 finished.

Front row: M Trintignant – 2m-09.4s (88.67mph); J Behra 0.8s; M Hawthorn 1.5s.

11-JUL: No Works Maseratis as, a week earlier, they'd had a bad French GP at Reims, and Mercedes was entering only World Championship rounds. Behra's Works Gordini had split the Works Ferraris of Hawthorn and Trintignant on the grid. However, it was the Ferraris which duelled ahead of Behra until brake trouble dropped him back. Hawthorn's engine blew up with ten laps to go and spread oil on the track, on which Behra spun. Both he and Mike Hawthorn got their teammates to push them back into motion which got them disqualified, to the benefit of the privateer Maseratis.

1st	M Trintignant (W)	Ferrari 625 in 3h-40m-34.5s	82.37
2nd	B Bira	Maserati 250F	1 lap
3rd	R Salvadori (GE)	Maserati 250F	5 laps
F lap	M Trintignant	Ferrari 625 in 2m-09.9s	88.33r

✳✳✳ (WC4) IX British Grand Prix (Silverstone)

90 laps of 2.927 miles = 263.43 miles.

32 entries – 30 starters – 15 finished.

Front row: J-M Fangio – 1m-45s (100.35mph); F González 1s; M Hawthorn 1s; S Moss 2s.

17-JUL: Just two cars from Mercedes were here to battle with three-car teams from Ferrari, Maserati and Gordini, one from Vanwall, plus loads of privateers. The Maserati Works cars started from the back having missed practice. González and Moss led away, but Hawthorn and Fangio passed Moss. Fangio took second from Hawthorn but couldn't make any impression on González. The massive streamlined Mercedes was a handicap around the Silverstone marker barrels, and it hit a few. Moss passed Hawthorn and they both overtook Fangio who had various troubles and eventually lost out to Marimón on lap 77. Moss' transmission failed on lap 80, so González repeated his 1951 triumph unchallenged. The point for fastest lap (whole second increments) was shared by Ascari, Behra, Fangio, González, Hawthorn, Marimón and Moss. This made a complete mockery of the timing system, and a farce of the points system. So who actually did it? That one seventh of a point might prove vital.

1st	F González (W)	Ferrari 625 in 2h-56m-14s	89.69
2nd	M Hawthorn (W)	Ferrari 625	1m-10s
3rd	O Marimón (W)	Maserati 250F	1 lap
F lap	See text	See text in 1m-50s	95.79

Championship positions:
Fangio 28.14; González 14.64; Trintignant 11.

✳ III Grand Prix de Caen

60 laps of 2.187 miles = 131.2 miles.
10 entries – 9 started – 5 finished.
Front row: M Trintignant – 1m-26.0s (91.55mph); S Moss 0.4s. Row two: J Behra 0.4s.

25-JUL: Moss was Maserati's only Works entry to challenge Trintignant's Works Ferrari and three Works Gordinis. Moss led away from the 2 x 1 x 2 grid from Trintignant, with Behra running them close, but on lap four Behra went off the road, damaging his steering. Pollet was called in from seventh place, and Behra took over the car. He passed Bira and then recovered to third on lap 39, whereupon Manzon retired. Rain started about this time and Trintignant now began to catch Moss, whose handling had deteriorated due to a lighter rear fuel tank. A real battle followed and the lead changed hands on laps 46, 53 and 56. Few starters but a good race.

1st	M Trintignant (W)	Ferrari 625 in 1h-29m-01.1s	88.46
2nd	S Moss (W)	Maserati 250F	3.6s
3rd	J Pollet/J Behra (W)	Gordini T16	2 laps
F lap	S Moss	Maserati 250F in 1m-25,7s	91.87

✳✳✳ (WC5) XVII Grosser Preis von Deutschland (N Nürburgring)

22 laps of 14.17 miles = 311.7 miles.
24 entries – 20 started – 10 finished.

10-AUG: Front row: J-M Fangio – 9m-50.1s (86.47mph); M Hawthorn 3.2s; S Moss 10.6s.

Ferrari, Mercedes, Gordini and Maserati entered four cars each, although Moss' Maserati was technically a private entry, Works supported. Onofre Marimón was arguably Maserati's main driver now, but was sadly killed in practice on his first visit to this very challenging circuit: the first driver to die at a Championship event. His distraught compatriots Fangio and González raced in his honour, and led on lap one, but Moss soon retired. Mercedes was 1, 2, 3 by lap seven, as Lang and Kling had passed González. Lang spun and retired, but Kling actually led on laps 15 and 16 as Fangio refuelled, before stopping for fuel himself. On lap 16 Hawthorn replaced González, whose heart just wasn't in it. He never recovered from the loss of his friend.

1st	J-M Fangio (W)	Mercedes W196 in 3h-45m-45.8s	82.87
2nd	González/ Hawthorn (W)	Ferrari 625	1m-36s
3rd	M Trintignant (W)	Ferrari 625	5m-09s
F lap	K Kling (W)	Mercedes W196 in 9m-55.1s	85.74

Championship positions:
Fangio 36.14; González 17.64; Trintignant 15.

✳ 1st International Gold Cup (Oulton Park)

36 laps of 2.678 miles = 96.4 miles.
28 entries – 19 started – 9 finished.
Front row: R Gerard – 1m-59.4s (80.75mph); J Behra 0.0s; R Parnell 0.2s.

07-AUG: A great new circuit came on the international scene here. A Works Ferrari for Hawthorn didn't materialise, and Moss' Maserati was too late for practice, so he had to start from the back. Bob Gerard, in a Cooper-Bristol, had beaten Jean Behra's Works Gordini to pole! The grid indicated a very close race, and Behra led for two laps but then retired, handing over to Parnell. However, Parnell was just a caretaker of this position until Moss assumed charge having taken just four laps to overtake 18 cars! Roy Salvadori in a new Maserati 250F lay second until lap 15 when a sticking throttle put him into a tree, luckily without injury. Moss 'strode' majestically on untroubled, his race average being faster than pole speed. He was never beaten here!

1st	S Moss (W)	Maserati 250F in 1h-11m-27.0s	80.98
2nd	R Parnell (SA)	Ferrari 625	1m-20s
3rd	R Gerard	Cooper T23-Bristol	1m-24s
F lap	S Moss	Maserati 250F in 1m-56.8s	82.55

1st	J-M Fangio (W)	Mercedes W196 in 3h-00m-34.5s	99.20
2nd	F González (W)	Ferrari 625	57.8s
3rd	H Herrmann (W)	Mercedes W196	1 lap
F lap	J-M Fangio (W)	Mercedes w196 in 2m-39.7s	101.97r

✳ XXIII Circuito di Pescara
16 laps of 15.88 miles = 254.1 miles.
15 starters – 5 finished.
Front row: S Moss – 10m-23.0s (91.77mph); R Manzon 21.3s: C Bucci (Gordini) 23.0s.

15-AUG: Marimón's death in Germany made Moss de facto team leader, and pole was easily won on his debut at this 16 mile circuit! Though Ferrari's only Works driver Maglioli was unable to drive, due to family reasons. Moss led easily from Manzon's Ferrari 625, which retired on lap two. Moss' great drive ended on lap four with a split oil pipe. So now Bira's private Maserati looked set to win, but exhaust problems handed victory to Moss' teammate Luigi Musso. Five cars on this long circuit meant a car only every two minutes, but the sight and sound of a Grand Prix car on a country road would be well worth waiting for, especially when driven by the likes of Moss. A win for Bira would have been quite a surprise as his practice time was well over 11 minutes – he had learned the circuit quickly, as the race progressed, though, and had posted the fastest lap!

1st	L Musso (W)	Maserati 250F in 2h-55m-54.51s	86.73
2nd	B Bira	Maserati 250F	2m-56s
3rd	H Schell	Maserati A6GCM	6m-47s
F lap	B Bira	Maserati 250F in 10m-46.39s	88.45

✳✳✳ (WC6) XIV Grosser Preis der Schweiz (Bremgarten Berne)
66 laps of 4.524 miles = 298.6miles.
18 entries – 16 started – 8 finished.
Front row: F González – 2m-39.5s (102.10mph); J-M Fangio 0.2s; S Moss 1.9s.

22-AUG: González' pole was wasted at the start, beaten by Fangio and Kling, but soon he and Moss passed Kling who then spun. Next lap Moss was second, chasing Fangio, but his oil pump failed. Hawthorn came through to second at that point, but his oil pump soon failed, too. Trintignant was now behind Fangio and González but suffered engine failure, leaving third to Kling whose injector pump failed. So it was Hans Herrmann who got the final podium spot. Fangio was beyond catching as champion now.

Championship positions:
Fangio 42 (WC); González 23.64; Trintignant 15.

✳✳✳ (WC7) XXIV Gran Premio d'Italia (Monza)
80 laps of 3.915 miles = 313.2 miles.
30 entries and starters – 20 finished.
Front row: J-M Fangio – 1m-59.0s (119.43mph); A Ascari 0.2s; S Moss 0.3s.

05-SEP: No fewer than six cars from Ferrari and Maserati were here, including, at last, Alberto Ascari, this time for Ferrari, and he almost stole pole from Fangio. The first two rows were covered by just 1.2 seconds on the grid, so a true Monza slipstreamer was on the cards. It was Kling's Mercedes from row two that led the first two laps, then spun leaving Fangio, Ascari, Moss and González scrapping away. Ascari led from lap six to 48 except for Fangio who led lap 23 and Moss lap 45. Then Ascari retired with engine trouble. Moss took over, pulling out 20 seconds over Fangio, when a split oil tank made him stop near the finish line ten laps from the finish; to huge cheers. This enabled him to push over the line after the winner; required in those days to be classified. So the results suggest a dominant victory by Fangio, but this was not so much the case.

1st	J-M Fangio (W)	Mercedes W196 in 2h-47m-47.9s	111.98
2nd	M Hawthorn (W)	Ferrari 625	1 lap
3rd	Maglioli/González (W)	Ferrari 625	2 laps
F lap	F González (W)	Ferrari 625 in 2m-00.8s	116.66

Championship positions:
Fangio 42 (WC); González 25.14; Trintignant 17.

V Circuit de Cadours
15-lap heats + 30 lap final of 2.495 miles = 112.3 miles.
12 started – 5 finished.
No grid positions available.

12-SEP: A strange 'little' event. The circuit was 2.5 miles long, yet each heat had just six cars starting! There being three retirements all remaining nine started the final. Heat winners Jean Behra and Harry Schell (Maserati A6GCM) led the way, with Behra in hot form, and breaking the lap record.

Schell eventually retired, so Pilette took over second place, equalled the new record but couldn't challenge Behra. Louis Rosier's plodding in a new Maserati 250F was rewarded with third, repeating the heat one result.

1st	J Behra (W)	Gordini T16 in 58m-49.8s	76.32
2nd	A Pilette (W)	Gordini T16	14.0s
F lap	Behra/Pilette	Gordini T16 in 1m-55.0s	78.12r

Grosser Preis von Berlin (Avus)
60 laps of 5.157 miles = 309.4 miles.
14 entries – 10 started – 7 finished.

Front row: J-M Fangio – 2m-12.3s (140.34mph); H Hermann 1.3s; K Kling 2.8s.

19-SEP: Mercedes had entered only World Championship rounds so far, and had not been invincible. Beaten in Britain by González' Ferrari, and in Italy 'morally' by Moss' Maserati, which didn't arrive here. But, on the flat-out long straights down each side of an Autobahn, with the high-banked north turn of Avus, superfunded streamlined Mercedes-Benz, against cash-strapped Gordini and a few also-rans, wasn't a race: it was a demonstration pure and simple. Behra's time for fourth on the grid was ten seconds slower than Kling's third place time, yet he slipstreamed into second before blowing up on lap 14! Heroism. The post-war German East/West border crossed the track, cutting it in half. It was 12 miles long and Lang had lapped at 172mph!

1st	K Kling (W)	Mercedes W196 in 2h-19m-59.8s	132.62
2nd	J-M Fangio (W)	Mercedes W196	0.5s
F lap	J-M Fangio	Mercedes W196 in 2m-13.4s	139.18

✳ VII Goodwood Trophy (Goodwood)
21 laps of 2.4 miles = 50.4 miles.
23 entries – 21 started – 14 finished.

Front row: S Moss – 1m-32.2s (93.71mph); P Collins 4.0s; R Gerard 5.6s; R Parnell 6.1s.

25-SEP: At last, a decent length race at Goodwood. Moss' status was crystal clear now, and he was on pole position by four seconds – the rest just happy to be on the front row, I guess – and led by the British Vanwall. Reg Parnell's Ferrari 625 was best away, but Moss and Collins were past him within the lap. Parnell then had a piston failure, handing third place to Salvadori who had just passed Bob Gerard (Cooper-Bristol). Moss pulled away from Collins' now 2.5-litre Vanwall, and Salvadori couldn't challenge Collins. A

good omen for the Vanwall, which had averaged a second a lap better than its practice time?

1st	S Moss (W)	Maserati 250F in 33m-03.2s	91.48
2nd	P Collins (W)	Vanwall	20.4s
3rd	R Salvadori (GE)	Maserati 250F	1m-17s
F lap	S Moss	Maserati 250F in 1m-33.0s	92.90

✳ *Daily Telegraph* Trophy (Aintree)
17 laps of 3.00 miles = 51 miles.
24 entries – 19 started – 13 finished.

Front row: S Moss – 2m-03.6s (87.38mph); J Behra 1.4s; M Hawthorn 2.4s; HSchell 4.8s.

02-OCT: This new circuit – intertwined with the famous Grand National horse racecourse – had hosted a Formule Libre meeting, won by Moss, earlier in the year, and running anticlockwise. This first F1 race was run clockwise. Moss was on pole again but only by 1.4 seconds from Behra's Works Gordini. Away went Moss, never to be headed, while Hawthorn and Behra scrapped strongly for second place. Schell's private Maserati passed Moss' Works teammate Mantovani and then Behra. He even passed Hawthorn, but spun on the last bend. In a later Formule Libre race, Moss' Maserati lapped four seconds faster than before – and won of course!

1st	S Moss (W)	Maserati 250F in 35m-49.0s	85.43
2nd	M Hawthorn (W)	Vanwall	14.4s
3rd	H Schell	Maserati 250F	15.4s
F lap	Moss/Hawthorn	Maserati/Vanwall in 2m-04.8s	86.54

✳✳✳ (WC8) XII Gran Premio d'Espagna (Pedralbes)
80 laps of 3.925 miles = 314 miles
25 entries – 21 starters – 8 finished.

Front row: A Ascari – 2m-18.1s (102.30mph); J-M Fangio 1.0s; M Hawthorn 2.5s; H Schell 2.5s.

24-OCT: At long last, the Lancia D50 arrived for Ascari and Villoresi. This car significantly raised the challenge to Mercedes, though Moss' Maserati had so nearly beaten its cars at Monza. Hawthorn's Ferrari was the type 553 'Squalo' – lower than the 625. Four different marques were on the front row! Schell's lightly fuelled Maserati led for two laps, before Ascari passed followed by a Schell, Hawthorn and Trintignant scrap, with Moss and Fangio close behind. (Mercedes only sixth?) Six laps later, Ascari's Lancia was out with clutch slip after its very serious challenge. Moss soon had oil pump failure and Schell spun down to fourth place. Trintignant dropped out of the hunt so now Hawthorn led from lap 24 to the finish, with Fangio closing then falling back with litter in the air intakes. Newcomer Luigi Musso took second from Fangio with six laps to go. What a great race!

1st	M Hawthorn (W)	Ferrari 553 in 3h-13m-52.1s	97.17
2nd	L Musso (W)	Maserati 250F	1m-13s
3rd	J-M Fangio (W)	Mercedes W196	1 lap
F lap	A Ascari (W)	Lancia D50 in 2m-20.4s	100.63

Championship positions:
Fangio 42 (WC); González 25.14; Hawthorn 24.64.

Winners of the 23 graded F1 races of 1954 – quantity & quality of success

6 wins	J-M Fangio (6A)	9 wins	Ferrari (4A, 3B, 2C)
4 wins	F González (2A, 2B)	7 wins	Maserati (2A, B, 4C)
3 wins	M Trintignant (A, B, C) S Moss (3C)	5 wins	Mercedes-Benz (4A, D)
2 wins	J Behra (B, D)	2 wins	Gordini (B, D)
1 win	M Hawthorn (A) O Marimón (B) G Farina (C) L Musso (C) K Kling (D)		

1954 seasonal review

There had been 21 good races, including eight Championship rounds, but excepting inferior Cadours and Avus. Maserati and Ferrari were seen to be on fairly level terms, and both were capable of beating Mercedes at the right venue. Ferrari had beaten Mercedes at the British and Spanish GPs, the latter with the new type 553 'Squalo,' so it wasn't necessary for Mercedes to be present to appreciate the speed of the new F1 car. The streamlined Mercedes W196 was generally seen as a technical step too far, being more often a handicap than an asset. Stirling Moss had been advised by Mercedes to prove himself in a Maserati before being considered for a Mercedes drive, and his subsequent performances did just that – a seat now secured alongside Fangio for 1955. What a shame that the Lancia D50 arrived so late, as it had shown great speed at the year's end. Gordini, unsurprisingly, achieved little, with the single exception of a win at Pau due to the brilliance of

Jean Behra. He had shown his mettle and surely deserved a seat with a top team. BRM had not appeared with a new car, but one was expected in 1955; BRM's history requiring patience before performance. Connaught had used the F2 type 'A' car with no international success, but was known to be developing a new car looking very different but known simply as the 'Type B.' The Vanwall had appeared, and was fast, but as yet unreliable – would it have a future? Froilán González had four victories which placed him among the elite of this year, and his friend and compatriot Onofre Marimón had shown real potential to join the men at the top. But 1954 had shown what a lethal game racing could be when, very sadly Marimón lost his life at the Nürburgring; the first fatality in Championship history after four years.

World Championship review

This was the year of crazy scores. During the years 1950 to 1957, cars could be shared by any number of drivers during a Grand Prix, splitting the points between them. This would create fractions of a point, and was exacerbated to a significant degree by Silverstone timing being only to the nearest whole second. With, not surprisingly, seven drivers sharing a single point for fastest lap at the British Grand Prix the points system became truly bizarre. Jean Behra's only score that season was a share of that point, so his total was just one seventh of a point. An all-time record low score for a season, and one which will indeed last for evermore! Ask that in a motor sport quiz and see if anyone knows!

A little maths: In the following season two drivers had a third share of both second and third places in the same event! If that had happened at Silverstone – and it could – and one had also been amongst those who shared the fastest lap – what would be the scores? There were no calculators then, so they're not allowed now.

Amazingly, Ascari went from total domination in 1952/3 to only scoring from fastest lap points. His score of 1½ points is still the lowest ever score by a defending champion. It's often quoted as Jody Scheckter's 1980 season total of two for a fifth place finish. So Alberto Ascari created and still holds the records for most successive GP wins and worst title defence in successive seasons! He did start only four GP races, though. However, it should be noted that the two retirements from the lead in Italy and Spain cost many points. He would have been fourth instead of nineteenth – a classic case of statistics misrepresenting skill.

Fangio had regained the title with a race to spare, and had won in a Maserati as well as a Mercedes, so was clearly the benchmark for everyone to follow. If Stirling Moss had had the reliability enjoyed by Fangio he would have finished second in the table, not tenth. Mercedes was obviously aware of that fact when it engaged him for 1955, proving that it's potential score not actual score that determines a driver's worth. Mike Hawthorn had won his second Championship Grand Prix, so was not a one-hit-wonder. Giuseppe Farina, however, was past his best now, and, in fact, had never been as good as in his Championship winning year.

Answer to the question above: ⅓ share of six points +

⅓ share of four points + ½ share of one point = 3.476190 ... or, $3\frac{10}{21}$ points. That sort of thing could have happened in any Grand Prix prior to 1958. In fact, Hawthorn had shared fourth place at Belgium and was amongst the British GP fastest lappers. His final total was $24\frac{9}{14}$ points.

VISIT VELOCE ON THE WEB – WWW.VELOCE.CO.UK
All current books • New book news • Special offers • Gift vouchers • Forum

95

Chapter 14

1955
The outlook is bright

Fangio had won the 1954 World Drivers' Championship with Mercedes, and this was seen as a Championship victory for the Mercedes-Benz marque, even though no such Championship existed, and Juan-Manuel Fangio had taken his first two wins at the wheel of a Maserati. So no major changes happened to the W196 car except the abolition of the streamliner, which had not exhibited any real benefit. Fangio's striking of the marker barrels at Silverstone displayed the difficulty in positioning the car as accurately as the open wheeled version. Stirling Moss was a significant addition to the driver squad, having now proved himself to the team through his performances in his own Maserati 250F the previous year.

Lancia was expected to provide the main challenge, with Alberto Ascari at the wheel of the D50. The combination had been leading when they retired from the Spanish Grand Prix the previous year. Ascari was supported by Luigi Villoresi and new find Eugenio Castellotti.

Ferrari had been working on a revised type 553, the 555 called 'Super Squalo' which was ready by mid-April. Froilán González was team leader as Hawthorn had gone to Vanwall, and was supported by Giuseppe Farina and Maurice Trintignant.

Maserati had recognised the skills of Jean Behra and signed him up as leader, with Luigi Musso and Roberto Mieres plus various others from race-to-race. The type 250F was unchanged except for a five-speed gearbox.

Gordini, ever cash-strapped, was all the French could provide, and was led by Robert Manzon plus Elie Bayol (re-instated) and Jacques Pollett. A new car was essential and for Monza 'Le Sorcier' produced a wide-bodied car with a straight-eight engine, looking rather like a broad

250F Maserati. This was the type 32. If it went as well as it looked then Gordini fortunes might change, and Formula One would be the better for it. However, that engine configuration was somewhat outdated now, and the car was clearly not a lightweight in the Gordini tradition.

Vanwall was the main British hope now, with Mike Hawthorn signed in an admirable act of patriotism, and supported by Ken Wharton and Harry Schell.

Connaught had a new 'type B' but was without any top flight drivers, and entered few races outside England (one of them, though, would never be forgotten).

BRM, still damaged by the legacy of the V16, didn't arrive with its four-cylinder P25 car until September at Aintree and Oulton Park. Meanwhile, the BRM owner, the Owen Racing Organisation, ran a Maserati 250F in a privateer capacity, Peter Collins being the pilot for both marques. The P25 BRM would be slow to develop being hindered by a serious car accident to designer Peter Berthon which kept him away for most of the year, but BRM stuck with it throughout the 1950s.

There were now eight constructors involved in Formula One, and no fewer than ten rounds were scheduled for the World Championship, with extra events taking the total to twenty-six, so the outlook was very rosy.

The Grand Prix driver's diary of single-seater racing for the 1955 season

16th January	**Gran Premio do Argentina** at Buenos Aires (No 2) (Ag) – 233.4 miles
30th January	Gran Premio di Buenos Aires (No 4 layout) (Ag) – 175.4 miles
27th March	Gran Premio del Valentino at Torino (I) – 234.8 miles

11th April	Glover Trophy at Goodwood (UK) – 50.4 miles
11th April	Grand Prix de Pau (F) – 189.3 miles
24th April	Grand Prix de Bordeaux (F) – 187.8 miles
7th May	*Daily Express* International Trophy at Silverstone (UK) – 175.6 miles
8th May	Gran Premio di Napoli at Posillipo (I) – 152.9 miles
22nd May	**Grand Prix de Monaco** (M) – 195.4 miles
30th May	Cornwall MRC F1 Race at Davidstow (UK) – 37 miles*
29th May	Grand Prix d'Albi (F) – 195.1 miles
5th June	**Grand Prix de Belgique** at Spa Francorchamps (B) – 315.5 miles
19th June	**Grote Prijs van Nederland** at Zandvoort (N) – 260.5 miles
3rd July	**Grand Prix de l'ACF** at Reims (F) – 313 miles**
16th July	**British Grand Prix** at Aintree (UK) – 270 miles
30th July	London Trophy at Crystal Palace (UK) – 34.8 miles
31st July	**Grosse Preis von Deutschland** at Nürburgring (D) – 311.7 miles**
6th August	*Daily Record* Trophy at Charterhall (UK) – 70 miles*
13th August	Redex Trophy at Snetterton (UK) – 677.5 miles
21st August	**Grosse Preis der Schweiz** at Bremgarten (S) – 240.3 miles**
3rd September	Daily Telegraph Trophy at Aintree (UK) – 51miles
11th September	**Gran Premio d'Italia at Monza** (I) – 310.8 miles
24th September	International Gold Cup at Oulton Park (UK) – 144.6 miles
1st October	Avon Trophy at Castle Combe (UK) – 101.2 miles
23rd October	Gran Premio di Siracusa (I) – 239.2 miles
23rd October	**Gran Premio d'Espagna** (E) – 313.2 miles**

26 events of total race mileage = 4873 miles but only 22 run. Events in bold are World Championship rounds – but only six were run = 28.6 per cent of F1 races.

* See Appendix A for these ungraded race results.

** Race cancelled in the wake of the Le Mans disaster.

✱✱✱ (WC1) IX Gran Premio de la Republica Argentina (Buenos Aires No 2)

96 laps of a 2.431-mile circuit = 233.4 miles.
21 entries and starters – 7 finished.

Front row: F González – 1m-43.1s (84.88mph); J-M Fangio 0.5s; A Ascari 0.5s; J Behra 0.7s.

16-JAN: A race in extreme heat saw only two drivers able to complete the full distance without relief: Fangio and §Mieres, who was fifth. The team leaders of the top four marques were on the front of the grid, and covered by just 0.7 seconds, so a great race was expected. Fangio led away, while Behra and Villoresi crashed. Ascari led lap three, González lap six, and Ascari again lap 11 from González, Fangio and Moss. Ten laps later Ascari spun on oil, crashed and retired. Whether the following drivers avoided the oil having seen Ascari spin is open to conjecture, but he had the misfortune to be first on the scene. González now led but handed the car over to Trintignant. Moss stopped on lap 29 with fuel trouble, lay down to relax and was promptly carted off by ambulance men who thought he had heat stroke! He took over another car and shared the fourth place Mercedes with Herrmann and Kling. Still mourning the death of his friend Marimón – González hung up his helmet after this.

1st	J-M Fangio (W)	Mercedes W196 in 3h-00m-38.6s	77.51
2nd	González/Farina/Trintignant (W)	Ferrari 625	1m-30s
3rd	Farina/Maglioli/Trintignant (W)	Ferrari 625	2 laps
F lap	J-M Fangio	Mercedes W196 in 1m-48.3s	80.80

Championship positions:
Fangio 9; Trintignant and Farina 3.33.

X Gran Premio de Buenos Aires (Buenos Aires No 4)

2 x 30 laps of 2.924 miles = 175.4 miles.
17 finished.

Front row: J-M Fangio; Trintignant; González; Behra.

30-JAN: All but Lancia were here from two weeks previously, but when is Formula One not Formula One? Answer: When the cars are fitted with oversize engines, as were the Mercedes (300SLR units); Farina's Ferrari (3-litre sports engine) and Behra's Maserati (2.7 litres). This was a designated Formule Libre race so this was allowed, but sadly that disqualifies this event from the F1 list of this book (indicated by the lack of bold type in the race title). In the first part Fangio and Moss swapped the lead twice, but the star was Farina whose Ferrari 625/750 stormed past Trintignant and González' Ferrari 625s, then Kling, Moss and Fangio to see off the Mercedes trio and win. He fluffed his start in the second part, though, and it was the star Mercedes pair who held sway. Trintignant used González' car for this part, but Farina spun on lap one and handed over to González, losing a lap. It was Trintignant's turn to be the hero now as he passed Menditeguy and Behra's Maseratis and took up the chase of the Mercs. He made up 14 seconds on Fangio just as Moss took the lead to win by three seconds. It was Fangio's two second places, however, which gave the overall win – he knowing perfectly well what the situation was. Interestingly, it is recorded that the crowd for this non-Championship, non-F1 race was way bigger than that for the Argentine GP. This was an event worthy of recording.

1st	J-M Fangio (W)	Mercedes W196 (3000) in 2h-23m-18.9s	73.45
2nd	S Moss (W)	Mercedes W196 (3000)	11.9
3rd	González/ Trintignant (W)	Ferrari 625 (2500)	34.2s
F lap	G Farina/S Moss	Ferrari 625/Mercedes in 2m-19.5s	75.46

✸✸✸ VII Gran Premio del Valentino (Torino)
90 laps of 2.609 miles = 234.8 miles.
18 entries – 15 started – 7 finished.
Front row: A Ascari – 1m-42.0s (92.11mph); J Behra (0.2s); L Musso 1.1s.
27-MAR: No Mercedes or Gordini, but five Works Maseratis, three from Ferrari and Lancia. Maserati lost Mantovani in practice, crashing and sadly losing a leg. A Maserati trio – Musso, Mieres and Behra – led Ascari at first, Mieres dropping to fourth after five laps. Behra's deDion tube broke and Ascari needed ten laps to wipe out the four second gap to Musso, who retired due to oil loss. From then Ascari led with ease. When being lapped, Castellotti tucked in behind his team leader, and they caught up with Villoresi's Lancia. Castellotti unlapped himself and the whole Lancia team crossed the line together; Ascari to win just behind his teammates setting off to complete their final lap, just 0.4 seconds apart for third and fourth. Schell was fifth for Ferrari, three laps down. So Lancia had found speed and reliability here – a very good omen for it and for Formula One.

1st	A Ascari (W)	Lancia D50 in 2h-40m-21.1s	87.86
2nd	R Mieres (W)	Maserati 250F	27.2s
3rd	L Villoresi (W)	Lancia D50	1m-45s
F lap	J Behra (W)	Maserati 250F in 1m-43.1s	91.13

✸✸ XVI Grand Prix du Pau
110 laps of 1.721 miles = 189.3 miles.
16 entries and starters – 10 finished.

Front row: A Ascari – 1m-34.5s (65.55mph); J Behra 0.9s. Row two R Mieres 1.1s; L Villoresi 2.2s.
11-APR: Scuderia Ferrari skipped this race after its poor Turin showing, but the full Gordini team arrived. Behra led Ascari, Castellotti, Mieres and Villoresi (Lancia). The lead scrap settled in Ascari's favour on lap 11, and his lead was held at four seconds for the next 30 laps when Ascari pulled away. Castellotti pulled clear of the duelling Mieres and Villoresi. All was set for another Ascari victory, but a split brake pipe on lap 90 meant a long pit stop, so grateful French hero Behra won. Villoresi and Ascari were a lap down in fourth and fifth, but Lancia again had a 100 per cent finish.

1st	J Behra (W)	Maserati 250F in 3h-02m-09.6s	62.34
2nd	E Castellotti (W)	Lancia D50	1m-1s
3rd	R Mieres (W)	Maserati 250F	1m-31s
F lap	A Ascari (W)	Lancia D50 in 1m-35.3s	65.00r

✸ III Glover Trophy (Goodwood)
21 laps of 2.4 miles = 50.5 miles.
22 entries – 10 started – 6 finished.
Front row: S Moss; R Salvadori; D Beauman; W Holt. No times are available.
11-APR: Running on the same day as Pau made this a British affair. The Vanwalls withdrew but the new Connaught B type made its debut with all-enclosed body and huge fin, like the 'D' type Jaguar. Tony Rolt was at the wheel. Also debuting was a chap from Australia called Brabham. Moss headed Salvadori at the start, with Brabham sliding his way in sixth place. Salvadori spun back to sixth at the chicane, but took just two laps to regain second. He was rewarded when Moss retired. Brabham chased Gerard and Beauman, hard but ran out of fuel.

1st	R Salvadori (GE)	Maserati 250F in 33m-53.0s	89.26
2nd	R Gerard	Cooper T23-Bristol 2.0	27.4s
3rd	D Beauman	Connaught 'A' type	33.0s
F lap	R Salvadori	Maserati 250F in 1m-33.8s	92.11

✸✸ IV Grand Prix de Bordeaux
123 laps of 1.527 miles = 187.8 miles.
12 entries and starters.
Front row: J Behra 1m-21.7s (67.29mph); L Musso (0.4s); S Moss (0.6s).
24-APR: No Lancias, but Ferrari had new type 555 cars for Farina and Trintignant, and the Gordini pair of Manzon and Bayol were present. Behra made a great start, with Musso and

Moss behind. Moss' privateer Maserati had brake problems, though, and he dropped to eighth, but the problem cured itself and he was fifth by lap 23. Trintignant had passed Musso for second, but the heat made him hand over to Farina. A tank strap repair for Moss cost almost three laps, but after smashing the lap record by almost two seconds, he finished fourth – just one lap down to the cruising formation Maserati team. Ferrari still had not made its new car perform, both cars retiring by lap 70. Where was Ferrari's 1952/3 form?

1st	J Behra (W)	Maserati 250F in 2h-54m-12.6s	64.70
2nd	L Musso (W)	Maserati 250F	0.2s
3rd	R Mieres (W)	Maserati 250F	1.2s
F lap	S Moss	Maserati 250F in 1m-20.9s	67.96r

✳ VII *Daily Express* International Trophy (Silverstone)

60 laps of 2.927 miles = 175.6 miles.
26 entries – 22 started – 10 finished.

Front row: R Salvadori – 1m-48s (97.57mph); M Hawthorn 0s; S Moss 2s; J Fairman 3s.

07-MAY: As ever a large entry at Silverstone, and a longer race this year, but only Gordini of the continental teams arrived to battle with the Vanwall and Connaught Works teams, and private Maseratis and Connaughts. Salvadori led from the start, from Peter Collins, Jack Fairman (Connaught 'B'), Hawthorn (Vanwall), and Moss (Maserati). The latter three had retired by lap 28. The lead swapped three times but Collins led from lap 34. After a very long stop to repair throttle linkage trouble, Wharton's Vanwall re-entered the fray but spun off when attempting a pass on Salvadori. The car ran off course and took a leap when on the grass. This split the fuel tank and a fire ensued in which Wharton suffered slight burns. Third place, just a lap down, was Bira's fine career swansong, after 20 years in the sport. Fairman's Connaught had run well in third place, having qualified well. What would a top driver have done in this beautiful, but perhaps overweight, streamlined car?

1st	P Collins (ORO)	Maserati 250F in 1h-49m-50s	95.94
2nd	R Salvadori (GE)	Maserati 250F	39s
3rd	B Bira	Maserati 250F	1 lap
F lap	Collins/Salvadori	Maserati 250F in 1m-47s	98.48

I think it's clear that Formula One might not have survived as the senior category without the Maserati 250F at this time, as the supply of competitive cars has to match the talent needing it.

✳✳ VIII Gran Premio di Napoli (Posillipo)

60 laps of 2.548 miles – 152.9 miles.
10 entries and starters – 6 finished.

Front row: A Ascari – 2m-08.1s (71.61mph); L Musso 1.4s; J Behra 2.8s.

08-MAY: Lancia and Maserati were here instead of at Silverstone, and without any serious opposition. Ferrari had seemed to feel the need to recoup for Monaco in two weeks. Ascari, as expected, led throughout virtually unopposed, with Musso steadily losing ground. Behra overtook Villoresi for third but struck a kerb, the ensuing repair stop costing him five laps. His spirited recovery netted fastest lap, but Ascari was taking it easy. Lancia now looked a good bet for a battle with Mercedes when it arrived.

1st	A Ascari (W)	Lancia D50 in 2h-13m-03.6s	68.94
2nd	L Musso (W)	Maserati 250F	1m-17s
3rd	L Villoresi (W)	Lancia D50	1 lap
F lap	J Behra (W)	Maserati 250F in 2m-09.4s	70.89

✳✳✳ (WC2) XIII Grand Prix de Monaco (Monte Carlo)

100 laps of a 1.954-mile circuit = 195.4 miles.
24 entries – 20 started – 10 finished.

Front row: J-M Fangio – 1m-41.1s (69.59mph); A Ascari 0.0s; S Moss 0.1s.

22-MAY: Fangio and Ascari had two World Championships each, and now their teams met at last and they had identical practice times, both smashing the record set in 1937 by the 646bhp Mercedes of Rudi Caracciola. Only 20 were allowed to start, and it was Fangio who was first out of the hairpin at the start, followed by Castellotti, Moss and Ascari. Moss took second on lap five, and Ascari took third, five laps later. Ascari, Castellotti, and Behra battled for 30 laps while Moss drew close to Fangio. Castellotti hit a kerb and pitted for a wheel and fuel, and soon after Behra stopped and lost two laps, changing cars with Perdisa. Lap 49 saw Fangio's transmission fail, and Moss then had a full minute lead over Ascari, extending it until lap 80 when his engine expired in smoke near the pits. The race was Ascari's, him not knowing of Moss' demise at that point, but a seized front brake caused a striking blow to the chicane and a plunge into the sea, so he never actually crossed the finish line in the lead. He escaped unscathed as Trintignant proved the adage that 'to finish first – first you have to finish.' Behra was back to third in Perdisa's car to retire on lap 84, but hey! He still shared third place …

1st	M Trintignant (W)	Ferrari 625 in 2h-58m-09.7s	65.81
2nd	E Castellotti (W)	Lancia D50	20.2s
3rd	J Behra/C Perdisa (W)	Maserati 250F	1 lap
F lap	J-M Fangio (W)	Mercedes W196 in 1m-42.4s	68.70r

Championship positions:
Trintignant 11.33; Fangio 10; Farina 6.33.

The relief of the motor racing world at Alberto Ascari's escape at Monaco was shattered beyond belief by the tragedy of his death a few days later, in a Ferrari sports car test at Monza. He'd been asked along to observe, but wanted to drive to prove his recovery from Monaco. The crash has never been explained.

✳ XVII Grand Prix d'Albi
105 laps of 1.858 miles = 195.1 miles.
12 entries – 11 started – 5 finished.
Front row: A Simon – 1m-18.1s (85.64mph); R Manzon 0.1s; L Rosier 0.3s.
29-MAY: The circuit had been considerably shortened from the traditional five-miler. Three Gordinis were the only Works cars here, against four Maseratis, one belonging to Stirling Moss and driven by Lance Macklin, and assorted others. Practice times had indicated a close race, as André Simon, who had driven for Mercedes-Benz at Monaco the week before, led away but pitted after 20 laps. He soon passed Rosier to retake the lead and pulled away. The Gordinis now couldn't even do well against this lesser level of competition. Macklin was second when retiring on lap 36. Hose split = water spilt.

1st	A Simon (ER)	Maserati 250F in 2h-23m-22.1s	81.66
2nd	L Rosier (ER)	Maserati 250F	1 lap
3rd	H Gould	Maserati 250F	2 laps
F lap	A Simon	Maserati 250F in 1m-17.1s	86.75

✳✳✳ (WC3) XVII Grand Prix de Belgique (Spa)
36 laps of 8.774 mile circuit = 315.9 miles.
23 entries – 13 started – 10 finished.
Front row: E Castellotti – 4m-18.1s (122.39mph); J-M Fangio 0.5s; S Moss 1.1s.
05-JUN: In the aftermath of Ascari's death, Lancia had decided to stop racing, but brave Castellotti talked them into entering a single car for him, despite the dangerous

circuit being new to him – and he went and got pole position! Fangio beat him away from the line, however, soon followed by Moss, the pair never to be headed. Castellotti retired from third place on lap 16 with gearbox failure, handing the place to Farina. Behra crashed badly on lap three, approaching La Source, but was unhurt, and then ran to the pits and took over Mieres's car. He failed to catch the Works Ferrari of journalist/driver Paul Frére, though, who raced infrequently in Formula One but drove very well when he did, and finished fourth only 1m-40s behind team-leader Farina.

1st	J-M Fangio (W)	Mercedes W196 in 2h-39m-29.0s	118.83
2nd	S Moss (W)	Mercedes W196	8.1s
3rd	G Farina (W)	Maserati 250F	1m-40s
F lap	J-M Fangio (W)	Mercedes W196 in 4m-20.6s	121.21r

Championship positions:
Fangio 19; Trintignant 11.33; Farina 10.33.

Just 16 days after the sadness of Ascari's demise came the greatest catastrophe in motor racing history, with the slaughter of over 80 spectators and a driver in the Le Mans Disaster, about which much has already been and will be written. Many races were cancelled while safety issues were addressed. Switzerland banned motor sport altogether, and, unfortunately, still adheres to that decision today.

✳✳✳ (WC4) V Grote Prijs van Nederland (Zandvoort)
100 laps of a 2.605-mile circuit = 260.5 miles.
16 entries and starters – 11 finished.
Front row: J-M Fangio – 1m-40.0s (93.80mph); S Moss 0.4s; K Kling 1.1s.
19-JUN: The week following Le Mans this race went ahead, safety being thought no problem. Lancia would not be seen again this year, so Castellotti had joined Ferrari, as had Hawthorn, being disillusioned with Vanwall progress. This was at the expense of Farina who, non-starting at Monza, had now driven his last World Championship race. The front grid row was all Mercedes, with Musso leading the rest. He followed Fangio on lap one but Moss got past him on lap two. The podium positions remained unaltered from then on. Behra took fourth pace from Kling, who spun his Mercedes and retired on lap 21. Mieres passed Behra, and Castellotti gained from Behra's and Hawthorn's pit stops.

1st	J-M Fangio (W)	Mercedes W196 in 2h-54m-23.8s	88.64
2nd	S Moss (W)	Mercedes W196	0.3s
3rd	L Musso (W)	Maserati 250F	57.1s
F lap	R Mieres (W)	Maserati 250F in 1m-40.9s	92.95r

Championship positions:
Fangio 27; Moss 13; Trintignant 11.33.

✱✱✱ 03-Jul (WC) XLII Grand Prix de l'ACF (Reims)
-----*CANCELLED FOLLOWING LE-MANS*-----

✱✱✱ (WC5) X British Grand Prix (Aintree)
90 laps of a 3.00-mile circuit = 270 miles.
25 entries – 24 starters – 9 finished.
Front row: S Moss – 2m-0.4s (89.70mph); J-M Fangio 0.2s; J Behra 1.0s.
16-JUL: Aintree provided a very well-equipped alternative to Silverstone, having the facilities of the Grand National horse racecourse. Mercedes-Benz provided a fourth car for veteran Piero Taruffi. Fangio and Moss stormed away and swapped places on laps three, 17 and 28, with Moss leading from then on. Behra lay third for nine laps, and retired to be replaced by Kling who battled with Mieres. When Mieres retired the whole Mercedez-Benz team was in complete charge. Did Fangio let Moss win? I don't believe so. With the cancellation of other Grands Prix, only the Italian remained in the Championship, so Fangio had sewn up the title at Aintree – the only time the Championship has been won in England; though no-one knew that at the time.

1st	S Moss (W)	Mercedes W196 in 3h-07m-21.2s	86.47
2nd	J-M Fangio (W)	Mercedes W196	0.2s
3rd	K Kling (W)	Mercedes W196	46.2s
F lap	S Moss (W)	Mercedes W196 in 2m-0.4s	89.70r

Championship positions:
Fangio 33 (WC); Moss 22; Trintignant 11.33.

III London Trophy (Crystal Palace)
10-lap heat +15-lap final of 1.39 miles = 34.8 miles.
23 entries – 20 started – 8 finished.
Poles: Heat one – M Hawthorn – 1m-05.8s (76.05mph); Heat two – H Schell – 1m-04.4s (77.70mph).
30-JUL: A pity the final wasn't longer, which would have elevated its status. Hawthorn drove Moss' private Maserati,

Moss being committed to Mercedes, and headed a trio of Maserati 250Fs in his heat from Salvadori and Gould, while Schell took heat two from lesser opposition. Someone called Jack Brabham was third in a Cooper-Bristol. Schell was slow away in the final and failed to catch Hawthorn. Salvadori was third, ahead of Tony Brooks' Connaught. Brooks and Vanwall – names to watch.

1st	M Hawthorn	Maserati 250F in 16m-10.0s	77.38
2nd	H Schell (W)	Vanwall VW/55	1.4s
F lap	M Hawthorn	Maserati 250F in 1m-03.4s	78.93

✱✱✱ 31-Jul (WC) XVIII Grosser Preis von Deutschland (N Nürburgring)
-----*CANCELLED FOLLOWING LE-MANS*-----

✱ Redex Trophy (Snetterton)
25 laps of 2.71 miles = 67.75 miles.
25 entries – 15 started – 11 finished.
Front row: S Moss – H Schell; H Gould; K Wharton. No times known.
13-AUG: A milestone was reached in this damp race: the first victory by a British car over a good Italian one. The Vanwalls held the top two spots all the way. Behind was a great battle between Moss' overgeared Maserati and the amazingly driven Cooper 40-Bristol of Jack Brabham. The car was based on the 1100cc Cooper 'Bobtail' centre-seat sports car, with a two-litre engine. They swapped places frequently until Brabham lost it with four laps to go, but he recovered to finish fourth. This convinced him that his future was in Europe, and, thankfully, he returned the following year to mould a very great career.

1st	H Schell (W)	Vanwall VW/55 in 50m-07.4s	80.80
2nd	K Wharton (W)	Vanwall VW/55	11.0s
3rd	S Moss	Maserati 250F	18.6s
F lap	S Moss	Maserati 250F in 1m-56.0s	84.10

✱✱✱ 21-Aug (WC) XV Grosser Preis der Schweiz (Bremgarten Berne)
-----*CANCELLED FOLLOWING LE-MANS*-----

✱ II *Daily Telegraph* Trophy (Aintree)
17 laps of 3.00 mile circuit = 51 miles.
20 entries – 17 started – 10 finished.
Front row: S Moss – 2m-06.4s (85.44mph); R Salvadori 0.6s; H Gould 2.6s.

03-SEP: The BRM type 25 finally appeared for Peter Collins, but oil-on-tyres made it disappear into the foliage, and, sadly, became a non-starter. Reg Parnell in the streamlined 'B' type Connaught made a great start from the second row. Moss' private Maserati couldn't challenge, and retired on lap 13 with engine trouble. A first win for the new Connaught was denied with two laps to go, but Brooks was fourth in an 'A' type. Compensation was not far away; big-time.

1st	R Salvadori (GE)	Maserati 250F in 36m-33.0s	83.72
2nd	R Gerard	Cooper T23-Bristol 2.0	15.2s
3rd	H Gould	Maserati 250F	25.6s
F lap	R Salvadori	Maserati 250F in 2m-05.2s	86.26

✳✳✳ (WC6) XXV Gran Premio d'Italia (Monza – combined)
50 laps of a 6.214-mile circuit = 310.7 miles.
23 entries – 20 starters – 9 finished.
Front row: J-M Fangio – 2m-46.5s (134.35mph); S Moss 0.3s: K Kling 1.8s.

11-SEP: This was everyone's introduction to the bumpy banked track. Ferrari and Maserati each had six cars, and Mercedes sent four (two streamlined). Behra's Maserati had bodywork shielding the wheels. Three came from Gordini, including the new eight-cylinder type 32, and Vanwall sent two. Lancia had handed all its cars to Ferrari, but the Lancias didn't suit the banking. The Mercedes team promptly led away, headed by Fangio and Moss. Lap 19 and Moss pitted for repairs to his windscreen. While recovering, however, his engine expired. Kling was second when his gearbox packed up on lap 32. So crumbs were handed to the others. Castellotti had been closest chaser and Behra next up. Fifth was another Argentinian – Carlos Menditeguy – who had clawed his way from the very back in his works Maserati. Might he be a future star? It had been hoped that the French GP might be reinstated, but it was now known that this was not to be. So, with the Spanish race cancelled, Mercedes-Benz had now retired.

1st	J-M Fangio (W)	Mercedes W196 in 2h-25m-04.4s	128.49
2nd	P Taruffi (W)	Mercedes W196	0.7s
3rd	E Castellotti (W)	Ferrari 555	46.2s
F lap	S Moss (W)	Mercedes W196 in 2m-46.9s	134.03

Championship positions:
Fangio 40 (WC); Moss 23; Trintignant 12.

✳✳✳ 2nd International Gold Cup (Oulton Park)
54 laps of 2.678 miles = 144.6 miles.
23 entries – 19 started – 11 finished.
Front row: M Hawthorn – 1m-52.4s (85.78mph); S Moss 0.2s; L Musso 0.4s; E Castellotti 0.4s.

24-SEP: Mercedes had retired and Lancia gone bust, its cars now part of Scuderia Ferrari. So, in just its second running, this race had attracted all the world's best teams with their top pilots. The front of the grid was all Italian cars separated by just 0.4 seconds – the Italians had learned this driver's circuit very well. Castellotti and Hawthorn led off in their Lancias, but Moss had passed both within a lap. Musso took second, but Moss drew away by a second a lap. Collins in the new BRM stormed through from 13th grid spot to third on lap nine, and closed up to Musso's Maserati when his oil pressure failed. Castellotti pitted for a suspension check, and Harry Schell's Vanwall was now up to fourth, but he retired on lap 16, handing the spot to Parnell's Connaught. Parnell was then passed by the Vanwall of Titterington, who then claimed third, when Musso's Maserati retired from second place with just five laps to go. Moss had led all the way, and was 'Il Supremo' at this challenging, 'proper road' circuit.

1st	S Moss (W)	Maserati 250F in 1h-44m-05.4s	83.36
2nd	M Hawthorn (W)	Lancia D50	1m-6s
3rd	D Titterington (W)	Vanwall VW/55	1 lap
F lap	S Moss	Maserati 250F in 1m-53.2s	85.18

✳ Avon Trophy (Castle Combe)
55 laps of 1.84 miles = 101.2 miles.
20 entries – 14 started – 10 finished.
Front row: H Schell – 1m-14.4s (89.03mph); H Gould 0.6s; R Gerard 0.6s; CAS Brooks 2.6s.

01-OCT: The promising entry included two of Scuderia Ferrari's Lancias, but they were withdrawn and BRM wasn't ready but entered Collins, who started from the back, in its Maserati. Vanwall, unlike BRM, was always ready with one car. Connaught was planning for Siracuse, and one type 'B' was run by the impressive Rob Walker team. So it was just the British teams here, plus plodder Rosier in his Maserati 250F. Schell's Vanwall dominated all the way. Gerard's amazing start gave second, but he was reined back by Gould and Collins (the latter retiring from second place). Gerard just held off Salvadori for third.

1st	H Schell (W)	Vanwall VW/55 in 1h-10m-32.8s	86.07
2nd	H Gould	Maserati 250F	20.0s
3rd	R Gerard	CooperT23-Bristol 2.2	32.6s
F lap	H Schell	Vanwall VW/55 in 1m-13.6s	90.00

✳✳✳ (WC) V Gran Premio d'Espagna (Pedralbes)
-----CANCELLED FOLLOWING LE-MANS-----

✳✳ V Gran Premio di Siracusa
70 laps of 3.418 miles = 239.2 miles.
15 entries and starters – 9 finished.
Front row: L Musso – 2m-03.4s (99.54mph); L Villoresi
(1.1s); CAS Brooks (1.8s).

23-OCT: This race was the stuff of fantasy! Charles Anthony Standish Brooks was working on a dental patient when he was offered this drive by telephone. So shocked, he handed over the patient to a colleague so he could accept the offer to do this race! He had never driven the F1 Connaught 'B type' before, and only twice the old 'A' type. There were no Works Ferraris but five Works Maseratis, two works Gordinis, the two Connaughts and six private Ferraris and Maseratis. Connaught arrived late, so Tony Brooks and Les Leston learnt the circuit on hired scooters! Their cars arrived for the final practice, and Tony Brooks made the front row of the grid! He had a cautious start but then picked off the experienced Maserati stars one by one, and stunned the home crowd by taking the lead on lap 15. Luigi Musso fought back but was repassed a lap later. Worse than that for the Italians, Brooks pulled away almost unchallenged. His lap record was no less than five seconds better than his practice time. A British driver and car wins a major Grand Prix. The first for thirty two years! A star driver is discovered. And a star car?

1st	CAS Brooks (W)	Connaught 'B' type in 2h-24m-55.7s	99.04
2nd	L Musso (W)	Maserati 250F	50.5s
3rd	L Villoresi (W)	Maserati 250F	2 laps
F lap	CAS Brooks	Connaught 'B' type in 2m-00.2s	102.36r

1955 seasonal review – life after Ascari, Le Mans and Mercedes
Most Formula One records say that Alberto Ascari won no F1 race after 1953, his second Championship winning year. It should be noted that, in fact, he won twice with the Lancia D50, in Turin and Naples early in 1955. Not Championship races, but the entries were good. The records do not show either that he retired from a winning position in the last

four Championship rounds he drove, and in the presence of Mercedes and Fangio. This shows that his death robbed Grand Prix racing of a towering talent at the peak of its powers.

The death of Ayrton Senna in 1994 was a shock to the motor racing fraternity because drivers were seen to survive almost unscathed from extremely damaged cars, and no Grand Prix driver had lost his life since Elio deAngelis eight years before. Yet Senna died not from the impact but from flying suspension debris. His now legendary fatal accident was surely no more traumatic for Formula One than that of two-times World Champion Alberto Ascari in 1955. People were still talking about his survival from crashing into the sea at Monaco just four days earlier. No-one would have known that he was back on a race track so soon – it was a private test session to which, only that morning, he had been invited to observe.

The whole world of motor racing was shattered by Le Mans 1955, and a re-evaluation took place which meant the loss of some races. In Switzerland this meant a cessation of motor and motorcycle racing permanently – not surprising, as the Bremgarten circuit of Berne was amongst the most dangerous for drivers and spectators, and no purpose-built tracks existed there. The fact was that the people who died were not standing at the edge of the track, but behind a safety bank. This proved useless in stopping a car which had flown through the air at the very point where the track kinked slightly to the right, which took the car's trajectory right over and into the crowd. To put it in perspective, in 1955 a passenger airplane crash would not have killed more people. Spectator safety was now of prime importance, and tracks running on public roads were particularly at risk. Britain, by law, had no such circuits, so the British season was little affected.

Winners of 20 graded F1 races of 1955 – quantity & quality of success

5 wins	J-M Fangio (4A, D)	8 wins	Maserati: (A, 2B, 4C, D)
2 wins	S Moss (2A) A Ascari (A, B) J Behra (2B) H Schell (2C) R Salvadori (2C)	6 wins	Mercedes (5A, D)
1 win	M Trintignant (A) T Brooks (B) P Collins (C) A Simon (C) Hawthorn (D)	2 wins	Lancia (A, B) Vanwall (2C)
		1 win	Ferrari (A) Connaught (B)

World Championship review
A complete success for Mercedez-Benz was assisted by the signing of Stirling Moss, who proved his worth throughout the season by providing close support for Fangio, and even better at Aintree. The one double-failure at Monaco stopped

a clean sweep from occurring. If the original ten rounds of the Championship had been run, Fangio would almost certainly have sewn up the title even earlier than he did. Lancia had produced the D50, a car that, with Ascari at the wheel, looked likely to take the challenge to the Mercedez-Benz team, and all was set for a great year. Instead, Lancia's finances were so depleted that it felt that the loss of Ascari, following the retirement of González, made success unlikely, and its continuation, therefore, financially unviable. However, Lancia handed its whole outfit to Ferrari, who accepted keenly as the Lancia D50 was clearly superior to its type 555 'Super Squalo.' The good-looking Gordini 32 had flattered to deceive at Monza, having been at the very back and lasting just seven laps.

VISIT VELOCE ON THE WEB – WWW.VELOCE.CO.UK
All current books • New book news • Special offers • Gift vouchers • Forum

104

Chapter 15

1956
Recovery from catastrophe

Mercedes-Benz's withdrawal from Formula One at the previous season's end made 1956 prospects feel more open, and, while the grandeur of the cars' performances had been wonderful to behold, most racing fans would always be drawn to the teams that raced 'for racing's sake,' and that was just about any of the others. Even after Red Bull won the Constructors' Championship four times in a row, because it serves to publicise their caffeine-laced drinks, they don't have the same fanbase as the traditional 'racing teams' for whom racing is their 'raison d'etre seulement,' and this was proved by the reaction to Williams' resurgence in 2014.

The anticipated battle between Mercedes and Lancia had sadly been shortened by Ascari's death, but what could Ferrari do with the gift bestowed on it following Lancia's withdrawal? The cars, now known as Lancia-Ferraris, should give some idea of what sort of battle had been missed, especially as Juan-Manuel Fangio had signed for Ferrari, supported by Peter Collins, Eugenio Castellotti, and Luigi Musso. From July, the Spanish Marquis Alfonso 'Fon' dePortago was added to the squad. The cars were modified during the year to reposition the fuel from the mid-wheel sponsons to the tail, but their appearance was virtually unaltered.

Maserati had signed Fangio's principal team rival Stirling Moss, so now they would be true competitors, Moss' principal teammate being Jean Behra, with Luigi Villoresi and Cesare Perdisa also regulars. But no less than nine other drivers were used by the Works team, seemingly on an ad hoc basis at various races! Maserati's car was still the 250F, now in its third year of development.

Gordini was struggling on as usual, but its new Type 32 car hadn't gone nearly as well as it looked at Monza, and had been right at the back. The team still used Robert Manzon and Elie Bayol, and also the Type 16.

The British teams of Vanwall and Connaught had shown promise, particularly at home events, plus the amazing Siracuse performance of Tony Brooks and Connaught.

Vanwall had signed Harry Schell and Maurice Trintignant, but would use some significant others. It planned a full European campaign, and now used a larger, yet more slippery body by Frank Costin, and the suspension was reworked by Lotus' Colin Chapman.

BRM had appeared only near the season's end, and seemed quick but unreliable, but, with its long background in racing, better was expected in 1956. BRM had the services of Mike Hawthorn and Tony Brooks, who just had to have a regular Works drive after his Siracuse GP triumph. How many of the European events would the cars appear at?

Connaught had the services of the amazing one-handed Archie Scott Brown, but Europeans thought his handicap a danger – quite mistakenly as his record at home proved. So Connaught was unable to secure entries on the continent, and stayed at home. What a disappointment, particularly after Siracuse. This year, then, should see the beginnings of a shift from relying on the two Italian marques towards better involvement of the British who now had three Works teams.

Fortunately, in those days contracts were rather more flexible than today, to say the least, as a driver could be found driving for an opposing marque if his regular team was unable to provide him with a car for any reason: Mike Hawthorn's Maserati appearances in Argentina and Moss' Vanwall drives in England are just two examples of this.

The Grand Prix driver's diary of single-seater racing for 1956

22nd January   **Gran Premio do Argentina** at Buenos Aires (Ag) – 238.2 miles

5th February	Gran Premio Ciudad do Buenos Aires at Mendoza (Ag) – 156 miles
2nd April	Glover Trophy at Goodwood (UK) – 76.8 miles
15th April	Gran Premio di Siracusa (I) – 273.4 miles
21st April	Aintree '200' (UK) – 201 miles
5th May	*Daily Express* International Trophy at Silverstone (UK) – 175.6 miles
6th May	Gran Premio di Napoli at Posillipo (I) – 152.9 miles
13th May	**Grand Prix de Monaco** (M) – 195.4 miles
20th May	Gran Premio di Valentino at Turin (I) (cancelled due to withdrawals)
3rd June	**Grand Prix de Belgique** at Spa Francorchamps (B) – 315.5 miles
23rd June	Aintree '100' (UK) – 102 miles
1st July	**Grand Prix de** l'ACF at Reims (F) – 313 miles
14th July	**British Grand Prix** at Silverstone (UK) – 295.6 miles
22nd July	Vanwall Trophy at Snetterton (UK) – 40.8 miles*
5th August	**Grosse Preis von Deutschland** at Nürburgring (D) – 311.7 miles
26th August	Grand Prix de Caen (F) – 153.1 miles
2nd September	**Gran Premio d'Italia at Monza** (I) – 310.8 miles
14th October	BRSCC F1 race at Brands Hatch (UK) –18.6 miles*

17 events of total race mileage = 3349 miles.
Events in bold are World Championship rounds – 41.2 per cent of F1 races run.
* See appendix 'A' for these ungraded race results.

✷✷ (WC1) X Gran Premio de la Republica Argentina (Buenos Aires No 2)

98 laps of 2.431 miles = 238.2 miles.
13 entries and starters – 6 finished.
Front row: J-M Fangio – 1m-42.5s (85.38mph); E Castellotti 2.2s; L Musso 2.2s; J Behra 2.7s.

22-JAN: A race thankfully not run in extreme heat this year. Only Maserati and Ferrari attended, but supplied all but two of the field. Maserati's team included three 'locals,' one of which was the great Froilán González, out of retirement for one race – who could blame him? Musso led off but was passed by González by the end of the lap. Another 'local,' Carlos Menditeguy, then overtook both and led on lap four. He held it for almost 40 laps before a half-shaft failed – a great one-off drive. Fangio had been fifth at the start, and passed by Moss on lap two, but came through to second on lap nine. Next lap he dropped right back, to stop on lap 22.

Fangio and Musso swapped cars on lap 27, so Fangio had second place behind Moss after Menditeguy retired. A misfire caused Moss to lose ground, so Fangio had the race in the bag from lap 66. Retirements helped Hawthorn to third place in the 'BRM team' Maserati. Strangely, though, the man who took the flag was not leading the Championship ...

1st	L Musso/J-M Fangio (W)	Lancia-Ferrari in 3h-00m-03.7s	79.38
2nd	J Behra (W)	Maserati 250F	24.4s
3rd	M Hawthorn (ORO)	Maserati 250F	2 laps
F lap	J-M Fangio	Lancia-Ferrari in 1m-45.3s	83.10r

Championship positions:
Behra 6; Fangio 5; Hawthorn 4.

✷✷ XI Gran Premio de Buenos Aires (Mendoza)

60 laps of 2.6 miles = 156 miles.
13 entries – 12 started – 10 finished.
Front row: J-M Fangio; E Castellotti; L Musso. No times available.

05-FEB: Strange title for this race, as Mendoza is 600 miles from Buenos-Aires! This race had exactly the same entry as the Championship Argentine GP two weeks previously, so, unlike the previous year, this was a proper F1 race. Castellotti took the lead, but soon Fangio was in his familiar position at the head. His teammates Castellotti and Musso were out by lap 14. On lap 23 Moss took up the Maserati chase of Fangio from Menditeguy and closed, but Fangio had every answer to Moss who eased when he realised the hopelessness of his task. Menditeguy stopped to cure a misfire, spoiling another good drive and dropping to fourth, so handing third to Behra with a few laps to go. An unlucky driver clearly much better than his results show.

1st	J-M Fangio (W)	Lancia-Ferrari D50 in 1h-52m-38.9s	83.10
2nd	S Moss (W)	Maserati 250F	38.6s
3rd	J Behra (W)	Maserati 250F	1m-46s
F lap	J-M Fangio	Lancia-Ferrari D50 in 1m-49.2s	85.72

✷ IV Glover Trophy (Goodwood)

32 laps of 2.4 miles = 76.8 miles.
14 entries – 12 started – 8 started.
Front row: S Moss – 1m-32.0s (93.92mph); A Scott-Brown 0.6s; M Hawthorn 1.8s; R Gerard 2.2s.

02-APR: The Maseratis of Moss, Salvadori and Jack Brabham faced the British teams here. Hawthorn (BRM) led from the amazing one-handed Archie Scott Brown (Connaught) and Moss. They passed the BRM on lap two, and Moss was shown the way by Scott-Brown until failing brakes led to his retirement, and Moss was past. Hawthorn's BRM had suspension seizure, slid off and overturned, fortunately without serious injury to him. The BRMs had plenty of speed, but reliability was still lacking for the British marques.

1st	S Moss	Maserati 250F in 48m-50.4s	94.35
2nd	R Salvadori (GE)	Maserati 250F	1m-03s
3rd	L Leston (W)	Connaught 'B' type	1m-35s
F lap	S Moss	Maserati 250F in 1m-30.2s	95.79r

✷✷ VI Gran Premio di Siracusa
80 laps of 3.418 miles = 273.4 miles.
15 entries and starters – 7 finished.
Front row: J-M Fangio – 1m-58.0s (104.26mph); E Castellotti 0.9s; J Behra 1.6s.
15-APR: Works cars from Ferrari (four), Gordini (two), Maserati (one) and Connaught (two) made for a good entry. There was no Connaught fairytale here again, but an expected domination by Scuderia Ferrari. Apart from Behra's Works Maserati getting amongst them for a few laps before retiring, the Scuderia mixed it together until Castellotti hit a wall on lap 40. Might BRM and Vanwall have worried them? Brooks' Connaught had held the race record and the World Champion had broken it by just 0.4s, but his race record wasn't approached. Connaught had used Desmond Titterington and Piero Scotti – neither one a Tony Brooks.

1st	J-M Fangio (W)	Lancia-Ferrari D50 in 2h-48m-59.9s	97.07
2nd	L Musso (W)	Lancia-Ferrari D50	0.2s
3rd	P Collins (W)	Lancia-Ferrari D50	0.5s
F lap	J-M Fangio	Lancia-Ferrari D50 in 1m-59.8s	102.67

✷ 1st Aintree 'International 200'
67 laps of 3.00 miles = 201.0 miles.
17 entries – 13 started – 5 finished.
Front row: A Scott-Brown – 2m-03.8s (87.24mph); M Hawthorn 2.2s; D Titterington 2.4s.
21-APR: Vanwall withdrew its entries for Moss and Schell, leaving Works entries from only BRM and Connaught. Stirling Moss reverted to his old, private, drum-braked Maserati, but was on the grid second row. Scott-Brown was on pole by over two seconds, and shot into the lead, followed by the BRMs of Hawthorn and Brooks. Hawthorn took

over on lap three, but his BRM's brakes vanished only two laps later. Scott-Brown now led Brooks by six seconds, but sadly, on lap 13, piston failure put him out. As at Goodwood, though, he had made his presence felt in a big way, despite his 'handicap'; his prowess in sports cars clearly translating to Formula One. So, the second BRM of Brooks now led Moss by 28 seconds on lap 30, but his brakes faded and he pitted on lap 47 for advice but maintained second place in this race of attrition – a poor showing with serious brake problems.

1st	S Moss	Maserati 250F in 2h-23m-06.4s	84.27
2nd	CAS Brooks (W)	BRM P25	1 lap
3rd	J Brabham	Maserati 250F	3 laps
F lap	CAS Brooks	BRM P25 in 2m-04.6s	86.68

✷✷✷ VIII *Daily Express* International Trophy (Silverstone)
60 laps of 2.927 miles = 175.6 miles.
25 entries – 20 started – 8 finished.
Front row: S Moss – 1m-42s (103.31mph); H Schell 0s; J-M Fangio 1s; M Hawthorn 1s.
05-MAY: Ferrari split its forces and entered two cars in this race, for Fangio and Collins, and two at Naples the day after. There were no Works Maseratis, but three 250Fs were in experienced British hands. Maserati allowed Moss to drive for Vanwall, and he and teammate Schell headed the grid with the now Costin-bodied cars, despite Fangio's presence. Connaught had five of its promising 'B' type cars. Fangio's Lancia-Ferrari led as the flag dropped, but Hawthorn's BRM led until lap 13 – magneto failure and yet another lead lost. Moss had passed Schell and Fangio, so now led, and he romped away to a 58 second lead by lap 30! Fangio had clutch trouble, though, and took over Collins' Lancia-Ferrari, only to suffer clutch trouble again. Salvadori and Scott-Brown had the best battle of the race, ending on lap 48 when Salvadori overshot Stowe corner, slid into a barrier and overturned. He was pinned inside the car and sustained leg damage. Vanwall's first race of 1956 saw it easily beat the Championship's leading driver and car. A very significant race in British F1 history.

1st	S Moss (W)	Vanwall VW/56 in 1h-44m-53s	100.47
2nd	A Scott-Brown (W)	Connaught 'B'type	1 lap
3rd	D Titterington (W)	Connaught 'B' type	2 laps
F lap	Moss/Hawthorn (W)	Vanwall/BRM in 1m-43s	102.30r

✴ **Gran Premio di Napoli (Posillipo)**

60 laps of 2.548 miles = 152.9 miles.

10 started – 4 finished.

Front row: E Castellotti – 2m-07.7s (71.83mph); L Musso 0.1s; R Manzon 4.4s.

06-MAY: A day after Silverstone, and Ferrari's other drivers were here with no real opposition – apparently – and over four seconds clear in practice from Manzon. A retirement on lap two for Castellotti still left Musso to cruise to victory. Only he didn't ... retiring on lap 37 with engine trouble. This left Manzon enjoying the lead, and holding it until the end. Double gloom for Ferrari this weekend.

1st	R Manzon (W)	Gordini T16 in 2h-20m-43.8s	65.19
2nd	H Gould	Maserati 250F	11s
3rd	G Gerini	Maserati 250F	3 laps
F lap	L Musso (W)	Lancia-Ferrari D50 in 2m-12.3s	69.33

✴✴✴ **(WC2) XIV Grand Prix de Monaco (Monte Carlo)**

100 laps of a 1.954-mile circuit = 195.4 miles.

18 entries – 14 started – 9 finished.

Front row: J-M Fangio – 1m-44.0s (67.65mph); S Moss 0.6s; E Castellotti 0.9s.

13-MAY: Vanwall and BRM entered, but the BRMs non-started, as a result of their eternal brake troubles. Schell's Vanwall got onto the second row, though. The chicane had been tightened to prevent a repetition of Ascari's 1955 accident, so speeds were slightly down. Moss made a great start, and, on lap two, Fangio spun at St Devote trying to stay with him. While re-joining the circuit Musso and Schell were forced off-track to retire. Fangio regained second but forceful driving gave his car front end damage and he dropped to fourth. He took over Collins' second-place car, his battered one given to a retired Castellotti. Fangio closed on Moss who had everything in hand and had led all the way in an imperious drive. Not one of Fangio's best days despite a strenuous fight to catch Moss. Castellotti brought the damaged ex-Fangio car into fourth place, six laps down.

1st	S Moss (W)	Maserati 250F in 3h-00m-32.9s	64.94
2nd	P Collins/J Fangio (W)	Lancia-Ferrari D50	6.1s
3rd	J Behra (W)	Maserati 250F	1 lap
F lap	J-M Fangio	Lancia-Ferrari D50 in 1m-44.4s	67.39

Championship positions:
Behra 10; Fangio 9; Moss 8.

✴✴✴ **(WC3) XVIII Grand Prix de Belgique (Spa)**

36 laps of 8.774 mile circuit = 315.9 miles.

18 entries – 15 started – 8 finished.

Front row: J-M Fangio – 4m-09.8s (126.44mph); S Moss 4.9s; P Collins 5.5s.

03-JUN: Two Vanwalls and three BRMs were entered to challenge the Italians, but, surprise-surprise, the BRMs didn't arrive. Fangio's pole lap was 8.8 seconds faster than the previous year in the Mercedes, so a real challenge would surely have happened that year if only Ascari hadn't died. Moss was fastest away, with Fangio third behind Castellotti. By lap five Fangio led, and, on a drying track, began pulling away. Moss then lost his left rear wheel on lap ten approaching Eau Rouge (of all places) and, with amazing skill, parked the car just off the track and ran back to take over Perdisa's already lapped car. Castellotti retired at the same time. Fangio was well ahead of Collins and Behra when his transmission failed on lap 23, so Collins now led Behra and Frére, with Moss now unlapped. Behra retired so Moss got home third, with Schell's Vanwall next. The Vanwall was so fast on the straight that Schell flew past Moss after being overtaken – brilliant aerodynamics – but not for long.

1st	P Collins (W)	Lancia-Ferrari D50 in 2h-40m-00.3s	118.44
2nd	P Frére (W)	Lancia-Ferrari D50	1m-51s
3rd	C Perdisa/S Moss (W)	Maserati 250F	3m-17s
F lap	S Moss (W)	Maserati 250F in 4m-14.7s	124.01r

Championship positions:
Collins and Moss 11; Behra 10.

Aintree '100' (Aintree)

34 laps of 3.00 miles = 102 miles.

12 entries – 8 started – 7 finished.

Front row: A Scott-Brown – 2m-05.8s (85.85mph); R Salvadori 4.8s; H Gould; W Holt.

23-JUN: BRM and Connaught sent a Works car each. Brooks' BRM set a time of 2m-04.8s, but the engine failed so the door was open for Scott-Brown. Second grid slot was excellent for Salvadori's Connaught 'A' type. Scott-Brown led after half a lap, but he became the race's only retirement on lap nine due to oil loss. Places were static thereafter. The privateer finishing rate of 100 per cent was extraordinary. Salvadori would have won in his Maserati 250F, surely, but he was fourth behind Halford's 250F.

1st	H Gould	Maserati 250F in 1h-13m-39.8s	83.08
2nd	R Gerard	Cooper-Bristol	35.2s
F lap	H Gould	Maserati 250F in 2m-06.0s	85.71

✱✱✱ (WC4) XLII Grand Prix de l'ACF (Reims)
61 laps of a 5.158-mile circuit = 314.6 miles.
24 entries – 19 started – 11 finished.
Front row: J-M Fangio – 2m-23.3s (129.60mph); E Castellotti 1.3s; P Collins 1.6s.

01-JUL: Three Vanwalls and two BRMs were listed this time to challenge the Italians, but the BRMs didn't arrive – yet again. Hawthorn was loaned to Vanwall for this race, and he and teammate Schell were closest to the three front row Ferraris, even beating Moss' Maserati. Collins led lap one but was behind his two teammates next lap. The Fangio, Castellotti, Collins train commanded the podium spots until lap 30. Behind them Hawthorn had handed his fourth place Vanwall to the retired Harry Schell as he had driven the 12-hour sports car race before the Grand Prix and was tiring. Schell was now eighth, but Moss' retirement benefitted him. Then Schell began what would become a famous drive. By lap 30 he was worrying the leaders and used the Vanwall's slippery shape to gain second place on lap 31 – he had gained 25 seconds in just eight laps! Collins and Castellotti re-passed Schell on the bends and teamed up to keep him back and help Fangio pull away. Fuel pump trouble interrupted Schell's wonderful drive, though, and soon after, Fangio pitted to repair a fuel pipe, finishing fourth. A repeat victory for Peter Collins.

1st	P Collins (W)	Lancia-Ferrari D50 in 2h-34m-23.4s	122.29
2nd	E Castellotti (W)	Lancia-Ferrari D50	0.3s
3rd	J Behra (W)	Maserati 250F	1m-30s
F lap	J-M Fangio (W)	Lancia-Ferrari D50 in 2m-25.8s	127.37r

Championship positions:
Collins 19; Behra 14; Fangio 13.

✱✱✱ (WC5) XI British Grand Prix (Silverstone)
101 laps of 2.927 miles = 295.6 miles.
31 entries – 28 starters – 12 finished.
Front row: S Moss – 1m-41.0s (104.33mph); J-M Fangio; M Hawthorn 2.0s; P Collins 2.0s.

14-JUL: The British teams were here, so there was hope for a British/Italian inter-marque battle. Hawthorn's BRM was third on the grid, behind Fangio. Schell and González were

on the second row for Vanwall. The BRMs of Hawthorn and Brooks (from row three) amazingly led for six laps, then Fangio passed Brooks but spun. Moss and Salvadori (private Maserati) came through to head the field by lap 20 as Hawthorn retired. Brooks held fifth to lap 39, whereupon he pitted with throttle trouble. A botched repair caused him to crash and overturn in flames, luckily escaping serious injuries. Trouble for Salvadori let Fangio and Collins pass, but Collins retired and took over dePortago's car. Moss lost the lead to Fangio on lap 68, the gearbox playing up, retiring from second on lap 95. This was Fangio's first solo win of the year, but a Brit was leading the championship with two rounds left.

1st	J-M Fangio (W)	Lancia-Ferrari D50 in 2h-59m-47.0s	98.66
2nd	DePortago/ Collins (W)	Lancia-Ferrari D50	1 lap
3rd	J Behra (W)	Maserati 250F	2 laps
F lap	S Moss (W)	Maserati 250F in 1m-43.2s	102.10

Championship positions:
Collins 22; Fangio 21; Behra 18.

✱✱ (WC6) XVIII Grosser Preis von Deutschland (N Nürburgring)
22 laps of 14.17 miles = 311.7 miles.
21 entries – 19 started – 5 finished.
Front row: J-M Fangio – 9m-51.2s (86.31mph); P Collins 0.3s; E Castellotti 3.2s; S Moss 12.2s.

05-AUG: No British cars (why not, after a promising Silverstone?) And no Hawthorn, as he had shamefully been banned by the German club for breaking pit area regulations in the sports car race in May. Fangio led flag-to-flag, with Collins close behind for eight laps. Collins stopped, dizzy with fumes, taking over from dePortago, but crashed trying to catch up. Moss and Behra followed for the rest of the race. Castellotti was 16th on lap one, and his magneto failed after five laps. He took over Musso's car but, like Collins, spun out of the race. Salvadori was fifth on lap two when his suspension failed – a good performance in his non-Works Maserati. Four cars had stopped or pitted after lap one, so this was more like an endurance race. Even Bruce Halford's Maserati would have been fourth but had had outside help to regain the track so was disqualified, handing the place to Francesco Godia-Sales – two laps down – both were amateurs, really. Lang's lap record from 1939 was shattered by Fangio, Collins and Moss.

1st	J-M Fangio (W)	Lancia-Ferrari D50 in 3h-38m-43.7s	85.54
2nd	S Moss (W)	Maserati 250F	46.4s
3rd	J Behra (W)	Maserati 250F	7m-38s
F lap	J-M Fangio (W)	Lancia-Ferrari D50 in 9m-41.6s	87.73r

Championship positions:
Fangio 30; Collins and Behra 22.

✴ IV Grand Prix de Caen
70 laps of 2.187 miles = 153.1 miles.
13 entries & starters – 7 finished.
Front row: R Salvadori; L Rosier. Row two: B Halford; R Manzon. No times available.

26-AUG: Four Works Gordinis were here, so they fancied their chances, and, with Schell's Works Maserati plus four regular privateers, made up the serious entries. Salvadori, Schell and Gould led the way, then Gould took second place but crashed off the wet track into the fields. Halford, in fourth place, also crashed. Salvadori spun handing the lead to Schell, and eventually lost second to Simon on lap 52; the Gordini suited the awful conditions. Rosier and Manzon also crashed, but there were no injuries.

1st	H Schell	Maserati 250F in 1h-54m-19.4s	80.36
2nd	A Simon	Gordini T16	1m-10s
3rd	R Salvadori	Maserati 250F	1 lap
F lap	R Salvadori	Maserati 250F in 1m-26.2s	91.35

✴✴✴ (WC7) XXVI Gran Premio d'Italia (Monza – Combined)
50 laps of 6.214 mile circuit = 310.7 miles.
27 entries – 24 starters – 12 finished.
Front row: J-M Fangio – 2m-42.6s (137.57mph); E Castellotti 0.8s; L Musso 1.1s.

02-SEP: This was again on the combined banked track where the track leaving the banking adjoined the outside of the road circuit as it passed the pits and entered the banking. The Lancia-Ferraris had steering arms break and tyres throw treads on the banking, yet still filled the front grid row. Vanwall had Piero Taruffi for this race, and he was next fastest. Connaught was here, but BRM was absent again! Musso and Castellotti scorched away from Fangio who was soon overtaken by Schell's Vanwall. The two leaders' tyres shredded after only four laps, though, so now it was Moss shadowed by Schell with Fangio and Collins close. Castellotti and dePortago both had tyres fail

on the banking, and were lucky to escape injury. Lap 11 saw Collins pit for tyres and Schell passed Moss, so, for the first time ever, a Vanwall led a Grand Epreuve, but just for a lap. He fell back and retired on lap 32. Fangio's steering broke on lap 17, and Musso was now third but soon to be second. Collins pitted, famously handing his car to Fangio. Moss ran short of fuel on lap 45, and Musso now led. A push from Piotti's Maserati helped Moss to reach the pits to refuel – so it would seem that only manual assistance was banned? With three laps to go a thrown tread broke Musso's steering as he came off the banking, and he spun across both track widths to finish against the pit end, uninjured! Moss cruised to victory and Fangio was Champion for the fourth time. Today, Musso would have been classified fifth. And through all that came the Connaught of Ron Flockhart which had started on the back row of the grid and had overtaken nine cars on the opening lap. He was only lapped once and his only stop was precautionary, for fuel on the penultimate lap!

This was the first World Championship podium finish for a British F1 constructor; also the only one ever for Connaught or Ron Flockhart in their brief F1 histories. No fluke either, as, although he'd qualified at only 3m-08.1s (118.92mph) he averaged 125.67mph for the race! An improvement of a full ten seconds per lap. A bit of forgotten history worth recalling.

1st	S Moss (W)	Maserati 250F in 2h-23m-41.3s	129.73
2nd	Collins/Fangio (W)	Lancia-Ferrari D50	5.7s
3rd	R Flockhart (W)	Connaught 'B'	1 lap
F lap	S Moss (W)	Maserati 250F in 2m-45.5s	135.16r

Final Championship positions:
Fangio 30 (WC); Moss 27; Collins 25.

Winners of the 15 graded F1 races of 1956 – quantity & quality of success

5 wins	S Moss (3A, B, C) J-M Fangio (3A, 2B)	7 wins	Lancia-Ferrari (5A, 2B)
2 wins	P Collins (2A)	6 wins	Maserati (2A, B, 2C, D)
1 win	H Schell (C) R Manzon (C) H Gould (D)	1 win	Vanwall (A); Gordini (C)

1956 seasonal review
Motor racing recovered this year from the dreadful 1955,

when some were even questioning its morality following the Le Mans slaughter. The total number of Formula One races was still down at about two thirds that of the 1954 figure. Sadly, the Swiss Grand Prix was lost forever. In spring each year a mini-season, mostly in Britain, was now being established, with races being precursers to the Championship battle in Europe. Aintree's '200' event was of almost Grand Prix length, and it attracted a good field, but Silverstone's now well established International Trophy was slightly better, with two Lancia-Ferraris present, and was won much faster than the British Grand Prix itself two months later. There always seemed more privately run Formula One cars from Britain than the rest of Europe, which made for good grids in Britain and fostered driving talent.

The Lancia-Ferraris had the lion's share of wins in the Championship, and shared with Maserati in other races. Gordini had scraped up a win against the odds at Naples, thanks to unexpected Lancia failures and an unusually reliable car for Robert Manzon, Gordini's only entry. Maybe there was still life in the underdog. At Reims, Bugatti re-emerged with a radical new car, having a rear-mounted transverse straight-eight-cylinder engine to be driven by Maurice Trintignant. It didn't work and was not seen again.

Vanwall had made real progress with its new Costin-bodied and Chapman-suspended car, the Silverstone victory being augmented by Harry Schell's great drives at Reims and Monza. Vanwall was now a front runner, to be taken seriously. BRM was absent so often yet had flown at the British Grand Prix before failing. It had taken far too long to get any reliability into the V16 BRM; we hoped it wasn't repeating this with the new obviously fast car, brakes seeming to be an Achilles Heel. Three years of this formula had passed and BRM had nothing to show for itself. Archie Scott-Brown had shown the speed of the Connaught, at least when *he* drove it, in the British races. What a travesty it was that he couldn't race abroad where its one Championship foray into Europe, at Monza, produced such a great result.

Britain's drivers were making their presence felt more, as Peter Collins had now joined Mike Hawthorn and Stirling Moss in the elite of Formula One winners, not forgetting Tony Brooks and his 1955 win at Siracuse. BRM's problems perhaps prevented him from making his name bigger at that time.

1956 Championship review

This year showed just how versatile Fangio was, as he secured yet another title in yet another marque. But let's not assume

from the points chart that this result was inevitable. Two other outcomes involving two other drivers could, and some might say should, have eventuated.

At Monaco, Peter Collins yielded second place to Fangio when the team leader was making up ground from an earlier spin, which had caused Musso and Schell to crash when taking avoiding action. Fangio still pressed on hard, and damaged a wheel exiting Tabac corner. He retired his battered car on lap 40. On lap 54, Collins was in a secure second place and closing on leader Moss when called to hand over his car at Fangio's request. The World Champion then regained second place and finished the race in the same position as Collins would likely have done, although closer to Moss maybe. This meant that Collins received only three points for a share of second place instead of the six points. Fangio ended the year five points ahead of Collins. Swap three points from Fangio to Collins and a new result emerges. Fangio had caused his retirement and had been missing from the race for 14 laps! Hmmm ...

Collins' magnificent gesture: he would have been Champion at Monza if he had won the race even without fastest lap and had Fangio not scored. He would have had equal points but scored three victories to Fangio's two, and one shared. He clearly recognised the fact that his position was due to Fangio's mechanical misfortunes in Belgium and France, and felt that he kept the Championship's credentials intact by handing over his car to the superior driver. It was a rare gesture, which would no doubt attract derision in the twenty-first century's unsporting sports world – were it still allowed.

At Silverstone, Moss had been leading on lap 67 when a visit to the pits to investigate loss of power dropped him to second place. Soon after, a transmission problem caused him to lose ground, and he was in danger of losing second to Collins on lap 95 of 101 when the gearbox cried enough. If he had finished even third, those four points would have given him the title by one point from Fangio. It's not often realised how close Moss came in 1956.

It is a reflection of the credentials of Collins and Moss that either of the above scenarios may easily have come about. The former, in my opinion, should have, and the latter very nearly did. This was clearly not the most dominant of Fangio's title years. He was, of course, gentleman enough to have acknowledged that fact. Next year would clearly be no walkover for Ferrari or Maserati, with Vanwall heading the British challenge.

VISIT VELOCE ON THE WEB – WWW.VELOCE.CO.UK
All current books • New book news • Special offers • Gift vouchers • Forum

111

Chapter 16

1957

Italy v Britain; battle truly engaged

Both Vanwall and Connaught had each now won international Formula One races against the best of the present opposition: Connaught at Syracuse in 1955 against a host of Works Maseratis; and Vanwall at Silverstone the previous May against Lancia-Ferraris driven by Fangio and Collins. Those two Italian marques were the only serious opposition the British teams were likely to face in 1957, with Gordini (despite the Naples win when the Lancia-Ferraris surprised by retiring), were not expected to last long due to funds running out. Could BRM sort itself out and get the reliability required to achieve the results suggested by the speed demonstrated at the British Grand Prix? If so, then a really close battle between Italy and Britain should happen. Although Connaught had produced the best finishes in the Championship in 1956, Vanwall was probably the strongest British team, as Connaught was known to be struggling financially.

Ferrari was continuing with the Lancia D50, but had removed the bodywork from between the wheels so they looked more conventional, and they were redesignated Ferrari 801. The driver lineup was now: Mike Hawthorn; close friend Peter Collins; Eugenio Castellotti, and Luigi Musso.

Maserati had secured Juan-Manuel Fangio from Ferrari as he hadn't liked Enzo Ferrari's attitude to his drivers, and clearly thought the 250F had plenty to offer in its new lightweight form. He was supported by Jean Behra, Harry Schell and Carlos Menditeguy. Stirling Moss would drive for Maserati until Vanwall was ready.

Gordini still had Robert Manzon, but its survival was known to be on the very edge.

Vanwall had convinced Stirling Moss of its cars' potential winning form, and at last it looked as though he had the

British team of his desire. Tony Brooks' potential was recognised by Mr Vandervell, and was expected to provide strong support to Moss. BRM's 1956 performance probably made his decision to accept rather easy.

BRM had revised its suspension and re-bodied the cars in the final, beautiful, form now familiar in historic racing. It had the services of Roy Salvadori and Ron Flockhart; maybe Hawthorn and Brooks had had enough of the crashes, brake failure and unreliability which had destroyed any possible power advantage.

Connaught retained the brilliant Archie Scott Brown (for British events only – shame on the FIA), Stuart Lewis-Evans, and Jack Fairman. Les Leston and Ivor Bueb were also on the list, but how long could the team last? Connaught had looked at a rear-engined design, but lacked the resources to see it into the flesh. So that tactic was pioneered by ... Cooper Cars, with Climax power. One is apt to say this tiny outfit was 'under-the-radar,' except that it was very conspicuous by its size – or lack of it! The Works team had Jack Brabham and Roy Salvadori as main drivers, though the former twice drove for Rob Walker, who had also employed Tony Brooks at the late season International Trophy at Silverstone.

At Easter, the Pau GP always clashed with Goodwood, and Connaught ran no fewer than five cars on Easter Monday. How strange for a team short of funds to field so many cars, but retirement rates in those days suggested that safety was in numbers financed by starting money. This was often a crucial source of income, which was why more than Championship races alone were essential as part of the Formula One scene. Without the inducement of World Championship points, organisers would frequently offer greater starting money than Championship rounds to ensure a good field. A huge crowd would attend, as a well-supported Formula One race was a top event in its own right – Championship or not.

The Championship was now expanding, with eight rounds chosen from of a total of 18 scheduled F1 events, and with the Dutch Grand Prix back on the Championship schedule. So, despite Mercedez-Benz' withdrawal at the end of 1955, motor racing in 1957 was looking healthy. However, there was a sword hanging over the whole of the sport at that time due to the unfortunate events at Suez in 1956. Egypt's leader Colonel Abdul Nasser had nationalised the Suez Canal, and Britain and France had been humiliated in their futile attempt to wrest control of it from him. The canal was now blocked by sunken ships, and the supply of vital oil was threatened, so petrol was in short supply to the point, in Britain, of rationing. How would motor sport weather this difficult problem? Silverstone announced as early as February that its famous International Trophy race would be postponed from its usual May date to a date as yet unconfirmed.

In February a meeting of National automobile clubs took place in Brussels to decide a scale of starting money to be used by World Championship race organisers; it seems that no delegation from Italy attended, so Italian races were exempt. Here's what was agreed. Drivers: Grade 1 – the World Champion £180 (Fangio); Grade 2 – the next three in the Championship £100 (Moss, Collins, Behra); Grade 3 – other points scorers £40 (Castellotti, Musso, Hawthorn, Schell, Frére, Fairman, Flockhart, etc). Omissions, such as Brooks, suggest that 'likely performance' was not taken into account, though it was the sole criterion with the cars (three per team): £700 per Ferrari and Maserati; £540 each Vanwall; £350 to all others. What's that today? Multiply by 22.7, it seems, which would give £636,000 per two-car top team for a 20-race season. Out by a factor of hundreds? All this shows how sponsorship and TV advertising has influenced 'who races and how' beyond imagination.

After the Monaco Grand Prix came the bombshell that, in dispute over the agreed scale, Ferrari and Maserati stated that they would not compete in the forthcoming Belgian and Dutch Grands Prix, or the German Grand Prix in August. Without the Italian teams the races would be meaningless in World Championship terms, and financially unviable, so the organisers withdrew them. This would leave just the French, British and Italian races yet to be run, giving only five Championship rounds; less than the minimum required to be run according to Championship rules. The organisers in this dispute must have believed that this fact would bring the Italian teams to heel. It didn't, so, in June, the Belgian and Dutch races were lost. However, just before the French Grand Prix, it was announced that the August Pescara F1 race – in Italy, no surprise – would be elevated to World Championship status, thus saving the situation for 1957 – and for Ferrari and Maserati.

The Grand Prix driver's diary of single-seater racing for 1957

13th January	**F1 – Gran Premio do Argentina** at Buenos Aires (Ag) – 243.1 miles
27th January	F1 – Gran Premio Ciudad do Buenos Aires (Ag) – 175.5 miles
7th April	F1 – Gran Premio di Siracusa (I) – 273.4 miles
13th April	F1 – Aintree '200' (UK) – 201 miles*
22nd April	F1 – Glover Trophy at Goodwood (UK) – 76.8 miles
22nd April	F1 – Grand Prix de Pau (F) – 188.5 miles
28th April	F1 – Gran Premio di Napoli at Posillipo (I) – 152.9 miles
4th May	F1 – *Daily Express* Internat'l Trophy at Silverstone (postponed to 14th September)
19th May	**F1 – Grand Prix de Monaco** (M) – 205.2 miles
2nd June	**F1 – Grand Prix de Belgique** at Spa Francorchamps (B) – 315.5 miles**
16th June	F1 – **Grote Prijs van Nederland** at Zandvoort (N) – 312.6 miles**
7th July	**F1 – Grand Prix de l'ACF** at Rouen-les-Essarts (F) – 313 miles
14th July	F2 – Coupe International de Vitesse at Reims (F) – 190.9 miles
14th July	F1 – Grand Prix de Reims (F) – 314.6 miles
20th July	**British F1 – Grand Prix** at Aintree (UK) – 225 miles
28th July	F1 – Grand Prix de Caen (F) – 188.1 miles
4th August	F1 – **Grosse Preis von Deutschland** at Nürburgring (D) – 311.7 miles
18th August	**F1 – Grand Premio di Pescara** (I) – 286.1 miles
8th September	**F1 – Gran Premio d'Italia at Monza** (I) – 310.8 miles
14th September	F1 – *Daily Express* International Trophy at Silverstone (UK) – 146.4 miles
22nd September	F1 – Gran Premio di Modena (I) – 117.7 miles
5th October	F2 – International Gold Cup at Oulton Park (UK) – 133.9 miles
27th October	F1 – Grand Prix de Maroc at Ain Diab, Casablanca (Mo) – 259.8 miles

25 events of total planned race mileage = 4943 miles, but only 22 run of 4113 miles – 4037 max due to simultaneous events.
* = Cancelled due to fuel shortage caused by Suez crisis.
** = Cancelled due to start money dispute.
Events in bold are World Championship rounds. However, only seven were run = 38.9 per cent of F1 races run.

✴✴ (WC1) XI Gran Premio de la Republica Argentina (Buenos Aires No 2)

100 laps of 2.431 miles = 243.1 miles.
14 entries and starters – 10 finished.

Front row: S Moss – 1m-42.6s (85.29mph); J-M Fangio 1.1s; J Behra 1.4s: E Castellotti 1.6s.

13-JAN: As per the previous year, only the Italian Works teams and the non-Works Scuderia Centro-Sud entered. With Vanwall being absent, Moss was free to be drafted into the Maserati team, and he out-qualified Fangio by over a second! The starter fumbled the start, though, causing Moss to make a jolted start which bent a throttle link. He pulled straight into the pits and lost eight laps before setting off again. Meanwhile, Behra led Castellotti, and swapped the lead twice before Collins came through to lead from lap 13, before retiring on lap 25 with clutch slip. Fangio now led Behra, except when refuelling, until the end. The clutch problem also put Musso and Hawthorn's Lancia-Ferraris out. Moss finished eighth but seven laps down, so he'd gained a lap on the leaders! Was this a victory gone begging? Maybe, but he states in his book All My Races that he'd been told not to beat Fangio. Clearly surprised by his pole time, they felt the need to issue the order, but where does that leave an honest driver's Championship?

1st	J-M Fangio (W)	Maserati 250F in 3h-00m-55.9s	80.61
2nd	J Behra (W)	Maserati 250F	18.3s
3rd	C Menditeguy (W)	Maserati 250F	1 lap
F lap	S Moss (W)	Maserati 250F in 1m-44.7s	83.52r

✴✴ XI Grand Prix de Buenos Aires (Buenos Aires No 4)

2 x 30 laps of 2.925 miles = 175.5 miles.
15 entries and starters – 10 finished.

Front row: J-M Fangio – 2m-17.9s (76.36mph); S Moss 0.3s; M Hawthorn 0.6s; J Behra 1.0s.

27-JAN: As in 1954, the Argentine GP field returned to the Buenos Aires autodrome for its eponymous GP in two 88 mile parts. Castellotti's Ferrari led off from Fangio, Moss and Collins, who both then passed Fangio. Moss took the lead but stopped with heat exhaustion, the same causing Collins to hand over to Masten Gregory. So Fangio won heat one from Behra, Castellotti, Hawthorn and Musso. Many drivers were treated for the heat before the second part. Moss recovered to drive Menditeguy's Maserati and Collins took over Musso's car as he had not recovered. Hawthorn led well after Castelotti spun, but the heat got to him again and he dropped back, while Collins passed Behra to lead. Fangio took

Hawthorn for third, but his aggregate times would have given him the overall win anyway. Once again, he was the one who coped with the heat – a real advantage here.

1st	J-M Fangio (W)	Maserati 250F in 2h-22m-30.3s	73.89
2nd	J Behra (W)	Maserati 250F	24.5s
3rd	Musso/Collins (W)	Ferrari 801	1m-27s
F lap	J-M Fangio/P Collins	Ferrari 801 in 2m-19.6s	75.43r

Just before the previous Formula One race came news of the death of former F1 driver Ken Wharton, in a sports car race in New Zealand. Never a top line F1 driver, he was, nevertheless, a great all-rounder, gifted in all branches of motor sport and well liked. Then, early in March, Eugenio Castellotti died in a testing accident at Modena autodrome. He was seen as better than Musso, and a likely replacement for Ascari. This bitter blow left Luigi Musso as the only Italian star remaining in Formula One. Still the Italian cars dominated, but now, Fangio apart, British drivers were well in the ascendancy. Many had bemoaned the lack of public-road racing in Britain, but the purpose-built closed circuit scene had created a breeding ground second to none.

✴✴✴ VII Gran Premio di Siracusa

80 laps of 3.418 miles = 273.4 miles.
19 entries – 17 started – 6 finished.

Front row: P Collins: 1m-55.5s (106.54mph); L Musso 0.4s; S Moss 0.8s.

07-APR: Back from Argentina, the Italian teams were joined by Connaught, with three cars, and Vanwall's two, so the Italy vs Britain battle started here. Fangio was absent, so Jean Behra led the Maserati effort which included the first appearance of the V12-engined 250F but not used in the race. Two cars from Ferrari, Vanwall and Maserati made up the top six grid places, so a great race was on the cards. Musso led at first with teammate Collins close but Moss passed them both within three laps. Brooks soon made it a Vanwall one-two as they drew away from the Ferrari duo. Schell and Behra's Maseratis both retired by lap 18. Collins passed Musso and chased after Brooks, gaining second place, but Moss was now clear until a cracked injector pipe stopped him for five laps. Soon afterwards Brooks retired on lap 34 with head gasket failure. Moss rejoined, then blew the lap record away whilst recovering a whole lap, having smashed Fangio's 1956 time by over five seconds! If this was the season's warm-up race, it was already red hot, and Vanwall was now the fastest car ... if only it could keep going.

1st	P Collins (W)	Ferrari 801 in 2h-40m-11.9s	102.40
2nd	L Musso (W)	Ferrari 801	1m-15s
3rd	S Moss (W)	Vanwall VW/57	3 laps
F lap	S Moss	Vanwall VW/57 in 1m-54.3s	107.64r

✳✳✳ Aintree International '200'

13-APR: Cancelled due to fuel rationing in Britain following the Suez crisis. This event had been included in a list of government-approved events for fuel supply, but the organisers felt that fuel rationing would prevent many people from attending, so making the event financially unviable.

✳ XVII Grand Prix de Pau

110 laps of 1.714 miles = 188.5 miles.
16 entries – 14 started – 8 finished.
Front row: J Behra – 1m-35.7s (64.48mph); H Schell 2.2s; M Gregory 3.5s.

22-APR: Following Le Mans 1955, Pau had to make changes to regain its licence, and was now back in business. Ferrari was preparing for Naples, so Maserati (1), Connaught (2) and Gordini (4!) were the Works teams. Behra took five laps to take the lead from the Scuderia Centro Sud car of Harry Schell. He then pressed on unnecessarily hard and nearly lost the race against straw bales at one point. A highlight of this dull race was Masten Gregory's chase of Le Mans winner Ivor Bueb. This was Gregory's Formula One debut, and he had made the front row of the grid. His fourth place marked him as a potential star with his three-year-old Maserati 250F in American colours of white with blue stripe – a first for Formula One.

1st	J Behra (W)	Maserati 250F in 3h-00m-13.7s	62.70
2nd	H Schell (SCS)	Maserati 250F	2 laps
3rd	I Bueb (W)	Connaught 'B' type	3 laps
F lap	J Behra	Maserati 250F in 1m-35.9s	64.34

✳ V Glover Trophy (Goodwood)

32 laps of 2.4 miles = 76.8 miles.
13 entries – 10 started – 6 finished.
Front row: S Moss – 1m-28.2s (97.96mph); A Brooks 0.8s; A Scott-Brown 3.0s; R Flockhart 4.4s.

22-APR: Only British Works teams here, so, on paper, Vanwall should walk it, particularly as Moss shattered the lap record in practice. Sure enough, Stirling Moss led away from Archie Scott-Brown (Connaught), Brooks and Flockhart, but the BRM bogie – brakes – put Salvadori out on lap one. Scott-Brown spun as did Flockhart so a Vanwall one-two

looked certain. However, familiar throttle linkage trouble delayed first Brooks and then Moss' Vanwall. So Stuart Lewis-Evans won in the new rebodied 'toothpaste tube' Connaught on its debut. It was also his international F1 debut. Very few have done that.

1st	S Lewis-Evans (W)	Connaught 'B' type in 50m-49.8s	90.66
2nd	J Fairman (W)	Connaught 'B' type	24.4s
3rd	R Flockhart (W)	BRM P25	43.2s
F lap	CAS Brooks (W)	Vanwall VW/57 in 1m-29,6s	96.43r

✳ X GP di Napoli (Posillipo)

60 laps of 2.548 miles = 152.9 miles.
9 F1 entries and starters – 6 finished.
Front row: M Hawthorn – 2m-08.0s (71.66mph); P Collins 0.0s; L Musso 1.2s.

28-APR: The Works Ferrari team vs private Maseratis, a Connaught and a Gordini was on offer here, so a Ferrari party was likely. There were seven others in various sports or old F2 cars, but they kept out of the way. Horace Gould's Maserati made a great start, but was soon swallowed by Collins, Hawthorn and Musso as expected. Musso was debuting the new Ferrari Dino 156 F2 car – nimble and suited to the twisty course. Hawthorn led but pitted on lap 13 with fuel pressure trouble costing him just over a lap. Lewis-Evans' Connaught passed Musso for second, but hub failure stopped him. Hawthorn's great recovery netted him second place on the last lap, and wowed the crowd. His new record lap much faster than pole is testament to that.

1st	P Collins (W)	Ferrari 801 in 2h-10m-31.2s	70.28
2nd	M Hawthorn (W)	Ferrari 801	30.9s
3rd	L Musso (W)	Ferrari Dino 156 (F2)	31.2s
F lap	M Hawthorn	Ferrari 801 in 2m-05.6s	73.03r

✳✳✳ (WC2) XV Grand Prix de Monaco (Monte Carlo)

105 laps of 1.954 mile circuit = 205.2 miles.
24 entries – 16 qualified – 7 finished.
Front row: J-M Fangio – 1m-42.7s (68.50mph); P Collins 0.6s; S Moss 0.9s.

19-MAY: With Gordini gone a new team appeared, with a tiny 1900cc rear-engined car. This was Cooper, and was not regarded seriously at the time. But it qualified for the limited spaces on the grid. Fangio set a new record for pole, but was beaten at the start by Moss, who led until crashing at the chicane on lap four with brake failure. Flying poles hit Collins, and Hawthorn struck the back of Collins' car so they were also out – and lucky not to end up in the sea. Fangio and Brooks now had the first two places sewn up, but the race was now all about the cheeky Cooper-Climax of Jack Brabham. He started almost at the back, was sixth by lap ten, fourth by lap 25 and, after von Trips' Ferrari retired on lap, was all set for a podium finish. This year's race was five laps longer than before and, on the one hundredth lap, Brabham's engine expired. He pushed home to sixth place. All this helped Masten Gregory gain a podium place on his World Championship debut. A rare achievement.

1st	J-M Fangio (W)	Maserati 250F in 3h-10m-12.8s	64.73
2nd	CAS Brooks (W)	Vanwall VW/57	25.2s
3rd	M Gregory (SCS)	Maserati 250F	2 laps
F lap	J-M Fangio	Maserati 250F in 1m-45.6s	66.62

Championship positions:
Fangio 17; Brooks and Behra 6.

With the loss of start money from the Belgian and Dutch GPs on top of the Aintree cancellation, Connaught announced that it would cease racing with immediate effect, and placed its cars and equipment for sale.

Gordini and Connaught were now gone. It wouldn't be very long until the situation was reversed, and British teams would dominate the grid. As it was, English was becoming the dominant language in the driver market.

✳✳✳ 02-Jun-1957 (WC3) XVIII Grand Prix de Belgique (Spa)
-----*CANCELLED*-----

✳✳✳ 16-Jun-1957 (WC4) VI Grote Prijs van Nederland (Zandvoort)
-----*CANCELLED*-----

✳✳✳ (WC3) XLIII Grand Prix de l'ACF (Rouen-les-Essarts)
77 laps of a 4.065 mile circuit = 313.0 miles.
15 entries and starters – 7 finished.
Front row: J-M Fangio – 2m-21.5s (103.42mph); J Behra 1.1s; L Musso 1.2s.
07-JUL: This was held on an extended and faster Rouen circuit than in 1952. Vanwall had replaced Moss, suffering sinusitis, with Stuart Lewis-Evans and Brooks, the latter recovering from Le Mans injuries, with Roy Salvadori who had now left BRM. Musso and Behra led Fangio for

a lap, whereupon the great man, after slight contact with Behra, passed both to lead lap four – the dent on Fangio's car becoming an iconic image of this race. BRM's leading driver, Ron Flockhart, crashed on oil on lap two, suffering burns and injuries which affected the rest of his and BRM's season. Collins soon passed Behra, and, on lap 14, Musso also. Lap 28 and Musso took back second place, and began catching Fangio, but spun after at the hairpin after a 40-lap chase. The Vanwalls didn't feature much, though Lewis-Evans made fifth by lap 27 before retiring just after Salvadori retired from ninth.

1st	J-M Fangio (W)	Maserati 250F in 3h-07m-46.4s	100.02
2nd	L Musso (W)	Ferrari 801	50.8s
3rd	P Collins (W)	Ferrari 801	2m-06s
F lap	L Musso (W)	Ferrari 801 in 2m-22.4s	102.77

Championship positions:
Fangio 25; Musso 7; Behra 6.

✳✳✳ XXIII Grand Prix de Reims
61 laps of 5.158 miles = 314.6 miles.
20 entries – 18 started – 12 finished.
Front row: J-M Fangio – 2m-23.3s (129.60mph); S Lewis-Evans 0.2s; J Behra 0.8s.
14-JUL: A full Grand Prix length, and the whole Rouen field arrived plus extra Maseratis. The new Vanwall duo was still in place, and Lewis-Evans flew in practice almost equalling Fangio. It was 'L-E' who stormed off at the chaotic start, though, 'Toto' Roche dropping the flag too early. He pulled away for 20 laps when oil spray on his goggles necessitated easing off. Musso passed on lap 34, and a great Fangio/Behra duel caught him on lap 48. Locking brakes caused Fangio to spin at Thillois, so 'L-E' salvaged third from his deserved winning position. Stuart Lewis-Evans is, undeservedly, almost a forgotten man of Grand Prix racing. BRM's season got much worse as, with Salvadori at Vanwall and Flockhart injured, the replacement driver Herbert Mackay-Fraser, who had driven well at Rouen, died in a preliminary F2 race. BRM was now without drivers.

1st	L Musso (W)	Ferrari 801 in 2h-33m-02.6s	123.40
2nd	J Behra (W)	Maserati 250F	27.5s
3rd	S Lewis-Evans (W)	Vanwall VW/57	1m-16s
F lap	J Behra (W)	Maserati 250F in 2m-27.8s	125.68

✲✲✲ (WC4) XII British Grand Prix (Aintree)
90 laps of a 3.00 mile circuit = 270 miles.
19 entries – 18 starters – 7 finished.
Front row: S Moss – 2m-00.2s (89.85mph); J Behra 0.2s;
A Brooks 0.2s.

20-JUL: Aintree provided the setting for a famous race – on four wheels not legs this time. The Vanwall team was back to strength, with Stuart Lewis-Evans being made a permanent member. BRM had engaged Jack Fairman and Les Leston, second string drivers for this race. Moss pulled away by a second a lap for ten laps, with Behra in pursuit. Brooks was third at first, but dropped back, still recovering from his Le Mans crash. At lap 22 the order was Moss, Behra, Hawthorn, Collins, Lewis-Evans and Brooks. Moss then pulled in with mis-firing and took over Brooks' car, but now down in ninth place. Behra led comfortably until his clutch exploded on lap 69. Hawthorn punctured on the debris, and, at the same time, Moss passed Lewis-Evans to lead the race. Now it was a Vanwall one-two. But Vanwall's throttle linkage jinx made Lewis-Evans pit and drop to seventh and last. Musso was the fortunate recipient of second place, while Moss even had time for a quick 'splash-n-dash' stop.

This was the first Championship win for a British car – a watershed moment in the Italian Red vs British Green battle.

1st	Brooks/Moss (W)	Vanwall VW/57 in 3h-06m-37.8s	86.80
2nd	L Musso (W)	Ferrari 801	25.6s
3rd	M Hawthorn (W)	Ferrari 801	42.8s
F lap	S Moss (W)	Vanwall VW/57 in 1m-59.2s	90.60r

Championship positions:
Fangio 25; Musso 13; Brooks 1.

✲ V Grand Prix de Caen
86 laps of 2.187 miles = 188.1 miles.
11 entries & starters – 7 finished
Front row: J Behra – 1m-21.1s (97.09mph); CAS Brooks 2.5s.
Row two: R Salvadori 3.4s; B Halford 4.1s.

28-JUL: How's this for flexibility! Maserati was hors de combat after Aintree, so Behra was freed from his contract, and persuaded BRM to enter as a top flight driver was now available ... him. Harry Schell's Maserati blew up in practice, and he was loaned the car taken by BRM as a spare. So, unexpectedly, a BRM Works team was there to oppose the Cooper Works. Tony Brooks' Rob Walker-entered Cooper bolstered the entry. Behra led Brooks and Salvadori at first, but soon Schell joined Behra at the front and they swapped the lead as they pulled away. BRM's one-two was spoiled

when Schell's engine blew up and Brooks retired, but Behra had gear problems so Salvadori closed up. Could he have won if he'd been aware of Behra's problem?

1st	J Behra (W)	BRM P25 in 2h-01m-35.0s	92.82
2nd	R Salvadori (W)	Cooper T43-Climax 2.0	12.2s
3rd	B Halford	Maserati 250F	27.0s
F lap	J Behra	BRM P25 in 1m-20.7s	97.57r

✲✲✲ (WC5) XIX Grosser Preis von Deutschland (N Nürburgring)
22 laps of 14.173 miles = 311.7 miles.
27 F1/F2 entries – 15 F1 started – 11 F1 finished.
First row: J-M Fangio – 9m-25.6s (90.2mph); M Hawthorn 2.8s; J Behra 4.9s; P Collins 9.1s.

04-AUG: An historic race. The lap record was smashed in practice by no less than sixteen seconds! The first seven cars on the grid were below it, but the Vanwalls were on the second row. This race was between three people – Hawthorn and Collins led Fangio for two laps, but on lap three it was Fangio, Collins and Hawthorn. Fangio had pulled out a lead of 28 seconds when he pitted for fuel and tyres on lap 11. The Ferrari team wasn't stopping, so by the time Fangio restarted he was almost 50 seconds behind, and in third place. What happened next has passed into legend. Fangio said afterwards that he never wanted to drive that hard again – his motto being: "Win at the slowest possible speed." His win at a greater speed than the previous lap record, and setting a new record no less than 24.2 seconds better than before, almost beggars belief! Musso won the other race: that is the one for fourth place, and was three minutes behind Collins, with Moss a further minute back. This drive had sealed Fangio's fifth World Championship with two races remaining – and he was 46 years old! That's old for a star racing driver on peak form, and unlikely ever to be beaten.

1st	J-M Fangio (W)	Maserati 250F in 3h-30m-38.3s	88.82
2nd	M Hawthorn (W)	Ferrari 801	3.6s
3rd	P Collins (W)	Ferrari 801	35.6s
F lap	J-M Fangio (W)	Maserati 250F in 9m-17.4s	91.54r

Championship positions:
Fangio 34 (WC); Musso 16; Hawthorn 13.

✲✲ (WC6) XXV Gran Premio di Pescara
18 laps of 15.89 miles = 286.1 miles.
16 entries and starters – 7 finished.

First row: J-M Fangio – 9m-44.6s (97.87mph); S Moss 10.1s; L Musso 15.4s.

18-AUG: How many races give rise to a book about just that one event? Richard Williams' evocative *The Last Road Race* is about this special one-off event. A substitute for the cancelled Dutch and Belgian GPs, it used the longest circuit ever for a Formula One race. Two long, mostly straight sections connected by a twisty, bumpy mountainous section suitable for a modern rally! After Castellotti's death at Modena in March, and the Mille Miglia tragedy in May, in which dePortago, his co-driver and nine spectators died, Enzo Ferrari felt aggrieved that officialdom wanted him blamed. His response was to officially boycott the race. After much pleading by Luigi Musso, who wished to defend his Championship runner-up position, a car was supplied for him. Maserati, Vanwall and Cooper sent teams, plus there were six non-Works Maseratis. Musso led off and retained the lead for a lap before Moss' slippery Vanwall went past and was untouchable on the fast straights. Fangio was only third ahead of Behra which did nothing to alter the suspicion that a special brew of fuel had been used in practice – not illegal but unusual. Musso's chase ended on lap ten when his oil tank split. Fangio spun on the oil and pitted to replace two buckled wheels. Behra lasted just four laps in fourth place, so when Musso stopped it was Schell who was chasing Fangio, having passed Bonnier's and Gregory's Maseratis. Brooks retired after a lap and Lewis-Evans experienced thrown tyre treads on lap three at 170mph! The Aintree victory had been repeated and Moss exactly matched Fangio's great pole lap.

1st	S Moss (W)	Vanwall VW/57 in 2h-59m-22.7s	95.69
2nd	J-M Fangio (W)	Maserati 250F	3m-14s
3rd	H Schell (W)	Maserati 250F	6m-47s
F lap	S Moss (W)	Vanwall VW/57 in 9m-44.6s	97.87r

Championship positions:
Fangio 40 (WC); Moss 17; Musso 16.

*** (WC7) XXVII Gran Premio d'Italia (Monza-Road)

87 laps of a 3.573 mile circuit = 310.84 miles.
18 entries and starters – 11 finished.
Front row: S Lewis-Evans – 1m-42.4s (125.61mph); S Moss 0.3s; A Brooks 0.5s; J-M Fangio 0.7s.

08-SEP: Four cars from each Italian marque, plus three Vanwalls made up the Works entries, plus there was the usual clutch of non-Works Maseratis (some grids would

have been sparse without them). Behra this time raced the V12 Maserati, but still the Vanwall team occupied the top three places on the grid. So much happens at Monza that it's easiest to list the race lead shared by five drivers as follows: Laps 1-3 Moss; lap four Behra; lap five Moss; lap six Behra; 7-10 Fangio; 11 Moss; 12-15 Brooks; 16-20 Lewis-Evans; 21-finish Moss chased by Fangio. Brooks suffered a sticking throttle, pitting on lap 19, and Lewis-Evans had engine trouble when leading and pitted on lap 23, so it was all down to Moss in the end. Vanwall was riding high with its cars unbeaten on the grid, held the lap record, and the team shared the lead for the last 76 laps. But for reliability issues, it would almost certainly be the team to beat in '58. Absent BRM must have been feeling sore at Vanwall's success.

1st	S Moss (W)	Vanwall VW/57 in 2h-35m-03.9s	120.28
2nd	J-M Fangio (W)	Maserati 250F	41.2s
3rd	W von Trips (W)	Ferrari 801	2 laps
F lap	CAS Brooks (W)	Vanwall VW/57 in 1m-43.7s	124.04r

Final Championship positions:
Fangio 40 (WC); Moss 25; Musso 16.

✳ IX International Trophy (Silverstone)

15 lap heat+35 lap final of 2.927 miles = 146.4 miles.
17 entries – 14 started – 9 finished.
Poles: Heat one – CAS Brooks – 1m-43.0s (102.30mph). Heat two – H Schell – 1-44.8s (100.54mph).

14-SEP: The combination of being put back from May because of fuel restrictions following the Suez crisis and being only six days after Monza reduced the Works entries. Maserati and Ferrari didn't enter, and Vanwall withdrew, so Brooks was in the Walker Cooper again, and Behra and Schell were available. So BRM, having skipped races and being without a top flight driver, now had a full house. It would have wanted to show its worth against Vanwall, though. Brooks, amazingly, produced the fastest pole with his 1960cc Cooper, and with just 176bhp against 250+ for the BRMs and Maseratis. Sadly, though, his final drive broke on the line in heat one, which Behra won easily, from Flockhart (in the process breaking the Vanwall lap record from 1956). Schell won heat two by seven seconds from Brabham, so the final looked like a BRM benefit. But would the BRMs last? Amazingly, they all did, and gave a demonstration that might well have challenged Vanwall. Bonnier's Maserati lost to Flockhart by one second, but led a trio of 250Fs, with Gregory fifth.

1st	J Behra (W)	BRM P25 in 1h-01m-30s	99.96
2nd	H Schell (W)	BRM P25	1m-30s
3rd	R Flockhart (W)	BRM P25	1m-36s
F lap	J Behra (heat 1)	BRM P25 in 1m-42.0s	103.31r

1st	J Behra (W)	Maserati 250F in 2h-18m-23.0s	112.65
2nd	S Lewis-Evans (W)	Vanwall VW/57	30.1s
3rd	M Trintignant (W)	BRM P25	1m-26s
F lap	J-M Fangio (W)	Maserati 250F in 2m-25.6s	116.80

✳ V Gran Premio di Modena

2x 40 laps of 1.471 miles = 117.7 miles.

14 entries – 10 started – 7 finished.

Front row: J Behra; L Musso; H Schell (no times available).

22-SEP: Maserati (4), BRM (2), and Ferrari (2) were the Works teams. Stuart Lewis-Evans agreed to drive for BRM here, thinking that Mr Vandervell had agreed. He hadn't been asked, so declined to release him. A pity, as he'd allowed Brooks to drive at Silverstone. Ferrari used F2 type Dino 156s, with two-litre engines, as a trial for 1958, and Musso was only 20 secconds behind Behra in heat one. Heat two was an exact repeat, with Collins (Ferrari) fourth each time. BRM had Flockhart and Lewis-Evans' replacement, Joachim Bonnier, but they were sixth and seventh in heat one, and retired from heat two.

1st	J Behra (W)	Maserati 250F in 1h-24m-47.9s	83.42
2nd	L Musso (W)	Ferrari Dino 196 1.96 ltr	40.3s
3rd	H Schell (W)	Maserati 250F	1m-9s
F lap	Behra/Musso	Maserati / Ferrari in 1m-02.2s	85.14

✳✳✳ VI Grand Prix de Maroc (Ain Diab)

55 laps of 4.724 miles = 259.8 miles.

16 entries – 14 started – 8 finished

Front row: CAS Brooks – 2m-23.3s (116.80mph); J Behra 0.2s; S Lewis-Evans 2.9s

27-OCT: This was a trial for World Championship status the following year, and every major team entered. Ferrari debuted its Dino 246 V6 cars, now with 2.2- and 2.4-litre engines for Hawthorn and Collins respectively. Sadly, flu affected Moss after he'd recorded third fastest time, but Fangio and Hawthorn managed to race. Collins' light-fuelled Ferrari led lap one from Behra, Brooks, Lewis-Evans and Fangio. Lap eight saw Collins spin, so Behra led with Brooks close on Collins' tail. Collins hit the straw bales on lap 16, and Brooks pitted, so both were out. Fangio went into second only to spin and having to pit for repairs. Behra then cruised to a great victory. Formula One records cover only World Championship races, and suggest that Jean Behra was not of a Formula One winner's calibre. He now has a hat-trick against all-comers, proving the falsehood of this – as his contemporaries well knew.

1957 seasonal review

Notwithstanding the fuel shortage, a good season's racing took place, with decent non-Championship races again outnumbering the World Championship rounds 10 to 7, so participation was important for a Formula One entrant. The Aintree '200' was lost to organisational nervousness due to fuel rationing in Britain following the Suez crisis. Fortunately, though, the Silverstone International Trophy was run later, but its entry suffered due to proximity with Championship rounds. Jean Behra was dominant in this branch of the Formula One scene, with five wins and two seconds from eight starts; an amazing result. His true credentials showed in the Grand Prix in Morocco, where the field was of World Championship quality; definitely better than the Argentine GP – as was Reims.

In early December came the unsurprising but disappointing news that Maserati had withdrawn from Works participation in F1, and maybe all racing. The 250F was now four years old, yet had just powered Fangio to the Championship, but the V12 engine had disappointed, and sports car racing had soaked up funds. Ferrari's new V6 car had shown Maserati that a new car was needed, but Maserati couldn't afford it (Ferrari was funded by Fiat). This meant that of the six Works teams in January only half remained: Ferrari, Vanwall and BRM, none of which sold cars like Maserati. Formula One could have been poor but for those customer Maseratis.

The Ferrari Dino 246 had proved a potentially good replacement for the outdated Lancia-derived car in Morocco, so a poor year ended on an optimistic note. As did BRM, following its Silverstone result, which, while not against top opposition, produced a lap record and reliability not seen before. Vanwall's late Championship performances with speed and reliability had shown clearly that it was now the team to beat. Thank goodness Cooper had joined in with cars run by the Works and Rob Walker. Cooper's lucky but amazing Monaco performance was not repeated, so it was still an unknown quantity and not thought a threat. Little did people know what was around the corner! At the year's end Ferrari was the only non-British manufacturer in Formula One, so no serious F1 race could take place without the British who had now learned how to win.

*Winners of the 17 F1 races of 1957 –
quantity & quality of success*

5 wins	J-M Fangio (3A, 2B) J Behra (A, 4C)	8 wins	Maserati (5A, B, 2C)
3 wins	S Moss (2A, B)	3 wins	Vanwall (2A, B) Lancia-Ferrari (2A, C)
2 wins	P Collins (A, C)	2 wins	BRM (2C)
1 win	L Musso (A) S Lewis-Evans (C)	1 win	Connaught (C)

World Championship review

After a good 1956, what a shame that the Championship
was in turmoil again, reducing from the eight original
rounds to five, then recovering to seven. It is an indication
of the strength of the two Italian marques at that time that
the Belgian and Dutch Grands Prix were cancelled because
of their non-participation, yet the Argentine GP had been
accepted as Championship standard despite only those
two Works teams sending cars. British Works teams from
Vanwall, Connaught, BRM and now Cooper, plus some
good private Maseratis, would have provided a larger field
in Belgium and the Netherlands than had taken part in
Argentina, but organisers clearly didn't believe they had the
crowd pulling power. The likes of Hawthorn, Behra and even
Fangio were known to have had contracts releasing them
to drive for other teams when their principal employers
didn't race, but there doesn't seem to be any record of any
approaches in the cases of Belgium and Holland at the
time. So there was no Championship rule as to what was a
minimum required level of competition for either drivers or
entrants.

Ferrari failed to win a Championship race for the first
time since 1950, while Vanwall won three of the last four.
Maserati won the remaining four rounds thanks to Fangio,
who won his fifth World Title. No one else has won three
successive Championships in three different cars, and maybe
never will since the driver's contribution to victory in the
twenty-first century, it must be admitted, is less than it was
then. His victory was achieved with two of the seven rounds
left, and included a performance in Germany which was
his best ever, and has rightly attained legendary status. His
position was now rather ambiguous, though, as he hadn't
signed with any team, and it was thought he might be on the
point of retiring. Stirling Moss had lost two potential wins
at the start of his campaign, missed the French GP through
illness, and could have won at Aintree on his own if his
Vanwall had performed as well as the one he took over from
Brooks. These losses amounted to a massive 20 points, and
he was 15 points adrift of Fangio's 40 at the end of the season,
yet still runner-up. You have to say that his potential to take
the Championship from Fangio, if he'd shared his reliability,
is self-evident.

VISIT VELOCE ON THE WEB – WWW.VELOCE.CO.UK
All current books • New book news • Special offers • Gift vouchers • Forum

120

Varzi leads Wimille in Alfa-Romeo 158s at the 1947 Belgian GP. Sommer's Maserati is about to split them.

Monaco 1948. Wimille, second on the grid, actually led for a while in the little Simca-Gordini before dropping back.

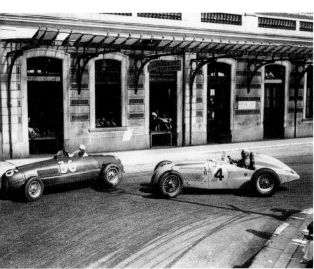

The first Ferrari in a classic GP, driven by Count Troubetskoy, about to fall to the Talbot of Yves Giraud-Cabantous at Monaco in 1948.

Chaboud's Delahaye leads Rosier's Talbot 26 into Tabac at Monaco, 1948. The latter retired and Chaboud was seventh.

Maestro of the Alfa-Romeo team Jean-Pierre Wimille winning at Reims in 1948.

Ascari leads Villoresi in the first Silverstone British GP, in October 1948, but gave best to his mentor, losing by five seconds.

Count Trossi's Alfa-Romeo 158 heading for victory in the 1948 Swiss GP. Dodgy surface – close crowd – 100mph track!

Celebrations afterwards at Silverstone '48. Blackened faces told that they'd been in a race in those days.

1949 Jersey Road Race – Peter Whitehead's Ferrari leads Villoresi's Maserati at St Helier's West Park hairpin,

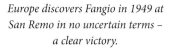

Bira leads Villo (Maseratis) at the unpopular Club Corner hairpin in the 1949 British GP.

Europe discovers Fangio in 1949 at San Remo in no uncertain terms – a clear victory.

deGraffenried heads for an unexpected victory in the 1949 British Grand Prix, as others encounter trouble.

Monza 1949. The Maestro listens to 'Phi-phi' Etancelin, who's wearing his race headgear reversed – really – well yes!"

At Bremgarten, 1949, deGraffenried leads Villoresi after the start. Ascari has passed and soon Villoresi will.

Chiron heads 'Levegh' in Talbots at the 1949 French GP. Bira lost the race to Chiron after needing to refuel.

Reg Parnell's Maserati 4CLT/48 vainly chases Whitehead's Ferrari (out of shot) at St Helier in 1950 – a fast street circuit.

Monaco 1950. Ascari gets through the mayhem. "Stop the race! Never!" Note the absence of shrapnel.

Ascari and Ferrari at Pedralbes in 1950 – so often unbeatable. Note human crash barrier: not even a rope!

Dorino Serafini leads the Ferraris away best at Pedralbes in 1950, but soon Ascari is ahead for good.

In 1950, Manzon's Gordini got to fourth before retirement at Pedralbes. Almost a 'lion dressed as a lamb.'

1950. Fangio about to pass Fagioli on the Reims-Gueux circuit and take up the chase of Farina.

No hesitation in those days. Even hailstones weren't stopping the 1951 International Trophy final at Silverstone.

Parnell masters the conditions best.

Reg Parnell congratulates the 1951 Ulster victor 'Nino' Farina – in his own way.

1951 British GP. Fangio holds off González' Ferrari but pit stops meant he couldn't prevent his historic victory.

Stirling Moss in a HWM-Alta at San Remo in 1951. Fifth in an F2 car was very creditable and marked him out.

International Trophy, 1951, and Parnell's 'Thinwall Special' is about to pass Bonetto's Alfa-Romeo for second in heat one.

The Ferraris of Villoresi, Ascari and González, and Chiron's Talbot-Lago, lead off at Pescara in 1951.

1951 British GP. Reg Parnell gets the leading V16 BRM into fifth place despite being scalded by inboard exhaust pipes.

At Boreham in 1952, Harry Schell controls a slide in his Maserati-
Platé in a very wet F1/F2, race only to retire.

Behra's performance at Spa in 1952, in his 'cute' Gordini astonished as he
mixed it with the Ferraris, only to be taken out by Taruffi's spin.

Hawthorn's Cooper-Bristol amazed with a front row position then matching Ascari at the start of the 1952 Dutch GP. A Ferrari Works drive was his reward.

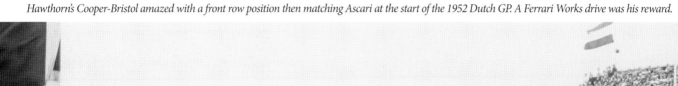

Froilán González gets the best result for Maserati all year, with second to Ascari in the 1952 Italian GP.

Felice Bonetto's Maserati did get the better of Andre Simon's Ferrari, though, for fifth.

'Smile please!' Was he really using a flash in Bonetto's face? And our cameraman?

Andre Simon's Gordini about to be caught by Ascari's Ferrari at Pau, in 1953. How little lateral support!

Argentina 1953. Ascari and Fangio, now recovered, meet at last in the latter's homeland, but a 'local' victory didn't occur.

At Ulster, in 1953, Ken Wharton's Cooper-Bristol leads Mike Hawthorn's Ferrari – but not for long.

A rare F1 race in 1953. Rosier's Ferrari was swallowed by Fangio's BRM at Albi, but his reliability prevailed.

In Holland in 1953, Moss' Connaught 'A' made a good start to seventh place, but a long pit stop spoiled his race.

Fangio leads Ascari away, but only for half a lap, at the 1953 German GP ...

... he lost a wheel, handing victory to Farina.

González wins the 1954 Daily Express International Trophy – a feat he would repeat in the British GP in July.

At Reims in 1954, a bulky, but great, man, about to occupy a bulky, but not-so-great, Ferrari Squalo.

When it's wet at Silverstone IT'S WET. Start of heat one in the 1954 International Trophy – González already out of view.

1954 International Trophy. Moss' Maserati and Behra's Gordini battled for second in the final, until Moss retired.

Fangio and Kling in the Mercedes streamliners which suited the superfast Reims course in 1954.

Moss and Maserati master Oulton Park Gold Cup in 1954. Winning from the back on this new circuit.

1954 British GP. Not Fangio's best race. His streamliner unsuited to the circuit and striking marker barrels.

A great study of Moss about to fly through Eau Rouge at Spa, 1954 – suspension fully compressed.

At the 1954 Spanish GP, Moss and Fangio swapped places five times in 16 laps before Moss retired.

1955 Buenos Aires GP, and Farina flings his car ahead of Kling, then Moss and Fangio, to win part one.

Stirling Moss and his blackened face celebrate his maiden Championship win, beating Fangio at Aintree in 1955.

Monaco 1955. Ascari's Lancia retrieved from its resting place after his crash at the chicane. He was about to lead.

At Zandvoort in 1955, Fangio and Moss' Mercedes gobble up Manzon's Gordini at Tarzan.

Behra's #2 Maserati split the Mercedes at the 1955 British GP grid, and hung on for nine laps before retiring.

The great Archie Scott-Brown leads Moss at Goodwood, Easter 1955, both having disposed of Hawthorn ...

... whose car disposed of itself after suspension seizure. He was thrown out. That was how to survive then.

Collins' BRM and Hawthorn's Lancia D50 battle for third early in the 1955 Gold Cup at Oulton Park.

Fangio's Lancia-Ferrari at Silverstone in May '56. Clutch trouble spoiled a battle with Moss' Vanwall.

The start of the legendary 1956 International Trophy at Silverstone. Moss on pole, Schell, Fangio, Hawthorn. The Brits mean business.

A beautiful 4-wheel drift (now sadly a lost art) from Moss before gearbox problems cost him his lead in the 1956 British GP.

British GP, and Fangio and Lancia make up for International Trophy defeat with a little help from Moss' Maserati gearbox.

British GP, 1956. It looks worse than it was as Tony Brooks was thrown out and not seriously hurt. Seat belts no use then.

A plane with wheels for wings. The beautiful lines of the Vanwall show why it was fast at Silverstone in May International Trophy, 1956.

But Moss had to pass teammate Harry Schell, who was no slouch, to win at Silverstone.

Afterwards, Moss addresses the 100,000-strong crowd, while others hold the loot! F3 winner Jim Russell is next to Moss.

…unlike earlier at the chicane. Fangio passes
Hawthorn and Collins' crashed Ferraris.

Fangio, Collins and Moss with six, eight and four
cylinders respectively at Monaco, 1957. The age of
motor racing music. Now it's pure monotony.

Monaco 1957, and Brooks' Vanwall follows Flockhart's BRM in an almost serene scene ...

Monza 1957. A front row lock-down, with Fangio
just visible and seemingly a support act. He did lead
for a while, though.

At the delayed 1957 International Trophy, Brooks
took over Fairman's car, made up all the time from
the stop, and chased Bueb's Maserati, but retired.

Monaco 1957, and Brabham pushes home after over three hours of racing, as a podium finish
had been snatched away.

'The Kansas Flash' Masten Gregory's Maserati wears American colours en-route to fourth place at Pescara in 1957.

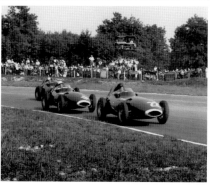

Italian GP 1957, and three Vanwalls shared the lead – Brooks here leading Moss and Lewis-Evans. But only Moss survived.

The 1957 International Trophy and, in heat one, Brooks' Cooper from pole is about to lose his transmission, to the benefit of Behra and Flockhart.

International Trophy 1958, Moss #7 takes McLaren and catches Allison after his bad start, but retired on lap 18 with gearbox trouble.

Moss just holds off Brabham at the 1958 Aintree '200,' despite a slipping clutch.

1958 Easter Goodwood. Brake failure caused Behra's BRM to swipe the solid chicane. He lost a wheel ... gaining (thankfully) just bruises.

In the 1958 Morocco GP, Phil Hill leads team leader Hawthorn before yielding to help his #1 to the world title.

Goodwood 1958. Hawthorn exits the now revised chicane and shows the quality of the Ferrari Dino 246 with a win.

Chapter 17

1958

Almost a new formula

A real shake-up occurred when it was announced that, from 1958, engines would have to run on 'pump fuel.' This meant aviation spirit of 130 octane. Roadside petrol varied between countries, so they weren't using what you put in your car. This caused problems for Vanwall and BRM in particular, as the engines were losing the cooling properties of alcohol-based fuels for which they were originally designed. Ferrari's new V6 had been designed with 130 octane in mind, and the Coventry Climax engine used by Cooper was also suitable. Championship rounds were reduced in length from 500km to 300km, or two hours' duration, so refuelling would be less frequent (if required at all).

The number of F1 races beyond the Championship had reduced after 1957 because, with the arrival of Climax-powered Cooper and Lotus cars, Formula Two cars looked and sounded just like their Formula One 'elder sisters,' were driven by many of the Grand Prix stars of the day, and, with them at the wheel, were only about four per cent slower. Formula Two was also cheaper to put on, not governed by any F1 type starting money scale, and cars were plentiful. Ferrari's F2 car had won the 190-mile Reims F2 race after a battle with the Works Coopers. This started the movement of Formula Two into a major category, in which newcomers would compete with top F1 stars.

A new World Championship of Constructors was introduced, but drivers would not be allowed to share a drive on penalty of losing any Championship points gained. This sorted out the strange business of there being only a Driver's Championship, yet a driver taking over a car might not have completed the whole race distance but could score points – it was the car which went the distance but there had been no Championship to recognise that. The Championships now encompassed ten rounds with the best six results to count.

The Vanwall driver strength remained unaltered, with Stirling Moss, Tony Brooks and Stuart Lewis-Evans. The car was as per the previous year, with just detail improvements. They provided the only driver team to match …

Ferrari had Mike Hawthorn, Peter Collins and Luigi Musso. The car was the 2417cc Dino 246, as had been tested in the previous year's Moroccan GP, and been impressive.

BRM had recruited Jean Behra and Harry Schell as regulars, with a varying driver for a third car when entered. The Type 25 was also developed from the 1957 car.

Cooper had retained the superb technical and driving skills of Jack Brabham and the very experienced Roy Salvadori. A new T45 car for a 2.2-litre engine would appear.

Newcomer Team Lotus was known to be adapting its Formula Two car, the tiny Type 12 to take the larger Climax engine, and was entering the Formula One scene with Cliff Allison and Graham Hill. Later in the year Lotus introduced the smart-looking 16 – a miniature Vanwall, some said, and with justification, as Colin Chapman of Lotus and aerodynamicist Frank Costin had been heavily involved in both. So those were all the Works teams.

Of the non-Works teams, the Connaughts were welcomed back on the grid, the whole outfit having been bought by a 27 year-old car salesman called Bernard Ecclestone, but it was now a non-Works team. The main driver was Archie Scott-Brown. Non-Works teams would begin to feature more than recently, particularly the brilliant team of RRC (Rob) Walker who had the latest Coopers to be driven by Maurice Trintignant and, thankfully when not required by Vanwall, Stirling Moss or Tony Brooks. Disappointingly, I think, Vanwall was only interested in World Championship events, so Moss and a Walker Cooper were seen quite often early on – in one case very memorably!

Stirling Moss' father, along with manager Ken Gregory, formed a team called 'British Racing Partnership,' also using Coopers. Maseratis would still be seen in some quantity, run by the independent team Scuderia Centro-Sud and individual privateers. Masten Gregory had driven for SC-S in 1957, and was in demand. The Works must have provided some support.

The Championship got off to a shaky start when the first round in mid-January in Argentina was thought to have been cancelled and then reinstated. Vanwall and BRM only got to hear of this reinstatement in mid-December, which was too late to prepare the cars and arrange shipment. Were they slow in adapting their engines to the new fuel, thinking they still had a couple of months more before the season started? It's not as though this was a new event on the calendar, as it had occupied the same week in January since 1953. *Autosport* magazine in Britain was adamant that the race should be stripped of its Championship status, but failed. Hindsight is happy about that as a piece of Grand Prix heritage would have been lost. Certainly its entry quality was beaten by many a non-Championship race, but it wasn't as bad as the 2005 USGP – but then nothing could ever be.

The Grand Prix driver's diary of single-seater racing for 1958

19th January	F1 – **Gran Premio do Argentina** at Buenos Aires (Ag) – 194.5 miles
2nd February	F1 – Grand Prix de Buenos Aires (Ag) – 175.5 miles
7th April	F1 – Glover Trophy at Goodwood (UK) – 100.8 miles
7th April	F2 – Lavant Cup at Goodwood (UK) – 36 miles
13th April	F1 – Gran Premio di Siracusa (I) – 205.1 miles
19th April	F1/2 – Aintree '200' (UK) – 201 miles
3rd May	F1/2 – *Daily Express* International Trophy at Silverstone (UK) – 146.4 miles
18th May	F1 – **Grand Prix de Monaco** (M) – 195.4 miles
25th May	F1 – **Grote Prijs van Nederland** (N) – 195.4 miles
15th June	F1 – **Grand Prix de Belgique** at Spa Francorchamps (B) – 210.3 miles
6th July	F1 – **Grand Prix de l'ACF** at Reims(F) – 257.9 miles
6th July	F2 – Coupe International de Vitesse at Reims (F) – 154.7 miles
19th July	F1 – **British Grand Prix** at Silverstone (UK) – 219.5 miles
20th July	F1 – Grand Prix de Caen (F) – 188.1 miles
27th July	F2 – Trophée d'Auvergne at Clermont

Ferrand (F) – 100.1 miles

3rd August	F1 – **Grosse Preis von Deutschland** at Nürburgring (D) – 309.4 miles
4th August	F2 – Kent Trophy at Brands Hatch (UK) – 52.1 miles
24th August	F1 – **Grande Premio de Portugal** at Oporto (P) – 230.1 miles
30th August	F2 – 'Kentish 100' at Brands Hatch (UK) – 104.1 miles
7th September	F1 – **Gran Premio d'Italia at Monza** (I) – 257.3 miles
19th October	F1 – **Grand Prix de Maroc** at Casablanca (Mo) – 250.9 miles

21 events of total race mileage = 3794 miles.
Events in bold are World Championship rounds – 62.5 per cent of F1 races run.
Formula Two dates above are those with a strong F1 driver contingent.

✳ (WC1) XII Gran Premio de la Republica Argentina (Buenos Aires No 2)
80 laps of 2.431 miles = 194.5 miles.
17 entries – 10 started – 9 finished.

Front row: J-M Fangio – 1m-42.0s (85.79mph); M Hawthorn 0.6s; P Collins 0.6s; J Behra 0.7s.

19-JAN: A Works Ferrari and three Maseratis were still en-route, and Centro-Sud withdrew its cars, which left only ten. Vanwall and BRM weren't ready, so the three Ferraris were the only Works cars, plus six Maseratis and a little Cooper-Climax which gave away half a litre to the others. Collins' Ferrari broke a drive-shaft at the start, so only nine cars left the line – and they all finished – unheard of in that era! Behra's Maserati led for a lap, and was passed by Hawthorn's Ferrari who led for eight laps, then it was Fangio until he pitted on lap 34. By this time Moss had passed Musso and Behra, and Hawthorn had pitted to check something. So it was Moss who assumed the lead from Musso. Ferrari wasn't worried as the Cooper would have to make a long stop for tyres, each wheel having four bolts to undo. The fresh tyres were out ready and waiting – but Moss didn't stop and a piece of simple gamesmanship and superb tyre management by Moss produced an historic and prophetic victory.

1st	S Moss (RW)	CooperT43-Climax 2.0 in 2h-19m-33.7s	83.60
2nd	L Musso (W)	Ferrari Dino 246	2.7s
3rd	M Hawthorn (W)	Ferrari Dino 246	12.6s
F lap	J-M Fangio (SSA)	Maserati 250F in 1m-41.8s	85.96r

✶✶ XII Grand Prix de Buenos Aires (Buenos-Aires No 4)
2 x 30 laps of 2.925 = 175.5 miles.
12 F1 starters – 5 finished.

Front row: J-M Fangio – 2m-14.8s (78.11mph);
C Menditeguy; S Moss – times unknown.

02-FEB: The Works Ferrari for von Trips, and Bonnier's Maserati had now arrived. A wet start saw Hawthorn lead from Fangio while Collins' drive failed again. Moss was T-boned from fifth by a local on lap two – a favourite out in heat one. Hawthorn took the flag 31 seconds ahead of Fangio, with Musso third. Part two, and Hawthorn had Collins' start-line jinx so a duel with Fangio didn't happen. On lap three Musso took the lead and started to draw away, but spun, retaining his lead. But he was cautious after the spin, and Fangio passed to win heat two from Menditeguy, Musso and Behra. So a second and first gave Fangio the aggregate win; second and third produced second for Musso; and fifth and second gave Menditeguy third overall. Jean Behra and Joakim Bonnier's Maseratis completed the F1 finishers. Behra had missed the start of heat one due to a misunderstanding over the start time, and took over the Godia Maserati after a lap. Six local Formule Libre cars started – the best finishing sixth, a lap behind Bonnier. Would anyone have beaten Moss in this rain affected two-parter? Doubtful. The F1 brigade had a clear run – this was a true Formula One race.

1st	J-M Fangio (SSA)	Maserati 250F in 2h-37m-48.3s	66.73
2nd	L Musso (W)	Ferrari Dino 246	1m-9s
3rd	C Menditeguy (SSA)	Maserati 250F	1 lap
F lap	S Moss (RW)	CooperT43-Climax2.0 in 2m-34.0s	68.37

✶✶✶ VI Glover Trophy (Goodwood)
42 laps of 2.4 miles = 100.8 miles.
24 entries – 17 started – 11 finished.

Front row: S Moss; J Behra; M Hawthorn; R Salvadori. No times available.

07-APR: No F1 clash with Pau this time, so a top entry, better than the Argentine GP, was received. Ferrari entered two cars, but sent just one for Hawthorn. BRM and Cooper teams were there, and a new Works team called Team Lotus made its F1 debut. Moss stalled on pole position, so Behra's BRM led the first four laps, when total brake failure produced a collision with the solid chicane. He was lucky to escape with bruising whilst ripping off a front wheel. Hawthorn led from Brabham with Moss amazingly already third. Soon after Schell's BRM stopped with the rear brake stuck on – brakes again! Moss took second on lap ten, but his chase of

Hawthorn ended on lap 22 when his engine blew-up and almost took out Brabham. Allison's Lotus 12 was fourth, beating the Connaughts of Lewis-Evans and Scott-Brown. A good win for Ferrari, but the Vanwalls were absent.

1st	M Hawthorn (W)	Ferrari Dino 246 in 1h-03m-44.4s	94.89
2nd	J Brabham (W)	Cooper T45-Climax 2.0	36.0s
3rd	R Salvadori (W)	Cooper T45-Climax 2.0	1 lap
F lap	Moss/Hawthorn	Cooper T43 / Ferrari in 1m-28.8s	97.30r

VIII Gran Premio di Siracusa
205.1m – 60 laps of 3.418 miles = 205.1 miles.
14 entries – 12 started – 6 finished.

Front row: L Musso – 1m-58.4s (103.91mph); G Scarlatti 3.3s; J Bonnier 3.5s.

13-APR: One Works Ferrari, a Works OSCA and a ten private Maseratis made up the field – much reduced in quality from 1957. Musso was fastest in practice, but midfield was Maria-Therese deFillipis, the first woman to start a Formula One race. Musso led all the way, while Jo Bonnier and Giorgio Scarlatti fought for second until Scarlatti spun out. Masten Gregory lost third with engine failure. The lady was fifth, four laps down. Times were way off the record. Just about qualifies for this list.

1st	L Musso (W)	Ferrari Dino 246 in 2h-2m-44.5s	100.23
2nd	J Bonnier	Maserati 250F	1 lap
F lap	L Musso	Ferrari Dino 246 in 1m-59.1s	103.30

✶✶ 2nd International 'Aintree 200'
67 laps of 3 miles = 201 miles.
14 F1+17 F2 entries – 12 F1 started – 6 F1 finished.

Front row: J Behra – 1m-59.8s (90.15mph); R Salvadori 0.4s; S Moss 0.8s.

19-APR: A lone BRM plus a few Connaughts and Maseratis were against the Cooper and Lotus 'new boys.' However, on this 'point and squirt' circuit, nimbleness paid off. Moss led away from Behra and Salvadori, but soon Brabham was second, chased by Behra who took his place on lap 16 but failed to close on Moss and retired on lap 29 with the usual brake trouble. After a 57 second pit stop Brabham charged after Moss, whose clutch was slipping, and produced a gripping finish. Tony Brooks' finish, just 65 seconds behind in 67 laps, in a car giving away 500cc or more to the others, can only be described as amazing. His fastest lap was 2m-04.4s ... would have been fifth on the grid! In 13th place on his British debut came Bruce McLaren.

1st	S Moss (RW)	CooperT45-Climax 2.0 in 2h-20m-47.0s	85.66
2nd	J Brabham (W)	Cooper T45-Climax 2.0	0.2s
3rd	CAS Brooks (RW)	Cooper T45-Climax 1.5 (F2)	1m-5s
F lap	J Brabham	Cooper T45-Climax 2.0 in 2m-01.4s	88.96

✱✱✱ X *Daily Express* International Trophy (Silverstone)

50 laps of 2.927 miles = 146.4 miles.

18 F1+15 F2 entries – 18 F1 started – 11 F1 finished.

Front row: R Salvadori – 1m-40.8s (104.54mph); J Brabham 0.6s; S Moss 1.0s; P Collins 1.0s.

03-MAY: An excellent entry for this important race, but this time Collins had the Ferrari. Moss was in Rob Walker's Cooper, again with 2.2-litre Climax engine, but stalled on the line as at Goodwood. Collins led away from Behra, Flockhart and Gregory on lap one, but Behra passed on lap five, having already smashed the lap record. On lap ten, a stone smashed his goggles and cut his eye. Brabham had come through to challenge Collins for the lead, but pitted to clear his carburettor, so Flockhart's BRM was second from Salvadori. Collins had a 15-second lead, but spun at Copse corner, losing just a few seconds but not the lead. A near disaster occurred when Halford's Maserati spun and was being push-started by marshals (on the track!) when a Cooper and Flockhart arrived. They missed the Maserati and marshals, but Flockhart hit wheels with the swerving Cooper, was launched, hit the bank and was out. Moss recovered to sixth on lap 18, but retired. Graham Hill's Lotus 12 was fourth at half way, but suffered fuel starvation. A very entertaining race, with Gregory proving that the 250F Maserati was not quite finished yet, and Lotus was looking serious. Behra's charge back to fourth was a very brave effort. After his brake problems at Goodwood and Aintree, this was incredibly bad luck for him, and BRM's woes were compounded by Flockhart's misfortune. Jean Behra set the new track record on lap two – the first flying lap! How was it possible then? It's impossible now.

1st	P Collins (W)	Ferrari Dino 246 in 1h-26m-14.6s	101.82
2nd	R Salvadori (W)	Cooper T45-Climax 2.0	23.4s
3rd	M Gregory (SCS)	Maserati 250F	36.4s
F lap	J Behra/P Collins	BRM P25/ Ferrari Dino in 1m-40.0s	105.37r

✱✱✱ (WC2) XVI Grand Prix de Monaco (Monte Carlo)

100 laps of 1.954 mile circuit = 195.4 miles.

28 entries – 16 qualified – 6 finished

Front row: CAS Brooks – 1m-39.8s (70.49mph); J Behra 1.0s; J Brabham 1.2s.

18-MAY: A huge entry was received for just the 16 allowed starters. All 14 Works cars qualified, with Ron Flockhart, driving a Cooper T43 for Rob Walker, just failing with 1m-45.9s. The first three grid rows were all under Fangio's Mercedes 1955 record, and Brooks was fastest by a whole second. It was Behra, though, who led Brooks for 19 laps when the latter retired with no ignition. Eight laps later Behra's BRM brakes failed, and Hawthorn now led, having come through from eighth. Four laps later Moss took over, but his engine failed on lap 38, then Hawthorn's fuel pump packed in nine laps after that. So, steady Trintignant, in the well-prepared Walker Cooper, led from the two Ferraris, and that's how it stayed for the last half of the race. The Argentine surprise was no fluke at all, and never again would a private team beat the world's best in successive Championship races.

1st	M Trintignant (RW)	Cooper T45-Climax2.0 in 2h-52m-27.9s	67.99
2nd	L Musso (W)	Ferrari Dino 246	20.2s
3rd	P Collins (W)	Ferrari Dino 246	38.8s
F lap	M Hawthorn	Ferrari Dino 246 in 1m-40.8s	69.93r

Championship positions:
Musso 12: Moss and Trintignant 8.

✱✱✱ (WC3) VI Grote Prijs van Nederland (Zandvoort)

75 laps of a 2.605 mile circuit = 195.4 miles.

17 entries and starters – 11 finished.

Front row: S Lewis-Evans – 1m-37.1s (96.60mph); S Moss 0.9s; CAS Brooks 1.0s.

25-MAY: This race was by invitation only. The top teams, of course, but Dutchman deBeaufort in a Porsche RSK sports car? Needless to say he was last on the grid. An all-Vanwall front row led to a flag-to-flag victory for Stirling Moss. Behind him Lewis-Evans held off Schell until lap 12, and retired from third place on lap 46 with a dropped valve. Brooks dropped from fourth on lap two with axle trouble, his place taken by Salvadori, until deprived of it by Behra on lap 21. So the Cooper-Climax show came to an end and had to settle for fourth with Salvadori. Hawthorn's fifth place for Ferrari was the only point scorer in a non-British car. He'd never been higher in the race at any point. This was a great result for BRM – at last.

1st	S Moss (W)	Vanwall VW/57 in 2h-04m-49.2s	93.93
2nd	H Schell (W)	BRM P25	47.9s
3rd	J Behra (W)	BRM P25	1m-42s
F lap	S Moss (W)	Vanwall VW/57 in 1m-37.6s	96.10r

Championship positions:
Moss 17; Musso 12; Trintignant 8.

✱✱✱ (WC4) XIX Grand Prix de Belgique (Spa)
24 laps of 8.761 mile circuit = 210.3 miles.
21 entries – 19 started – 11 finished.

Front row: M Hawthorn – 3m-57.1s (133.03mph); L Musso 0.4s; S Moss 0.5s.

15-JUN: The track had been slightly eased since 1956, but no one expected that all the Ferraris and Vanwalls would be under four minutes. The front row was covered by half a second in a four-minute lap. A fourth car was entered by Scuderia Ferrari for Belgian Olivier Gendebien, who had raced twice for Ferrari in 1956. He was the lap record holder on this revised circuit, with a time of 4m-09.8s (126.26mph) in a 4.1-litre Ferrari from the previous year year. He was sixth on the grid and the last man under four minutes. A very long wait on the grid caused Collins' car to overheat. Moss led away, but a missed gear change on the first lap over-revved the engine and finished his race. Then Brooks and Collins mixed it for a few laps but then Collins' engine cried 'enough.' Gendebien acquitted himself very well, being in third place after a lap, and fourth behind Hawthorn a lap later. Braking for La Source hairpin on lap four, he was tapped in the rear by Lewis-Evans, contacted the inside barrier and stalled. Brooks, Hawthorn and Lewis-Evans then held the podium places unchanged until the end – but only just! Brooks' gearbox was seizing, Hawthorn's engine had a piston break, and Lewis-Evans' Vanwall finished with broken suspension. Cliff Allison's tiny, fragile-looking Lotus 12, in fourth place, nearly won, as all ahead finished crippled. Gendebien recovered from the very back to finish sixth, behind Schell's BRM. This had been by far the shortest Championship race duration yet, and ended in near farce. If it had been run over 36 laps like the following year (in 1960), how many would have finished?

1st	CAS Brooks (W)	Vanwall VW/57 in 1h-37m-06.3s	129.93
2nd	M Hawthorn (W)	Ferrari Dino 246	20.7s
3rd	S Lewis-Evans (W)	Vanwall VW/57	3m-01s
F lap	M Hawthorn (W)	Ferrari Dino 246 in 3m-58.3s	132.36r

Championship positions:
Moss 17; Hawthorn 14; Musso 12.

The new race length rule hadn't meant to produce such a race time, but it was entirely foreseeable here. The race time had been almost half an hour less than any previous Championship round, and the general reaction was that this was not how premier Grand Prix racing should be. *MotorSport* magazine reported that many wondered if that had been the main event – surely not, as the usual duration was an hour longer. Note was duly taken, and it would be eight years before another Championship race was completed in less than two hours. Yet 1.5 hours has been the norm in Formula One for years since two hours became the maximum duration. Television, of course, is to blame (if that's the right word), as it's TV audiences and the attraction to advertisers that produces the huge funds for the modern era. With the reliability of modern cars, would it not be preferable to return to two hours minimum? Surely viewers would accept that, as many other major sports last rather longer.

✱✱✱ (WC5) XLIV Grand Prix de l'ACF (Reims)
50 laps of a 5.158 mile circuit = 257.9 miles.
24 entries – 19 started – 11 finished.

Front row: M Hawthorn – 2m-21.7s (131.06mph); L Musso 0.7s; H Schell 1.4s.

06-JUL: Fangio was back, with a self-entered Maserati, his first race since February. The Dino 246 had closed the gap on Vanwall as regards straight line speed, and took the first two grid slots, with a BRM alongside. Moss was sixth. Schell and Brooks were fastest away, but Hawthorn was soon past, never to be headed. He was followed by teammates Musso and Collins, but the latter spun at Muizon when a small air-scoop dropped under his brake pedal. Dropping to 18th, he threw it at the pit as he passed. Behind Musso was Brooks and a battle with Moss, Fangio and Schell. On lap ten, Musso was trying to keep up with Hawthorn nut crashed at the notorious high speed first bend. He was thrown out and died soon after. Italy had lost its only top flight driver. Brooks dropped out, and Schell fell back to retire. Moss and Behra had a great scrap for second, swapping the lead every lap for 12 laps, but Behra's fuel pump put an end to that. Moss followed Hawthorn home, with Ferrari new recruit Wolfgang von Trips third, having come through from the back. Fangio was fourth – his final race. He had first raced in Europe at this track ten years earlier in a Simca-Gordini, and had gone unnoticed …

1st	M Hawthorn (W)	Ferrari Dino 246 in 2h-03m-21.3s	125.46
2nd	S Moss (W)	Vanwall VW/57	24.6s
3rd	W von Trips (W)	Ferrari Dino 246	59.7s
F lap	M Hawthorn (W)	Ferrari Dino 246 in 2m-24.9s	128.17r

Championship positions:
Moss and Hawthorn 23; Musso 12.

✱✱✱ (WC6) XIII British Grand Prix (Silverstone)

75 laps of 2.927 miles = 219.5 miles.
21 entries and starters – 9 finished.
Front row: S Moss – 1m-39.4s (106.01mph); H Schell 0.4s;
R Salvadori 0.6s; M Hawthorn 1.0s.

19-JUL: The Championship battle was now red-hot, and practice indicated a great race. The front row order being Moss (Vanwall), Schell (BRM), Salvadori (Cooper), and Hawthorn (Ferrari); all different marques and separated by a single second! But it was Collins from the second row who stormed off and led from Moss, Hawthorn and Schell. Then came Brooks and Salvadori. This was the first World Championship race I had attended, and I remember that the opinion of the crowd was that Collins' function was to entice Moss to burst his engine and then allow Hawthorn through to assist his Championship hopes. On lap 24 Moss' engine duly expired in smoke, but Collins was 23 seconds ahead of Hawthorn by then and led all the way home. Hawthorn pitted for oil on lap 44 but Collins' engine was okay. Salvadori and Lewis-Evans' long scrap was won by Salvadori by 0.2 seconds. No joy for Moss or Vanwall – fourth not good with a constructors title now on offer, but Moss must have been relieved that Collins and not Hawthorn had won the race, though Hawthorn also had fastest lap point.

1st	P Collins (W)	Ferrari Dino 246 in 2h-09m-04.2s	102.05
2nd	M Hawthorn (W)	Ferrari Dino 246	24.2s
3rd	R Salvadori (W)	Cooper T45-Climax 2.2	50.6s
F lap	M Hawthorn (W)	Ferrari Dino 246 in 1m-40.8s	104.54

Championship positions:
Hawthorn 30; Moss 23; Collins 14.

✱ VI Grand Prix de Caen

86 laps of 2.187 miles = 188.1 miles.
12 entries and starters – 7 finished.
Front row: S Moss: 1m-23.8s (93.95mph); J Behra 2.9s. Row two: B Halford 3.6s; M Trintignant 4.3s.

20-JUL: This race was the day after the British GP, yet two BRMs and the Rob Walker Coopers were here. A special practice was put on for the seven arrivals from Silverstone on a drying track. Moss and Behra fought for the lead early on, but Moss' car now had a 2.2-litre engine, and he pulled away. Behra's engine failed at half distance, and his teammate, Schell, retired with an oil leak. Bonnier and Halford scrapped

mightily, with the former always ahead at the line, but were no challenge to the leader. Three F2 cars also started, with Trintignant, also for Rob Walker, the winner of the three, in fourth place overall. Weren't they busy in those days?

1st	S Moss (RW)	Cooper T45-Climax 2.2 in 2h-00m-09.7s	93.93
2nd	J Bonnier	Maserati 250F	1 lap
3rd	B Halford	Maserati 250F	1 lap
F lap	J Behra (W)	BRM P25 in 1m-20.8s	97.43

✱✱ (WC7) XX Grosser Preis von Deutschland (N Nürburgring)

15 laps of 14.173 miles = 212.6 miles.
16 F1 + 14 F2 entries – 12 F1 started – 5 F1 finished.
Front row: M Hawthorn – 9m-14.0s (92.10mph); CAS Brooks 1.0s; S Moss 5.1s; P Collins 7.9s.

03-AUG: There were few F1 starters, as only two Vanwalls arrived, plus one each from the Cooper and Lotus Works, and four Centro-Sud Maseratis. In the F2 class, however, there was a Ferrari, a Lotus, and two Coopers, each from their respective Works. Moss made a great start, with Hawthorn's and Collins' Ferraris sandwiched between his and Brooks' Vanwalls. On lap three Moss put in a tremendous lap – eight seconds under Fangio's fantastic 1957 figure – and then, with a 17 second lead, retired with magneto trouble. In two years over half a minute had been taken off the lap record! The Ferraris were now in charge, Hawthorn leading lap four and Collins fove-ten. However, soon Brooks would do to them what Fangio did the year before, and took the lead from Collins during lap 11. Before the lap was over Collins had run wide trying to hold on to Brooks, crashed and suffered fatal head injuries on being thrown out. Hawthorn retired soon after with clutch trouble (or, since he had seen his closest friend crash, it might it have been with worry). Tony Brooks 'stepped-up-to-the-plate' wonderfully after Moss retired, and produced a near Moss-quality performance.

1st	CAS Brooks (W)	Vanwall VW/57 in 2h-21m-15.0s	90.31
2nd	R Salvadori (W)	Cooper T45-Climax 2.2	3m-30s
3rd	M Trintignant (RW)	Cooper T45-Climax 2.2	35.6s
F lap	S Moss (W)	Vanwall VW/57 in 9m-09.2s	92.90r

Championship positions:
Hawthorn 30; Moss 24; Brooks 16.

✳✳✳ (WC8) VII Grande Premio de Portugal (Oporto)

50 laps of 4.603 miles = 230.1 miles. 17 entries – 15 started – 10 finished.

Front row: S Moss – 2m-34.21s (107.46mph); M Hawthorn 0.05s; S Lewis-Evans 0.39s.

24-AUG: The first F1 race in Portugal was on a long street circuit, with tram-lines, cobbles, roundabouts, etc. How this new circuit came to have the facility to time cars fifty times more accurately than Silverstone is baffling. Moss led Hawthorn, lost the lead, claimed it back on lap eight, and just drove away easily as Hawthorn's brakes lost effectiveness. Schell, von Trips and Lewis-Evans scrapped for third but were soon passed by Behra. Hawthorn pitted for brake adjustment on lap 34, and repassed Behra in just six laps. The Vanwall pit hung a 'HAW-REC' (for record) sign to Moss as there was a point for fastest lap, but Moss thought it read 'HAW-REG' (regular) and ignored it. Lewis-Evans tucked in behind his team leader on being lapped, and, when Moss lapped Behra, Lewis-Evans followed him past Behra and into third place. Moss entered the last lap with Hawthorn the only unlapped runner just ahead. Hawthorn thought it was Lewis-Evans, slid wide on trying hard and Moss lapped him – and then let Hawthorn back ahead again. Now Hawthorn knew who was who. The two Vanwalls completed their race as Hawthorn started his last lap. He spun where he had slid last time, restarting on the slope by running off-track in reverse to the circuit. This accounts for the apparent massive winning margin achieved by Moss. Hawthorn was disqualified but reinstated when Moss explained that Hawthorn wasn't on the track – he'd seen him – which meant that Hawthorn retained his six points. This magnanimous gesture shows the code of honour that prevailed those days. Another example: Allison crashed his Lotus in practice, thankfully without injury, and was then offered a drive by Scuderia Centro-Sud chief 'Mimo' Dei' in his spare Maserati, the obscure driver of which hadn't turned up. It did 15 laps. Anything for pursuit of the game!

1st	S Moss (W)	Vanwall VW/57 in 2h-11m-27.80s	105.04
2nd	M Hawthorn (W)	Ferrari Dino 246	5m-13s
3rd	S Lewis-Evans (W)	Vanwall VW/57	1 lap
F lap	M Hawthorn (W)	Ferrari Dino 246 in 2m-32.37s	108.75

Championship positions:
Hawthorn 36; Moss 32; Brooks 16.

Stirling Moss lost the World Championship to Hawthorn by a single point. He says that it was his misreading of the pit sign that cost him that point. I rather think his sporting gesture cost much more – but integrity ruled then.

Either way, those factors caused Stirling Moss to miss the World Championship in 1958.

✳✳✳ (WC9) XXVIII Gran Premio d'Italia (Monza-Road)

70 laps of a 3.573 mile circuit = 250.1 miles.
21 entries and starters – 7 finished.

Front row: S Moss – 1m-40.5s (127.98mph); CAS Brooks 0.9s; M Hawthorn 1.3s; S Lewis-Evans 1.9s.

07-SEP: As per the previous year, the grid front row consisted of three Vanwalls and the Championship leader. It was Ferrari new-boy Phil Hill, though, who led for four laps, from Moss, Lewis-Evans, and Hawthorn (who passed one per lap to lead lap five). A tussle with Moss lasted eight laps when Moss lost second to Behra, got it back then retired (gearbox). Hawthorn led until lap 60 except when pitting for tyres, when Phil Hill led prior to his stop – he had recovered from an early loss of a tyre tread. Lewis-Evans had stopped on lap 30 from second, the order then Hawthorn, Hill, Gregory (old Maserati) and Brooks. Hill's tyre stop put Brooks into second on lap 46. Gregory, recovering from a Silverstone crash, handed over to Shelby late in the race, their shared fourth place gaining no points now. By lap 61 Brooks had eaten up Hawthorn's lead, and led with help from Hawthorn's slipping clutch.

1st	CAS Brooks (W)	Vanwall VW/57 in 2h-35m-03.9s	121.20
2nd	M Hawthorn (W)	Ferrari Dino 246	24.2s
3rd	P Hill (W)	Ferrari Dino 246	28.3s
F lap	P Hill (W)	Ferrari Dino 246 in 1m-42.9s	125.00r

Championship positions:
Hawthorn 40; Moss 32; Brooks 24.

✳✳✳ (WC10) VII Grand Prix de Maroc (Ain Diab)

53 laps of 4.734 miles = 250.9 miles.
20 F1 + 9 F2 entries – 19 F1 started – 12 F1 finished.

Front row: M Hawthorn – 2m-23.1s (119.08mph); S Moss 0.1s; S Lewis-Evans 0.6s.

19-OCT: This was the only Championship event ever held in North Africa. Moss had to win with fastest lap to take the crown, with Hawthorn not second. It was Phil Hill who led away from the second row, but Moss stamped his authority by the end of lap one and was never threatened. Hill, Hawthorn and Bonnier (BRM) followed. Lap three saw Hawthorn second but, four laps later, let Hill through to challenge and break Moss. Things got bad for Hawthorn's title bid when Brooks passed him on lap 16. They fought for ten laps, whereupon Brooks' engine failed. That was bad for Moss, whose lead was now well over a minute. Hill, inevitably, made way for Hawthorn on lap 39, and tailed him to the finish, so Hawthorn's second place gave him the title. Bonnier had followed all this to claim fourth place, but, just behind him, tragedy took place as Lewis-Evans' engine blew up and crashed on its oil. The driver jumped out ablaze and died a few days later from his burns. Triumph soiled by tragedy.

1st	S Moss (W)	Vanwall VW/57 in 2h-09m-15.1s	116.46
2nd	M Hawthorn (W)	Ferrari Dino 246	1m-25s
3rd	P Hill (W)	Ferrari Dino 246	1m-26s
F lap	S Moss (W)	Vanwall VW/57 in 2m-22.5s	119.59r

Final Championship positions:
Hawthorn 42(WC); Moss 41; Brooks 24.

Winners of the 16 F1 races of 1958 –
quantity & quality of success

6 wins	S Moss (3A, B, 2C)	6 wins	Vanwall (5A, B)
3 wins	T Brooks (2A, B)	5 wins	Ferrari (4A, D)
2 wins	M Hawthorn (2A) P Collins (2A)	4 wins	Cooper-Climax (A, B, 2C)
1 win	M Trintignant: (A) J-M Fangio (B) L Musso (D)	1 win	Maserati (B)

1958 seasonal review

The seeds of change were firmly sown in 1957, and the efforts of British constructors and drivers now bore rich fruit. The surprise win (to put it mildly) by Moss and the Rob Walker Cooper in Argentina was, with hindsight, even more of an achievement. Although its effectiveness against Vanwall and BRM remained unproven by their absence, the Ferrari Dino 246 it beat was soon proven to be a formidable race car – one of which was driven by the 'champion-to-be.' Yes, it was on a twisty track suited to a lightweight car, but he had only 176bhp against 260+ of the Ferrari. Yet after a whole season there was no sign of anyone taking note of the obvious potential of a Cooper-type car with Ferrari-type power. At Goodwood, Siracuse and Silverstone in April/May, Scuderia Ferrari entered only a single car, and it won on each occasion with different drivers so Ferrari was sure the Cooper wasn't a threat. It had however beaten BRM at Aintree with a little help from BRM's braking system, though the BRM had

never led the race. With the 2.2-litre Climax engine it was competitive everywhere and made the point at Caen when the Moss/Walker Cooper combo beat the BRM cleanly. BRM was well up to speed now, but brakes were still its Achilles' heel. After Goodwood and Aintree, Jean Behra must have been brave to get in it. No brake trouble at Silverstone, but the stone-in-the-face incident must have made him feel jinxed. When Vanwall finally appeared at Monaco, Stirling Moss was, of course, not available to Rob Walker, yet in an act of some irony it was Moss' Vanwall engine failure which let the Walker Cooper win again. One more lap at Spa would have seen Lotus in the winner's circle in its first season.

This is still one of the most tragic of all years, and saw the loss of three drivers: Luigi Musso, Peter Collins, and Stuart Lewis-Evans, each a proven or potential Grand Prix winner; the latter quality also applying to Archie Scott-Brown, killed by a sign post when leading in a sports racing car at Spa when Europeans wouldn't let him race in Formula One because of his handicap. If he'd survived surely they would have relented.

World Championship review

What a great two-way scrap for the title this year was. The Championship now expanded to ten races, and included what is still the only round ever run in North Africa, at Morocco on the Ain Diab circuit near Casablanca. The 'best six of ten' system in place this year kept the Championship alive until the last round, the first time since 1951, otherwise Hawthorn would have sealed it with a round to spare.

Terrific reliability and consistency for Hawthorn's Ferrari saw him score points in all but one race, which was exceptional in a year when only just over half the starters finished on average. He had fastest laps in five to Moss' two – the single point for which was scrapped in 1960 and given to sixth place – and Moss lost the title by 1 point! Tony Brooks on the other hand scored only three times, and was winner each time which gave him third place at the season's end. True, this was with a little help from Moss' retirements, but at Nürburgring and Monza his victories were hard earned indeed. This was a victory for consistency over speed, won fair and square by Mike Hawthorn, but which purists might say was not what the crowds ought to want. Are they right?

In terms of Championship rounds won and lost the score was: Mike Hawthorn – won one, lost one; Stirling Moss – won four, lost three; Tony Brooks – won three, lost zero. Clearly the top three.

The inaugural World Championship for Constructors was a clear victory for Vanwall with six wins to two for Ferrari, but only the best finishing car counted then, so Vanwall had 48 points from its six wins and Ferrari had 40 from two wins and four second places – closer than most people think. If the best two finishing cars had counted, as they do today, then Vanwall would have been beaten by 66 points to 56. Well I'm glad it was as it was.

Mike Hawthorn announced his (expected) retirement as soon as the last race was over, but Tony Vandervell also declared himself unfit to continue to run Vanwall on medical grounds, so Formula One was losing both its champions. It's believed, though, that racing fatalities had a bearing on both announcements.

I had seen two masterly drives by Collins at Silverstone, my first F1 experience, he was a star character and now he was dead. It affects me now to write it. Coming so soon after Musso's crash and the loss of another hero of mine – Archie Scott-Brown at Spa in May, I began to wonder what sort of a sport I had got hooked on. I knew it was dangerous, and that was part of the thrill, but this level of loss could hardly be accepted for long. However, I realised that this season was exceptionally bad, that luck played a part, and that only Marimón had died since the Championship started four years earlier. Life goes on.

A bright new future for Formula One?

In October at the annual RAC presentation evening, Mike Hawthorn was presented with a commemoration plaque on becoming Britain's First World Champion. Then the CSI president Augustin Pérouse dropped a bombshell, and created the biggest hoo-ha in F1 history when he announced the FIA's decision on the new Formula One for 1961. It was a very significant moment indeed in F1 history. Engine size would be restricted to just 1500cc, with a 500kg minimum weight limit. This tactless speech caused howls of derision all around the room, destroying the celebratory atmosphere.

Strangely, at the same time, an attempt was announced to lure America into European racing, also in 1961, by creating a new formula called 'The Inter-Continental Formula' (ICF). Italy and Britain had expressed an interest. This was for single-seater cars of 3000cc, but would not be part of any Championship. This meant that 1960 F1 cars could continue in this new series, but the World Championship would now seem to be aimed at 1960's F2 cars(!) which were already 1500cc.

The British believed that if they ignored the silly new F1 it would be killed off by the success of ICF. The weight limit compounded the annoyance, since existing F1 cars by Cooper and Lotus had been weighed at less than 400kg and no minimum weight had ever been introduced in F1 before. The new F1 would surely be simply unworthy of being a proper challenge at the premier level. The British thought it a German/French stitch-up to suit the new F2 Porsche and maybe a French F2 car. It was in two years, so surely there was time to get rid of it.

VISIT VELOCE ON THE WEB – WWW.VELOCE.CO.UK
All current books • New book news • Special offers • Gift vouchers • Forum

145

Chapter 18

1959

The rear-engine threat is realised

The year started with yet more tragic news when, on 22nd of January, Mike Hawthorn lost his life in a road accident on the Guildford bypass. This loss was huge to Britain as a sporting nation, as we had now lost our golden boy, our first World Motor Racing Champion, and the gloom around the racing fraternity must have been immense – five great names gone in nine months. Oh, for a safe year's racing!

The World Championship was reduced this year with the loss of races from the start, middle and end of the season: the Argentinian, Belgian and Moroccan Grands Prix. Thankfully, the Moroccan race was being replaced by the first American Grand Prix, a very welcome addition. After ten years in existence, the Championship was having difficulty in achieving dominance in F1. The number of rounds was still fluctuating: six in 1950; seven in 1951/52; eight in 1953/54; six in 1955; seven in 1956; eight in 1957; ten in 1958, and now eight in 1959. Four good and one minor extra F1 races would be run in Britain, giving a reasonable season with thirteen races. Twenty-one had taken place back in 1954, so surely it couldn't survive any more shrinkage. While drivers had the extra business of Formula Two (and sports cars) to keep them busy, pure Formula One constructors like BRM must not have wanted the fixture list to have shrunk any further, since Formula One was their sole raison d'être: racing equals revenue. So, F1 races beyond the Championship were still important, though Vanwall, having been one man's indulgence, was the sole absentee. Vandervell didn't enter non-Championship races in 1958/9.

Vanwall's withdrawal meant that a lot of team changes were bound to take place. Stirling Moss' decision was fundamental to everything, being the biggest winner of the previous year – though not of the World Championship. His decision was made without fanfare: he would drive Coopers

for the RRC Walker Racing Team with Maurice Trintignant as support. Both had already won a World Championship race with Walker, and driven for him with success in other F1 events. Their rapport was legendary, and Rob Walker probably had more funds, from his family connection to the famous whisky enterprise, than the Cooper Works did. Another legend associated with this outfit was the great mechanic Alf Francis. Cooper would almost certainly supply the latest model, as would Coventry Climax the best engines, but would Cooper supply its updated gearbox? It was a great team, and Stirling would remain with it for the rest of his career, though he was free to drive a BRM for BRP (see below) when he chose.

Ferrari enrolled Tony Brooks, who'd had a great 1958, Jean Behra and Cliff Allison. American Phil Hill was naturally retained after his 1958 performances, and he would be joined later in the year by his compatriot Dan Gurney. There was a new car, slightly larger than the previous year's 246, denoted 256 with full 2.5-litre engine. So that was five drivers on Ferrari's books. There was no limit as to how many cars a team could enter in those days as there were only a few constructors.

BRM had lost Behra, but kept Harry Schell, Joakim Bonnier and Ron Flockhart, and would continue to develop the Type 25 car. Surely a Championship win was overdue if only the brake problems were solved. Early in the season the team formed by Stirling Moss' father, along with manager Ken Gregory, and called the British Racing Partnership (BRP), arranged to buy a BRM, so they had plenty of faith in it.

A very welcome new marque to F1 this year, effectively replacing Vanwall, was Aston Martin, the renowned sports car marque. It had signed Roy Salvadori and American sports car ace Carroll Shelby. With its success in sports car racing it was thought to possess the ability to rise to the occasion in F1. However, its entrance into F1 had been put on hold in 1958 to concentrate on the sports car World Championship, and the F1 car it had for 1959, the DBR4/250, was now looking rather 'old school' (a front-engined car of some bulk powered by Aston's own straight-six). Those three – Ferrari, BRM and Aston-Martin – were the thoroughbreds; they made the whole car.

The new breed of chassis-engine combination teams, disparagingly referred to by Ferrari as 'garagistes,' was, of course, led by Cooper-Climax. Jack Brabham was retained as leader, and, with his brilliant technical ability, he was perhaps also chief engineer. Masten Gregory, whose drives in a Maserati 250F and Lister-Jaguar had been well noted, was engaged. Young New Zealander Bruce McLaren had arrived the previous year and driven well in F2, so he was promoted to Formula One driver. A new car, the Type 51, would appear, with the revised Climax FPF engine which was now fully 2.5-litre but of only 239bhp. However, the rear-engine layout helped to make the cars very light.

Lotus-Climax had lost Cliff Allison to Ferrari, but Graham Hill, who had driven well the previous year was promoted to leader, with Innes Ireland and Alan Stacey, excellent sports car drivers, completing the team.

The Grand Prix driver's diary of single-seater racing for 1959

10th January	FL – New Zealand Grand Prix at Ardmore (NZ) – 178.9 miles
24th January	FL – Lady Wigram Trophy Christchurch (NZ) – 150.3 miles
7th February	FL – Teretonga Trophy at Invercargill (NZ) – 72 miles
30th March	F1 – Glover Trophy at Goodwood (UK) – 100.8 miles
30th March	F2 – Lavant Cup at Goodwood (UK) – 36 miles
11th April	F2 – British Empire Trophy at Oulton Park (UK) – 107.1 miles
18th April	F1 – Aintree '200' (UK) – 201 miles
25th April	F2 – Gran Premio di Siracusa (I) – 188 miles
2nd May	F1 – *Daily Express* International Trophy at Silverstone (UK) – 146.4 miles
10th May	F1 – **Grand Prix de Monaco** (M) – 195.4 miles
18th May	F2 – Grand Prix de Pau (F) – 137.1 miles
31st May	F1 – **Grote Prijs van Nederland** (N) – 195.4 miles
5th July	F1 – **Grand Prix de l'ACF** at Reims (F) – 257.9 miles
5th July	F2 – Coupe International de Vitesse at Reims (F) – 128.9 miles
12th July	F2 – Grand Prix de Rouen at Rouen-les-Essarts (F) – 142.3 miles
18th July	F1 – **British Grand Prix** at Aintree (UK) – 225 miles
26th July	F2 – Trophy d'Auvergne at Clermont-Ferrand (F) – 130.2 miles
2nd August	F1 – **Grosse Preis von Deutschland** at Avus Berlin (D) – 309.4 miles
3rd August	F2 – John Davy Trophy at Brands Hatch (UK) – 62 miles
23rd August	F1 – **Grande Premio de Portugal** at Monsanto (P) – 209.6 mile
29th August	F2 – 'Kentish 100' at Brands Hatch (UK) – 104.2 miles
13th September	F1 – **Gran Premio d'Italia at Monza** (I) – 257.3 miles
26th September	F1 – International Gold Cup at Oulton Park (UK) – 147.3 miles
10th October	F1 – Silver City Trophy at Snetterton (UK) – 67.7 miles
12th December	F1 – **United States Grand Prix** at Sebring (US) – 218.4 miles

25 events of total race mileage = 3961 miles.
Events in bold are World Championship rounds – 61.5 per cent of F1 events run.
Formula Two dates above are those with a strong F1 driver contingent.

Keeping busy in the off-season

There was an unbreakable connection between Australia, New Zealand and Great Britain through the British Commonwealth. Motor racing in Britain had been enriched with the arrival in 1955 of Aussie Jack Brabham, and Bruce McLaren from New Zealand. Naturally, in the European off-season, the Australasian drivers would wish to return home and demonstrate their prowess, accompanied by some of the best opposition they had encountered. A series of races was run in each new year which, while technically Formule Libre, were invariably contested by Formula One cars and their regular drivers. Some races were virtually indistinguishable from Formula One, as was the first of these (see below), with a Works BRM for Le Mans winner Ron Flockhart, and Stirling Moss present with Rob Walker's Cooper. No less than seven Maserati 250Fs were there, with French-American Harry Schell, Swede Jo Bonnier and American Carroll Shelby (all F1 Works drivers) among the pilots. Any cars using motors greater than the 2.5-litre F1 limit, usually 3-litre, were in the possession of the 'locals,' for whom the chance to compete with 'the best' was not to be missed. There was little, if any, trade in up-to-date Formula One machinery with those far-off places then, so it was absolutely right to allow them to take their place on the grids with whatever they had. Invariably, the visitors had the upper hand, even when learning new tracks, perhaps because the machinery used by the 'locals' was European and older so new spares were not as easy to come by. Finishing well and being around to benefit from any of the visitors' misfortune would be important.

✶ VI New Zealand GP (Ardmore)
15+75 laps of 1.988 miles = 178.9 miles.
33 entries – 22 started final – 15 finished.
Front row for final : R Flockhart in 1m-23.6s (85.62mph); J Brabham; B McLaren; J Bonnier.
10-JAN: Brabham won heat one and Flockhart heat two, after Moss' driveshaft failed with 400 metres to go. There now came a famous sporting gesture indicative of the atmosphere of those times, and of events unencumbered by Championship points. Jack Brabham 'loaned' Moss one of his shafts to allow him to start from the back in the final. On the wide track it took Moss just two laps to lead the race and disappear at the rate of over a second a lap. Poleman Flockhart stalled at the start with help from an incompetent starter (a politician!) who raised but didn't drop the flag. He recovered spectacularly to fourth by lap six, aided by a McLaren spin, but sadly retired on lap 24 whilst in third place. Schell also stopped at this point, took over Shelby's third-placed car later when he suffered leg cramp, and brought it to fourth place a lap behind McLaren. It was reported that Moss' practice lap of 1m-21.5s had been missed by timekeepers. It was suggested that because it was off their speed/time chart they didn't believe it. His performance suggests they were almost certainly wrong.

1st S Moss (Cooper T45-Climax 2.0) in 1h-48m-24.4s = 82.55mph
2nd J Brabham (Cooper T45-Climax 2.2) @ 1m-29s
3rd B McLaren (Cooper T45-Climax 2.0) @ 1 lap
Fastest lap Moss/Flockhart in 1m-24.2s = 85.01mph

✶ Lady Wigram Trophy (Christchurch)
71 laps of 2.116 miles = 150.24 miles.
33 entries – 22 started – 15 finished.
Front row: R Flockhart in 1m-21.6s (93.35mph); J Brabham; B McLaren; R Jensen (Maserati 250F).
24-JAN: No Moss here, having left for Sebring, nor most of the Maseratis. Moss was effectively replaced by Ron Flockhart who showed what might have happened had the starter at Ardmore done his job. He stormed off to lead Brabham by 1.8 seconds after a lap. Lap seven saw Brabham take the lead, and a titanic battle begin which lasted all race. The lead changed hands on laps 25, 39 and 60. In the end it was the BRM's straight-line

speed which decided it as Brabham was signalled 'faster,' but he was flat out. Ross Jensen's Maserati expired with transmission trouble after four laps, to be replaced in fourth place by the other Jensen – Syd – in a Formula Two Cooper T45 who finished a lap behind McLaren.

1st R Flockhart (BRM P25) in 1h-41m-04.0s = 82.57mph
2nd J Brabham (Cooper T45-Climax 2.2) @ 2.7s
3rd B McLaren (Cooper T45-Climax 2.0) @ 2 laps
Fastest lap R Flockhart in 1m- 22.2s = 92.67mph

31-Jan

Bruce McLaren accepted an invitation and cruised to a win in a street race at Waimate from Ross Jensen's Maserati. No other F1 stars were present so it wasn't an international event – more a demonstration.

✶ Teretonga International (Invercargill)
8+40 laps of 1.5 miles = 72 miles.
15 started.
Front row: R Flockhart in 1m-09.3s (77.92mph); B McLaren; J Brabham; R Jensen (Maserati 250F).
07-FEB: Flockhart couldn't find first gear at the start, and was fifth after a lap. McLaren and Brabham headed into the first bend abreast with only room for one and Brabham conceded – an unusual occurrence. McLaren pulled away with his car handling better than Brabham's. Flockhart took second from Brabham on lap 12, and closed on McLaren, but front tyre problems left him second. Flockhart was a Scot and was very popular there – the town (and winner) having somewhat Scottish names.

1st B McLaren (Cooper T45-Climax 2.0) in 48m-38.4s = 74.01mph
2nd R Flockhart (BRM P25)
3rd J Brabham (Cooper T45-Climax 2.2)
Fastest lap R Flockhart in 1m-10.0s = 77.14mph

✶✶ VII Glover Trophy (Goodwood)
100.8m – 42 laps of 2.4 miles = 100.8 miles.
14 entries – 13 started – 9 finished.
Front row: H Schell – 1m-39.0s (87.27mph); R Salvadori 3.0s; J Brabham 3.0s; J Bonnier 3.8s.
30-MAR: Unusually for a wet practice Moss was only fifth, whereas Harry Schell took pole for BRM, easily beating the Maserati-engined Cooper of Roy Salvadori. Harry Schell made the best start, while Moss came from the second row for second. He was followed by BRM new boy Joakim Bonnier and Brabham. Lap three saw Brabham take third from Bonnier, and things stayed the same until lap ten when Moss found a way past Harry Schell. Soon Brabham followed suit but never got close to Moss, who then led to the finish on a drying track. Brabham, Schell and Bonnier were separated

by just over a second at the end, followed by Masten Gregory, having his first drive in a Works Cooper but a lap down. Team Lotus never featured.

1st	S Moss (RW)	Cooper T51-Climax 2.5 in 1h-06m-58.0s	90.31
2nd	J Brabham (W)	Cooper T51-Climax 2.5	16.6s
3rd	H Schell (W)	BRM P25	17.6s
F lap	S Moss	Cooper T51-Climax 2.5 in 1m-31-8s	94.12

✶✶ III International 'Aintree 200'
67 laps of 3.00 miles = 201 miles.
15 F1+ 19 F2 entries – 12 F1 started – 5 F1 finished.
Front row – M Gregory – 1m-59.6s (90.30mph); J Behra 0.4s; H Schell 0.4s.

18-APR: The established teams were here, but Aston-Martin wasn't ready. The Rob Walker stable had fitted a BRM engine and Colotti gearbox to the Cooper of Stirling Moss, who was back on the third row. Cooper recruit Masten Gregory stormed off from pole as Behra faltered, leading from the BRM of Bonnier then Moss and Schell's BRM. Bonnier's engine failed on lap two, so Moss was second, but Gregory drew steadily clear from him! Schell in third was followed by Brabham, Salvadori's Cooper-Maserati, Behra, McLaren and Brooks. Things were not looking well for Ferrari as Behra was 22 seconds behind leader Gregory on lap ten. Salvadori soon retired, then Brabham on lap 18, immediately followed by Gregory, whose clutch had failed. Moss now led Schell and Behra, but Behra got the better of Schell whose engine promptly failed. A few laps more and Moss' gearbox broke, so Ferrari was now one-two from nowhere. Behra eased up – a pity about his start. Moss' Cooper-BRM was never raced again despite a record lap. His inability to challenge Gregory surely played a part in that decision.

1st	J Behra (W)	Ferrari Dino 256 in 2h-15m-52.0s	88.76
2nd	CAS Brooks (W)	Ferrari Dino 256	10.4s
3rd	B McLaren (W)	Cooper T45-Climax2.2	1m-58s
F lap	S Moss (RW)	Cooper T45-BRM in 1m-58.8s	90.91r

✶✶✶ XI *Daily Express* International Trophy (Silverstone)
50 laps of 2.927 miles = 146.4 miles.
16 F1 + 9 F2 entries – 15 F1 started – 8 finished.
Front row – S Moss – 1m-39.2s (106.22mph); CAS Brooks 0.8s; R Salvadori 1.2s; J Brabham 1.2s.

02-MAY: Now Aston-Martin joined the fray, and for sight and sound matched the Ferraris of Phil Hill and Tony Brooks.

Moss had tried a BRM and the BRP stable bought one for him to race when suitable. This was its first outing, but run here by the Works. Amazingly, Moss beat his own pole time in Flockhart's BRM with 1m-38.6s (106.87mph) to Flockhart's 1m-41.2s. Brabham led Salvadori away, but Moss led by lap three, only to lose all brakes at Copse the next lap. He produced one of the great escapes of Formula One with a brilliantly executed spin to a standstill without hitting anything or stalling. Third place Brooks (Ferrari) retired on lap 29, thus benefitting Flockhart. Shelby was challenging Flockhart for third place, but retired on lap 48. So the best Ferrari could do was fourth for Phil Hill, a lap down. Aston-Martin's great debut, equalling the lap record and beating Ferrari, sadly also flattered to deceive. Aston never did nearly as well again.

1st	J Brabham (W)	Cooper T51-Climax 2.5 in 1h-25m-28.6s	102.73
2nd	R Salvadori (W)	Aston-Martin DBR4	17.6s
3rd	R Flockhart (W)	BRM P25	24.6s
F lap	R Salvadori	Aston-Martin DBR4 in 1m-40.0s	105.37

✶✶✶ (WC1) XVII Grand Prix de Monaco (Monte Carlo)
100 laps of a 1.954 mile circuit = 195.4 miles.
20 F1 + 9 F2 entries – 13 F1 qualified – 5 F1 finished.
Front row – S Moss – 1m-39.6s (70.63mph); J Behra 0.4s; J Brabham 0.5s.

10-MAY: A huge entry, but not including Aston-Martin, was received for just the 16 allowed starters. Three F2 cars qualified (a Lotus, Porsche and Ferrari) and they promptly tangled together at the back of the field on lap two, neatly arranged in line after St Devote bend (that was the end of the F2 race). In the main race, the order for 20 laps was Behra, Moss, Brabham, and Phil Hill, whereupon Behra's engine failed. Moss led easily until lap 81; gearbox failure. Hill held third until passed on lap 27 by Schell (BRM) and Brooks (Ferrari). Schell dropped out on lap 48, and Hill dropped down to sixth. Salvadori used a Cooper-Maserati, and was third after Moss retired, but his transmission failed soon after handing the place to the previous year's winner Trintignant. Phil Hill was fourth and McLaren fifth. All finishers gained points; not untypical at Monaco.

1st	J Brabham (W)	Cooper T51-Climax 2.5 in 2h-55m-51.3s	66.67
2nd	CAS Brooks (W)	Ferrari Dino 256	20.4s
3rd	M Trintignant (RW)	Cooper T51-Climax 2.5	2 laps
F lap	J Brabham (W)	Cooper T51-Climax 2.5 in 1m-40.4s	70.09r

✱✱✱ (WC2) VII Grote Prijs van Nederland (Zandvoort)

75 laps of a 2.605 mile circuit = 195.4 miles.
15 entries and starters – 10 finished.
Front row – J Bonnier – 1m-36.0s (97.70mph); J Brabham 0.0s; S Moss 0.2s.

31-MAY: This race was by invitation only – top teams yes, but Dutchman de Beaufort in a Porsche RSK sports car? I said exactly that of the previous year's race. Why they were allowed to do this? There were howls of protest as surely a World Championship by definition should be an open competition for all to enter. There were two cars each from Cooper, BRM, Lotus, and Aston-Martin, yet four from Ferrari! The Rob Walker stable was the only non-Works outfit invited – Moss drove for it so it couldn't refuse. From pole Bonnier's BRM took off to be passed by Gregory a lap later, regaining the lead on lap 12 as Gregory had gear selector trouble. Moss was eighth at first, but gained third on lap 28 behind Bonnier and Brabham. Brabham was overtaken on lap 49 and Bonnier on lap 60, so a fairytale first win for BRM seemed over. Two laps later Moss' gearbox failed again, and lo, the fairytale BRM maiden victory happened and everyone was pleased. But would they be happy ever after?

1st	J Bonnier (W)	BRM P25 in 2h-05m-26.8s	93.46
2nd	J Brabham (W)	Cooper T51-Climax 2.5	14.2s
3rd	M Gregory (W)	Cooper T51-Climax 2.5	1m-23s
F lap	S Moss (W)	Cooper T51-Climax 2.5 in 1m-36.7s	97.00r

Championship positions:
Brabham 15; Bonnier and Brooks 8.

✱✱✱ (WC3) XLV Grand Prix de l'ACF (Reims)

50 laps of a 5.158 mile circuit = 257.9 miles.
22 entries – 21 started – 10 finished.
Front row – CAS Brooks – 2m-19.4s (133.22mph); J Brabham 90.3s; P Hill 0.4s.

05-JUL: Top speed was always a factor at Reims, and the powerful Ferraris had 180+mph, so Cooper produced a streamlined car. The front lifted at high speed, so it was abandoned for the race, yet in the normal car Brabham was, amazingly, only 0.3 seconds behind Brooks on the grid, despite a much lower top speed. The Cooper's acceleration and handling on the few corners must have been quite superior to that of the Ferraris. After race director Raymond Roche produced another crazy start – just avoiding being run over (!) it was a flag-to-flag victory for Brooks, the real battle being for second. Moss, driving the BRP entered BRM, had this first, then it was Gregory, but he suffered heat exhaustion

in the scorching day and retired. Behra had stalled at the start, yet was third on lap 24 only to retire (he then had a scuffle with the team manager, involving fisticuffs, and was sacked!). Trintignant's Rob Walker Cooper took over second from Gregory until he spun on lap 19, handing the place to Brabham. Six laps later, Phil Hill overtook Brabham, and held second place until the end. Moss passed Brabham for third on lap 38, but had been without a clutch for most of the race and spun on lap 42, exiting Thillois hairpin. He attempted to push start in the extreme heat, but it was futile and he was out. Cars and drivers had been roasted and spattered by stones and melting tar, many ending with blooded faces. For many it wasn't over yet, though, as they still had a 25-lap Formula Two race to do! Busy, eh!

1st	CAS Brooks (W)	Ferrari Dino 256 in 2h-01m-26.5s	127.44
2nd	P Hill (W)	Ferrari Dino 256	27.1s
3rd	J Brabham (W)	Cooper T51-Climax2.5	1m-38s
F lap	S Moss (BRP)	BRM P25 in 2m-22.8s	130.04r

Championship positions:
Brabham 19; Brooks 14; P Hill 9.

✱✱✱ (WC4) XIV British Grand Prix (Aintree)

75 laps of a 3.00 mile circuit = 225 miles.
20 F1 + 12 F2 entries – 18 F1 starters – 10 F1 finished.
Front row: J Brabham – 1m-58.0s (91.53mph); R Salvadori 0.0; H Schell 1.2s.

18-JUL: Ferrari withdrew even before the entry list in the programmes had been printed, because, it said, of a strike. However, Centro-Sud managed to arrive from Italy while Ferrari did not. Ferrari was not unfamiliar with making excuses. Brooks avoided idleness by accepting a drive in a lightened and lowered Vanwall (a one-off occasion) and qualified amid the F2 cars, some five seconds off the pace. Aston-Martin had missed France, but was on the front row here with Salvadori, who had equalled the pole time. Moss had chosen BRP's BRM again, but was on row three. As in France it was a flag-to-flag victory, but for Brabham this time, chased at first by Schell, Bonnier and Gregory. Both Astons pitted early on with fuel splashing the drivers from full tanks, which put them out of the running. Moss came through to lie second on lap nine, and the chase of Brabham, 13 seconds ahead, began. By lap 50 Moss had gained only three seconds, and he made an unscheduled stop for a left rear tyre. He retained second place but was now 51 seconds adrift of Brabham. With nine laps left the gap was 30 seconds, but Moss' engine fluffed and he pitted for a 'splash and dash' fuel stop. McLaren passed as Moss left the pits, but was relegated within a lap, from which point on they were tied together. Both smashed the lap record in their battle, beating the pole time by a whole second! Schell and Trintignant followed, with Salvadori's Aston sixth after a good recovery.

1st	J Brabham (W)	Cooper T51-Climax 2.5 in 2h-30m-11.6s	89.88
2nd	S Moss (BRP)	BRM P25	22.2s
3rd	B McLaren (W)	Cooper T51-Climax 2.5	22.4s
F lap	Moss/McLaren	BRM/Cooper in 1m-57.0s	92.31r

Championship positions:
Brabham 27; Brooks 14; P Hill 9.

✳✳✳ (WC5) XX Grosser Preis von Deutschland (Avusring)

2 x 30 laps of 5.157 miles = 309.4 miles.
17 entries – 15 started – 6 finished.
Front row: CAS Brooks – 2m-05.9s (147.47mph); S Moss 0.9s; D Gurney 1.3s: J Brabham 1.5s.

02-AUG: Politics and money moved the race this year to the AVUS in West Berlin, the most unsuitable track ever used for Formula One. It involved both sides of an Autobahn, massive high-banked bend one end, and a tight loop the other. It was really a high-speed test track. Tragically, Jean Behra had been killed the day before, when he went over the top of the banking in a sports car race and struck a flag pole. A charismatic character sadly gone. Amazingly, de Beaufort, of Dutch GP fame, survived doing exactly the same thing, and re-joined the race! No such luck for poor Behra who had departed Ferrari in France and entered in his own Behra-Porsche. No one was going to challenge Ferrari here. Brooks seemed to excel on fast tracks, and won both halves. Masten Gregory was the only driver to mix it with the Ferraris in the first heat, but he retired. Moss' Cooper retired (gearbox again) on lap two. Hans Hermann's works BRM lost its brakes approaching the sharp loop at very high speed, hit the bales and somersaulted spectacularly, throwing him out more-or-less unharmed! Newcomer Dan Gurney was an excellent second in only his second F1 race. He would become one of the best ever Americans to race in Formula One.

1st	CAS Brooks (W)	Ferrari Dino 256 in 2h-09m-31.6s	143.34
2nd	D Gurney (W)	Ferrari Dino 256	2.9s
3rd	P Hill (W)	Ferrari Dino 256	1m-5s
F lap	CAS Brooks (W)	Ferrari Dino 256 in 2m-04.5s	149.13r

Championship positions:
Brabham 27; Brooks 23; P Hill 13.

✳✳✳ (WC6) VII Grande Premio de Portugal (Monsanto)

62 laps of 3.380 miles = 209.6 miles.
17 entries – 16 started – 10 finished.
Front row: S Moss – 2m-02.89s (99.02s); J Brabham 2.06s; M Gregory 3.44s.

23-AUG: This was a driver's circuit, and Moss had been here before, albeit in a 1955 sports car race, so he was untouchable throughout the weekend. On pole by two seconds over Brabham's identical car, he led every lap, and had the rare distinction of lapping the entire field near the finish. The troublesome Colotti box used by the Rob Walker team had been sorted out now. Its problems had cost Moss dearly, and this result showed by just how much. The Cooper Works team dominated the situation behind Moss, until Brabham crashed when lapping a slower car, hit a telegraph pole, and was dumped on the road as the car overturned. He was very nearly run over by Masten Gregory. He was not seriously hurt, thankfully. McLaren retired from third place on lap 38, handing the position to Gurney. Ferraris hadn't offered a challenge here, but Gurney had been best of the Ferrari team. However, when lapping fourth-placed Trintignant he touched the back of the Cooper as Trintignant surprised him by lifting off to allow him through, so they were both nearly out. Brooks had had an awful race, and felt that his car was quite unsuitable.

1st	S Moss (W)	Cooper T51-Climax 2.5 in 2h-11m-27.80s	95.32
2nd	M Gregory (W)	Cooper T51-Climax 2.5	1 lap
3rd	D Gurney (W)	Ferrari Dino256	1 lap
F lap	S Moss (W)	Cooper T51-Climax 2.5 in 2m-05.07s	97.30r

Championship positions:
Brabham 27; Brooks 23; Moss 17.5.

✳✳✳ (WC7) XXIX Gran Premio d'Italia (Monza-Road)

72 laps of a 3.573 mile circuit = 257.3 miles.
22 entries – 21 starters – 15 finished.
Front row: S Moss – 1m-39.7s (129.01mph); CAS Brooks 0.1s; J Brabham 0.5s.

13-SEP: A Ferrari circuit this, isn't it? The Scuderia probably thought so, but that "... damn little car is on pole even here now"! BRM produced a new rear-engined car for trial, showing that it had seen the light. Moss led from Brabham at first, but Brooks' clutch failed. Hill came to lead lap two, and Gurney lay third ahead of Brabham. It was two Coopers and three Ferraris in the first five places all the way. The Ferraris all pitted for tyres about halfway, whereupon Moss now led.

Tyre stops would surely mean the Coopers would drop back, what with their four-bolt wheels. Moss' car had been fitted with knock-off hubs at the back to reduce the time loss. But no, it was Argentina 1958 all over again – the Coopers had fooled everyone. They were lighter and less powerful, so fresh tyres were not needed if a little caution was used; and they were just as fast down the straights as well. Moss lapped Allison's Ferrari but let him unlap himself so he could cruise along in the slipstream, saving tyres and fuel. Ferrari was fourth (Gurney), fifth (Allison) and sixth (Gendebien), so four finished, but victory on their home soil was denied.

1st	S Moss (W)	Cooper T51-Climax 2.5 in 2h-04m-05.4s	124.38
2nd	P Hill (W)	Ferrari Dino 256	46.7s
3rd	J Brabham (W)	Cooper T51-Climax 2.5	1m-13s
F lap	P Hill (W)	Ferrari Dino 256 in 1m-40.4s	128.11r

Championship positions:
Brabham 31; Moss 25.5; Brooks 23.

A three-way battle for the world crown was now enticingly set up. The best five scores from the eight Championship rounds counted. A points reminder: eight, six, four, three, two for the first five places, plus one for fastest lap. Brabham had scored five podium finishes, so only a second place finish in America would add to his total. Moss also had five scores, but two were single-pointers for fastest laps. A second place with fastest lap would give him 31.5 points and the title, if neither Brabham nor Brooks won. The latter had only three point scores from the seven rounds to date, so a win for him would catch Brabham, but his three wins to Brabham's two would make him Champion if neither of the others finished second. A win for any of them, therefore, would secure the Championship ... or would it? There was till the joker in the pack of a point for fastest lap. There's little doubt that Brooks' situation would have been rather better had Ferrari turned up at Aintree.

✳ VI Oulton Park Gold Cup
152m – 55 laps of 2.678 miles = 147.05 miles.
18 entries – 13 started – 9 finished.
Front row: S Moss – 1m-42.4s (94.16mph); J Brabham 0.2s; C Bristow 1.6s; G Hill 1.8s.
26-SEP: For the first time since 1955, the Gold Cup returned to Formula One – where it should be. A car from BRM for Jo Bonnier and from Lotus for Graham Hill, Coopers for Brabham and McLaren, Walker's Cooper for Moss and BRP's Cooper for new discovery Chris Bristow, plus Roy Salvadori's Cooper-Maserati, were the 'Championship quality' entrants,

but then BRM withdrew. As mentioned previously, the BRP car was sponsored by the Yeoman Credit finance company, and was the first example of sponsorship in the modern manner in Formula One. The cars showed the advances made over the past four years as Moss' pole time was exactly ten seconds faster than Hawthorn's Lancia D50 had been. But it was Brabham who led at first, and Moss took five laps to take the lead from him. Brabham then chased hard all the way nut to no avail. Chris Bristow was a talented new find, and finished a lap ahead of experienced Roy Salvadori, and Hill was fifth. Moss' fastest lap even bettered his pole time, so these two World Championship contenders were really at it – race speed being close to pole speed!

1st	S Moss (RW)	Cooper T51-Climax in 1h-34m-37.2s	93.40
2nd	J Brabham (W)	Cooper T51-Climax	5.2s
3rd	C Bristow (YCB)	Cooper T51-Climax	1m-37s
F lap	S Moss	Cooper T51-Climax 1m-41.8s	94.71r

Silver City Trophy (Snetterton)
25 laps of 2.71 miles = 67.7 miles.
8 F1 + 17 F2 entries – 8 F1 started – 5 F1 finished.
Front row: R Flockhart – 1m-34.8s (102.91mph); R Salvadori 0.2s; G Hill 0.4s; B Halford 1.6s; I Ireland 1.8s.
10-OCT: BRM gave its main drivers a break, entering Flockhart who knew Snetterton well. Brabham drove his own car, but factory entered. Lotus had regular drivers Graham Hill and Innes Ireland. A five-car front row was very rare, yet Brabham wasn't on it. Flockhart led from Halford and Hill, but, on lap seven, a Lotus led a Formula One race for the first time thanks to Graham Hill. Brabham had taken third from Halford on lap three, and Hill retired after leading for just two laps, and that was that.

1st	R Flockhart (W)	BRM P25 in 39m-58.0s	101.71
2nd	J Brabham	Cooper T51-Climax 2.2	same lap
F lap	R Flockhart	BRM P25 in 1m-33.6s	104.23r
Pole	R Flockhart	BRM P25 in 1m-34.8s	102.91

✳✳✳ (WC8) 2nd United States Grand Prix (Sebring)
42 laps of a 5.20 mile circuit = 218.4 miles.
20 entries – 17 starters – 7 finished.
Front row: S Moss – 3m-00.0s (104.00mph); J Brabham 3.0s; H Schell 5.2s.
12-DEC: A famous circuit in sports car racing, this was, in fact, the inaugural Formula One race in the USA, and what a

crucial one it was! Moss was on pole by a full three seconds! The three-way battle seemed likely to be resolved rather quickly. Schell's practice time raised a few eyebrows (Harry had taken a small shortcut on the five-mile circuit unseen by officials!) as Brooks' 3m-05.9s should have placed him at the front. Harry Schell, ever the joker, had short-cut the circuit for a laugh but no-one had noticed. The entries included Indianapolis star Roger Ward in a dirt-track midget racer. He was quoted as saying, "I'll teach these guys how to corner." His qualifying time of 3m-43.8s shows that it was rather the other way round. He accepted with good grace. Moss was ten seconds ahead when his gearbox failed on lap five, having survived the last few outings. Brooks was rammed by teammate von Trips on lap one, and, perhaps overcautious, pulled in to be checked out. His title hopes virtually gone right at the start. Everything was going Brabham's way until the last lap when he ran out of fuel. Teammate McLaren slowed but was waved past to beat Trintignant by a small margin while Brabham pushed his car home for fourth. Brooks' drive to third was a fine effort indeed – but for that start-line nudge …

1st	B McLaren (W)	Cooper T51-Climax 2.5 in 2h-12m-35.7s	98.83
2nd	M Trintignant (RW)	Cooper T51-Climax2.5	0.6s
3rd	CAS Brooks (W)	Ferrari Dino 256	3m-01s
F lap	M Trintignant (RW)	Cooper T51-Climax 2.5 in 3m-05.0s	101.19r

Championship positions:
Brabham (WC) 31; Brooks 27; Moss 25.5.

1959 seasonal review

Since the arrival of Cooper on the Grand Prix scene two years earlier, its rise had been steady without faltering. Now the truth was obvious – front-engined cars had had it. No amount of extra horsepower was going to make up for being heavier, with a larger frontal area, and being less nimble than the Coopers. More weight meant more fuel to power it, so compounds the problem. The full-size 2475cc Climax produced 240bhp, some 30 or 40 less than Ferraris or BRMs, but Coopers were winning easily with it. Even the front-engined Lotus 16, which was as small as a front-engined car could be, and as light as the Cooper with the same engine, failed completely. Ferrari won with luck at Aintree and at the out-and-out speed tracks of Reims and Avus, but at the end of the year was equalled even on top speed. BRM at last won a top class event, which pleased everyone, other teams included, as competition is vital for the health of the sport. BRM's win at Snetterton, however, was in an event lacking

in any competitive depth, and therefore isn't included below. It was difficult to understand Aston-Martin's year. A long-established and respected marque was expected to add real variety and colour to the sport. Its debut at Silverstone in May had been a real success: lap record with second and nearly fourth place in top company. This suggested that it was on a par with Ferrari at that point, maybe better since both cars had a Ferrari behind them. Yet Aston-Martin entered only five races all season, and that promise never came near to being fulfilled. If it wasn't going to race regularly, then only four marques would be left in Formula One racing. Thank goodness for the 'garagistes' Cooper and Lotus, without whom proper racing wouldn't have happened.

The Formula One 'family' had lost a valuable member with the death of Jean Behra in August. His win in Aintree might have had a degree of good fortune about it, but it was felt that it was some compensation for losing the British GP there in 1957. His Championship record bears little resemblance to his true ability. His wins in races for World Championship cars is actually in double figures. Who's the best driver never to win a Championship Grand Prix? The name Chris Amon rightly comes to mind but so does that of Jean Behra.

Thirteen races was the shortest season in Grand Prix racing to date, and it was hoped that more races, Championship or not, would take place the following year. Despite his gearbox woes, Stirling Moss still won most races during the year, but only two were Championship rounds.

Winners of the 13 graded F1 races of 1959 –
quantity & quality of success

4 wins	S Moss (2A, B, C)	8 wins	Cooper (6A, B, C)
3 wins	J Brabham (3A)	3 wins	Ferrari (2A, B)
2 wins	T Brooks (2A)	2 wins	BRM (A, D)
1 win	J Bonnier (A) J Behra (B) B McLaren (A) R Flockhart (D)		

World Championship review

Stirling Moss must have started this year as hot favourite for the title, but his campaign began as badly as it had in 1957, with no finishes in the first three Grands Prix, and just a couple of crumbs for fastest laps. Under the 2015 scoring system his title hopes would have been over already, with a 65 point deficit and only five races to go. However, thanks to the 'best five scores count' system he was able to climb back into contention, and was just 5.5 points down going into the last round. The fight to the finish involved three drivers: Brabham, Moss and Brooks. Although neither Moss nor Brooks achieved their necessary results at Sebring, it's worth noting that each could have won the title with their Sebring result, but for a loss in just one previous round. Brooks only needed to have finished in third place at Monza, a distinct likelihood, for the crown to have been his at Sebring, but his clutch failed on the line; a rare occurrence. Any one of Moss' lost victories would have given him the crown, so maybe he lost the title three times. However, everyone recognised Jack Brabham's due for brilliantly bringing himself and Cooper to the point where this result was possible; and fully deserved. He finished the last race pushing his car to the line protected by police motorcyclists. Does this mean that he was the only World Champion ever to win on foot, and with a police escort?

VISIT VELOCE ON THE WEB – WWW.VELOCE.CO.UK
All current books • New book news • Special offers • Gift vouchers • Forum

154

Chapter 19

1960

Who has learned last year's lesson?

Now that Cooper's Championship victory had 'moved the goalposts' for Formula One design, what would the other teams produce to compete with Cooper?

At the Boxing Day Brands Hatch meeting of 1959 there arrived a new Lotus, the Type 18: a tiny rear-engined, minimalist car that *Autosport* magazine described as having an "... extremely ugly – and we hope temporary – tank-like body." The 500cc Formula Three, which had been around virtually since the war, was being replaced by a new minor formula called 'Formula Junior,' and a race for these cars with production-based 1100cc engines was on that programme. Little did racegoers know that this was the first view of the (with larger engine) 1960 Grand Prix Lotus, and that it would 'move the goalposts' even further. Team Lotus would have Innes Ireland as leader, with Alan Stacey as strong support – a brave driver with a prosthetic leg! A third car would be available to Jim Clark and/or motorcycle multi-World Champion and four-wheeled new-boy John Surtees.

The present World Champion, Cooper, retained Champion Jack Brabham, of course, and Bruce McLaren, restricting itself mainly to a two-car team, but a new car would be needed.

BRM had shown a rear-engined car at Monza the previous year, and now it was official – it had joined the new breed. BRM's driver line-up was Graham Hill, Jo Bonnier and Dan Gurney.

The RRC Walker Racing Team retained Stirling Moss and Maurice Trintignant. Because of the presence of the former it would probably have whatever machinery from the above teams it wanted.

Ferrari retained Phil Hill, Cliff Allison and Wolfgang von Trips, adding American Ritchie Ginther. Trouble was that it also retained the previous year's car, which was almost

obsolete. Enzo Ferrari's statement that, "The horse pulls the cart, not the cart pushes the horse," clouded his judgement of rear-engine design – he still believed the engine was the most important part of the car. His statement didn't make sense anyway, as, wherever the engine was placed, it would drive the rear wheels, so the cart always had pushed the horse.

Aston-Martin continued despite a disappointing 1959, but, unfortunately, like Ferrari, it stuck to an outdated model (the DBR4/250) which, in its case, hadn't been raced outside England. Roy Salvadori and Maurice Trintignant drove the few outings Aston had before it disappeared from the scene without making a mark.

A new marque from the USA, Scarab, featured drivers Chuck Daigh and Lance Reventlow. The latter was the team owner and heir to the Woolworth fortune. A new nation being involved was a great thing, but it was a pity the car was as obsolete as the Aston-Martin. Scarab had produced a sports-racer which had done well in America, but perhaps it was too influenced by Indianapolis, where front engines were embedded in the culture. There'd never been anything else – or was there likely to be.

The one name amongst the 'great and good' not mentioned so far is the runner-up in the World Championship, Tony Brooks, who, having missed out on a Works drive while Vandervell made up his mind about continuing, joined the British Racing Partnership. And here we have a new dimension in racing: Sponsorship. The BRP was approached in 1959 by financier Yeoman Credit wanting publicity relating to motoring. So came about the first fully sponsored racing team in F1. BRP, renamed the Yeoman Credit Racing Team, purchased four Cooper T51s, and, in addition to Brooks, took on Harry Schell and Chris Bristow. The first race for this entity had been in the Oulton Park Gold Cup with Bristow at the wheel. Now it was a full-time business proposition. So popular were Coopers that Scuderia Centro-Sud fitted Maserati four-cylinder sports engines to them, with Masten Gregory and Maurice Trintignant as main pilots. There was even a Cooper-Ferrari squad called Scuderia Eugenio Castellotti, using four-cylinder Squalo engines from 1955. So Coopers would dominate most grids. But in the Manufacturers' Championship all those Coopers would be separated by engine – a Cooper-Climax being regarded as a different marque from a Cooper-Maserati, etc.

Great news on the British scene was that popular Brands Hatch was being increased in length (now quoted at 2.65 miles*). It had been referred to as a stadium and was now a proper road track in the style of Oulton Park, with plentiful variety of bends and elevation changes. Now it qualified for a full Formula One race, and promptly got one on August 1st to inaugurate the track.

On the Championship front; the German Grand Prix was lost to Formula Two, probably because of a good chance of a German win, namely Porsche. Thankfully, the Belgian Grand Prix was back on the agenda, as was the Argentine Grand Prix. This was now in February, and gave teams a better chance to be ready and provide an appropriate field. So now the Championship was back to nine rounds, but it was still thanks to the extra races in Britain that a decent calendar of F1 races existed. The Championship points system changed, with the single point re-allocated to the sixth place finisher. This year was the only year when the maximum score available to a winner was eight points.

The Grand Prix driver's diary of single-seater racing for 1960

9th January	FL – New Zealand Grand Prix at Ardmore (NZ) – 178.9 miles
23rd January	FL – Lady Wigram Trophy at Christchurch (NZ) – 150.3 miles
7th February	**F1 – Gran Premio do Argentina at Buenos Aires (Ag)** – 194.5 miles
14th February	F1 – Gran Prix do Buenos Aires at Cordoba (Ag) – 144.5 miles
19th March	F2 – Gran Premio di Siracusa (I) – 191.4 miles
2nd April	F2 – Oulton Park Trophy (UK) – 67 miles
8th April	F2 – Grand Prix de Bruxelles at Heysel (B) – 198 miles
18th April	F2 – Grand Prix de Pau (F) – 154.4 miles
18th April	F1 – Glover Trophy at Goodwood (UK) – 100.8 miles
30th April	F2 – Aintree '200' (UK) – 150 miles
14th May	F1 – *Daily Express* International Trophy at Silverstone (UK) – 146.4 miles

29th May	**F1 – Grand Prix de Monaco (M)** – 195.4 miles
6th June	**F1 – Grote Prijs van Nederland at Zandvoort (N)** – 195.4 miles
19th June	**F1 – Grand Prix de Belgique at Spa Francorchamps (B)** – 315.4 miles
3rd July	**F1 – Grand Prix de l'ACF at Reims (F)** – 257.9 miles
16th July	**F1 – British Grand Prix at Silverstone (UK)** – 225.4 miles
24th July	F2 – Grosse Preis der Solitude (D) – 141.8 miles
31st July	F2 – Grosse Preis von Deutschland at Nürburgring (D) – 154.1 miles
1st August	F1 – Silver City Trophy at Brands Hatch (UK) – 123.5 miles
14th August	**F1 – Grande Premio de Portugal at Oporto (P)** – 253.2 miles
28th August	F2 – 'Kentish 100' at Brands Hatch (UK) – 104 miles
4th September	**F1 – Gran Premio d'Italia at Monza (I)** – 310.7 miles
10th September	F2 – Danske Grand Prix at Roskilde (Dk) – 74.6 miles
17th September	F1 – Lombank Trophy at Snetterton (UK) – 100.3 miles
18th September	F2 – Flugplatzrennen at Zeltweg (A) – 117 miles
24th September	F1 – International Gold Cup at Oulton Park (UK) – 160.7 miles
2nd October	F2 – Gran Premio di Modena (I) – 147 miles
20th November	**F1 – United States Grand Prix at Riverside (US)** – 244.3 miles

28 events of total race mileage = 4797 miles, but 4643 max with simultaneous races.

Events in bold are World Championship rounds – 60 per cent of F1 races run.

Formula Two dates above are those with a strong F1 driver contingent.

Off-season in New Zealand 1960

There were only four weeks between the American Grand Prix of the previous year and the first of these races. Run technically to Formule Libre, as were the 1959 races, so they don't form part of the mainstream F1 scene, hence the results are not in boxed format. But it was regular F1 cars which provided the real competition, so they deserve to be included 'wherever the great and good met.' As per the previous year, it was New Zealand where this racing took place.

Stirling Moss had a Yeoman Credit-entered Cooper,

while Jack Brabham and Bruce McLaren comprised the regular Works Cooper team in the World Championship. Also from England were David Piper with his Lotus 16 and Ian Burgess with a Cooper-Maserati. Regulars on the F1 scene, and not amongst the elite, maybe, but could give the 'locals' a hard time.

✶ VI New Zealand GP (Ardmore)
15+75 laps of 1.988 miles = 178.9 miles.
33 entries – 22 started final – 15 finished.

Front row: J Brabham in 1m-20.1s (89.37mph): S Moss 0.3s; D Piper 2.5s; I Burgess 2.8s.

09-JAN: Moss and Burgess won the heats, but Brabham retired from heat two because of a fire! He was allowed to start the final from the back, though. It was McLaren, Moss and Brabham after a lap, followed by Piper, Stillwell and Burgess. Brabham stormed past into the lead on lap four. Moss regained second soon, and, after chasing Brabham hard, led on lap 16, but clutch failure put him out on lap 27. McLaren then closed on Brabham and they scrapped well, but Brabham had the best of it – he was reigning World Champion after all.

1st J Brabham (Cooper T51-Climax 2.5) in 1h-43m-49.2s = 86.19mph

2nd B McLaren (Cooper T45-Climax 2.5) @ 0.6s

3rd B Stillwell (Cooper T45-Climax 2.2) @ 3 laps

Fastest lap Moss in 1m- 20.7s = 88.70mph (heat one)

✶ Lady Wigram Trophy (Christchurch)
71 laps of 2.116 miles = 150.24 miles.
21 entries – 16 started – 11 finished.

Front row: J Brabham; I Burgess; D Piper, P Hoare. No times are available.

23-JAN: No Moss here, and McLaren drove Malcolm Gill's 4733cc aero-engined Lycoming special of only four cylinders – 1183cc per cylinder! He started from the back. Pat Hoare had a 1959 Ferrari 256, with a four-cylinder, three-litre engine from an older sports Ferrari. Although it wasn't as powerful as the 2.5-litre six-cylinder normally fitted, it was, perhaps, more durable. McLaren came through to deprive him of fourth place, while Piper easily had the better of Burgess. A win for Brabham was almost a formality. The star 'local' wasn't the expected Pat Hoare, or Bib Stillwell, but Denny Hulme, who, with only a two-litre motor, lost sixth place to Jim Palmer after retiring with lost oil pressure. He was still classified seventh on the same lap as Palmer (68), but might have been fifth. A new discovery?

1st J Brabham (Cooper T51-Climax 2.5) in 1h-40m-42.0s = 89.52mph

2nd D Piper (Lotus 16-Climax 2.5) @ 9.8s

3rd I Burgess (Cooper T51-Climax 2.2) @ 2m-01s

Fastest lap J Brabham in 1m- 20.8s = 94.28mph

✶✶✶ (WC1) XIII Gran Premio de la Republica Argentina (Buenos Aires No 2)
80 laps of 2.431 miles = 194.5 miles.
24 entries – 22 started – 14 finished.

First row: S Moss – 1m-36.9s (90.31mph); I Ireland 1.6s; G Hill 2.0s; J Bonnier 2.0s.

07-FEB: Lotus brought a single new model 18 for Innes Ireland, and a 16 for Stacey. All other entries were for the previous year's cars. A welcome addition was the very popular Froilán González, out of retirement for a single Works Ferrari drive. He acquitted himself well on the third grid row. Moss took pole easily, but it was Innes Ireland who led from the BRMs, with Moss eighth! Ireland spun, dropping to sixth. Bonnier's BRM now led, joined by Moss on lap ten. The two swapped three times before Moss' suspension broke on lap 40 when leading. Now it was Bonnier, from a recovered Ireland, McLaren, Allison and Moss (who'd taken over Trintignant's car). On lap 67 Bonnier had engine trouble and fell back. But Ireland led for only a few seconds before his gear selectors jammed, dropping to sixth. McLaren won his second GP, aged just 22; a record that would remain unbroken for 49 years! Cliff Allison had been 12th on lap one – a very good drive. In fourth came 'local hero' Menditeguy's Cooper-Maserati from von Trips' Ferrari. Surely Menditeguy could have had a great F1 career – his Maserati engine not on-a-par with Climax. No points were awarded now for shared drives which applied to third place.

1st	B McLaren (W)	Cooper T51-Climax in 2h-17m-49.5s	86.64
2nd	C Allison (W)	Ferrari Dino 256	26.3s
3rd	Trintignant/Moss (RW)	Cooper T51-Climax	36.9s
F lap	Moss (RW)	Cooper T51-Climax in 1m-38.9s	88.48r

Championship positions:
McLaren 8; Allison 6; Menditeguy 3.

✶ XIII GP do Buenos Aires (Cordoba)
144.5m – 75 laps.
16 entries – 15 started – 7 finished.

First row: J Brabham 1m-27.9s (78.91mph); M Trintignant 0.1; J Bonnier 0.3s; D Gurney 0.7s.

14-FEB: This was a true F1 race. BRM, Cooper and Lotus Works teams were there, the only non-F1 car being González' old Ferrari-Chevrolet. Moss skipped this race – wary of the locals – 'once bitten, twice shy.' Ireland's Lotus 18 broke a driveshaft at the start, so no flying start this time. Brabham, McLaren and Trintignant led the way from the BRMs of Gurney and Bonnier. Gurney passed Trintignant, then led after both Works Coopers retired with water pump trouble. Gear problems let Trintignant catch him, though, and take the lead. Innes Ireland had taken over from Alan Stacey (Lotus 16) but ran out of fuel on lap 68. Mentiteguy had retired five laps before, so, surprisingly, Ireland was fourth as only Munaron passed him after he stopped.

1st	M Trintignant (RW)	Cooper T51-Climax in 1h-53m-50.9s	76.14
2nd	D Gurney (W)	BRM P25	47.6
3rd	G Munaron	Maserati 250F	5 laps
F lap	B McLaren (W)	Cooper T51-Climax in 1m-27.2s	79.56

∗∗ VII Glover Trophy (Goodwood)

42 laps of 2.4 miles = 100.8 miles.
14 entries and starters – 7 finished.
First row: C Bristow – 1m-24.8s (101.89mph); S Moss 0.2s; H Schell 0.2s; I Ireland 1.2s.

18-APR: Ferrari and Brabham's Cooper were missing. BRM had the rear-powered P48, and Tony Brooks drove a 'lightweight' front-engined Vanwall, breaking the lap record in practice by a whole two seconds yet still two seconds off pole! Mercurial Bristow now had a pole position to his credit, and led away but was soon passed by Moss. Ireland took Bristow and then Moss on successive laps to lead. The ensuing Moss/Ireland scrap is legend, and Ireland made no mistakes despite Moss' pressure, even pulled away slightly at the end. Glory for Lotus and Ireland. Gurney tangled with Salvadori on lap two and was out, leaving Bristow on his own, 13 seconds ahead of McLaren. Moss' new record lap was 4.4 seconds inside the old time: that's how fast this new breed of small, lightweight car was. Ireland also beat Moss in the F2 race in a similar works Lotus 18! How would others respond to this?

1st	I Ireland (W)	Lotus 18-Climax in 1h-00m-14.8s	100.39
2nd	S Moss (RW)	Cooper T51-Climax	2.8s
3rd	C Bristow (YCB)	Cooper T51-Climax	1m-05s
F lap	S Moss (RW)	Cooper T51-Climax in 1m-24.4s	102.13r

∗∗∗ XII *Daily Express* International Trophy (Silverstone)

50 laps of 2.927 miles = 146.4 miles.
29 F1/F2 entries – 21 F1 started – 13 F1 finished.
First row: S Moss – 1m-50.4s (95.44mph); J Bonnier 2.2s; D Gurney 3.4s; P Hill 5.2s.

14-MAY: Harry Schell's fatal crash in the wet practice marred this event; a great character, very popular, and a very good driver lost.

Ferrari was here, and Cooper had responded very fast to Lotus with its 'low-line' Type 53. Would Goodwood be repeated? Practice was so wet it proved little except that Moss was still '*Der Regenmeister,*' and that the rear-engined BRMs were good. In the middle of the second row in a Works Lotus 18 was John Surtees, on his F1 debut, having out-qualified his leader Ireland who was on the outside of row 3! The two BRMs led from Moss, Graham Hill's BRM, Ireland, Surtees and Brabham. By lap three the order was Moss, Ireland, Bonnier, Brabham, Gurney, Surtees, and Hill – every place having changed. Surtees rose to fourth but lost oil on lap nine; a superlative F1 intro. Now it was Moss, Ireland (rekindling their Goodwood bash), Brabham, Hill and Bonnier's BRMs, and Stacey. Ireland took the lead on lap 25 but Moss retook it on lap 29 in his 'old type' Cooper T51 (only he could do that), but broken suspension put him out. Brabham chased Ireland in vain. Another Ireland-Lotus triumph, this time against the cream of F1. Stacey's Works Lotus was fourth, a lap down, beating Phil Hill's Ferrari. The lap record here was smashed by six seconds – an increase never seen before. The race speed and record lap proved faster than in the British GP in July, which shows that people were not messing about in these extra races.

1st	I Ireland (W)	Lotus 18-Climax in 1h-20m-04.4s	108.82
2nd	J Brabham (W)	Cooper T53-Climax	1.6s
3rd	G Hill (W)	BRM P48	1m-12s
F lap	I Ireland	Lotus 18-Climax in 1m-34.2s	111.86r

∗∗∗ (WC2) XVIII Grand Prix de Monaco (Monte Carlo)

100 laps of 1.954 mile circuit = 195.4 miles.
24 entries – 16 qualified – 5 finished.
First row: S Moss – 1m-36.3s (73.06mph); J Brabham 1.0s; C Bristow 1.4s.

29-MAY: As per the previous year, a huge entry for 16 places including – out of the blue – a rear-engined Ferrari for Ginther! Moss was 4.1 seconds below the lap record, and the whole grid separated by just 2.8 seconds! Bonnier's new BRM P48 showed its credentials by leading from row two from Brabham and Moss. It was Moss who passed him on lap 17 and held the lead until lap 34 when Brabham took over, but he spun out of the race six laps later. Brooks should have been third then, in the Yeoman Credit Cooper after Bonnier, but had spun on lap 30. So it was Phil Hill but he, too, spun, and now it was McLaren and Graham Hill chasing Bonnier.

1st	J Brabham (W)	Cooper T53-Climax in 2h-01m-47.2.s	96.25
2nd	I Ireland (W)	Lotus 18-Climax	24.0s
3rd	G Hill (W)	BRM P48	56.6s
F lap	S Moss (W)	Lotus 18-Climax in 1m-33.8s	99.98r

Championship positions:
McLaren 14; Moss 11; Brabham 8.

✱✱✱ (WC4) XX Grand Prix de Belgique (Spa)
36 laps of a 8.761 mile circuit = 315.4 miles.
20 entries – 17 started – 6 finished.
Front row: J Brabham – 3m-50.0s (137.13mph); CAS Brooks 2.5s; P Hill 3.3s.

19-JUN: Apart from those involving spectator fatalities, only the San Marino GP of 1994 came anywhere near this dreadful event. The race at this super fast, dangerous road circuit was 50 per cent longer than last time. Moss produced a time of 3m-52.6s to set the ball rolling, but, trying to beat Brabham's time, a lost rear wheel at 140mph resulted in him being thrown him out, causing leg and back injuries. Soon after, Mike Taylor's broken steering caused him very serious injuries. Both were in Lotus 18s. With Moss out the race was Brabham's all the way, at first from the Belgian Gendebien, then Ireland whose clutch played up, then Phil Hill was second until a fuel leak on lap 28. Graham Hill was set for second when his crankshaft broke on the final lap. So it was a Works Cooper one-two, followed by a customer Cooper. Today, Graham Hill would have held his third place, as Gendebien never caught him, but you had to cross the line after the winner then. Phil Hill and Jim Clark followed. Two disasters further marred the event: Chris Bristow crashed fatally on lap 19 after a battle with Mairesse for sixth; and Alan Stacey, hit in the face at well over 100mph by a bird, crashed and also died. Both these men were carving good reputations in Grand Prix racing.

1st	J Brabham (W)	Cooper T53-Climax in 2h-21-37.3s	133.63
2nd	B McLaren (W)	Cooper T53-Climax	1m-03s
3rd	O Gendebien (YCB)	Cooper T51-Climax	1 lap
F lap	Brabham/Ireland/P Hill	Cooper T53-Climax in 3m-51.9.s	136.02r

Championship positions:
McLaren 20; Brabham 16; Moss 11.

✱✱✱ (WC5) XLVI Grand Prix de l'ACF (Reims)
50 laps of a 5.158 mile circuit = 257.9 miles.
24 entries – 20 started – 10 finished.

Bonnier passed Moss who pitted for plugs on lap 60, but he regained his lead on lap 67 to the end. Bonnier lost second place on lap 78 with broken suspension. The attrition left just four cars running, but six scored points now, so Bonnier and Ginther dragged their crippled cars onto the track to finish behind Brooks in fourth, the last fit runner. Thus came about the idea of *parc fermé*.

1st	S Moss (RW)	Lotus 18-Climax in 2h-53m-45.5s	67.47
2nd	B McLaren (W)	Cooper T53-Climax	52.1s
3rd	P Hill (W)	Ferrari 256	1m-02s
F lap	B McLaren (W)	Cooper T53-Climax in 1m-36.2s	73.13r

Championship positions:
McLaren 14; Moss 8; Allison 6.

✱✱✱ (WC3) VIII Grote Prijs van Nederland (Zandvoort)
75 laps of a 2.605 mile circuit = 195.4 miles.
20 entries – 17 starters – 8 finished.
First row: S Moss – 1m-33.2s (100.62mph); J Brabham 0.2s; I Ireland 0.7s.

06-JUN: The Dutch ran their own show to their own unfair rules as usual. All could start but only 15 (+ de Beaufort, of course) got starting money! That pleased one person. Aston-Martin and Scarab promptly withdrew, and Centro Sud entered only Trintignant, with the strange proviso that starting money would be paid if he got to tenth spot early on (whenever that was).

Moss chased Brabham closely for 17 laps when a piece of kerb was flicked up by Brabham and punctured Moss' tyre. The resultant stop cost him almost two laps. Ireland and Stacey fought over third place and then second when Moss pitted. Meanwhile Trintignant, last man on the grid, started on little fuel – a good idea that paid off by lap ten. Then he stopped to fuel up properly. Gurney lost fifth place on lap 12 when yet another BRM brake failure occurred. In the ensuing crash a young boy watching from a banned area was tragically killed. Teammate Graham Hill was now fifth. Stacey retired from third with transmission failure, so now Moss, who had unlapped himself, was fourth and on the same lap as the leader.

A very great F1 career started here as, on lap 42, and from fifth place, having risen from 11th on the grid, Jim Clark retired on his Championship debut. The new 'lowline' Cooper T53 was clearly a swift and effective reply to the Lotus 18 – unless Moss was driving it.

Front row: J Brabham – 2m-16.8s (135.75mph); P Hill 1.4s; G Hill 1.6s.

03-JUL: As at Spa, Brabham set pole easily by over a second. A front-engined car was on the front grid row at Spa (and here) so Vandervell must have thought he still had a chance, but the new Vanwall prepared for Brooks was well off the pace. Roche messed the start again – the '30 second to go' signal became two seconds. Graham Hill was still finding a gear and was hit by Trintignant – both out. A huge Brabham/Phil Hill battle on another fast circuit took place at, in places, close to 190mph. It seemed that whoever led from Thillois was second at the line. Where maximum speed was important, Ferrari was still in the game. When Brabham pulled a little clear, Hill was challenged by teammate von Trips. Then both Ferraris' transmissions broke by lap 30, as had teammate Mairesse's car. Ireland was then second but for only a lap. Gendebien and McLaren took second and third, in the reverse of Belgium. The Yeoman Credit cars – operated by the BRP – might have been the previous year's models, but they were doing very well, also taking fourth place with Henry Taylor. Coopers got the top four places, followed by three Works Lotus of Clark, Flockhart and Ireland, who had pitted with suspension trouble. Both BRMs failed before half distance, so only Climax-engined cars were running at the end. Jim Clark now had his first Championship points.

1st	J Brabham (W)	Cooper T53-Climax in 1h-57m-24.9s	131.79
2nd	O Gendebien (YCB)	Cooper T51-Climax	48.3s
3rd	B McLaren (W)	Cooper T53-Climax	51.9s
F lap	J Brabham (W)	Cooper T53-Climax in 2m-17.5s	135.06r

Championship positions:
Brabham and McLaren 24; Moss 11.

✳✳✳ (WC6) XV British Grand Prix (Silverstone)
77 laps of 2.927 miles = 225.4 miles.
25 entries – 24 starters – 16 finished.
Front row: J Brabham – 1m-34.6s (111.39mph); G Hill 1.0s: B McLaren 1.4s; J Bonnier 1.6s.

16-JUL: Brabham was on pole again by a clear margin – his superiority in Moss' absence beyond doubt. Another starting disaster for Graham Hill as he stalled on the line, perhaps provoked one of the almost great drives of all time. By lap 55 he had passed the whole field to lead the race! Brabham had led up until then, hotly pursued by Ireland, and with Bonnier, Surtees, Clark and McLaren swapping the next places. However, through them all came Hill – seventh on lap 11; sixth lap 20; fifth lap 25; fourth lap 30; third lap 32,

and second on lap 37. The chase for the lead was hard and took 18 laps to complete – to huge cheers. Surtees had by then the better of his battles and was third. Soon afterwards, Clark pitted for suspension repairs from fourth. The Hill/Brabham battle was unrelenting, and Hill was pressured into a late attempt to overtake a lapped runner into Copse on lap 72, but his brakes weren't up to it and he spun off. Victory to Brabham – but perhaps moral victory to Graham Hill and BRM. With this 'result,' Graham Hill showed himself to be Champion material, and hugely popular at that. What a fantastic race! It should be recalled that this was only John Surtees' second Championship Grand Prix, and the first time he and Clark (joint No.3s [?]) had met, and he led Team Lotus home ahead of team leader Innes Ireland! He had been missing since Monaco to go winning for MV Agusta on two wheels (including the Isle-of-Man TT). **No-one will ever do that again.**

1st	J Brabham (W)	Cooper T53-Climax in 2h-04m-24.6s	108.70
2nd	J Surtees (W)	Lotus 18-Climax	49.6s
3rd	I Ireland (W)	Lotus 18-Climax	1m-30s
F lap	G Hill (W)	BRM P48 in 1m-34.4s	111.62

Championship positions:
Brabham 32; McLaren 27; Moss 11.

✳✳✳ Silver City Trophy (Brands Hatch)
50 laps of 2.46 miles = 123 miles.
23 entries and starters – 14 finished.
Front row: J Clark – 1m-39.4s (89.09mph); J Brabham 0.2s; I Ireland 0.4s; G Hill 0.8s.

01-AUG: A longer Brands Hatch, and its first F1 race. This was the day after the F2 German GP in which most of the F1 teams had been involved, yet everyone wanted to be here. More teams entered than had the Portugese GP two weeks later! Sadly, Moss was still recovering. BRM entered one car, so Dan Gurney was snapped up by Yeoman Credit/BRP, which also had Tony Brooks and Henry Taylor. This was Jim Clark's first F1 pole position – of many. Brabham stormed away, though, followed closely by Clark and Graham Hill, who dropped back after a few laps. Surtees pitted after a lap but continued. Lotus team leader Ireland stopped after six laps with no oil pressure. A great Brabham/Clark lead battle ensued for a dozen laps when Clark began to drop back to retire on lap 21 with gearbox trouble. Graham Hill was now 30 seconds down, but inexorably closed when oil surge caused Brabham to ease up about lap 30 – the chase became a major factor of the race. By this time McLaren had got the better of Phil Hill's Ferrari for fourth becoming third when Clark stopped. Then came Henry Taylor and Surtees, both one lap down, the latter had made a great recovery from his early pit stop. A great start for a track clearly fit for Grand Prix racing.

1st	J Brabham (W)	Cooper T53-Climax in 1h-25m-36.6s	86.20
2nd	G Hill (W)	BRM P48	4.4s
3rd	B McLaren (W)	Cooper T53-Climax	49.4s
F lap	Brabham/Clark	Cooper/Lotus 18 in 1m-40.6s	88.03

✱✱✱ (WC7) IX Grande Premio de Portugal (Oporto)
55 laps of 4.603 miles = 253.2 miles.
16 entries – 15 started – 7 finished.
Front row: J Surtees – 2m-25.56s (11.84mph); D Gurney 0.07s; J Brabham 0.49s.

14-AUG: This year the race returned to Oporto as in 1958 but the greatest return was by Stirling Moss, amazingly recovered from his crash at Spa. Like the Dutch, the organisers invited only the top drivers, plus local hero Mario Cabral. He was last on the grid, though over two seconds slower than anyone. Monaco runner-up Richie Ginther wasn't there. How the FIA allowed organisers to dictate is unbelievable. Surtees had his first pole position, but Brabham was first away, soon passed by Gurney, who held the lead for ten laps. Brabham slid wide and lost six places, so Moss and Surtees now chased Gurney who gave up the lead after sliding on what he thought was his own oil. Surtees had passed Moss, so it was he who led after Gurney's problem. He led well and looked set for a victory in his 'rookie' year, but fuel had been seeping onto his pedals, and, on lap 36, his foot slipped and a visit to the straw bales damaged his radiator. Moss' stop for plug changes on lap 20 allowed Brabham's recovery to be complete, when taking advantage of Surtees' misfortune. Moss ended fifth, but was disqualified as, after a spin, he had pushed his car in the wrong direction on the footpath. In 1958 Hawthorn had done this here, Moss had spoken up for him and got Hawthorn reinstated. What irony! von Trips, Brooks and Ireland completed the points scorers. Brabham was now World Champion again, after six successive F1 wins (including Brands Hatch, of course).

1st	J Brabham (W)	Cooper T53-Climax in 2h-19m-00.03s	109.27
2nd	B McLaren (W)	Cooper T53-Climax	57.97s
3rd	J Clark (W)	Lotus 18-Climax	1m-53s
F lap	J Surtees (W)	Lotus 18-Climax in 2m-27.53s	112.31

Championship positions:
Brabham (WC) 40; McLaren 33; Ireland 12.

✱ (WC8) XXX Gran Premio d'Italia (Monza – Combined)
50 laps of a 6.214-mile circuit = 310.7 miles.
18 F1/F2 entries – 9 F1 started – 5 F1 finished.
Front row: P Hill – 2m-41.4s (138.60mph); R Ginther 1.9s; W Mairesse 2.5s.

04-SEP: This was again on the combined banked track not used since 1956. The British teams felt that the cars now in use, designed for a road circuit, weren't suitable for the bumpy banked track, with its compound loadings. Since Ferrari was the only team using a car of 1956 style, the decision was a stitch-up to favour the obsolete Ferrari. As a result, all the other teams boycotted it. Three Works Ferraris faced no opposition at all. As a race it didn't exist. No front-engined car has won a Championship Formula One race since – if you can really call it a victory. It must have been the longest bore ever – not worthy of any of my grades really, but as a Championship round I have to accede to its 'status.'

1st	P Hill (W)	Ferrari 256 in 2h-21m-09.2s	132.07
2nd	R Ginther (W)	Ferrari 256	2m-28s
3rd	W Mairesse (W)	Ferrari 256	1 lap
F lap	P Hill (W)	Ferrari 256 in 2m-43.6s	136.76r

Championship positions:
Brabham (WC) 40; McLaren 33; P Hill 15.

✱ Lombank Trophy (Snetterton)
37 laps of 2.71 miles = 100.3 miles.
26 F1 + F2 entries – 11 F1 started – 8 F1 finished.
Front row: G Hill – 1m-34.6s (103.13mph); J Clark 0.0s; J Bonnier 0.2s; J Surtees; I Ireland.

17-SEP: Back to some proper racing. Three-car teams from BRM and Lotus, a new teammate, Denny Hulme, for Henry Taylor in the BRP team, and a Cooper for Roy Salvadori formed the main field. An intriguing entry was for a Vanwall-powered Lotus 18 for Brooks. Was Vanwall returning? We hoped so, and, with 280bhp, it should be fast. It was, but it non-started due to engine problems, as had Dan Gurney's BRM. Lotus drivers Clark, Surtees and Ireland led the pack. Ireland passed Surtees, who was soon chased by Hill and Bonnier. Surtees couldn't hold off the BRMs and soon retired with mechanical maladies. Hill overshot The Esses on lap seven, and Clark did likewise on lap 13, so Ireland took the lead and won. Salvadori was fourth.

1st	I Ireland (W)	Lotus 18-Climax in 58m-33.8s	102.73
2nd	J Clark (W)	Lotus 18-Climax	13.0s
3rd	J Bonnier (W)	BRM P48	1m-03s
F lap	J Clark	Lotus 18-Climax in 1m-32.6s	105.36r

✱✱✱ VII International Gold Cup (Oulton Park)

60 laps of 2.678 miles = 160.7 miles.
21 entries – 18 started – 8 finished
Front row: S Moss – 1m-40.4s (96.03mph); J Clark 1.2s;
J Brabham 1.2s; G Hill 1.2s.

24-SEP: A superb entry with only Ferrari not attending, as it didn't for the remainder of the Championship race. This was Oulton Park – Moss' track – and he duly dominated practice. He was rarely a good starter, though, and Brabham led from Ireland, Clark, McLaren, Moss and Bonnier after a lap. By lap seven it was Ireland, Clark, Brabham, Moss and Bonnier. On lap 14 Clark followed Ireland to lap Brian Naylor's JBW, and was eliminated when Naylor failed to realise he was there. The great three-way lead battle from lap 15 with Ireland, Brabham and Moss produced every permutation over the next few laps. Lap 30 saw Ireland's gearbox break after leading for ten laps. Moss had passed Brabham on lap 24, and soon led the race with a fair margin from Brabham, Hill and McLaren. Things remained this way to the end, so Moss was still unbeaten at this drivers' circuit! Bonnier's and Gurney's BRMs followed. A great race, better than many a Championship round. Ferrari wasn't missed.

1st	S Moss (RW)	Lotus 18-Climax in 1h-45m-54.0s	91.03
2nd	J Brabham (W)	Cooper T53-Climax	22.8s
3rd	G Hill (W)	BRM P48	47.4s
F lap	J Clark (W)	Lotus 18-Climax in 1m-42.4s	94.16

✱✱✱ (WC9) 3rd United States Grand Prix (Riverside)

75 laps of a 3.275 mile circuit = 244.3 miles.
25 entries – 23 starters – 16 finished.
Front row: S Moss – 1m-54.4s (103.06mph); J Brabham 0.6s;
D Gurney 0.8s.

20-NOV: The Grand Prix moved from Florida to California for the last race of the successful 2.5-litre formula. Ferrari was absent, but Phil Hill drove for BRP and von Trips for Centro-Sud. Brabham made his normal great start, leading Moss, Gurney, Ireland and Bonnier, while behind them Surtees and Clark had a coming-together. After four laps

Brabham had a scare when fuel overflow in an undertray hit the exhaust on acceleration and the explosion scorched Brabham's back. The pits found nothing. It happened again four laps later and then the cause was found. Moss now led from Gurney and Bonnier but Gurney retired on lap 19. Bonnier, Ireland and McLaren held position behind Moss until lap 59 when Bonnier's engine went rough and he slipped back. Brabham recovered to fourth place ahead of Jim Hall (later of Chaparral fame) and Bonnier, but Hall's transmission failed near the end. Graham Hill retired from fourth on lap 36, so a poor race for BRM. That was it for 2.5-litre F1.

1st	S Moss (RW)	Lotus 18-Climax in 2h-28m-52.2s	99.00
2nd	I Ireland (W)	Lotus 18-Climax	38.0s
3rd	B McLaren (W)	Cooper T53-Climax	52.0s
F lap	J Brabham (W)	Cooper T53-Climax in 1m-56.3s	101.38

Championship positions:
Brabham (WC) 43; McLaren 34; Moss 19.

*Winners of the 15 F1 races of 1960 –
quantity & quality of success*

6 wins	J Brabham (6A)	8 wins	Cooper-Climax (7A, C)
3 wins	S Moss (3A) I Ireland (A, B, C)	6 wins	Lotus-Climax (4A, B, C)
1 win	B McLaren (A) P Hill (C) M Trintignant (C)	1 win	Ferrari (C)

1960 seasonal review

The emergence of John Surtees as a major talent in Formula One in his first ever season in cars, whilst simultaneously winning World Championships for MV Agusta on two wheels, must rank as one of the most astonishing feats in the history of motor sport. Fate alone surely robbed him of the Portuguese Grand Prix. It was surely the best 'rookie' F1 season until Lewis Hamilton's in 2007. The comparison between Surtees and fellow F1 rookie Jim Clark was fascinating, each having the better of the other at times. There were now four good Americans in F1 (in order of arrival in Europe): Masten Gregory, Phil Hill, Dan Gurney and Richie Ginther. How good that would be in the 21st century. Moss' recovery was thankfully complete, and he finished the year as strongly as he started it. With the loss of three F1 talents (Harry Schell, Alan Stacey, and the young and exciting Chris Bristow) this was one of Formula One's two worst ever years, matching that of only two years before.

The nine Championship rounds (or was it really 8½?) were supported by six non-Championship races, which produced some of the best F1 racing of the year. Lotus had come from nowhere in 1959 to take over in the early part of the year, and forced Cooper to do something about it, which it did remarkably quickly with the T53. The Ferrari win at Monza meant nothing as to its competitiveness. The new 1500cc Formula One for 1961 was a certainty now, and the domination of British cars would be severely tested. Ferrari had won in F2 with both front- and rear-engined cars – the latter on its debut at Solitude – so it was obviously ready, as was Porsche. There was no sign of an available new F2 engine from any British engine supplier, despite the existence of Formula Two to test them in advance of the new F1. The engine situation in F1 was that, without Coventry Climax, the formula would be near to the inadequate situation that occurred in 1952, when F2 had to take over. But the availability of Cooper and Lotus for purchase created a new era of 'anyone can do it.'

1960 Championship review

This season is generally looked back on as a runaway one for Jack Brabham. The fact is, though, that he did not take the overall lead in the title race until after the sixth of the nine rounds. Consistency on Bruce McLaren's part saw him in the Championship lead after each of the first four rounds and still share it after round five of nine. He had competed in only 12 GPs in an F1 car, but had won twice, at the age of just 22, and was set to hold the 'youngest winner' record for 43 years. He even just led Stirling Moss after round three! Moss, unfortunately, and through no possible fault of his own, was to miss the next three rounds due to the infamous crash in practice for the Spa race when a wheel fell off. His subsequent return to winning ways by the year's end was amazing, in a manner similar to that of Niki Lauda in 1976.

The 'best six points' system meant that after Oporto, McLaren could beat Brabham's score if he won the remaining two Grands Prix and Brabham gained only a single point. Regrettably, this interesting potential scenario was thwarted when the Italian GP was boycotted by all the main teams but Ferrari, and that sealed the Championship prematurely in Jack Brabham's favour. However, with five successive Championship wins, his right to the title was beyond dispute.

The 'Hard Luck Trophy,' if there had been one, was a battle between the BRM team drivers, Graham Hill and Dan Gurney. I give it to Gurney, for losing 14 points and failing to get on the score sheet at all. Graham Hill lost 24 points while securing only four. Both had retired from a race when leading.

The value of nearly winning a race can be measured by the fact that at season's end, apparently, it was John Surtees and not Jim Clark that was offered the team leadership for 1961 by Colin Chapman, replacing Innes Ireland. Surtees had shown a potential 15 points from four starts to Clark's ten from six starts. From John Surtees autobiography, I discover Chapman even asked Surtees who he wanted as teammate and he replied: "I'd take Jimmy, but what about Innes?" Chapman assured him that, "Innes is all organised. It's all fixed." Why didn't it happen? Because Ireland called Surtees to ask "What's going on, you're taking my place?" Surtees was told by Chapman that Innes Ireland's contract was being transferred to a second Works team run by BRP and everything was sorted. It clearly wasn't, though, so Surtees said to Chapman "Enough is enough – count me out." Naiveté? No ... integrity ... a much rarer commodity now, sadly. Surely this is one of the biggest 'What if's' in motor racing.

VISIT VELOCE ON THE WEB – WWW.VELOCE.CO.UK
All current books • New book news • Special offers • Gift vouchers • Forum

163

Chapter 20

1961
Formula wars – ICF v F1

Inter-Continental Formula – The kiss-of-life for 2.5-litre F1?

The CSI (now FIA) decision in 1958 to convert the 1500cc Formula Two into Formula One for 1961 had caused uproar. The British constituted all of the F1 marques except Ferrari, and felt their weight of numbers could overturn the decision. However, during 1959, Porsche developed an F2 car with which it could join Ferrari in Grand Prix racing in 1961. At the same time as the announcement of the new F1, the CSI had sanctioned this single-seater series to attract the Americans into Grand Prix type circuit racing. If successful, it would create a more 'world-wide' competition than the new Formula One so, though welcomed by everyone, the logic was difficult to understand. The series was called the 'Inter-Continental Formula,' and was for 3-litre cars, but no Championship was established. Ferrari had supported it originally, but now withdrew as it had sold its obsolete 1960 cars and the Scuderia knew it was better prepared for Formula One as the British had distracted themselves with this formula.

All the British teams and the American Scarabs, which had joined F1 in 1960, competed with their regular drivers, so the outgoing Formula One of 1960 effectively continued. Even Vanwall, Constructor Champion of 1958, came back to the tracks with a rear-engined car powered by its own engine stretched to 2.6 litres, and more powerful than the ubiquitous Climax FPF. Tony Vandervell must have felt that his presence would give this series clout or he would be wasting his time. However, Coventry Climax and BRM were well into new V8 designs for Formula One, so they couldn't have wanted this series to be too successful could they? Only Ferrari was missing from the ICF grids – as it had also been from the American GP the year before, so ICF was top class serious racing.

The first of these races were, I feel, in the Antipodes.

Although not designated as ICF races, a 3-litre limit was used, so they conformed to the ICF and should be regarded as such. Stirling Moss classifies them as ICF in his *All my Races* book, so no argument there. The first official ICF race was at Snetterton – a pathetic event mixed with F1 – but these Antipodean events were patently better than that.

Formula One
Less (power) gives more (racing)

A British appeal in May 1960 to the FIA to think again was thrown out, so now there was nothing to do but get on with trying to win. As Formula Two, engines had been restricted to six cylinders, but now, promoted to Formula One, the number of cylinders was unrestricted. The British set about their V8 units, but were about nine months behind Porsche and Ferrari, who had developed highly competitive cars in the 1960 F2 season. At Monaco, Coventry Climax produced an interim revised 1500cc FPF engine with 152bhp to power all the British 'fleet,' which now included BRM. The British would need to continue their superiority in the chassis department, as power was still some way off that of the flat-four Porsche, which had 160bhp, and far away from Ferrari's V6 with almost 180bhp. The new V8 engines would not be seen until late in the season. Since the 1500cc Formula Two had been created in 1957, 'extra' F1 races had dwindled because F2 was cheaper, and the F1 stars competed in it. In 1961, however, the flood gates were opened, as all of those races were now full-blown Formula One events. This gave a season of some thirty two races, of varying standard, from South Africa to Sweden, of which just eight were rounds of the World Championship (the Portuguese GP having dropped from the calendar). The 'one round per nation' rule was preventing a representative Championship. A Championship win was now nine points.

The Formula One constructors

Scuderia Ferrari sprang a surprise with the 'shark-nose' Tipo 156. Initially featuring a 65°V6 engine, it was soon updated with a 120°V version. The drivers would be Wolfgang von Trips, Phil Hill and Richie Ginther. A few races would also involve a hitherto unknown Italian: Giancarlo Baghetti. What could he do?

Porsche had recruited Dan Gurney to join Joakim Bonnier, and tried updated suspension on the previous year's cars; now called the Type 787.

Team Lotus produced an even smaller car than the Type 18, with a sleek, smoother body: the Type 21. After the off-season mix up, the team leader was still Innes Ireland, with Jim Clark as number two.

The Cooper team remained unchanged, with Jack Brabham and Bruce McLaren, but its chances of a third title were extremely slim, due to the first V8 Climax not arriving until the German GP.

BRM had retained Graham Hill, and taken on Tony Brooks, but would have to use Climax engines in the Type 57 until the arrival of the V8, which was hoped for Monza.

The independents

The RRC Walker Racing Team was the independent most likely to worry the Works teams, simply because it had Stirling Moss. It would run Lotus-Climax cars, but wasn't supplied with the latest models; instead updating the cars with bodywork similar to that of the Lotus 21. The cars were designated 18/21s.

The British Racing Partnership lost its sponsor after a dispute between another firm run by Ken Gregory and Yeoman Credit, but found a new sponsor and entered as UDT-Laystall Racing, with Henry Taylor and Cliff Allison (others being used after Allison's Monaco accident).

A new team to Formula One was Reg Parnell Racing, which had taken over the Yeoman Credit funds lost by the BRP. Reg Parnell, a former top-line driver himself, had taken Aston Martin to World Sports Car Championship victory, and managed its F1 project. He attracted a strong driver line-up. After the mix-up over his contract with Chapman and Lotus, John Surtees – all other works seats having been taken – signed with this team as the best available. Veteran Roy Salvadori was strong support.

Another interesting new team in Formula One was Camoradi International. Although it sounds Italian, the name is a catchy contraction of Casner Motor Racing Division, run by the American Lloyd 'Lucky' Casner, who also ran a successful team of Maserati 'Birdcage' sports-racing cars. It had won the Nürburgring '1000km' race with Moss at the

wheel. Clearly, Camoradi knew what it was doing. It had a Cooper T53 for the skilful Masten Gregory, and Britisher Ian Burgess drove a Lotus 18.

The Grand Prix driver's diary of single-seater racing for the 1961 season

Series were run in South Africa spanning New Year 1960/1 and 1961/2. These anticipated the 1961 season and stretched into January 1962, but belong to the 1961 season. They were run as Formule Libre, but all serious competitors were in cars conforming to 1961 F1, so they were de facto F1 races.

A proper race series took place 'down-under' this year. Seven events involving F1 stars and run to the usual 'down-under' series format, which had a 3-litre limit so now matched the new Intercontinental Formula (ICF). Indeed, Stirling Moss classifies them as such in his book *All My Races*. No Championship was run, though, and fuel was less restricted than in ICF, so methanol, which produced more power, was allowed.

17th Dec '60	F1 – Cape Grand Prix at Killarney (SA) – 148.3 miles
27th Dec '60	F1 – South African Grand Prix at East London (SA) – 195.2 miles
7th January	FIC – New Zealand Grand Prix at Ardmore (NZ) – 180 miles
14th January	FIC – Levin International (NZ) – 32.5 miles
21st January	FIC – Lady Wigram Trophy at Christchurch (NZ) – 150.2 miles
29th January	FIC – Australian Grand Prix at Warwick Farm (Au) – 101 miles
4th February	FIC – Teretonga Trophy at Invercargill (NZ) – 75 miles
12th February	FIC – Victoria Trophy at Ballarat (Au) – 117 miles
5th March	FIC – Longford International (Au) – 108 miles
26th March	F1/FIC – Lombank Trophy at Snetterton (UK) – 100.3 miles
3rd April	F1 – Glover Trophy at Goodwood (UK) – 100.8 miles
3rd April	FIC – Lavant Cup at Goodwood (UK) – 50.4 miles
3rd April	F1 – Pau Grand Prix (F) – 171.5 miles
9th April	F1 – Grand Prix de Bruxelles at Heysel (B) – 186.6 miles
16th April	F1 – Preis von Wien at Aspern (A) – 9.33 miles*
22nd April	F1 – Aintree '200' (UK) – 150 miles
25th April	F1 – Gran Premio di Siracusa (I) – 191.4 miles
6th May	FIC – *Daily Express* International Trophy at Silverstone (UK) – 234.2 miles

14th May	F1 – **Grand Prix de Monaco** (M) – 195.4 miles
14th May	F1 – Gran Premio di Napoli at Posillipo (I) – 92.9 miles
22nd May	F1 – **Grote Prijs van Nederland** at Zandvoort (N) – 195.4 miles
22nd May	F1 – London Trophy at Crystal Palace (UK) – 51.4 miles
3rd June	F1 – Silver City Trophy at Brands Hatch (UK) – 187.6 miles
18th June	F1 – **Grand Prix de Belgique** at Spa Francorchamps (B) – 262.8 miles
2nd July	F1 – **Grand Prix de l'ACF** at Reims (F) – 268.2 miles
8th July	FIC – British Empire Trophy at Silverstone (UK) – 152.2 miles
15th July	F1 – **British Grand Prix** at Aintree (UK) – 225 miles
23rd July	F1 – Grosser Preis der Solitude (D) – 177.3 miles
6th August	F1 – **Grosse Preis von Deutschland** (D) at Nürburgring – 212.5 miles
7th August	FIC – Guards Trophy at Brands Hatch (UK) – 201.4 miles
20th August	F1 – Kanonloppet at Karlskoga (S) – 55.9 miles
26th August	F1 – Danske Grand Prix at Roskilde (Dk) – 59.7 miles
3rd September	F1 – Gran Premio di Modena (I) – 147.1 miles
10th September	F1 – **Gran Premio d'Italia** at Monza (I) – 262.7 miles
17th September	F1 – Flugplatzrennen at Zeltweg (A) – 159.1 miles
23rd September	F1 – International Gold Cup at Oulton Park (UK) – 160.7 miles
1st October	F1 – Lewis-Evans Trophy at Brands Hatch (UK) – 79.5 miles*
8th October	F1 – **United States Grand Prix** at Watkins Glen (US) – 230 miles
12th October	F1 – Coppa Italia at Vallelunga (I) – 66.2 miles*
9th December	F1 – Rand Grand Prix at Kyalami (SA) – 190 miles
17th December	F1 – Natal Grand Prix at Westmead (SA) – 195.8 miles
26th December	F1 – South African Grand Prix at East London (SA) – 194.9 miles
2nd January '62'	F1 – Cape Grand Prix at Killarney (SA) – 123.4 miles

43 events of total race mileage = 5905 miles, or 5661 max due

to simultaneous events.

Events in bold are World Championship rounds – 25.8 per cent of F1 races run.

* See Appendix A for these ungraded race results.

(F1) Cape Grand Prix (Killarney)
72 laps of 2.06 miles = 148.3 miles.
21 started – 10 finished.

No grid details available.

17-DEC-1960: Moss and Bonnier were in their regular cars, but von Trips drove a Lotus-Climax and came third. European regular Count Godin de Beaufort had a Cooper-Climax), and was fifth behind Bruce Johnston. Moss recalls winning this with ease, though Jo Bonnier was close.

1st	S Moss (RW)	Porsche 718 in 1h-57m-40.8s	75.61
2nd	J Bonnier (W)	Porsche 718	0.4s
F lap	J Bonnier	Porsche 718 in 1m-31.1s	81.39

✱ (F1) VII South African GP (East London)
80 laps of 2.44 miles = 195.2 miles.
25 started – 18 finished.

Front row: S Moss – 1m-38.0s (89.62mph). No other information

27-DEC-1960: Clearly the country's most prestigious event. Jack Brabham joined the party for this race, elevating its status to grade C. Again the top ten finishers' cars would all be F1 cars in just five days. The same assortment of local hybrids as earlier also entered, yet only six of the large field retired. The Porsche threat was now obvious.

1st	S Moss (RW)	Porsche 718 in 2h-11m-02s	89.36
2nd	J Bonnier (W)	Porsche 718	14.0s
3rd	J Brabham (W)	Cooper T53-Climax	1 lap
F lap	J Bonnier	Porsche 718 in 1m-35.7s	91.77

✱✱✱ (ICF) VIII New Zealand GP (Ardmore)
15 + 75 laps of 1.988 miles = 178.9 miles.
38 entries – 24 started final – 14 finished.

Poles: Heat one: S Moss – 1m-20.2s (89.27mph). Heat two – J Brabham – 1m-20.4s (89.01mph).

07-JAN: The cream of the 1960 F1 World Championship was here, with Works teams from Lotus, Cooper and BRM, plus the RRC Walker team. Even the Italian GP winning Ferrari was here, driven by the experienced Pat Hoare. Moss, McLaren, Brabham and Hill formed the front row for the final. It was McLaren, Brabham and Moss on lap one, but after five more Moss led and pulled away. Drive failure put

Moss out on lap 32, though, and Brabham led but nursed a rough motor at the end. After Hill, two laps down, were Ron Flockhart, Denny Hulme. Jim Clark was sixth, Salvadori retired on lap 36 from fourth, and Dan Gurney, John Surtees, Innes Ireland and Jo Bonnier also failed to finish.

1st	J Brabham (W)	Cooper T53-Climax in 1h-42m-30.0s	87.82
2nd	B McLaren (W)	Cooper T53-Climax	1.7s
3rd	G Hill (W)	BRM P48	1 lap
F lap	S Moss (RW)	Lotus 18-Climax in 1m-19.6s	89.94r

(ICF) 2nd Levin International
25 laps of 1.3 miles = 32.5 miles.
16 entries – 14 started – 12 finished.
No grid positions available.

14-JAN: Clark's transmission played up on the rough surface, and he took it easy after Roy Salvadori's Lotus 18 had retired after five laps due to the same thing. Clark's teammate Surtees retired on lap 17 with radiator trouble. All this aided Bonnier's win. In third place, 30 seconds behind Clark, came a name that would become familiar soon – Denny Hulme in a Cooper.

1st	J Bonnier	Cooper T51-Climax in 24m-21.5	80.05
2nd	J Clark (W)	Lotus 18-Climax	8.4s
F lap	J Bonnier	Cooper T51-Climax in 55.7s	84.02

✳ (ICF) Lady Wigram Trophy (Christchurch)
71 laps of 2.116 miles = 150.24 miles.
23 entries – 20 started – 12 finished
Front row: J Surtees: J Brabham; J Bonnier; J Clark. No times available.

21-JAN: In dreadful conditions, Brabham led Moss and McLaren, who collided at the first corner. Moss' car suffered damaged intake trumpets and visibly bent rear suspension yet finished second! Jo Bonnier's Lotus chased Brabham, but spun twice and retired. McLaren brilliantly led on lap 34 but spoiled it with a spin, dropping to sixth. Clark spun and stalled, unable to restart, while Surtees and Salvadori both retired. It had been hoped that a 100mph lap would occur, but all weekend that was impossible. McLaren recovered to fourth behind the well-driven Cooper of Angus Hyslop, who had survived conditions which had caught out some of the best of F1. There had been huge accidents in practice when a TecMec, Ferrari and Maserati filled a ditch together. In the race, Jim Clark spun and miraculously missed a timekeeper's

car, but a Ferrari 625 collided with it, taking off the doors and throwing the occupants out and almost cutting the Ferrari in half. Amazingly no serious injuries resulted. This farcical race was stopped early.

1st	J Brabham (W)	Cooper T53-Climax 47 laps in 1h-16m-33.9s	77.19
2nd	S Moss (RW)	Lotus 18-Climax	48.5s
3rd	A Hyslop	Cooper T45-Climax 2.0	1m-22s
F lap	J Brabham (W)	Cooper T53-Climax in 1m-33.0s	81.91

✳ (ICF) Australian Grand Prix (Warwick Farm)
45 laps of 2.25 miles = 101.2 miles.
14 started – 5 finished.
Front row: S Moss – 1m-39.2s (81.65mph); D Gurney 0.1s; G Hill 0.9s; I Ireland 1.0s.

29-JAN: The front row consisted of Moss and the BRMs of Gurney and Graham Hill. On lap six Moss led from Hill and Gurney, but the heat, combined with the alcohol fuel used, melted a seam in Hill's fuel tank and all fuel was lost. Jack Brabham retired on lap 25 with fuel trouble. Four laps to go and Gurney lost second place with a split fuel pipe. So local man Bib Stillwell got third.

1st	S Moss (RW)	Lotus 18-Climax in 1h-16m-33.9s	79.34
2nd	I Ireland (W)	Lotus 18-Climax	1m-50s
3rd	B Stillwell	Cooper T51-Climax	2 lap
F lap	S Moss (RW)	Lotus 18-Climax in 1m-40.3s	80.76

(ICF) IV Teretonga Trophy (Invercargill)
50 laps of 1.5 miles = 75 miles.
16 entries – 14 started – 12 finished.
Front row: J Bonnier; D Hulme; P Hoare; A Shelly. No times available.

04-FEB: Bonnier and Salvadori were the only F1 stars here, but a new name showed his real promise when Denny Hulme again finished third (again, 30 seconds adrift in a Cooper identical to that of the winner, so only 0.5s a lap slower). One of the 1960 F1 Ferrari 256s with a 3-litre engine was fourth, in the hands of local man Pat Hoare, also on the lead lap.

1st	J Bonnier	Cooper T51-Climax in 1h-00m-55.0s	73.87
2nd	R Salvadori	Lotus 18-Climax	5.0s
F lap	J Bonnier	Cooper T51-Climax in 1m-08.4s	78.95

(ICF) Victorian Trophy (Ballarat)
6 + 33 laps of circa 3 miles = 18 + 99 miles.
15 entries – 12 started – 9 finished.
Front row: R Flockhart – 1m-52s (95.40mph); D Gurney 1s;
G Hill 2s.

12-FEB: The BRM Works team faced no real opposition
beyond Flockhart. Gurney took the first heat from
Flockhart, and Hill the second from Stillwell. In the final
Gurney took off never to be headed, while Hill had a
disastrous start and had to chase Flockhart. He only just
'succeeded' after the last bend as Flockhart's engine went
off song after a very good drive by him. This was a one-off
event at this simple airfield track. Rudimentary timing only
done to the whole second.

1st	D Gurney (W)	BRM P48 in 1h-02m-52s	94.50
2nd	G Hill (W)	BRM P48	40s
F lap	D Gurney (W)	BRM P48 in 1m-51s	104.23

(ICF) Longford International (Tasmania)
24 laps of 4.5 miles = 108.0 miles.
19 entries – 14 started – 10 finished.
Front row: J Brabham; W Patterson; S Jones. No times
available.

05-MAR: Just Jack Brabham and Roy Salvadori of the visitors
stayed on for this race. Yes Brabham was regarded as an
'overseas' driver, being domiciled in England. Salvadori had
an easy time after Brabham suffered a broken half-shaft on
lap 16.

1st	R Salvadori	Cooper T51-Climax in 1h-01m-43.4s	104.98
2nd	W Patterson	Cooper T51-Climax	13.8s
F lap	n/a		

(ICF) Lombank Trophy (Snetterton)
37 laps of 2.71 miles = 100.3 miles.
7 ICF/12 F1 entries – 5 ICF started – 2 ICF finished.
Front row: I Ireland – 1m-34.4s 103.35mph; J Brabham 1.4s;
C Allison 1.4s.

26-MAR: Combining ICF and the new F1 did no good
for either class. If it was to show how much faster ICF was
then it was proven as Ireland was almost four seconds
faster than Surtees' F1 in practice. Apart from the three
stars above, no other competitive ICF cars were present.
Allison led away, but by the end of the first lap Brabham
and Ireland were ahead. Ireland took the lead on lap four,
with Brabham happy to wait. On lap 15 Ireland retired and
that was that.

1st	J Brabham	Cooper T53-Climax in 59m-31.6s	102.67
2nd	C Allison (BRP)	Lotus 18-Climax	1m-22s
F lap	I Ireland (W)	Lotus 18-Climax in 1m-33.6s	104.23

(F1) Lombank Trophy (Snetterton)
37 laps of 2.71 miles = 100.3 miles.
12 F1 entries – 9 F1 started – 6 F1 finished.
Front row: ICF car; ICF car; ICF car; J Surtees – 1m-38.2s
(99.35mph): R Salvadori 1.6s.

26-MAR: Combining ICF and the new F1 did no good for
either class. If it was to show how much faster ICF was then
it was proven, as Ireland's pole time was almost four seconds
better than Surtees' F1 in fourth spot on the grid. Surtees led
the F1 class all the way, but was lapped by the ICF winner.
Roy Salvadori pitted twice yet recovered to beat Jim Clark
near the finish but failed to catch Henry Taylor. If it had been
run for a single category it might have had status. Run as it
was, both classes were unworthy.

1st	J Surtees (YCP)	Cooper T53-Climax 1.5 in 1h-00m-35.2s	96.61
2nd	H Taylor (UDT)	Lotus 18-Climax 1.5	31.6s
F lap	R Salvadori (YCP)	Cooper T53-Climax 1.5 in 1m-38.0s	99.55

(ICF) Lavant Cup (Goodwood)
21 laps of 2.4 miles = 50.4 miles.
9 entries and starters – 9 finished.
Front row: B McLaren – 1m-24.2s (102.61mph); S Moss 0.4s;
G Hill 0.6s; CAS Brooks 1.0s.

03-APR: This was a supporting race to the main F1 event.
Gurney's Lotus 18 came through from the second row to
lead from McLaren. Moss' car slipped out of gear at the
start, but was fifth by lap three, and soon on the tail the
leaders. McLaren led on lap nine until 15 when Moss took
over. McLaren challenged hard, but Moss held on. Hill's
BRM took third from Gurney who tried to retake it on the
last lap but crashed (without injury). A pity the race was
wet, for they were three seconds a lap faster than Formula
One.

1st	S Moss (RW)	Cooper T53-Climax in 33m-25.6s	90.47
2nd	B McLaren	Cooper T53-Climax	0.6s
F lap	B McLaren	Cooper T53-Climax in 1m-30.4s	95.57

✷✷ (F1) IX Glover Trophy (Goodwood)

42 laps of 2.4 miles = 100.8 miles.
15 entries – 14 started – 12 finished.
Front row: S Moss – 1m-27.8s (98.41mph); J Surtees 1.0s;
R Salvadori 1.0s; G Hill 1.0s.

03-APR: Pau and Goodwood clashed, but the best entry
was here. Lotus entered both events, with Ireland driving.
Surtees stormed off, and a Surtees/Moss duel followed for
21 laps. Moss failed to get by on the outside at Lavant; a rare
occurrence! His engine went off song soon after, and he fell
back to fourth when passed by Salvadori, who had recovered
after spinning on lap three. He was almost lapped by Surtees
at the end. Brooks' BRM passed Ireland's Lotus 18 for fifth,
but then crashed. This was a deserved first F1 victory for
Surtees, and not too soon; he was unlucky not to have won in
Portugal the previous year.

1st	J Surtees (YCP)	Cooper T53-Climax in 1h-03m-10.0s	95.76
2nd	G Hill (W)	BRM P57-Climax	26.6s
3rd	R Salvadori (YCP)	Cooper T53-Climax	1m-09s
F lap	J Surtees	Cooper T53-Climax in 1m-28.0s	98.18

✷ (F1) XXI Grand Prix de Pau

100 laps of 1.714 = 171.4 miles.
19 entries – 16 started – 6 finished.
Front row: **J Brabham** – 1m-32.7s (66.56mph); J Clark 0.2s;
M Trintignant 1.8s.

03-APR: It may have had a long history but Goodwood was
attracting the better entry now on this annual day of clashes.
Porsche, surprisingly, didn't enter, so Bonnier drove a private
Lotus 18. Brabham's sole Works Cooper was the only worry
that Clark had, but he expired on lap nine. Bonnier hung on
for a few laps but then dropped back and the race was then
all but over. Trintignant had clutch trouble, which made him
last away, but a great drive took the Pau specialist back to
fifth place before retiring. Clark's teammate Trevor Taylor
fought from a poor start to fourth, before retiring on lap 41.
The excellent privateer Jack Lewis lost a secure third place
because of fuel fumes making him drowsy. He lost a whole
lap, and ended up fifth behind Cabral's Cooper.

1st	J Clark (W)	Lotus 18-Climax in 2h-42m-00.3s	63.48
2nd	J Bonnier	Lotus 18-Climax	1m-31s
3rd	L Bandini (SCS)	Cooper T51-Maserati	3 laps
F lap	J Clark	Lotus 18-Climax in 1m-34.1s	65.57r

✷✷ (F1) III Grand Prix de Bruxelles (Heysel)

3 x 22 laps of 2.828 miles = 186.6 miles.
24 entries – 19 started – 8 finished.
Front row: J Bonnier – 2m-02.7s (82.99mph); B McLaren
1.7s; D Gurney 2.0s.

09-APR: A three-parter, with points for first = 1; second =
2, etc. But aggregate times gave the same result, thankfully.
Ferrari and BRM were the only absentees. Bonnier led from
Gurney, McLaren, Clark, Surtees and Brabham, but Clark and
Gurney soon retired, and Surtees' gear lever broke. By lap eight
Brabham was second, ahead of McLaren, having been seventh
on lap one, but both had a 60 second penalty for a jumped
start, which surprised everyone and elevated Salvadori to
second. Heat one winner Bonnier led again, and Surtees came
from sixth to attack Bonnier for the lead on lap 12, but touched
the back of his car and both retired damaged, to Brabham's
advantage. Moss' misfire was cured in heat three, so he was no
threat despite finishing only 0.1 second behind Brabham.

1st	J Brabham (W)	Cooper T53-Climax in 2h-19m-21.8s	80.37
2nd	B McLaren	Cooper T53-Climax	1m-7s
3rd	A Marsh	Lotus 18-Climax	3m-08s
F lap	J Surtees (YCP)	Cooper T53-Climax in 2m-02.6s	83.06r

✷✷ (F1) V International 'Aintree 200'

50 laps of 3.0 miles = 150 miles.
31 entries – 28 started – 17 finished.
Front row: G Hill – 2m-00.2s (89.85mph); J Brabham 0.4s;
B McLaren 1.2s.

22-APR: Ferrari and Porsche were absent, but Gurney had a
Lotus 18 so the driver entry was great. Dunlop had a new wet
weather tyre, and so began the 'tyre choice problem' in F1 racing.
It was wet throughout, and Cooper made the right choice.
Brabham led all the way, from Clark, who was soon passed by
McLaren, Hill and Surtees. Surtees took third from Hill, but, on
lap 16, was deprived of it again. The top four places remained
unaltered from then. Perhaps the best drive of the day was by
Masten Gregory who, from the very back of the grid (he had not
posted a practice time), was 17th on lap one, but sixth on lap 18
and took fifth from Clark on lap 42 – a storming drive in adverse
conditions. Clark dropped to ninth with electrical trouble.

1st	J Brabham (W)	Cooper T55-Climax in 1h-55m-17.2s	78.06
2nd	B McLaren (W)	Cooper T55-Climax	28.4s
3rd	G Hill (W)	BRM P57-Climax	1m-10s
F lap	J Brabham	Cooper T55-Climax in 2m-15.0s	80.00

✱✱✱ (F1) XI Gran Premio di Siracusa

56 laps of 3.418 miles = 191.4 miles.
26 entries – 19 started – 11 finished.
Front row: D Gurney – 1m-56.9s (105.24mph); G Baghetti
0.1s; J Surtees 0.9s.

25-APR: Just three days after Aintree and Ferrari (just one), and Porsche were here, as were all the British teams. The new amazing-looking Ferrari was driven by an unknown in his first F1 race. Why choose an unknown? He'd won an Italian competition in lesser formulae to find a new Italian star. And he was almost on pole position! Next to him was Surtees in the Yeoman Credit Cooper with extra-sleek bodywork – called the VR (very rapid). Surtees led away, and he and Gurney swapped the lead for four laps. Baghetti spun down to seventh but, by lap six, he had bagged the lot. Gurney led one lap (25), then that was it. Surtees had his fuel pump drive fail on lap ten, so only Gurney challenged the precocious newcomer. Moss had carburation problems and never featured. Brabham was fourth; Salvadori fifth; Clark sixth. No one had ever won their debut F1 race before, and against all the main opposition. What could the regular drivers do with this Ferrari? The British had been caught napping.

1st	G Baghetti (W)	Ferrari 156-65° in 1h-50m-08.2s	104.38
2nd	D Gurney (W)	Porsche 718	5.0s
3rd	J Bonnier (W)	Porsche 718	1 lap
F lap	D Gurney	Porsche 718 in 1m-54.9s	107.08

✱✱✱ (ICF) XIII *Daily Express* International Trophy (Silverstone)

80 laps of 2.927 miles = 234.2 miles.
24 entries – 19 started – 9 finished.
Front row: B McLaren – 1m-34.2s (111.86mph); S Moss 0.6s;
J Brabham 1.2s; G Hill 1.4s.

06-MAY: A great field arrived for this long race, which saw the only ever outing of the rear-engined Vanwall, with John Surtees at the wheel, and fifth on the grid. The dreadful conditions were perfect for Moss, but it was Brabham, McLaren, Moss and Surtees as they departed. Clark and Ireland spun at Abbey on the opening lap but restarted. On lap six McLaren spun off and Surtees passed Moss for second. Moss soon rectified that and Brabham lost the lead to Moss on lap 23. Surtees spun the Vanwall on lap 14, pitted, and lost two laps, brilliantly fighting back to fifth – if only it had been dry for this powerful car's unique outing? By lap 53 Moss had lapped the World Champion – in an identical car! Chuck Daigh started the Scarab from near the back and survived to be seventh, three laps down. Drawn-out ... dull? No ... genius is never dull. Moss rates this as one of his finest drives.

1st	S Moss (RW)	Cooper T53-Climax in 2h-41m-19.2s	87.15
2nd	J Brabham (W)	Cooper T53-Climax	1 lap
3rd	R Salvadori (RP)	Cooper T53-Climax	2 laps
F lap	S Moss	Cooper T53-Climax in 1m-52.4s	93.75

✱✱✱ (F1) (WC1) XIX Grand Prix de Monaco (Monte Carlo)

100 laps of a 1.954-mile circuit = 195.4 miles.
21 entries – 16 qualified – 10 finished.
Front row: S Moss – 1m-39.1s (70.98mph); R Ginther 0.2s;
J Clark 0.5s.

14-MAY: As always there was an oversize entry for 16 places. The new Climax FPF Mk2 was now available, and Moss' and Clark's new Lotus 21s sandwiched Ginther's Ferrari using it. This new Lotus was even smaller than the 18; such sleek bodywork and fitting Clark like a glove. Unfortunately, team-leader Innes Ireland selected a wrong gear in the tunnel (the gate was the reverse from usual) and broke a leg when ejected in the ensuing crash. The first lap order was Ginther, Clark, Moss and Gurney, but Clark immediately pitted with fuel pump trouble. Lap 13, and Ginther was passed by Moss and Bonnier, with Phil Hill now fourth. The latter became second on lap 26, while Ginther dropped to fifth. On Lap 41 Ginther recovered to third, and the top three stayed that way until lap 74 when Ginther was invited to pass Hill to see if he could do anything about Moss as Hill was unable to do so. Ginther closed up in a tremendous fight, but Moss held on to claim a fabulous win; in a year-old car against a new car with 20 per cent more horsepower! The fastest lap was just 0.1 second off the record lap set the previous year by Moss, in an identical car but with 58 per cent more power than he had this time! The race average lap time was just 0.39 seconds off the pole time! The race record had been broken by seven minutes! Did someone say these little cars were going to be slow? Moss was driving a Lotus 18/2,1 which was the previous year's car updated with 21-style bodywork. A truly historic drive.

1st	S Moss (RW)	Lotus 18-Climax in 2h-45m-50.1s	70.70
2nd	R Ginther (W)	Ferrari 156-120°	3.6s
3rd	P Hill (W)	Ferrari 156-65°	41.3s
F lap	Moss/Ginther	Lotus/Ferrari in 1m-36.3s	73.06

(F1) Gran Premio di Napoli (Posillipo)

60 laps of 1.548 miles = 92.9 miles.
20 entries – 13 qualified – 8 finished.
Front row: G Ashmore (68.53mph); R Salvadori 0.0s;
G Baghetti 0.1s.

14-MAY: This took place on Monaco Grand Prix day, there being so many Formula One cars now. Salvadori was favourite, despite Ashmore's pole. No other stars here. Future star Lorenzo Bandini led at first, from the second row, but soon Salvadori and Baghetti passed him. On lap four Baghetti had found his confidence on this tight street circuit and now led. Salvadori's pursuit ended on lap 26 with a puncture. Now Baghetti led easily, and recovered from a spin on lap 53 without worry; he'd been two laps ahead. He had now won his first two F1 races, but this one was easy. Will that ever be beaten?

1st	G Baghetti (W)	Ferrari 156-65° in 1h-22m-46.5s	67.31
2nd	G Ashmore	Lotus 18-Climax	1 lap
F lap	G Baghetti	Ferrari 156 in 1m-20.2s	69.47

✶✶✶ (F1) (WC2) IX Grote Prijs van Nederland (Zandvoort)

75 laps of a 2.605-mile circuit = 195.4 miles.
17 invited – 15 started and finished.
Front row: P Hill – 1m-35.7s (98.01mph): W von Trips 0.0s;
R Ginther 0.2s.

22-MAY: The Dutch invited two entries per Works team, yet three for Ferrari and two extra locally-entered Porsches for deBeaufort (of course) and Herrmann. Reg Parnell Racing wasn't a Works team, so Surtees' teammate Salvadori was excluded, yet two were accepted from Camoradi International for Gregory and Burgess (who wasn't in Salvadori's class). When were these organisers going to be brought into line? It wasn't their Championship. An all-Ferrari front row confirmed what was suspected – that Monaco would not be repeated. Von Trips led the whole way, with Phil Hill and Jim Clark battling for second place, swapping six times. Clark was showing how effective the Lotus 21 was. Moss' Lotus 18 just beat Ginther on the last lap, for fourth place. No retirements or a single pit visit made this a unique race – unrepeatable as pit visits are now routine.

1st	W von Trips (W)	Ferrari 156-120° in 2h-01m-52.1.s	96.21
2nd	P Hill (W)	Ferrari 156-120°	0.9s
3rd	J Clark (W)	Lotus 21-Climax	13.1s
F lap	J Clark (W)	Lotus 21-Climax in 1m-35.5s	98.22

Championship positions:
Moss and von Trips 12; P Hill 10.

(F1) IX London Trophy (Crystal Palace)

37 laps of 1.39 miles = 51.4 miles.
17 entries – 13 started – 11 finished.
Front row: R Salvadori – 59.0s (84.81mph); H Taylor 0.6s;
J Lewis 1.2s; C Allison 1.4s.

22-MAY: This provided small consolation for Roy Salvadori and the UDT team of Henry Taylor and Cliff Allison, all three of whom were prevented by the unfair Dutch system from being at Zandvoort today. These three had the only Mk2 Climax engines. Taylor started best, but was passed by Salvadori after two laps. Then it was a slow stretching of his lead. Tony Marsh was third, 20 seconds back.

1st	R Salvadori (YCP)	Cooper T53-Climax in 37m-22.8s	82.55
2nd	H Taylor (UDT)	Lotus 18-Climax	8.0s
F lap	Salvadori/Taylor	Cooper/Lotus in 59.6s	83.96

✶✶✶ (F1) VI Silver City Trophy (Brands Hatch)

76 laps of 2.46 miles = 187 miles.
26 entries – 24 started – 9 finished.
Front row: S Moss – 1m-42.8s (86.14s); J Surtees 0.0s; J Clark 0.2s; G Hill 0.4s.

03-JUN: Neither Ferrari nor Porsche entered, but the latter's drivers, Bonnier and Gurney, did. Gurney had a Lotus 18 owned by American Mrs Louise Bryden-Brown. BRP had updated its Lotus 18s with type 21-style bodywork and suspension, designated 18/21. Moss and Henry Taylor were joined by Bonnier, so a great field was present. Tragedy struck early on in practice when promising newcomer Shane Summers crashed fatally at Paddock Bend. Pole at Brands was not an advantage owing to the camber of the track giving the 'pole-squatter' a steeper climb to Paddock Bend. Surtees led from second grid slot, followed by Clark, Moss, Hill, Brabham, McLaren, Salvadori and Brooks. Almost a stalemate between them occurred for 23 laps, broken when Brabham passed Hill, only to retire two laps later. Hill pitted for throttle linkage repair, and, soon after, Surtees lost the lead to Clark and spun out of the race. Soon afterwards McLaren was forced off by a backmarker, and Moss took Clark to lead at half distance. Salvadori lost third to Brooks, falling back to be lapped, and was followed by Dan Gurney in fifth.

1st	S Moss (BRP)	Lotus 18/21-Climax in 2h-11m-40.6s	85.19
2nd	J Clark (W)	Lotus 21-Climax	10.0s
3rd	CAS Brooks (W)	BRM P57-Climax	1m-28s
F lap	S Moss	Lotus 18/21-Climax in 1m-42.0s	86.82

✱✱✱ (F1) (WC3) XXI Grand Prix de Belgique (Spa)

30 laps of a 8.761-mile circuit = 262.8 miles.
25 entries – 21 started – 13 finished.
Front row: P Hill – 3m-59.3s (131.80mph); W von Trips 0.8s; O Gendebien 3.7s.

18-JUN: Ferrari entered a fourth car in the Belgian colour of yellow for Olivier Gendebien. Ferrari duly occupied the grid front row, with John Surtees in the sole Reg Parnell-run Yeoman Credit Cooper just beating Ginther's Ferrari for fourth grid spot. Surtees' time of 4m-06.0s was easily the best of the British cars, and was 2.6 seconds better than World Champion Brabham's Works Cooper and the Porsches. The UDT-Laystall team, run by BRP, was given only one place, for which its two drivers had to compete, using just one car. However, Allison crashed on his first lap, suffering career-ending leg injuries. In the end it was a Ferrari demonstration, with Gendebien following Ginther home by 26 seconds to complete a four-car Ferrari whitewash, with all but Ginther leading the race at some point. Surtees' Cooper and Graham Hill's BRM battled furiously for fifth. The BRM developed ignition trouble, so Surtees was 'best-of-the-rest,' followed un-challenged by Dan Gurney's Porsche. Porsche wasn't doing as well as the previous year had suggested it would.

1st	P Hill (W)	Ferrari 156-120° in 2h-03m-03.8.s	128.15
2nd	W von Trips (W)	Ferrari 156-120°	0.7s
3rd	R Ginther (W)	Ferrari 156-120°	19.5s
F lap	R Ginther (W)	Ferrari 156-120° in 3m-59.8s	131.53

Championship positions:
P Hill 19; von Trips 18; Moss 12.

✱✱✱ (F1) (WC4) XLVII Grand Prix de l'ACF (Reims)

52 laps of a 5.158-mile circuit = 268.2 miles.
27 entries – 26 started – 14 finished.
Front row: P Hill – 2m-24.9s (128.17mph); W von Trips 1.5s; R Ginther 1.9s.

02-JUL: The fourth Ferrari was this time driven by Giancarlo Baghetti, the wonder-boy of Siracusa. Moss, in fourth spot was best non-Ferrari driver here, and Baghetti was on the fifth row, so the 'rookie' looked no threat here. The Ferrari main trio set off in command, but Ginther spun letting Moss into a temporary third place. Von Trips' engine expired on lap 18, so Phil Hill took over for 20 laps before spinning on the melting surface; the race held in the usual cauldron heat. Two laps later Baghetti had come through the meleé to lie a useful second to Ginther. Two more laps and Ferrari's

fortunes were in his hands as Ginther's engine failed. A famous battle with Gurney's Porsche followed for the final ten laps, places swapping very often. Baghetti timed his slipstream of Gurney perfectly to win at the line. Now he's won his first Championship event and his first three F1 races.

1st	G Baghetti (W)	Ferrari 156-65° in 2h-14m-17.5s	119.84
2nd	D Gurney (W)	Porsche 718	0.1s
3rd	J Clark (W)	Lotus 21-Climax	1m-01s
F lap	P Hill (W)	Ferrari 156-120° in 2m-27.1s	126.25

Championship positions:
P Hill 19; von Trips 18; Moss 12.

✱✱✱ (ICF) XXXII British Empire Trophy (Silverstone)

52 laps of 2.927 miles = 152.2 miles.
22 entries – 18 started – 10 finished.
Front row: J Surtees – 1m-33.0s (113.30mph); S Moss 0.6s; B McLaren 0.8s; J Brabham 0.8s.

08-JUL: The ICF was back at Silverstone with a similar entry to before, but this time with a similar entry, but this time the 4WD Ferguson replaced the Vanwall. It was entered by Rob Walker and driven by Jack Fairman. The Scarab had crashed in practice, and driver Chuck Daigh was hospitalised. A record pole lap from Surtees, but, on yet another damp track, Moss took the lead from Surtees after half a lap; he was never bothered thereafter. Hill took third from McLaren on lap 15, but made no headway on catching Surtees, while Moss went on his merry way. Jack Brabham drove the 2.75-litre Indianapolis Cooper, but dropped to the back of the field on lap four with suspension problems, and retired on lap 16. McLaren was fourth and Clark fifth, a lap down. Another Moss demonstration – on a dry track the record would surely have gone. The Ferguson disappointed but, in truth, Fairman was not amongst the elite.

1st	S Moss (RW)	Cooper T53-Climax in 1h-27m-19.2s	104.58
2nd	J Surtees (RP)	Cooper T53-Climax	50.6s
3rd	G Hill (W)	BRM P48	1m-17s
F lap	S Moss	Cooper T53-Climax in 1m-35.4s	109.31

✱✱✱ (F1) (WC5) XVI British Grand Prix (Aintree)

75 laps of a 3.0-mile circuit = 225.0 miles.
31 entries – 30 started – 16 finished.

Front row: P Hill – 1m-58.8s (90.91mph); R Ginther 0.0s; J Bonnier 0.0s.

15-JUL: On this circuit of mostly slow bends – a point and squirt type of race – Ferrari's power would dominate, though not by much. The top four had identical times, and the first three grid rows were separated by just 0.4 seconds! The closest grid ever, with all three Ferraris on identical times. The race was wet, though, and the Ferrari trio duly took off in formation thanks to their extra power. Moss was in hot pursuit from row two, and, on lap three, passed Ginther, while P Hill and von Trips swapped places at the front. Hill fell to rainmaster Moss on lap ten. Moss now had leader von Trips in his sights, and another famous Moss drive was under way. He hauled him in, but fresh standing water at the superfast Melling Crossing kink caused Moss to spin – he caught it, deliberately re-spun to complete 720° and face the right way, losing only a few seconds (to massive cheers – some of them mine – and all of us on our feet); pure genius at work. He was still second, but the track dried a bit, and this didn't help him. On lap 44 his race was run, due to brake trouble. Near the end, Tony Brooks, in ninth place, and bored after pitting early in the race, decided (his autobiography says) "... to enjoy himself." He left the fastest lap a whole second faster than pole on a drying track with just a narrow dry line. He was known not to like these 'underpowered' Formula One cars, but rain made a difference.

1st	W von Trips (W)	Ferrari 156-120° in 2h-40m-53.6.s	83.91
2nd	P Hill (W)	Ferrari 156-120°	46.0s
3rd	R Ginther (W)	Ferrari 156-120°	46.8s
F lap	CAS Brooks (W)	BRM P57-Climax in 1m-57.8s	91.68

Championship positions:
von Trips 27; P Hill 25; Ginther 16.

✳✳✳ (F1) X Grosser Preis der Solitude

25 laps of 7.092 miles = 177.3 miles.
22 entries – 17 started – 10 finished.

Front row: J Bonnier – 4m-01.s (105.89mph); D Gurney 0.4s; B McLaren 0.8s.

23-JUL: Back to this challenging, 'half-Nürburgring' track. This was no relaxation from the World Championship rounds. Porsche home territory here, so it had four cars, but Ferrari withdrew late on. No less than 300,000 people attended – this was a major race all right! Bonnier, Gurney and McLaren had the front row, but it was four-abreast into the first corner. At the end of the lap, Ireland led McLaren and the Porsche brigade, then Brabham and Moss. Brabham was soon amongst them, and actually led lap 11 – just the

one lap – but on lap 20 a misfire dropped him back, to be overtaken by McLaren. Moss' Lotus 18/21 was now at a disadvantage to the latest Lotus 21s. He qualified fifth, but was never higher than seventh, being down on speed. He retired with gearbox trouble near the end. One lap to go and Bonnier passed Ireland to lead, to huge cheers from the crowd. Ireland immediately retook the lead, almost on the grass, and just held on to beat Porsche on its home ground in one of the best races of 1961 – probably his best win. McLaren and Brabham were fourth and fifth. Clark was only seventh on the grid and finished in that place! Looking back, it seems strange that, on this demanding track, and with Ferrari absent, Moss and Clark didn't make hay. Moss had engine and gear trouble throughout, but Clark, in his book *Jim Clark at the wheel*, expressed annoyance with himself for allowing a road accident on the way home from Aintree to affect his driving. Swerving into railings to avoid an errant motorist had required stitches to a head wound. He was up to the leaders' pace at the end, so any idea that non-Championship status reduced his, or anyone else's, determination is completely unfounded. The result itself proves that.

1st	I Ireland (W)	Lotus 21-Climax in 1h-41m-04.6s	105.24
2nd	J Bonnier (W)	Porsche 718	0.1s
3rd	D Gurney (W)	Porsche 718	0.3s
F lap	D Gurney	Porsche 718 in 3m-58.6s	107.01r

✳✳✳ (F1) (WC6) XXIII Grosse Preis von Deutschland (Nürburgring)

15 laps of 14.173 miles = 212.5 miles.
34 entries – 26 started – 17 finished.

Front row: P Hill – 8m-55.2s (95.37mph); J Brabham 6.2s; S Moss 6.5s; J Bonnier 9.6s.

06-AUG: Back to the Nordschlief for the first time since 1958, and the small-engined cars produced the first ever sub-nine-minute lap. This was, of course, a Ferrari, but it was the only one on the front row. Next to it was Brabham's Cooper, the only car with the long-awaited V8 Climax engine, but handling problems made him only 0.3 seconds better than Moss, with Bonnier's Porsche over three seconds adrift. Moss started on the new wet-weather tyres which others thought would wear out in the dry. Brabham led at first, but, after a mile, hit a puddle and went off. Moss now led, lost it to Phil Hill, took it back and led after a lap. He was never seriously challenged, and completed another superb victory – Moss (the man) beating Ferrari (the machine) on the supreme driver's circuit. Clark, Surtees and McLaren finished the point-scoring places. Gurney's Porsche in seventh led that marque's surprisingly poor race.

173

1st	S Moss (RW)	Lotus 18/21-Climax in 2h-18m-12.4s	92.29
2nd	W von Trips (W)	Ferrari 156-120°	21.4s
3rd	P Hill (W)	Ferrari 156-120°	22.5s
F lap	P Hill (W)	Ferrari 156-120° in 8m-57.8s	94.88r

Championship positions:
von Trips 33; P Hill 29; Moss 21.

✱✱✱ (ICF) Guards Trophy (Brands Hatch)
76 laps of 2.46 miles = 187 miles.
20 entries – 17 started – 6 finished.
Front row: S Moss – 1m-37.4s (90.92mph); B McLaren 1.4s; J Surtees 1.6s; G Hill 1.8s.

07-AUG: As per the previous year, this was the day after the German GP, and another full Grand Prix length race within 24 hours; not allowed now. Surtees shot away, with Moss, Hill and Brabham in pursuit. Lap 17 saw Moss pass Surtees, who then crashed on oil two laps later. Brabham had taken Hill, and Moss led him until retiring with gearbox trouble on lap 24. Brabham now led Hill, Clark and Brooks, the latter retiring with throttle linkage trouble. Hill needed to refuel, so Brabham won by a lap. McLaren was fourth.

1st	J Brabham (W)	Cooper T53-Climax in 2h-10m-53.6s	85.70
2nd	J Clark (W)	Lotus 18-Climax	1 lap
3rd	G Hill (W)	BRM P48	1 lap
F lap	B McLaren (W)	Cooper T53-Climax in 1m-40.2s	88.38r

That was it for the Inter-Continental Formula. Only six events were worthy of good grading, with the New Zealand GP and the last three in England being the best. Only the Scarab had appeared from the USA, and it was little better than in 1960. The rear-engined Vanwall driven by John Surtees had shown promise in May, but in July Brabham and Surtees had tried it and chose to race Coopers. The unique 4WD Ferguson had been converted to F1, and from the main teams there was nothing new, nor was there likely to be, as the derided but now established F1 demanded all their attention. What had probably sealed the formula's fate was the fact that the Dutch, Germans and Italians had stated early on that they would hold their Grands Prix for the small-engined cars anyway, as the chance of a German or Italian win would double the spectator numbers. ICF evaporated, having actually facilitated Ferrari's domination in the new Formula One this year. Would the British make up the gap to Ferrari the following year? New engines had arrived too late for 1961.

✱ (F1) IX Kanonloppet (Karlskoga)
30 laps of 1.864 miles = 55.9 miles.
14 entries – 11 started – 5 finished.
Front row: J Clark – 1m-30.1s (74.18mph); J Bonnier 0.5s; J Brabham 0.9s.

20-AUG: A small invited band of star drivers competed for these two Scandinavian races, taking on 'local aces.' Some had been at the Goodwood Tourist Trophy the day before, but TT winner Moss started from the back, not having practiced. It didn't matter, though, as he was third after one lap behind Clark and Bonnier. Then came Brabham, driving his own car, Surtees, Ireland and Salvadori. Moss led on lap three and pulled away. Surtees passed Brabham for fourth, before Ireland's gearbox failed on lap ten, and Clark retired with suspension failure shortly after. Brabham's gearbox failure on lap 26 gave his fourth place to Salvadori, whose engine failed in sight of the line. He pushed over to retain the place, a lap down ahead but of Tim Parnell, Reg's son.

1st	S Moss (UDT)	Lotus 18/21-Climax in 46m-16.8s	72.50
2nd	J Bonnier (W)	Porsche 718	12.0s
3rd	J Surtees (YCP)	Cooper T53-Climax 'VR'	22.7s
F lap	S Moss	Lotus 18/21-Climax in 1m-30.4s	74.23

✱ (F1) II GP van Danske (Roskilde)
20+30+30 laps of 0.746 miles = 59.65 miles.
12 entries – 11 started – 6 finished.
Front row: S Moss – 42.8s (62.75mph); J Brabham 0.2s; J Surtees 0.5s.

26/27-AUG: The same 'team' minus Bonnier contested this race on the strangest circuit ever to have a F1 race. Built in a gravel pit, it was 'U' shaped, with banked bends and no straights. More of a stadium than a circuit really. Moss won all three heats, holding off Brabham in the first, but had to pass Ireland in the last two. Brabham and Ireland fought for second in heat two until Brabham retired. Salvadori took third, from Surtees' rough-sounding engine, but then non-started heat three, the result of which was a repeat of heat two.

1st	S Moss (UDT)	Lotus 18/21-Climax in 59m-28.5s	60.21
2nd	I Ireland (W)	Lotus 21-Climax	1m-14s
3rd	R Salvadori (YCP)	Cooper T53-Climax	2m-07s
F lap	S Moss	Lotus 18/21-Climax in 42.8s	62.75

✱✱✱ (F1) VII Gran Premio di Modena

100 laps of 1.471 miles = 147.1 miles.

33 entries – 14 qualified – 8 finished.

Front row: S Moss – 58.6s (90.39mph); J Bonnier 0.4s; D Gurney 0.4s.

03-SEP: Ferrari and Bruce McLaren were the only absentees, even though this was on Ferrari's doorstep. Only 14 could start, with three Italians guaranteed, the best of which was Lorenzo Bandini whose 59.8s gave him eighth spot. Ireland lost out through the system. Fangio dropped the flag and Gurney, Moss, G Hill, Salvadori and Surtees led off. Bonnier lost fifth gear and dropped to 12th. Moss led lap 12 and was never headed. Surtees took Hill for third on lap seven, and Gregory also passed him. On lap 25 Gregory inherited third when Surtees stopped, but fuel starvation ruined things and he dropped right back. Bonnier had found fifth gear, fought right through to pass Hill, and deprived Gurney of second on lap 60. Clark and Brabham became fourth and fifth on lap 95, after Graham Hill punctured on the debris of Bandini's engine. Only Moss could beat the Porsches here.

1st	S Moss (RW)	Lotus 18/21-Climax in 1h-40m-08.1s	88.16
2nd	J Bonnier (W)	Porsche 718	7.0s
3rd	D Gurney (W)	Porsche 718	7.3s
F lap	S Moss	Lotus 18/21-Climax in 59.2s	89.48

✱✱✱ (F1) (WC7) XXXI Gran Premio d'Italia (Monza – Combined)

43 laps of a 6.214-mile circuit = 267.2 miles.

37 entries – 32 started – 12 finished.

Front row: W von Trips – 2m-46.3s (134.51mph); P Rodriguez 0.1s. Row two: R Ginther 0.5s; P Hill 0.9s.

10-SEP: There were no accidents the previous year, so there were no objections to the banked track this time. Five Ferraris were there, including one driven by 19-year-old Ricardo Rodriguez having his Grand Prix debut; and he was second on the grid. Only Graham Hill's new V8-powered BRM P578, in fourth place, had got amongst the Ferraris. Hill reverted to the old car for the race, though, whereas Brabham's Cooper did use the V8 Climax. Clark was the fastest of the Climax four-cylinder cars, in seventh. Lap one was Phil Hill, Ginther, Rodriguez, Clark, Brabham and von Trips (who'd made a bad start). Lap two, von Trips passed Clark, Clark challenged under braking for Parabolica, then von Trips moved across to him. Their wheels touched, von Trips spun away to the left, across the run-off grass area, and up the bank to where the crowd was pressed against a chain-link fence. The Ferrari spun like a top along the

fence, killing 14, and somersaulted back to the track, throwing its driver out to his death. The race continued ... they always did. Bonnier slowed near the crash site and was hit by Surtees. By lap 25 only Phil Hill's Ferrari remained of the five that started. Gurney and Moss pursued the leader, swapping places a few times until Moss suffered wheel bearing failure on the banking – not a good place for that. In a very fine fourth place, just 12 seconds behind McLaren came the private Cooper of Welsh farmer Jack Lewis – one of the best 'one-man-bands' in F1. He just beat a slip-streaming Tony Brooks by 0.1 seconds. Phil Hill thus became America's first World Champion in the most tragic Formula One race ever.

1st	P Hill (W)	Ferrari 156-120° in 2h-21m-09.2s	130.11
2nd	D Gurney (W)	Porsche 718	31.2s
3rd	B McLaren (W)	Cooper T55-Climax	2m-28s
F lap	G Baghetti (W)	Ferrari 156-120° in 2m-48.4s	132.84

Championship positions:

P Hill 34 (WC); von Trips 33; Moss 21.

✱ (F1) IV Flugplatzrennen (Zeltweg)

80 laps of 1.988 miles = 159.1 miles.

19 entries – 16 started – 9 finished.

Front row: I Ireland – 1m-15.6s (94.69mph): J Clark 0.7s; J Surtees 1.0s; J Brabham 1.6s.

17-SEP: Won by Stirling Moss the year before, as a minor F2 race, now it was F1, with a slightly better entry (although the track was still as bad: a bumpy, featureless airfield circuit using runways and straw bales). Ferrari, which had finished for the season, BRM and Moss were all absent. Porsche sent one car, and Brabham raced his ex-works car. Clark led off, followed by Surtees, Brabham and Salvadori. Ireland had too much wheelspin yet still led from lap four. This was one of his 'on' days. A backmarker sent Salvadori flying, Surtees pitted, fought back, but retired, and Clark had steering problems but was fourth, three laps down.

1st	I Ireland (W)	Lotus 21-Climax in 1h-44m-22.2s	91.45
2nd	J Brabham	Cooper T53-Climax	1 lap
3rd	J Bonnier (W)	Porsche 718	1 lap
F lap	I Ireland	Lotus 21-Climax in 1m-13.6s	97.26r

*** (F1) VIII International Gold Cup (Oulton Park)

60 laps of 2.678 miles = 160.7 miles.
30 entries – 23 started – 12 finished.
Front row: B McLaren – 1m-44.6s (92.17mph); S Moss 0.2s;
G Hill 0.4s; J Clark 0.6s.

23-SEP: This was an historic race. Porsche didn't turn up, but the unique 4WD Ferguson more than compensated. Moss had tried it at Aintree, after retiring during the British GP, and he liked it. On a damp track Clark led from Hill (BRM) and Ireland, but on lap six Moss took the Ferguson ahead. This unique car was perfect for this damp race and he drew inexorably away. Brabham came from sixth to third on lap nine, while Clark dropped back to fifth, holding the place until lap 32, when his suspension failed. Lap 31 and Brabham was second after overtaking Graham Hill, who retired ten laps later with engine trouble, just after Surtees had. This was the last front-engined F1 win, and the only ever 4WD F1 win, and the car never raced again! Ferguson's research department had proved all it needed. "Racing improves the breed" they say. Moss won every single-seater race he started at this track!

1st	S Moss (RW)	Ferguson-Climax 4WD in 1h-51m-53.8s	86.16
2nd	J Brabham (W)	Cooper T53-Climax	46.0s
3rd	B McLaren (W)	Cooper T53-Climax	53.6s
F lap	S Moss	Ferguson-Climax 4WD in 1m-46.4s	90.62

*** (F1) (WC8) 4th United States Grand Prix (Watkins Glen)

100 laps of 2.30 miles = 230 miles.
20 entries – 19 started – 11 finished.
Front row: J Brabham – 1m-17.0s (107.53mph); G Hill 1.1s.
Row two: S Moss 1.2s; B McLaren 1.2s.

08-OCT: The American GP found its regular home here. No Ferraris, but Brabham and Moss had V8s, though Moss raced with the four-cylinder for reliability. The pair battled for the lead, swapping eight times before Brabham's V8 overheating problem occurred again. He pitted on lap 44, and dropped out on lap 57. Moss now led by 45 seconds but, on lap 58, retired with bearing failure. This gave Ireland a lead he kept to the end, helped when Graham Hill's challenge ended on lap 73 – pitting to fix the dynamo. Salvadori assumed a great second place having charged through from ninth, but he retired when within four seconds of Ireland with just four laps remaining. Ireland was nursing his car with dropping fuel pressure so did well to hold off Gurney's charge. Team Lotus and Ireland had won their first Championship race. McLaren was fourth, and Graham Hill fifth … he might have won.

1st	I Ireland (W)	Lotus 21-Climax in 2h-13m-45.8s	103.17
2nd	D Gurney (W)	Porsche 718	4.3s
3rd	CAS Brooks (W)	BRM P57-Climax	49.0s
F lap	J Brabham (W)	Cooper T58-Climax V8 in 1m-18.2s	105.88

Championship positions:
P Hill 34 (WC); von Trips 33; Moss 21.

After the success of the previous year's mini-series of Formula Two races, a larger series was laid on in South Africa this year, attracting Team Lotus and Works Porsches for Joakim Bonnier and Edgar Barth. BRP, sponsored by UDT, had Masten Gregory and, for two races, Stirling Moss. Reg Parnell Racing sponsored by Yeoman Credit gave drives to two of the best South Africans: Tony Maggs and Bruce Johnstone. Both would drive F1 in Europe in 1962. The East London venue chosen for the South African GP was selected after this to host the first World Championship race in South Africa, to finish the 1962 year; and a famous one it would turn out to be.

* (F1) IV Rand Grand Prix (Kyalami)

75 laps of 2.545 miles = 190.9 miles.
28 entries – 24 started – 11 finished.
Front row: J Clark – 1m-38.5s (92.96mph); T Taylor 0.3s;
M Gregory 0.4s.

09-DEC: A series of four races was run this year, now attracting Team Lotus and Porsche. UDT-BRP and Yeoman Credit-Parnell Racing were here, too. Porsche arrived so late that its cars were still being fuelled in the pits when the race started. Clark took an immediate lead, shadowed all the way by teammate Trevor Taylor. Masten Gregory, driving a BRP-entered Lotus, overtook Tony Maggs' Cooper to lie third until half way, when passed by a determined Bonnier, who made no inroads into Clark's lead.

1st	J Clark (W)	Lotus 21-Climax in 2h-06m-26.27s	90.55
2nd	T Taylor (W)	Lotus 21-Climax	0.14s
3rd	J Bonnier (W)	Porsche 718	23.16s
F lap	J Bonnier	Porsche 718 in 1m-39.1s	92.40

* (F1) 1st Natal Grand Prix (Westmead)

89 laps of 2.20 miles = 195.8 miles.
29 entries – 22 started – 10 finished.
Front row: J Clark – 1m-26.10s (93.95mph); J Bonnier 0.69s;
T Taylor 2.92s.

17-DEC: Would things change as Moss had now joined the

party? He had missed practice, having been in London to receive the 'Sports-Personality-of-the-Year' award, so he started from the back of the grid. Clark stormed off, followed by Taylor, Bonnier and Gregory, but Moss was soon with them. On lap 14 Gregory retired and Taylor's suspension failed, the car rolled over but Taylor was unhurt. Moss was second soon after, but made no ground on Clark – "The engine wouldn't rev," he said.

1st	J Clark (W)	Lotus 21-Climax in 2h-13m-58.4s	89.57
2nd	S Moss (UDT)	Lotus 18/21-Climax	31.9s
3rd	J Bonnier (W)	Porsche 718	1 lap
F lap	S Moss	Lotus 18/21-Climax in 1m-24.8s	95.39

✳ (F1) VIII South African GP (East London)
80 laps of 2.436 miles = 194.9 miles.
26 entries – 23 started – 15 finished.
Front row: J Clark – 1m-33.9s (93.39mph); S Moss 0.2s: T Taylor 0.3s.
26-DEC: Now they were adjacent on the grid. Clark and Taylor led away, but Moss soon passed Taylor. Lap six saw Clark spin to avoid a stalled car. This made Moss leader by 15 seconds over Taylor and Clark. Taylor slid off the track and Moss admits there was nothing he could do about Clark's brilliant recovery, and was unable to hold him off. He now knew what he was up against for 1962. Tony Maggs was fourth for the YC/RPR team. These drives earned him a Works Cooper drive for 1962.

1st	J Clark (W)	Lotus 21-Climax in 2h-06m-49.2s	92.20
2nd	S Moss (UDT)	Lotus 18/21-Climax	15.7s
3rd	J Bonnier (W)	Porsche 718	1 lap
F lap	J Clark	Lotus 21-Climax in 1m-33.1s	94.20

✳ (F1) V Cape Grand Prix (Killarney)
60 laps of 2.058 miles = 123.4 miles.
23 entries – 19 started – 14 finished.
Front row: J Clark – 1m-28.4s (83.81mph); T Taylor (0.9s): J Bonnier (1.6s).
02-JAN-1962: Yes, this race belongs to the 1961 season. No Moss here. Clark was easily fastest in practice, but Bonnier was best away and led lap one from Clark, Taylor, Gregory and the best 'locals': Tony Maggs (now signed by Cooper this year), and John Love. Maggs was soon fourth but Love spun. Clark took the lead and Bonnier fell briefly to fourth behind Maggs. Taylor led from Clark on lap 19 and held it to

lap 30. Clark later spun and just failed to catch Taylor by the flag. Bonnier must have been fed up with third, but was 30 seconds ahead of Gregory and Maggs, and all on the lead lap.

1st	T Taylor (W)	Lotus 21-Climax in 1h-30m-54.0s	81.50
2nd	J Clark (W)	Lotus 21-Climax	0.6s
3rd	J Bonnier (W)	Porsche 718	6.6s
F lap	J Clark	Lotus 21-Climax in 1m-28.9s	83.34

Winners of the 41 graded F1 & ICF races of 1961 – quantity & quality of success

13 wins	S Moss (7A, 4C, 2D)	15 wins	Lotus-Climax (6A-9C)
6 wins	J Brabham (2A, 2B, C, D)	15 wins	Cooper-Climax (4A, 3B, C, 7D)
4 wins	J Clark (4C)	7 wins	Ferrari (6A, D)
3 wins	I Ireland (2A, C) G Baghetti (2A, D)	2 wins	Porsche (C, D)
2 wins	P Hill (2A) W von Trips (2A) J Surtees (B,D) J Bonnier (2D) R Salvadori (2D)	1 win	Ferguson (A); BRM (D)
1 win	T Taylor (C) D Gurney (D)		

1961 seasonal review
A huge Formula One season lasting slightly over 12 months had shown that fears of duller, significantly slower racing were unfounded. The sights and sounds of the new F1 were virtually indistinguishable from those of the previous year, and speeds were only about four per cent slower – not an obvious difference to the observer. In fact, a new race record was set at Monaco, and almost a new lap record. The Ferrari Dino V6 was, as expected, the dominant car in its early 65˚V arrangement, let alone the 120˚ version, except, that is, on circuits where driver skill was at a premium (and that was when Stirling Moss came into his own). Porsche had the next most powerful engine yet failed to win a single top race in 1961. Lotus and Cooper scored so many victories thanks to Ferrari not competing outside Italy in non-Championship races. I think it's reasonable to say, though, that neither of Ferrari's top drivers were quite of the calibre of Moss, Brabham or Clark, so the win list is not misleading. The arrival of the V8 engines for Cooper and BRM proved that things would be different in 1962, when reliability could be found. Coventry Climax was choosing the recipients carefully, so Cooper had the first, and the next

was for the Walker equipe, because of Moss's presence there, in preference to the Lotus Works team. BRM's new P578, first seen in practice at Monza, was a wonderfully slim and sleek car, beautifully co-ordinated and packaged as only a thoroughbred (maker of the whole car) can be. For me this is the best looking F1 car ever – beautiful from any angle. If it went as well as it looked and sounded, the others should really worry. Also new at Monza were de Tomasos – Cooper copies with Alfa Romeo or OSCA engines. One qualified mid-field in Vaccarella's hands, retiring in 11th place. Of the others the less said the better.

This uniquely huge season was supplemented by the Inter-Continental Formula (ICF), which had been approved by the FIA back in 1958, and used the same pool of drivers as F1. Combining the ICF and F1 races gives an amazing 41 possible events, of which Moss competed in 28, covering over 5000 racing miles and taking the chequered flag 14 times! These were just the single-seater formulae with which this book is concerned. He also took part in supporting races for sports cars at some of those venues, and on many other dates, including endurance events such as the Sebring 12hr, Targa Florio, Le Mans, and the Nürburgring 1000km. Do drivers of today wish they had the opportunity to race so often I wonder?

1961 Championship review
Never has a Championship battle been settled in such an horrific manner. The death at Monza of the Championship leader Wolfgang von Trips and 14 spectators brought a very tragic end to the year-long battle between him and Phil Hill. The lack of any new engines to challenge Ferrari meant that Jack Brabham was denied any chance of defending his title. This turned into a year of Ferrari power vs Moss' skill, as he was the only person to challenge Ferrari, and displayed his credentials as one of the all-time greats. Much has been written about his superb drives at Monaco and the Nürburgring but his drive in the wet at Aintree where he was so far ahead of all the other Climax-powered cars gave a clear sign of the standard of his Monaco drive.

Despite the power advantage of the Ferraris – 180bhp to 152bhp of the four-cylinder Coventry Climax, the fact is that the 13 points lost by Stirling Moss, in Italy from fourth and USA from the lead, may well have cost him this year's title. He would have had equal points, but three wins to Phil Hill's two. However, had Moss not retired at Monza, and, therefore, got within touching distance of Phil Hill, then Ferrari would surely have entered the American GP. Moss would then have had to beat the Ferrari, with Phil Hill being on home soil and needing a second place to increase his total. Moss raced in America with a four-cylinder engine, but perhaps he would have been offered a Climax V8 as he had been at Monza. The race report shows that this was not beyond possibility, but the V8 Climax was unreliable then. It could be said, therefore, that it was Moss' retirement at Monza, not just the dreadful accident, which sealed the title for Phil Hill.

VISIT VELOCE ON THE WEB – WWW.VELOCE.CO.UK
All current books • New book news • Special offers • Gift vouchers • Forum

178

Chapter 21

1962

Now the 1.5-litre battle is truly joined

In 1960, the British had taken control of F1 through the efforts of Cooper, Lotus and BRM. The willingness of the former two to sell their products encouraged the creation of independent teams, and Ferrari didn't get a look in. Then, in 1961, the whole show was turned upside down by Ferrari having the only car designed to the new formula. This year the battle for supremacy should be fascinating, now that the British V8 engines were on the scene. Power they had, but not yet proven reliability. At the start of 1962, both Climax and BRM engines were about to become available to non-Works teams depending on the team's driver. Climax used carburettors, while the BRM had fuel injection and a few more horsepower. These 'customer' engines did give useful power, so provided a chance to be competitive, but they were initially few, so a split between 'have V8s' and 'have not V8s' occurred early in 1962. This imbalance led the organiser at the Goodwood Easter International, the BARC, to run a one-off supporting race exclusively for the 'have-not V8s.'

The constructors

Ferrari retained World Champion Phil Hill, of course, and French GP winner Giancarlo Baghetti. They were supported by Ricardo Rodriguez, and newcomers Lorenzo Bandini and Willy Mairesse. Italy had just one team, but up to five drivers. However the team's organisation was in some disarray as, disillusioned with the lack of developement, team manager Romolo Tavoni and chief designer Carlo Chiti had left, along with a few others, to form a new team which would not be seen until the following year. Its car was virtually the same as the previous year's, so it was hoping the British hadn't been too clever (although the BRM V8 had been seen at Monza).

Team Lotus had a new leader in Jim Clark, supported by Trevor Taylor, and produced the Type 24 to take the V8

engine. It sold it to independents, but unknown to them, the Type 25 would soon make it obsolete.

Cooper Cars was led now by Bruce McLaren, and had taken on South African Tony Maggs. The T60 was available to accept the V8 – when it arrived. After the previous year, Cooper wasn't Coventry Climax's preferred team.

BRM would, of course, have its own V8s in the P578 car from the start of 1962. Was it the most beautiful and co-ordinated rear-engine F1 design ever? BRM continued to be led by Graham Hill, but now supported by diminutive ex-Ferrari pilot, American Ritchie Ginther. The cockpit opening narrowed over the driver's shoulder, and seeing Graham Hill climb aboard with his arms above his head, to feed them below that narrow screen, made it look as though he was putting on clothing.

Porsche retained Dan Gurney and Joakim Bonnier, and would produce a flat-eight engine – air-cooled of course – to join the new multi-cylinder culture.

Lola Cars was a welcome newcomer to the ranks of manufacturers. It had built a brilliant 1100c sports-racing car in 1959, which had shattered all the competition, including Lotus and Cooper, then built fairly successful Formula Junior cars. It had been commissioned to design a Formula One car by Reg Parnell Racing, which was now sponsored by Yeoman Credit and Bowmaker; the team known as Bowmaker-Yeoman Racing. Lola was headed by John Surtees, at last getting a Works drive again, and the very experienced Roy Salvadori. Thanks to its signing of Surtees, it was given one of the first batch of Climax V8s.

Brabham Racing Organisation initialy used a Lotus-Climax 24, and had priority over Cooper for the Climax V8, as did Lola thanks to the status of Surtees. The racing world awaited the first Brabham Formula One car which would bring the total of major marques to seven – a very healthy situation. Brabham Racing was originally going to be called Motor Racing Developments, but was advised to use another as the sound of the initials, to the French, sounded like an rather undesirable word.

Other one-off, self-built cars, such as Gilby and Emeryson, were small outfits, and would never challenge the magnificent seven.

The independents

The British Racing Partnership was led by Innes Ireland, who had lost the leadership of Lotus, and supported by Masten Gregory. However, in reality, Stirling Moss would be leader of BRP until RRC Walker Racing was ready to run the Ferrari that had been promised by Enzo. Sadly, this never happened due to the Goodwood crash. Maurice Trintignant was then the main driver for Walker.

Formula One had rarely been in better shape than in 1962. The cars were super-looking, tightly packaged gems of engineering, their sound was almost as good as anything heard before, and they were plentiful. There were twenty-eight F1 races this year, but only nine were World Championship rounds. Prospects were good.

The Grand Prix driver's diary of single-seater racing for 1962

6th January	FL – New Zealand GP at Ardmore (NZ) – 150 miles
13th January	FL – International at Levin (NZ) – 30.8 miles
20th January	FL – Lady Wigram Trophy at Christchurch (NZ) – 150.2 miles
27th January	FL – Teretonga Trophy at Invercargill (NZ) – 75 miles
4th February	FL – Warwick Farm '100' (Au) – 101.3 miles
11th February	FL – Lakeside International (Au) – 45.0 miles
5th March	FL – South Pacific Trophy at Longford (Au) – 90 miles
11th March	FL – Sandown Park Trophy (Au) – 115.7 miles
1st April	F1 – Grand Prix de Bruxelles at Heysel (B) – 186.7 miles
14th April	F1 – Lombank Trophy at Snetterton (UK) – 135.5 miles
23rd April	F1 – Lavant Cup at Goodwood (UK) – 50.4 miles
23rd April	F1 – Glover Trophy at Goodwood (UK) – 100.8 miles
23rd April	F1 – Grand Prix de Pau (F) – 171.5 miles
28th April	F1 – Aintree '200' (UK) – 150 miles
12th May	F1 – *Daily Express* International Trophy at Silverstone (UK) – 152.2 miles
20th May	F1 – **Grand Prix van Nederland** at Zandvoort (N) – 208.4 miles
20th May	F1 – Gran Premio di Napoli at Posillipo (I) – 92.9 miles
3rd June	F1 – **Grand Prix de Monaco** (M) – 195.4 miles
11th June	F1 – '2000 Guineas' at Mallory Park (UK) – 101.3 miles
11th June	F1 – Crystal Palace Trophy (UK) – 50.04 miles
17th June	F1 – **Grand Prix de Belgique** at Spa (B) – 280.4 miles
1st July	F1 – Grand Prix de Reims (F) – 257.9 miles
8th July	F1 – **Grand Prix de l'ACF** at Rouen les Essarts (F) – 219.5 miles
15th July	F1 – Grosse Preis der Solitude (D) – 177.3 miles
21st July	F1 – **British Grand Prix** at Aintree (UK) – 225 miles
5th August	F1 – **Grosse Preis von Deutschland** at N Nürburgring (D) – 212.6 miles
12th August	F1 – Kanonloppet at Karlskoga (S) – 55.9 miles
19th August	F1 – Gran Prem del Mediterraneo at Enna-Pergusa (I) – 149.4 miles
25th August	F1 – Danske Grand Prix at Roskilde (Dk) – 59.7 miles
1st September	F1 – International Gold Cup at Oulton Park (UK) – 195.6 miles
16th September	F1 – **Gran Premio d'Italia** at Monza (I) – 307.3 miles
7th October	F1 – **United States Grand Prix** at Watkins Glen (US) – 230 miles
4th November	F1 – **Gran Premio de Mexico** at Mexico City (Mx) – 186.4 miles
18th November	FL – Australian GP at Caversham, Perth (Au) – 123.5 miles
15th December	F1 – Rand Grand Prix at Kyalami (SA) – 127.5 miles
22th December	F1 – Natal Grand Prix at Westmead (SA) – 123.6 miles
29th December	F1 – **South African Grand Prix** at East London (SA) – 199.8 miles

37 events of total race mileage = 5488 miles or 5191 max due to simultaneous events.

Events in bold are World Championship rounds – 35.6 per cent of F1 races run.

Keeping busy in the off-season 1962

The following series of races was still run generally to the now expired 'Inter-Continental Formula' of 1961 for up to three litres, so these cars were faster than the new V8 powered F1 cars, the Climax 2.5 having a third more power – 240bhp against 180 for the 1.5 V8s. Rob Walker took a Lotus 21, probably the tiniest car ever to house the 2.5-litre Climax FPF unit, and the regular Cooper for Stirling Moss, while Jack Brabham, now having left Cooper to form his own team, put a 2.7-Climax in the latest Cooper T55. John Surtees' 2.7-litre Cooper was entered by Bowmaker-Yeoman, for whom he would drive the works Lola F1 cars later in the year. Bruce McLaren, also with a 2.7 unit, was entered by the respected Tommy Atkins outfit, whose preparation matched that of the Works cars. These four were among the elite drivers of the time (perhaps in that order). Veteran Roy Salvadori was teammate to Surtees and capable of running them close, as could Ron Flockhart in best form. Flockhart had a Lotus 18-Climax. Extra international status was added this year with the Italian team Scuderia Centro-Sud sending two 2.8-litre Maserati-powered Coopers for Italian Lorenzo Bandini, who was on his way up in F1, and New Zealander Johnny Mansel.

✳ New Zealand GP (Ardmore)
75 laps of 1.988 miles = 149.1 miles.
30 entries – 21 started – 15 finished.
Front row: B McLaren in 1m-25.4s (83.82mph); J Brabham 0.3s: J Surtees 1.4s.
06-JAN: Practice took place on a wet Thursday, but Moss was delayed en-route from Europe due to snow. A special session was arranged on Friday, though, as he had arrived. On the dry track he recorded 1m-17.1 s but was beaten by Brabham who posted 1m-16.3s (94.36mph). Grid positions, were, however, arranged using the Thursday times, so Moss was at the back. On race day the weather was atrocious, and the race was abandoned after 50 laps. Brabham had retired after 32 laps with gear selector problems. Salvadori and Bandini were fourth and fifth, so the 'locals' didn't get a look in. Moss' pre-eminence in these conditions was amply demonstrated.
1st S Moss (Lotus 21-Climax) in 1h-23m-14.3s = 71.66mph
2nd J Surtees (Cooper T53-Climax) @1m-40s
3rd B McLaren (Cooper T53-Climax) @ 2 laps
Fastest lap S Moss in 1m-32.8s = 77.14mph

✳ 3rd Levin International
28 laps of 1.1 miles = 30.8 miles.
12 entries – 11 started – 8 finished.
Front row: J Brabham (no other information).
13-JAN: On a shortened course (as if the previous wasn't short enough), Moss chose to run his Cooper and finished second to Brabham in the preliminary heat. The race was stopped after eight laps due to the conditions. A decision Stirling Moss was not happy with. Surely, the most dangerous

time in any race is the beginning when cars are bunched up. Why stop so soon when, according to Moss' reflections in *All my Races*, the conditions weren't worse. This is the shortest ever race time.
1st J Brabham (Cooper T55-Climax) in 7m-52.0s = 67.12mph
2nd S Moss (Cooper T55-Climax) @7.5s
3rd J Surtees (Cooper T53-Climax) @ 27.0s
Fastest lap J Brabham in 56.8s = 69.72mph

✳ Lady Wigram Trophy (Christchurch)
71 laps of 2.116 miles = 150.2 miles.
20 entries – 18 started – 14 finished.
Front row: B McLaren; J Brabham; S Moss; J Surtees. No times available.
20-JAN: The lesser event at Levin had also been stopped due to torrential rain so a hot day was welcomed. Moss was just at home in the intense heat as the rain. Surtees pressed Brabham strongly while McLaren was fourth over half a minute back. Surtees' teammate Salvadori was fifth. All finished on the same lap. First 'local' home was Angus Hyslop's Cooper T53-Climax, two laps back.
1st S Moss (Lotus 21-Climax) in 1h-36m-38.7s = 93.27mph
2nd J Brabham (Cooper T55-Climax) @ 16.3s
3rd J Surtees (Cooper T53-Climax) @ 17.7s
Fastest lap Moss/Surtees in 1m-20.1s = 95.10mph

✳ Teretonga Trophy (Invercargill)
50 laps of 1.5 miles = 75.0 miles.
14 started – 12 finished.
Front row: B McLaren; S Moss; J Brabham; L Bandini. No times available.
27-JAN: This was an anticlockwise track, and McLaren had removed the right-hand fuel tank for this shorter race on a track with predominantly left-hand corners, giving a handling advantage. He made a demon start and, run in intense heat on his home track, was never headed, almost lapping Brabham. His idea proved right.
1st B McLaren (Cooper T53-Climax)
2nd S Moss (Cooper T55-Climax) @ 40s
3rd J Brabham (Cooper T55-Climax) @ 1m-18s
Fastest lap B McLaren in 1m-06.2s = 81.57mph

✳ Warwick Farm '100' (Sydney)
45 laps of 2.25 miles = 101.25 miles.
16 entries – 11 started – 7 finished.
Front row: S Moss in 1m-37.5s (83.08mph); J Brabham 0.6s; B McLaren 1.6s; J Surtees 3.1s.
04-FEB: A great scrap with Brabham leading Moss, Surtees and McLaren ensued until Surtees' crownwheel broke. McLaren spun but recovered and, on lap 21, Brabham's gearbox failed. Moss took an easy win from McLaren. Moss

had used his Cooper to prove the 'pundits' wrong after they had claimed his Lotus 21 was unbeatable, proving it was him that was unbeatable.

1st S Moss (Cooper T53-Climax) in 1h-14m-36.6s = 81.49mph

2nd B McLaren (Cooper T53-Climax) @ 20.2s

3rd B Stillwell (Cooper T53-Climax) @ 2 laps

Fastest lap B McLaren – no time available

✳ Lakeside International
30 laps of 1.5 miles = 45 miles.
13 entries – 10 started – 7 finished

Front row: B McLaren in 59.8s (90.30mph); J Brabham 0.0s; L Bandini 1.4s.

11-FEB: Moss was absent at Daytona this weekend. Bruce McLaren retired and Ron Flockhart crashed, leaving Brabham to fend off the attentions of Bib Stillwell without much trouble. The truth was that none of the residents ever presented a serious challenge, even on their own tracks. The result on paper was slightly misleading.

1st J Brabham (Cooper T55-Climax) in 30m-50.0s = 87.57mph

2nd B Stillwell (Cooper T53-Climax) @ 1.0s

3rd A Hyslop (Cooper T53-Climax) @ 6.0s

Fastest lap B McLaren – no time available

✳ South Pacific Trophy (Longford)
20 laps of 4.5 miles = 90 miles.
12 entries – 10 started – 7 finished.

Front row: J Brabham in 2m-21.3s 114.65mph; J Surtees 0.1s; W Patterson 0.4s.

05-MAR: Surtees and Brabham were the star visitors here on this dangerous fast road circuit, which included crossing a wooden-sided bridge across a valley and zig-zagging under a railway bridge. Bill Patterson's promising practice time didn't translate into the expected result, finishing sixth. Bib Stilwell and Angus Hyslop were fourth and fifth, over a minute adrift of the winner.

1st J Surtees (Cooper T53-Climax) in 48m-31.0s = 111.30mph

2nd J Brabham (Cooper T55-Climax) @ 22.5s

3rd B Stillwell (Cooper T53-Climax) @ 1m-08.2s

Fastest lap J Brabham – no time available

✳ Sandown Park Trophy
60 laps of 1.928 miles = 115.7 miles.
21 entries – 18 started – 11 finished.

Front row: J Brabham in 1m-08.1s (101.92mph); J Surtees 0.8s; S Moss 1.3s; B McLaren 1.3s.

11-MAR: A new track around Melbourne's horse racecourse, like Aintree in England. Moss chose the Lotus 21 for this race, but was over a second off pole time. A great scrap

ensued, but Moss was strangely off the pace, while the other three had a great scrap, led mostly by Brabham. Moss' troubles caused him to be lapped by Brabham, Surtees and McLaren, and beaten by a 3.9-litre Scarab driven by Chuck Daigh which had been two seconds slower in practice!

1st J Brabham (Cooper T55-Climax) in 1h-10m-08.6s = 98.95mph

2nd J Surtees (Cooper T53-Climax) @ 0.8s

3rd B McLaren (Cooper T53-Climax) @ 4.1s

Fastest lap: not available

✳✳✳ IV Grand Prix de Bruxelles (Heysel)
3 x 22 laps of 2.828 miles = 186.7 miles.
21 entries – 19 started – 8 finished.

Front row: J Clark – 2m-03.1s (82.76mph); S Moss 0.2s; G Hill 0.8s.

01-APR: This was the first real test of the Climax and BRM V8s against Ferrari, albeit one of the older 65° cars. Only Moss and Clark had the Climax V8, though. Works Coopers were absent, being without a V8. Having lost the services of Jack Brabham, Cooper wasn't given priority. Here we saw Lotus' 1962 car designed for the V8, or so we were meant to think. This would be available to buy soon. Moss shot away, but messed up at the hairpin and was now last. Clark's V8 valve gear lasted less than a lap, so Hill's new BRM won from an amazingly recovered Moss, Mairesse and Tony Marsh's privately-run 1961 BRM V8. In heat two, both BRMs failed to start, and were push started after the field had left – believing this to be allowed – this was not so, and both were disqualified. Moss passed Mairesse and Surtees by lap three to lead but retired; Salvadori (Lola four-cylinder), Bonnier, then Mairesse led. Heat three and Bonnier soon lost out to Mairesse again. Unreliability had stopped a maiden British V8 victory.

1st	W Mairesse (W)	Ferrari 156 (65°V6) in 2h-18m-37.1s	80.85
2nd	J Bonnier (W)	Porsche 718	1m-50s
3rd	I Ireland (UDT)	Lotus 21-Climax 4	2m-40s
F lap	S Moss (RW)	Lotus 18/21-Climax V8 in 2m-00.0s	84.90r

✳✳ I Lombank Trophy (Snetterton)
50 laps of 2.71 miles = 135.5 miles.
21 entries – 15 started – 8 finished.

Front row: S Moss – 1m-34.2s (103.57mph); J Clark 0.2s; G Hill 0.4s; J Surtees 0.6s.

14-APR: BRM, Lotus, Lola, Porsche, Brabham and UDT (for which Moss drove) were represented, but no new Coopers yet. Brabham non-started his Lotus 21 after a fire. Once again, only Moss and Clark had Climax V8 power. Hill had a gap to Moss, Clark and Surtees after a lap. UDT's Gregory and Ireland collided when Gregory spun on oil. Moss took the lead on lap six from Hill, whose car was losing some of its eight stackpipe exhausts. Clark had passed the ailing Hill and took Moss on lap 19, who soon pitted losing five laps. He rejoined, then shredded the lap record for the new F1, equalling the old 2.5-litre F1 time!

1st	J Clark (W)	Lotus 24-Climax V8 in 1h-20h-25.6s	101.09
2nd	G Hill (W)	BRM P578 V8	58.4s
3rd	J Bonnier (SV)	Porsche 718	1 lap
F lap	S Moss (UDT)	Lotus 18/21-Climax V8 in 1m-33.6s	104.23r

XIV Lavant Cup (Goodwood)
21 laps of 2.4 miles = 50.4 miles.
14 entries – 11 started – 7 finished.

Front row: B McLaren – 1m-37.0s (89.07mph); J Surtees 0.8s; A Shelly 5.8s.

23-APR: The status of this race is reduced since it was a supporting event for four-cylinder cars only, all of which were eligible for the main race above. Surely the only F1 race ever to specifically exclude the fastest cars. Surtees had a four-cylinder engine in his Lola for this race. McLaren made another great start, but Surtees took the lead from him on lap three, while Salvadori spun but had little difficulty in recovering to second on lap 11. Lap five saw the leaders coming to lap the hopeless Gunther Seifert (grid time 2m-10.8s), Surtees tried to pass at the chicane entrance but collided with the crawler. So McLaren cruised comfortably home.

1st	B McLaren (W)	Cooper T55-Climax 4 in 30m-31.8s	99.05
2nd	R Salvadori (BYP)	Lola T4-Climax 4	45.8s
F lap	B McLaren (W)	Cooper T55-Climax4 in 1m-25.4s	101.17

✱✱ X Glover Trophy (Goodwood)
42 laps of 2.4 miles = 100.8 miles.
18 entries – 15 started – 11 finished.

Front row: S Moss – 1m-34.2s (91.72mph); G Hill 2.0s; B McLaren 2.8s.

23-APR: Cooper arrived, but Lotus and Brabham went to Pau, but a debut in F1 for the new Lola marque took place. Practice was wet, producing the usual dominance by Moss in those conditions, but two seconds is enormous. The times served for the grids in this and the Lavant Cup race. Only Moss and Surtees had Climax V8s. Race day was dry, and

McLaren, in a four-cylinder car, made a super start from to lead from Hill, Moss, Ireland and Surtees. But it was Hill who led lap three from McLaren, Surtees and Moss. Moss retook third, then pitted on lap nine with gear selector trouble, while Surtees took second on lap 18, then spun and pitted with a sticking throttle. Both continued, and then Surtees blew the outright record apart, matched by Moss, but Surtees retired just before Moss' awful career-ending crash. A fierce battle between Ireland and Salvadori was settled by a whisker in favour of Ireland – both given identical race times. So Hill and BRM won a sadly overshadowed victory. The V8s were clearly fast even, in Moss's basically two-year old Lotus. McLaren's race speed was 101.40mph – faster than his fastest lap in the 'pseudo Formula One' Lavant Cup. The previous year's 1.5-litre F1 record had been smashed by six seconds, and the 2.5-litre F1 outright record of 1960 had also been consigned to history. However, events were overshadowed by Moss' awful accident, which has never been explained as Moss' memory of it is lost. The departing crowd must have left hoping and praying for his survival.

1st	G Hill (W)	BRM P578 V8 in 58m-55.2s	102.65
2nd	B McLaren (W)	Cooper T55-Climax 4	43.4s
3rd	I Ireland (UDT)	Lotus 18/21-Climax4	1 lap
F lap	Moss/Surtees (BYP)	Lotus/Lola T4-Climax V8 in 1m-22.0s	105.37r

✱✱ XXII Grand Prix de Pau
100 laps of 1.715 miles = 171.5 miles.
19 entries – 16 started – 10 finished.

Front row: J Clark – 1m-30.6s (68.15mph); R Rodriguez 1.9s; J Bonnier 2.1s.

23-APR: Clashing with Goodwood as usual, Moss preferred Goodwood so Rob Walker entered Trintignant here. Only the Works Lotuses for Jim Clark and Trevor Taylor were this year's cars. Brabham's Lotus 21 and Trintignant were on row two and on row three were Bandini Ferrari V6) and the two ex-Works BRMs with V8 power of Jack Lewis and Tony Marsh. Rodriguez led from Bonnier (Porsche) and Clark, whose teammate Taylor dropped to the back. Clark passed Bonnier on lap three and led on lap nine but began having selector trouble. Pau was Trintignant's stamping ground, and he amazed by passing from fourth on lap 11 to take the lead from Clark on lap 16 – with a four-cylinder car! Clark's gear problems caused his retirement on lap 24. Jack Lewis and Tony Marsh did brilliantly, with Lewis almost getting Rodriguez for second, and Marsh passing Bandini's Ferrari for fourth. Trintignant's drive matched that of his win at Monaco in 1958 – both on 'round-the-house circuits.

1st	M Trintignant (RW)	Lotus 18/21-Climax 4 in 2h-39m-35.5s	64.48
2nd	R Rodriguez (W)	Ferrari 156 (120˚V6)	33.6s
3rd	J Lewis	BRM P57 V8	34.6s
F lap	J Clark (W)	Lotus 24-Climax V8 in 1m-33.4s	66.10r

✱✱✱ VI International 'Aintree 200'

50 laps of 3.0 miles = 150 miles.

26 entries – 23 started – 11 finished.

Front row: J Clark – 1m-53.8s (94.91mph); G Hill 1.2s; J Surtees 1.2s.

28-APR: Everyone was here, and, while BRMs had shown form at Goodwood, Clark hadn't been there. This was a Jim Clark benefit, and he dominated throughout. Though beaten off the line, he passed the BRMs on lap two and pulled out over a second for the next 25 laps. Ginther took second from G Hill on lap 16, and retired five laps later. Surtees' Lola V8 had recovered from a bad start and was now third, but stopped on lap 37. Hill's BRM engine failed on lap 45, so McLaren's four-cylinder inherited second and beat the Ferraris, with Baghetti just behind Phil Hill! With these retirements, McLaren's Works non-V8 Cooper was chalking up some decent results. This also showed that the Ferraris were unlikely to be a threat this year. Three seconds was taken off the old 2.5-litre F1 record from 1959 – and was left untouched at the British GP here in July.

1st	J Clark (W)	Lotus 24-Climax V8 in 1h-37m-08.2s	92.65
2nd	B McLaren (W)	Cooper T55-Climax 4	1m-30s
3rd	P Hill (W)	Ferrari 156 (120˚ V6)	1m-34s
F lap	J Clark	Lotus 24-Climax V8 in 1m-54.0s	94.74r

✱✱✱ XIV International Trophy (Silverstone)

52 laps of 2.927 miles = 152.2 miles.

26 entries – 24 started – 18 finished.

Front row: G Hill – 1m-34.6s (111.39s); J Clark 0.2s; J Surtees 0.8s; R Ginther 2.2s.

12-MAY: Ferrari sent a car for UDT to run and Ireland to drive, as homage to critically injured Moss who, it had been hoped, would drive a Ferrari this year. Climax V8s were available now to Brabham for his Lotus 24 and to UDT for Masten Gregory, but still not Cooper. Clark led by a second from Ireland and the BRMs on lap one. Surtees came from sixth on lap one and third on lap four to take Hill for second on lap 18, but was third again after four laps. McLaren's four-cylinder Cooper followed Ireland, with Brabham now in sixth. Drizzle started about mid-race but Clark held his

lead steady over Hill's BRM, now losing exhaust stack-pipes again. It didn't seem to matter, though, as the BRM went just as well without them. On the damp track Clark eased up with a lead of 17 seconds with four laps to go, but then with three to go it was 12; two to go – six; and at the start of the last lap – three seconds; Clark seemingly unaware of the danger. The finish line at Silverstone then was at the very exit from the challenging and fast Woodcote bend. Hill's memorable lunge around the outside to beat Clark on the line was the stuff of legend! Anyone who still thinks non-Championship Formula One races unimportant should find a time-machine – go back – and think again.

1st	G Hill (W)	BRM P578 V8 in 1h-31m-34.2s	99.73
2nd	J Clark (W)	Lotus 24-Climax V8	0.0s
3rd	J Surtees (BYP)	Lola T4-Climax V8	1m-56s
F lap	J Clark	Lotus 24-Climax V8 in 1m-36.4s	109.31

After a busy pre-Championship season in which the new BRMs and Lotus proved about equal, and Ferrari had produced nothing new, the forthcoming Championship opener at Zandvoort was eagerly anticipated. The conversion of Climax powered teams to V8 was almost complete – the only major teams still using the Climax FPF four-cylinder were the second cars of the Cooper Works team and UDT-Laystall, run by the BRP. It was known that Porsche had produced a flat-eight engined car, still air-cooled as was Porsche's 'religion,' but it was not known whether Ferrari had anything new. All would come together in Holland – only six of the entry having four-cylinder engines – including Porsche 718s for Dutch no-hopers. Jack Lewis and Tony Marsh with BRM V8s weren't invited; Zandvoort still a law unto itself.

✱✱✱ (WC1) XI Grote Prijs van Nederland (Zandvoort)

80 laps of a 2.605-mile circuit = 208.4 miles.

20 invited and started – 11 finished.

Front row: J Surtees (Lola-Climax) – 1m-32.5s (101.38mph); G Hill 0.1s; J Clark 0.7s.

20-MAY: The Lotus 25 with monocoque chassis arrived completely out of the blue – a brilliant master stroke. Those customer Type 24s were not the same as the Works cars after all – well, they were when they bought them. Ferrari, however, had nothing new. For all that, though, it was Surtees' Lola on pole by 0.1 seconds from Graham Hill's BRM, with Phil Hill's Ferrari (the oldest) in ninth place and lowest of all the marques. Clark led from G Hill, Gurney, Surtees, P Hill, Ireland and McLaren – six makes in the top seven. Clark pulled away, but Hill's BRM caught him on lap 11 and he pitted with clutch trouble. Gurney pitted with a broken gear lever. Behind them, Surtees had had a scare when a wishbone collapsed, and he'd crashed at high speed; thankfully without injury. Teammate Salvadori was withdrawn in consequence. Hill's BRM was well ahead of McLaren, who retired eight laps later, so now G Hill led P Hill by plenty. Lotus No 2 Trevor Taylor took second place from Phil Hill on lap 60. Ferrari finished third and fourth but was never a threat. Ginther spun and Rodriguez crashed near the end, so after all that de Beaufort in his old Porsche took sixth but four laps down. Hill's and BRM's win was very popular, but hopefully not a one-off, unlike 1959.

1st	G Hill (W)	BRM P578 V8 in 2h-11m-02.1s	95.44
2nd	T Taylor (W)	Lotus 24-Climax V8	27.2s
3rd	P Hill (W)	Ferrari 156-120°	1m-21s
F lap	B McLaren (W)	Cooper T60-Climax V8 in 1m-34.4s	99.36

Gran Premio di Napoli (Posillipo)
60 laps of 1.548 miles = 92.9 miles.
24 entries – 10 qualified – 7 finished.
Front row: L Bandini – 1m-18.7s (70.81mph); W Mairesse 0.2s. Second row – K Greene 2.5s; T Parnell 2.5s.
20-MAY: As per the previous year, this Grand Prix accepted the left-overs from the day's Dutch GP. The Ferrari duo had no opposition in truth. Everyone else had four-cylinder engines. Bandini led until baulked when lapping a backmarker, braked hard and was passed by Mairesse who had the 120° engine so Bandini stood little chance. He would take Mairesse's place at Ferrari.

1st	W Mairesse (W)	Ferrari 156-120° in 1h-19m-36.1s	70.01
2nd	L Bandini (W)	Ferrari 156-65°	3.3s
F lap	Mairesse/Bandini	Ferrari 156s in 1m-18.1s	71.35r

✱✱✱ (WC2) XX Grand Prix de Monaco (Monte Carlo)
100 laps of a 1.954-mile circuit = 195.4 miles.
23 entries – 16 qualified – 7 finished.
Front row: J Clark – 1m-35.4s (73.74mph); G Hill 0.4s; B McLaren 1.0s.
03-JUN: As usual, an oversize entry for 16 places, but guarantees to Works teams meant that it wasn't the fastest 16 that started – Jack Lewis and newcomer Jo Siffert missing out despite being over three seconds faster than Jo Bonnier's Works Porsche 718. The pile-up at the hairpin yards from the start line, begun by Mairesse, eliminated Gurney, Trintignant

and Ginther – and any idea of starting from there again. From the melee, McLaren led G Hill, and the two swapped places three times in 11 laps. P Hill was third, but spun on lap 12, and both Brabham and Clark passed. At lap 31 it was G Hill, Clark, McLaren, Brabham and P Hill. This changed when Clark's clutch failed on lap 55, and G Hill was half a lap ahead of McLaren. Phil Hill passed Brabham on lap 75 and set off after McLaren, but Graham Hill's BRM was sick and retired with eight laps left, so it was a lead battle which McLaren was able to control. Brabham retired, Surtees was fourth, and Bonnier fifth but seven laps down. Jack Lewis would have done better. Ferrari may have lost any performance advantage now, but reliability might still bring some compensation.

1st	B McLaren (W)	Cooper T60-Climax V8 in 2h-46m-29.7s	70.42
2nd	P Hill (W)	Ferrari 156-120°	3.3s
3rd	L Bandini (W)	Ferrari 156-65°	1m-24s
F lap	J Clark (W)	Lotus 25-Climax V8 in 1m-35.5s	73.66r

Championship positions:
G Hill and P Hill 10; McLaren 9.

✱ '2000 Guineas' (Mallory Park)
75 laps of 1.35 miles = 101.3 miles.
16 entries – 13 started.
Front row: J Clark – 51.0s (95.29mph); J Brabham 0.6s; G Hill 1.0s; J Surtees 1.6s.
11-JUN: Two British F1 races took place today. The absence of BRM allowed Graham Hill to race for Rob Walker, but he only had a four-cylinder car. The top four drivers of the day occupied the front row, with Clark looking very good (0.6 seconds on such a short track is quite a margin). It was Surtees, though, who led from Brabham and Gregory's BRP-entered Lotus 18/21. He was soon passed by Hill and Clark. Strangely, Clark, in the super Lotus 25 V8, was unable to pass Hill, and low oil pressure him put out of the race. Mike Parkes had a good F1 debut driving for Yeoman Credit, passing Gregory for fourth on lap 28, settling the places.

1st	J Surtees (BYP)	Lola T4-Climax V8 in 1h-05m-03.6s	93.39
2nd	J Brabham	Lotus 24-Climax V8	18.2s
3rd	G Hill (RW)	Lotus 18/21-Climax 4	28.2s
F lap	J Surtees	Lola T4-Climax V8 in 50.8s	95.67

✳ X Crystal Palace Trophy
36 laps of 1.39 miles = 50.04 miles.
13 entries – 12 started – 8 finished.
Front row: R Salvadori – 58.0s (86.28mph); B McLaren 0.2s;
T Taylor 0.4s.

11-JUN: Lotuses fitted with BRM's customer engine appeared here first, even used in Trevor Taylor's Works Lotus. Cooper gave McLaren one of the previous year's car, with the four-cylinder motor. Roy Salvadori, Bruce McLaren, Innes Ireland was the original order, but Ireland, who started at the back, came right through in just three laps and the order remained unchanged. Taylor's engine expired on the last lap but he was classified fourth. Ireland beat 'Master of the Palace' Salvadori. It must be said that Innes Ireland wasn't always on top form, but when he was he could be superb.

1st	I Ireland (UDT)	Lotus 24-BRM V8 in 34m-46.4s	86.34
2nd	R Salvadori (BYP)	Lola T4-Climax V8	20.2s
3rd	B McLaren (W)	Cooper T55-Climax 4	23.6s
F lap	I Ireland	Lotus 24-BRM V8 in 57.2s	87.48r

✳✳✳ (WC3) XXII Grand Prix de Belgique (Spa)
32 laps of an 8.761-mile circuit = 280.4 miles.
25 entries – 19 started – 10 finished.
Front row: G Hill – 3m-57.0s (133.08mph); B McLaren 1.8s;
T Taylor 2.3s.

17-JUN: Porsche was strike-ridden (not expected of a German company) and, therefore, absent. Jim Clark's engine failed in practice, and he cautiously qualified in Taylor's car while awaiting a new one. This placed him on the fifth row, while teammate Taylor's 'old' type 24 was at the front with Hill and McLaren. Lap one order was G Hill, Taylor, McLaren, Clark and Mairesse. This group pulled clear as G Hill dropped to the back of the group, while Taylor and Mairesse fought over, and swapped, the lead until Clark came through on lap nine. He drew away to a brilliant dominant maiden Championship victory. Taylor and Mairesse's fight, now for second, came to a near disastrous conclusion on lap 26 when Mairesse touched the back of the Lotus, putting it out of gear and both were lucky to survive the fiery crash: Taylor unscathed and Mairesse injured. This left G Hill second and P Hill and Rodriguez swapping third place, just 0.1 seconds apart at the end. McLaren had retired with engine failure from fifth on lap 19, while Surtees and Brabham, in fifth and sixth places, were lapped. Jim Clark's race speed was within two mph of the race record on this superfast track, and shows how technology had now compensated for power losses in this formula.

1st	J Clark (W)	Lotus 25-Climax V8 in 2h-07m-32.3s	131.89
2nd	G Hill (W)	BRM P578 V8	44.1s
3rd	P Hill (W)	Ferrari 156-120°	2m-06s
F lap	J Clark (W)	Lotus 25-Climax V8 in 3m-55.6s	133.87

Championship positions:
G Hill 16; P Hill 14; McLaren 9.

✳✳✳ XXVIII Grand Prix de Reims
50 laps of 5.158 = 257.9 miles.
23 entries – 20 started – 8 finished
Front row: J.Clark – 2m-22.9s (129.94mph); G.Hill (0.6s);
J.Surtees (0.8s)

01-JUL: The Championship race had gone to Rouen this year, but Reims was not to be outdone, and ran its race anyway. A rehearsal for the following week's French Grand Prix? Ferrari missed both races, and Porsche this one (both strike-bound?). Surtees went clear on this slipstreaming circuit after a lap. McLaren, Clark, Brabham, Hill and Ireland followed. Clark lost coolant and stopped. The pursuers were then McLaren, Hill and Brabham, while Surtees pulled away to a huge 20 second lead on lap 20 – brilliant! On lap 28 he was robbed by a broken valve spring. New leader McLaren overdid Muizon on lap 33 and was passed by Brabham and Hill who swapped the lead. By lap 37 McLaren was ahead again. Brabham forgot to switch fuel lines on the last lap and lost third place to Ireland. The previous year's speeds were demolished, but were still six seconds short of Brabham's 1960 record. Unlike Spa, this track relied on sheer power, so improvements in cornering produced less resultant increase in lap speeds.

1st	B McLaren (W)	Cooper T60-Climax V8 in 2h-02m-30.2s	126.32
2nd	G Hill (W)	BRM P578 V8	8.0s
3rd	I Ireland (UDT)	Lotus 24-Climax V8	1m-36s
F lap	G Hill	BRM P578V8 in 2m-24.0s	128.95

Ferrari had withdrawn from Reims and now, disappointingly, also the World Championship round at Rouen. A strike at home was the official reason, but one cannot help thinking that perhaps Ferrari was licking its wounds after having been unable to challenge for the lead at Spa – fast tracks being its favoured stamping ground. The win at Brussels at the start of the season had been fortunate, and the 'win' at the Naples non-event was worthless. Now Ferrari's superiority from the previous year had clearly been more than wiped out. It had rested on its laurels and been found out. It had done that in 1960, but had reaped a major dividend in 1961. It must be recognised, however, that Ferrari was just as interested, perhaps more so, in success in the World Sports Car Championship – most of all Le Mans. No other Formula One team had such diverse racing activities, so perhaps Formula One was not the 'be-all-and-end-all' that it was for everyone else. Having said that, all racing followers wanted a competitive Ferrari, the strongest non-British F1 marque, as it gave credence to the World Constructor's Championship. Ferrari provided the spice – the frisson – that Formula One needed for survival.

✱✱✱ (WC4) XLVIII Grand Prix de l'ACF (Rouen-Les-Essarts)

54 laps of a 4.065 mile circuit = 219.5 miles.

21 entries – 17 started – 9 finished.

Front row: J Clark – 2m-14.8s (108.56mph); G Hill 0.2s; B McLaren 0.6s.

08-JUL: Back to the Rouen circuit of 1957. Hill stormed away, while teammate Ginther was left on the grid for electrical repairs. Surtees challenged Hill while Clark was being left behind. Surtees pitted on lap 13, giving Hill a healthy lead. Having lapped Lewis, the latter's brakes failed at Nouveau Monde hairpin, and he rammed Hill who then spun, losing the lead to Clark. Soon afterwards, though, Clark's suspension failed. Hill led Gurney, but not for long as, on lap 41, his fuel system played up and he stopped. Gurney now led a revived Surtees who was soon coping with gearbox trouble. The problems suffered by most of the main runners produced a very spread out result, with even McLaren, in fourth place, a lap behind Ginther. So occurred the only ever Championship win for Porsche, and a first for Dan Gurney. Surtees headed for the paddock, only to find the entrance inexplicably blocked by a phalanx of gendarmes. A slow finishing Trintignant swerved in avoidance and was collected by a fast finishing Trevor Taylor. Both cars were completely wrecked, but fortunately the drivers were uninjured. Had Taylor opted for swerving either way the result could have been much worse, probably involving many innocent people. It takes the likes of a motor racing driver to make such a quick, clear and cool decision which presents risk to himself. Why police, clearly ignorant of motor race matters, were given such marshalling roles in continental races is beyond me.

1st	D Gurney (W)	Porsche 804 in 2h-07m-35.5s	103.23
2nd	T Maggs (W)	Cooper T60-Climax V8	1 lap
3rd	R Ginther (W)	BRM P578 V8	2 laps
F lap	G Hill (W)	BRM P578 V8 in 2m-16.9s	106.90r

Championship positions:
G Hill 16; P Hill 14; McLaren 12.

✱ XI Grosse Preis von Solitude

25 laps of 7.092 miles = 177.3 miles.

23 entries – 14 started – 7 finished.

Front row: J Clark – 3m-53.9s (109.16mph); D Gurney 0.9s; J Bonnier 1.9s.

15-JUL: The third race in as many weeks, Lotus and Porsche were the only major teams able to attend after the technical carnage of the Rouen race. Porsche was on a high from its French GP win a week before, though Clark's ill-fortune had assisted in that win; did Porsche need it again? The answer was, surprisingly, no. Gurney led from the start as Clark suffered wheelspin, with Taylor third and Bonnier fourth. At two thirds distance rain put all three front runners onto the grass, Clark hitting a bank and retiring. Bonnier was, no doubt, very grateful, as were the 300,000 German spectators who, perhaps, were also there for the World Championship bikes. Porsche must have been happy, being, apparently, competitive with Lotus – all to play for now.

1st	D Gurney (W)	Porsche 804 F8 in 1h-45m-37.2s	100.72
2nd	J Bonnier (W)	Porsche 804 F8	1m-47s
3rd	T Taylor (W)	Lotus 24-Climax V8	3m-55s
F lap	D Gurney	Porsche 804 F8 in 3m-55.6s	108.37r

✱✱✱ (WC5) XVII British Grand Prix (Aintree)

75 laps of a 3.0-mile circuit = 225.0 miles.

27 entries – 21 started – 16 finished.

Front row: J Clark – 1m-53.6s (95.07mph); J Surtees 0.6s; I Ireland 0.8s.

21-JUL: The British GP returned to Aintree to celebrate the golden jubilee of the BARC, which ran Aintree races; much to the chagrin of Silverstone's BRDC. They weren't rewarded with a memorable race, save for the sheer domination of Jim Clark. Ferrari had entered three cars, but sent only one for Phil Hill who was over a second faster in practice than he had been here at the end of April. Unfortunately, this netted him only 12th place on the grid, not sixth as before – everyone else had eight cylinders now. From the start it was Clark, Surtees, Gurney and McLaren for 12 laps, then McLaren passed Gurney and that was it for the podium places. Graham Hill took Brabham and Gurney to gain fourth place by lap 17 – that was his place settled. Gurney's Porsche dropped from third at the start to a sad ninth at the end due to clutch slip – the 'Porsche Purple Patch' was over.

1st	J Clark (W)	Lotus 25-Climax V8 in 2h-26m-20.8s	92.25
2nd	J Surtees (W)	Lola T4-Climax V8	49.2s
3rd	B McLaren (W)	Cooper T60-Climax V8	1m-45s
F lap	J Clark	Lotus 25-Climax V8 in 1m-55.0s	93.91

Championship positions:
G Hill 19; J Clark 18; McLaren 16.

✷✷✷ (WC6) XXIV Grosse Preis von Deutschland (N Nürburgring)

15 laps of 14.173 miles = 212.5 miles.
33 entries – 26 started – 16 finished.
Front row: D Gurney – 8m-47.2s (96.74mph); G Hill 3.0s;
J Clark 4.0s; J Surtees 10.3s.

05-AUG: There's rarely a run-of-the-mill race here, and this was no exception. Gurney gave Porsche its first World Championship pole position. At the back was Jack Brabham in the first F1 car driven by its creator, having been unable to complete a lap in dry conditions. Graham Hill had survived an argument with a film camera which had fallen of the back of deBeaufort's Porsche sending him through the trees. Jim Clark forgot to switch on his fuel pumps, so was left at the start as Gurney, Graham and Phil Hill and Surtees stormed off in the awful weather. Graham Hill passed Gurney on lap three, as did Surtees on lap five, with McLaren in fourth place. However, on lap eight, he was relieved of that place by Jim Clark. The leading three were never far apart, and Jim Clark closed to within 14 seconds when he had a monumental slide on lap 11 which took over 100 metres to control. He then wisely settled for his position on the soaked track. A backmarker interfered with Surtees' attempt to pass Hill after slipstreaming him on the final long straight. Awful weather for the whole race will always produce a very worthy winner.

1st	G Hill (W)	BRM P578 V8 in 2h-38m-45.3s	80.35
2nd	J Surtees (W)	Lola T4-Climax V8	2.4s
3rd	D Gurney (W)	Porsche 804 F8	4.4s
F lap	G Hill (W)	BRM P578 V8 in 10m-12.2s	83.39

Championship positions:
G Hill 28; J Clark 21; Surtees 19.

✷ X Kanonloppet (Karlskoga)

30 laps of 1.864 miles = 55.9 miles.
14 entries – 10 started – 6 finished.

Front row: J Surtees – 1m-25.4s (78.58mph); I Ireland 0.1s;
J Bonnier 0.4s.

12-Aug: No BRMs, so Graham Hill drove Rob Walkers' Lotus 24 again. One Works Porsche and the Works Lolas, plus UDT cars for Ireland and Gregory, were the top entries. Surtees led away, followed by Gregory from third grid row. A melee put Ireland in a ditch, from which he extricated himself. Then he stormed to fourth, just 36 seconds adrift. Surtees struck a puddle when attacked on lap two by Gregory, retiring on lap ten, as did Hill. Salvadori took second from Bonnier's eight-cylinder Porsche near the end.

1st	M Gregory (UDT)	Lotus 24-BRM V8 in 42m-51.3s	78.30
2nd	R Salvadori (YCP)	Lola T4-Climax V8	7.3s
3rd	J Bonnier (W)	Porsche 804 F8	7.5s
F lap	I Ireland (UDT)	Lotus 24-Climax V8 in 1m-24.1 s	79.79r

1mo GP del Mediterraneo (Enna-Pergusa)

50 laps of 2.982 miles = 149.1 miles.
16 entries – 11 started.
Front row: L Bandini – 1m-21.5s (131.68mph); G Baghetti
1.4s; J Siffert 2.4s.

19-AUG: This is the fastest track of them all, around a lake, almost oval in shape. The poor entry consisted of two Ferraris driven by second string drivers with zero opposition. The Ferrari boys had a point to prove between them, though. Jo Siffert (Lotus 21 four-cylinder) actually led lap one, but finished fourth behind Carlo Abate's Porsche 718 – both lapped. He developed a taste for this track in the next few years. Yes, I notice this race was slower than Spa but when the stars got hold of it, it speeded up by 10mph.

1st	L Bandini (W)	Ferrari 156-120° in 1h-09m-25.8s	128.81
2nd	G Baghetti (W)	Ferrari 156-120°	0.9s
F lap	Bandini/Baghetti	Ferrari 156-120° in 1m-20.9s	132.65

✷ III GP van Danske (Roskilde)

59.7m – 20+30+30 laps of 0.746 miles = 59.7 miles.
13 entries – 11 started – 8 finished.
Front row: J Brabham – 43.4s (61.88mph); M Gregory 0.7s;
J Surtees 0.7s; I Ireland 0.8s.

25/26-AUG: Brabham and Trevor Taylor in a Works Lotus joined the Karlskoga field at this tiny, twisty track. Another interesting addition was Gary Hocking (World 500cc motorcycle champion) who made his four-wheel debut in Parnell's Lotus 18/21. Brabham won all three heats, while

Ireland, Surtees and Gregory battled every time. Surtees retired in heat three with suspension trouble. Hocking impressed greatly, and finished fourth overall after mixing it strongly with Ireland, Taylor and Salvadori. Surtees dropped out with suspension trouble, so losing a likely podium place. Brabham had saved his new Brabham-Climax for Oulton Park.

1st	J Brabham	Lotus 24-Climax in 59m-14.1s	60.42
2nd	M Gregory (UDT)	Lotus 24-BRM	20.8s
3rd	I Ireland (UDT)	Lotus 24-Climax	33.2s
F Lap	J Brabham	Lotus 24-Climax in 42.7s	62.89

✱✱✱ IX International Gold Cup (Oulton Park)
73 laps of 2.678 miles = 195.6 miles.
26 entries – 23 started – 10 finished.
Front row: R Ginther – 1m-38.6s (97.79mph); J Clark 0.0s; G Hill 0.4s; B McLaren 1.4s.

01-SEP: No Ferraris or Porsches (as was the case for the later South African GP) and full GP length for this major race. Ginther beat Clark to the same practice time ahead of Hill and McLaren. It was Clark who stormed off at the start and won as he pleased, with Hill second throughout. McLaren, Ginther and Surtees chased, all three retiring around half distance. McLaren, with his bodywork on fire, coasted into the pits and calmly vacated the cockpit. The fire was easily extinguished but a zealous marshal thought otherwise, and soon a 'snowstorm' of foam had erupted. Ireland ran sixth but was penalised one minute when his clutch caused him to jump the start. The penalty proved unnecessary as his clutch gave up on lap 28. Gary Hocking (four-cylinder Lotus) amazingly kept up with the eight-cylinder boys in ninth, until engine failure on lap 62 – his potential now obvious to all. Brabham gained from dropouts to be third ahead of BRM 'rookie' Bruce Johnstone. UDT had a bad day, with Gregory's clutch causing a stall on the line – his charging recovery netting sixth after a pit stop – he could well have been third. Rob Walker had Jo Bonnier in his Lotus 24-V8 but he was beaten by Hocking's four-cylinder car in practice, and retired on lap 13. A disappointing race for many.

1st	J Clark (W)	Lotus 25-Climax in 2h-03m-46.6s	94.77
2nd	G Hill (W)	BRM P578	1m-18s
3rd	J Brabham (W)	Brabham BT3-Climax	3 laps
F lap	J Clark	Lotus 25-Climax in 1m-40.0s	96.42r

✱✱✱ (WC7) XXXII Gran Premio d'Italia (Monza-Road)
86 laps of 3.573 mile circuit = 307.3 miles.
31 entries – 21 qualified – 12 finished.
Front row: J Clark – 1m-40.35 (128.18mph); G Hill 0.03s.
Row two: R Ginther 0.75s; B McLaren 1.45s.

16-SEP: A six-week wait between Championship rounds due to swapping dates with Oulton Park. Damn it! This meant I missed both. Only the road circuit was used this year. The banking was never raced on again, thankfully, except for record attempts.
Clark and Graham Hill were separated by using 0.01 second increments! Why not the rest? Clark led away, but the first lap was led by Hill from Clark, Ginther, Surtees, McLaren and Bonnier. Clark pitted on lap two with gearbox seizure, leaving Ginther and Surtees to scrap for second, swapping often until Surtees retired at half distance. Behind them McLaren and Gurney were joined on lap 23 by Maggs. Bonnier, Baghetti, Rodriguez and Mairesse formed the third battling group. This became a seven-some by lap 50, while the BRMs went their serene way ahead untroubled. Rodriguez stopped on lap 63 and, three laps later, Gurney succumbed to axle trouble. McLaren and Mairesse pulled away from their group, and McLaren slipstreamed past Mairesse on the last lap. This was a BRM triumph. Ferrari was well beaten at home, and was not seen again that season.

1st	G Hill (W)	BRM P578 V8 in 2h-29m-08.4s	123.62
2nd	R Ginther (W)	BRM P578 V8	29.8s
3rd	B McLaren (W)	Cooper T60-Climax V8	57.8s
F lap	G Hill (W)	BRM P578 V8 in 1m-42.3s	125.73

Championship positions:
G Hill 36: McLaren 22; Clark 21.

✱✱✱ (WC8) 5th United States Grand Prix (Watkins Glen)
100 laps of 2.30 miles = 230 miles.
25 entries – 18 started – 12 finished.
Front row: J Clark – 1m-15.8s (109.24mph); R Ginther 0.8s.
Row two: G Hill 0.8s; D Gurney 1.1s.

07-OCT: Ferrari didn't turn up – another strike it was said (or was it sour grapes?). Surtees had survived a scary crash when suspension failure sent him into bushes and trees. He took over Salvadori's car but started at the back. Ginther was ahead of team-leader Hill and next to Clark at the front – perhaps the American knew this track better. A win for Hill would secure the World Championship, but Clark had to win to keep his hopes alive. Sure enough it was Clark and Hill who battled for the lead, with Hill ahead from lap 12 to 18. Ginther, Gurney and Brabham fought over third place until McLaren joined in. Ginther retired at one third distance, and McLaren got the better of the other two by two thirds distance. Apart from that, the top seven places remained the same, with Hill unable to mount a strong challenge to Clark. Brabham's fourth place was the first instance of points scored by the builder of the car. Gurney was within a second of Brabham, thus claiming the last points ever for a Porsche single-seater.

1st	J Clark (W)	Lotus 25-Climax V8 in 2h-07m-13.0s	108.48
2nd	G Hill (W)	BRM P578 V8	9.2s
3rd	B McLaren (W)	Cooper T60-Climax V8	1 lap
F lap	J Clark	Lotus 25-Climax V8 in 1m-15.0s	110.40r

Championship positions:
G Hill 39; Clark 30; McLaren 24.

If Hill had won the USGP, the title would have been settled then, even with Clark coming second. But the title race was going 'down to the wire' this year because of the 'best 5 of 9' scoring system. Hill had by now grossed 43 points to Clark's 30, and I believe this was thought fair to compensate for unreliability factors not of a driver's making, and to benefit winning over point-accumulation. The modern system introduced for 1991 of counting every score would have made Graham Hill Champion at this point, with a race to go. Which is best?

✳ Gran Premio de Mexico (Mexico City)
60 laps of 3.107 miles = 186.4 miles.
19 entries – 17 started – 9 finished.
Front row: J Clark – 2m-00.1s (93.13mph); I Ireland 1.0. Row two: T Taylor 1.9s; J Surtees 2.0s.
04-NOV: This was a trial to qualify for a World Championship round in 1963. No BRMs, Porsches or Ferraris, so rising star Ricardo Rodriguez was free to drive Walker's Lotus-Climax V8. Sadly, though, he tried too hard in an unfamiliar car for his home crowd, and died in practice at the notorious Peraltada banked turn. A real lost talent. The race was held up for Clark's battery to be replaced, but he was still push started. The start was a shared affair – one man had his foot on Jim Clark's wheel while giving signals as another one dropped the flag – he leapt off smartly. Clark led off, but on lap five was black-flagged for a push start, handing the lead to Brabham. Surtees, in a Reg Parnell-entered Lotus (Salvadori had the Lola), was out on lap one with ignition trouble. Clark took over Taylor's third place car on lap ten,

without losing the place. Now Brabham led McLaren, who soon took the lead but retired on lap 36. Brabham lost the lead again a couple of laps later, this time to Clark, who cruised to victory. After the start fiasco, Mexico was still awarded a Championship race the following year!

1st	T Taylor/J Clark (W)	Lotus 25-Climax V8 in 2h-03m-50.9s	90.31
2nd	J Brabham (W)	Brabham BT3-Climax V8	1m-02s
3rd	I Ireland (UDT)	Lotus 24-Climax V8	1 lap
F lap	J Clark (W)	Lotus 25-Climax V8 in 1m-59.7s	93.44

✳ Australian GP (Caversham-Perth)
18-NOV: On the way to South Africa for the end of the Formula One season, Brabham and McLaren took their 'Tasman' cars to compete in this race – an important one for the region. The cars could then remain there for the start of the series on the fifth of January. See the 'Down-Under' series for 1963 for which this was a precursor.

✳ V Rand Grand Prix (Kyalami)
50 laps of 2.550 miles =°127.5 miles.
40 entries – 17 qualified – 14 finished.
Front row: J Clark – 1m-35.0s (96.63mph); T Taylor 0.2s; G Hill 0.4s.
15-DEC: Two cars from Team Lotus and three from BRM – one for South African Bruce Johnstone, a single Lola, and Lotus-Climax V8s for Ireland and Hocking were the top entries. There were so many local entries that a qualifying standard of ten per cent from pole was set. Clark and Taylor led Surtees and Ireland but soon Hocking, in Walker's Lotus 24, joined them and passed Ireland into fourth. Graham Hill was making up for a bad start and was setting about Surtees for third when his race ended with engine failure. Teammate Ginther's BRM retired after gearbox trouble. Hocking was fourth, a lap down – but impressing again.

1st	J Clark (W)	Lotus 25-Climax V8in 1h-20m-47.42s	94.69
2nd	T Taylor (W)	Lotus 25-Climax V8	0.05s
3rd	J Surtees (YCP)	Lola T4-Climax V8	50.18s
F lap	J Clark	Lotus 25-Climax V8 in 1m-35.3s	96.33r

✳ II Natal Grand Prix (Westmead)
22-lap heat + 33-lap final of 2.247 miles = 123.6 miles.
39 entries – 22 started final – 16 finished.
Poles: Heat one – J Clark – 1m-22.11s (98.52mph). Heat two – G Hill – 1m-22.67s (97.85mph).

22-DEC: The entry was as Kyalami, except for the absence of John Surtees. Clark and Ginther swapped the lead in heat one, but Clark retired, and Bruce Johnstone was second in a Works BRM. Graham Hill and Trevor Taylor fought for the second heat, which went to Taylor. However, all V8s were assured of a place in the final, so Clark was at the back on the grid. Taylor led the final, followed by Johnstone, who was soon passed by teammates Hill and Ginther. By lap 13 the order was Taylor, Clark, Ginther and Hill, the latter retiring four laps later. That was it. Fourth place went to Neville Lederle's Lotus 21 four-cylinder, almost lapped by the top three.

1st	T Taylor (W)	Lotus 25-Climax in 48m-08.67s	93.36
2nd	J Clark (W)	Lotus 25-Climax	6.16s
3rd	R Ginther (W)	BRM P578	22.11s
F lap	T Taylor	Lotus 25-Climax in 1m-24.20s	96.07r

Having lost Ricardo Rodriguez there was a double tragedy for the Walker team as Gary Hocking crashed fatally in practice, having set a time good enough for the front row. The Rhodesian World 500cc Motorcycle Champion never drove an F1 Championship Grand Prix, but would have in a week's time, and doubtless would have made his mark. Therefore, he is missing from Grand Prix records. An unfortunate anomaly – he mixed it with the best from the start, and may well have emulated John Surtees' feat and achieved the highest glory on both two and four wheels. That he was a truly major lost talent is beyond dispute.

*** (WC9) IX South African Grand Prix (East London)

82 laps of 2.436 miles = 199.8 miles.
26 entries – 23 started – 10 finished.
Front row: J Clark – 1m-29.3s (98.30mph); G Hill 0.3s. Row two: J Brabham 1.7s; I Ireland 1.8s.
29-DEC: After almost a three month wait, finally the Championship finale took place. If Clark won, he was Champion – as simple as that. Porsche was absent, as was Ferrari, so there was little to get in the way of the two protagonists. Sure enough, they were in line abreast on the front row of the 2x2 grid. Clark took off, with Hill in close attendance. McLaren, Maggs and Surtees formed a group behind them, changing place frequently until Surtees retired on lap 26 with valve trouble. Meanwhile, Clark inexorably drew out a lead over Hill, and it looked to be all over. Then, at two-thirds distance, oil smoke was coming from Clark's car, and the Championship was Hill's when Clark retired on lap 62 with oil loss. Brabham picked up more points in

his own car again. People remarked that Hill was lucky to be Champion, whereas Clark was lucky to still be in with a chance – see the review.

1st	G Hill (W)	BRM P578 V8 in 2h-08m-03.3s	93.59
2nd	B McLaren (W)	Cooper T60-Climax V8	49.8s
3rd	A Maggs (W)	Cooper T60-Climax V8	50.3s
F lap	J Clark	Lotus 25-Climax V8 in 1m-31.0s	96.37r

Championship positions:
G Hill (WC) 42; Clark 30; McLaren 27.

Winners of the 28 graded F1 races of 1962 – quantity & quality of success

8 wins	J Clark (5A, B, 2C)	11 wins	Lotus-Climax (5A, 2B, 4C)
6 wins	G Hill (5A, B)	6 wins	BRM (5A, B)
3 wins	B McLaren (2A, D)	3 wins	Cooper-Climax (2A, D); Ferrari (A, 2D)
2 wins	D Gurney (A, C) W Mairesse (A, D)	2 wins	Porsche (A, C); Lotus-BRM (2C)
1 win	M Trintgnant (B) T Taylor (C) J Surtees (C) I Ireland (C) J Brabham (C) M Gregory (C) L Bandini (D)	1 win	Lola-Climax (C)

A record 12 winners!

1962 seasonal review

This was another very full season, with 25 good Formula One races plus a few lesser events, but just nine Championship rounds. Every marque had some share of the spoils sometimes; when Lotus and BRM let them. This was a healthy state of affairs, and would improve if Ferrari got back into the game.

The new breed of car for this 'underpowered' Formula One had, within two years, made up for an engine size reduction of 40 per cent! More power had been found, but they still had a deficit to 1960 F1 cars of 25 per cent. The standard set by Colin Chapman with the Lotus 21 had been taken up, and the cars were now 'bullets-on-wheels,' but fired with less powder, and were, perhaps, some of the best-looking and sounding of all Formula cars, ever. At Goodwood, Aintree and Oulton Park new outright records were set. Even at speedy Silverstone, the International Trophy pole was identical to the 1960 British GP pole time. The April Aintree '200' was run faster than the British GP there later in the year, and these were all non-Championship races. In the Championship itself, the Monaco GP had race and lap records reset. But what about the fastest of all – Belgium? The 1962 race was won at 98.7 per cent of the 1960 figure – Clark would have been within 50 seconds of second place in that race! Fears of slow cars had been well assuaged. But Ferrari had failed miserably in 1962, after the loss of key personnel. Would it recover in 1963? Phil Hill was made a scapegoat and lost his seat. Porsche had recognised that its victory in France owed something to fortune, and, sadly, gave up – six foot three inch Dan Gurney had never looked comfortable in the tiny car. Promising Lola had also stopped, though the 1962 cars would continue to be operated by Reg Parnell. However, an exciting newcomer had emerged in the ranks of F1 marques when Jack Brabham produced his eponymous car and soon scored points with it. This was in complete contrast to the very brief 'career' of the deTomaso Flat 8 car which appeared at Monza, did one practice lap, and made the previous year's de Tomaso look good. Formula One was too healthy too worry about that.

1962 Championship review

Four marques shared the winners' spoils. The race list clearly shows the well-remembered last race agony for Jim Clark in South Africa. Was the Championship stolen from him? No ... luck had evened out. Take a look back at Monaco. Graham Hill's BRM had let him down at 93 per cent race distance, presenting Bruce McLaren with the sole victory for the Cooper marque. Although Hill finished sixth, those eight lost points would have sealed the Championship for him at Watkins Glen with a race to spare! So any idea that Jim Clark was the moral victor in 1962 should be re-thought.

The potential gross scores of both Hill and Clark are interesting. Graham Hill grossed 52 points, but the system allowed for retention of only 42. However, he had lost 18 points from retirements, so his highest gross potential was 70, the system allowing 45 of those to be retained. Clark had 30 points from just four finishes, but he had lost 39 points giving a gross potential of 69 points of which 45 would have been retained – little to choose between them then. They could have won all the races between them. Even Dan Gurney's victory at Rouen was achieved after both of the main protagonists had retired from the lead with machinery problems. No-one can deny a manufacturer's win is well deserved when a rival's machinery has failed, but it's tough on the driver. Interestingly, the Cooper team had been so strong at the end of the 2.5-litre Formula One just two years previously, and was now beginning to struggle, having lost the skills of Jack Brabham. Reliability was good – no retirements in the last six GPs – but that would not bring glory. Ferrari's team leader, reigning Champion Phil Hill, led the title race after the first two rounds, but that was flattery as a third place in the next race was all he scored for the season; his services being dispensed with after the Italian GP.

VISIT VELOCE ON THE WEB – WWW.VELOCE.CO.UK
All current books • New book news • Special offers • Gift vouchers • Forum

192

Picture gallery 2

A 140mph full drift at Spa by Mike Hawthorn on his way to second place; a sight to behold.

Aintree '200' in 1959. Gregory #11 and Schell #14 were not too quick away, but Behra #2 faltered. He would win, though.

A very fine driver winning the 1959 Aintree '200' in a very handsome car. Behra and Ferrari in the Aintree '200.'

The first US Grand Prix, at Sebring, in 1959. A superb action shot of Jack Brabham, as young Bruce McLaren follows ...

... and studies Brabham very hard indeed. Moss had retired, leaving the race to the two of them.

Oulton Park 1959, and Brabham leads away from Moss, Bristow and Hill. Once he had the lead, Moss was untouchable.

International Trophy 1959. BRM, Ferrari, Aston Martin and Cooper get away together. Moss' BRM brakes failed on lap three.

At Goodwood in 1959, Schell's BRM is soon to be passed by the Coopers of Moss and Brabham.

But fortune favoured McLaren, as did the girl. Brabham had to settle for the World Championship.

1960 International Trophy. Alan Stacey's Lotus 18 laps Cliff Allison's battered Ferrari, and eventually Phil Hill's as well.

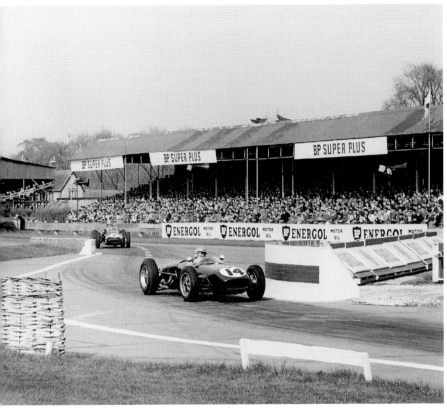

Goodwood 1960, and Innes Ireland shows the true speed of the Lotus 18 as Moss is unable to retake the lead he lost.

In the 1960 Dutch GP, Ginther's Ferrari gives Jim Clark something to think about.

International Trophy 1960, with Moss leading Ireland before suspension trouble took him out.

At Monza a taster for 1961 with von Trips' F2-engined Ferrari 246P in the Italian GP 'non-event.'

195

A neat start in the 1961 Goodwood Glover Trophy. Surtees #11 takes his first F1 win.

British GP. Tony Brooks is about to be lapped by Graham Hill, in his great but unfortunate drive at Silverstone.

The 1961 Silverstone International Trophy race, and Brabham has the only clear view ahead of Ireland, Moss and McLaren.

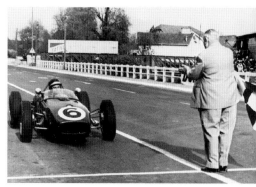

A lonely finish at Pau for Jim Clark, who, like Surtees, won his first F1 race on this same day. But who was first first?

But Moss later took command in the '61 International Trophy, and lapped the field. Here, showing true poise at Stowe.

Moss was at home in any car. A perfect study of the Maestro and Ferguson winning an historic 1961 Oulton Park Gold Cup.

1962 International Trophy. Amazing start by Clark. Ireland's green Ferrari (in honour of Moss) is directly behind.

Zandvoort 1962. A perfect fit for Jim Clark in the revolutionary Lotus 25. Winning would wait until Belgium.

Graham Hill in BRM 'stackpipe' phase chases Clark, losing second near the end of the 1962 Aintree '200.' The straw bale protected the tree rather than the driver?

1962 Aintree '200.' Ireland and Gregory's BRP Lotus 18/21s sandwich Baghetti's Ferrari for seventh place at Anchor turn.

Jim Clark's hand aloft at the start of the 1963 Aintree '200.' He later took over Taylor's car and claimed third with an amazing record lap.

'Open wide.' Shortened noses were often used at Monaco. Innes Ireland's Lotus-BRM leads Gurney in 1963.

I've heard of 'Smile please,' but 'Slide please' is new to me. Not to Graham Hill, though, at East London in December 1963.

The 1964 Mexican GP has a strange podium. Winner Gurney on step two, second place Surtees is now World Champion. The girl feels on top of the world in such company. Where's third-placed Bandini ... keeping a low profile?

Andre Pilette has baulked Jim Clark and caused the crash at the 1964 Aintree '200.' Does he know?

Gurney had the 1964 Belgian GP completely sewn up, with time for a refuel, but no fuel was available. Oh for a radio!

Jim Clark leads Phil Hill's Cooper at Teretonga, New Zealand, 1965, to claim a Tasman hat-trick.

A new series gets under way in 1965 as Clark heads the field at the 1st 'Race of Champions' start.

Spa 1966. Now that's a close-up! Frankenheimer's 'Grand Prix' is filmed during the actual race as Brabham passes.

199

Rindt leads Bonnier in Cooper-Maseratis in the 1966 International Trophy. Oversteer leads understeer – understeer won this battle.

Mike Parkes springs ahead of Stewart, Spence and Hulme – never to be headed in the 1967 International Trophy.

Brands Hatch '67. All friends together – Gurney, Brabham, McLaren, Ginther, Hulme, Rindt and Graham Hill share a joke before action. Fun and danger went together then. Today there's almost neither.

But Gurney led the 1967 Race of Champions flag-to-flag at Brands. Here, Ginther's Eagle and Surtees' Honda lead the chasers.

How small Graham Hill's Lotus 33-BRM looks against 1967 cars. But he put up fastest lap after pitting for plugs at the International Trophy.

At the 1968 Brands Hatch 'Race of Champs,' if exhaust pipes equals power then Ferrari has the rest beaten.

Graham Hill heads Amon's Ferrari in the 1968 International Trophy. Track limits were not open for discussion in 1968.

Clark's Lotus practised with the BRM H16 engine at the 1966 Gold Cup at Oulton Park, but used the Lotus 33 in the race.

A new era for racing, New Zealand, 1968: sponsor colours replacing the traditional national colours.

McLaren's eponymous car just beat Spence and Stewart off the line at the 1968 Brands Hatch RoC, and led throughout.

Pole man Denny Hulme in contemplation on the 1968 International Trophy grid, ahead of Chris Amon's Ferrari.

Worth the ticket price alone: Lap after lap artistry from Chris Amon at the 1968 Gold Cup at Oulton Park.

Chased by Brabham, Ickx and Oliver into 'Deer's leap' at Oulton Park chasing Amon for second place.

Rindt wins 1969 Lady Wigram Trophy over teammate Hill and Amon's Ferrari.

'Wings above the clouds' as the 1969 International Trophy field gets away. Courage #16 and Siffert #12 from second row lead Bell's Ferrari.

Last year's British GP winner Jo Siffert back at Brands in March 1969, with extra wings. Fourth was the best he could manage.

1969 'Race-of Champs.' Jackie Oliver's BRM lifts its wheels despite wings, en route to fifth two laps down.

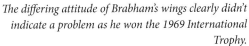

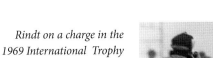

The differing attitude of Brabham's wings clearly didn't indicate a problem as he won the 1969 International Trophy.

Rindt on a charge in the 1969 International Trophy recovering from a misfire.

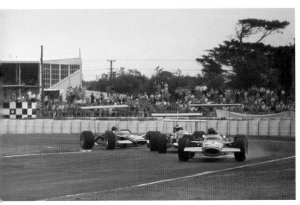

At Lakeside, 1969, Graham Hill holds off Courage and Rindt who both retired. Chris Amon took the race and the Tasman title.

203

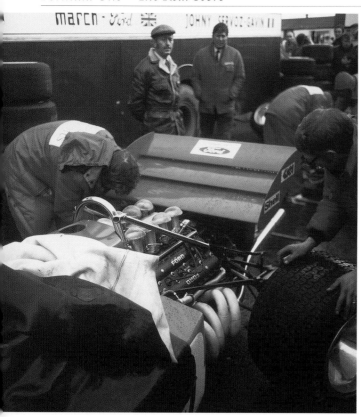

A tri-plane worked magic for the 'Red Baron,' so it's bound to make the Lotus 72 fly at the 1970 International Trophy.

Surtees' Surtees leads the 1970 Oulton Park Gold Cup field from Oliver's BRM, with Rindt lying fifth.

There's fun to be had at the 1970 'RoC.' That's what Bruce McLaren thinks.

The shock arrival of the Tyrrell, and its sheer speed in Stewart's hands, at the 1970 Oulton Park Gold Cup ...

... here chasing Rindt after losing a lap at the start.

Stewart, Hulme and Regazzoni lead off the 1971 'RoC' at Brands Hatch. Tyres played a part in Regga's favour at half distance.

Hill's 'Lobster-claw' Brabham made fastest lap at the 1971 Brands RoC, but retired. They won at Silverstone in May, though: Graham Hill's final F1 triumph.

Fittipaldi debuts the unique Lotus 56 turbine in the 1970 RoC. A brave but eventually fruitless innovation. The race went to Beltoise's BRM.

1971 International Trophy, and Fittipaldi's 4wd Lotus turbine leads Pescarolo's 'Spitfire-winged' March 711. Pescarolo was sixth – the Lotus failed.

After the unique F1-v-F4 Questor GP, American Mario Andretti holds the trophy after he and his Ferrari beat the – er – Americans.

The race went to Beltoise's BRM – its final victory in F1. Small consolation after last year's tragedy.

The front row of Fittipaldi and Peterson take off in-line at the 32-car 1972 Brands Hatch 'Victory Race.' Wrong tyres cost them both.

Lauda has won 100 bottles of Champers in practice at 1974 'RoC.' No need for an ice-bucket by the looks of things.

Beltoise and Gethin's BRMs lead the 1972 International Trophy field towards Stowe. Fittipaldi in third would take the honours.

Jacky Ickx lines up his famous outside pass on Lauda at Paddock Bend in the 1974 Brands RoC.

Hunt's Hesketh hounds Peterson's Lotus at Silverstone in 1974 – successfully. They had been the 'Talk-of-the-Grid.'

75 'RoC' and Schekter leads the formation lap, though Pryce is on pole. The last race before relocation of the paddock.

A Gladiator prepares – Hunt takes up pole position in the 1976 International Trophy.

Villeneuve attacks Andretti at Druids in the 1979 'Race of Champions,' eventually succeeding ...

"Who is he?" asked Fittipaldi when unknown rookie Keke Rosberg won the 1978 International Trophy. Theodore owner 'Teddy' Yip seems rather pleased.

... having stretched his lead and the track width a little.

1983 'RoC,' and Arnoux's Ferrari leads champion Keke Rosberg, Danny Sullivan and Alan Jones. The very final 'extra' race.

Chapter 22

1963
Domination not seen for ten years

The Hill/Clark and BRM/Lotus year-long battle the year before had promoted F1 well, and crowds were plentiful with lots to look forward to in 1963. Porsche had withdrawn, sadly, so it was back to Britain versus Ferrari, and it was crucial that Ferrari upped its game to give Formula One credibility as a world sport. Happily, a great new signing helped no end. Several of Ferrari's key personnel had left early in 1962 to form a new F1 marque called ATS – Automobili Turismo e Sport – so Italy had two marques with which to attack the British ... or did it? More competition from outside the UK was needed now without Porsche, and surely in Italy there was a sufficient automotive skill base to produce more than one marque; Ferrari had flown the Italian flag alone for too long. There would be twenty-four Formula One races this season, but only ten World Championship rounds.

The constructors

The main protagonists from the previous year continued unaltered, with BRM retaining Graham Hill and Richie Ginther, whilst Team Lotus continued with Jim Clark and Trevor Taylor. It's always good to see a great battle re-engaged without change. This would now be 'Round two.'

Cooper Cars continued with Bruce McLaren and Tony Maggs. It was hoped by most followers that they would recover some of their lost form.

Jack Brabham's Works team, called Brabham Racing Organisation, had himself, of course, and would soon be joined by Dan Gurney. Everyone was pleased to see that the latter had a good seat for 1963 after Porsche's withdrawal.

Ferrari had a new chassis to mount the V6 engine, and its great new signing was John Surtees, who brought his technical skills to bear in the new design, which looked

rather more like those of Ferrari's challengers than before. His teammate would be Willy Mairesse and/or Ludovico Scarfiotti.

ATS (Automibili Turismo e Sport) was created by the Ferrari defectors in 1961, and had shown its sleek new car, with a V8 engine and a claimed 190bhp, at the end of 1962. ATS had hired 1961 World Champion Phil Hill and 1961 French GP winner Giancarlo Baghetti, and was expected to be a useful addition to the field that year. Brabham was the only other marque employing two GP winners.

BRP (British Racing Partnership) now operated without sponsorship, and, tired of being a customer, introduced its own monocoque design based on Lotus 24 suspension geometry. Innes Ireland would drive the new BRM-powered car, which first appeared in Belgium. American Jim Hall, famous now as creator of the ground-breaking Chaparral sports cars, would drive the existing Lotus 24-BRM.

The last marque is the American Scirocco of Scirocco-Powell Racing, which had bought out the former unsuccessful Emeryson cars made on a shoestring by Englishman Paul Emery. The driver line-up was the experienced but none-too successful Ian Burgess, and unknown young American Tony Settember, whose guardian, Hugo Powell, had set up the team to provide him with a car.

That was eight Works teams – now to the best independents who could be relied upon to keep the factories on their toes.

The independents

Reg Parnell Racing had purchased two of the Lolas of the previous year, thus putting a ninth marque on the grid, and had signed New Zealander Chris Amon, not yet 20 years old (!) as leader.

Another Lola was sold to motorcycle racer Bob

Anderson, who would make good use of it and become a leading privateer.

The RRC Walker Racing team had disastrously lost Stirling Moss, but continued by taking on Jo Bonnier, and was using a 1962 Cooper T60-Climax V8.

Scuderia Centro-Sud had purchased a BRM P578 for Lorenzo Bandini. A rare sale of a BRM to an unconnected team, with owner Guglielmo Dei happy to provide opposition to Ferrari who never sold his F1 cars.

The Grand Prix driver's diary of single-seater racing for 1963

5th January	FL – New Zealand GP at Pukekohe (NZ) – 165.7 miles
12th January	FL – Levin International (NZ) – 30.8 miles
19th January	FL – Lady Wigram Trophy at Christchurch – 150.2 miles
26th January	FL – Teretonga Trophy at Invercargill – 75 miles
10th February	FL – Australian GP at Warwick Farm (Au) – 101.3 miles
17th February	FL – Lakeside International (Au) – 99 miles
4th March	FL – South Pacific Trophy at Longford (Au) – 112.5 miles
11th March	FL – Sandown Park Trophy (Au) – 115.7 miles
30th March	F1 – Lombank Trophy at Snetterton (UK) – 135.5 miles
15th April	F1 – Glover Trophy at Goodwood (UK) – 100.8 miles
15th April	F1 – Grand Prix de Pau (F) – 171.5 miles
21st April	F1 – Gran Premio Citta di Imola (I) – 155.9 miles
25th April	F1 – Gran Premio di Siracusa (I) – 191.4 miles
27th April	F1 – International 'Aintree 200' (UK) – 150 miles
11th May	F1 – *Daily Express* International Trophy at Silverstone (UK) – 152.2 miles
19th May	F1 – Gran Premio di Roma at Vallelunga (I) – 159 miles*
26th May	F1 – **Grand Prix de Monaco** (M) – 195.4 miles
9th June	F1 – **Grand Prix de Belgique** at Spa (B) – 280.4 miles
23rd June	F1 – **Grote Prijs van Nederland** at Zandvoort (N) – 208.4 miles
30th June	F1 – **Grand Prix de l'ACF at Reims** (F) – 273.4 miles
20th July	F1 – **British Grand Prix** at Silverstone (UK) – 240 miles
28th July	F1 – Grosse Preis von Solitude (D) – 177.3 miles
4th August	F1 – **Grosse Preis von Deutschland** at Nurburgring (D) – 212.5 miles
11th August	F1 – Kanonloppet at Karlskoga (S) – 74.6 miles
18th August	F1 – Gran Premio del Mediterraneo at Enna-Pergusa (I) – 179.2 miles
1st September	F1 – Grosse Pries von Osterreich at Zeltweg (A) – 159.1 miles
8th September	F1 – **Gran Premio d'Italia** at Monza (I) – 307.3 miles
21st September	F1 – International Gold Cup at Oulton Park (UK) – 195.6 miles
6th October	F1 – **United States Grand Prix** at Watkins Glen (US) – 253 miles
3rd November	F1 – **Gran Premio de Mexico** at Mexico City (Mx) – 201.9 miles
14th December	F1 – Rand Grand Prix at Kyalami (SA) – 127.3 miles
28th December	F1 – **South African Grand Prix** at East London (SA) – 207.1 miles

32 events of total race mileage = 5359 miles – 5258 max due to simultaneous races.
Events in bold are World Championship rounds – 41.7 per cent of F1 races run.
* See Appendix 'A' for this ungraded race result.

Keeping busy in the off-season 1963 – a race ahead of schedule?

Brabham and McLaren slotted this race in their schedules before the final F1 races in South Africa in December '62. I feel it belongs here as they were no doubt using it as preparation for their New Zealand/Australia campaign starting in January. The title was also a great incentive I'm sure, and would be repeated before they returned to Europe.

✱ Australian GP (Caversham-Perth)
60 laps of 2.056 miles = 123.5 miles.
11 entries – 10 started – 5 finished.
Front row: B McLaren in 1m-19.6s (92.98mph); J Brabham 0.5s; B Stillwell 0.7s.
18-NOV 1962: McLaren had a crash in practice, and Brabham blew an engine. McLaren's car was repaired, and he loaned a spare engine to Brabham, emulating Braham's generosity to Moss in 1959. McLaren led throughout, but Brabham challenged hard. However, a misunderstanding by a lapped driver put him into a fence and out of the race on lap 50. McLaren cruised home.
1st B McLaren (Cooper T62-Climax) in 1h-21m-50.8s = 90.43mph
2nd J Youl (Cooper T55-Climax) @ 41.6s
3rd B Stillwell (Cooper T55-Climax) @ 46.3s

Fastest lap J Brabham (Brabham BT4-Climax) in 1m-20.0s = 92.52mph

Heading the line-up for the now regular 'Down Under' series was new World Champion Graham Hill, driving for Rob Walker who had bought the Ferguson four-wheel drive car and entered it for him or, in New Zealand, Innes Ireland. John Surtees was driving for the Reg Parnell-run Yeoman-Credit team, despite having signed for Ferrari for the coming F1 season, so presumably his contract hadn't started yet. Yeoman Credit had Lola T4-Climax cars for Surtees, and McLaren's Cooper F1 teammate Tony Maggs. Jack Brabham had his own Brabham BT4, and Bruce McLaren his self-built and run Cooper T62. All the cars were developed from the latest Works F1 cars, and powered by Climax engines, expanded, with the exception of the Ferguson, to 2.75 litres with about 255bhp. The latest Formula One cars had about 195bhp by then, so these were the fastest single-seaters in road racing.

✴ New Zealand GP (Pukekohe)
75 laps of 2.21 miles = 165.75 miles.
26 entries – 17 started – 5 finished.
Front row: B McLaren in 1m-26.8s (91.66mph); J Surtees 1.4s; J Brabham 1.5s.
05-JAN: The visitors occupied the first five grid slots, but McLaren had wheelspin so Surtees led him and 'local' Tony Shelly, Maggs, and Hill, while Brabham had overshot the hairpin. Hill was clutchless but soon third, and Brabham seventh. Maggs retired with a seized engine, and Brabham overheated. McLaren led on lap eight, but magneto trouble spoiled his race on lap 20. Hill nursed his car until the last lap, when his gearbox cried enough. Modern rules would rightly credit the retired Hill with third ... so have I.
1st J Surtees (Lola T4-Climax) in 1h-56m-32.7s = 85.33mph
2nd A Hyslop (Cooper T53-Climax) @1m-24s
3rd G Hill (Ferguson P99-Climax) @ 1 lap
Fastest lap B McLaren (Cooper T62-Climax) in 1m-29.5s = 88.89mph

✴ 4th Levin International
28 lap final of 1.1 miles = 30.8 miles.
14 entries – 14 started – 8 finished.
Front row: J Brabham, A Hyslop, D Young; C Amon (no times available).
12-JAN: Brabham was the only visitor on the front row, as McLaren, Maggs and Surtees all had trouble in their heats, and Ireland, in the Ferguson, replacing Hill, was on the second row. Brabham made a good start, yet Ireland's Fergie came wafting past by the first corner. The race was his but he got stuck in fourth gear near the end and dropped right back. Within a few laps McLaren was catching Brabham, but

overdid it on lap 18 and clouted tyre markers and damaged his suspension. Surtees had gearbox trouble soon after the start, so Jack Brabham scored the first win for his eponymous marque.
1st J Brabham (Brabham BT4-Climax) in 24m-50.6s = 74.39mph
2nd A Maggs (Lola T4-Climax) @26.3s
3rd I Ireland (Ferguson P99-Climax) @ 48.9s
Fastest lap J Brabham in 51.8s = 76.45mph

✴ Lady Wigram Trophy (Christchurch)
71 laps of 2.116 miles = 150.2 miles.
20 entries – 18 started – 14 finished.
Front row: J Brabham, J Surtees; B McLaren; A Maggs (no times available).
19-JAN: A structural failure stopped Ireland from practising, so he was at the back with the other visitors on the front row. He had warned others about the Ferguson's amazing starting, and was fourth by the first bend, behind Surtees, McLaren and Brabham. Oil on the track in an awkward place allowed McLaren to pass Surtees on lap two, and pulled away. Soon, though, the Ferguson was overheating, and McLaren was aided by Surtees stopping on lap 33 with gearbox trouble. Brabham had to stop for oil, so McLaren was able to cruise home having over a minute's lead. He was also losing oil!
1st B McLaren (Cooper T62-Climax) in 1h-36m-04.7s = 93.82mph
2nd J Brabham (Brabham BT4-Climax) @ 30.3s
3rd A Maggs (Lola T4-Climax) @ 1 lap
Fastest lap J Brabham in 1m-18.4s = 97.16mph

✴ Teretonga Trophy (Invercargill)
50-lap final of 1.5 miles = 75.0 miles.
17 entries – 16 started – 9 finished.
Front row: J Brabham, J Surtees; B McLaren; A Maggs (no times available).
26-JAN: McLaren led Ireland in heat one, with Brabham heading Surtees in heat two. The Lolas started well, and Surtees and Maggs led Brabham and McLaren. Surtees spun on oil and later pitted, while Brabham took Maggs for the lead. McLaren passed Maggs and took the lead when Brabham went a little wide. The pressure was eased when Brabham's tyre wore out right at the end and deflated. He finished on the rim behind the Ferguson of Ireland, but a lap down.
1st B McLaren (Cooper T62-Climax) in 55m-43.1s = 80.76mph
2nd A Maggs (Lola T4-Climax) @ 10.1s
3rd I Ireland (Ferguson P99-Climax) @ 18.6s
Fastest lap J Brabham in 1m-03.6s = 84.91mph

✳ Australian GP (Warwick Farm)
45 laps of 2.25 miles = 101.25 miles.
17 entries – 16 started – 11 finished.

Front row: J Surtees in 1m-38.1s (82.57mph); B McLaren 0.7s; D McKay 0.8s; A Maggs 1.9s.

10-FEB: Surtees had a new Lola, and was on pole ahead of McLaren and David McKay, who had bought Brabham's car. Maggs was behind, with Chris Amon equalling his time – one to watch. Graham Hill was back in the Ferguson, while Brabham, having reached Australia too late for practice, was at the back with his new car. Surtees stormed off from McKay and McLaren, who was soon second but spun, losing many places. Brabham fought to second spot but wasn't catching Surtees until the said leader spun. He recovered but lost most of his lead. Brabham battled to within striking distance, and did just that on lap 30. McKay was fourth, ahead of Stillwell and Graham Hill. So Brabham won his home GP in his own, brand new car.

1st J Brabham (Brabham BT4-Climax) in 1h-16m-34.1s = 79.34mph
2nd J Surtees (Lola T4A-Climax) @ 8.0s
3rd B McLaren (Cooper T62-Climax) @ 54.0s
Fastest lap J Brabham in 1m-40.3s = 80.77mph

✳ Lakeside International
66 laps of 1.5 miles = 99 miles.
19 entries – 15 started – 9 finished.

Front row: B McLaren in 59.4s (90.91mph): J Youl (0.2s); J Surtees (0.2s).

17-FEB: For some reason there was no Jack Brabham here. John Youl's Cooper was just 0.2 seconds slower than McLaren in practice, so perhaps a 'local' was going to worry the visitors. Instead it was the weather which worried everybody, and took Youl out after seven laps. It did the same for McLaren and Maggs, but Graham Hill used the Ferguson to good effect. John Surtees, however, was in command throughout the rain-sodden event.

1st J Surtees (Lola T4A-Climax) in 1h-19m-26.6s = 74.77mph
2nd G Hill (Ferguson P99-Climax) @ 31.1s
3rd B Stillwell (Brabham BT4-Climax) @ 51.0s
Fastest lap n/a
B McLaren (Cooper T62-Climax) in 59.4s = 90.91mph

✳ South Pacific Championship (Longford)
25-lap final of 4.5 miles = 112.5 miles.
16 entries – 15 started – 9 finished.

Front row: B McLaren in 2m-22.6s (113.60mph); B Stillwell 0.4s.

04-MAR: John Surtees was required for testing by Ferrari, so the only visitors were Brabham, McLaren and Maggs. Despite problems in their heats, it was McLaren, and Brabham who fought out this race. McLaren used harder 'dry' tyres, but Brabham had softer 'wet' ones, which should last the race. This meant he was faster on slow corners while McLaren had a benefit on the straights. The two battled furiously for 15 laps, whereupon Brabham lost his oil with a split oil pipe. McLaren cruised home from then. Maggs' Lola was sixth, three minutes behind, having had suspension trouble.

1st B McLaren (Cooper T62-Climax) in 1h-01m-03.8s = 110.54mph
2nd B Stillwell (Cooper T53-Climax) @ 1m-02s
3rd J Youl (Cooper T55-Climax) @ 1m-55s
Fastest lap n/a

✳ Sandown Park Trophy
60 laps of 1.928 miles = 115.7 miles.
21 entries – 18 started – 11 finished.

Front row: B McLaren in 1m-10.4s (98.56mph); J Brabham 0.8s; A Maggs 1.4s.

11-MAR: The three visiting internationals from Longford were supplemented by former Cooper Works driver, American Masten Gregory, driving John Surtees' latest Lola T4A. He was seventh fastest on this circuit new to him, while the other three monopolised the top spots. It was the 'Jack and Bruce show' for nearly all race, though, and Brabham looked to have it until, on the penultimate lap, his engine blew up. McLaren then romped home. Gregory made it to fourth, but his car failed near the end leaving him and Brabham pushing home together for eighth and ninth places.

1st B McLaren (Cooper T55-Climax) in 1h-10m-03.8s = 99.06mph
2nd A Maggs (Lola T4-Climax) @ 1 lap
3rd D McKay (Brabham BT4-Climax) @ 1 lap
Fastest lap – not available

Note: Coventry Climax engines were now almost all of V8 configuration, as were all BRM engines (Ferrari was still using V6s). For the sake of brevity, then, only exceptions to this are identified from now on.

✳ IV Lombank Trophy (Snetterton)
50 laps of 2.71 miles = 135.5 miles.
17 entries – 10 started – 7 finished.

Front row: J Clark – 1m-44.4s (93.45mph); R Ginther 2.4s; B McLaren 4.4s; I Ireland 4.8s.

30-MAR: Two cars from BRM, a single car from Lotus and Cooper, and Lotus-BRM V8s for Ireland and American Jim Hall were the main entries. Hill started at the back, having missed the wet practice. Ginther (BRM) led on the slippery track until overtaken by Clark on lap three. Clark spun on the wet track but brilliantly saved the situation, dropping only behind Ginther, then retaking the lead on lap 15. Hill passed McLaren for fourth at this time, and was on new R6

Dunlops, so was well suited to the conditions. He came right through to lead from lap 33. A mistake by Ginther let Ireland and McLaren through to battle to the end for third.

1st	G Hill (W)	BRM P578 in 1h-25m-29.6s	95.47
2nd	J Clark (W)	Lotus 25-Climax	11.2s
3rd	I Ireland (BRP)	Lotus 24-BRM	1m-34s
F lap	J Clark	Lotus 25-Climax in 1m-38.2s	99.35

✻✻ XI Glover Trophy (Goodwood)
42 laps of 2.4 miles = 100.8 miles.
12 entries – 10 started – 8 finished.
Front row: G Hill – 1m-22.0s (105.37mph); B McLaren 1.0s; J Brabham 1.0s.

15-APR: Once again the available field was split between Goodwood and Pau, with Ferrari at neither. The field was as Snetterton, with Brabham replacing Clark. McLaren led the first lap from Ginther and Hill's BRMs and Brabham's self-built car. By lap four the order was Hill, Ginther, McLaren and Brabham, with Ireland closing. McLaren soon gained second, and then Brabham pitted on lap eight with a loose wire. Ireland took Ginther and, on lap 24, McLaren, to claim second place. Ginther retired on lap 30, and Hill's engine faltered, starved of fuel, on lap 36, so the earlier BRM 1-2 had evaporated. Ireland had shown that even in a non-Works Lotus-BRM he still had plenty of challenge to offer the others. The previous year's records were not broken, though.

1st	I Ireland (BRP)	Lotus 24-BRM in 59m-02.4s	102.44
2nd	B McLaren (W)	Cooper T66-Climax	5.0s
3rd	A Maggs (W)	Lotus 24-Climax	1 lap
F lap	G Hill (W)	BRM P578 in 1m-22.4s	104.85

✻ XXIII Grand Prix de Pau
100 laps of 1.715 miles = 171.5 miles.
16 entries – 15 started – 7 finished.
Front row: J Clark – 1m-30.5s (68.22mph); J Bonnier 2.7s; T Taylor 3.0s.

15-APR: Only Rob Walker's entries for Bonnier (Cooper) and Pau specialist Trintignant (Lotus) presented any challenge to the Works Lotus duo. Clark was way fastest in practice, but come the race he and Taylor drew away tied together. Trintignant was third but pitted on lap eight, retiring on lap 15. Bonnier took over third place, but retired on lap 73. Neither offered any real challenge. Goodwood was 59 minutes of action – Pau was 2hr-47 minutes of boring near-inaction. A pity Lotus wasn't at Goodwood.

1st	J Clark (W)	Lotus 25-Climax in 2h-46m-59.7s	61.62
2nd	T Taylor (W)	Lotus 25-Climax	0.1s
3rd	H Schiller (SF)	Porsche 718	5 laps
F lap	J Clark (W)	Lotus 25-Climax in 1m-35.5s	64.65

✻ IV Gran Premio Citta di Imola
50 laps of 3.118 miles = 155.9 miles.
18 entries – 13 started – 8 finished.
Front row: J Clark – 1m-48.3s (103.63mph); T Taylor 2.5s; J Bonnier 3.5s.

21-APR: Most of the Pau entrants headed off to Imola, 750 miles away, to meet a challenge from Surtees' Ferrari, but it didn't arrive. Clark again secured pole by a 2.5 second margin! This time he was five seconds ahead after a lap from teammate Taylor and Bonnier (Cooper). Taylor had a long pit stop with a gearbox problem after two laps, and Bonnier retired on lap 20, so now Siffert was second. Privateer Bob Anderson, who had dropped from fifth to ninth, had fought back to third by this time – a terrific drive in his 'new' car. Another doddle for Clark and Lotus, but I suppose concentration was easy to lose in those situations.

1st	J Clark (W)	Lotus 25-Climax in 1h-34m-07.4s	99.36
2nd	J Siffert (SF)	Lotus 24-BRM	1m-16s
3rd	R Anderson	Lola T4-Climax	1 lap
F lap	T Taylor (W)	Lotus 25-Climax in 1m-48.3s	103.63

XII Gran Premio di Siracusa
56 laps of 3.418 miles = 191.4 miles.
15 entries – 10 started – 6 finished.
Front row: J Siffert – 1m-59.0s (103.40mph); R Anderson 1.1s. Row two: J Bonnier 1.3s; G deBeaufort 2.3s.

25-APR: This was run on a Thursday, it being a national holiday. The Works Lotus were entered but scratched, it being too close to the Aintree race, and even the Ferrari for Surtees wasn't ready. This left a field devoid of factory entries or first grade drivers, except, perhaps, for Bonnier in the Walker Cooper. He was third after one lap behind Bob Anderson and Jo Siffert. Siffert took over the lead on lap two, and, midrace, Anderson slipped back to fourth. Bonnier's poor race yielded only fifth. A not so Gran Premio after all, and made worse by rain after lap 20. DeBeaufort must have been well pleased with second – his best ever placing.

1st	J Siffert (SF)	Lotus 24-BRM in 2h-06m-25.4s	90.84
2nd	Ct G deBeaufort	Porsche 718	1m-21s
F lap	J Siffert	Lotus 25-Climax in 2m-00.4s	102.20

✱✱✱ VII International 'Aintree 200'

50 laps of 3 miles = 150 miles.
21 entries – 16 started – 9 finished.
Front row: J Clark – 1m-52.4s (96.09mph); J Brabham 0.8s;
I Ireland 1.0s
27-APR: A great entry, with all but Ferrari present. Brabham
was second on the grid, but non-started. His car was already
better than the Coopers which he had left a year before. Clark
was left on the line with a flat battery, losing a lap, while
the BRMs took the lead from Ireland, McLaren and Taylor.
Ireland split the BRMs, and Ginther fell behind McLaren for
a few laps. Lotus swapped its drivers on lap 16, putting Clark
into fifth who then gave a great drive to take fourth from
McLaren on lap 39, and third from Ginther with three laps
to go. In so doing he took over two seconds off the lap record
set in this race the previous year, and beating his own pole
time – all without fuel-injection! A heroic drive inspired by
the car swap which would not be allowed in a Championship
event, but here enlivened the race no end. A great race also
from Innes Ireland, beating many Works cars.

1st	G Hill (W)	BRM P578 in 1h-35m-20.8s	94.39
2nd	I Ireland (BRP)	Lotus 24-BRM	15.0s
3rd	T Taylor/J Clark (W)	Lotus 25-Climax	28.6s
F lap	J Clark	Lotus 25-Climax in 1m-51.8s	96.60r

✱✱✱ XV *Daily Express* International Trophy (Silverstone)

52 laps of 2.927 miles = 152.2 miles.
20 entries and starters.
Front row: I Ireland – 1m-34.4s (111.62mph); G Hill 1.0s;
B McLaren 1.2s; J Brabham 1.2s.
11-MAY: Ferrari arrived so all serious contenders are here.
Ireland's great season nets pole by a whole second from
Hill, and just 0.2 seconds from the track record here! Clark
came from the second row to follow McLaren, ahead of
Hill, Ireland and Surtees' Ferrari. Clark soon took the lead
and never lost it. Surtees got second on lap 11, but 20 laps
later oil loss finished his race. Hill battled for fourth with
Taylor, then stopped on lap 30 with electrical trouble. Exiting
Woodcote Bend Ireland, after a bad start, spun all the way

down the finishing straight on lap seven, from fourth place
to eighth, then repassed Maggs and Brabham, and left them
for dead, lapping them well before the end. He finished just
six seconds behind Taylor having been catching him at three
seconds a lap, and making the fastest lap on the final lap – a
performance not far short of Clark's at Aintree. Why was
he not in a Works team? A customer BRM engine, a Lotus
24 (not 25) and Ireland was clearly a strong combination.
Perhaps this was his best period.

1st	J Clark (W)	Lotus 25-Climax in 1h-24m-27.6s	108.13
2nd	B McLaren (W)	Cooper T66-Climax	24.6s
3rd	T Taylor (W)	Lotus 25-Climax	34.0s
F lap	I Ireland (BRP)	Lotus 24-BRM in 1m-35.4s	110.45

✱✱✱ (WC1) XXI Grand Prix de Monaco (Monte Carlo)

100 laps of a 1.954-mile circuit = 195.4 miles.
24 entries – 15 qualified – 7 finished.
Front row: J Clark – 1m-34.3s (74.60mph); G Hill 0.7s. Row
two: J Surtees 0.9s; R Ginther 0.9s.
26-MAY: Seven non-arrivals, including the ATS and
Scirocco, meant 17 cars chasing 16 places. After engine
failures for the Brabham team, Chapman loaned a Lotus
25 to Brabham for the race. Clark was passed by Hill and
Ginther off the line, and took 17 laps to claim the lead from
Hill. The race was his from then on apparently, but cautious
gear changing (firmness was required) caused two ratios to
engage at once, and he was out with locked transmission.
Surtees was fourth until passing Ginther on lap 28, then
second on passing Hill on lap 57. Hill retook second six
laps later, and Surtees started having varying oil pressure,
dropping to fifth behind McLaren just before Clark's demise
from the race. The problem seemed over, so he chased
McLaren for third place and, with a record last lap, was just
a second away at the end. It was good to see Ferrari back in
the competition.

1st	G Hill (W)	BRM P578 in 2h-41m-49.7s	72.45
2nd	R Ginther (W)	BRM P578	4.6s
3rd	B McLaren (W)	Cooper T66-Climax	12.8s
F lap	J Surtees (W)	Ferrari 156/63 in 1m-34.5s	74.45r

✱✱✱ (WC2) XXIII Grand Prix de Belgique (Spa)

32 laps of an 8.761-mile circuit = 280.4 miles.
28 entries – 20 started – 6 finished.

Front row: G Hill – 3m-54.1s (134.73mph); D Gurney 0.9s; W Mairesse 1.2s.

09-JUN: ATS and Scirocco appeared, but were not near being competitive – the ATS being particularly tatty. How ex-Ferrari people could be satisfied with this car was baffling. A poor practice, as per the previous year, saw Clark eighth on the grid, with Hill, Gurney and Mairesse at the head, and the Works Coopers behind. Ahead of Clark was Innes Ireland in the new BRP-BRM, so he was now a Works driver. The start then was after La Source, but by Eau Rouge Clark was in front of Hill, Brabham, Gurney and Mairesse. Two laps gone and Clark and Hill were 22 seconds ahead of the rest! Mairesse spun and Brabham dropped out, so by lap eight Surtees was third ahead of McLaren. He retired on lap 14, so Gurney was third. At half way a cloudburst occurred and Clark relished it. Hill's gearbox failed, and Gurney was now second from Maggs, who crashed on lap 28. McLaren came through for second, un-lapping himself. Yes, Clark had been a whole lap ahead on an almost nine-mile long circuit that he hated – a performance in the wet which, in Championship history, can surely be described as without any obvious parallel!

1st	J Clark (W)	Lotus 25-Climax in 2h-27m-47.6s	113.82
2nd	B McLaren (W)	Cooper T66-Climax	4m-54s
3rd	D Gurney (W)	Brabham BT7-Climax	1 lap
F lap	J Clark (W)	Lotus 25-Climax in 3m-58.1s	132.47

Championship positions:
B McLaren 10; G Hill, J Clark, R Ginther 9.

✳✳✳ (WC3) XII Grote Prijs van Nederland (Zandvoort)
80 laps of a 2.605-mile circuit = 208.4 miles.
21 invited – 19 started – 10 finished.
Front row: J Clark – 1m-31.6s (102.40mph); G Hill 0.6s; B McLaren 0.7s.

23-JUN: The first six on the grid were below Moss' 1960 lap record from the 2.5-litre era. Arriving at the Tarzan hairpin in line abreast, Clark was able to use his poleman's advantage and claim a lead he never lost. Then came Graham Hill, McLaren, Brabham, Maggs, Ginther, Surtees and Bonnier, Amon and ... Phil Hill's ATS! McLaren's gearbox failed on lap two, and Brabham headed Hill for second from laps five to 20. Surtees was fourth on lap 14, aided by Maggs' retirement. Gurney had started from 14th place after a fraught practice, and carved his way up to fifth by lap 16, passing Surtees for fourth seven laps later. Lap 54 and Brabham pitted with throttle trouble. Soon after Hill's BRM overheating caused

his departure from second on lap 59, and retirement from third ten laps later. Now Surtees was second, but an 'on-fire' Gurney relieved him of that position on lap 63. And of Jim Clark ... well he just went further and further away and saved his closest pursuers from having to bother completing the whole distance by lapping them all. Gurney in a Brabham was now very strong, and clearly the best of the other Climax-powered cars.

1st	J Clark (W)	Lotus 25-Climax in 2h-08m-13.7s	97.53
2nd	D Gurney (W)	Brabham BT7-Climax	1 lap
3rd	J Surtees (W)	Ferrari 156/63	1 lap
F lap	J Clark (W)	Lotus 25-Climax in 1m-33.7s	100.10r

Championship positions:
J Clark 18; R Ginther 11; B McLaren 10.

✳✳✳ (WC4) XLIX Grand Prix de l'ACF (Reims)
53 laps of a 5.158-mile circuit = 273.4 miles.
25 entries – 19 started – 11 finished.
Front row: J Clark – 2m-20.2s (132.46mph); G Hill 0.7s; D Gurney 1.5s.

30-JUN: This saw the debut of a semi-monocoque BRM for Graham Hill. Surtees was without teammate Scarfiotti who had crashed in practice. Hill stalled on the grid, was push started on the instructions of starter Toto Roche, and promptly incurred a one-minute penalty. Roche, standing slightly in front of Clark's front wheel, then dropped the red flag to start the race – thank goodness they all ignored its real meaning and departed together. Off went Jim Clark on his merry way, despite Roche having been in front of him when dropping the flag! Behind him eight cars scrapped away, including the BRMs, Coopers, Brabhams, Taylor's Lotus and Surtees. Second place was shared for eight laps by Gurney, Ginther, Surtees, Gurney again (pitting with a broken gear lever), and Surtees who stopped with fuel pump failure. Hill had dropped to seventh on lap three, but retook third from Taylor on lap 33, and second when Brabham lost four places with a loose lead. Maggs inherited third when McLaren retired on lap 42, becoming second with a lap to go when Hill's clutch slipped. After applying the extra minute to Hill (included below) Brabham finished only 1.3 seconds behind him. If he'd known about Hill's penalty, surely he would have tried harder. Gurney was fifth, recovered from 16th. Clark wasn't so 'kind' this time, so four unlapped others had to do the whole distance. This was somewhat due to the fact that his engine was off peak form for most of the race, and he nursed it at the end!

1st	J Clark (W)	Lotus 25-Climax in 2h-10m-54.3s	125.32
2nd	A Maggs (W)	Cooper T66-Climax	1m-05s
3rd	G Hill (W)	BRM P61 (push started so no points)	2m-14s
F lap	J Clark (W)	Lotus 25-Climax in 2m-21.6s	131.15

Championship positions:
J Clark 27; D Gurney 12; R Ginther 11.

✳✳✳ (WC5) XVIII British Grand Prix (Silverstone)

82 laps of 2.927 miles = 240.0 miles.
26 entries – 23 starters – 13 finished.
Front row: J Clark – 1m-34.4s (111.62mph); D Gurney 0.2s; G Hill 0.4s; J Brabham 0.6s.

20-JUL: Another Jim Clark benefit was expected and was duly delivered by him – or was it the opposition? Surtees was Ferrari's only entry – Mairesse and Scarfiotti being hors de combat – and ATS didn't turn up. BRM dropped the new P61 for a while. Surprisingly, Clark's pole just equalled the time set in May by Innes Ireland's Lotus 24-BRM, but another five were within a second of him, so a good race was in prospect. It looked exciting when Clark was only fifth on lap one behind the Brabhams, McLaren and Hill. But he led lap four easily, and that was that as far as the lead was concerned! Behind him the Brabhams fought over second place, McLaren retired from fourth on lap seven, and his place was fought over by Hill and Surtees. Brabham's engine expired when third on lap 27, and Gurney lost second on lap 59 for the same reason. So the Brabham challenge expired. Hill lost second place when he ran out of fuel on the last lap, while Ginther's fourth place brought him into second Championship spot. Bandini brought the Centro-Sud BRM home in fifth. The Championship battle behind Clark was very strong.

1st	J Clark (W)	Lotus 25-Climax in 2h-10m-54.3s	107.34
2nd	J Surtees (W)	Ferrari 156/63	25.8s
3rd	G Hill (W)	BRM P578	37.6s
F lap	J Surtees (W)	Ferrari 156/63 in 1m-36.0s	109.76

Championship positions:
J Clark 36; R Ginther 14; G Hill and J Surtees 13.

✳ XII Grosser Preis von Solitude

25 laps of 7.092 miles = 177.3 miles.
29 entries – 27 started – 14 finished.

Front row: J Clark – 3m-50.2s (110.91mph); J Brabham 1.6s; J Bonnier 4.2s.

28-JUL: No BRM, Ferrari or Cooper Works teams, but Lotus added Formula Junior star Peter Arundell for a three-man squad for this race. Clark's car was fitted with experimental driveshafts, which failed on the line, so Brabham led, followed by Taylor, Bonnier (Rob Walker Cooper), Ireland, Amon and Arundell. Amon brought the Parnell Lola into third on lap two, but was soon retaken by Bonnier, and followed by Arundell and Ireland. Taylor and Amon both retired on lap six. Clark joined in after ten laps to have some fun, and smashed the lap record at the very end to huge cheers from the crowd – just as Moss was doing when he crashed at Goodwood. Bonnier lost second place spot with just a lap to go, so Arundell had a fine race. Brabham won unworried, having led throughout; and in the previous year's car. This was the first win by a driver/constructor combination in Formula One.

1st	J Brabham (W)	Brabham BT3-Climax in 1h-40m-06.9s	106.26
2nd	P Arundell (W)	Lotus 25-Climax	24.7s
3rd	I Ireland (BRP)	BRP 1-BRM	2m-30s
F lap	J Clark (W)	Lotus 25-Climax in 3m-49.1s	111.44r

✳✳✳ (WC6) XXV Grosse Preis von Deutschland (N Nürburgring)

15 laps of 14.173 miles = 212.5 miles.
29 entries – 22 started – 8 finished.
Front row: J Clark – 8m-45.8s (97.04mph); J Surtees 0.9s; L Bandini 9.5s; G Hill 11.4s.

04-AUG: Surtees was Clark's closest challenger on the grid, with Bandini's Centro-Sud BRM beating Graham Hill's Works car for third! However, it was Ginther who chased Clark off the grid, passing after half a lap, as did Surtees – Clark was intermittently running on seven cylinders. These three were followed by McLaren and Hill – all five separated by a single second after a nine minute lap! Bandini had collided with Ireland, putting both out. Mairesse, recovered from Le Mans burns, crashed on lap two and ended his career. Hill's gearbox failed on lap three, and McLaren crashed on lap four. Clark led lap four but no other so the podium places remained unaltered to the end. Many retirements gave fourth to Gerhard Mitter's old Porsche 718, over eight minutes behind Surtees. His first Championship win was overdue for a driver of his talent – three years after Portugal.

1st	J Surtees (W)	Ferrari 156/63 in 2h-13m-06.8s	95.83
2nd	J Clark (W)	Lotus 25-Climax	1m-18s
3rd	R Ginther (W)	BRM P578	2m-45s
F lap	J Surtees (W)	Ferrari 156/63 in 8m-47.0s	96.82r

Championship positions:
J Clark 42; J Surtees 22; R Ginther 18.

Graham Hill's defence of his title had been disastrous so far. He was 29 points down now, having lost two second places and a likely podium place here. Also, his points for third in France were taken away due to the push start, despite a one minute penalty having been applied as the actual punishment. He would have still been nine points adrift of Clark who could have won the first five. One more win was all Clark needed to be Champion if Surtees failed to score. This was domination by a great man/machine combo.

✳ XI Kanonloppet (Karlskoga)

2 x 20 laps of 1.864 miles = 74.56 miles.
19 entries – 14 started – 11 finished.
Front row: J Brabham – 1m-22.4s (81.24mph); J Clark 0.5s.
Row two: T Taylor 2.1s; J Bonnier 2.4s.
11-AUG: Lotus and Brabham were the major Works teams entered. Brabham added Denny Hulme to its line-up for his first Brabham F1 drive, but Gurney's new BT7 wasn't ready. Brabham, Clark, Taylor was the order at the start of the first heat, but Brabham's engine cut out – it restarted but Clark and Taylor had passed 60 seconds earlier. He still finished third. The second heat finished Brabham, Taylor, Clark, but Brabham's advantage wasn't enough to overhaul the others. Hulme was fourth overall.

1st	J Clark (W)	Lotus 25-Climax in 1h-04m-26.7s	69.42
2nd	T Taylor (W)	Lotus 25-Climax	36.0s
3rd	J Brabham (W)	Brabham BT7-Climax	46.5s
F lap	J Clark	Lotus 25-Climax in 1m-30.6s	74.07

✳ II GP del Mediterraneo (Enna-Pergusa)

60 laps of 2.982 miles = 178.9 miles.
18 entries – 15 started – 11 finished.
Front row: J Surtees – 1m-16.1s (141.02mph); L Bandini 0.3s; T Taylor 1.3s.
18-AUG: A Ferrari for Surtees, Works Lotus for Taylor and Arundell (Clark was in the USA), a Brabham for 'the boss,'

and some very good privateers. Bandini's BRM was Works supported, and he was second on the grid ahead of Taylor. After a lap Surtees led Taylor and had the power to get clear of slip-streamers – at no point were cars below 120mph here. Siffert, Bonnier, Brabham, Arundell and Bandini followed. The latter two passed Siffert and Bonnier, Brabham clearly in trouble. Bandini took third and challenged Taylor, got ahead but both crossed the edge of the track. Taylor was showered with dust and stones, hit the bank, flew across the track to smash the barriers. He was thrown out and was lucky to survive as the car cartwheeled to destruction. The big boys had now shown how fast this track was – within 10mph of Indianapolis yet with half the power!

1st	J Surtees (W)	Ferrari 156/63 in 1h-18m-00.8s	137.56
2nd	P Arundell (W)	Lotus 25-Climax	17.4s
3rd	L Bandini (SCS)	BRM P578	17.7s
F lap	J Surtees	Ferrari 156/63 in 1m-15.9s	141.39r

✳ Grosse Preis von Osterreich (Zeltweg)

80 laps of 1.988 miles = 159.1 miles.
19 entries – 17 started – 7 finished.
Front row: J Clark – 1m-10.20s (101.97mph); J Brabham 1.24s; J Hall 1.91s; I Ireland 2.49s.
01-SEP: A tester for a Championship round the following year on this bumpy, shortish, airfield track. Single cars from Brabham and Lotus, and two for the BRP team, plus Bonnier (Walker Lotus) and Amon in Parnell's Lola were the main entries. Brabham led Clark and Ireland away, but on lap four Clark led only to retire with a split oil pipe eight laps later. Ireland now led, but spun, recovered, and he and Brabham fought for an hour until Ireland retired, having pulled clear. Chris Amon, Bonnier and Siffert all retired from second or third place, so the Scirocco (never a real challenger) benefitted having been push-started at the start. An unknown having his first F1 race in an 1100cc Cooper-Cosworth was a certain Jochen Rindt. He retired, but might well have inherited second place – they'd have noticed him then. Only one serious runner finished, netting the biggest winning margin ever in F1.

1st	J Brabham (W)	Brabham BT3-Climax in 1h-39m-06.33s	96.30
2nd	A Settember (W)	Scirocco-BRM	5 laps
3rd	G deBeaufort	Porsche 718	5 laps
F lap	J Brabham	Brabham BT3-Climax in 1m-11.39s	100.27r

✲✲✲ (WC7) XXXIII Gran Premio d'Italia (Monza-road)

86 laps of a 3.573-mile circuit = 307.3 miles.
28 entries – 20 qualified – 12 finished.
Front row: J Surtees – 1m-37.3s (132.19mph); G Hill 1.2s.
Row two: J Clark 1.7s; R Ginther 1.9s.

08-SEP: Ferrari had a new car designed for a V8, but fitted with the usual V6, and Surtees put it on pole by over a second from Hill. From the start, it was Hill's BRM, Surtees and Clark. From lap four Surtees led, with Clark stuck to his tail. The Ferrari failed on lap 14, however, and, without a tow, Clark fell back into the clutches of Hill and Gurney. Those three had a mammoth Monza-style scrap until Hill had clutch slip on lap 49. When Gurney retired on lap 63, Clark had it all his own way to the end. Bandini's Ferrari retired from fourth place on lap 37 when leading a scrap with Ireland, Ginther and Brabham. Ireland took Brabham's third place on lap 80 when Brabham stopped for fuel, but his engine seized with two lap left. The rules now allowed a retired car to retain its place if not overtaken by anyone before the race was concluded, so Ireland still had fourth place. Jim Clark was now uncatchable for the title with three rounds remaining. His score just three less than the perfect maximum of 54.

1st	J Clark (W)	Lotus 25-Climax in 2h-24m-19.6s	127.74
2nd	R Ginther (W)	BRM P578	1m-35s
3rd	B McLaren (W)	Cooper T66-Climax	1.lap
F lap	J Clark	Lotus 25-Climax in 1m-38.9s	130.05r

Championship positions:
J Clark 51 (WC); R Ginther 24; J Surtees 22.

✲✲✲ X International Gold Cup (Oulton Park)

73 laps of 2.678 miles = 195.6 miles.
23 entries – 22 started – 12 finished.
Front row: J Clark – 1m-39.0s (97.39mph); G Hill 0.0s;
R Ginther 0.6s; T Taylor 0.6s.

21-SEP: The whole World Championship field was here with the exception of Ferrari (which wasn't a rare thing anyway). Jim Clark's drive truly showed why he was now World Champion. He led easily all the way, chased by Ginther, Hill and, at first, Maggs, but the latter soon fell to Ireland, Taylor, Brabham and McLaren. Hill took second place on lap 21, and looked secure, but lost third gear 40 laps later, giving Ginther second place again. Brabham and Ireland battled for fourth, but the latter's race was run on lap 56. Gurney was on the fifth grid row and was left at the start, never getting into the race and retiring on lap 16. He would have stirred it up at the

front if his car had been okay. Brabham finished fourth ahead of Maggs and McLaren who were lapped.

1st	J Clark (W)	Lotus 25-Climax in 2h-02m-58.6s	95.39
2nd	R Ginther (W)	BRM P578	22.6s
3rd	G Hill (W)	BRM P578	28.2s
F lap	J Clark	Lotus 25-Climax in 1m-39.2s	97.19r

✲✲✲ (WC8) 5th United States Grand Prix (Watkins Glen)

110 laps of 2.30 miles = 253 miles.
25 entries – 21 started – 7 finished.
Front row: G Hill – 1m-13.4s (112.81mph); J Clark 0.1s. Row two: J Surtees 0.3s; R Ginther 0.6s.

06-OCT: The Championship may have been settled, but a good race took place, just as it often did, in non-Champ events. Lotus had added Pedro Rodriguez, the late Ricardo's brother to the team, fielding three cars. He started on the seventh of 11 rows. Clark lost a lap at the start with fuel pump trouble, while Hill, Ginther, Surtees and Gurney scrapped away, with Brabham joining after a few laps. Hill held the lead until Surtees deprived him of it on lap seven. Gurney took over the challenge from Hill for a few laps, but it was Hill who swapped the lead with Surtees four times from lap 20 to 26. Gurney retired on lap 42, so the BRMs were second and third. Surtees then held the lead until retiring on lap 82 when set for victory. Just before this, Clark had overtaken Brabham's misfiring car so held third on the demise of Surtees' Ferrari. He had clearly matched the race leaders' pace throughout, though the rate of attrition helped. The second one-two result for BRM still left Hill chasing his 'number two' for points.

1st	G Hill (W)	BRM P578 in 2h-07m-13.0s	108.92
2nd	R Ginther (W)	BRM P578	34.2s
3rd	J Clark (W)	Lotus 25-Climax	1 lap
F lap	J Clark	Lotus 25-Climax in 1m-14.5s	111.14r

Championship positions:
J Clark 51 (WC); R Ginther 28; J Surtees and G Hill 22.

✲✲✲ (WC9) II Gran Premio de Mexico (Mexico City)

65 laps of 3.107 miles = 201.9 miles.
25 entries – 21 started – 10 finished.
Front row: J Clark – 1m-58.8s (94.15mph); J Surtees 1.7s.
Row two: G Hill 1.8s; D Gurney 2.8s.

03-NOV: This was the first Championship event in Mexico and, after the previous year's tragedy, everyone was praying that Pedro Rodriguez wasn't as hot-headed as his younger brother had been. Clark was on pole position by 1.7 seconds (!) from Surtees, and pulled away from everyone at almost that rate throughout the race. It was a trouncing, and he now had a perfect score under the 'best six' system. Gurney took second from Surtees early on, and pulled away as Ferrari had over-inflated Surtees' tyres. When he called at the pits to have them reduced the car failed to start, was push started and promptly disqualified. Brabham was now third from sixth at the start, but some way behind his 'employee' Gurney. McLaren and Ginther fought over fourth, and Graham Hill and Bandini over sixth, but McLaren and Bandini retired near half-distance. Gurney had fuel starvation, lost second to Brabham, and tried to cure his problem by turning on a fuel tap to which no tank had been fitted. The subsequent stop to cure things dropped him to sixth, three laps down at the end. Hill's disastrous start meant he finished behind Ginther yet again.

1st	J Clark (W)	Lotus 25-Climax in 2h-09m-52.2s	93.29
2nd	J Brabham (W)	Brabham BT7-Climax	1m-41s
3rd	R Ginther (W)	BRM P578	1m-55s
F lap	J Clark (W)	Lotus 25-Climax in 1m-58.1s	94.71r

Championship positions:
J Clark 54 (WC); R Ginther 29; G Hill 25.

✳ VI Rand Grand Prix (Kyalami)
2 x 25 laps of 2.550 miles = 127.50 miles.
26 entries – 22 started – 14 finished.
Front row: J Surtees – 1m-34.1s (97.56mph); T Taylor 1.9s; L Bandini 2.1s.

14-DEC: A Lotus/Ferrari battle was on the cards. Could any 'locals' get involved? DeKlerk and Love were within a second of Clark in fifth/sixth grid slots. Lotus suffered from the altitude (5000ft) more than Ferrari, and so didn't offer real opposition to a Ferrari one/two in both parts, Surtees being dominant. The Lotuses failed in the first heat, so they were out of the running. John Love (Cooper Climax 4) was fourth, having failed by 0.1 second to overturn deKlerk's heat one advantage.

1st	J Surtees (W)	Ferrari 156/63 in 1h-20m-11.0s	95.41
2nd	L Bandini (W)	Ferrari 156/63	1m-16s
3rd	P deKlerk	Alfa Romeo Special 4	2m-19s
F lap	J Surtees	Ferrari 156/63 in 1m-34.8s	96.84

✳✳✳ (WC10) X South African Grand Prix (East London)
85 laps of 2.436 miles = 207.1 miles.
22 entries – 20 started – 12 finished.
Front row: J Clark – 1m-28.9s (98.65mph); J Brabham 0.1s; D Gurney 0.2s.

28-DEC: The organisers invited only the Works teams, plus Rob Walker's car for Bonnier and deBeaufort with his old Porsche, to battle with the locals; unfair to points scorers. Another Jim Clark runaway happened, as was now expected. First it was Surtees who chased, then Brabham for a lap, then Gurney who held second place to the flag. Brabham dropped back with an over-revved engine, retiring on lap 70. On lap 43 Surtees' engine failed when in third place, as did Ginther's transmission from fifth. The BRMs hadn't been in the picture here, but Graham Hill came from tenth on lap two to third on Surtees' retirement, followed by McLaren, Bandini and Bonnier. Jim Clark's record seven Championship wins in a year would be unbroken for 25 years (!) and his 70 per cent strike rate unbeaten until 2004! (Perhaps I forgot Ascari's 100 per cent in 1952.)

1st	J Clark (W)	Lotus 25-Climax in 2h-10m-36.9s	95.11
2nd	D Gurney (W)	Brabham BT7-Climax	1m-07s
3rd	G Hill (W)	BRM P578	1 lap
F lap	J Clark	Lotus 25-Climax in 1m-29.1s	98.43r

Championship positions:
J Clark 54 (WC); G Hill and R Ginther 29,

*Winners of the 23 graded F1 races of 1963 –
quantity & quality of success*

12 wins	J Clark (9A,3 C)	12 wins	Lotus-Climax (9A, 3C)
4 wins	G Hill (3A, C)	4 wins	BRM (3A, C)
3 wins	J Surtees (A, 2C)	3 wins	Ferrari (A, 2C)
2 wins	J Brabham (2C)	2 wins	Brabham-Climax (2C); Lotus-BRM (B, D)
1 win	I Ireland (B) J Siffert (D)		

1963 seasonal review
A strong year of 22 good F1 races was run, excepting the poor Syracuse GP which lost its main entries and the Rome GP which never invited the stars. Extra races still well out-numbered Championship rounds. This was the year that established Team Lotus as the predominant team of

the 1.5-litre F1 era, and Jim Clark a superstar. He saw the chequered flag first in 12 of the 19 F1 races he entered in 1963 – a total only broken 41 years later in 2004 by Michael Schumacher. So now Alberto Ascari's total of 11 F2 wins from 15 starts in 1952 had been broken. It's worth noting that, in 1963, the Championship finish rate was 52.5 per cent, but by 2004 had steadily increased to 72.2 per cent, so Clark's and Lotus' achievement is all the more remarkable.

The Brabham team, with two non-Championship wins, now clearly had the better of Cooper, which was the only previously winning marque not to claim a victory this year. Brabhams had shown signs of being close to Jim Clark's Lotus on speed, and with a year of development and better reliability, things could get rather interesting the following year. Unusually no team provided wins for more than one of its drivers, as is shown by the lists below.

1963 Championship review

This year no change in the fortune of others would have prevented Clark and Lotus taking this title. Indeed, his record of seven victories stood for 25 years until broken by Ayrton Senna in 1988, despite the number of rounds increasing from ten to as many as 17 in the intervening years. In fact, Clark's 70 per cent success rate was only marginally beaten 41 years later in 2004 by Michael Schumacher, with 13 out of 18 races: ie, 72 per cent. However, if you look at the two-car team picture a different perspective emerges. Has there ever been such a disparity between the drivers in a two-car team as occurred in 1963? Trevor Taylor scored his only point of the year – one for sixth place – in the first round where Jim Clark retired. So Team Lotus never brought both cars home in the points in any Championship round, whereas BRM did so on four occasions, each driver amassing 29 points (best six counting). So this gives BRM a better team result with 29+29 beating 54+1. In those days the Constructor's Championship took only the score from the leading car of each marque. Today, scores from each car count, making for a better inter-team competition. Therefore, under the 'best 6' system, BRM would have been Constructors' Champion not Lotus; and with the previous year's car! In that situation, would Chapman have put more effort into his second car? It was good to see Surtees' maiden Championship victory, and also to see Ferrari back on the top step in Germany. Of the new ATS outfit the least said the better. The car which emerged at Spa looked like a back-yard special, and went little better than one. A sad sight to see was the 1961 World Champion Phil Hill in this unworthy car. No progress was made during the year, so it was as well ATS packed up.

VISIT VELOCE ON THE WEB – WWW.VELOCE.CO.UK
All current books • New book news • Special offers • Gift vouchers • Forum

220

Chapter 23

1964
More competition hoped for

After the previous year, some real competition was hoped for. After the 'mauling' dished out by Jim Clark and Lotus, had the opposition responded for the new season? Probably even Jim Clark himself hoped so, as competition is the life-blood of any sport.

The constructors

Team Lotus produced a revised car specifically for the new tyres (see below) designated the Lotus 33, but outwardly similar to the 25. Jim Clark was retained as team leader, of course, but his number two was now Peter Arundell, who had been a real star in Formula Junior.

BRM had its established duo of Graham Hill and Richie Ginther, and a completely redesigned car. After the previous year's failure of the semi-monocoque car mid-season, now a full monocoque type 261 of almost tubular shape appeared. This would be called 'The flying cigar.' Would it light-up the track, burn steadily and smoothly, and give lasting satisfaction?

Brabham Racing had the strongest driver pairing of any Climax-powered team, with 'The Boss' and Dan Gurney, who, Jack Brabham probably realised, was now the faster driver. The BT7 car from the year before had been developed throughout the year.

Cooper Cars had recruited Phil Hill to accompany Bruce McLaren now the ATS debacle had, thankfully, disappeared, and would introduce a slimmer T73 Climax-powered car. Would it halt Cooper's apparent decline with a World Champion once again at the wheel?

Scuderia Ferrari retained John Surtees and Lorenzo Bandini to drive the new semi-monocoque 158 car, which had a V8 engine, the V6 now only used as a reserve power unit. It would also produce a Flat 12 engine, and provide a choice that no other marque ever had. Power was always a Ferrari obsession – was it enough, though?

BRP developed its 1963 BRM-powered design, and produced a second car. The cars would be driven by Innes Ireland and Trevor Taylor.

The six Works teams were shortly to become seven, as, on the horizon was the exciting prospect of Honda entering Formula One – small capacity, high-revving engines being its forte from motorcycle experience. Who would drive the Honda, and when, wasn't yet known.

The independents

RRC Walker Racing was still providing Jo Bonnier with a Cooper-Climax. It has to be said, though, that Stirling Moss had proved, not surprisingly, impossible to replace: the team now a mid-field outfit, though still popular.

Reg Parnell Racing sadly suffered the sudden loss of founder Reg Parnell – a true grandee of British racing – who died in January, aged only 52, after complications following an operation. His son Tim took the reins, providing Lotus 25-BRMs for Chris Amon and motorcycle supremo Mike Hailwood (also a director), seeing if he could 'do-a-Surtees' while still racing for MV Agusta.

Scuderia Centro-Sud used BRM 578s, now discontinued by the Works, and provided berths for Giancarlo Baghetti and Tony Maggs, both former Works drivers.

Privateers to look out for were Bob Anderson with his Brabham BT11-Climax and Jo Siffert with a Lotus 24-BRM. Everyone likes a good underdog, and these two might surprise.

New to everyone this year were wider Dunlop tyres running on 13in wheels, often referred to as 'balloon tyres,' and started the inevitable trend to more and more rubber on the track. However, while lap speeds rose, the proportional difference in speed between dry and wet weather performance also started to increase – 10 to 15 per cent having been the usual difference in any conditions short of the monsoon of 1951 Silverstone.

The season started with the usual eight race series in the Antipodes, now titled the 'Tasman Championship.' A new Formula Two of just 1000cc was introduced this year, and was bound to eat into those F1 races not part of the World Championship, yet there were still 17 good F1 races this year, of which ten were World Championship rounds.

The Grand Prix driver's diary of single-seater racing for 1964

4th January	Tas – Levin International (NZ) – 39.6 miles
11th January	Tas – New Zealand GP at Pukekohe (NZ) – 136.4 miles
18th January	Tas – Lady Wigram Trophy at Christchurch (NZ) – 127.5 miles
25th January	Tas – Teretonga Trophy at Invercargill (NZ) – 84 miles
9th February	Tas – Australian GP at Sandown Park (Aus) – 121.5 miles
16th February	Tas – Warwick Farm '100' (Aus) – 101.3 miles
23rd February	Tas – Lakeside International (Aus) – 99 miles
2nd March	Tas – South Pacific Trophy at Longford (Aus) – 157.5 miles
14th March	F1 – *Daily Mirror* Trophy at Snetterton(UK) – 135.5 miles
30th March	F1 – *News of the World* Trophy at Goodwood (UK) – 100.8 miles
5th April	F2 – Grand Prix de Pau (F) – 137.7 miles
12th April	F2 – Preis von Wien at Aspern (A) – 101.8 miles
12th April	F1 – Gran Premio di Siracusa (I) – 191.4 miles
18th April	F1 – Aintree '200' (UK) – 201 miles
26th April	F2 – Eifelrennen at SNurburgring (D) – 72.2 miles
2nd May	F1 – *Daily Express* International Trophy at Silverstone (UK) – 152.2 miles
10th May	F1 – **Monaco Grand Prix** (M) – 195.4 miles
17th May	F2 – Grovewood Trophy at Mallory Park (UK) – 40.5 miles
18th May	F2 – London Trophy at Crystal Palace (UK) – 83.4 miles
24th May	F1 – **Grote Prijs van Nederland** at Zandvoort (N) – 208.4 miles
14th June	F1 – **Grand Prix de Belgique** at Spa Francorchamps (B) – 280.4 miles

28th June	F1 – **Grand Prix de l'ACF** at Rouen-les-Essarts (F) – 231.7 miles
5th July	F2 – Grand Prix de Reims (F) – 190.9 miles
11th July	F1 – **British Grand Prix** at Silverstone (UK) – 234.2 miles
19th July	F1 – Grosser Preis von Solitude (D) – 141.8 miles
2nd August	F1 – **Grosser Preis von Deutschland** at Nurburgring (D) – 212.6 miles
3rd August	F2 – British Eagle Trophy at Brands Hatch (UK) – 49.4 miles
9th August	F2 – Kanonloppet at Karlskoga (S) – 65.2 miles
16th August	F1 – Gran Premio del Mediterraneo at Enna Pergusa (I) – 179.2 miles
23rd August	F1 – **Grosser Preis von Osterreich** at Zeltweg (A) – 208.8 miles
6th September	F1 – **Gran Premio d'Italia** at Monza (I) – 278.7 miles
13th September	F2 – Grand Prix d'Albi (F) – 192 miles
19th September	F2 – Oulton Park Gold Cup (UK) – 107.1 miles
26th September	F2 – Grand Pris de l'Ile de France at Montlhéry (F) – 154.9 miles
4th October	F1 – **United States Grand Prix** at Watkins Glen (US) – 253 miles
25th October	F1 – **Gran Premio de Mexico** at Mexico City (Mx) – 201.9 miles
12th December	F1 – Rand Grand Prix at Kyalami (SA) – 127.25 miles

36 events of total race mileage = 5494 miles or 5392 max due to simultaneous races.

Events in bold are World Championship rounds – 55.5 per cent of F1 races run.

Formula Two dates above are those in which top Formula One drivers entered.

Tasman Championship 1964

The annual series of races early each year in New Zealand and Australia, where visiting major world stars had produced great racing and had helped establish Antipodean stars in Europe, was formalised into the annual Tasman Championship.

A formula was drawn up for 2.5-litre cars but fuel was now restricted to that available at the roadside – 93 octane – so the formula was virtually identical to the Formula One of 1954-60. The Climax FPF engine was ubiquitous, powering all competitive cars. The 1500cc Formula One cars of this year produced about 210bhp, so were still down on the simpler four-cylinder Climax unit which declared 239bhp, but perhaps losing a little to the octane rating. I am not aware of any minimum weight limit for this series, so it's likely that they would be under the 450kg dry-weight limit for F1 cars. The Lotus 18 of 1960 was quoted at 390kg, and the Cooper T53 of that year at 430kg, and both powered by this same Climax engine. A 400kg Tasman car would, therefore, have a power-to-weight ratio of 597bhp/tonne, while a 1964 F1 car would be 467. So, for the first few years, this was a 'Faster-than-Formula One' series. This is borne out by the wonderful Goodwood Revival race series started in 1998 which often has a combined race for 1500cc F1 and Tasman cars of this period. The Tasman cars nearly always win.

The visiting stars were eligible for points for what was an international series, where before they were excluded from National Gold Star entry. Twice World Champion Jack Brabham naturally entered, and engaged Denny Hulme, who had established a reputation in Europe as a fast rising star, perhaps ready for F1. Bruce McLaren operated a slick team with two Cooper T70s built for McLaren Racing, which included American Tim Mayer who was signed to the Cooper Formula One team for 1964. Chris Amon had a season of F1 under his belt, driving for Reg Parnell's team, was now an international name, and so was regarded as a visitor himself. He drove a two-year-old Lola T4. These would be joined in Australia by 1962 World Champion Graham Hill.

This was the first of an annual series which world stars would grace until the end of the decade. Points were awarded as the F1 Championship, ie, 9, 6, 4, 3, 2, 1. The two national Grands Prix and the best two other scores from each country counted, so giving a max of six scores out of eight rounds.

❋ 5th Levin International
8-lap heats + 28-lap final of 1.1 miles = 39.6 miles.
14 started – 11 finished.
Front row: D Hulme – 50.7s (78.11mph); B McLaren 0.7s; T Mayer 1.0s.
04-JAN: Heat times determined the grid, and Hulme was on pole. It was Mayer, though, who stole the lead at the first corner from Hulme. The two scrapped furiously for eight laps, whereupon Hulme took advantage of a slight slip by Mayer and began to pull away. McLaren closed on Mayer but never got close enough to strike, while Hulme took a great win. This did great things for his reputation, while Mayer had beaten his 'team leader' in an identical car, proving that his selection for the Cooper F1 team was wise. Chris Amon's Lola T4 went out on lap 17 with gearbox trouble. Brabham had skipped this race.
1st D Hulme (Brabham BT4) in 24m-36.8s = 75.08mph
2nd T Mayer (Cooper T70) @ 15.4s
3rd B McLaren (Cooper T70) @ 19.0s
Fastest lap D Hulme in 50.3 = 78.73mph (heat two)

❋ New Zealand Grand Prix (Pukekohe)
12-lap heats + 50-lap final of 2.20 miles = 136.4 miles.
19 started – 14 finished.
Front row: B McLaren – 1m-25.2s (92.96mph); J Brabham 0.3; F Matich 0.8s.
11-JAN: Frank Matich had shown his form by coming second to Brabham in their heat, the other won by McLaren. But it was Mayer who came from the second row to lead Brabham, Matich and Hulme, while McLaren made a poor start. On lap two it was Brabham, Mayer, McLaren, Matich and Hulme. McLaren took Mayer, and soon 'old adversaries' Brabham and McLaren were at it until they swapped places on lap nine and Matich took Mayer. At half way Matich's engine blew and Mayer slid on the oil so Hulme was through to third. This became second when Brabham clashed with a backmarker and was airborne and out of the race. McLaren then had an easy ride allowing Hulme to close. Amon had a bad race with brake trouble and retired again.
1st B McLaren (Cooper T70) in 1h-14m-20.7s = 88.76mph
2nd D Hulme (Brabham BT4) @ 4.4s
3rd T Mayer (Cooper T70) @ 15.7s
Fastest lap D Hulme and F Matich (Brabham BT7A) in 1m-26.2s = 91.88mph

❋ Lady Wigram Trophy (Christchurch)
11 lap heats + 44 lap final of 2.318 miles = 127.5 miles.
13 started – 11 finished
Front row: D Hulme – 1m-27.7s (95.15mph); J Brabham 1.3s; T Mayer 1.5s; B McLaren 1.9s.
18-JAN: The track was lengthened with a loop, avoiding a chicane but including a hairpin bend. Brabham and McLaren led off, but a sticking throttle cause McLaren to slip to eighth. Hulme, Youl and Mayer now chased Brabham, but Mayer pitted after a mishap at the loop. McLaren dealt with Youl, and, on lap 23, Hulme also. Now the Brabham/McLaren duo led again, but, as at Pukekohe, a backmarker gave Brabham a problem and he slid wide, dropping to third behind Hulme. A failing engine cost the unlucky Hulme second on the last lap. Amon had an awful race, again, stopping on lap 28 with suspension trouble this time. A truly dreadful series.
1st B McLaren (Cooper T70) in 1h-05m-00.8s = 94.13mph
2nd J Brabham (Brabham BT7A) @ 8.0s
3rd D Hulme (Brabham BT4) @ 23.2s
Fastest lap D Hulme in 1m-26.7s = 96.25mph (heat one)

❋ Teretonga International (Invercargill)
6-lap heats + 50-lap final of 1.5 miles = 84.0 miles.
14 started – 11 finished.
Poles: Heat one – T Mayer – 1m-07.5s (80.00mph). Heat two – D Hulme – 1m-06.3s (81.45mph).
25-JAN: Brabham was away for this round. The first heat was Mayer and Amon, while the second, with McLaren and

Hulme, was faster. Hulme beat polesitter McLaren away, with Amon, Palmer and Mayer behind, but Mayer was soon third. Hulme pulled away, and was eight seconds up after six laps, but unexpectedly spun and hit a fence, putting himself out. McLaren now led Mayer, Amon and Palmer. Amon tried everything to get Mayer, but spun into a ditch, leaving the top three as they finished. This wasn't without drama, though, as the teammates put on a great show, swapping the lead often before McLaren completed his hat-trick.

1st B McLaren (Cooper T70) in 58m-24.5s = 77.04mph
2nd T Mayer (Cooper T70) @0.1s
3rd J Palmer (Cooper T53) @ 11.5s
Fastest lap D Hulme (Brabham BT4) in 1m-05.7s = 82.19mph

✶ Australian GP (Sandown Park)
63 laps of 1.928 miles = 121.46 miles.
24 started – 9 finished.
Front row: B McLaren – 1m-09.7s (99.58mph); F Matich 0.4s; J Brabham 0.8s; T Mayer 1.0s.

09-FEB: McLaren led Matich, Davison and Brabham into the first bend, but sudden braking by Matich caused Davison to swerve and spin to the back. Brabham was soon second and Matich was out with gearbox trouble on lap four. On lap 24 Brabham took the lead from McLaren and a great scrap ensued, the lead swapping until Brabham led from lap 31. It was lap 39 when McLaren's chase came to an end with a rod through the block, and Brabham now led Mayer by 34 seconds. With ten laps to go Mayer's engine suffered fuel starvation, and Stillwell and Youl passed to claim the podium slots ahead of Mayer and Hulme.

1st J Brabham (Brabham BT7A) in 1h-15m-19.2s = 96.76mph
2nd B Stillwell (Brabham BT4) @ 11.9s
3rd J Youl (Cooper T55) @ 14.9s
Fastest lap J Brabham & B McLaren in 1m-09.5s = 99.87mph

✶ Warwick Farm '100'
45 laps of 2.25 miles = 101.25 miles
19 started – 12 finished
Front row: F Matich – 1m-36.6s (83.85mph); D Hulme (0.4s); J Brabham (0.4s)

16-FEB: Graham Hill had been engaged to drive David McKay's Brabham BT4 for this race and Longford, so there were two World Champions on the grid again. It was Matich's later Brabham BT7A on pole, but he spun his wheels and Hulme stalled, so it was Brabham from the outside who led away from Matich, Hill, McLaren and Mayer. On lap four Matich took the lead, but two laps later he spun off, dropping to fifth behind Brabham, Hill, McLaren and Mayer. A chassis member had been damaged and he retired on lap 16. Lap 22 saw Hill passed by McLaren and Mayer when he took a wide line. McLaren then caught Brabham for another tussle, but Brabham held him off to win. Australia was Brabham

territory, and New Zealand McLaren's.

1st J Brabham (Brabham BT7A) in 1h-13m-45.1s = 82.37mph
2nd B McLaren (Cooper T70) @ 0.4s
3rd T Mayer (Cooper T70) @ 11.8s
Fastest lap B McLaren in 1m-37.4s = 83.16mph

✶ Lakeside International
66 laps of 1.5 miles = 99 miles.
14 started – 8 finished.
Front row: F Matich – 58.7s (91.99mph); T Mayer (0.1s).

23-FEB: Another pole for Frank Matich, who was clearly the most serious challenger to the star visitors. Mayer was alongside him on the two by two grid. It was Matich, Mayer, Brabham, Youl and McLaren for the first few laps. The front two drew away a bit, but on lap eight Matich's engine blew after swallowing a stone. Mayer's lead vanished seven laps later at the same spot with another blow-up. Not until lap 44 did McLaren and Hulme manage to pass Youl, and soon after the stars collided and Youl passed McLaren. Hulme had suffered a tyre valve problem in the contact, though, and was out on lap 62. McLaren settled for third.

1st Brabham (Brabham BT7A) in 1h-06m-46.4s = 88.96mph
2nd J Youl (Cooper T55) @ 25.0s
3rd B McLaren (Cooper T70) @ 55.0s
Fastest lap Brabham in 58.7s = 91.99mph

✶ South Pacific Championship (Longford)
10-lap heats + 25-lap final of 4.5 miles = 157.5 miles.
18 entries – 17 started – 12 finished.
Front row: F Matich – 2m-23.5s (112.89mph); J Brabham 0.0s; B Stillwell 1.5s.

02-MAR: Practice was marred by a dreadful accident to Tim Mayer, who landed awkwardly after the King's Bridge hump, hitting a tree. This very promising driver died on the way to hospital. He had proved his credentials as worthy F1 Works driver material. Matich's third pole was wasted a little, and he was third behind Brabham and Hill after two laps. McLaren passed Stillwell and Matich for third, and then Brabham when his gearbox failed after 22 laps. Hill now led McLaren. So a clean sweep of the Australian races by Brabham was foiled. Matich's engine was off-song, and he was almost caught by Stillwell.

1st G Hill (Brabham BT4) in 1h-00m-25.8s = 111.70mph
2nd B McLaren (Cooper T70) @ 9.3s
3rd F Matich (Brabham BT7A) @ 37.5s
Fastest lap n/a

Tasman Champion:
1st Bruce McLaren (Cooper-T70) – 39
2nd Jack Brabham (Brabham BT7A) – 33
3rd Denny Hulme (Brabham BT4) – 23

✳✳ **2nd *Daily Mirror* Trophy (Snetterton)**

50 laps of 2.71 miles = 135.5 miles.
25 entries – 17 started – 7 finished.

Front row: J Clark – 1m-32.8s (105.13mph); G Hill 0.4s;
P Arundell 0.6s.

14-MAR: Every team entered, but Ferrari withdrew, and
BRM, Brabham and Cooper had a single car each. With
torrential rain the race was cut to 35 laps. The use of a
'dummy grid' was first used here to allow the cars to get into
formation before slowly moving to the starting grid. This
was to obviate any problems with a car engine failing to start.
Clark's wheels spun, so Hill led Arundell, Brabham, Bonnier,
Clark and Ireland. Lap seven saw Hill crash into a bank,
launching it but thankfully not inverting it. This was despite
his special 'spinning rain visor.' Arundell now led until his
gearbox failed on lap 22. Clark and Brabham had spun on
their 'balloon' tyres and retired. Bonnier had taken the lead
at Arundell's retirement, but was deprived of it on lap 25,
so a brilliant drive by Ireland, returning after injury, was
rewarded, as was BRP – its only ever victory.

1st	I Ireland (W)	BRP-BRM in 1h-12m-53.4s	78.08
2nd	J Bonnier (RW)	Cooper 66-Climax	20.0s
3rd	B McLaren (W)	Cooper 66-Climax	1m-03s
F lap	P Arundell (W)	Lotus 25-Climax in 1m-51.2s	87.73

✳✳ *News Of The World* **Trophy (Goodwood)**

42 laps of 2.4 miles = 100.8 miles.
22 entries – 16 started – 11 finished.

Front row: J Brabham – 1m-21.0s (106.67mph); J Clark 0.2s;
G Hill 0.4s.

30-MAR: The same entry and starters as Snetterton, except
Richard Attwood was BRMs number two. Again Hill led
away from Clark, Ireland and Brabham. The latter two
swapped places, but then, on lap eight, Ireland, challenged by
Arundell, spun and took out McLaren. Clark had dropped
back with a difficult clutch, and was passed on lap 28 by
Brabham, only for him to suffer a broken wheel, a lost tyre,
and strike the bank. A seemingly assured victory was then
denied Hill as, on lap 40, his distributor failed exiting the
chicane, and a surprised Clark won. Twice now Hill and
BRM had had Lotus beaten. Attwood was fourth.

1st	J Clark (W)	Lotus 25-Climax in 57m-39.0s	104.91
2nd	P Arundell (W)	Lotus 25-Climax	21.6s
3rd	T Taylor (BRP)	Lotus 24-BRM	1 lap
F lap	G Hill (W)	BRM P261 in 1m-21.0s	106.67r

✳ **XIII Gran Premio di Siracusa**

40 laps of 3.418 miles = 136.7 miles.
19 entries – 14 started – 9 finished.

Front row: L Bandini – 1m-50.5s (111.34mph); J Surtees 1.7s;
M Hailwood 6.3s.

12-APR: Lotus and Ferrari Works teams and Parnell
and Walker cars were the main contenders. Italian legal
repercussions of the tragic 1961 Monza crash meant that
Clark was not available, so Spence had his chance. During
practice, spilt oil after Siffert's car overturned was burned off
using petrol – not the best idea as the track surface melted,
unsurprisingly. The Lotus drivers missed the only dry
practice period, so were mid-field. Race day dawned wet, and
the drivers' union got the race shortened from 56 laps, yet
it soon dried – unions are very effective in Italy. Surtees had
the new V8 engine, soon passed Bandini, and shot off out
of any danger. Arundell had gearbox problems, was put in
Spence's car and fought back to regain third. Bandini stopped
for fresh goggles and re-passed Arundell with only three laps
to go. Bonnier (Walker Cooper) and Amon (Parnell Lotus)
followed. Surtees could clearly have gone faster if needed.
The record was seven years old!

1st	J Surtees (W)	Ferrari 158 V8 in 1h-19m-51.8s	102.70
2nd	L Bandini (W)	Ferrari 156/63 V6	37.3s
3rd	Spence/Arundell (W)	Lotus 25-Climax	37.4s
F lap	L Bandini	Ferrari 158 V8 in 1m-53.9s	108.02r

✳✳✳ **VIII International 'Aintree 200'**

67 laps of 3 miles = 201 miles.
23 F1 entries – 16 F1 started – 8 F1 finished.

Front row: G Hill – 1m-52.8s (95.74mph); J Brabham 0.2s;
P Arundell 1.0s.

18-APR: Ferrari again failed to turn up. Ginther survived a
scary high speed sliding inversion at Melling Crossing during
practice and non-started – his diminutive stature maybe
saved him – no seat belts then. It was Hill's turn for pole,
and he led the way, again with Brabham and McLaren close,
and Clark only ninth! Brabham led lap six, while McLaren
was out with overheating. Lap eight and Clark was second
after taking Hill. It took 18 laps to steal Brabham's lead, and
15 more for Brabham to snatch it back. The battling pair
came to lap Rees and Pilette at Melling Crossing – a very fast
left-right kink. Brabham made it through, but the leading
lapped car of Pilette braked (in panic?), causing Rees to
swerve and Clark to crash heavily into the bales at speed,
thankfully unhurt. Gurney had started on the eighth grid row
behind some of the nine F2 cars in this race. He was fifth by

lap seven, and retired on lap 37 with driveshaft failure. Soon after, Ireland's BRP had a wishbone break and he crawled in from sixth. After Clark's misfortune Brabham was untroubled giving his team its best win to date, and the Clark-Lotus combo more trouble.

1st	J Brabham (W)	Brabham BT7-Cl'x in 2h-09m-02.6s	93.46
2nd	G Hill (W)	BRM P261	34.0s
3rd	P Arundell (W)	Lotus 25-Climax	1m-31s
F lap	J Clark (W)	Lotus 33-Climax in 1m-52.2s	96.26

✴✴✴ XVI *Daily Express* International Trophy (Silverstone)

52 laps of 2.927 miles = 152.2 miles.
24 entries – 22 started – 14 finished.
Front row: D Gurney – 1m-33.4s (112.82mph); J Brabham 0.2s; G Hill 0.4s; J Clark 0.8s.

02-MAY: A cool wet morning; a non-Championship race, and still over 100,000 people came! This was normal. At last a Ferrari was in attendance. Hill was best away again, but on lap one it was Clark, Hill, Brabham, Arundell, Gurney, and, on lap eight: Gurney, Brabham, Hill, Arundell and Clark. Soon Clark's engine was cooked, giving fifth to Surtees who soon dropped back, then out, with fuel pump trouble. Ferrari had finally taken on the challenge of the full F1 circus, and found it tougher than expected. Lap 25 saw Gurney out with brake problems, and teammate Brabham had the lead but was deprived of it by Hill on lap 29. The ensuing Hill/Brabham scrap went all the way, with Brabham glued to Hill's gearbox, and finally to the last few yards when the 1962 finish was repeated with Brabham's last bend lunge on the outside. But this time it was Graham Hill on the receiving end of this manoeuvre ... fabulous! Their battle had taken them well away. Phil Hill's fourth-place Cooper being lapped. At last, the four year old outright record had gone – only superfast Spa was left to be conquered by the 1.5-litre cars.

1st	J Brabham (W)	Brabham BT7-Cl'x in 1h-22m-45.2s	110.35
2nd	G Hill (W)	BRM P261	0.0s
3rd	P Arundell (W)	Lotus 25-Climax	1m-29s
F lap	J Brabham	Brabham BT7-Climax in 1m-33.6s	112.58r

The pre-Championship 'season' was over, and had shown that there was now nothing to choose between a BRM with Hill at the helm, a Brabham with either of its pilots, or the new Lotus 33/Clark duo. However, BRM had yet to win. The Ferrari win at Syracuse had proved to be misleading, and showed that Ferrari had done itself no favours by avoiding the real competition. It and Alfa Romeo before had a habit of doing this, and it's one of the blessings of the 'Ecclestone era' that entries always materialise and no longer are crowds lured with false promises. The World Championship was about to begin, and, if 'preserving points' took over from the winner-takes-all culture seen so far this year, then Formula One and fans would lose. Thankfully it wasn't so yet.

✴✴✴ (WC1) XXII Grand Prix de Monaco (Monte Carlo)

100 laps of a 1.954-mile circuit = 195.4 miles.
23 entries – 16 qualified – 6 finished.
Front row: J Clark – 1m-34.0s (74.84mph); J Brabham 0.1s.
Row two: G Hill 0.5s; J Surtees 0.5s.

10-MAY: Clark was on pole despite having little practice due to being at Indianapolis! Non-qualifiers included Ireland, who'd crashed, and Amon, who was out qualified by teammate Hailwood. The Centro-Sud team didn't arrive at all. Clark shot off at the start and led by five seconds on lap three, despite a glancing blow with the bales at the chicane. The chasing group was Brabham, Graham Hill, Gurney, Surtees and Ginther. Gurney took Hill and Brabham on successive laps and chased after Clark's nine second lead. Surtees lost fifth place with gearbox maladies, and Brabham dropped to fifth behind Ginther, soon to stop with fuel trouble. Clark's anti-roll bar was broken on that first lap, and was now loose, so he pitted for repairs on lap 26. Gurney took the lead, but Hill took that from him on lap 52, and, ten laps later, Gurney's gearbox failed. Now Clark was second but no oil pressure on lap 96 finished his race. So as per the previous year it was a BRM one-two, with Clark classified fourth. Every finisher scored points.

1st	G Hill (W)	BRM P261 in 2h-41m-19.5s	72.68
2nd	R Ginther (W)	BRM P261	1 lap
3rd	P Arundell (W)	Lotus 25-Climax	3 laps
F lap	G Hill (W)	BRM P261 in 1m-33.9s	74.92r

✴✴✴ (WC2) XIII Grote Prijs van Nederland (Zandvoort)

80 laps of a 2.605-mile circuit = 208.4 miles.
18 invited – 17 started – 10 finished.
Front row: D Gurney – 1m-31.2s (102.85mph); J Clark 0.1s; G Hill 0.2s.

24-MAY: Gurney was credited with pole from Clark despite doubt in some minds. But, in any case, Clark out-dragged Gurney at the start, and that was that. He drew away just as he'd done the year before: this was a perfect Jim Clark circuit. Hill, Gurney, Arundell and Surtees were the chasing bunch, but Surtees worked through to second by lap 22. Gurney retired on lap 23 with a broken steering wheel. Hill suffered fuel vaporisation later and lost third to Arundell on lap 46. Brabham lost fifth on lap 44 due to ignition drive failure. He had 'nipped' over to Indianapolis between first practice and the race to qualify for the '500.' How very busy drivers were then! Chris Amon's Parnell Racing Lotus was fifth, ahead of privateer Bob Anderson – a Championship point for a one-man band – terrific!

1st	J Clark (W)	Lotus 25-Climax in 2h-07m-35.4s	98.02
2nd	J Surtees (W)	Ferrari 158	53.6s
3rd	P Arundell (W)	Lotus 25-Climax	1 lap
F lap	J Clark (W)	Lotus 25-Climax in 1m-32.8s	101.06r

Championship positions:
J Clark and G Hill 12; P Arundell 8.

✳✳✳ (WC3) XXIV Grand Prix de Belgique (Spa)

32 laps of an 8.761-mile circuit = 280.4 miles.
28 entries – 18 started – 10 finished.
Front row: D Gurney – 3m-50.9s (136.60mph); G Hill 1.8s; Brabham 1.9s.

14-JUN: Spa – super fast, dangerous and unpredictable. Dan Gurney surprised all with an early time which no-one approached – Clark was on the third row behind his number two Arundell! Yet it was Clark who led at Eau Rouge, but was soon swallowed by Gurney, Surtees, Clark and Hill. Surtees led lap three, then retired with piston trouble. Gurney charged away at two seconds a lap – his pole time no fluke. McLaren joined Hill and Clark, who swapped places many times until backmarkers helped Hill pulled away on lap 20. Both Lotuses pitted for water, with Clark doing it on lap 28. Gurney's 50-second lead seemed sufficient to stop for fuel on lap 29 – but the pit team didn't have any! The last lap finale. It was now Hill, McLaren, Gurney and Clark, but Gurney's fuel ran out. Hill's lead evaporated like the last drops of his fuel. Now McLaren led, but coasted down from La Source, the last corner, with a dead engine, as Clark flashed past to win. His fuel ran out as he arrived where Gurney was stopped, not knowing of his victory! It was like 1958 where the first three had broken cars but now the 'fourth man' had won. The 2.5-litre Formula One lap record from 1960 had also gone, so the new F1 breed was on top of all the speed charts now. The records show Clark as the victor, but, in truth, he was well beaten by Gurney who was robbed by his own team! No radios then.

1st	J Clark (W)	Lotus 25-Climax in 2h-06m-40.5s	132.79
2nd	B McLaren (W)	Cooper T73-Climax	3.4s
3rd	J Brabham (W)	Brabham BT7-Climax	48.1s
F lap	D Gurney (W)	Brabham BT7-Climax in 3m-49.2s	137.61r

Championship positions:
J Clark 21; G Hill 14; R Ginther 9.

✳✳✳ (WC4) L Grand Prix de l'ACF (Rouen-les-Essarts)

57 laps of a 4.065-mile circuit = 231.7 miles.
25 entries – 23 started – 13 finished.
Front row: J Clark – 2m-09.6s (112.92mph); D Gurney 0.5s; J Surtees 1.5s.

28-JUN: The fast downhill sweeps of this track, high bank on the left and drop on the right, were the preserve of the brave and skilful. Clark and Gurney mastered these best, and were a second ahead of the rest. Clark, Gurney and Surtees led the first two laps from Brabham, Phil Hill and Graham Hill. Surtees pitted with a split oil pipe, and Graham hill spun, losing seven places. Clark led Gurney by 15 seconds after 20 laps. Gurney held the deficit, and was gifted the lead ten laps later, when Clark's engine failed. Graham Hill pulled back from his mistake to claim second on lap 37 from Brabham, with Arundell in close attendance. For the last 20 laps, Gurney was able to take it easy, while a Hill/Brabham battle raged right to the end. Arundell, Ginther and McLaren completed the point scorers. Gurney's win was just recompense for his brilliant-but-losing drive at Spa.

1st	D Gurney (W)	Brabham BT7-Climax in 2h-07m-49.1s	108.77
2nd	G Hill (W)	BRM P261	24.1s
3rd	J Brabham (W)	Brabham BT7-Climax	24.9s
F lap	J Brabham (W)	Brabham BT7-Climax in 2m-11.4s	111.37r

Championship positions:
J Clark 21; G Hill 20; R Ginther 11.

✳✳✳ (WC5) XIX British Grand Prix (Brands Hatch)

80 laps of 2.46 miles = 196.8 miles.
25 entries – 23 started – 13 finished.
Front row: J Clark – 1m-38.1s (90.28mph); G Hill 0.2s; D Gurney 0.3s.

11-JUL: The first visit by the British GP to this great undulating road-style circuit, replacing flat, unloved

Aintree, saw Jim Clark complete his third win. It also saw the first entry of a 4WD car in the Championship. This was from BRM for Attwood, but was only exploratory, and was withdrawn after practice. Bob Anderson amazingly got in with the Works cars in the middle of row three. Graham Hill split Clark and Gurney on the grid, but Gurney and Clark fought for the first bend with Clark winning out. Gurney clung on, but fate, in the form of electrical trouble, intervened again for him. Hill closed on Clark and the pair gave a great demonstration of a dog-fight for 30 laps, but Clark always led. Better handling of back markers allowed Clark to draw a few seconds away, but Hill was always ready for any mistake – it didn't come. Surtees had a lonely drive into third, and Brabham took fourth place from Bandini with nine laps left, both a lap down. Anderson lost his long battle with Phil Hill for sixth. Anderson had now been given the popular role of favourite underdog. It was looking now that Clark might take hold of this Championship.

1st	J Clark (W)	Lotus 25-Climax in 2h-15m-07.0s	87.39
2nd	G Hill (W)	BRM P261	2.8s
3rd	J Surtees (W)	Ferrari 158	1m-21s
F lap	J Clark (W)	Lotus 25-Climax in 1m-38.8s	89.64

Championship positions:
J Clark 30; G Hill 26; R Ginther, P Arundell, J Brabham 11.

✱✱✱ XIII Grosser Preis von Solitude
20 laps of 7.092 miles = 141.8 miles.
20 entries – 18 started – 10 finished.
Front row: J Clark – 3m-49.6s (111.23mph); J Surtees 0.2s; G Hill 3.2s.

19-JUL: Only Cooper didn't enter. BRM and Brabham had one car, but Lotus had three – an extra 25 for Gerhard Mitter. Mike 'the bike' Hailwood was on the second row in Reg Parnell's Lotus 25-BRM. A brilliant effort helped, perhaps, in having won the 500cc World Championship bike race beforehand. Not even Surtees raced on two and four wheels on the same day! Clark led away on a flooded track, but John Surtees passed before the end of the long lap in which Bandini spun and was collected by Brabham, Amon, Mitter and a backmarker. Then Hill felled a telegraph pole, Ireland went off avoiding a spinner, and seven cars had been eliminated. Surtees led by 20 seconds on lap four, but on the drying track Clark led lap ten. Surtees reclaimed it two laps later for four laps. Privateer Bob Anderson had ditched on that awful opening lap, bent a chassis tube, yet was thi3rd after lap eight! Fortune favours the brave. Oh, and Hailwood finished ninth, and, no doubt, disappointed, unclassified after spinning off.

1st	J Clark (W)	Lotus 33-Climax in 1h-33m-02.2s	91.50
2nd	J Surtees (W)	Ferrari 158	10.4s
3rd	R Anderson	Brabham BT11-Climax	1 lap
F lap	J Clark	Lotus 33-Climax in 3m-58.7s	106.99

✱✱✱ (WC6) XXVI Grosse Preis von Deutschland (N Nürburgring)
15 laps of 14.173 miles = 212.5 miles.
28 entries – 22 started – 10 finished.
Front row: J Surtees – 8m-38.4s (98.43mph); J Clark 0.4s; D Gurney 0.9s; L Bandini 4.2s.

02-AUG: The big news was the arrival of the Honda, and its transverse V12 engine. But its driver was an unknown American, Ronnie Bucknum, with no single-seater experience. It overheated badly and was last by 20 seconds on the grid! BRP didn't agree starting money terms, so was missing. Very sadly, regular privateer Count Godin de Beaufort was killed after hitting a tree in practice in his old Porsche. Clark led lap one, but Surtees, Gurney and Hill passed him by lap four, and valve trouble stopped him at half distance. The problem with such a long circuit is that position changes within a single lap are often not shown. This was the case here, as Gurney and Surtees swapped the lead often in the next few laps. It was Surtees to the end after Gurney's 1964 jinx intervened to halt this great battle on lap ten with overheating. A 'triumph' for the underdog occurred when privateer Jo Siffert came fourth, ahead of Trintignant who had been racing since the war (almost 20 years). So, from the last two Grands, Prix John Surtees had now become a possible Championship contender.

1st	J Surtees (W)	Ferrari 158 in 2h-12m-04.8s	96.58
2nd	G Hill (W)	BRM P261	1m-16s
3rd	L Bandini (W)	Ferrari 156/63	4m-23s
F lap	J Surtees (W)	Ferrari 158 in 8m-39.0s	98.31r

Championship positions:
G Hill 32; J Clark 30; J Surtees 19.

✱ III GP del Mediterraneo (Enna-Pergusa)
60 laps of 2.982 miles = 178.9 miles.
19 entries – 14 started – 9 finished.
Front row: J Siffert – 1m-17.1s (139.19mph); T Taylor (0.1s); J Clark (1.1s)

16-AUG: Lotus and BRP were the only Works teams, so many privateers shared the generous start money. Clark and Spence led off, but by lap three Siffert had slip-streamed past. Ireland came from fourth to lead Siffert on lap 17, but only for two laps. Clark and Ireland then battled for second for many laps until Clark secured it on lap 52. He closed the three-second gap to Siffert, but this track suited Siffert's style and bravery, and he parried Clark's every move, winning by half a length – in truth probably 0.01 of a second. A privateer beating Jim Clark on such a fast track showed what a great chassis and engine this combination was.

1st	J Siffert	Brabham BT11-BRM in 1h-17m-59.3s	137.60
2nd	J Clark (W)	Lotus 25-Climax	0.1s
3rd	I Ireland (W)	BRP 2-BRM	2.1s
F lap	M Spence (W)	Lotus 25-Climax in 1m-16.0s	141.21

✳✳✳ (WC7) II Grosse Preis von Osterreich (Zeltweg)

105 laps of 1.988 miles = 208.7 miles.
20 entries and starters – 8 finished.
Front row: G Hill – 1m-09.84s (102.49mph); J Surtees 0.28s; J Clark 0.37s; D Gurney 0.56s.
23-AUG: An inadequate circuit for Championship Formula One: short, featureless, and with a bumpy concrete surface. The operational airfield using runways was converted with straw bales, and had two hairpins and two 90° bends giving an 'L' shape. That was it! Some cars had structural repairs in order to start. Clark started in second gear, and Graham Hill spun his wheels madly, so the other two front row men, Gurney and Surtees, led the first lap, with Surtees taking over for six laps before his suspension collapsed. Graham Hill retired on lap five. Bandini took over his teammate's second place for one lap when Clark passed, having come from 13th on lap one. The top three remained until lap 40 when Clark's drive failed. Six laps later Gurney's suspension failed and he lost yet another race. Bandini and Ginther held their places the rest of the way. Phil Hill crashed his Cooper and it burned out when in seventh place. Through the attrition came Bob Anderson for a podium. A feat by a privateer never repeated.

1st	L Bandini (W)	Ferrari 156/63 in 2h-06m-18.23s	99.18
2nd	R Ginther (W)	BRM P261	6.18s
3rd	R Anderson	Brabham BT11-Climax	3 laps
F lap	D Gurney (W)	Brabham BT7-Climax in 1m-10.56s	101.45r

Championship positions:
G Hill 32; J Clark 30; J Surtees 19.

✳✳✳ (WC8) XXXIV Gran Premio d'Italia (Monza)

78 laps of a 3.573-mile circuit = 278.7 miles.
30 entries – 20 qualified – 13 finished.
Front row: J Surtees – 1m-37.4s (132.06mph); D Gurney 0.8s; G Hill 1.3s.
06-SEP: Ferrari introduced its new flat 12 engine in a standard chassis, but didn't race it. Just as the year before, Surtees was on pole by a good margin, this time from Gurney and Hill, but Hill's clutch burnt out at the start so it was Gurney and Surtees, as in Austria, that battled; the lead changing 27 times by lap 56! Twelve laps later Gurney dropped out with a flat battery, leaving Surtees well clear of the field. McLaren and Clark swapped third place seven times, before Clark's piston broke – unlucky him! Bandini and Ginther had fought strongly over fourth place and now for third. It went to Bandini by a whisker giving the *tifosi* a very good day. Ireland's BRP was fifth, and Spence's Lotus sixth. This was Clark's third consecutive non-finish, while Surtees was now a hot challenger in the title race. Poor Gurney's hopes were now finished.

1st	J Surtees (W)	Ferrari 158 in 2h-10m-51.8s	127.77
2nd	B McLaren (W)	Cooper T73-Climax	1m-06s
3rd	L Bandini (W)	Ferrari 156/63	1 lap
F lap	J Surtees	Ferrari 158 in 1m-38.8s	130.19r

Championship positions:
G Hill 32; J Clark 30; J Surtees 28.

✳✳✳ (WC9) 7th United States Grand Prix (Watkins Glen)

110 laps of 2.30 miles = 253 miles.
24 entries – 19 started – 8 finished.
Front row: J Clark – 1m-12.65s (113.97mph); J Surtees 0.13s.
Row two: D Gurney 0.25s: G Hill 0.27s.
04-OCT: Ferrari was in dispute with the FIA Italian delegation over homologation of the 250LM, and, in a fit of pique, raced here in American colours entered by NART, Ferrari's representative in America. For four laps the order was Surtees, Spence, Hill and Clark – a Lotus No 2 ahead of Clark? Things sorted out, and laps 13 to 30 it was Clark, Surtees, Hill, Gurney, Spence. Clark had injection trouble on lap 44 which put him out of contention. Hill and Surtees had swapped second place many times, now it was for the lead, which Graham Hill secured from lap 48 to the end. Gurney took second place from Surtees a few times before retiring yet again with oil loss. Clark had taken over Spence's car but retired, and Hailwood was fourth on retiring on lap 101. This was Hill's seventh point score, so he dropped his lowest (fifth in Belgium) but was now in the hot seat for the title.

229

1st	G Hill (W)	BRM P261 in 2h-07m-13.0s	111.10
2nd	J Surtees (W)	Ferrari 158	30.5s
3rd	J Siffert (RW)	Brabham BT11-BRM	1 lap
F lap	J Clark	Lotus 33-Climax in 1m-12.7s	113.89r

1st	D Gurney (W)	Brabham BT7-Climax in 2h-09m-05.32s	93.32
2nd	J Surtees (W)	Ferrari 158	1m-08.9s
3rd	L Bandini (W)	Ferrari 1512	1m-09.6s
F lap	J Clark (W)	Lotus 25-Climax in 1m-58.37s	94.49

Championship positions:
G Hill 39; J Surtees 34; J Clark 30.

Championship positions:
J Surtees (WC) 40 ; G Hill 39; J Clark 32.

Now was the day the permutations of the possibilities the three-way title battle presented came into play. If John Surtees won he was Champion with 43, as Hill's then maximum was 42, but second would do if Hill didn't win. Jim Clark simply had to win with Hill lower than fourth and Surtees lower than second. If Graham Hill won he was uncatchable despite dropping three points won at Holland on the 'best six' system, but third would do even if Surtees was second. Scores would then be level at 40, as would finishes, so Graham Hill would then reintroduce the Dutch GP points for fourth as a tie-breaker. I hope that's clear. The fact was that Surtees and Clark had to score.

✱✱✱ (WC10) III Gran Premio de Mexico (Mexico City)

65 laps of 3.107 miles = 201.9 miles.
24 entries – 19 started – 13 finished.
Front row: J Clark – 1m-57.24s (95.40mph); D Gurney (0.86s) Row two: L Bandini (1.36s); J Surtees (1.46s)
25-OCT: Jim Clark's ability, when on the rack, to do what had to be done is now legendary. He just went away from the field, chased by Gurney. His task was aided by very poor starts by both his opposition – Hill had a broken goggle strap (tenth on lap one), while Surtees' car misfired (13th on lap one). However, on lap 18, it was Clark, Gurney, Hill, Bandini and Surtees, so Hill just had to finish now. Lap 30 saw a dramatic twist when Bandini, driving the flat 12 Ferrari, tried an impossible manoeuvre to cut inside Hill at the hairpin and hit Hill's car, sending it backwards into the guard rail, and bending the exhaust pipes at 90°. The title was now Clark's – or was it? With less than a lap to go it was 1962 all over again, as a steady oil leak finally caught up with him and his engine died. Gurney went past and Bandini had done his duty by yielding second to team leader Surtees, just as Phil Hill had done for Hawthorn in 1958. So came about John Surtees' unique achievement of becoming World Champion on two and four wheels. It was sad that Gurney's second win of the year was overshadowed by the events of those behind. He'd had an absolutely rotten year, having lost more points (50) than Surtees had scored.

VII Rand Grand Prix (Kyalami)

2 x 25 laps of 2.545 miles = 127.25 miles.
26 entries – 22 started – 12 finished.
Front row: J Stewart – 1m-35.0s (96.44mph); M Spence 0.6s.
Row two: A Maggs 1.1s; P Hawkins 1.7s.
12-DEC: A slipped disc for Clark made room for F3 star Jackie Stewart's F1 debut, joining Spence at Lotus: the only Works team here. The John Willment team entered the realms of Formula 1 here, and attracted the services of Graham Hill and South African Paul Hawkins. Pole in his first F1 race for one JY Stewart – terrific, but a broken driveshaft at the start did for him. Part one was won by Graham Hill from the back of the grid, beating Spence by three seconds. In part two, with the shaft repaired, Stewart emulated Hill from the back to lead in only seven laps! Hill, of course, knew that Stewart was no threat. Jackie Stewart won part two by ten seconds from Graham Hill, but the Willment cars finished one-two on aggregate – what a start!

Quiz point: When did Jackie Stewart first lead a Formula One field to the chequered flag? Was part two his first F1 win?

1st	G Hill (JW)	Brabham BT11-BRM in 1h-22m-48.7s	92.20
2nd	P Hawkins (JW)	Brabham BT10-Ford t/c	53.0s
F lap	J Stewart (W)	Lotus 33-Climax in 1m-36.0s	95.44

Winners of the 18 F1 races of 1964 – quantity & quality of success

5 wins	J Clark (4A, B)	5 wins	Lotus-Climax (4A,B)
3 wins	J Surtees (2A, C)	4 wins	Brabham-Climax (4A); Ferrari (3A,C)
3 wins	G Hill (2A, D)	2 wins	BRM (2A); Brabham-BRM (C,D)
2 wins	J Brabham (2A) D Gurney (2A)	1 win	BRP-BRM (B)
1 win	L Bandini (A) I Ireland (B) J Siffert (C)		

1964 seasonal review

The early season pre-Championship races showed that the spoils were likely to be shared this year, and so it proved. Eight drivers scored wins, but yet again Jim Clark did all the winning for Lotus, though Peter Arundell had provided better support than anyone before until his awful accident in the Reims F2 race. His replacement, Mike Spence, wasn't bad either. Possibly the fastest trio (car and drivers) of all the Works teams was the Brabham team. But for their lack of finishes they could have beaten the lot. Their victory with pole and fastest lap at Silverstone's International Trophy in May must have surprised many, since they had not joined the 'monocoque club,' as had BRM, BRP and (semi) Ferrari. Even Brabham's customer cars did very well for Bob Anderson, and particularly Jo Siffert, daring to beat Clark in Sicily. BRM's monocoque P261 was a match for the Lotus 25 and 33. If the Clark genius factor is taken out of the Lotus/Clark equation, how quick was the Lotus really? Cooper was now clearly ceasing to be a serious threat, which was sad to see as it had been the game-changer only a few years before; even newcomer BRP had won something at the start of the year. The fact was that Brabham's engineering prowess had not been replaced.

1964 Championship review

What a great battle for the title this year was. The result went right to the end, and, like any good Grand Prix, saw someone fighting from well behind to challenge at the end. John Surtees' title was not a given at mid-season. If Ferrari had taken on the British earlier than Silverstone in May, then maybe Surtees' late challenge could have begun sooner. But were the best three drivers involved in that final shootout? This Championship campaign produced one of the worst bad luck stories in Championship history, even to this day. One man lost more points from the top two race positions than Champion John Surtees scored all year, and never, apparently, due to his fault! Dan Gurney was regarded by Jim Clark as his greatest adversary – the one he feared the most. We can now see why. He could have won the title before the final race if he'd had the same reliability as Graham Hill. Yet he wasn't even in the picture. In fact, he never led the title race or even challenged for the lead at any point in the year! It was poetic justice that he won the final race when the title contenders fell by the wayside. This level of cruel luck has, surely, to be remembered, and proves that in motor racing the result is so often not the full story. Every time Dan Gurney crossed the finish line he won. How much – if any – responsibility a driver has for each misfortune is impossible to say, and, therefore, it's unwise to speculate. Clark lost 38 points, Surtees himself 24, and Graham Hill 15. This simply shows that the potential of each of these four was very similar.

Dan Gurney's disaster year: Monaco GP – gearbox (when second); Dutch GP – broken steering wheel (when fourth); Belgian GP – no fuel at pits (when leading) but classified sixth; British GP – electrical wiring (when second); German GP – overheating (when second); Austrian GP – suspension (when leading); Italian – misfire (when second); American GP – low oil pressure (when second). Total loss = 50 points and no consistent failings!

Let not people conclude that John Surtees was a lucky Champion. He was the changing factor in Ferrari's Formula One fortunes, and drove for a team that, at that time, concentrated more on sports car racing than Formula One until Le Mans was out of the way – which was about the time that results started coming in. Yes Bandini's clumsy thumping of Graham Hill in Mexico was a help, as was Clark's oil loss. But it's the whole season that counts, and no-one was in any doubt that becoming Champion confirmed his known ability. Remember that it was he that was Colin Chapman's first choice as leader for Lotus in 1961, not Jim Clark.

VISIT VELOCE ON THE WEB – WWW.VELOCE.CO.UK
All current books • New book news • Special offers • Gift vouchers • Forum

231

Chapter 24

1965

Swansong with a surprising finale

This was the final year of this, originally unwanted, formula, which had proved that technology would always find a way around problems to move the sport forward – for that's what racing's all about. The previous year ended with Brabham, Ferrari, BRM, and Lotus in a tremendous battle. The first named winning the final race, while the others fought over which of their drivers would claim the Driver's World Championship. There was no reason to think the same might not continue in 1965. Horsepower was now around 215bhp, or 140bhp/litre, a figure never seen in unsupercharged engines burning pump fuel, except for multi-cylinder motorcycle racing, that is. In that discipline, Honda's 250cc four-cylinder engine was achieving no less than 200bhp/litre, and now Honda had entered Formula One with a 12-cylinder unit. No serious challenge to the Europeans had occurred in 1964, but for this year might Honda up the power stakes? If it did, and produced a good chassis, and with a top driver aboard, the established teams had better look out.

Coventry Climax, which had supported Formula One so reliably for years, announced in February of '65 that it would be withdrawing from racing at season's end, stating that a completely new design would be required for the incoming 3-litre formula, and this would be beyond its budget. 'Would 'blowing' the existing V8 be possible?' was a question asked by a few teams, but the lack of a suitable turbo at that time prevented that. People often forget that racing engines were a sideline to Coventry Climax's main business of mobile water pump units and forklift trucks. To ameliorate this bad news, a new flat-16 engine, which it had been working on during 1964, should be available to a few select clients to see off any challenge in 1965, so Coventry Climax expected to go out on a high note – which, of course, goes with high revs. A great final season was in prospect for this formula.

The constructors

Ferrari had finally finished on top of both Driver's and Constructor's Championships in 1964, so, naturally, continued with Champion John Surtees and Lorenzo Bandini.

BRM had lost Ginther to Honda, but found a very good replacement to accompany Graham Hill by signing the 'find of '64,' Jackie Stewart – BRM would not regret it.

Team Lotus continued with Mike Spence as support to the great Jim Clark. Peter Arundell was still recovering from serious injuries from his Reims smash. It was very much hoped he would be back before long.

Brabhams were, not surprisingly, the same as the year before. Reliability would surely improve and produce the results that Dan Gurney and 'The Boss' deserved.

Cooper had signed up the other 'find of '64,' Jochen Rindt, to join Bruce McLaren. Could they turn around Cooper's failing results – two lucky second places being its best Championship finishes the previous year.

Honda had now expanded its operation to a two-car team, and acquired Richie Ginther as team leader to Ronnie Bucknum. Honda was quoted as having 225bhp to power them – 150bhp/litre – and 93 per cent of the final 2.5-litre Championship winner in 1960. The V12 was placed, very unusually, across the chassis, and sloping forward, which suggests a rather wide car in this 'slim-car' era, but it wasn't any wider than Ferrari's flat-12.

BRP had ceased operations, never having acquired the status of other marques.

The independents

RRC Walker had Joakim Bonnier and Josef Siffert to drive the Climax-powered Brabham BT7 and BRM-powered BT11 respectively.

Reg Parnell Racing had Lotus 25-BRMs, to be driven by Richard Attwood, Innes Ireland and Mike Hailwood, but only entered all three at the British Grand Prix.

Scuderia Centro Sud continued with its ageing BRM 578s, using Masten Gregory and a variety of others.

The best privateer of the previous year, Bob Anderson, continued with his Brabham-Climax.

Formula Two had eaten into the Formula One diary a little more, but there were still 15 good F1 races, and the 'big guns' were still allowed to compete in 14 F2 races. All this was after a busy Tasman series of seven races, which filled the gap between the South African GP on New Year's Day and the start of the European F1 season in mid-March. This series was run to an engine limit of 2500cc, so the latest F1 technology was married to the extra power of the previous F1 which had expired in 1960. Lotus, BRM and Cooper Works teams took part, so it's easy to see that it was attractive to those F1 big guns – and, no doubt, paid well.

So, a mammoth season of 36 events was now available to those invited, of which just ten were F1 World Championship rounds. This shows how much of a Grand Prix driver's single-seater racing from this period has been missing from the records. This still, of course, doesn't cover the racing they did in other categories.

The Grand Prix driver's diary of single-seater racing for 1965

1st January	F1 – **South African Grand Prix** at East London (SA) – 207 miles
9th January	FT – New Zealand Grand Prix at Pukekohe (NZ) – 136.4 miles"
16th January	FT – Levin International (NZ) – 30.8 miles^"
23rd January	FT – Lady Wigram Trophy at Christchurch (NZ) – 127.5 miles^"
30th January	FT – Teretonga International at Invercargill (NZ) – 84 miles^"
14th February	FT – Sydney Grand Prix at Warwick Farm (Au) – 101.3 miles
21st February	FT – Sandown '100'at Sandown Park (Au) – 104.1 miles
1st March	FT – Australian Grand Prix at Longford (Au) – 117 miles
13th March	F1 – Race of Champions at Brands Hatch (GB) – 197.5 miles
20th March	F2 – BARC '200' at Silverstone (GB) – 125.9 miles
3rd April	F2 – Spring Trophy at Oulton Park (GB) – 107.1 miles*
4th April	F1 – Gran Premio di Siracusa (I) – 191.4 miles^

10th April	F2 – *Autocar* Trophy at Snetterton (GB) – 135.5 miles
19th April	F1 – *Sunday Mirror* Trophy at Goodwood (GB) – 100.8 miles
25th April	F2 – Grand Prix de Pau (UK) – 137.7 miles
25th April	F2 – Eifelrennen at S. Nurburgring (G) – 96.3 miles*^"
15th May	F1 – *Daily Express* International Trophy at Silverstone (GB) – 152.2 miles*
16th May	F2 – Gran Premio di Roma at Vallelunga (I) – 119.3 miles*^"
30th May	F1 – **Monaco Grand Prix** (M) – 195.4 miles*
7th June	F2 – London Trophy at Crystal Palace (GB) – 69.5 miles
13th June	F1 – **Grand Prix de Belgique** at Spa Francorchamps (B) – 280.4 miles
27th June	F1 – **Grand Prix de l'ACF** at Clermont Ferrand (F) – 200.4 miles
4th July	F2 – Grand Prix de Reims (F) – 190.9 miles
10th July	F1 – **British Grand Prix** at Silverstone (GB) – 234.2 miles
11th July	F2 – Grand Prix de Rouen (F) – 187.2 miles
18th July	F1 – **Grote Prijs van Nederland** at Zandvoort (N) – 208.4 miles"
1st August	F1 – **Grosser Preis von Deutschland** at Nurburgring (D) – 212.6 miles
8th August	F2 – Kanonloppet at Karlskoga (S) – 55.9 miles
8th August	F2 – Gran Premio di Pergusa (I) – 144.4 miles*^"
15th August	F1 – Gran Premio del Mediterraneo at Enna Pergusa (I) – 179.2 miles^
30th August	F2 – British Eagle Trophy at Brands Hatch (GB) – 49.4 miles
12th September	F1 – **Gran Premio d'Italia** at Monza (I) – 271.5 miles
18th September	F2 – International Gold Cup at Oulton Park (GB) – 107.1 miles
26th September	F2 – Grand Prix d'Albi (F) – 192 miles
3rd October	F1 – **United States Grand Prix** at Watkins Glen (US) – 253 miles
24th October	F1 – **Gran Premio de Mexico** at Mexico City (Mx) – 201.9 miles

36 events of total race mileage = 5506 miles – 5354 max (simultaneous events).

Events in bold are World Championship rounds – 66.7 per cent of F1 races run.

Formula Two and FT (Tasman Formula) dates are those which offered the prospect of a battle involving top Formula One drivers. Below shows how very busy they were.

Busy drivers
* Races in which Jim Clark did not compete – just six. But he was at Indianapolis in May.
^ Races in which Graham Hill did not compete – just eight.
" Races in which Jack Brabham did not compete – just eight.

Tasman Championship 1965

Two other World Champions were present this year, with 1963 Champion Jim Clark in a Works Lotus 32B (effectively a Formula Two car with twice the power), and 1961 Champion Phil Hill in a Cooper T70 that McLaren Racing ran last year. Hill's team leader, Bruce McLaren, had a Cooper T79 based on the previous season's T73 F1 car. Unfortunately, the Coopers were hampered by having to use 15-inch wheels for their Firestone tyres when the cars had been designed for 13 inch ones – it took a while to sort. Graham Hill was engaged again by the Australian team Scuderia Veloce in its Brabham BT11A. Jack Brabham only raced in the Australian rounds, but the Braham marque was well represented, fields being fairly evenly split between Brabham, Lotus and Cooper. So every World Champion from 1959 to 1963 took part this season. As per previous years, the Climax FPF engine was universal.

* New Zealand Grand Prix (Pukekohe)
12-lap heats + 50-lap final of 2.20 miles = 136.4 miles.
19 started – 14 finished.
Poles: Heat one – G Hill – 1m-25.0s (93.18mph). Heat two – J Clark – 1m-25.5s (92.63mph).
09-JAN: Graham Hill took one heat from Phil Hill, but Clark was much faster in winning his heat from Davison after McLaren had crashed out. Phil Hill gave up his car so the locals would see their hero. Clark led the final from McLaren who shunted the back of the Lotus when trying to pass putting Clark out. Hill now led, but McLaren was recovering and closing when his gearbox packed up on lap 14. From then Hill was untroubled and nearly lapped the rest, being the only international star left in the field. Hill's pole position lap suggested that Clark wasn't going to have things his own way.
1st G Hill (Brabham BT11A) in 1h-13m-43.4s = 89.52mph
2nd F Gardner (Brabham BT11A) @ 1m-23s
3rd J Palmer (Brabham BT7A) @ 1 lap
Fastest lap G Hill in 1m-26.3s = 91.77mph

* 6th Levin International
8-lap heat + 28-lap final of 1.1 miles = 39.6 miles.
15 started – 13 finished.
Front row: J Clark – 49.4s (80.16mph); G Hill (0.6s).
16-JAN: Graham Hill had gone to Australia after the NZ GP, so Jim Clark had an easier time. It was Clark, Phil Hill and McLaren on the front row for the final, and duly led in that order at first, but NZ resident Kerry Grant in a Brabham

took second place on lap two, with the Coopers handling badly on their 15 inch wheels. However, after ten laps Grant spoiled his glory with a spin onto the rough, dropping right back. Before long Gardner and Palmer had embarrassed the Cooper pilots further, leaving Hill and McLaren to settle for fourth and fifth. Clark, like Graham Hill at Pukekohe, won at ease. A battle between the world stars was needed.
1st J Clark (Lotus 32B) in 24m-05.9s = 76.69mph
2nd F Gardner (Brabham BT11A) @ 11.3s
3rd J Palmer (Brabham BT7A) @ 16.0s
Fastest lap J Clark in 49.9s = 79.36mph

* Lady Wigram Trophy (Christchurch)
11-lap heats + 44-lap final of 2.318 miles = 127.5 miles.
16 started – 10 finished.
Poles: Heat one – B McLaren – 1m-1m-29.4s (93.34mph).
Heat two – J Clark – 1m-26.0s (97.04mph).
23-JAN: McLaren and Clark won the preliminary heats, with McLaren the faster, but it was Clark all the way in the final without a serious challenge from McLaren. Phil Hill was slow away due to gearbox trouble, and took Grant for fifth place after 12 laps. That was as far as he got, retiring from that position on lap 25, having been unable to challenge Palmer and Gardner. Clark had falling oil pressure and was 'soft-pedalling' for the last few laps while passing the pits on full power to hide the fact.
1st J Clark (Lotus 32B) in 1h-04m-19.3s = 95.15mph
2nd B McLaren (Cooper T79) @10.2s
3rd J Palmer (Brabham BT7A) @ 38.7s
Fastest lap J Clark and B McLaren in 1m-25.9s = 97.15mph

* Teretonga International (Invercargill)
Six-lap heat + 50-lap final of 1.5 miles = 84.0 miles.
14 started – 11 finished.
Poles: Heat one: J Clark – 1m-01.2s (88.24mph). Heat two: B McLaren 1m-02.5s (86.40mph).
30-JAN: Lap times were way faster than the previous year, with Clark's pole having bettered the lap record by over four seconds! No doubt the new 'balloon' tyres used this year had a large part to play. He was over a second better than the Coopers, which were trying to sort out their tyre problem. Clark and McLaren again won the heats, but it was Clark on pole for the final; something of a repeat of Wigram. Hill had to pass Grant again, but this time for third place, and he kept going but his ill-handling car was lapped. Clark was troubled by overheating, but again brought the car home to win. Clark completed a hat-trick, which might not have been so easy had Graham Hill or Jack Brabham been present.
1st J Clark (Lotus 32B) in 52m-58.9s = 84.94mph
2nd B McLaren (Cooper T79) @13.5s
3rd P Hill (Cooper T70) @ 1 lap
Fastest lap J Clark in 1m-01.7s = 87.52mph

✴ Warwick Farm '100'

45 laps of 2.25 miles = 101.25 miles.
19 started – 12 finished.
Front row: F Matich – 1m-34.7s (85.53mph); G Hill (0.2s);
J Clark (0.2s)

14-FEB: Into Australia, and Jack Brabham and Graham Hill were there to stop Clark's monopoly. It was Aussie Frank Matich who led from pole, though. He was soon passed by Clark and Hill, and then Hill led as Clark lost third gear. Brabham passed Matich for third on lap nine, as Phil Hill retired with suspension bothers. Next lap and McLaren was out with engine trouble, never having been in the main chase. Clark led Hill, and Matich was catching Brabham as the latter's tyres were badly worn. Hill spun down to fifth place on the last lap, so Clark continued collecting the laurels despite the better competition in Australia. All records were shattered.

1st J Clark (Lotus 32B) in 1h-11m-06.8s = 85.42mph
2nd J Brabham (Brabham BT11A) @1m-01.3s
3rd F Matich (Brabham BT7) @1m-06.7s
Fastest lap J Clark in 1m-33.7s = 86.45mph

✴ Sandown '100' (Sandown Park)

54 laps of 1.928 miles = 104.12 miles.
14 started – 9 finished.
Front row: J Brabham – 1m-08.8s (100.88mph); J Clark;
F Matich.

21-FEB: Tragically, popular Aussie Lex Davison, one of the best resident drivers, was killed in practice. Brabham had new Firestones, and McLaren and Phil Hill's Coopers were now shod with 13 inch tyres from the same supplier, and were much happier. Matich led off the line again, but it was Clark ahead by the first corner. Soon all the overseas stars had passed Matich, led by Brabham who passed Clark on lap eight to lead the race. The two Hills, McLaren and Stillwell were battling, so World F1 Champions held the first four places – this was a true 'battle of the greats.' I bet reigning Champion John Surtees would have liked to have been involved. The two leaders swapped places twice, while Bib Stillwell got himself into fourth, then third when Graham Hill retired. Sadly, Stillwell's great drive was spoiled by a bad misfire. So Jim Clark's 'reign' came to an end, and, again, records were broken.

1st J Brabham (Brabham BT11) in 1h-02m-57.7s = 99.22mph
2nd J Clark (Lotus 32B) @ 4.6s
3rd P Hill (Cooper T70) @ 1 lap
Fastest lap J Brabham in 1m-08.6s = 101.18mph

✴ Australian Grand Prix (Longford, Tasmania)

26 laps of 4.5 miles = 117.0 miles.
18 started – 11 finished.
Front row: B McLaren – 2m-18.5s (116.97mph); J Brabham;
G Hill.

01-MAR: Low profile tyres and short-stroke engines made the Coopers come good, and McLaren's pole time was five seconds better that the previous year's. It was McLaren, Brabham, G Hill, Clark, Matich, Stillwell and P Hill at first. Local driver Rocky Tresise, trying to pass in midfield, crashed, went through a fence and was killed – another tragedy on this fast and unforgiving public road circuit. Phil Hill took Matich and Stillwell, closing on Clark. He and Clark swapped places often, as and when Clark's misfire intervened. Matich suffered collapsed suspension at half distance, and was lucky to stop without damage. Brabham had contact with a backmarker and pitted for a check, dropping to fifth. Soon he was carving his way back, and he and Phil Hill scrapped strongly, gaining and swapping second and third places to the detriment of Graham Hill. This was Phil Hill's best performance in this class of company since his Championship win in 1961, beating Graham by 3.0 seconds. Just over eight seconds covered the five world class performers at the finish, with Clark fifth. Not that many World Championship races have bettered this.

1st B McLaren (Cooper T79) in 1h-01m-10.9s = 114.74mph
2nd J Brabham (Brabham BT11) @ 3.3s
3rd P Hill (Cooper T70) @ 4.9s
Fastest lap J Brabham in 2m-18.0s = 117.39mph

Clark had taken New Zealand, while Jack Brabham's win and two seconds made him the top scorer in Australia. If Brabham had gone to New Zealand, the fight for the Championship would have been tremendous in these 'faster-than-F1' cars. Same goes if the Cooper duo had not had tyre issues at the start of the campaign. Maybe next year.

Tasman Champion:
1st Jim Clark (Lotus 32A) – 35
2nd Bruce McLaren (Cooper T79) – 24
3rd Jack Brabham (Brabham BT11) – 21

✴✴✴ (WC1) XI South African Grand Prix (East London)

85 laps of 2.436 miles = 207.1 miles.
31 entries – 20 started – 11 finished.
Front row: J Clark – 1m-27.2s (100.57mph); J Surtees 0.9s;
J Brabham 1.1s.

01-JAN: The race was put back a week thus making it the start of the '65 campaign. Clark and Spence (from the second row) took off as if tied together, followed by Brabham and McLaren, while Gurney's 1964 bad luck continued with electrical trouble. Surtees and Hill soon passed McLaren, and Surtees took Brabham a lap later. Spence spun at half distance at Beacon Bend, which had caught him out in practice, just keeping his second place.

Brabham had a flat battery, so Surtees and Hill chased Spence, to be rewarded when Spence spun again at Beacon Bend, dropping to fourth but clear of McLaren and Jackie Stewart. Stewart was having a great Championship debut, gaining a point. Clark was shown the flag at lap 84, but, being unsure, stopped at his pit a lap later to check, then continued to the line for a second chequered flag. He had time in hand.

1st	J Clark (W)	Lotus 33-Climax in 2h-06m-46.0s	98.00
2nd	J Surtees (W)	Ferrari 158	29.0s
3rd	G Hill (W)	BRM P261	31.8s
F lap	J Clark	Lotus 33-Climax in 1m-27.6s	100.11r

✳✳✳ 1st 'Race of Champions' (Brands Hatch)
2 x 40 laps of 2.46 miles = 196.8 miles.
25 entries – 20 started – 10 finished.
Front row: J Clark – 1m-34.9s (93.32mph); G Hill 0.7s; M Spence 1.2s.

13-MAR: A new event on the calendar, and very early in the year, yet every team arrived; Ferrari sending one car. The lap record was demolished in practice by over three seconds. Clark won the first half from Gurney, who had been on fifth grid row, by 21 seconds. Would he stroke it to an easy win in the second half? Never – he was a racer – so a great battle ensued in which Clark was pressured by Gurney into going off at Bottom Bend, hitting the bank hard and lucky to escape injury– a very rare event. Two laps later Gurney's engine failed, having got the better of Clark again. Brabham led but retired, gifting part two and overall win to Mike Spence. Surtees' Ferrari and Hill's BRM retired in part two. Seventh and fourth places gave Stewart second overall – strange races these two-part affairs sometimes. However, it's better than a points system I think.

1st	M Spence (W)	Lotus 33-Climax in 2h-11m-42.0s	89.64
2nd	J Stewart (W)	BRM P261	59.6s
3rd	J Bonnier (RW)	Brabham BT7-Climax	1 lap
F lap	J Clark	Lotus 33-Climax in 1m-35.4s	92.83r

✳ XIV Gran Premio di Siracusa
191.4m – 56 laps of 3.418 miles = 191.4 miles.
16 entries – 15 started – 5 finished.
Front row: J Clark – 1m-46.5s (115.52mph); J Surtees 0.3s; J Bonnier 0.5s.

04-APR: Having missed Brands Hatch, the 12-cylinder Ferrari was here for Bandini. This was expected to be a Ferrari/Lotus event, as no other Works teams entered. Instead, Jo 'Seppi' Siffert in Rob Walker's Brabham-BRM was the hero here. He and Surtees ganged up and left Clark at the start. 'Seppi' had twice retaken the lead from Surtees when, on lap 45, over-revving with a missed gear change blew his engine and he retired, to huge cheers. Clark had remained close to the lead battle and was beginning to look a threat, when Surtees unluckily lost his new lead just a lap later due to misfiring on two cylinders. He lost 42 seconds in the last ten laps, but still Bandini's 12-cylinder Ferrari couldn't challenge, despite having got the better of Spence earlier.

The result doesn't indicate the fierceness of the competition that took place. It only takes two but three's even better.

1st	J Clark (W)	Lotus 33-Climax in 1h-43m-47.0s	110.64
2nd	J Surtees (W)	Ferrari 158	42.1s
3rd	L Bandini (W)	Ferrari 1512	56.3s
F lap	J Clark	Lotus 33-Climax in 1m-46.0s	116.07r

✳✳✳ *Sunday Mirror* Trophy (Goodwood)
42 laps of 2.4 miles = 100.8 miles.
19 entries – 18 started – 12 finished.
Front row: J Stewart – 1m-19.8s (108.27mph); G Hill 0.8s; J Clark 0.8s.

19-APR: Only Ferrari absented, so Stewart's pole by 0.8 seconds was amazing, as was Bob Anderson beating the Works Brabhams to fifth on the grid. Spence non-started due to fuel injection trouble, while Clark took the lead from Graham Hill on lap six and pulled away. Hill's engine was off-song, and Gurney and Stewart went by. Luck fell Hill's way when both retired on lap 38. Brabham had been on 'wet' tyres on a dry track. Anderson arrived too fast at the chicane, diverted through the weaker part, stopped to remove wood from his suspension, and continued. The same befell Rindt later, but wood wasn't involved as he used 'Anderson's hole.' Both were disqualified. Siffert was catching his teammate Bonnier, but a wheel touched the right-hand entry wall to the chicane and he smacked the facing wall head-on, bending his car double (fortunately, without serious injury). One braking problem might have been due to the wind blowing towards the chicane. I was spectating at that point, and well remember the chicane wall being blown a few yards down the track earlier in the day during a hailstorm.

1st	J Clark (W)	Lotus 33-Climax in 57m-33.8s	105.07
2nd	G Hill (W)	BRM P261	24.2s
3rd	J Brabham (W)	Brabham BT11-Climax	50.8s
F lap	J Clark/J Stewart	Lotus/BRM in 1m-20.4s	107.46r

But for his Brands mishap, with a win seemingly 'in the bag', Clark would have won four-out-of-four, even before the Championship had really got under way. A repeat of 1963 was looking very possible already.

✳✳✳ XVII *Daily Express* International Trophy (Silverstone)

152.2m – 52 laps of 2.927 miles = 152.2 miles.
22 entries – 21 started – 13 finished.
Front row: G Hill – 1m-31.4s (115.28mph); J Stewart 0.2s; J Surtees 0.7s; L Bandini 0.9s.

15-MAY: All the Works teams here in full, but Clark and Gurney were at Indianapolis, so they were replaced by Rodriguez and Hulme. Graham Hill's pole time smashed the previous year's lap record by over two seconds. Hill led Surtees and Brabham, the latter then passing both by lap eight. Surtees had led off the line, but was fourth behind Stewart by lap five. Lap 16 saw Hill retire with engine trouble, so Brabham looked secure. Surtees took second from Stewart on lap 21, losing it as they closed on Brabham on lap 35. Lap 39 and Brabham was out, and Stewart held on for his maiden F1 win. His career was rising steadily but he had yet to beat his team leader.

1st	J Stewart (W)	BRM P261 in 1h-21m-47.0s	111.66
2nd	J Surtees (W)	Ferrari158	3.0s
3rd	M Spence (W)	Lotus 33-Climax	56.4s
F lap	J Surtees	Ferrari158 in 1m-33.0s	113.30r

✳✳✳ (WC2) XXIII Grand Prix de Monaco (Monte Carlo)

100 laps of a 1.954-mile circuit = 195.4 miles.
17 entries – 16 qualified – 9 finished.
Front row: G Hill – 1m-32.5s (76.06mph); J Brabham 0.3s.
Row two: J Stewart 0.4s; L Bandini 0.5s.

30-MAY: Clark and Gurney were still at Indianapolis, so Lotus engaged Pedro Rodriguez as substitute, but the organisers wouldn't guarantee him a start, as this depended on 1964's results. Lotus withdrew in disgust, which didn't do Spence any favours. Denny Hulme replaced Gurney, and qualified eighth. Rindt was the only non-qualifier, yet was two seconds faster than Ginther's Honda which was guaranteed a start and then failed on the line! Hill had

smashed Clark's pole time of the year before, so speed would not be missing. He led for 24 laps, before taking the escape road at the chicane, when inadvertently baulked by Anderson, slowing with driveshaft failure. A magnificent drive back ensued to recover the lead 40 laps later – and this was at impossible-to-pass Monaco! Stewart, Bandini and Brabham had all led meanwhile. Surtees lost second – out of fuel – but was classified fourth. Paul Hawkins dived into the sea, as Ascari had in 1955, and also without injury. It's difficult to see that Clark would have spoiled Hill's Monaco hat-trick – he was absolutely at home here – his fastest lap well beating his pole time and reducing the record by over two seconds!

1st	G Hill (W)	BRM P261 in 2h-37m-39.6s	74.37
2nd	L Bandini (W)	Ferrari 1512	1m-04s
3rd	J Stewart (W)	BRM P261	1m-42s
F lap	G Hill (W)	BRM P261 in 1m-31.7s	76.72r

Championship positions:
G Hill 13; J Clark and J Surtees 9.

✳✳✳ (WC3) XXV Grand Prix de Belgique (Spa)

32 laps of a 8.761-mile circuit = 280.4 miles.
22 entries – 20 started – 13 finished.
Front row: G Hill – 3m-45.4s (139.93mph); J Clark 2.1s; J Stewart 3.4s.

13-JUN: Graham Hill improved on the previous year's lap record by almost four seconds: a lap at almost 140mph with just 1500cc and a hairpin bend! However, on race day it rained and rained. This was Jim Clark territory now, and he made use of it. Hill led through Eau Rouge, but Clark passed and drew away, leading by three seconds after a lap. Hill's car was handling badly in the wet, and Stewart passed him on lap three, Hill dropping to fifth behind Brabham at the end. Clark led by 45 seconds at half distance, but lost much of that due to clutch trouble with a few laps left. It cleared, and he regained time lost. Stewart's debut was very impressive, though. Ginther's new Honda was now looking sorted, and was fourth on the grid and finished sixth – a first point for Honda.

1st	J Clark (W)	Lotus 33-Climax in 2h-23m-34.8s	117.16
2nd	J Stewart (W)	BRM P261	44.8s
3rd	B McLaren (W)	Cooper T77-Climax	1 lap
F lap	J Clark (W)	Lotus 33-Climax in 4m-12.9s	124.72

Championship positions:
J Clark 18; G Hill 15; J Stewart 11.

With four wins in four years here, it's obvious that Spa was Clark's territory, though he hated it. Monaco was Hill's domain, having very nearly achieved the same in the Principality. No superfast tracks, like Spa, Reims and Monza exist now. A Spa type circuit would produce lap speeds of 180+mph, with maximum speeds of 240mph, and would be great to see but difficult to accommodate safely ... for drivers and spectators.

✱✱✱ (WC4) LI Grand Prix de l'ACF (Clermont-Ferrand)

40 laps of 5.005 mile circuit = 200.2 miles
25 entries – 17 started – 9 finished.
Front row: J Clark – 3m-18.3s (90.87mph); J Stewart 0.5s; L Bandini 0.8s.

27-JUN: The first visit of F1 to this mini-Nürburgring proved to be another Clark benefit, setting pole with an old car after a blow-up of his new 32-valve motor. Brabham gave Hulme his car due to his prior knowledge of the circuit. Hill hurt his neck after a spin caused him to hit a rock face. Clark led off from Bandini, who held up Stewart, Gurney and Surtees. Stewart was second on lap two, and pursued Clark vainly. Gurney and Surtees passed Bandini but plug trouble dropped Gurney way back, and Surtees pitted to remove a loose rectifier. Hulme used his knowledge to good effect with fourth place after a poor start from 14th on lap one. Bandini lost a wheel after striking a bank, so Hill and Siffert completed the point scorers. A great circuit but a dull race.

1st	J Clark (W)	Lotus 25-Climax in 2h13m-38.4s	89.22
2nd	J Stewart (W)	BRM P261	26.3s
3rd	J Surtees (W)	Ferrari 158	2m-33s
F lap	J Brabham (W)	Brabham BT7-Climax in 3m-18.9s	90.59

Championship positions:
J Clark 27; G Hill and J Stewart 17.

✱✱✱ (WC5) XX British Grand Prix (Silverstone)

80 laps of 2.927 miles = 234.2 miles.
25 entries – 21 starters – 12 finished.
Front row: J Clark – 1m-30.8s (116.05mph); G Hill 0.2s; R Ginther 0.5s; J Stewart 0.5s.

10-JUL: Only one Honda was entered, and it was on the front row between the BRMs. With Ginther aboard it led for half a lap, but was soon second, then was swallowed up by Hill and Surtees after lap two. Ten laps later it lost power

and dropped out, but it had shown its hand. Stewart was now fourth, with Spence in hot pursuit, passing after a few laps and then catching and scrapping furiously with Surtees who had 12-cylinder power at last. Clark had done his usual disappearing trick once the Honda was disposed of. The Brabhams weren't in it; Gurney's engine had failed after the warm-up lap. Brabham gave him his car on the grid, but he was 14th from second grid row while getting used to a different set up – making sixth at the end, a lap down. Clark's 20-second lead was threatened by misfire and oil loss, and it looked like May '62 all over again, but this time he held on by coasting around the corners! Clark had missed Monaco, but had won every Championship race he had started, and four British Grands Prix in a row.

1st	J Clark (W)	Lotus 33-Climax in 2h-05m-25.4s	112.02
2nd	G Hill (W)	BRM P261	3.2s
3rd	J Surtees (W)	Ferrari 1512	27.6s
F lap	G Hill (W)	BRM P261 in 1m-32.2s	114.29r

Championship positions: J Clark 36; G Hill 23; J Stewart 19.

✱✱✱ (WC6) XIV Grote Prijs van Nederland (Zandvoort)

80 laps of a 2.605-mile circuit = 208.4 miles.
19 invited – 17 started – 13 finished.
Front row: G Hill – 1m-30.7s (103.51mph); J Clark 0.3s; R Ginther 0.3s.

18-JUL: Two from each marque, plus the Walker, Willment and Parnell teams, was the limit for the Dutch this year. But Honda entered only one, so Bob Anderson was let in. A repeat of the previous week occurred when Ginther's Honda was on the front row and led away, but this time it took two laps for the rest to get to grips with it. By lap six it was Clark, Hill, Gurney, Ginther, Stewart and Spence. Gurney took second from Hill, but soon both lost out to a determined Stewart. Ginther was passed by Hulme and Surtees, but retook sixth on lap 52, and that was it to the end. Stewart was again the strongest challenger to Clark, his fourth podium in six Grands Prix. The Honda had again shown speed, but not the ability to retain it during a race.

1st	J Clark (W)	Lotus 33-Climax in 2h-03m-59.1s	100.87
2nd	J Stewart (W)	BRM P261	8.0s
3rd	D Gurney (W)	Brabham BT11-Climax	13.0s
F lap	J Clark (W)	Lotus 33-Climax in 1m-30.6s	103.53r

Championship positions:
J Clark 45; G Hill 26; J Stewart 25.

✳✳✳ (WC7) XXVII Grosse Preis von Deutschland (N Nürburgring)

15 laps of 14.173 miles = 212.5 miles.
24 entries – 19 started – 8 finished.

Front row: J Clark – 8m-22.7s (101.50mph); J Stewart 3.4s; G Hill 4.1s; J Surtees 5.1s.

01-AUG: No less than a quarter of a minute was taken from the track records this year as the little cars got faster and faster. Clark was well on top in practice, and Hill was beaten by his young teammate. Honda, however, decided to skip this race to prepare for the power circuit of Monza. Clark's supremacy translated to the race and he won without serious challenge, though Hill tried his best all the way. Stewart put a wheel in the grass when third on lap two, hit something and retired. Apart from that it was Clark, Hill and Gurney all the way. Surtees had gearbox trouble from his front row start, while teammate Bandini was fifth but dropped to 12th after a spin due to contact with Rindt. Surtees recovered to sixth behind Rindt and Brabham thanks to retirements. So Clark had now finally conquered the Nürburgring in F1. Of the seven rounds run, he had missed one while at Indianapolis and won the other six. This exactly matched Alberto Ascari's 1952 campaign. The title was Clark's with a maximum score.

1st	J Clark (W)	Lotus 33-Climax in 2h-07m-52.4s	99.76
2nd	G Hill (W)	BRM P261	15.9s
3rd	D Gurney (W)	Brabham BT11-Climax	21.4s
F lap	J Clark (W)	Lotus 33-Climax in 8m-24.1s	101.22r

Championship positions:
J Clark (WC) 54; G Hill 30; J Stewart 25.

✳ GP del Mediterraneo (Enna-Pergusa)

60 laps of 2.982 miles = 178.9 miles.
19 entries – 15 started – 6 finished.

Front row: J Clark – 1m-15.8s (141.09mph); M Spence 0.4s; J Siffert 0.7s.

15-AUG: A similar entry quality to the previous year, with Lotus and Brabham being the only Works teams, plus all the best non-Works teams. A chaotic start as the starter dropped the flag while the cars rolled up from the dummy grid. How on earth was such a crucial role handed to an incompetent! Perhaps a local dignitary ... Clark was in neutral, rushed and found third, and was swamped, so teammate Spence led with Siffert heading the chasing pack of Hulme, Gardner, Ireland and Bonnier. Siffert took Spence and they pulled away by eight

seconds, while Clark managed to join them on lap 26. Spence, hit in the face by stones, somersaulted into the lakeside, landing upside down but, amazingly, without serious injury. Siffert then fended off Clark just as he had the year before.

1st	J Siffert (RW)	Brabham BT11-BRM in 1h-17m-05.2s	139.00
2nd	J Clark (W)	Lotus 25-Climax	0.3s
3rd	F Gardner (JW)	Brabham BT11-BRM	1 lap
F lap	J Clark	Lotus 25-Climax in 1m-15.8s	141.09

✳✳✳ (WC8) XXXVI Gran Premio d'Italia (Monza-road)

78 laps of a 3.573-mile circuit = 278.7 miles.
26 entries – 23 started – 9 finished.

Front row: J Clark – 1m-35.9s (134.12mph); J Surtees 0.2s; J Stewart 0.7s.

12-SEP: Surtees had clutch slip at the start and was 13th on lap one, but then it gripped solid and, despite changing gear without it, he came through to join the lead scrap involving Clark, Stewart and Hill, with Gurney, Siffert and Spence in close attendance. This being Monza the first four shared the lead – slipstreaming and leapfrogging each other, and drawing away from the others. Surtees' clutch failed on lap 34 when in fifth place, as Gurney joined the back of the lead group, getting third ahead of Clark briefly. Fuel pump trouble stopped Clark on lap 63, and the BRMs drew away from Gurney to fight it out alone. Entering the very final bend – the famous Parabolica – Graham Hill surprisingly left sufficient room for Stewart to dive past on the inside, to achieve his maiden World Championship victory in his first Formula One season. He now challenged Hill's second spot again.

1st	J Stewart (W)	BRM P261 in 2h-04m-52.8s	130.46
2nd	G Hill (W)	BRM P261	3.3s
3rd	D Gurney (W)	Brabham BT11-Climax	16.5s
F lap	J Clark (W)	Lotus 33-Climax in 1m-36.4s	133.43r

Championship positions:
J Clark (WC) 54; G Hill 34; J Stewart 33.

✳✳✳ (WC9) 8th United States Grand Prix (Watkins Glen)

110 laps of 2.30 miles = 253 miles.
19 entries – 18 started – 13 finished.

Front row: G Hill – 1m-11.25s (116.21mph): J Clark 0.10s.
Row two: R Ginther 0.15s; M Spence 0.25s.

03-OCT: Ferrari engaged Pedro Rodriguez to stand in for a seriously injured John Surtees who had crashed badly in his Lola T70 at Toronto. Hill took his fourth pole of the year – the only person to beat Clark to pole all year. The leaping, lavender suited Tex Hopkins dropped the flag, and Hill beat Clark at the first corner but Clark led laps two, three and four. Then it was Hill all the way, Clark's engine failing on lap 11. Stewart was third for three laps, but pitted with a broken throttle cable. He had bent a wishbone when Ginther forced him onto the grass. Rain fell as Gurney and Brabham made their way to second and third places by lap 16 ahead of Bandini. The track dried fairly soon, and the podium places were settled. Rindt got ahead of Bandini for a few laps and, near the end, lost his fifth place to Rodriguez's Ferrari 1512. Ginther's third grid slot wasn't rewarded due to excursions.

1st	G Hill (W)	BRM P261 in 2h-20m-36.1s	107.98
2nd	D Gurney (W)	Brabham BT11-Climax	12.5s
3rd	J Brabham (W)	Brabham BT11-Climax	57.5s
F lap	G Hill (W)	BRM P261 in 1m-11.90s	115.16r

Championship positions:
J Clark (WC) 54; G Hill 40; J Stewart 33.

✳✳✳ (WC10) IV Gran Premio de Mexico (Mexico City)

65 laps of 3.107 miles = 201.9 miles.
24 entries – 19 started – 13 finished.
Front row: J Clark – 1m-56.17s (96.28mph); D Gurney 0.07s.
Row two: R Ginther 0.32s; J Brabham 0.61s.

24-OCT: At this high altitude track – 7000ft – Honda had retained more of its power than others, and this showed from the start as Ginther 'did a Clark' and pulled well away. Clark's engine was losing power, and he stopped on lap eight. Stewart lost second to Spence on lap three, and Hill and Gurney passed five laps later. Stewart retired on lap 35. Gurney took third from Hill, closed on Spence, and, after scrapping for a few laps, drew away securely in second place. He then began to challenge the 'threat from the East,' but was held off as Ginther achieved his, Honda's, and Japan's first Formula One World Championship Grand Prix victory.

1st	R Ginther (W)	Honda RA272 in 2h-08m-32.10s	94.28
2nd	D Gurney (W)	Brabham BT11-Climax	2.89s
3rd	M Spence (W)	Lotus 33-Climax	1m-00s
F lap	D Gurney (W)	Brabham BT11-Climax in 1m-55.84s	96.55r

Championship positions:
J Clark (WC) 54; G Hill 40; J Stewart 33.

Winners of the 15 F1 races of 1965 – quantity and quality of success

8 wins	J Clark (7A, C)	9 wins	Lotus-Climax (8A, C)
2 wins	G Hill (2A) J Stewart (2A)	4 wins	BRM (4A)
1 win	R Ginther (A) M Spence (A) J Siffert (C)	1 win	Honda (A); Brabham-BRM (C)

1965 seasonal review

Now the World Championship rounds were truly, and rightly, dominating the Formula One scene, but a pre-Championship season was still very vibrant, with the 'Race of Champions' at Brands Hatch having replaced Aintree's role after it had closed for car racing the year before. Personally, I hate pompous race titles (it wasn't reserved for Champions), but it wasn't that far out, actually, as the cream had entered. Jackie Stewart's heady climb can be seen with a second at Brands Hatch, pole position and lap record at Goodwood, and then a maiden F1 victory at Silverstone. The best 'extra' F1 races were all in Britain, where all but Ferrari were based.

Sadly, the Climax F16 engine didn't deliver its theoretical promise, possibly because its design was compromised to enable it to be fitted into the existing chassis of its clients with minimal alteration – the monocoque of the Lotus 33 being a particular difficulty. Nevertheless, the updated V8 was sufficient to power Jim Clark to domination again.

1965 Championship review

This year is easy to sum up as Jim Clark won the first six races he entered, missing the second round at Monaco whilst at Indianapolis. This exactly matches Alberto Ascari's season in 1952, and a score of six wins from six starts to begin a season is a record still standing. Ascari, however, didn't win at Indy as Clark did. If Indy had still had the complimentary status of a World Championship round, as in the 1950s, then Clark could have been said to have won his first seven rounds. Strangely, though, Clark, having won the title, then failed to finish in any of the three remaining Grands Prix, and in none of them did he dominate as before. Still, only the best six scores counted, so he had a maximum score anyway. Clark's winnings for Indianapolis were seventy times what the winnings for the Monaco GP were, so no wonder they went there. It should be recalled how close Jim Clark had come to winning the Championship four times in a row, having lost a Championship winning race lead in the final event in 1962 and 1964. Once again, despite the Clark/Lotus domination, if the Constructors' title had run to the modern format of counting all finishes, then BRM, not Lotus, would have been crowned, with 73 points to Lotus' 64 – just as 1963. I sincerely suggest that the Lotus won because Jim Clark was in it, and that maybe the BRM was the better car actually – and a true thoroughbred, not a hybrid chassis-engine combination.

The season, and the 1.5-litre Formula One era, ended on an intriguing historical note, when Richie Ginther drove to a first victory for Honda and himself. Another year of this formula and maybe a Honda era would have emerged. This car was an entire Honda design, and is the only ever victory for a transverse engine – and a V12 at that! This was even more amazing in an era of super-slim cars, but it was the most powerful. The car had made little impact on the score sheets prior to Mexico, but had been on pole position for the British Grand Prix. The fact was that Honda came good too late, and the new Formula One would not be a tiny-cylinder affair. Given one more year of this formula, would Honda have beaten a developed Climax F16? We'll never know.

The best team of the 1.5-litre era (modern reckoning)

The Clark-Lotus duo was undeniably the greatest of the last five years, but as for best team? The chart below has been created by applying modern scoring to the Constructor's World Championship, and an interesting picture has emerged. From each Works team the best two scores count, as today's teams score both cars.

* Stirling Moss drove for Rob Walker not Team Lotus.

And the winner is ... (drum roll) ... BRM

Question: If Jim Clark didn't have the best car after all, how did he win so often? Answer ... Genius.

Or does this prove that Chapman deliberately produced only one good car – for Jim Clark?

Either way, since a team consists of two cars, the winner of 'Best Team' remains unaltered.

	1st	2nd	3rd	4th	5th
1961	Ferrari 71	Porsche 24	**Lotus** 23*	Cooper 13	**BRM** 7
1962	**BRM** 62	**Lotus** 43	Cooper 40	Ferrari 30	Lola 19
1963	**Lotus** 74	**BRM** 63	Brabham 33	Ferrari 27	Cooper 26
1964	**BRM** 64	Ferrari 63	**Lotus** 49	Brabham 30	Cooper 14
1965	**BRM** 81	**Lotus** 64	Brabham 34	Ferrari 32	Cooper 14

VISIT VELOCE ON THE WEB – WWW.VELOCE.CO.UK
All current books • New book news • Special offers • Gift vouchers • Forum

241

Chapter 25

1966

A new era dawns with the 'Return of Power'

The F1 of 1961-65 may have lacked raw power, but it produced sophisticated machinery which created a thrilling sound; the high speed engines now approaching 150bhp/litre. Now came the formula hoped for back in 1958, and which the failed Intercontinental Formula of 1961 ran to. Sadly, Coventry Climax had stopped new F1 engine design but, like BRM, modified the V8 to two litres as an interim engine solely for Lotus, leaving Climax's other customers to source their own, a very unsettling situation. A few teams had enquired whether the existing V8 could be 'blown,' but lack of a suitable turbocharger put paid to that, so that idea disappeared for 11 years. Two new marques entered the scene: Eagle – the marque name for Anglo-American-Racing, run by Dan Gurney; and Bruce McLaren had now added Formula One to his sports-racing construction activities. Honda had ended 1965 on a high, but disappeared until Monza in September.

The World Championship was reduced to nine rounds, fewer than 1958, while the extra races were also reduced to five as Formula Two could produce decent fields and was cheaper to run. The extra events were needed particularly to develop the many new designs in preparation for the Championship. Unfortunately, the spring season lost Goodwood to F1, which banned the supposedly 'too fast' cars, and changed to F2 – sadly closing in July – but only for 32 years. Team un-readiness reduced the number and quality of entries, with only Silverstone able to attract a field of real depth. Of course, this race had a long history – stronger than some of the Championship Grands Prix.

The constructors

BRM retained Graham Hill and Jackie Stewart, and produced an amazing H-16 engine consisting of two 1.5-litre flat-8 engines based on the V8, one above the other, and with geared crankshafts. Would it have twice the power – 440bhp – of the previous year's engine, to offset the extra weight? It supplied one to Lotus. BRM also enlarged the previous year's V8 unit to two litres, and had just 270bhp but a known package. Time would tell which was most effective.

Lotus was able to supply Jim Clark and a recovered Peter Arundell with a choice of 2.0 V8 Climax-engined Type 33, or BRM H-16-powered Type 43. Each was a different marque in the Constructor's Championship.

Ferrari had no engine problem thanks to its racing sports prototypes, so John Surtees and Lorenzo Bandini should be at an advantage with, it was assumed, about 360bhp.

Brabham had commissioned an engine from the Australian firm of Repco, based on an aluminium Oldsmobile block he had sourced. It was a single-cam two-valve unit with about 290bhp: not a lot, but light, uncomplicated, and with plenty of torque. 'The Boss' and Denny Hulme felt reasonably well positioned. A 2.5-litre unit would be available for the Tasman Series before the F1 season began.

Cooper, now owned by Maserati's British importer and run by Roy Salvadori, used an enlarged version of the V12 from the 250F car of 1957. This was reckoned to have over 330bhp. It retained Jochen Rindt, and Richie Ginther joined, until needed by Honda. John Surtees also joined Cooper after leaving Ferrari.

McLaren Racing joined the constructors, and had a V8 Ford engine based on one used at Indianapolis, but reduced to three litres, and also tried a Serenissima V8 sports car engine – unknown quantities, but at least Bruce McLaren and Chris Amon were up and running.

The Eagle for Dan Gurney was powered by the old Coventry Climax FPF four-cylinder unit stretched to its limit of 2.7 litres, with just 255bhp but good torque. He had commissioned the V12 Gurney-Weslake engine made in Harry Weslake's premises at beautiful Rye in East Sussex, England and available mid-year.

Honda didn't appear until Monza, when it produced its V12 car, not transverse this time, for Richie Ginther and later Ronnie Bucknum. They were expected to be serious contenders before long.

The independents

RRC Walker Racing was supplied with a Cooper-Maserati for Jo Siffert, as were privateers Joakim Bonnier and Guy Ligier. The former being Dutch GP winner in 1959.

Reg Parnell Racing used Lotuses powered by V8 BRM or four-cylinder Climax engines, and a BRM P261 was used by Mike Spence and a second driver. Top privateer Bob Anderson had a 2.7-litre Climax FPF in his Brabham, and monopolised the underdog support. So, after some worry, a good turnout was pretty well assured.

The total single-seater events available to a top-flight F1 driver had now risen to 36 with F2 and Tasman Series activity. But only 25 per cent of them were World Championship rounds. This ignores Indianapolis oval racing which Clark, Hill and Stewart also did to great effect. Just six weeks elapsed between the seasons.

The Grand Prix driver's diary of single-seater racing for 1966

4th Dec '65	F1 – Rand Grand Prix at Kyalami (SA) – 127.2 miles
1st January	F1 – South African Grand Prix at East London (SA) – 146.2 miles
8th January	Tas – New Zealand Grand Prix at Pukekohe (NZ) – 88 miles
15th January	Tas – Gold Leaf Trophy at Levin (NZ) – 30.8 miles
22nd January	Tas – Lady Wigram Trophy at Christchurch (NZ) – 127.5 miles
29th January	Tas – Teretonga International at Invercargill (NZ) – 69 miles
13th February	Tas – Sydney Grand Prix at Warwick Farm (Au) – 101.3 miles
20th February	Tas – Australian Grand Prix at Lakeside (Au) – 99 miles
27st February	Tas – Exide International Cup at Sandown Park (Au) – 100.3 miles
7th March	Tas – South Pacific Trophy at Longford (Au) – 117 miles
2nd April	F2 – BARC '200' at Oulton Park (UK) – 107.1 miles
11th April	F2 – *Sunday Mirror* Trophy at Goodwood (UK) – 100.8 miles

17th April	F2 – Grand Prix de Pau (F) – 137.7 miles
24th April	F2 – Gran Premio de Barcelona at Montjuic (E) – 141.3 miles
1st May	F1 – Gran Premio di Siracusa (I) – 191.4 miles
8th May	F2 – Grote Prijs van Limborg at Zolder (B) – 125.3 miles
14th May	F1 – International Trophy at Silverstone (UK) – 152.2 miles
22nd May	F1 – **Monaco Grand Prix** (M) – 195.4 miles
30th May	F2 – London Trophy at Crystal Palace (UK) – 83.4 miles
12th June	F1 – **Grand Prix de Belgique** at Spa Francorchamps (B) – 245.3 miles
2nd July	F2 – Grand Prix de Reims (F) – 190.9 miles
3rd July	F1 – **Grand Prix de l'ACF** at Reims (F) – 247.6 miles
10th July	F2 – Grand Prix de Rouen (F) – 187.2 miles
16th July	F1 – **British Grand Prix** at Brands Hatch (UK) – 197.5 miles
24th July	F1 – **Grote Prijs van Nederland** at Zandvoort (N) – 234.5 miles
7th August	F1 – **Grosser Preis von Deutschland** at Nurburgring (D) – 212.6 miles
21st August	F2 – Kanonloppet at Karlskoga(S) – 55.9 miles
24th August	F2 – Suomen Grand Prix at Keimola (Fn) – 71.4 miles
4th September	F1 – **Gran Premio d'Italia** at Monza (I) – 243 miles
11th September	F2 – Grand Prix de l'Ile de France at Montlhéry (F) – 160 miles
17th September	F1 – International Gold Cup at Oulton Park (UK) – 107.1 miles
18th September	F2 – Trophée Craven 'A' at Le Mans (F) – 164.9 miles
25th September	F2 – Grand Prix d'Albi (F) – 192.3 miles
2nd October	F1 – **United States Grand Prix** at Watkins Glen (US) – 248.4 miles
23rd October	F1 – **Gran Premio de Mexico** at Mexico City (Mx) – 201.9 miles
30th October	F2 – Motor Show '200' at Brands Hatch (UK) – 132.5 miles

36 events of total race mileage = 5335 miles.

Events in bold are World Championship rounds – 64.3 per cent of F1 races run.

Formula Two and Tas (Tasman Formula) dates are those which offered the prospect of a battle between top Formula One drivers, and they well outnumbered the Formula One races available.

Tasman Championship 1966

The status quo shifted this year from the ubiquitous and essential Coventry Climax FPF 2.5-litre engine powering every successful car. Formula One had changed to three litres, and the British were again, amazingly, not ready (as in 1961). BRM was awaiting its H-16 F1 engine, and decided, as an interim, to stretch the existing Formula One V8 engine to 1930cc, increasing its power from 210bhp to acound 260bhp, for use in the new F1. This was very useful for the Tasman series, as it beat the power of the Climax four-cylinder, which had 240. BRM hadn't entered the South African Grand Prix a week earlier, so this Tasman series saw the first running of BRMs team for the new 1966 Formula One, with regular drivers Graham Hill and Jackie Stewart. For the last three New Zealand races Hill would return home and be replaced by Richard Attwood, who had twice scored World Championship points in a Lotus-BRM in 1965. Lotus had won the aforementioned GP with Mike Spence powered by a two-litre Climax V8. Jim Clark's new Lotus 39 was originally designed for the aborted Flat 16 Climax F1 engine, but Lotus still used the 2.5 Climax FPF for this Tasman series, presumably thinking that its torque would suit the mostly medium-to-slow tracks. Jack Brabham would contest only the last two races in the series, with his car now powered by a 2.5 Repco V8. This was a smaller version of the Formula One unit with which he had almost won in South Africa and would conquer the F1 World Championship this year. His F1 unit had 295bhp, so the 2.5 would have had about 250 and good torque, I guess. So that's five F1 stars for this Tasman Championship, but only twice would four appear together.

✳ New Zealand Grand Prix (Pukekohe)

40 lap final of 2.20 miles = 88.0 miles.
19 started – 12 finished.

Front row: G Hill – 1m-25.2s (92.96mph); J Clark 0.3; S Martin 1.1s.

08-JAN: Spencer Martin's Brabham led the residents and gave the 'stars' something to think about by beating Stewart to the outside grid slot next to Clark. He worried them a little more by leading away as Jim Clark stripped first gear and was left on the line. He soon spoiled his glory by hitting an embankment and was out on lap one. Clark was push-started but lasted just six laps, so it was a BRM benefit from then on. Hill had set a new record on his first flying lap just as rain began falling. Stewart closed on Hill near the end but Hill was in command. Palmer's ex-Clark car was well ahead of Marwood's Cooper and not far off Stewart. Now any idea that the 'small-engined' BRMs weren't a challenge was wiped out in act one of this little saga.

1st G Hill (BRM P261) in 1h-02m-56.5s = 83.89mph
2nd J Stewart (BRM P261) @ 1.5s

3rd J Palmer (Lotus 32B-Climax 4) @ 13.8s
Fastest lap G Hill in 1m-25.7s = 92.42mph

✳ Gold Leaf Trophy (Levin)

8-lap heat + 28-lap final of 1.1 miles = 39.6 miles.
16 started – 10 finished.

Front row: F Gardner – 48.3s (81.99mph); J Stewart 0.2s; J Clark 0.7s.

15-JAN: It was the fastest laps of the runners in the two heats which formed the grid and Frank Gardner's Brabham took pole from Stewart and Clark. It was Gardner who led Stewart, Clark and Attwood and Spencer Martin after a lap. Stewart pressed Gardner hard but slipped up himself on lap seven and spun, losing out to Attwood. Gardner was now in command while Stewart stopped after 11 laps with gear selection troubles. Perhaps Jim Clark was wishing he had his old type 32B as, with the same power unit as Gardner, he couldn't challenge him. The race was Gardner's into the penultimate lap but no – his transmission failed and Richard Attwood and BRM took a lucky win. Maybe the Climax torque had real merit, but so did Gardner.

1st R Attwood (BRM P261) in 23m-12.0s = 79.65mph
2nd J Clark (Lotus 39-Climax 4) @ 12.1s
3rd S Martin (Brabham BT11A-Climax 4) @ 21.1s
Fastest lap F Gardner in 47.8s = 82.85mph

✳ Lady Wigram Trophy (Christchurch)

11-lap heats + 44-lap final of 2.318 miles = 127.5 miles.
16 started – 9 finished.

Poles: Heat one – R Attwood – 1m-25.1s (98.06mph). Heat two – J Stewart – 1m-23.9s (99.46mph).

22-JAN: Here it was heat times that determined the grid, and it was Stewart, Attwood, Gardner and Clark at the front. Clark made it into second place after the start, and he and leader Stewart pulled away by a second or two from Attwood who had Gardner in his slipstream. On lap five Gardner suffered total brake loss at the hairpin, shot past Attwood, and caught Clark in mid-turn, putting them both out. That was it for the main racing then, just as Jim Clark looked like putting the BRM hat-trick in danger. Palmer took the 'resident's honours' by taking Martin at two-third distance, but was no challenge. Now the BRM hat-trick has happened, yet, strangely, each with a different driver. Maybe a Clark/Stewart fight next time? It was hoped so.

1st J Stewart (BRM P261) in 1h-03m-44.1s = 96.02mph
2nd R Attwood (BRM P261) @16.4s
3rd J Palmer (Lotus 32B-Climax 4) @ 1m-06s
Fastest lap J Stewart in 1m-25.0s = 98.18mph

Let no-one think that Formula One Grand Prix racing had its own level of danger in those times. In these last three Tasman Championship series, 23 races were run and four of the resident drivers perished, along with two young spectators. Circuits were, naturally, more primitive than in Europe, but so were the safety features.

✱ Teretonga Trophy (Invercargill)

5-lap heats + 50-lap final of 1.5 miles = 82.5 miles.
19 started – 12 finished.

Front row: F Gardner – 1m-01.0s (88.52mph); J Clark 0.3s; R Attwood 0.3s.

29-JAN: Heat times set the grid, and Clark was on pole from Stewart and Gardner. Martin and Attwood were on row two. Gardner led Clark off the line, while Attwood, spinning wheels on the slippery new surface he was on, was caught by others. Entering the long Loop corner he was struck from behind, sending the car airborne and pinning him underneath on landing upside down; he escaped, battered and bruised, but otherwise okay. Clark soon led from Stewart, but he spun on oil at the Loop and crashed. It was Stewart from Gardner from then on. On lap 31 he had to adapt to only having third gear but stayed ahead. Two laps later tragedy struck as Bill Caldwell's throttle stuck open. He was launched off a ditch, becoming airborne, and struck a truck with spectators on it. He died, along with two boys. This tragic race was stopped on lap 46 as ambulances were now on the track.

1st J Stewart (BRM P261) in 49m-04.8s = 84.35mph
2nd F Gardner (Brabham BT11-Climax 4) @18.8s
3rd J Palmer (Lotus 32B-Climax 4 @ 2 laps
Fastest lap J Clark in 1m-01.0s = 88.52mph

✱ Warwick Farm '100'

45 laps of 2.25 miles = 101.25 miles.
19 started – 12 finished.

Front row: J Clark – 1m-33.0s (87.10mph); G Hill 0.6s; F Gardner 1.5s.

13-FEB: Hill was back to lead the BRM team, but they were beaten to pole by Clark; his Firestone-shod car bettering the Dunlop-tyred BRMs. Hill and Gardner completed the front row, with Stewart on row two. Clark led off the line then was passed on the straight by Hill. Clark's superior tyres helped him reclaim the lead under braking before the lap ended. Stewart was third, but spun, damaging a rear wheel rim. He restarted in ninth place, and, fortunately, the tyre remained inflated allowing him to claw his way back to fourth. Palmer and Martin had been picked off, but Gardner was out of reach. The BRM monopoly was broken now.

1st J Clark (Lotus 39-Climax 4) in 1h-11m-03.6s = 85.49mph
2nd G Hill (BRM P261) @ 20.9s
3rd F Gardner (Brabham BT11-Climax 4) @ 59.2s
Fastest lap J Clark in 1m-34.0s = 86.17mph

✱ Australian Grand Prix (Lakeside)

10-lap heats + 66-lap final of 1.5 miles = 114.0 miles.
14 started – 9 finished.

Poles: Heat one – J Stewart – 55.4s (97.47mph). Heat two – G Hill – 55.6s (97.12mph).

20-FEB: Stewart and Hill won the heats, but it was heat two winner Clark who was level with Stewart on the front row, Hill being on row two of this two x two grid. Hill shot past Clark to latch onto Stewart at the start, with Clark being chased by Gardner. On lap 28 leader Stewart stopped with gearbox failure, and Hill had it fairly easy from then on. His engine ran a little rough towards the end, and Clark was catching by over a second a lap, but he, too, had a rough motor, and Frank Gardner took second place with five laps left. Hill was safe but Clark was dropping way back, however Palmer was two laps down at the end. BRM was on top again.

1st G Hill (BRM P261) in 1h-02m-38.4s = 94.83mph
2nd F Gardner (Brabham BT11-Climax 4) @ 16.6s
3rd J Clark (Lotus 39-Climax 4 @ 58.6s
Fastest lap J Stewart 55.5s = 97.30mph

✱ Exide International Cup (Sandown Park)

10-lap prelim + 52-lap final of 1.928 miles = 119.5 miles.
16 started – 9 finished.

Front row of prelim: J Stewart – 1m-07.9s (102.22mph); J Clark 0.3s; G Hill 0.5s.

27-FEB: Jack Brabham was here with his new Brabham BT19-Repco, and finished fourth in the preliminary qualifying race, won by Stewart. But it was lap times from this that formed the grid, so Brabham was on pole, with Stewart and Clark next. It was Brabham, Stewart, Clark and Hill at first, but, on lap two, Stewart took the lead and Hill passed Clark for third. On lap six Brabham lost oil pressure and retired, leaving the BRMs in charge as Clark dropped back. Stewart pulled away while Clark battled to catch Hill and eventually take second by out-braking him on lap 32. The Tasman Championship was now Stewart's.

1st J Stewart (BRM P261) in 59m-37.1s = 100.90mph
2nd J Clark (Lotus 39-Climax 4) @ 23.8s
3rd G Hill (BRM P261) @ 50.1s
Fastest lap J Brabham (Brabham BT19-Repco) in 1m-07.6s = 102.67mph (prelim)

✱ S Pacific Championship Race (Longford)

10-lap prelim + 26 laps of 4.5 miles = 162.0 miles.
8 started final – 7 finished.

Front row of prelim: J Stewart – 2m-16.0s (119.12mph); G Hill 0.2s; J Clark n/a.

07-MAR: The 1500cc cars from previous races were prevented from racing here on grounds of speed differential, with the cars 'flying mile' average of 167mph. Stewart won the preliminary from Hill and Clark, with lap times from this forming the final grid. He duly led off, with Hill making a terrible start and dropping to sixth. Stewart drew away from Clark by two seconds a lap, while Hill battled back to take Brabham's third place on lap three, and Clark's second spot on lap six. They had a great scrap for a few laps until Clark pitted with misfiring. Stewart's debut on this dangerous track was simply imperious.

1st J Stewart (BRM P261) in 1h-02m-55.4s = 111.56mph
2nd G Hill (BRM P261) @ 1m-06s
3rd J Brabham (Brabham BT19-Repco) @ 1m-33s
Fastest lap J Stewart in 2m-17.7s = 117.65mph (prelim)

Tasman Champion:
1st Jackie Stewart (BRM P261 V8) – 45
2nd Graham Hill (BRM P261 V8) – 30
3rd Jim Clark (Lotus 39-Climax 4) – 25

VIII Rand GP (Kyalami)
50 laps of 2.544 miles = 127.2 miles.
19 entries – 16 started – 11 finished.

Front row: J Brabham – 1m-30.8s (100.86mph); J Love 0.1s.
Row two: P deKlerk 2.1s; R Anderson 2.4s.

04-DEC-1965: Just as in late 1960, South Africa ran a race to the new incoming formula ahead of time. Brabham borrowed an ex-Works car, and Ireland, now past his best, drove a Lotus-BRM for Reg Parnell. Siffert and Bonnier drove for Rob Walker, but were never higher than fifth. The battle was with 'local hero' John Love's Cooper. He and Brabham swapped the lead many times, but suspension trouble at half distance dropped him to fourth, behind Paul Hawkins but ahead of Siffert and Ireland. He was surely South Africa's top man. Brabham held off deKlerk without too much trouble.

1st	J Brabham (W)	Brabham BT11-Climax 2.7 in 1h-18m-11.2s	97.61
2nd	P deClerk	Brabham BT11-Climax 2.7	5.9s
F lap	J Brabham (W)	Brabham BT11-Climax 2.7 in 1m-31.5s	100.09

＊ XII South African GP (East London)
60 laps of 2.436 miles = 146.2 miles.
22 entries – 19 started – 10 finished.

Front row: J Brabham – 1m-25.1s (103.05mph); M Spence 0.9s; D Hulme 1.1s.

01-JAN: The South African GP had unfairly been denied Championship status because it was "too early," yet Works Lotus and Brabham teams joined the Rand GP field. Brabham's use of a Repco power unit, not known outside Australia, had people scratching their heads. He eased away at the start, unsure of the gearbox, but led from Spence on lap

two, and held him off until a backmarker caused him to spin on lap 51, failing to restart. Hulme's gearbox had expired two laps earlier, and de Klerk's followed suit on lap 51. So Spence was now miles ahead, with Siffert taking it easy. Brabham's secret was out now, though.

1st	M Spence (W)	Lotus 33-Climax 2.0 in 1h-29-39.4s	97.81
2nd	J Siffert (RW)	Brabham BT11-BRM 2.0	2 laps
3rd	P Arundell (W)	Lotus 33-Climax 2.0	2 laps
F lap	J Brabham (W)	Brabham BT19-Repco in 1m-25.2s	102.93

＊ XV Gran Premio di Siracusa
56 laps of 3.418 miles = 191.4 miles.
15 entries – 11 started – 5 finished.

Front row: J Surtees – 1m-42.3s (120.26mph); L Bandini 1.6s; J Siffert 1.9s.

01-MAY: Only Ferrari and Brabham sent Works teams, but Jack Brabham had the only Repco unit, Hulme having a 2.7 Climax. No Works Cooper-Maseratis, but Siffert and Ligier had new cars, so customer sales came first. The Brabhams missed practice so were at the back. Bandini led away from Siffert, with Brabham having charged into third only to retire on lap two. Surtees' engine now came on song, and he came through to win easily. Siffert dropped out from second with misfiring, and Bonnier's Walker-entered Brabham-BRM stopped due to vibration. A trial race really for many.

1st	J Surtees (W)	Ferrari 312 in 1h-40m-08.3s	114.67
2nd	L Bandini (W)	Ferrari 158/246	24.6s
3rd	D Hobbs (RP)	Lotus 25-BRM 2.0	2 laps
F lap	J Surtees	Ferrari 312 in 1m-43.4s	118.98r

＊＊ XVIII *Daily Express* International Trophy (Silverstone)
102.5m – 35 laps of 2.927 = 102.5 miles.
15 entries – 12 started – 8 finished.

Front row: J Brabham – 1m-29.8s (117.34mph): J Surtees 0.2s; J Rindt 1.0s; M Spence 1.4s.

14-MAY: A decent entry, with Brabham, Ferrari and Cooper Works cars. Lotus was absent, though, as Clark was at Indy and Arundell's engine, a BRM H-16, wasn't ready. Now Ferrari would show what the others were up against – well that's what it thought. However, it was Brabham who proved the worth of Repco power and led all the way, with Surtees struggling to stay in touch throughout, despite his car sounding okay. The Cooper-Maseratis were not fast enough, despite Rindt being a close third in practice. People still didn't realise the value of the Brabham-Repco solution to F1 – light, nimble and plenty of torque.

1st	J Brabham (W)	Brabham BT19-Repco in 52m-57.6s	116.06
2nd	J Surtees (W)	Ferrari 312	7.4s
3rd	J Bonnier	Cooper T81-Maserati	1m-25s
F lap	J Brabham	Brabham BT19-Repco in 1m-29.8s	117.34r

✳✳✳ (WC1) XXIV Grand Prix de Monaco (Monte Carlo)

100 laps of a 1.954-mile circuit = 195.4 miles.
20 entries – 16 qualified – 4 finished.
Front row: J Clark – 1m-29.9s (78.26mph); J Surtees 0.2s.
Row two: J Stewart 0.4s; G Hill 0.5s.

22-MAY: The Brabhams disappointed, with Hulme on row three and the Boss' Repco car on row six. Clark was stuck in gear at the start, and was last away, so Surtees led Stewart, Hill, Hulme and the amazing privateer Bob Anderson, who, unfortunately, retired on lap four. Rindt took his place and came through to third on lap eight, by which point Clark had astonishingly netted seventh place! Rindt was soon second as race leader Surtees stopped on lap 14 with drive failure. Bandini had almost matched Clark's progress from tenth on lap one, so on lap 20 it was Stewart, Bandini, Rindt, Hill and Clark, but Rindt was passed by the latter two, and retired with clutch trouble. Clark took third from Hill on lap 61, only to suffer suspension collapse before it registered on the lap chart. After all this attrition, BRM's client, Bob Bondurant, claimed fourth place, and last to be classified. The same three drivers claimed the podium positions as the year before, although only one stood with Prince Rainier actually. No three-litre car finished, so the first Championship race of the 'Return to Power' looked little different to the previous year at the end. Of the six marques on the grid, BRM provided three of the four finishers, achieving 100 per cent reliability to Ferrari's 50 per cent, and the others zero per cent. Thank God for BRM!

1st	J Stewart (W)	BRM P261 2.0 in 2h-33m-10.6s	76.55
2nd	L Bandini (W)	Ferrari 158/246	40.2s
3rd	G Hill (W)	BRM P261 2.0	1 lap
F lap	L Bandini (W)	Ferrari 158/246 in 1m-29.8s	78.34r

✳✳✳ (WC2) XXVI Grand Prix de Belgique (Spa)

28 laps of a 8.761-mile circuit = 280.4 miles.
19 entries – 15 started – 7 finished.

Front row: J Surtees – 3m-38.0s (144.68mph): J Rindt 3.2s; J Stewart 3.5s.

12-JUN: It was an easy pole for Surtees on this super fast circuit. He stormed away on a dry track, as Clark's engine blew up, and led easily on lap one from Brabham and Bandini. Way behind came Ginther, Rindt, Ligier and Gurney debuting his Eagle. That was it! Where were the rest? Serious rain at the back half of this long track had caused mayhem, with seven crashing out and having very lucky escapes. Even Rindt had spun a huge distance, but continued as if it was nothing. The Monaco BRM trio all crashed at the same spot, Stewart soaked in fuel. Hill could have continued, but saw his teammate's plight and helped to rescue him – fire would have killed him. Bandini led lap two, Surtees lap three, and, amazingly, Rindt lap four, after an astonishing recovery. Surtees saw Rindt slide again and kept out of his spray for 19 laps then passed as the rain eased a little, winning easily. Two great drives in almost impossible conditions. Thus began Stewart's campaign for safety – and much needed it was!

1st	J Surtees (W)	Ferrari 312 in 2h-09m-11.3s	113.94
2nd	J Rindt (W)	Cooper T81-Maserati	42.1s
3rd	L Bandini (W)	Ferrari 158/246	1 lap
F lap	J Surtees (W)	Ferrari 312 in 4m-18.7s	121.92

Championship positions:
L Bandini 10; J Stewart, J Surtees 9.

✳✳✳ (WC3) LII Grand Prix de l'ACF (Reims)

48 laps of a 5.158-mile circuit = 247.6 miles.
21 entries – 17 started – 9 finished.
Front row: L Bandini – 2m-07.8s (145.31mph); J Surtees 0.6s; M Parkes 1.3s.

03-JUL: Back at Reims after three years, and Surtees had defected to Cooper, after a famous spat with Ferrari after Le Mans (yes, Formula One men raced there as well). He split the Ferraris on the front row. Ginther, now at Honda, was replaced at Cooper by Amon. Clark was hit in the face by a bird – most thankfully not suffering the fate of his late teammate Alan Stacey at Spa 1960. A damaged left eye put him out, though. Surtees led for 200 yards before a fuel pump problem spoilt his revenge on Ferrari. Brabham slipstreamed Bandini, but slowly dropped back lacking sheer power. Bandini was leading easily on lap 32 when his throttle cable broke, and now Brabham led and, having had no trouble in seeing off Parkes, was able to ease to a famous win – the first for a driver/constructor in the World Championship – and on a power circuit where he would not have expected to challenge. Hulme finished after stopping to lift the front of his car to find enough fuel to complete his last lap! Odd fact: This was Mike Parkes' Championship debut. Had anything happened to Jack Brabham then he would have exactly emulated Baghetti's feat of 1961 and won his first ever Championship race on the same circuit with the same marque, and after the team leader's retirement. Nothing is too unusual as to be beyond repeat it seems. Five drivers separated by just three points showed what an intriguing title race this was turning out to be. Domination by no-one.

1st	J Brabham (W)	Brabham BT19-Repco in 1h-48m-31.3s	136.90
2nd	M Parkes (W)	Ferrari 312	9.5s
3rd	D Hulme (W)	Brabham BT19-Repco	2 laps
F lap	L Bandini (W)	Ferrari 312 in 2m-11.3s	141.44r

Championship positions:
J Brabham 12; L Bandini 10; J Stewart, J Surtees, J Rindt 9.

✲✲✲ (WC4) XXI British Grand Prix (Brands Hatch)
80 laps of 2.46 miles = 196.8 miles.
24 entries – 20 started – 13 finished.
Front row: J Brabham – 1m-34.5s (93.71mph); D Hulme (0.3s); D Gurney (1.3s)

16-JUL: Three driver/constructors were on the grid now, and two were on the front row. Ferrari was absent due to a strike, apparently. If patriotism could overcome a trade dispute anywhere surely it would be in Italy? Chris Amon made way for Surtees, and Brabham put Chris Irwin in its Climax-powered car. Hulme was slow away on the damp but drying track, so it was Brabham two seconds ahead of Gurney, Rindt, Clark, Surtees and Hill, before Hulme arrived at the end of lap one. Gurney lost out to Rindt, Surtees and Hill before retiring, the latter two having also passed Clark. Surtees soon led teammate Rindt, but on laps 28 to 32 both dropped behind Hill, Clark and Hulme. Brabham was well out of sight by now, and, on lap 40, it became a Brabham-Repco one-two as Hulme came through. The Cooper duo passed Clark as he had brake fluid loss. After pitting, though, Clark made up a whole lap on them to regain fourth as the Brabham-Repcos completed a comprehensive victory. Surtees' axle failed, so into sixth behind Rindt came Bruce McLaren in his McLaren-Serenissima. Another point for a second driver/constructor.

1st	J Brabham (W)	Brabham BT19-Repco in 2h-13m-13.4s	88.64
2nd	D Hulme (W)	Brabham BT19-Repco	9.6s
3rd	G Hill (W)	BRM 261 2.0	1 lap
F lap	J Brabham (W)	Brabham BT19-Repco in 1m-37.0s	91.30r

Championship positions: J Brabham 21; J Rindt 11; L Bandini 10.

✲✲✲ (WC5) XV Grote Prijs van Nederland (Zandvoort)
90 laps of a 2.605 mile circuit = 208.4 miles.
19 entries – 17 started – 9 finished.
Front row: J Brabham – 1m-28.1s (106.46mph); D Hulme 0.6s; J Clark 0.6s.

24-JUL: Brabham came limping to the grid and wearing a beard as, at 40 years old, he was the 'old man of the race,' so they said. It was youngster Clark who made a great start from the outside of the front row, but Brabham rescued the situation by the first corner. Soon Hulme passed Clark who clung on grimly, the three pulling away from Hill, Parkes and Stewart. Rindt crashed from eighth on lap two, and Parkes' race ended on lap ten by spinning off into Rindt's car. Hulme pitted with faulty ignition on lap 17, and, a few laps later, when lapping back markers, Clark found a way past Brabham to lead a race for the first time this year. He pulled out a gap of ten seconds before water loss, caused by a broken vibration damper, meant he had to replenish in the pits. This lost him a lap to Brabham, and the five seconds he was ahead of Hill disappeared within a few laps. Another stop almost lost him third place to Stewart. Brabham knew that his hat-trick had been nearly lost. Spence and Bandini were fifth and sixth.

1st	J Brabham (W)	Brabham BT19-Repco in 2h- 20m-32.5s	100.11
2nd	G Hill (W)	BRM 261 2.0	1 lap
3rd	J Clark (W)	Lotus 33-Climax 2.0	2 laps
F lap	D Hulme (W)	Brabham BT19-Repco in 1m-30.6s	103.53r

Championship positions:
J Brabham 30; G Hill 14; J Stewart 12.

✲✲✲ (WC6) XXVIII Grosse Preis von Deutschland (N Nürburgring)
15 laps of 14.173 miles = 212.5 miles.
19 entries – 18 started – 7 finished.
Front row: J Clark – 8m-16.5s (102.77mph); J Surtees 1.5s; J Stewart 2.3s; L.Scarfiotti 3.7s.

07-AUG: Ferrari supplied a V6 car for Ludovico Scarfiotti to supplement the team, and he beat both his teammates on the grid. On the wet track Clark struggled off the line on Firestone tyres, and was only fourth after the first lap, behind Brabham, Surtees, who had led most of the lap, and Rindt. By lap four he had also lost out to Hill and Gurney. Hulme came through taking Stewart, Clark and Hill on successive laps, only to retire with ignition trouble before he could tackle Gurney for fourth place. Clark retired from sixth on lap 11, and Gurney from fourth with a lap to go. Hill, Stewart and Bandini completed the points scorers, while the lead three had held station all race. A Formula Two class had taken part, and the outstanding star of them was Jacky Ickx in a French built Matra-Cosworth, who had almost matched Hulme's practice time. Sadly, though, soon after the start, a crash involving promising privateer John Taylor resulted in burns which proved fatal.

1st	J Brabham (W)	Brabham BT19-Repco in 2h- 27m-03.0s	86.75
2nd	J Surtees (W)	Cooper T81-Maserati	44.4s
3rd	J Rindt (W)	Cooper T81-Maserati	2m-33s
F lap	J Surtees (W)	Cooper T81-Maserati in 8m-49.0s	96.46

Championship positions:
J Brabham 39; G Hill 17; J Surtees, J Rindt 15.

After Jack Brabham's rare four-in-a-row run, the Championship seemed all over, but in those days the number of results counting was restricted to the next number above half the rounds run. This meant that of the nine rounds this year, only a driver's best five scores counted. Brabham had scored five times so would drop his lowest score if he scored again. But John Surtees and Jackie Stewart, on 14 points, were still in the game. Surtees had only scored twice so far, with a win and second, so wouldn't drop any further scores. To take the title would require a hat-trick of wins in the final three races from either, with Brabham failing to get a second place in Surtees' case and a fourth in Stewart's. This was very unlikely, but Surtees had won in 1964 with a late surge so who knows?

✱✱✱ (WC7) XXXVII Gran Premio d'Italia (Monza)
68 laps of a 3.573-mile circuit = 243.0 miles.
24 entries – 20 started – 10 finished.
Front row: M Parkes – 1m-31.3s (140.88mph); L Scarfiotti 0.3s; J Clark 0.5s.
04-SEP: There were new arrivals to take on as Honda arrived with a car for Ginther, and Dan Gurney's Eagle was now powered by an all-new Weslake V12 which, if it went as well as it looked, would surely challenge. BRM had finally developed its unique H-16 design to a point where it felt ready to run it, so left the V8s behind. Lotus also had a BRM H-16 unit in the back of Jim Clark's car. If a physically big engine has commensurately big power, then the rest didn't stand a chance. Now everything that had been in the 'pipeline' was on the grid, and the real 'return to power' would begin. Clark and Surtees were, with the

three Ferraris, filling the front two grid rows, the Honda in attendance just behind. Clark bogged down at the start, and Scarfiotti led away, but it was Bandini, Parkes, Surtees, Ginther, Brabham and Hulme after a lap – Scarfiotti seventh. Surtees led the next lap as Bandini pitted, Brabham led four laps and Surtees again for five as Brabham retired. Clark had launched into fifth from the very back by lap nine, but pitted for a new wheel balance weight. Now Scarfiotti led from Ginther's Honda, a lead that lasted three more laps. A single interruption by Parkes, who fell into the clutches of Hulme, was all that worried Scarfiotti. Surtees retired by half distance as Parkes and Hulme battled furiously, while Scarfiotti, having his first outing in the Ferrari 312, stayed out front and out of trouble. The Honda and the Lotus-BRM H-16 had threatened, but Gurney was nowhere. Brabham was Champion with two races remaining. Simplicity and reliability beating complexity.

1st	L Scarfiotti (W)	Ferrari 312 in 1h-47m-14.8s	135.92
2nd	M Parkes (W)	Ferrari 312	5.8s
3rd	D Hulme (W)	Brabham BT20-Repco	6.1s
F lap	L Scarfiotti (W)	Ferrari 312 in 1m-32.4s	139.20r

Championship positions:
J Brabham 39 (WC); J Rindt 18; G Hill 17.

✱ XIII International Gold Cup (Oulton Park)
40 laps of 2.678 miles = 107.1 miles.
15 entries – 10 started – 5 finished.
Front row: J Brabham – 1m-34.2s (102.35mph); D Hulme 0.6s; J Stewart 1.2s.
17-SEP: Lotus, Brabham and BRM entered teams. BRM had the H-16-engined cars which had failed in Italy, the unit having done better in Clark's Lotus, which was here. But his H-16's gearbox failed, meaning that Arundell was denied a start, his car taken over by Clark. I'll never forget standing near the H-16 BRM in the paddock, as you could in those 'good old days,' while the mechanics warmed it up at about 2000rpm. For a couple of minutes the engine was warmed and when the thumbs up signal to open it up was given the most heavenly exhaust note I'd ever heard emitted from those 16 cylinders. BRM improved on Monza, and a terrific race ensued, with the lead passing first to Brabham, then Hulme, then Brabham, then Stewart's H-16, then Brabham, then Hill's H-16 on lap ten. Hill then led all but one lap before retiring on lap 24 with camshaft failure. Clark's Lotus was, surprisingly, never in it. So the Brabhams deserved their demonstration finish. Only five cars finished, fourth being Ireland in a BRM 261. The H-16 BRM, though, had shown some form now, with maybe better to come. It had sounded wonderful. Could reliability be found

for this exciting, complicated engine? Would it overcome the weight disadvantage?

1st	J Brabham (W)	Brabham BT19-Repco in 1h-06m-14.2s	97.04
2nd	D Hulme (W)	Brabham BT20-Repco	0.1s
3rd	J Clark (W)	Lotus 33-Climax 2.0	25.2s
F lap	J Brabham	Brabham BT19-Repco in 1m-36.6s	99.80r

✳✳✳ (WC8) 9th United States Grand Prix (Watkins Glen)

108 laps of 2.30 miles = 248.4 miles.
20 entries – 19 started – 6 finished.

Front row: J Brabham – 1m-08.42s (121.02mph); J Clark 0.11s. Row two: L Bandini 0.15s; J Surtees 0.31s.

02-OCT: Ferrari sent just one car for Bandini and Honda two, while Lotus gave the H-16 BRM engine another chance in Jim Clark's car after its outing at Oulton Park – and it nearly took pole! After a lap it was Ferrari, Lotus-BRM, Honda, Brabham-Repco, Cooper-Maserati and BRM – six marques – what a variety! Then Ginther's third-placed Honda dropped back with gear trouble. Brabham led Bandini on lap ten from Surtees and Clark. Surtees and a lapped Arundell clashed and both spun on lap 16 – Surtees pitting for a checkup, and losing three laps. Bandini retook the lead on lap 20 holding it until retiring on lap 34. At half distance it was Brabham, Clark, Rindt, having inherited third as Stewart stopped, Siffert, McLaren, and an amazingly resurgent Surtees, who had already recovered one of his lost laps. Brabham's engine gave out next lap. Could the H-16 engine last? Well it did, and, one lap down, Surtees took third! He had unlapped himself twice since pitting! This was a win lost, and a sadly forgotten dazzling drive for John Surtees. It was also the only ever win in Formula One for a 16-cylinder car.

1st	J Clark (W)	Lotus 43-BRM H-16 in 2h-09m-40.1s	114.94
2nd	J Rindt (W)	Cooper T81-Maserati	1 lap
3rd	J Surtees (W)	Cooper T81-Maserati	1 lap
F lap	J Surtees (W)	Cooper T81-Maserati in 1m-09.67s	118.85r

Championship positions:
J Brabham 39 (WC); J Rindt 22; J Surtees 19.

✳✳✳ (WC9) V Gran Premio de Mexico (Mexico City)

65 laps of 3.107 miles = 201.9 miles.
19 entries – 18 started – 8 finished.

Front row: J Surtees – 1m-53.18s (98.82mph); J Clark 0.32s. Row two: R Ginther 0.38s; J Brabham 0.77s.

23-OCT: No Ferraris here – how often they failed to turn up at the year's end. At Watkins Glen Surtees' Cooper-Maserati had been the fastest car, and he took pole here ahead of Clark to reinforce the point. But a rough engine saw him fifth after a lap, behind Ginther, Rindt, Brabham and Hulme, but the Honda's lead lasted just a lap. Clark soon lost his sixth place to Stewart, and dropped out on lap eight. By then Surtees' engine had cleared and, being fired up again as at Watkins Glen, had disposed of all ahead, now leading the race untroubled to the end, and sealing Cooper's first win for over four years. Stewart retired from fourth on lap 30, and Rindt from third on lap 32. Pedro Rodriguez, given a drive by Lotus, was third on home ground, but lap 49 saw him stop with drive failure. Ginther's Honda gained his place, losing it to Hulme two laps from the end, but Honda was now back in the game, and with a fastest lap to its credit.

1st	J Surtees (W)	Cooper T81-Maserati in 2h-06m-35.34s	95.72
2nd	J Brabham (W)	Brabham BT20-Repco	7.88s
3rd	D Hulme (W)	Brabham BT20-Repco	1 lap
F lap	R Ginther (W)	Honda RA 273 in 1m-53.75s	98.33r

Championship positions:
J Brabham 42 (WC); J Surtees 28; J Rindt 22.

Winners of the 14 F1 races of 1966 – quantity and quality of success

7 wins	J Brabham (4A, B, C, D)	6 wins	Brabham-Repco (4A, B, C)
3 wins	J Surtees (2A, B)	3 wins	Ferrari (2A, B)
1 win	J Stewart (A) J Clark (A) L Scarfiotti (A) M Spence (C)	1 win	BRM (A); Cooper-Maserati (A); Lotus-Climax (C); Lotus-BRM (A) ; Brabham-Climax (D)

1966 seasonal review

With only 13 quality races in total this year for Grand Prix cars, this was the equal lowest number since Formula One had begun in 1947 (1959 had just 13). Even the inaugural year had seen 18! The presence, therefore, of the Tasman Series, and Formula Two being open to F1 stars, was essential for a full career. A weekend without racing was a disappointment to a star driver who pulled in the crowds. The Ferrari win at Syracuse had proved little as Surtees only led after Brabham's early demise. At Silverstone in May, in a better race, it was beaten by the Brabham-Repco, which had showed form in South Africa in January. The premature Rand Grand Prix in December '65, whilst run to the '66 F1 rules, was the sole minor event.

1966 Championship review

The doubling in engine size to three litres was welcomed by all, but the introduction of new engines was bound to be reflected in the retirement figures. Sure enough, average finishing rate for the season dropped from 57.2 per cent the previous year to only 42.5 per cent, the lowest since the Championship began in 1950. This makes Jack Brabham's four wins in a row quite remarkable, particularly since the Repco engine marque was new to Formula One. His record of six finishes, all in the points, was surprisingly matched by Jochen Rindt's Maserati-engined Cooper. This engine had the oldest history in the field, being based on the V12 unit used in 1957 in a Maserati 250F. So the newest and the oldest engines were the most reliable, but only for one member of each team. Five marques had won a major race, while, of those who hadn't, Honda was beginning to look a threat.

Dan Gurney's Eagle-Weslake looked and sounded great, and was expected to come good with his leadership, but Bruce McLaren had failed to achieve anything with either of his Ford Indianapolis or Serenissima-engined cars. However, his engineering skills were proven by the 'faster-than-F1' McLaren Can-Am cars, so his F1 fortunes were likely to turn around. All-in-all it was a very intriguing year, and the formula had a great future.

If (a big word) John Surtees had not had those two retirements early in the season a real fight for the title would have ensued, and subsequent events might have yielded him the title. His falling out with Ferrari after Le Mans and defection to Cooper-Maserati – a less fancied team by then – did not change his fortunes much, as he won a Grand Prix and lost a Grand Prix from the lead with each team. His performance in the last two Grands Prix of the year showed that the possibility of his taking a hat-trick of wins to worry Brabham was not as far-fetched as it had appeared at the time. For me, John Surtees is one of the most overlooked drivers in F1. Could he bring Cooper fully back into the big time where F1 heritage says it belongs? I hoped so.

VISIT VELOCE ON THE WEB – WWW.VELOCE.CO.UK
All current books • New book news • Special offers • Gift vouchers • Forum

251

Chapter 26

1967

Plenty of confidence all round

After the 'sorting-out' year of 1966 almost all teams could look back with some feeling of having achieved something which could be usefully developed. The exception would be McLaren Racing, whose Ford and Serenissima engines had failed to provide a reliable power unit for development of the car – a fresh start would be needed. The Championship was now extended to eleven rounds for the first time, but six extra races were held so the total F1 activity rose to 17. With the new power era came extra rubber to cope. Tyres got wider, as they had incrementally for the last few years, so speeds would increase significantly.

A new Formula Two started with as much power as the 1965 Formula One cars, and would eat into the F1 calendar. Nineteen F2 races would attract F1 stars, so provided more racing dates than F1. With the additional Tasman Formula races a massive season of 44 single-seater races was open to the Grand Prix elite.

The constructors

Team Lotus made the big news at the start of the year by signing Graham Hill to partner Jim Clark as joint number ones. The team was still in a state of flux, using the Type 43 with BRM H-16 power at first, then the older type 33s with Climax power for Clark and BRM for Hill. In June, at the Dutch GP, came the Type 49, with Cosworth DFV. It was seen that the engine constituted the back half of the new Lotus 49, performing the chassis function on which suspension was mounted. The combination changed racing car design forever – another Colin Chapman coup de foudre, and an instant success.

Brabham Racing continued with 'The Boss' and Denny Hulme using an updated Repco engine with four valves per cylinder, and exhausts in the centre of the vee. It had about

330bhp, less than many others, but could Brabham pull it off again? A 2.5-litre version would be used in the Tasman Series.

BRM had replaced Graham Hill with Mike Spence as number two to Jackie Stewart. Both the H-16-powered type P83 car and the P261 'cigar-shaped' car with 2010cc V8 engine would be used, the latter now having 280bhp. A V12 3-litre engine was also designed for use by customer teams.

Ferrari continued with Lorenzo Bandini as leader, supported by Mike Parkes, Chris Amon or Ludovico Scarfiotti. It often entered a three-car team, whereas others had two, but this was okay, as there was no rule on team numbers. The car was little altered from 1966, Le Mans being equally important to Ferrari then.

Honda had secured the services of John Surtees as sole driver. He had much faith in the Japanese to produce a winner – just look at the motorcycle record. Honda had the previous year's powerful but heavy car, but a new car with much input from Lola Cars was in the pipeline. This was often referred to as the 'Hondola.'

Cooper-Maserati had surprisingly finished on top at the end of the previous year, and now Jochen Rindt was joined by Pedro Rodriguez. They would have their work cut out to match Surtees' performances of America and Mexico the year before. Could the Maserati engine be persuaded to remain competitive?

Anglo-American Racing, using the Eagle name, and with boss Dan Gurney and Richie Ginther at the wheel, had reason to believe that the Weslake V12 engine was going to keep it in contention. The car looked great, and has recently been voted the prettiest Grand Prix car of all time (well nearly). In the 21st century looks are the last thing on a designer's mind. Technology demands ugliness now.

McLaren Racing was a single car team, with Bruce

McLaren using a new M4A car built for Formula Two, but accepting the 2-litre V8 BRM engine. This would be replaced as soon as the V12 BRM engine was available with the M5A chassis. Strangely, there would be a gap in July and August where McLaren, impatient for a V12 engine, would drive an Eagle for Dan Gurney, replacing Ginther who had, surprisingly, retired from racing after Monaco.

The independents

RRC Walker Racing, the most renowned independent of all, supplied Jo Siffert with a Cooper-Maserati, while Jo Bonnier operated as a privateer also with a Cooper-Maserati. Ever optimistic one-man-band Bob Anderson ran a Brabham-Climax 2.7.

The Grand Prix driver's diary of single-seater racing for the 1967 season

2nd January	F1 – **South African Grand Prix**(SA) at Kyalami – 203.5 miles
7th January	Tas – New Zealand Grand Prix at Pukekohe (NZ) – 120.8 miles
14th January	Tas – 'Wills International' at Levin (NZ) – 68.4 miles
21st January	Tas – Lady Wigram Trophy at Christchurch (NZ) – 127.9 miles
28th January	Tas – Teretonga Trophy at Invercargill (NZ) – 108.8 miles
12th February	Tas – Lakeside 99 International (Au) –99 miles
19th February	Tas – Australian Grand Prix at Warwick Farm (Au) – 101 miles
26th February	Tas – Sandown '100' at Sandown Park (Au) – 119.5 miles
6th March	Tas – South Pacific Trophy at Longford (Au) – 198 miles
12th March	F1 – 'Race of Champions' at Brands Hatch (UK) – 148.1 miles
24th March	F2 – Guards '100' at Snetterton (UK) – 135.5 miles
27th March	F2 – BARC '200' at Silverstone (UK) – 117.1 miles
2nd April	F2 – Grand Prix de Pau (F) – 120 miles
9th April	F2 – Gran Premio de Barcelona at Montjuic Pk (E) – 141.1 miles
15th April	F1 – Spring Trophy at Oulton Park (UK) – 133.9 miles
23rd April	F2 – Eifelrennen at SNurburgring (D) – 144.4 miles
29th April	F1 – *Daily Express* International Trophy at Silverstone (UK) – 152.2 miles
7th May	F1 – **Monaco Grand Prix** (M) – 195.4 miles
14th May	F2 – Guards' Int Trophy at Mallory Park (UK) – 114.8 miles
21st May	F1 – Gran Premio di Siracusa (I) – 194.8 miles*
21st May	F2 – Grote Prijs van Limborg at Zolder (B) – 125.3 miles
29th May	F2 – London Trophy at Crystal Palace (UK) – 118.2 miles
4th June	F1 – **Grote Prijs van Nederland** at Zandvoort (N) – 234.5 miles
18th June	F1 – **Grand Prix de Belgique** at Spa Francorchamps (B) – 245.3 miles
25th June	F2 – Grand Prix de Reims (F) – 190.9 miles
2nd July	F1 – **Grand Prix de l'ACF** at Le Mans (F) – 247.6 miles
9th July	F2 – Grand Prix de Rouen (F) – 160.3 miles
15th July	F1 – **British Grand Prix** at Silverstone (UK) – 234 miles
16th July	F2 – Flugplatzrennen at Tulln-Langenlebarn (A) – 83.9 miles
23rd July	F2 – Gran Premio de Madrid at Jarama(E) – 116.3 miles
6th August	F1 – **Grosser Preis von Deutschland** at Nurburgring (D) – 212.6 miles
13th August	F2 – Sveriges Grand Prix at Karlskoga (S) – 59.6 miles
20th August	F2 – Gran Premio del Mediterraneo at Enna-Pergusa (I) – 238.5 miles
27th August	F1 – **Grand Prix of Canada** at Mosport Park (C) – 221.3 miles
28th August	F2 – Guards Trophy at Brands Hatch (UK) – 123.5 miles
3rd September	F2 – Soumen Grand Prix at Keimola (Fn) – 73.9 miles
5th September	F2 – Hämeenlinnan Ajot at Ahvenisto (Fn) – 36.1 miles
10th September	F1 – **Gran Premio d'Italia** at Monza (I) – 243 miles
16th September	F1/2 – International Gold Cup at Oulton Park (UK) – 120.5 miles*
24th September	F2 – Grand Prix d'Albi (F) – 169.5 miles
1st October	F1 – **United States Grand Prix** at Watkins Glen (US) – 248.4 miles
8th October	F2 – Gran Premio di Roma at Vallelunga (I) – 116.2 miles
22nd October	F1 – **Gran Premio de Mexico** at Mexico City (Mx) – 201.9 miles
12th November	F1 – Gran Premio d'España at Jarama (E) – 190.4 miles

44 events of total race mileage = 6755 miles.

Events in bold are World Championship rounds – 64.7 per cent of F1 races run.
* See Appendix 'A' for these two ungraded race results. Formula Two dates are those in which top Formula One drivers competed and with the Tasman races (FT) they well outnumbered the Formula One races.

Tasman Championship 1967

BRM's dominance the previous season, with a multi-cylinder engine of just 1930cc, proved that a new era of Tasman racing had arrived, and the overseas drivers now all arrived with V8 power. The Repco V8 unit was full 2.5-litre, of around 250bhp, while BRM had enlarged its unit to 2070cc, giving over 270bhp. Jim Clark's Works Lotus was 1987cc with about 255bhp, and with only two-valve heads. This engine was produced solely for Lotus, as Climax had officially withdrawn from racing. BRM should be 'in the driving seat' for this campaign, then, but perhaps the Repco and Climax V8s might have better torque to suffice on the tighter circuits. Jack Brabham, now the reigning world F1 Champion, and Denny Hulme, would have Repco-powered Brabhams. BRM was headed by Jackie Stewart, who was now F1 team leader as Graham Hill had signed for Lotus. Richard Attwood was his support in New Zealand, and Piers Courage stood in for Stewart at Teretonga and Attwood at Lakeside. Chris Irwin was the support for the last three races. Though using four drivers, BRM always entered just two cars. Team Lotus had just a single entry for Jim Clark: a Type 33 as used in the previous year's F1 Championship, rather than the 39 as per the last Tasman season. Frank Gardner had a good reputation in Europe, and had driven a Brabham-BRM for John Willment in Formula One in 1966, so he was really a visitor himself now, and well capable of worrying the 'Tasman establishment' with his four-cylinder, Climax-powered car. Irwin and Courage, despite being Works drivers for BRM, were yet to have a regular F1 seat. The big tyre companies – Goodyear, Firestone and Dunlop – were taking this series seriously, so BRM was given the freedom by owner Sir Alfred Owen to fit whatever tyre it wanted.

The points system changed this year, with all scores accumulating except, for no reason I can find or think of, the races at Levin and Teretonga, which simply didn't count. How odd!

✳ **New Zealand Grand Prix (Pukekohe)**
12 prelim +57 laps of 1.75 miles = 120.75 miles.
24 entered – 20 started – 16 finished.
Front row of prelim: J Brabham – 1m-02.2s (101.29mph); J Clark 0.5s.
07-JAN: Brabham's BT23 had failed to arrive thanks to industrial action, so he had Hulme's BT19-Repco engined model from the previous year, while Hulme borrowed a

Brabham BT7A. The preliminary grid-decider put Stewart and Clark on the front of the grid for the final, with Brabham near the back as he had spun off. Stewart passed Clark soon after the start to lead, with Attwood following and heading Bartlett and Hulme. Soon Hulme was fourth and closing on Attwood, but Brabham broke a halfshaft on lap five. The leaders were glued together for the whole race, pulling away steadily. Hulme took Attwood on lap 29, but transmission failure stopped him with seven laps to go as a podium looked certain. A lap to go and Clark contacted a slow lapped car and lost his front bodywork and screen. Stewart won from the 'naked' Lotus of Clark.
1st J Stewart (BRM P261) in 59m-16.4s = 100.97mph.
2nd J Clark (Lotus 33-Climax V8) @ 4.5s.
3rd R Attwood (BRM P261) @ 1 lap.
Fastest lap J Clark in 1m-00.5s = 104.13mph.

✳ **Wills International at Levin**
14 +43 laps of 1.193 miles = 68.0 miles.
20 entries – 16 started – 9 finished.
Front row of prelim: J Clark – 48.6s (88.37mph); J Stewart 0.2s.
14-JAN: Brabham was at the Repco factory in Australia, so Hulme was now Repco V8-powered. The Clark/Stewart battle resumed, while Hulme lost third to Gardner and then to Attwood on lap two. Attwood forced an error from Gardner on lap 15 to claim third. Hulme dropped back to retire on lap 27. Clark and Stewart lapped Attwood on lap 30, and Clark held off Stewart easily.
1st J Clark (Lotus 33-Climax V8) in 34m-59.4s = 87.95mph
2nd J Stewart (BRM P261@ 3.0s
3rd R Attwood (BRM P261) @ 1 lap
Fastest lap J Clark in 47.5s = 90.42mph

✳ **Lady Wigram Trophy (Wigram Airfield)**
11-lap heats + 44-lap final of 2.318 miles = 127.5 miles.
16 started – 9 finished.
Front row of prelim: J Clark – 1m-21.8s (102.01mph); J Stewart 0.8s; J Brabham 2.0s; D Hulme 2.0s.
21-JAN: Clark was beaten by Stewart and Brabham in the 'big car' prelim, the other for 1500cc cars. In the final, Stewart led off the line, but Clark beat him into the first corner, with Brabham, Hulme and Attwood next. The lead two were set for a repeat lead battle but Clark clipped a course marker – an embedded half tyre. This flew into Stewart, smashing his screen. Even worse, it broke the oil line into his pressure gauge and hot oil sprayed him; he was out. Brabham's second place was lost after Attwood passed Hulme, who latched on behind, and the pair passed Brabham, who retired later. Clark had an easy run to win.
1st J Clark (Lotus 33-Climax V8) in 1h-03m-34.1s = 96.27mph

2nd R Attwood (BRM P261) @ 16.9s
3rd D Hulme (Brabham BT19-Repco) @ 1 lap
Fastest lap J Stewart in 1m-23.8s = 99.58mph (prelim)

✳ Teretonga Trophy (Invercargill)
8 prelim + 60 laps of 1.6 miles = 108.8 miles.
18 started – 8 finished.

Front row of prelim: J Clark – 1m-01.8s (93.20mph);
D Hulme (0.1s); F Gardner (0.7s)

28-JAN: Stewart and Brabham were absent, so this saw the BRM debut of Piers Courage, and the debut of a revised track. After the prelim it was Hulme on pole for the feature event, with Clark, Attwood and Courage on the outside. Clark shot away, Hulme stripped a gear on the line, and others dodged him. Courage spun on the first lap, and he, like Hulme, was lucky to avoid damage, resuming in eighth place. Clark led by ten seconds from Attwood on lap ten, with Gardner challenging. Courage had recovered well to fourth and was closing on Gardner. The titanic battle for second was over on lap 29 when Gardner stopped with an oil line split. Courage and Attwood were close, but the former retired on lap 53, having shown what his form was.

1st J Clark (Lotus 33-Climax V8) in 1h-04m-50.3s = 88.84mph
2nd R Attwood (BRM P261) @24.7s
3rd J Palmer (Brabham BT22-Climax 4) @ 2 laps
Fastest lap D Hulme in 1m-02.0s = 92.90mph

✳ Lakeside '99'
66 laps of 1.5 miles = 99.0 miles.
14 started – 8 finished.

Front row: J Clark – 54.1s (99.82mph); J Stewart 0.3s. Row two: J Brabham 0.7s; D Hulme 1.0s.

12-FEB: Stewart was back, supported by Courage, and Brabham was also present now that they were in Australia. Clark led off the line, but a poor gear change allowed Stewart past. Brabham and Hulme were next, with Leo Geoghegan in his ex-Clark Lotus ahead of Courage and Gardner. Courage took fifth from Geoghegan, but a cramp spasm caused a brief excursion along the Armco, dropping to ninth. Geoghegan retired on lap 29 after a great drive. Clark led on lap 39 as Stewart's gear-change gave trouble. He pulled steadily away, and Stewart's gearbox failed on lap 59. Hulme pitted for wheel-nut tightening so now Courage had recovered superbly to third place but his gearbox failed on lap 63. Clark lapped the field, and now had won four-in-a-row.

1st J Clark (Lotus 33-Climax V8) in 1h-0m-56.2s = 97.48mph
2nd J Brabham (Brabham BT23-Repco)@ 1 lap
3rd F Gardner (Brabham BT16-Climax 4) @ 2 laps
Fastest lap J Clark in 54.6s = 98.90mph

✳ Australian Grand Prix (Warwick Farm)
45 laps of 2.25 miles = 101.25 miles.
16 started – 8 finished.

Front row: J Stewart – 1m-30.8s (89.21mph); J Clark 0.8s;
G Hill 0.9s.

19-FEB: Chris Irwin now replaced Courage for the last three rounds, and Graham Hill was a welcome addition in the latest F2 Lotus 48 with its brilliant 220bhp Cosworth FVA engine. He promptly placed it third on the grid, behind Clark, but ahead of the Brabham-Repcos. This was the first indication of how fast these cars were – and how great the Ford Cosworth DFV would be. Stewart blasted clear at the start from Clark, Brabham, Hill, Gardner, Hulme, Martin and Geoghegan. Hill got third and latched onto Clark. Brabham was passed by Gardner then Hulme. Hill retired with gearbox trouble, and Hulme with a radiator hose split. Stewart won easily, while Brabham, in fourth, had a poor race.

1st J Stewart (BRM P261) in 1h-09m-17.3s = 87.68mph
2nd J Clark (Lotus 33-Climax V8) @ 16.7s
3rd F Gardner (Brabham BT16-Climax 4) @ 1m-12s
Fastest lap J Stewart in 1m-31.4s = 88.62mph

✳ Sandown '100' (Sandown Park)
10-lap prelim + 52-lap final of 1.928 miles = 119.5 miles.
16 started – 9 finished.

Front row of prelim: J Brabham – 1m-05.7s (105.64mph);
J Stewart 0.4s; D Hulme 0.9s.

26-FEB: Lap one, and it was Brabham, Stewart, Hulme, Clark, Martin, Gardner, Geoghegan and Irwin. After much trying on lap nine, Stewart passed Brabham, who then stopped with ignition trouble. Two laps later Stewart was out with transmission failure, so Hulme led and a ten-lap scrap with Clark ensued. Lap 23 saw Clark pass Hulme, who then retired three laps later. Geoghegan had passed Gardner, and, when Martin retired, he was now second. Irwin's BRM was fourth. So, the residents benefitted from visitor frailty.

1st J Clark (Lotus 33-Climax V8) in 59m-09.9s = 101.67mph
2nd L Geoghegan (Lotus 39-Climax 4) @ 49.6s
3rd F Gardner (Brabham BT16-Climax 4) @ 58.7s
Fastest lap J Brabham in 1m-05.7s (105.64mph)

✳ South Pacific Trophy (Longford)
8+8+28 laps of 4.5 miles = 198.0 miles.
9 started final – 6 finished.

Front row of prelim: J Brabham – 2m-13.4s = 121.44mph;
J Stewart 0.0s; D Hulme 2.2s.

06-MAR: Lap times in the prelims formed the final grid, which had Clark on pole ahead of Stewart. After a lap it was Brabham, Hulme. Clark, Stewart, Gardner and Irwin. By lap four Stewart was second, and soon Clark had taken Hulme who stopped with ignition trouble. At halfway Brabham led Stewart by five seconds, with Clark 25 seconds back, and

Irwin a further 26. No-one could challenge Brabham, and even when his exhaust split making his engine sound flat, he produced a new lap record. Stewart was all set for second, but another gearbox failure stopped him with two laps left. BRM's supposed power advantage didn't prevail.

1st J Brabham (Brabham BT23-Repco) in 1h-03m-25.6s = 119.19mph
2nd J Clark (Lotus 33-Climax V8) @ 14.8s
3rd C Irwin (BRM P261) @ 1m-38s
Fastest lap J Brabham in 2m-13.3s = 121.53mph

Tasman Champion:
1st Jim Clark (Lotus 33-Climax V8) – 45
2nd Jackie Stewart (BRM P261) – 18
3rd Frank Gardner (Brabham BT16-Climax 4) – 18

✳✳✳ (WC1) XIII South African Grand Prix (Kyalami)

80 laps of 2.544 miles = 203.5 miles.
19 entries – 18 started – 6 finished.

Front row: J Brabham – 1m-29-8.3s (103.72mph); D Hulme 0.6s. Row two: J Clark 0.7s; P Rodriguez 0.8s.

02-JAN: South Africa had a healthy domestic F1 series (not covered in this book). Could any of the locals get among the visiting elite?

It was too early in the year for any new cars, and the Brabhams had the front of the two-by-two grid, so was it Brabham domination again as last year? The Brabhams led the first two laps from Surtees and Rodriguez. Rindt came through and joined Surtees in passing Jack Brabham, but spun. Approaching half way and Hulme led Brabham and Rindt, but Rindt retired and Brabham's engine cut out. So who came through? Local hero John Love, and, when Hulme pitted for brake fluid and dropped to fourth, he had a clear lead! Sadly, though, a misfire used up fuel and he pitted on lap 74, so Rodriguez won for Cooper-Maserati. You can't beat unpredictability.

1st	P Rodriguez (W)	Cooper T81-Maserati in 2h- 05m-45.9s	97.10
2nd	J Love (W)	Cooper T79-Climax FPF	26.4s
3rd	J Surtees (W)	Honda RA 273	1 lap
F lap	D Hulme (W)	Brabham BT20-Repco in 1m-29.9s	101.87r

✳✳✳ II 'Race Of Champions' (Brands Hatch)

10 + 10 + 40-lap final of 2.46 miles = 147.6 miles.
22 entries – 18 started – 10 finished.

Front row: D Gurney – 1m-32.2s (96.05mph); J Surtees 1.2s; R Ginther 1.4s.

12-MAR: Back on the agenda, but without Team Lotus.

No Works BRMs either, but an H-16 was run by Parnell Racing for Mike Spence, and there were three Ferrari entries! Amon had an accident en route to the circuit, and decided to withdraw from his Ferrari debut after practice. Unusually, there were three races, two ten-lap preliminaries and a 40-lap final. The Eagles of Gurney and Ginther and Surtees' Honda made the best starts, but Gurney led flag-to-flag. Surtees retired and Brabham stormed into second on lap 11, but pitted on lap 17. Bandini forged his way into third from his ninth starting position and closed on the Eagles. An Eagle one/two failed as Ginther stopped on lap 35, and Bandini almost snatched victory. Close behind, Siffert just beat Rodriguez's Works Cooper for third. A great race – and great sound – with nine V12 cars and an H-16. This was also the first Formula One win for an American marque, though the power was English.

1st	D Gurney (W)	Eagle T1G-Weslake in 1h-04m-30.6s	91.53
2nd	L Bandini (W)	Ferrari 312	0.4s
3rd	J Siffert (RW)	Cooper T81-Maserati	13.0s
F lap	D Gurney	Eagle T1G-Weslake V12 in 1m-32.6s	95.64r

✳ International Spring Trophy (Oulton Park)

10 + 10 + 30 laps of 2.678 miles = 133.9 miles.
18 entries – 10 started – 8 finished.

Front row: J Stewart – 1m-32.2s (104.57mph); D Hulme 1.2s; J Surtees 1.6s.

15-APR: Run, like the 'Race of Champions,' in three parts, this was a fund-raiser for the 'Mobile Grand Prix Medical Unit' – brainchild of BRM boss Louis Stanley. Brabhams, BRMs, a Honda and a McLaren, plus a Team Lotus F2 car were the main field. Hulme won the preliminary races, from which any retirements were allowed to join the next grid at the back. This was just as well, as Brabham had retired from the first ten-lapper, but was third in the second one, so he was on the front of the grid for the final. In the final, it was Brabham who led from Hulme. Surtees took second on lap 13, and Hill's F2 car passed Hulme on lap 15. Hill was second as the Honda faltered, then his throttle failed. Hulme retook second from Surtees and then Brabham slowed for a team finish. Stewart's BRM suspension failed on lap ten, and Spence's BRM just disappointed. This was the best F1 race here this year. The corrected circuit length from 2.761 to 2.678 miles shows that this race was the first to register a 100mph race lap record – and by some considerable margin. Sadly, September's annual Gold Cup was a F1 non-event in comparison.

1st	J Brabham (W)	Brabham BT20-Repco in 47m-21.4s	101.79
2nd	D Hulme (W)	Brabham BT20-Repco	0.4s
3rd	J Surtees (W)	Honda RA273	22.4s
F lap	J Brabham	Brabham BT20-Repco (Heat 1) in 1m-32.4s	104.34r

✳ XIX *Daily Express* International Trophy (Silverstone)

52 laps of 2.927 miles = 152.2 miles.
17 entries – 12 started –8 finished.
Front row: J Stewart – 1m-27.8s (120.01mph); M Parkes 0.0s; M Spence 1.4s; D Hulme 1.4s.

29-APR: Single cars from Ferrari, BRM, Lotus and McLaren, plus the Brabham duo, but no Eagles or Works Coopers. Stewart and Parkes both did 120mph laps in practice, which everyone hoped would be replicated in the race. It promised to be a good race. The BRM H-16 engine now looked like a good idea, and chased the Ferrari for three laps, whereupon Stewart slid on oil deposited by Hulme's car which had contacted Bob Anderson's Cooper. Mike Parkes pulled easily away from then on. Brabham took Stewart on lap five and held on while Siffert came through to pass the ailing BRM and then Brabham on lap 24. But 25 laps later Brabham re-caught him for a final scrap to the flag. Graham Hill had pitted early on and dropped to tenth, re-joined and produced a storming recovery to fourth place, complete with fastest lap – and in a two-litre car! The track state precluded a repeat of the 120mph lap.

1st	M Parkes (W)	Ferrari 312 in 1h-19m-39.2s	114.65
2nd	J Brabham (W)	Brabham BT20-Repco	17.6s
3rd	J Siffert (RW)	Cooper T81-Maserati	18.4s
F lap	G Hill (W)	Lotus 33-BRM 2.0 in 1m-30.0s	117.08

✱✱✱ (WC2) XXV Grand Prix de Monaco (Monte Carlo)

100 laps of a 1.954-mile circuit = 195.4 miles.
22 entries – 16 qualified – 6 finished.
Front row: J Brabham – 1m-27.6s (80.31mph); L Bandini 0.7s. Row two: J Surtees 0.8s; D Hulme 1.2s.

07-MAY: Only five places were available to compete for as 11 were guaranteed starts, so Bob Anderson's great time of 1m-30.6s – faster than Amon, Rindt and Rodriguez – still left him out. Brabham's engine let go at the start and Clark took evasive action up an escape road. Bandini led lap one but Hulme and Stewart passed, as did Gurney who then retired. Stewart led laps seven to 14 in a 2-litre BRM when

his drive failed. Now Hulme drew away from Bandini, who was fighting off Surtees and McLaren. Surtees retired on lap 31 after McLaren and Clark passed. Lap 42 saw Clark's brilliant recovery halted by suspension problems. McLaren lost third, needing a new battery, and, ten laps later tragedy struck when Bandini crashed at the chicane, and struck the straw bales, which caught fire as did the car. He suffered injuries and serious burns before being extricated. The race continued – it always did. Amon, now second, punctured, and Hill passed him. McLaren was fourth, three laps down. Though Bandini was alive when removed from the wreckage, everyone knew he would be unlikely to survive – he didn't. A very sad race.

1st	D Hulme (W)	Brabham BT20-Repco in 2h-34m-34.3s	75.86
2nd	G Hill (W)	Lotus 33-BRM 2.0	1 lap
3rd	C Amon (W)	Ferrari 312	2 laps
F lap	J Clark (W)	Lotus 33-Climax 2.0 in 1m-29.5s	78.61r

Championship positions:
D Hulme 12; P Rodriguez 11; J Love, G Hill 6.

The next F1 race was the Siracuse Grand Prix on 21st May, but the serious entries there were reduced to just the two-car Ferrari team. Non-Works Cooper-Maseratis for Jo Siffert and Jo Bonnier weren't competitive. Only seven cars started, and the Ferraris lapped everyone twice before a slow last lap with the other three finishers crawling behind as they pre-arranged a dead-heat. So no individual won it! That's not a motor race is it? This event is reduced to unclassified status – see Appendix for result.

✱✱✱ (WC3) XVI Grote Prijs van Nederland (Zandvoort)

90 laps of a 2.605-mile circuit = 208.4 miles.
19 entries – 17 started – 9 finished.
Front row: G Hill – 1m-24.60s (110.87mph); D Gurney 0.5s; J Brabham 1.0s.

04-JUN: Here began the next phase of racing-car development, as Colin Chapman's creation arrived. Brabham's car had a new Repco engine, but was a second slower than poleman Graham Hill with the radical new Lotus 49-Cosworth, with Gurney's Eagle between them. Clark, surprisingly, was on the third row. Hill led off, with Brabham, Rindt and Gurney chasing. Soon Gurney was out, handing fourth to Clark. That became third when Hill retired with cam drive failure. Brabham led from Rindt, but Clark led lap 16, having passed them fairly easily. Hulme battled with Amon, and the pair were catching Brabham who responded.

Hulme had the better of Amon by 1.6 seconds, with Parkes not far back. The only place change in the last half of the race had been Surtees' retirement from sixth, making way for Scarfiotti's Ferrari. Clark's Lotus had won easily on its debut, but Hill might have felt robbed as both cars were so dominant. Given reliability the rest should worry – the game had changed now.

1st	J Clark (W)	Lotus 49-Cosworth in 2h-14m-45.1s	104.41
2nd	J Brabham (W)	Brabham BT19-Repco 740	23.6s
3rd	D Hulme (W)	Brabham BT20-Repco	25.7s
F lap	J Clark (W)	Lotus 49-Cosworth in 1m-28.08s	106.49r

Championship positions:
D Hulme16; P Rodriguez 11; J Clark 9.

✷✷✷ (WC4) XXVII Grand Prix de Belgique (Spa)
28 laps of an 8.761-mile circuit = 280.4 miles.
20 entries – 18 started – 11 finished.
Front row: J Clark – 3m-28.1s (151.57mph); D Gurney 3.1s; G Hill 4.8s.

18-JUN: Clark's pole was the first ever 150mph F1 lap: ten seconds faster than 1966 pole and three seconds ahead of Gurney (with Hill alongside and Rindt and Amon behind). Sure enough, while Hill's battery was flat, Clark led off from Rindt, Stewart and Parkes, but the latter crashed and suffered leg injuries. It was Clark, Stewart, Amon, Rindt and Gurney after a lap. Both Gurney and Brabham had passed Amon and Rindt by lap four. Clark's lead was lost on lap 12 with plug trouble, so now it was Stewart, Gurney and Brabham whose engine failed two laps later letting Rodriguez and Amon into fourth and fifth. A BRM H-16 victory looked on the cards now, but gear selector problems slowed Stewart, and Gurney swept past on lap 21. Rindt took over his teammate's fourth place when the latter retired. So, Dan Gurney became the second driver/constructor to win an F1 Championship Grand Prix. This race had begun a new era of over 140mph race speeds, and reports of speeds over 200mph are believable; after all, there is a slow hairpin, and there was no downforce for 4g cornering then. 200mph speeds are not a modern phenomenon.

1st	D Gurney (W)	Eagle T1G-Weslake in 1h-40m-49.4s	145.74
2nd	J Stewart (W)	BRM P83 H-16	1m-03s
3rd	C Amon (W)	Ferrari 312	1m-40s
F lap	D Gurney (W)	Eagle T1G-Weslake in 3m-31.9s	148.85r

Championship positions:
D Hulme 16; P Rodriguez, C Amon 11.

✷✷✷ (WC5) LIII Grand Prix dell'ACF (Le Mans)
80 laps of a 2.748-mile circuit = 219.8 miles.
20 entries – 15 started – 6 finished.
Front row: G Hill – 1m-36.2s (102.83mph); J Brabham 0.1s; D Gurney 0.8s.

02-JUL: This cobbled-up circuit used the first mile of the famous Le Mans 24hr track; peeling off right at the Esses, using triple hairpins behind the pits, then a 'wiggly' section to return to the main straight. Hill, Brabham and Gurney were in front and led off, but, by lap five Clark had the lead. Hill regained it on lap 11, but his final drive soon failed, as did Clark's ten laps later. Brabham led Gurney until lap 40, whereupon fuel pipe trouble gave Hulme second place. Amon was third, but his throttle cable broke. The Brabhams stroked home in a race of attrition, with Siffert fourth, three laps down, and a retired Irwin four laps back ahead of Rodriguez. Now it looked as though reliability was coming to the aid of the Brabham-Repcos against more powerful machinery, as per the year before.

1st	J Brabham (W)	Brabham BT24-Repco in 2h-13m-21.3s	98.90
2nd	D Hulme (W)	Brabham BT24-Repco	49.5s
3rd	J Stewart (W)	BRM P261 2.0	1 lap
F lap	G Hill (W)	Lotus 49-Cosworth in 1m-36.7s	102.29

Championship positions:
D Hulme 22; J Brabham 16; P Rodriguez 12.

✷✷✷ (WC6) XXII British Grand Prix (Silverstone)
80 laps of 2.927 miles = 234.2 miles.
22 entries – 20 started – 10 finished.
Front row: J Clark – 1m-25.3s (123.53mph); G Hill 0.7s; J Brabham 0.9s; D Hulme 1.0.

15-JUL: Hill's chance to match Clark's pole time was dashed when his rear suspension collapsed as he approached the pits, and he struck the entrance onto the new raised pit lane (a new car was built overnight). The Lotuses and Brabhams had the front row. Clark led off as Hill, getting used to a new car, battled with Brabham ahead of Amon and Gurney. On lap 26 Hill passed Clark for the lead, with Hulme having passed Amon and Brabham for third. Hill's drive was spoiled when a suspension link came loose, causing the left rear wheel to lean in at about 20 degrees. He struggled back for repairs, losing two laps. On lap 64 his engine failed – a great drive thwarted more than once. Amon took third from Brabham at Woodcote Bend with four laps to go. Rodriguez' Maserati and Surtees' Honda completed the points scorers. The 120mph lap barrier had been well shattered.

1st	J Clark (W)	Lotus 49-Cosworth in 1h-59m-29.6s	117.64
2nd	D Hulme (W)	Brabham BT24-Repco	12.8s
3rd	C Amon (W)	Ferrari 312	16.6s
F lap	D Hulme (W)	Brabham BT24-Repco in 1m-27.0s	121.12r

Championship positions:
D Hulme 28; J Clark and J Brabham 19.

This was the halfway point in the Championship, and the system was that each driver dropped their worst result from each half – six rounds had been run and five were to go. No-one had scored every time thus far, so all points accrued to date would count. Now, surely, the Lotus 49 would prevent another Repco-powered Champion.

An observation
The Lotus 49/Cosworth DFV had, in the last four races, shown itself to be the car to beat, and Jim Clark had, for the first time, a dangerous rival as a teammate. But Graham Hill had now retired from the lead in three races due to machinery failure, having deprived Clark of the lead twice. Hill had won two, so the records hide the fact that Clark, at this point, was not the dominant force in the team that he has been assumed to be. Of the four races with the Lotus 49, pole positions had been shared. Hill's contribution is often overlooked.

✳✳✳ (WC7) XXIX Grosse Preis von Deutschland (N Nürburgring)
15 laps of 14.173 miles = 212.5 miles.
17 F1 entries and starters – 8 finished.
Front row: J Clark – 8m-04.1s (105.52mph); D Hulme 9.4s; J Stewart 11.1s; D Gurney 12.8s.
06-AUG: The speed of the new cars past the pits had caused the ADAC to add a chicane on the approach to the pits at the end of the very long straight. To fill up the long track, a Formula Two race was held concurrently, but formed up to the rear of the F1 grid. Clark's pole time was massively ahead of next man Hulme! Perhaps equal to this was Jacky Ickx's 8m-14.0s in Ken Tyrrell's F2 Matra. He was third fastest overall, but way back on the F2 grid which formed up behind the F1 cars. Hill had crashed in practice and was on the fourth row. Clark, Hulme and Gurney led for three laps, whereupon Clark suffered a buckled front wishbone

and Gurney passed Hulme to lead until a halfshaft failed on lap 13. Hill had been contacted at the start and spun, but had risen to eighth on lap eight (mostly due to retirements) when suspension failure nearly caused another crash. The light but tough Brabhams had another one-two finish. Fourth was Surtees' Honda, sounding none-too-healthy. Fifth was Bonnier's Cooper-Mas, with the last points going to Guy Ligier in one of the previous year's Brabham-Repcos. Fifth on the road, though, was Jackie Oliver's F2 Lotus. Jacky Ickx's astonishing drive in the F2 Matra had ended on lap 12 with wheel bearing trouble, when he was in fourth place on the road ahead of Surtees' Honda. Next year Matra would be in F1, as would Tyrrell. It seems unfair that there were no points for F2 cars – weren't they supposed to be slower?

1st	D Hulme (W)	Brabham BT24-Repco in 2h-05m-55.7s	101.41
2nd	J Brabham (W)	Brabham BT24-Repco	38.5s
3rd	C Amon (W)	Ferrari 312	39.0s
F lap	D Gurney (W)	Eagle T1G-Weslake in 8m-15.1s	103.17r

Championship positions:
D Hulme 37; J Brabham 25; J Clark 1.

✳✳✳ (WC8) 1st Grand Prix Of Canada (Mosport Park)
90 laps of 2.459 miles = 221.3 miles.
21 entries – 18 started – 11 finished.
Front row: J Clark – 1m-22.4s (107.43mph); G Hill (0.3s); D Hulme (0.8s)
27-AUG: A welcome new venue outside Europe saw the inaugural Canadian GP. Unfortunately, supporting races followed by drizzle had made the track a grease-bowl – about as slippery as you can get. Clark, Hill and Hulme 'crawled' off in drizzle and soon rain, with Hulme leading lap four from Clark, Hill, Brabham and Stewart. McLaren, now powered by a V12 BRM unit, spun from fifth to 12th on lap four, yet was back to fourth on lap 12, then second to Hulme on lap 22. Clark soon got that place back as the track dried fast and hauled in Hulme to lead on lap 58. Then it rained again – hard – and damp ignition stopped his race. Brabham at the same time caught Hulme and led to the end for the third one-two finish for the Brabhams. McLaren stopped for a new battery, dropping to seventh. Until then, he had headed BRM's H-16s, so giving a message that the V12 was a better future proposition than the unique but monstrous H-16. Amon's lone Ferrari dropped to the back at the start, but recovered to sixth behind Hill, who'd had a poor race, and Spence.

1st	J Brabham (W)	Brabham BT24-Repco in 2h-40m-40.0s	82.65
2nd	D Hulme (W)	Brabham BT24-Repco	1m-02s
3rd	D Gurney (W)	Eagle T1G-Weslake	1 lap
F lap	J Clark (W)	Lotus 49-Cosworth in 1m-23.1s	106.53

Championship positions:
D Hulme 43; J Brabham 34; C Amon 20.

✳✳✳ (WC9) XXXVIII Gran Premio d'Italia (Monza)

68 laps of a 3.573-mile circuit = 243.0 miles.
20 entries – 18 started – 7 finished.
Front row: J Clark – 1m-28.5s (145.34mph); J Brabham 0.3s; B McLaren 0.81s.

10-SEP: Ferrari entered only one car – in Italy! – Chris Amon being the favoured conducente, and Honda, having missed Canada, appeared with a lighter car (with help from Lola Cars). Increments of 0.01 seconds were used to separate McLaren from Amon and Gurney, so close were the times. Gurney took the lead from Brabham, but was passed by Clark on lap three, having suffered an engine blow-up. A foursome of the Lotuses and Brabhams led for ten laps when Clark pitted with a puncture. The slow in-lap cost him over a lap, whence he produced a truly historic drive back to take the lead, having caught a whole lap back from Brabham. He'd just been gifted it by Hill's con-rod failure when well over a minute ahead having led since benefitting from Hulme's gasket problem on lap 28. Fatefully, on the very last lap, Clark suffered fuel starvation and was passed by Surtees and Brabham. Then Brabham tried to outbrake Surtees on the inside at Parabolica but slid on cement dust covering Hill's oil slick, as Surtees thought he might. So, a memorable win for Clark was replaced by one for Honda and Surtees. But Clark's drive will remain in motor sport folk lore ... but would Hill have felt robbed perhaps?

1st	J Surtees (W)	Honda RA300 in 1h-43m-45.0s	140.51
2nd	J Brabham (W)	Brabham BT24-Repco	0.2s
3rd	J Clark (W)	Lotus 49-Cosworth	23.1s
F lap	J Clark (W)	Lotus 49-Cosworth in 1m-28.5s	145.34r

Championship positions:
D Hulme 43; J Brabham 40; J Clark 23.

The next F1 race was the Oulton Park International Gold Cup on the 16th September, supposedly for Formula One but the entry was reduced to just the Brabham team with Frank Gardner replacing Denny Hulme (fourth on the grid), plus the slowest car in the field – local man, George Pitt, with a Climax-powered Brabham. This means there was no real F1 contest taking place. The actual racing was for F2 cars – Jackie Stewart second overall, only 5.4 seconds behind Jack Brabham after 120 miles. This event is given unclassified status – see Appendix for result.

✳✳✳ (WC10) 10th United States Grand Prix (Watkins Glen)

108 laps of 2.30 miles = 248.4 miles.
21 entries – 18 started – 7 finished.
Front row: G Hill – 1m-05.48s (126.45mph); J Clark 0.59s.
Row two: D Gurney 1.16s; C Amon 1.17s.

01-OCT: Another pole position for Hill, and he and Clark duly led away, but Clark was soon passed by Gurney, with Brabham, Amon and Hulme following. Clark recovered second spot a few laps later, while Hulme passed Amon and won a short battle with Brabham. Amon in the lone Ferrari replied by taking both Brabhams and Dan Gurney, who retired on lap 24. All was settled until lap 40, whereupon Hill had gear selection trouble which let Clark take the lead. On lap 65 this benefitted Amon, and he and Hill swapped places three times before Amon retired on lap 95. Hulme was now third, but a lap back, so out of contention. Clark had an upper suspension link fail with two laps left. Amazingly, he limped home ahead of the troubled Lotus of Hill, so Hulme was very nearly gifted this race. Surtees' Honda rose from 11th to sixth on lap 11, before pitting on lap 12, dropping to the very back. He was sixth when he stopped, with 12 laps left. But for the electrical troubles, Monza may have been repeated.

1st	J Clark (W)	Lotus 49-Cosworth in 2h-03m-13.2s	120.95
2nd	G Hill (W)	Lotus 49-Cosworth	6.3s
3rd	D Hulme (W)	Brabham BT24-Repco	1 lap
F lap	G Hill (W)	Lotus 49-Cosworth in 1m-06.00s	125.46r

Championship positions:
D Hulme 47; J Brabham 42; J Clark 32.

Despite the debut success of the brilliant DFV-powered Lotus 49 at Zandvoort, the Championship had finally come to a showdown between the Brabham-Repco pilots. Brabham had to drop his fifth place points from the previous round, so only a win would do, with Denny lower than fourth. How close Jack Brabham came to repeating 1966.

✱✱✱ (WC9) VI Gran Premio de Mexico (Mexico City)

65 laps of 3.107 miles = 201.9 miles.
21 entries – 19 started – 12 finished.
Front row: J Clark – 1m-47.56s (103.99mph); C Amon 0.48s.
Row two: D Gurney 0.54s; G Hill 1.18s.

22-OCT: Clark hesitated at the start, and Dan Gurney punctured his radiator on Clark's exhaust. By lap three Jim Clark had passed Amon and then Hill to lead, and pulled away to win despite an inoperative clutch! Hill retired on lap 18 with drive failure and water loss. Amon held second place ahead of Brabham and Hulme, but stopped with three laps to go with fuel shortage. Hulme had been one place behind Brabham since lap 13, after passing Mexican Moises Solana, an extra to the Lotus team for this race who retired from sixth. Denny Hulme just had to finish to become World Champion in only his second full F1 season.

1st	J Clark (W)	Lotus 49-Cosworth in 1h-59m-28.7s	101.41
2nd	J Brabham (W)	Brabham BT24-Repco	1m-25s
3rd	D Hulme (W)	Brabham BT24-Repco	1 lap
F lap	J Clark (W)	Lotus 49-Cosworth in 1m-48.13s	103.44r

Championship positions:
D Hulme (WC) 51; J Brabham 46; J Clark 41.

Gran Premio de España (Jarama)

60 laps of 2.115 miles = 126.9 miles.
6 F1 entries – 6 started – 4 finished.
Front row: J Clark – 1m-28.2s (86.33mph); G Hill 1.5s;
J Stewart 1.5s.

12-NOV: This was a trial for the first Championship race here in 1968. In truth, it wasn't a serious race, as the F1 field was Team Lotus, a single previous year's car for Brabham, and an old Ferrari for Andrea de Adamich. Two F2 Lola-BMWs of Siffert and Hahne had 2-litre engines, so were technically F1 cars – just 6 F1 starters. The rest were ballasted F2 cars to conform to the higher weight limit of F1, so they were handicapped further! Siffert retired from third on lap 48, to the benefit of Brabham. The Clark, Hill, Brabham result had been almost a formality. No better than the Oulton Park Gold Cup, in truth.

1st	J Clark (W)	Lotus 49-Cosworth in 1h-31m-10.1s	83.60
2nd	G Hill (W)	Lotus 49-Cosworth	15.2s
F lap	J Clark (W)	Lotus 49-Cosworth in 1m-28.8s	85.76

Winners of the 15 graded F1 races of 1967 – quantity & quality of success

5 wins	J Clark (4A, D)	5 wins	Brabham-Repco (4A, C); Lotus-Cosworth (4A, D)
3 wins	J Brabham (2A, C)	2 wins	Eagle-Weslake (2A)
2 wins	D Hulme (2A) D Gurney (2A)	1 win	Cooper-Maserati (A); Honda (A); Ferrari (C)
1 win	P Rodriguez (A) J Surtees (A) M Parkes (C)		

1967 seasonal review

Seventeen Formula One races heralded a decent season, with 11 Championship rounds for the first time. But the Siracuse GP was a farce, the Oulton Park Gold Cup turned out to be an F1 non-event, and the Spanish GP little more than a trial race, so the race calendar for an F1 driver was still insufficient to satisfy a racer's appetite. The Tasman series and F2 made up the shortfall in single-seater racing for some of them, though. In fact, there was more scope for good racing in the new F2, with its 1600cc engine limit, and these cars proved quite capable of giving a strong showing when mixed with F1 cars. These events brought the calendar up to a mammoth 41 races for the big boys, beating the thirty-eight of 1952. The busiest man of the year was Jack Brabham, who missed two Tasman races, the Siracuse GP, and one F2 race – a total of 37 appearances! Are 21st century F1 pilots jealous?

Dan Gurney's Eagle was a popular winner at Brands Hatch, and he followed it up with a win at Spa, thus adding a new marque to the F1 'Hall of Fame.' Ferrari, however, had had a terrible year, getting relatively small crumbs, with its only win a less-than-standard Silverstone International Trophy. This 3-litre formula had been expected to be something of a gift for Ferrari, with its expertise through endurance sports car racing, but it had wasted the opportunity by favouring that very thing over Formula One. The death of Bandini was devastating, of course, and compounded Ferrari's loss of John Surtees the year before due to Ferrari internal politics. By the end of this year, Surtees had produced victories in both of the marques he had driven for since leaving Ferrari.

1967 Championship review

The South African GP was restored to Championship status, and a newcomer was the Canadian GP, so, at last, the title race would occupy more than ten rounds. The year began with a repeat win for the Cooper-Maserati in South Africa, but that was soon shown to be a swansong for a team in decline again. Even after twelve months since the introduction of the 3-litre Formula 1, Team Lotus had still not got a full capacity engine, and was using the 2-litre Climax or BRM units. That situation was to change dramatically at the third round with an engine that changed the course of Formula One history! The wonderful 'bolt-on' Ford Cosworth DFV: the first 3-litre engine to have over 400bhp. The Brabham team continued to use the Repco engine, now uprated, and, by the end of the season, thanks to Lotus unreliability, were battling it out between themselves for the title, taking the chase to the final round. However, no less than three other drivers lost points sufficient to have won the Championship. Of those, Gurney and Hill finished the year as low as seventh and eighth places respectively! Hill had lost four rounds from the lead, almost as many points as Denny Hulme had accumulated to take the title, with

Gurney and Clark close behind in the bad-luck stakes. Lotus had produced one of the greatest new designs in Grand Prix to date, then almost monopolised the art of losing while leading. The 'honours' turned out at four losses for Hill and five for Clark, though he finished two of those. Not until round ten, the American GP, was a race run without a lead having been lost to ill fortune! The finishing rate for the year being 47.9 per cent, so the Brabham-Repco team triumphed again, with a new worthy Champion in Denny Hulme, by virtue of speed and consistency. Jack Brabham, however, almost took a fourth Championship crown. It would be another 26 years before Alain Prost would achieve that – not forgetting that Fangio had won five. Despite Lotus' losses, the DFV engine was clearly the one to have the folowing year (if Ford would let you).

VISIT VELOCE ON THE WEB – WWW.VELOCE.CO.UK
All current books • New book news • Special offers • Gift vouchers • Forum

262

Chapter 27

1968

Power spread is a good thing

The world of Formula One had changed with the arrival of the Ford-based Cosworth DFV engine. The deal with Lotus for its exclusive use had ended, and now it was available to others, as was the V12 BRM engine. But Cosworth was not a constructor, so all customers would receive the latest engines. Would that apply to BRM's customers? Tyres again increased in width to cope with the 400+bhp now needed to be competitive, so speeds would rise markedly. The formula was very strong and secure, with plenty of teams, including the welcome addition of Engins Matra, the French Aerospace company. The Championship now had twelve rounds with the addition of Spain, but the first round, the South African GP on New Year's Day, was far too early for new cars, so the season still really opened with the extra races at Brands Hatch and Silverstone; these races still had real importance. The mid-season Oulton Park Gold Cup brought the F1 calendar up to 15 races. The eight-race Tasman series filled in the gap before Brands Hatch, and Ferrari had now become involved, adding more caché to the series' status. Ferrari was also involved in Formula Two, which was still attracting F1 drivers, and the F2 calendar now included a revived four-race 'Argentine Temporada' series finishing on 22nd of December. So, from 1st of January to 22nd of December this was the longest racing year ever for some drivers.

The constructors

The Brabham Racing team, on the back of its second Championship success, continued with Repco, and an all-new 32v V8 engine with a quoted 380bhp. Jack Brabham had signed Jochen Rindt to replace World Champion Denny Hulme.

McLaren Racing had acquired Denny Hulme to partner Bruce McLaren, and the new M7A would have Ford Cosworth DFV power, so McLaren was in a much stronger position than hitherto. This was now an all-New Zealand team. That such a small country could produce such a team is extraordinary.

Team Lotus was on a high, certain now that it had a really great car, which, with reliability, would produce a world title for Jim Clark or Graham Hill – a very formidable duo, with three titles already.

The name Engins Matra, a French aerospace company, was a newcomer to the ranks of constructor, and operated a two-pronged approach. Matra Sport was the Works team for Engins Matra, and used the MS11 car driven by Jean-Pierre Beltiose. Designed for its own V12 engine, the MS11 possessed an unforgettably beautiful sound. An all-French outfit was on the grid for the first time since Gordini, but with better funding – an understatement. Matra International, run from England by renowned team operator Ken Tyrrell, had produced the MS10 chassis to be powered by the Ford Cosworth DFV engine, Jackie Stewart being the regular driver. Using a different engine meant that it was regarded as a separate marque, so there would be no point accumulation, but Matra would have two chances of a Constructor's title.

BRM, still owned and entered by the Owen Racing Organisation, had a new chassis, the P126, soon to be joined by a similar P133. The H-16 idea had been defeated by the DFV engine solution, and the previous year's V12 was the 'new' engine. Pedro Rodriguez and Mike Spence were the drivers. However, neither could be considered to be of the very top flight yet, so a difficult year lay ahead.

Cooper Cars had the type 86B, using the BRM V12 engine, but wasn't able to attract a top-flight driver. No-one had a permanent seat. Ludovico Scarfiotti, Brian Redman,

Lucien Bianchi, Vic Elford, Frank Gardner seemed to be selected on a race-by-race basis. Cooper was in serious trouble.

Ferrari, after a tragic 1967, continued developing the 312. It had lost Bandini (fatally) and Parkes (injured) but retained Chris Amon, who had rescued it and saw what it needed in Jacky Ickx, with Derek Bell and Andrea deAdamich occasionally piloting a third car.

Honda continued with John Surtees and had a lightened chassis, the type 301. The V12 engine was said to have 430bhp now.

The one team in real trouble was AAR Eagle, which had concentrated a lot on American USAC racing, and the Weslake engine hadn't been developed. Dan Gurney would even drive for Brabham and McLaren at times.

The independents

RRC Walker Racing was supplied with the latest Lotus 49 for the popular Josef 'Seppi' Siffert.

Reg Parnell Racing closely liaised with BRM, which supplied it with two cars for Richard Attwood, Chris Irwin and Piers Courage to share.

The Grand Prix driver's diary of single-seater racing for 1968

1st January	F1 – **South African Grand Prix** (SA) at Kyalami – 203.5 miles
6th January	FT – New Zealand Grand Prix at Pukekohe (NZ) – 101.5 miles
13th January	FT – Levin International (NZ) – 92.3 miles
20th January	FT – Lady Wigram Trophy at Christchurch (NZ) – 102 miles
27th January	FT – Teretonga Trophy at Invercargill (NZ) – 96 miles
11th February	FT – 'Rothmans 100' at Surfers Paradise (Au) –100 miles
18th February	FT – Sydney Trophy at Warwick Farm (Au) – 101.2 miles
25th February	FT – Australian GP at Sandown Park (Au) – 106 miles
4th March	FT – South Pacific Trophy at Longford (Au) – 67.5 miles
17th March	F1 – 'Race of Champions' at Brands Hatch (UK) – 123.5 miles
31st March	F2 – Gran Premio de Barcelona at Montjuic (E) – 141.3 miles
7th April	F2 – Deutschland Trophäe at Hockenheim (D) – 168.3 miles
15th April	F2 – BARC '200' at Thruxton (GB) – 162.6 miles
21st April	F2 – Grand Prix de Pau (F) – 120 miles
21st April	F2 – Eifelrennen at S Nürburgring (D) – 144.4 miles
27th April	F1 – *Daily Express* International Trophy at Silverstone (UK) – 152.2 miles
28th April	F2 – Gran Premio de Madrid at Jarama (E) – 126.9 miles
5th May	F2 – Grote Prijs van Limborg at Zolder (B) – 124.8 miles
12th May	F1 – **Gran Premio de España** at Jarama (E) – 190.4 miles
26th May	**Monaco Grand Prix** (M) – 195.4 miles
3rd June	F2 – London Trophy at Crystal Palace (UK) – 155.7 miles
9th June	F1 – **Grand Prix de Belgique** at Spa Francorchamps (B) – 245.3 miles
16th June	F2 – Rhein-Pokalrennen at Hockenheim (D) – 124.2 miles
23rd June	F1 – **Grote Prijs van Nederland** at Zandvoort (N) – 234.5 miles
7th July	F1 – **Grand Prix de France** at Rouen (F) – 243.9 miles
14th July	F2 – Flugplatzrennen at Tulln-Langenlebarn (A) – 117.5 miles
20th July	F1 **British Grand Prix** at Brands Hatch (UK) – 197.5 miles
4th August	F1 – **Grosser Preis von Deutschland** at Nürburgring (D) –198.4 miles
17th August	F1 – International Gold Cup at Oulton Park (UK) – 107.1 miles
25th August	F2 – Gran Premio del Mediterraneo at Enna-Pergusa (I) – 149.1 miles
8th September	F1 – **Gran Premio d'Italia** at Monza (I) – 243 miles
15th September	F2 –Grand Prix de Reims (F) – 180.6 miles
22nd September	F1 – **Grand Prix of Canada** at Mont Tremblant (C) –238.5 miles
6th October	F1 – **United States Grand Prix** at Watkins Glen (US) – 248.4 miles
13th October	F2 – Preis von Baden-Wurttemberg at Hockenheim (D) – 126.5 miles
20th October	F2 – Grand Prix d'Albi (F) – 192.3 miles
27th October	F2 – Gran Premio di Roma at Vallelunga (I) – 155.1 miles
3rd November	F1 – **Gran Premio de Mexico** at Mexico City (Mx) – 201.9 miles
1st December	F2 – Gran Premio de YPS at Buenos Aires (Ag) – 148.5 miles
8th December	F2 – Gran Premio de Ciudad de Cordoba (Ag) – 139.3 miles
15th December	F2 – Gran Premio de Ciudad San Juan (Ag) – 140.5 miles
22nd December	F2 – Gran Premio de Argentine Airlines (Ag) – 131 miles

42 events of total race mileage = 6539 miles but 6419 miles max.

Events in bold are World Championship rounds – 80 per cent of F1 races run.

Formula Two dates are those in which FIA graded Formula One drivers competed.

Tasman Championship 1968

The series stuck to the 2.5-litre limit chosen in 1964 due to the preponderance of Climax four-cylinder engines, despite them no longer being competitive. 1967 had shown that a smaller capacity F1 engine (from three litres to 2.5) was a better bet than a stretched 1.5-litre F1 unit (up to 2070cc at BRM), so reduced size motors appeared from BRM as well as Repco, Alfa and Cosworth. That special engines and cars were produced just for a series of only eight races of half Grand Prix length, and which would be little used anywhere else, shows the the constructors' opinion of the usefulness of this Championship prior to the main F1 season.

Power-to-weight ratio was a significant factor on these medium-to-slow tracks, and the lightweight F2 car, with 1600cc and 220bhp, had surprised everyone the season before, in Graham Hill's hands, so a few of these appeared.

The best was in the hands of reigning F1 World Champion Denny Hulme, with the ex-Jochen Rindt Brabham F2 car, while Piers Courage had an F2 McLaren – a bit strange, as Hulme had joined McLaren in F1 now.

New Zealand had become a big player on the world stage, boasting the reigning Champion Denny Hulme, and Chris Amon was leader for Ferrari after the tragic loss of Bandini in May.

Ferrari entered the scene with an F2-based car for Amon, using a 2417cc V6 with almost 300bhp. This exact engine size had powered Mike Hawthorn to the Championship in 1958. Bruce McLaren had been entered in New Zealand by BRM, driving a smaller capacity V12. This was the prototype P126 for this year's F1 campaign, and Richard Attwood replaced McLaren in Australia. Pedro Rodriguez had signed for BRM for 1968, and would drive the whole series mostly in a P261 2070cc V8: last year's car. Perhaps the star car of the series was the Lotus 49T (T for Tasman) with a reduced V8 DFW. World Championship leader, after winning the South African Grand Prix, Jim Clark, would drive it. The full-size DFV had 410bhp, so the Tasman DFW engine would have around 350bhp. Graham Hill would join the team in Australia and it would be the team to beat – and spring a surprise in New Zealand. Jack Brabham would appear only twice, in Australia naturally, with his usual Repco power. So that's ten stars competing this year. The Alfa V8 mentioned earlier would power a Brabham BT23 for Frank Gardner, a very interesting prospect. A great season was in prospect.

✳ **New Zealand Grand Prix (Pukekohe)**

58 laps of 1.75 miles = 101.5 miles.
21 entered and started – 14 finished.

Front row: J Clark in 59.8s (105.35mph); C Amon 0.1s. Row two: P Rodriguez 1.2s; F Gardner 1.2s.

06-JAN: It was Amon leading Clark, Gardner, Rodriguez, Hulme and McLaren off the line, but Clark led at the end of lap one. The leading duo pulled away from Gardner, while McLaren dropped into the clutches of Courage because of his own clutch trouble. Rodriguez pitted, also with clutch bothers, so the order was Clark, Amon, Gardner, Hulme and Courage. Amon had started closing on Clark when, on lap 44, Clark's motor died. Hulme's F2 Brabham began to challenge Gardner's Brabham-Alfa, but on lapping a backmarker for the fourth time there was contact and both cars flew off the track, overturned and broke up. Hulme was unhurt but Brownlie had serious leg injuries. So the Amon/Ferrari combination looked a good idea.

1st C Amon (Ferrari 246T) in 59m-20.1s = 100.97mph
2nd F Gardner (Brabham BT23-AlfaV8) @ 36.7s
3rd P Courage (McLaren M4A-FVA) @ 1 lap
Fastest lap C Amon in 59.3s = 106.24mph

✳ **9th Levin International**

14 + 63 laps of 1.193 miles = 91.8 miles.
18 entries – 17 started – 10 finished.

Prelim front row: F Gardner in 46.5s (92.36mph); C Amon 0.4s. Row two: P Rodriguez 0.4s; J Clark 0.5s.

13-JAN: Hulme was without a car, but all the other visitors were here. After the heats it was Clark, Gardner and Amon at the front, with Rodriguez, McLaren and Courage behind, with both BRMs being V12s. Gardner led Clark and Amon at first from Rodriguez. Clark passed Gardner on lap seven but, on lap 14, ran off at the hairpin, resuming in fourth. Gardner's new lead lasted only a lap as he hit a bank and was out. Clark took second from Rodriguez, closed on Amon but clipped a kerb bending a radius rod. Two errors from Clark! Both BRMs retired, handing second to Courage. A repeat win for Amon put pressure on Clark now.

1st C Amon (Ferrari 246T) in 50m-40.2s = 89.00mph
2nd P Courage (McLaren M4A-FVA) @ 50.3s
3rd J Palmer (McLaren M4A-FVA) @ 2 laps
Fastest lap J Clark (Lotus 49T DFW) in 46.2s = 92.96mph

✳ **Lady Wigram Trophy (Christchurch)**

11-lap heats + 44 lap final of 2.318 miles = 127.5 miles.
19 entries – 18 started – 14 finished.

Prelim front row: J Clark in 1m-20.0s (104.31mph); C Amon 0.6s. Row two: D Hulme 0.8s; F Gardner 0.9s.

20-JAN: Team Lotus was now Gold Leaf Team Lotus as the team appeared in the colours of its sponsor – a first outside the USA. After the heats it was Clark, Amon and Courage at the front, with Hulme and Courage behind. Rodriguez's V8 BRM was next, ahead of McLaren's V12. Gardner made a poor start as Clark and Amon shot away, glued together. Hulme and Courage followed, and the race order remained that way. Gardner had recovered to fifth, but retired after eight laps. Rodriguez pitted, handing fifth to McLaren, and followed in sixth, but at least they had finished – BRM's showing very poor so far.

1st J Clark (Lotus 49T-DFW) in 59m-10.6s = 103.41mph
2nd C Amon (Ferrari 246T) @7.9s
3rd D Hulme (Brabham BT23-FVA) @ 1 lap
Fastest lap J Clark & C Amon in 1m-19.6s = 104.83mph

✷ Teretonga Trophy (Invercargill)
8 prelim + 60 laps of 1.6 miles = 108.8 miles.
18 started – 8 finished.
Front row: C Amon in 1m-01.0s (94.43mph); J Clark 0.0s; P Rodriguez 0.2s; F Gardner 0.2s.

27-JAN: The preliminary heat times didn't produce the grid the organisers wanted, as heats were run in differing conditions, so practice times were used. Amon wasted his pole and was sixth behind Clark, Gardner, McLaren, Courage and Rodriguez, with Hulme and Palmer following after a lap. Amon was third on lap three and took Gardner on lap seven, but soon Clark was ten seconds ahead. Rain started to fall on lap 16. Rodriguez retired on lap 22, Amon and Gardner spun, so now McLaren was second. Lap 53 saw the defining moment when Clark slid onto the infield after a bump, losing the car's nose. BRM won after a poor start to the series, and McLaren won here for the fifth time.

1st B McLaren (BRM P126 V12) in 1h-08m-17.9s = 84.33mph
2nd J Clark (Lotus 49T-DFW) @ 10.6s
3rd F Gardner (Brabham BT23-Alfa V8) @ 51.6s
Fastest lap J Clark in 1m-01.0s = 94.43mph

✷ 'Rothman's 100' (Surfer's Paradise)
50 laps of 2.0 miles = 100.0 miles.
14 started – 10 finished.
Front row: C Amon in 1m-09.7s (103.30mph); J Clark 0.2s; G Hill 0.6s.

11-FEB: Clark was joined by Graham Hill, and Richard Attwood joined Rodriguez at BRM. Amon's Ferrari now had four-valve heads. This was the first time that the Tasman series had visited this track. Clark, Amon, Courage and Hill was the early order, but Courage's engine fluffed, dropping him to seventh, behind Hill, Gardner, Rodriguez, and Leo Geoghegan's Lotus-Repco V8. On lap ten Geoghegan and Courage deposed Gardner, but, at the front, Clark slid wide and Amon was through – not for long, though, as Clark recovered to pass on the straight. Slipstreaming caused the Ferrari to overheat, and Amon fell back on lap 22 and

Rodriguez pitted. Courage had taken Hill so was now third, but his motor fluffed and he spun, dropping him behind Geoghegan, but he was soon chasing Hill. Amon's great drive ended on lap 24, and Courage's super drive almost caught Hill.

1st J Clark (Lotus 49T-DFW) in1h-00m-22.2s = 99.39mph
2nd G Hill (Lotus 49-DFW) @ 6.4s
3rd P Courage (McLaren M4A-FVA) @ 7.9s
Fastest lap C Amon (Ferrari 246 V6) in 1m-11.1s = 101.27mph

✷ Warwick Farm '100'
45 laps of 2.25 miles = 101.25 miles.
16 started – 8 finished.
Front row: J Clark in 1m-27.4s (92.68mph); G Hill 0.6s; C Amon 0.8s.

18-FEB: Brabham had joined the party, but the order was Clark, Hill and Amon on the front row, with Courage and Hulme on row two, with their very zippy F2 cars. Grid order prevailed for a few laps, then Gardner headed Hulme on lap seven, with Brabham recovering from a bad start. Soon he passed Hulme but pitted for oil …" That's clear it's Brabham now and lost over a lap. Hulme took Gardner for fifth on lap 28, and was soon up to Amon, who had spun having let Courage through. Hill was pressured by Courage, and Hulme was giving Amon bother, but neither prevailed. Rodriguez's V8 BRM was sixth, ahead of Brabham, who'd made a lap record in his pursuit.

1st J Clark (Lotus 49T-DFW) in 1h-08m-17.2s = 88.96mph
2nd G Hill (Lotus 49-DFW) @ 11.7s
3rd P Courage (McLaren M4A-FVA) @ 20.0s
Fastest lap J Brabham (Brabham BT21-Repco) in 1m-29.0s = 91.01mph

✷ Australian Grand Prix (Sandown Park)
55 laps of 1.928 miles = 106.0 miles.
13 started – 9 finished.
Front row: J Brabham in 1m-06.7s (104.06mph); C Amon 0.1s; J Clark 0.7s.

25-FEB: Brabham, Amon and Clark, separated by 0.2s, comprised the front row, with Geoghegan and Hill behind. Brabham wasted his start, and was fifth behind Clark, Amon, Gardner and Hill after a lap. By lap eight, though, Brabham was third, and closing on the Clark/Amon scrap. Gardner and Hill had swapped places twice and repeated it by lap 19. A couple of laps later, Brabham's engine seized, leaving the leading four in two tremendous battles. Amon led at the line twice, but just failed at the end, and, a minute back, Hill beat Gardner by 0.2 seconds. A great race by three of the world's great drivers, and Gardner proving very worthy of being there.

1st J Clark (Lotus 49T-DFW) in 1h-02m-40.4s = 101.52mph

2nd C Amon (Ferrari 246 V6) @ 0.1s 3rd G Hill (Lotus 49-DFW) @ 59.3s

Fastest lap C Amon (Ferrari 246 V6) in 1m-07.0s = 103.59mph

✳ South Pacific Trophy (Longford)

15 laps of 4.5 miles = 67.5 miles.
9 started final – 6 finished.

Front row: J Clark in 2m-12.8s (121.99mph); G Hill 0.8s; C Amon 1.0s.

04-MAR: Atrocious conditions caused the race to be shortened. Clark, Rodriguez, Gardner, Courage, Hill, Attwood and Amon, after his trip down an escape road, was the order after a lap. Courage lived up to his name as he took the lead on lap four. Within a lap he had ten seconds on Gardner, Clark, Rodriguez, Attwood, Amon and Hill. Courage had narrow section tyres which were clearly perfect, as was the F2 car in these conditions. Rodriguez just took Gardner near the end from Attwood, Clark, Hill and Amon. Only Amon could have taken the Championship away from Clark, and it was clear that Clark didn't have to worry.

1st P Courage (McLaren M4A-FVA) in 41m-47.5s = 96.91mph

2nd P Rodriguez (BRM P261 V8) @ 55.9s

3rd F Gardner (Brabham BT23-Alfa) @ 56.5s

Fastest lap P Courage (McLaren M4A-FVA) in 2m-42.0s = 100.00mph

Tasman Champion:
1st Jim Clark (Lotus 49T-Cosworth DFW) – 44
2nd Chris Amon (Ferrari 246T) – 36
3rd Piers Courage (McLaren M4A-FVA) – 34

✳✳✳ (WC1) XIV South African Grand Prix (Kyalami)

80 laps of 2.550 miles = 204.0 miles.
25 entries – 23 started – 10 finished.

Front row: J Clark – 1m-21.6s (112.50mph); G Hill 1.0s; J Stewart 1.1s.

01-JAN: Being so early in the year, McLaren sent only Hulme's car, and BRM and Cooper each sent a new and old car – the Coopers for Scarfiotti and Redman, who had the new car. Brabham used the previous year's cars, too. However, a new name in Grand Prix – Matra – had arrived, and Stewart placed it on the front row (the front row was all Cosworth DFV powered). Stewart led the first lap from Clark, while Hill's poor start placed him behind Rindt, Surtees, Brabham and Amon. Clark led next time round, though, never to lose the lead, and Hill took Amon and Surtees, who had lost out to Brabham, for fifth. Before long Brabham had taken Rindt's third place, but dropped out with valve trouble soon after. Rindt then lost his regained third to

Hill, who made it a Lotus one-two by passing Stewart on lap 28. Twenty laps later Stewart was out with a connecting rod breakage. Surtees' Honda slowly dropped back and out of the running. Amon and Ickx's Ferraris ran fourth and fifth until Ickx retired, benefitting Hulme. All the top five then stayed put, but Beltoise's ballasted F2 Matra came through for the final point.

1st	J Clark (W)	Lotus 49-Cosworth in 1h-53m-56.6s	107.42
2nd	G Hill (W)	Lotus 49-Cosworth	25.3s
3rd	J Rindt (W)	Brabham BT24-Repco 740	30.4s
F lap	J Clark (W)	Lotus 49-Cosworth in 1m-23.7s	109.68r

✳✳ III 'Race Of Champions' (Brands Hatch)

50 laps of 2.46 miles = 123 miles.
21 entries – 14 started – 9 finished.

Front row: B McLaren – 1m-30.0s (98.40mph); M Spence (0.4s); J Stewart (1.0s)

17-MAR: This was really the first test for the 1968 cars, so the race had real significance. All teams entered, but the single entries from Brabham, Eagle and Honda weren't ready. Lotus had just one Type 49 for Hill, and Cooper one for Redman, yet Ferrari sent three cars. deAdamich's Ferrari, however, and Siffert's Rod Walker Lotus 49 both crashed and non-started. The race turned out to be all about the new constructor-driven McLaren, which led easily all the way. Spence's BRM P126 held second, but retired on lap 18. Stewart gave the Matra MS10 its debut, and was second on lap 23, but fell back with pedals fouling each other and needing attention! Hill ran fourth for ten laps when a driveshaft broke. Rodriguez was last away, but brilliantly fought through from 14th to second by half distance. Hulme had taken fourth from Amon's Ferrari, benefitting from Stewart's pedal problem which dropped him to sixth after a very necessary pit stop. Oddly, the previous year's F2 race speed wasn't bettered.

1st	B McLaren (W)	McLaren M7A-Cosworth in 1h-18m-53.4s	93.54
2nd	P Rodriguez (W)	BRM P133 V12	14.2s
3rd	D Hulme (W)	McLaren M7A-Cosworth	30.4s
F lap	B McLaren	McLaren M7A-Cosworth in 1m-31.6s	96.68r

II Deutschland Trophae (Hockenheim)

07-APR: Not a Formula One race, but a very significant and tragic event which shattered the racing world, and F1 in particular. Looking back, one has to ask why it was run?

Not just the extra race itself, but why such a lethal track as Hockenheim, with its long flat-out 'gentle' curves with no protection at all from the trees once the grass run-off area had been traversed, and which would be even more useless when wet. When Jim Clark's Lotus failed at the outbound curve on the damp track – believed to be due to a puncture – he stood virtually no chance of survival at all.

The yardstick by which all were measured was gone – and in his absolute prime.

✸✸ XX *Daily Express* International Trophy (Silverstone)

52 laps of 2.927 miles = 152.2 miles.
19 entries – 14 started – 7 finished.
Front row: D Hulme – 1m-24.3s (125.00mph); M Spence 0.6s; B McLaren 0.8s; P Rodriguez 1.0s.

25-APR: The racing world was still reeling from the loss of Jim Clark two weeks earlier. The Brabhams were still not ready, and Stewart's Matra was absent, so a similar field as at Brands came to Silverstone, and the McLarens continued to give the opposition plenty of worry. Now it was Frank Gardner's turn in a Cooper-BRM, but he was three seconds off the pace. McLaren led away but lost the lead to Spence on lap five, retook it, but lost again on lap 18 to teammate Hulme, who had fought back from seventh after a stone smashed his goggles. Hill came from sixth on lap one to second on lap eight, only to retire with fuel pipe trouble. Spence retired from second on lap 40, so now it was a McLaren one-two. Goggle strap breakage spoilt Amon's challenge to McLaren while he put on a spare pair, but he and Ickx's Ferraris were third and fourth. Race and lap records were smashed.

1st	D Hulme (W)	McLaren M7A-Cosworth 1h-14m-44.8s	122.18
2nd	B McLaren (W)	McLaren M7A-Cosworth	10.9s
3rd	C Amon (W)	Ferrari 312	16.5s
F lap	C Amon	Ferrari 312 in 1m-25.1s	123.82r

✸✸✸ (WC2) Gran Premio d'España (Jarama)

90 laps of 2.115 miles = 190.4 miles.
21 entries – 13 started – 5 finished.
Front row: C Amon – 1m-27.9s (86.63mph); P Rodriguez 0.2s; D Hulme 0.4s.

12-MAY: This was the first Championship race since Jim Clark died, and, to compound the misery, Mike Spence had been killed five days earlier at Indianapolis in a Lotus turbine. Hill has the sole Lotus, and Rodriguez the only BRM. Jackie Stewart had injured his hand a week earlier in F2 here, so Matra relied on Beltoise, making his GP debut in an F1 car. Non-arrivals and non-starters had reduced the field to less

than Monaco size. First lap order was Rodriguez, Beltoise and Amon, with Hill back in seventh. Lap 12 saw Beltoise lead, but soon oil smoke spoiled his race as he pitted to cure the leak. Amon led lap 16 from Rodriguez, but, 11 laps later, it was Hill chasing him from some distance as Rodriguez crashed. Lap 57 saw Amon's famous bad luck begin, retiring with fuel pump trouble. Hill won this attritional race, with Surtees and McLaren losing third in quick succession. Beltoise salvaged fifth eight, laps behind Scarfiotti's Cooper-BRM. He and teammate Redman had been on the back row, but had survived. Beltoise had won the F2 race here the week before, with a fastest lap 0.1 seconds better – as was the race speed.

1st	G Hill (W)	Lotus 49-Cosworth 2h-15m-20.1s	84.40
2nd	D Hulme (W)	McLaren M7A-Cosworth	15.9s
3rd	B Redman (W)	Cooper T86B-BRM	1 lap
F lap	JP Beltoise (MI)	Matra MS10-Cosworth in 1m-28.3s	86.23

Championship positions:
G Hill 15; J Clark 9; D Hulme 8.

✸✸✸ (WC3) XXVI Grand Prix de Monaco (Monte Carlo)

80 laps of a 1.954-mile circuit = 156.3 miles.
21 entries – 16 qualified – 5 finished.
Front row: G Hill – 1m-28.2s (79.76mph); J Servos-Gavin 0.6s. Row two: J Siffert 0.6s; J Surtees 0.9s.

26-MAY: Ferrari withdrew due to safety issues following Bandini's accident. The race was now 80 laps – two hours' duration deemed long enough here – Bandini had crashed on lap 81 (fatigue, perhaps?). Jackie Oliver had taken on the impossible task of replacing Jim Clark, and the unfit Jackie Stewart was replaced by F2 star 'Johnny' Servos-Gavin. Lotus sowed the seeds of downforce on Hill's car, with small wings on the nose and upswept rear bodywork – the reason quite obvious. The F2 whizz-kid promptly joined the front row alongside his number one, though Hill with his new 'aids' hadn't matched Brabham's pole time of the year before. The whizz-kid stormed off to lead the first three laps, until a driveshaft could stand no more – he'd clipped the chicane on the first lap. He never led a Grand Prix again. Four crashes, added to mechanical carnage, left just five cars running at just 20 per cent distance: Hill, Attwood, Hulme, Bianchi and Scarfiotti – thankfully, they all finished. Attwood chased Hill very strongly and achieved a podium finish and a lap record for a private team – very rare. Denny Hulme lost third place and ten minutes having a driveshaft replaced. Scarfiotti was fourth so, surprisingly, once again both slow Cooper-BRMs scored points. Lotus had now won five Championship rounds running, and Graham Hill looked very strong, as did Lotus despite losing Jim Clark.

1st	G Hill (W)	Lotus 49B-Cosworth in 2h-00m-32.3s	77.82
2nd	R Attwood (RP)	BRM P126	2.2s
3rd	L Bianchi (W)	Cooper T86B-BRM	4 laps
F lap	R Attwood	BRM P126 in 1m-28.1s	79.85r

Championship positions:
G Hill 24; D Hulme 10; J Clark 9.

✳✳✳ (WC4) XXVIII Grand Prix de Belgique (Spa)

28 laps of an 8.761-mile circuit = 280.4 miles.
19 entries – 18 started – 8 finished.
Front row: C Amon – 3m-28.6s (151.20mph); J Stewart 3.7s; J Ickx 5.7s.

09-JUN: Lotus was awaiting a new car, so missed the dry spell which put it near the back. Redman replaced Scarfiotti who was at Rossfeld hill-climb, and this terrible year continued with news of his death there. Ferrari had joined the downforce exploration with a small, gearbox-mounted wing. Amon took the 'Jim Clark role' and was on pole by quite a margin. He led Surtees' Honda for a lap and chased hard for six more but retired with a holed radiator. Surtees followed suit three laps later. Now it was Hulme and Stewart battling for seven laps, the lead changing three times before Hulme's halfshaft failed. McLaren and Rodriguez took up the chase, now of Stewart's Matra. A lap to go and Stewart pitted for fuel and, unlike Brabham in '64, there was some. But his final lap was disallowed for excess time so he was fourth. Bruce McLaren had drawn clear of Rodriguez so he won without knowing of Stewart's pit stop, so had a pleasant surprise on returning to the pits. McLaren was the third person to win driving a car of his own making, thus launching a magnificent and still expanding record. Redman's Cooper broke a wishbone, and also his arm in the ensuing crash. Oliver's Lotus was classified fifth, despite driveshaft failure. Bianchi's Cooper-BRM rolled in two laps down but in sixth place. Yet again in the points.

1st	B McLaren (W)	McLaren M7A-Cosworth in 1h-40m-02.1s	147.14
2nd	P Rodriguez (W)	BRM P133	12.1s
3rd	J Ickx (W)	Ferrari 312	39.6s
F lap	J Surtees (W)	Honda RA301 in 3m-30.5s	149.84r

Championship positions:
G Hill 24; D Hulme10; J Clark 9.

✳✳✳ (WC5) XVII Grote Prijs van Nederland (Zandvoort)

90 laps of a 2.605-mile circuit = 208.4 miles.
20 entries – 19 started – 10 finished.
Front row: C Amon – 1m-23.54s (112.28mph); J Rindt 0.26s; G Hill 0.30s.

23-JUN: Gurney's Eagle team was short of engines so Brabham offered a drive for him. What amazingly different times then! The regular drivers, Rindt and Brabham were second and fourth on the grid, so their poor year looked to improve. However, on the very wet track it was Hill and Stewart who led Rindt, Amon and Ickx. Rindt dropped five places, while the well-shod Beltoise amazingly climbed from 16th grid slot to third in four laps! Stewart had taken Hill at that point and, on lap 11, Beltoise followed suit. A Matra one-two was upset on lap 23 when Beltoise pitted after a spin due to throttle slides sticking. He lost five places, but was third again after just ten laps. It took him 17 laps to pass Hill for a second time, and Rodriguez helped himself to Hill's third place on lap 61. Ickx was handed fourth by Hill's crash on lap 81. While many were losing their heads in the awful conditions, a steady Silvio Moser kept his and made fifth place ahead of Amon. A great result in a private two year-old Brabham.

1st	J Stewart (MI)	Matra MS10-Cosworth in 2h-46m-11.26s	84.66
2nd	JP Beltoise (W)	Matra MS11-V12	1m-34s
3rd	P Rodriguez (W)	BRM P133	1 lap
F lap	JP Beltoise (W)	Matra-MS11-V12 in 1m-45.91s	88.56

Championship positions:
G Hill 24; J Stewart 12; P Rodriguez and D Hulme 10.

It was now becoming apparent that the new breed of wide tyres was more unsuitable to wet weather than those of a few years earlier. Speeds would now drop by over 20 per cent quite quickly, whereas 12 to 15 per cent had been more normal. Weather forecasting would play a bigger part in racing than had ever been necessary before.

✳✳✳ (WC6) LIV Grand Prix de France (Rouen-les-Essarts)

60 laps of 4.065 miles = 243.9 miles.
18 entries – 17 started – 12 finished.
Front row: J Rindt – 1m-56.1s (126.05mph); J Stewart 1.2s; J Ickx 1.6s.

09-JUL: The race title had changed from the 'Grand Prix de l'ACF' with an organisational change. A complete surprise was the arrival of a revolutionary new air-cooled V8 Honda for 41 year-old Jo Schlesser to make his debut in a Formula One car. John Surtees felt it not race-worthy, but Honda's hierarchy in France wanted it to be seen. Team Lotus had added large high-mounted aerofoils attached directly to the suspension uprights. Jackie Oliver survived unhurt from a massive unexplained crash in practice. Yet another wet race and Ickx led off from Stewart, Rindt, Surtees and Rodriguez. Lap three saw the fourth death of a Formula One driver in just over three months* when the radical Honda crashed in a horrendous ball of flames – poor Jo Schlesser had no chance. Looking back, it seems callous for a race to continue with the track a sheet of flame. No-one queried it, though, as it was the accepted culture. Rindt punctured on debris and dropped to the back while Ickx held his lead. Rodriguez and Surtees passed him for a single lap after which he pulled away, Rodriguez losing second place at three-quarter distance and falling right back. Graham Hill took Stewart for fourth on lap 14, but a driveshaft failed. Vic Elford brought more points for Cooper in fourth place, two laps down. Ickx and Beltoise proved the worth of F2 talent!

* This was the first of those four 'monthly' deaths during Formula One activity – F2, Indianapolis and Hill-climbing being the others.

1st	J Ickx (W)	Ferrari 312 in 2h-25m-40.9s	100.45
2nd	J Surtees (W)	Honda RA301	1m-59s
3rd	J Stewart (MI)	Matra MS10-Cosworth	1 lap
F lap	P Rodriguez (W)	BRM P133 in 2m-11.5s	111.28

Championship positions:
G Hill 24; J Ickx and J Stewart 16.

✱✱✱ (WC7) XXIII British Grand Prix (Brands Hatch)
80 laps of 2.46 miles = 196.8 miles.
23 entries – 20 started – 8 finished.
Front row: G Hill – 1m-28.9s (99.62mph); J Oliver 0.5s; C Amon 0.6s.

20-JUL: Only BRM had eschewed wings now. The 'bar being raised' in the most literal fashion. Dan Gurney's Eagle was back on the grid for only the third time this year, and was just 1.1 second from pole time. This race was all about the three Lotuses, though – the Works cars and Rob Walker's entry for Siffert. Hill took the lead from Oliver after three laps, and handed it back on lap 26 when the driveshaft jinx reared its head again. Siffert and Amon ran like a tandem not far behind Oliver, and Amon passed Siffert for second from

laps 37 to 41 when Siffert regained it. This became the race lead when Oliver suffered the Lotus jinx. Siffert kept Amon at bay, with a little help from a lapped Jackie Stewart, until the end for one of the most popular wins for many a year. Not because Hill or Oliver were unpopular but the British love of the underdog was personified by privateer Rob Walker's racing for 'love of the sport,' and affection for Jo'Seppi' Siffert. This was the very last time such an outfit would triumph in Grand Prix racing. Did Rob Walker fit stronger driveshafts – Lotus going for lightness? Hulme, Surtees and Stewart completed the points scores. Surtees had continued unperturbed by the collapse of his fragile wing. An omen for the future?

1st	J Siffert (RW)	Lotus 49B-Cosworth in 2h-01m-20.3s	97.30
2nd	C Amon (W)	Ferrari 312	4.4s
3rd	J Ickx (W)	Ferrari 312	1 lap
F lap	J Siffert (RW)	Lotus 49B-Cosworth in 1m-29.7s	98.73r

Championship positions:
G Hill 24; J Ickx 20; J Stewart 17.

After Jim Clark's win in S Africa, and Graham Hill's morale boosting winning of the next two GPs, the wheels seem to have come off Lotus, as Hill had now failed to score at all in the last four races. He still led the Championship, though, as no-one else had put a set of points together. Seven rounds to date had been shared by six drivers.

✱✱✱ (WC8) XXX Grosse Preis von Deutschland (N Nürburgring)
14 laps of 14.173 miles = 198.4 miles.
22 entries – 20 starters – 14 finished.
Front row: J Ickx – 9m-04.0s (93.90mph); C Amon 10.9s; J Rindt 27.9s.

04-AUG: Ickx was on pole position by over ten seconds at the end of a very wet practice, in which, perhaps, few tried very hard. At the soggy start Hill burst through between the Ferraris, followed by Stewart from row three, but soon it was the Matra that led, and pulled out 15 seconds on the opening lap! Since that wasn't enough, he continued to do it untroubled on every lap! Hill, Amon, Rindt, Gurney, Ickx and Surtees followed, but Surtees stopped on lap two, and Gurney dropped back on lap three. Amon crashed on lap 12, having chased Hill strongly. Hill then spun on the same lap, losing a minute, but rejoined just in time to fend off Rindt. Stewart's win is the stuff of legend, in the manner of Clark's 1963 Belgian victory, and repeated his Dutch demonstration in June. A true regenmeister in the homeland of the expression. Rain is a strange thing in racing – the finishing rate was 70 per cent, whereas the annual average to date had been exactly 40 per cent. The more rain the better? Maybe not.

1st	J Stewart (MI)	Matra MS10-Cosworth in 2h-19m-03.2s	85.71
2nd	G Hill (W)	Lotus 49B-Cosworth	4m-03s
3rd	J Rindt (W)	Brabham BT 26-Repco	4m-09s
F lap	J Stewart (MI)	Matra MS10-Cosworth in 9m-36.0s	88.68

Championship positions:
G Hill 30; J Stewart 26; J Ickx 23.

✳✳ XV International Gold Cup (Oulton Park)

40 laps of 2.678 miles = 107.1 miles.
16 entries – 13 started – 6 finished.
Front row: G Hill – 1m-29.2s (108.09mph); J Stewart 0.6s; C Amon 0.8s.

17-AUG: After the previous year's non-event, this time most of the main protagonists of the year were there, plus a third Ferrari for Derek Bell, but no Honda. McLaren entered Hulme, but its Can-Am activities now clashed – and certainly paid more. *MotorSport* magazine dubbed it "Grand Prix in the North." None other than Fangio himself dropped the flag, and Stewart, Amon, Hill and Ickx led off. Amon soon lost second, but regained it on lap six with Hill's drive failure – Lotus still not coping with the extra grip given by the wings this year. Ickx's Ferrari and Brabham battled over the following positions, but each retired at half distance. Jackie Oliver had split them just before this, and was a minute ahead of Rodriguez' BRM at the finish. Rindt, ninth on the grid, had never been in the hunt, retiring from sixth on lap 13. Bell had been with Rodriguez until pitting, stuck in fourth gear. Amon was drifting and sliding the Ferrari wonderfully, but Stewart kept him at bay. A very good race indeed.

1st	J Stewart (MI)	Matra MS10-Cosworth in 1h-00m-39.0s	105.98
2nd	C Amon (W)	Ferrari 312	4.6s
3rd	J Oliver (W)	Lotus 49B-Cosworth	49.6s
F lap	Stewart/Amon	Matra-Cosworth/Ferrari in 1m-30.0s	107.13r

✳✳✳ (WC9) XXXVIII Gran Premio d'Italia (Monza)

68 laps of a 3.573-mile circuit = 243.0 miles.
27 entries – 20 started – 6 finished.

Front row: J Surtees – 1m-26.07s (149.44mph); B McLaren 0.04s; C Amon 0.14s.

08-SEP: Lotus entered Mario Andretti and BRM Bobby Unser, but both abandoned Friday practice for a USAC event, which disqualified them, as a 'no race within 24 hours' rule had been implemented by the FIA. There was no consensus on wings on this superfast circuit, so some ran 'naked.' John Surtees claimed the first ever pole position for Honda, by a whisker, from McLaren, who then led the first six laps. Surtees held it for a lap, but was then taken out by a spinning Amon. Stewart, Siffert, Hulme and McLaren did the usual Monza slip-streaming exercise till lap 34 when McLaren retired. Ickx was now fourth, ahead of Servos-Gavin. Stewart retired on lap 42, having lost the lead to Hulme and second to Siffert. This brilliant privateer effort ended on lap 58 leaving Ickx an easy second, but he pitted for fuel on lap 62 emerging right behind Servos-Gavin to fight to the bitter end. To the eye it looked as though Servos-Gavin had won the GP, as winner Hulme was right behind the duo, but he was a lap ahead. Servos-G did win the race for runner-up spot a lap later, though. The World Championship was now wide open.

1st	D Hulme (W)	McLaren M7A-Cosworth in 1h-40m-14.8s	145.41
2nd	J Servos-Gavin (MI)	Matra MS10-Cosworth	1m-28.4s
3rd	J Ickx (W)	Ferrari 312	1m-28.6s
F lap	J Oliver (W)	Lotus 49B-Cosworth in 1m-26.5s	148.70r

Championship positions:
G Hill 30; J Ickx 27; J Stewart 26.

✳✳✳ (WC10) 2nd Grand Prix of Canada (Mont Tremblant)

90 laps of 2.65 miles = 238.5 miles.
23 entries – 20 started – 6 finished.
Front row: J Rindt – 1m-33.8s (101.71mph); C Amon 0.0s; J Siffert 0.7s.

22-SEP: Disaster befell Ickx in practice when a stuck throttle sent him into the barriers, causing a broken leg and ending his Championship hopes. Rindt, Amon and Siffert were the front row, but it was Amon, Siffert and Rindt for 19 laps, then Siffert stopped with oil loss. Gurney, whose F1 Eagle enterprise was now dormant, was driving for McLaren and holding fourth until passed by Hill on lap 13. This became third when Siffert stopped, and second when Rindt retired. Hill was worried about the rear end, and was unable to hold off Hulme and Mclaren. He stopped for a check, losing out to Rodriguez and Servoz-Gavin. The latter spun off a lap before Amon, who'd led all 72 laps, retired with transmission trouble; he'd been clutchless since lap 12! Hill nursed his car home in fourth, and discovered that the top engine mounts had broken, the car flexing in the middle!

1st	D Hulme (W)	McLaren M7A-Cosworth in 2h-27m-11.2s	97.22
2nd	B McLaren (W)	McLaren M7A-Cosworth	1 lap
3rd	P Rodriguez (W)	BRM P133	2 laps
F lap	J Siffert (RW)	Lotus 49B-Cosworth in 1m-35.1s	100.32r

Championship positions:
G Hill and D Hulme 33; J Stewart and J Ickx 27.

✳✳✳ (WC11) 11th United States Grand Prix (Watkins Glen)
108 laps of 2.30 miles = 248.4 miles.
21 entries – 20 started – 6 finished.
Front row: M Andretti – 1m-04.20s (128.97mph); J Stewart 0.07s. Row two: G Hill 0.08s; C Amon 0.17s.
06-OCT: Lotus added an American to its team – a good idea. Oliver non-started after a crash, but new teammate Mario Andretti made his GP debut, and promptly took pole. He led away, but Stewart led lap one and all the rest. Hill soon discovered that his steering wheel moved forward under braking, and his hands fouled the switches! Amon easily passed him for third. Hulme and Gurney (McLaren) followed. Andretti's car's nose started scraping the track: a mount had broken, and he pitted on lap 13. Amon had spun to ninth on lap ten, so Hill, coping with his problem, was now chasing Stewart. Hulme spun on oil and pitted for brake pipe repairs, now out of the picture. Surtees had come through and took Gurney's third spot from lap 26 to 32. Gurney retook third, but a slow puncture gave Surtees the place back with a lap to go. Siffert and McLaren were fifth and sixth.

1st	J Stewart (MI)	Matra MS10-Cosworth in 1h-59m-20.29s	124.89
2nd	G Hill (W)	Lotus 49B-Cosworth	6.3s
3rd	J Surtees (W)	Honda RA301	1 lap
F lap	J Stewart (MI)	Matra MS10-Cosworth in 1m-05.22s	126.96r

Championship positions:
G Hill 39; J Stewart 36; D Hulme 33.

As per the previous year, the Championship has gone down to the final round, but it was a three-way battle this year. Hulme had to win to stand any chance. Stewart had more wins than

Hill, so third with Hill sixth, or second with Hill fourth would do.

✳✳✳ (WC12) VII Gran Premio de Mexico (Mexico City)
65 laps of 3.107 miles = 201.9 miles.
21 entries – 19 started – 11 finished.
Front row: J Siffert – 1m-45.22s (106.30mph); C Amon 0.40s. Row two: G Hill 0.79s; D Hulme 0.82.
03-NOV: Moses Solana replaced Andretti for this race, so Lotus had three cars, but it was the non-Works Lotus on pole! When did that last happen? Solana made a poor start, and was seventh on lap one, behind Hill, Surtees, Stewart, Amon, Hulme and Rindt, who promptly retired. On lap six, though, the order was Stewart, Hill, Siffert, Hulme, Surtees, Brabham. Surtees' water pump packed up and he retired on lap 14. Hill regained the lead, while Siffert passed Stewart and then led the race on lap 22, but his heroism lasted just two laps; throttle trouble. Hulme had crashed due to a broken damper, so Hill just had to stay ahead of Stewart. Siffert's problem had put Dan Gurney's McLaren into third, but a wishbone broke, a lap later. Hill's Championship was secured on lap 50, when Stewart lost places with low fuel pressure.

1st	G Hill (W)	Lotus 49B-Cosworth in 1h-56m-43.95s	103.80
2nd	B McLaren (W)	McLaren M7A-Cosworth	1m-19s
3rd	J Oliver (W)	Lotus 49B-Cosworth	1m-41s
F lap	J Siffert (RW)	Lotus 49B-Cosworth in 1m-44.23s	107.31r

Championship positions:
G Hill (WC) 48; J Stewart 36; D Hulme 33.

Winners of the 15 F1 races of 1968 – quantity & quality of success

4 wins	J Stewart (3A, B)	5 wins	Lotus-Cosworth (5A); McLaren-Cosworth (3A, 2B)
3 wins	G Hill (3A) D Hulme (2A, B)	4 wins	Matra-Cosworth (3A ,B)
2 wins	B McLaren (A, B)	1 win	Ferrari (A)
1 win	J Clark (A) J Siffert (A) J Ickx (A)		

1968 seasonal review
Perhaps more change happened to Formula One this year than any other before or since – and none of it predictable. The worst was the dreadful accident to the fastest and safest

driver of the era: Jim Clark. The true yardstick had gone. He had taken over that mantle from Stirling Moss who had done the same on Juan Fangio's retirement. No-one would claim that status for many years – perhaps not until Ayrton Senna 20 years later. Clark's death in a Formula Two race, in hindsight, highlights the added danger faced those days in competing so frequently in an already potentially lethal sport. The added losses of Mike Spence at Indianapolis, Ludovico Scarfiotti at a hill climb and Jo Schlesser in F1, by early July made a lot of people take stock – particularly Jackie Stewart.

It was actually in the third race of the Tasman Series, the 'Lady Wigram Trophy,' that the racing world first saw the livery of the Gold Leaf Team Lotus cars – another Lotus introduction that changed racing forever – but no-one else followed suit with a change of livery for a couple of years. There were some mild reactions to the abandonment of the national racing colour at first, but it was fait accompli, as racing colours were not mandatory. In any case, everyone knew where each marque was from, and some vehicles were not entirely from a single nation: Cooper-Maserati and now Matra-Cosworth, for example. Matra had proved as serious a competitor in Formula One as it had in Formula Two, with four wins, thanks, to some degree, to Ken Tyrrell's organisational ability, and he was now a major F1 entrant. Four nations were now chasing the spoils (Eagle had finished), but Ferrari had to up its game, as it was no longer 'all about engines,' which was how Enzo Ferrari tended to see things, though the Cosworth engine was now ubiquitous: only a single Ferrari win stopping total Cosworth domination.

As inferred above, this was the year 'wings took off,' so to speak, and it was quickly realised that aerodynamically created downforce (weightless weight) was now the prime factor in reducing track times. The first manifestation was at Monaco, where Lotus had 40cm long inverted aerofoils either side of the nose, and an upswept engine cover. For Belgium, Ferrari mounted a wing half the width of the car well above the gearbox on Amon's car, but no significant front wings. It was in France where the wings went skyward on the Lotuses, became full width and mounted directly on the suspension uprights. Now things were serious. As with all things F1,

nothing was too heavy, and the wing mounting struts looked very fragile. Trouble was that some were just as fragile as they looked; the wing on Surtees' car collapsed at Brands Hatch. By Canada, these elevated wings appeared also on the front suspension on Brabhams, and looked, I thought, dangerous if one collapsed onto the driver – none did. The fundamentals of design and the financial structure of Formula One were now changing.

1968 Championship review

The Championship began with a win for Jim Clark – his Championship record breaking 25th, and, sadly, last. Given the safety and frequency of today's racing, he would probably have more than doubled that. His total Formula One win record, though, was 44 – standing for 25 years until broken by Alain Prost. After April 7th, Graham Hill 'stepped-up-to-the-plate' wonderfully, with victories in the next two rounds, and led the battle throughout, despite not scoring again for five rounds, and not winning again until the final crucial three-way shoot-out.

Despite supply of the Ford-Cosworth engine to any team, the finishing rate this year was an all-time low of 40.7 per cent. Lotus, particularly, suffered losses due to transmissions, notwithstanding extra forces created throughout the system by the wings. Once solved, Lotus began scoring again. Cooper picked up some crumbs due to others' retirements, and scored five times in the first four rounds, but the truth was that it was outclassed, and this was its final year in Formula One. Brabham had an awful year, having stayed with Repco a year too long, and scored only three times. It must have regretted not joining the Cosworth-powered squad.

Eagle had broken with Weslake and concentrated on USAC racing in America, so never gave a serious effort in F1 this year. It would not be seen again. Matra, however, nearly provided the car for a new Champion. If Stewart hadn't damaged his hand in an F2 race, would he have beaten Hill? The unluckiest was Chris Amon, down in tenth place at the season's end. His 38 lost points, including two lost wins, was the worst of anyone. This proves that not only could he have been a regular Grand Prix winner, but he was Champion quality as well.

VISIT VELOCE ON THE WEB – WWW.VELOCE.CO.UK
All current books • New book news • Special offers • Gift vouchers • Forum

273

Chapter 28

1969

More Cosworth power, yet fewer cars

The new season opened without Honda, which had given up; Eagle, which had left Formula One to concentrate solely in the USA; and Cooper, unable to find sponsorship. The latter was perhaps the most missed, as it was Cooper who had pioneered the rear-engine revolution so successfully, yet somehow never seemed to possess the technical facility to capitalise on the march it had stolen on its rivals in 1959. The Championship-winning car of 1960 had been a swift and effective reaction to Lotus' Type 18, yet Charles Cooper had been reluctant to keep up, once saying "Why change? We're winnin' aren't we?" This must have put the seed into Jack Brabham's mind to go-it-alone. Without him Cooper's technical know-how was damaged. Honda was in Formula One to sell cars in Europe, but success hadn't materialised as it had in motorcycle racing, where the engine was a greater part of the technical equation.

Matra had shelved its self-built engine in favour of the Cosworth, Ken Tyrrell running the whole show. Brabham had abandoned the Repco engine, which was never going to compete with the Cosworth unit, but one has to admire the team's hitherto patriotism. So now only Ferrari and BRM V12s provided any competition (and the best sound) to the Ford Cosworth. Without them there would be no need for Cosworth to develop the engine, except for reliability – so three cheers for Ferrari and BRM and their music. Thanks to this, power levels had increased to about 430bhp.

The start of the season was less intense than the year before, with the South African GP moving to March, after the Tasman Championship, which itself had dropped the race at Longford (the only one in Tasmania). No Belgian GP took place this year, principally due to safety considerations, thus reducing the Championship rounds to 11. The same three extra races took place in England, so 14 was the total number of Formula One

races on offer. With no Argentine Temporada, the total of F1, F2 and Tasman events involving contests between the elite F1 drivers reduced from 37 the previous year to 32.

The constructors

Team Lotus continued with the 49B and, naturally, the reigning World Champion Graham Hill was retained, but he was now teamed with Jochen Rindt.

McLaren Racing continued unchanged driver-wise with the founder Bruce McLaren and compatriot Denny Hulme, the 1967 World Champion. The car looked little changed but was now a full monocoque chassis designated M7C.

Engins Matra now used the team run by Ken Tyrrell as the sole entrant for the company, and provided a new more bulbous MS80 Cosworth DFV-powered car for Jackie Stewart and Jean-Pierre Beltoise, who had driven the Matra-engined car the year before. This was now the de facto Works team.

Brabham Racing had the Cosworth engine installed in its BT26 car driven by the boss Jack Brabham, who had signed Jacky Ickx to join him. He had also sold one of the latest cars to a new F1 entrant.

Scuderia Ferrari had, after another poor season, uprated its V12 engine, but little else, the car now designated the 312B, and the sole pilot being Chris Amon until joined by Pedro Rodriguez who arrived for the British GP. Le Mans, in particular, and other sports prototype racing took a lot of Ferrari's interest until then.

BRM was yet to win a race with a full three-litre-engined car, and now had a 48-valve engine for which 450bhp was claimed in a slightly revised car; the P139. A new driver line-up was forced on the team, and it was John Surtees and Jackie Oliver who joined. A revival of BRM fortunes would be popular with the public, but looked unlikely.

The independents

Reg Parnell Racing, run by his son Tim Parnell, was a customer of BRM. He employed Pedro Rodriguez, but this arrangement was wound up after Monaco when Tim Parnell replaced the architect of BRM's best years, Tony Rudd, who had gone to Lotus after disagreement. The BRM organisation was in some turmoil.

RRC Walker Racing continued to enter Jo Siffert in its Lotus 49B, and, following success in the British GP, would always be considered a significant threat.

Frank Williams Racing was the new F1 entrant mentioned above, running a new Brabham BT26 for his protégé, Piers Courage, who had driven so well in the Tasman Series.

The pool of top teams and drivers had reduced to just six marques and 14 drivers, from nearly twenty the year before, so Formula One was looking a bit shaky. Surely this would improve with a ready engine supply for any new constructor.

The Grand Prix driver's diary of single-seater racing for 1969

4th January	Tas – New Zealand Grand Prix at Pukekohe (NZ) – 101.5 miles
11th January	Tas – Levin International (NZ) – 75 miles
18th January	Tas – Lady Wigram Trophy at Christchurch (NZ) – 100.6 miles
25th January	Tas –Teretonga Trophy at Invercargill (NZ) – 99.2 miles
2nd February	Tas – Australian GP at Lakeside (Au) – 99.9 miles
9th February	Tas – Warwick Farm'100' (Au) – 101.2 miles
16th February	Tas – International '100' at Sandown Park (Au) – 106 miles
3rd March	F1 – **South African Grand Prix**(SA) at Kyalami – 203.5 miles
16th March	F1 – 'Race of Champions'at Brands Hatch (UK) – 123.5 miles
30th March	F1 – *Daily Express* International Trophy at Silverstone (UK) – 152.2 miles
7th April	F2 – BARC'200'at Thruxton (UK) – 153.1 miles
13th April	F2 – Deutschland Trophee at Hockenheim (D) – 168.3 miles
20th April	F2 – Grand Prix de Pau (F) – 120 miles
27th April	F2 – Eifelrennen at NNurburgring (D) – 142.6 miles
4th May	F1 – **Gran Premio de España** at Montjuic Park (E) – 212 miles
11th May	F2 – Gran Premio de Madrid at Jarama (E) – 126.9 miles
18th May	F1 – **Monaco Grand Prix** (M) – 156.3 miles
8th June	F2 – Grote Prijs van Limborg at Zolder (B) – 124.8 miles
21st June	F1 – **Grote Prijs van Nederland** at Zandvoort (N) – 234.5 miles
29th June	F2 – Grand Prix de Reims (F) – 180.6 miles
6th July	F1 – **Grand Prix de France** at Clermont-Ferrand (F) – 190.2 miles
13th July	F2 – Flugplatzrennen at Tulln-Langenlebarn (A) – 117.5 miles
19th July	F1 – **British Grand Prix** at Silverstone (UK) – 245.9 miles
3rd August	F1 – **Grosser Preis von Deutschland** at Nürburgring (D) –198.6 miles
16th August	F1 – International Gold Cup at Oulton Park (UK) – 107.1 miles
24th August	F2 – Gran Premio del'Mediterraneo at Enna-Pergusa (I) – 184.8 miles
7th September	F1 – **Gran Premio d'Italia** at Monza (I) – 243 miles
14th September	F2 – Grand Prix d'Albi (F) – 169.5 miles
20th September	F1 – **Grand Prix of Canada** at Mosport Park (C) – 221.3 miles
5th October	F1 – **United States Grand Prix** at Watkins Glen (US) – 248.4 miles
12th October	F2 – Gran Premio di Roma at Vallelunga (I) – 155.1 miles
19th October	F1 – **Gran Premio de Mexico** at Mexico City (Mx) – 201.9 miles

32 events of total race mileage = 5066 miles.
Formula Two dates are those in which graded Formula One drivers competed.
Events in bold are 11 World Championship rounds = 78.6 per cent of the 14 F1 races run.

Tasman Championship 1969

This was the last year in which major international stars took part, as the Tasman 2.5-litre formula came to an end. The next year would be for F5000 cars, and the lucrative starting money, needed to attract the European teams, was ended. Perhaps it was a victim of its own success, with the 'locals' being disadvantaged by the many visitors. This year's Championship had attracted Gold Leaf Team Lotus once again, with reigning World Champion Graham Hill and new signing Jochen Rindt, who was hot property. Scuderia Ferrari had loaned the same cars as the previous year to Chris Amon to run, but this year was supported by its F1 driver of the year before, Derek Bell. Brabham was represented by Frank Williams' car for Piers Courage, now an F1 driver, having driven a BRM for Parnell Racing the year before. The car was the first Brabham to be DFV-powered. Jack Brabham would only appear at the last race due to working on his F1 car. Frank Gardner was, perhaps, the best of the 'locals,' and, as usual, entered by Alex Mildren Racing, but this year with its own designed Mildren-Alfa V8. Resident Leo Geoghegan had shown well the previous year, and got among the stars, but reliability had scuppered his end result. This year he had the same Lotus 39-Repco V8, and was expected to challenge again. Unfortunately, BRM had lost money on the previous year's campaign, having needed so many hands to keep the new V12 cars running so far from home, so missed this campaign. Winged cars flew in from Europe – the Brabham with wings both front and rear. They should produce some great racing.

✳ New Zealand Grand Prix (Pukekohe)

58 laps of 1.75 miles = 101.5 miles.
21 entered – 20 started – 15 finished.
Front row: C Amon in 58.2s (108.24mph); J Rindt 0.2s. Row two: G Hill 0.6s: P Courage 0.8s.
04-JAN: Amon had pole and led after a lap from Rindt, Courage, Bell, Hill and Geoghegan, but Rindt was past on lap two. He slowly drew away from Amon, who also left Courage behind. Hill took Bell on lap eight, and was closing on Courage when front suspension trouble put him out on lap 13. Rindt had put up the fastest race lap on lap nine, but later spun off the course on oil when braking for the hairpin. Amon took the lead, but Rindt remained ahead of Courage. That was the way they finished, with everyone spread out. Derek Bell was lapped, and Australian Geoghegan was in fifth, a further lap back, but without challenging.
1st C Amon (Ferrari 246T) in 57m-55.4 s = 105.14mph
2nd J Rindt (Lotus 49T-DFW @ 20.1s
3rd P Courage (Brabham BT24-DFW) @ 50.8s
Fastest lap J Rindt in 58.9s = 106.96mph

✳ 10th Levin International

14 + 63 laps of 1.193 miles = 91.9 miles.
19 entries – 16 started – 10 finished.
Front row: J Rindt in 45.2s (95.02mph); C Amon 0.4s. Row two: D Bell 0.6s; F Gardner 0.8s.
11-JAN: Rindt beat Amon to pole this time. After a lap Rindt led Amon, Gardner, Hill, Bell and Geoghegan, and pulled out a two second lead. Bell passed Hill, though they and Gardner were falling away from the two leaders. On lap four Rindt spun and was sixth on recovery behind Courage. Two laps later he did the same thing again, and ended inverted but unhurt. Amon had a good lead from Gardner, and an even better one when Gardner spun down to sixth behind Bell, Hill and Courage. Hill had driveshaft trouble, so, when Bell spun, it was Courage who benefitted, closed on Amon and led on lap 26. His lead lasted just six laps when Courage spun, losing a few seconds. Bell retired on lap 41, so now

it was Amon, Courage, Gardner and Geoghegan. Courage looked like challenging Amon to the end, but putting a wheel in the rough put paid to that idea.
1st C Amon (Ferrari 246T) in 50m-08.8s = 89.93mph
2nd P Courage (Brabham BT24-DFW) @ 6.8s
3rd F Gardner (Mildren-Alfa V8) @ 1 lap
Fastest lap J Rindt (Lotus 49B DFW) in 45.3s = 94.81mph

✳ Lady Wigram Trophy (Christchurch)

11-lap heats, + 44-lap final of 2.318 miles = 127.5 miles.
19 entries – 18 started – 14 finished.
Prelim front row: J Rindt in 1m-18.5s (106.30mph); C Amon 0.9s; G Hill 1.1s.
18-JAN: After the heats it was Rindt, Hill and Courage ahead of Amon and Bell on the grid for the final. Rindt recovered from a sluggish start to lead lap one from Courage, Hill, Amon and Bell. By lap nine Courage was nine seconds adrift of Rindt and being caught by the Hill-Amon-Bell battle. On lap 18 Hill got by and on lap 29 Amon pushed Courage back to fourth. Rindt was almost half a minute ahead, though, so he had the comfort of a cruise to the finish. Amon ran out of time to catch Hill, having halved a seven second deficit by the flag, and no mistake was forthcoming from the reigning World Champion.
1st J Rindt (Lotus 49T-DFW) in 58m-53.6s = 103.91mph
2nd G Hill (Lotus 49T-DFW) @ 26.0s
3rd C Amon (Ferrari 246T)@ 29.9s
Fastest lap J Rindt/C Amon in 1m-18.8s = 105.90mph

✳ Teretonga Trophy (Invercargill)

8 + 62 laps of 1.6 miles = 112.0 miles.
20 started – 15 finished.
Prelim front row: P Courage in 57.2s (100.70mph); J Rindt 0.1s; G Hill 0.2s.
25-JAN: Rindt was on pole for the final, alongside Courage and Amon, but a driveshaft broke when the flag fell. This blocked Bell who literally pushed the Lotus away, suffering nose damage. Amon, Courage, Gardner and Hill was the first lap order, with Bell pitting for a new nose and now well out of things. Courage took the lead on lap three, with Gardner and Hill losing ground. Hill caught Gardner and took a few laps to pass him on lap 33. Bell was without a front spoiler, but from way back made fifth place by lap 16, but was unable to gain further. Hill clawed his way into Amon's slipstream and took second on lap 53.
1st P Courage (Brabham BT24-Cosworth) in 1h-01m-14.4s = 97.19mph
2nd G Hill (Lotus 49T-DFW) @ 18.4s
3rd C Amon (Ferrari 246T) @ 21.4s
Fastest lap J Rindt (Lotus 49T-DFW) in 57.9s = 99.48mph (prelim)

✴ 34th Australian Grand Prix at Lakeside

67 laps of 1.491 miles = 99.9 miles.
15 started – 8 finished.

Front row: C Amon; P Courage. Row two: G Hill; D Bell (no times available).

02-FEB: Amon and Courage headed the two-by-two grid, with Hill and Bell behind and ahead of Rindt and Gardner. The Lotuses had had little time for preparation. Amon shot away from the start and was never troubled thereafter. Hill, Courage, Bell, Gardner and Rindt followed. Courage's attempt to pass Hill on lap six failed and contact put him out. Bell took advantage, gaining second place. Rindt had lost places to Gardner and Geoghegan, but repassed the latter on lap 13 and Gardner on lap 19. Places held until lap 37 when Gardner retired, and, a few laps later, Rindt followed suit. Hill's rear wing partly collapsed, but he managed to get to the pits, allowing Geoghegan to claim the last podium spot. Hill recovered to fourth place, but had been lapped twice. Amon had lapped all but teammate Bell, and was now looking good for the Championship.

1st C Amon (Ferrari 246T) in 1h-00m-12.8s = 99.54mph
2nd D Bell (Ferrari 246T) @ 23.9s
3rd L Geoghegan (Lotus 39-Repco V8) @ 1 lap
Fastest lap C Amon in 52.8s = 101.68mph

✴ Warwick Farm '100'

45 laps of 2.25 miles = 101.25 miles.
16 started – 8 finished.

Front row: J Rindt in 1m-23.8s (96.66mph); C Amon 0.7s. Row two: G Hill; P Courage (no times available).

09-FEB: Rindt's pole lap was over three seconds faster than the previous year's pole, showing the effect of the wings clearly. Amon had been pipped to pole at the last moment. Hill and Courage were behind on the two-by-two grid, chosen at the last minute because of the weather. Amon led Rindt, Courage, Hill and Bell off the line, but Rindt got to grips with the rain best and led at the end of the first lap. Amon ran a little wide on lap two, and Courage took the chance to pass but spun on exiting Polo corner. Amon was unable to avoid contact and both were out. The irony was that Courage had been his only challenger for the title, and so Amon was now Tasman Champion for 1969. Hill's engine suffered from the wet and he pitted a couple of times, rejoining last and then setting the fastest lap (for the hell of it, I guess). Frank Gardner was lapped on lap 29, but no disgrace in the awful conditions.

1st J Rindt (Lotus 49T-DFW) in 1h-18m-12.8s = 77.67mph
2nd D Bell (Ferrari 246T) @ 44.9s
3rd F Gardner (Mildren-Alfa V8) @ 1 lap
Fastest lap G Hill (Lotus 49B-DFW) in 1m-40.3s = 80.76mph

✴ International '100' (Sandown Park)

55 laps of 1.928 miles = 106.0 miles.

19 started – 11 finished.

Front row: J Rindt; C Amon. Row two: G Hill; P Courage (no times available).

16-FEB: This was the final Tasman race to have international significance, and a huge crowd came, even though the title had been settled the week before. Brabham arrived with a Repco V8 shoehorned into the back of an F3 car, but was short on power compared to Lotus and Ferrari. Rindt just beat Amon to pole, and led through the first tight corner from Amon, Courage, Hill, Brabham and Bell. On the first straight Amon went past Rindt with ease, better gearing. Before the lap was over, Hill had throttle linkage trouble, then, two laps later, Courage was out with a halfshaft failure. Brabham couldn't hold on to the leaders, and Bell was deprived of fourth by Gardner towards the end. Graham Hill had lost four laps repairing his linkage, and recovered to sixth, four laps adrift. So that ends a super Amon-Rindt battle for the title – only Courage ever getting the better of both.

1st C Amon (Ferrari 246T) in 1h-00m-10.6s = 105.73mph
2nd J Rindt (Lotus 49T-DFW) @ 7.3s
3rd J Brabham (Brabham BT31-Repco) @ 1 lap
Fastest lap C Amon in 1m-04.5s = 107.61mph

Tasman Champion:
1st Chris Amon (Ferrari 246T) – 44
2nd Jochen Rindt (Lotus 49T-DFW) – 30
3rd Piers Courage (Brabham BT24-DFW) – 22

Tasman epilogue

Were the Tasman Championships internationally important? Well, major F1 marques produced special cars and engines for this series, which shows that it was serious for them, and sometimes useful for pre-season Formula One testing. Up to four World Champions had sometimes been on the grid, and the eventual involvement of Ferrari took it above the realms of a 'British Commonwealth Affair'. The 'Down Under' tradition involved every F1 World Champion of the period. Chris Amon's credentials showed in his beating of Rindt in '69 and almost Clark in '68. He was of true World Champion calibre – QED.

✴✴✴ (WC1) XV South African Grand Prix (Kyalami)

80 laps of 2.550 miles = 204.0 miles.
18 entries and starters – 9 finished.

Front row: J Brabham – 1m-20.0s (114.75mph); J Rindt 0.2s; D Hulme 0.3s.

01-MAR: Lotus and BRM both entered three cars, but Brabham now discovered the power of the DFV engine and took pole from Rindt, Hulme, Stewart and Amon – just half a second separated them. The three BRMs were very near the back. Brabham's good start was negated by Stewart very soon, and then it was the Scot all the way. Brabham's rear wing collapsed on lap six, leaving Stewart clear. Rindt led Hill for second now, but dropped back with a misfire and was replaced by Hulme. The action was all about third place now, and Hulme was overtaken by Siffert and Andretti, the latter taking third from Siffert on lap 21. However, ten laps later Andretti's transmission failed, and he handed the place back to Siffert in Rob Walker's Lotus 49B. Two laps later, Hulme had retaken the last podium place. McLaren and Beltoise followed Siffert home.

1st	J Stewart (W)	Matra MS10-Cosworth in 1h-50m-39.1s	110.62
2nd	G Hill (W)	Lotus 49B-Cosworth	18.8s
3rd	D Hulme (W)	McLaren M7A-Cosworth	31.8s
F lap	J Stewart	Matra MS10-Cosworth in 1m-21.6s	112.50r

✳✳✳ IV 'Race Of Champions' (Brands Hatch)

50 laps of 2.46 miles = 123 miles.
17 entries – 12 started – 6 finished.
Front row: G Hill – 1m-28.2s (100.41mph); J Stewart 0.1s; J Siffert 1.1s.

16-MAR: All the main teams entered, but Ferrari was victim to a strike by Italian customs. Matra unveiled its squat new car here. A chaotic one-at-a-time qualifying system was used, and produced a record-smashing pole by Hill. It was Stewart, though, who stormed off best and led throughout, winning at a faster race speed than pole position! Rindt followed in Hill's exhaust for the early part of the race, with Brabham threatening the Lotus duo, but Hill escaped when they lapped Oliver's BRM. Brabham retired on lap 16 with fuel trouble. The lap record was constantly being improved upon, and, during Rindt's chase of Hill, he set what is, with the now corrected lap length, the first 100mph lap record for the circuit, only to retire with falling oil pressure on lap 38. The McLarens were surprisingly outpaced all weekend, but salvaged a podium finish. Jo Siffert's Lotus 49 followed, so the first four places replicated the South African GP. How close to a Championship quality race could it be?

1st	J Stewart (W)	Matra MS80-Cosworth in 1h-13m-10.4s	100.86
2nd	G Hill (W)	Lotus 49B-Cosworth	7.0s
3rd	D Hulme (W)	McLaren M7A-Cosworth	57.9s
F lap	J Rindt (W)	Lotus 49B-Cosworth in 1m-26.8s	102.03r

✳✳✳ XXI *Daily Express* International Trophy (Silverstone)

52 laps of 2.927 miles = 152.2 miles.
17 entries – 14 started – 12 finished.

Front row: J Stewart – 1m-20.9s (130.25mph); J Brabham 0.1s; C Amon 0.2s; J Ickx 1.6s.

30-MAR: Two Ferraris arrived for a complete field. Stewart's pole lap was over four seconds under the record, as wings were now causing records to be shattered. However, he chose the old car for the wet race and started from the back. The Brabham trio of Brabham, Ickx and Courage led off from Siffert, Amon, Rindt and Bell. Rindt suffered misfiring, dropping him to 11th place on lap six before it cleared. A magnificent charge followed. In five laps he despatched Bell, Siffert, Hill, McLaren and Rodriguez – Siffert and Hill in identical machinery so Rindt was simply the master of it. Fourteen laps later he caught the Ickx/Courage battle as it also caught the lapped but battling Hill and Rodriguez. Rindt's answer was to pass all four of them into Stowe in one move! He was back to second by halfway. Siffert and Amon dropped right back early on as Hulme came from ninth to fourth in two laps only to retire on lap 16. Stewart claimed third at three-quarter distance from Courage and Ickx. Brabham's lead was cut from 28 to 12 seconds with three laps left, so Rindt's task looked hopeless. However, Brabham was short of fuel, so now clearly Rindt's misfire cost him the race. But for that he would have romped home.

1st	J Brabham (W)	Brabham BT26-Cos in 1h-25m-20.8s	107.00
2nd	J Rindt (W)	Lotus 49B-Cosworth	2.2s
3rd	J Stewart (W)	Matra MS10-Cosworth	1m-11s
F lap	J Rindt	Lotus 49B-Cosworth in 1m-30.6s	116.30

✳✳✳ (WC2) Gran Premio d'Espaňa (Montjuic)

90 laps of 2.356 miles = 212.0 miles.
14 entries and starters – 6 finished.
Front row: J Rindt – 1m-25.7s (98.97mph); C Amon 0.5s; G Hill 0.9s.

04-MAY: Rindt tore off at the start gaining a second a lap on Amon, Siffert, Hill, Brabham and Stewart. Lap seven saw Hill take third, and a lap later survive unscathed a huge crash as his sky-high wing collapsed on cresting a rise – saved by Armco fencing. Stewart had also taken fifth from Brabham, and was now fourth. Nine more laps and he was third as Rindt suffered a repeat of Hill's disaster, but he suffered facial injuries. Now Amon led easily, but his jinx awoke on lap 53 with an engine failure. Brabham had departed a few laps earlier, so Ickx was second until he was passed by McLaren and retired. The Lotus crashes heralded the death knell for high wings. The forces induced in the supports had never been truly understood by Lotus. The bizarre attitudes adopted by some wings under cornering forces made it seem that a failure was never far away. With the proliferation of front and rear elevated wings, sometimes one couldn't see the cars for the wings. It was good riddance with a huge sigh of relief that it hadn't ended in total catastrophe. It so very nearly did – drivers had been guinea-pigs. I suppose they had no choice. Phew!

1st	J Stewart (W)	Matra MS80-Cosworth in 2h-16m-53.9s	92.92
2nd	B McLaren (W)	McLaren M7A-Cosworth	2 laps
3rd	JP Beltoise (W)	Matra-MS80-Cosworth	3 laps
F lap	J Rindt (W)	Lotus 49B-Cosworth 1m-28.3s	96.04r

Championship positions:
J Stewart 18; B McLaren 8; D Hulme 7.

✳✳✳ (WC3) XXVII Grand Prix de Monaco (Monte Carlo)

80 laps of a 1.954-mile circuit = 156.3 miles.
16 entries and starters – 7 finished.
Front row: J Stewart – 1m-24.6s (83.15mph); C Amon 0.4s.
Row two: JP Beltoise 0.8s; G Hill 1.2s.
18-MAY: Richard Attwood replaced Rindt, who was recovering, while Lotus used modified Tasman cars. High wings still appeared, but after first practice they were banned by the CSI as fears of a repeat of the Spanish chaos was obvious. Stewart, Amon, Beltoise and Hill was the order after the start. Hill passed Beltoise on lap three but, by lap 23, only Hill was left, transmission trouble the common cause. Ickx, Courage, Siffert and McLaren now followed Hill. Ickx and Courage swapped places a couple of times before Ickx retired with rear suspension trouble. Hill then continued his untroubled journey to an amazing fifth win in his old stamping ground, but it was a pity Rindt was absent. Hill's record went to Senna in 1993 after 24 years.

1st	G Hill (W)	Lotus 49B-Cosworth in 1h-56m-59.4s	80.18
2nd	P Courage (W)	Brabham BT26-Cosworth	17.3s
3rd	J Siffert (RW)	Lotus 49B-Cosworth	34.6s
F lap	J Stewart (W)	Matra MS80-Cosworth in 1m-25.1s	82.67r

Championship positions:
J Stewart 18; G Hill 15; B McLaren 10.

✳✳✳ (WC4) XVIII Grote Prijs van Nederland (Zandvoort)

90 laps of a 2.605-mile circuit = 234.5 miles.
17 entries – 15 started – 10 finished.
Front row: J Rindt – 1m-20.85s (116.01mph); J Stewart 0.29s; G Hill 1.16s.

21-JUN: Rindt was back to form, and produced a great pole time. The cars now had various rear body attachments to replace the wings. Hill led the first two laps, then dropped to third behind Rindt and Stewart, who led lap 17 as Rindt's driveshaft cried enough. Siffert had brilliantly risen from ninth on lap one to follow Stewart on lap 14, by passing Hill, so he was now second. This drive easily matched his British GP win. Amon took third from Hulme with seven laps to go, Ickx and Brabham also scoring.

1st	J Stewart (W)	Matra MS80-Cosworth in 2h-06m-42.08s	111.04
2nd	J Siffert (RW)	Lotus 49B-Cosworth	24.52s
3rd	C Amon (W)	Ferrari312	30.51s
F lap	J Stewart	Matra MS80-Cosworth in 1m-22.94s	113.09r

Championship positions:
J Stewart 27; G Hill 15; J Siffert 13.

✳✳✳ (WC5) LV Grand Prix de France (Clermont-Ferrand)

38 laps of a 5.005-mile circuit = 190.2 miles.
14 entries – 13 started – 9 finished.
Front row: J Stewart – 3m-00.6s (99.77mph); D Hulme 1.8s.
Row two: J Rindt 1.9s; J Ickx 2.0s.
06-JUL: BRM withdrew to sort out its car, and Brabham was lucky to survive a shunt in testing at Silverstone – a foot injury putting him out until Monza. Lotus produced a four-wheel drive car – the Type 63 – to be tried out by John Miles. Another Stewart benefit followed without any real challenge, even by Rindt, who felt unwell, the circuit contours aggravating his condition; he stopped on lap 22. It was Hulme who was nearest to Stewart, but a broken roll-bar mount stopped him. Beltoise chased Ickx who was being booed by the crowd and shown the blue flag, yet he wasn't being lapped. He was Belgian, though, not French. Did this affect him? He slid wide on the last lap and Beltoise was past for a one/two for Matra. McLaren and Elford followed.

1st	J Stewart (W)	Matra MS80-Cosworth in 1h-56m-47.4s	97.71
2nd	JP Beltoise (W)	Matra MS80-Cosworth	57.1s
3rd	J Ickx (W)	Brabham BT26-Cosworth	57.3s
F lap	J Stewart	Matra MS80-Cosworth in 3m-02.7s	98.62r

Championship positions:
J Stewart 36; G Hill 16; J Siffert and B McLaren 13.

✱✱✱ (WC6) XXIV British Grand Prix (Silverstone)

84 laps of 2.927 miles = 245.9 miles.
19 entries – 17 started – 10 finished.

Front row: J Rindt – 1m-20.8s (130.41mph); J Stewart 0.4s;
D Hulme 0.7s.

19-JUL: Stewart actually set the fastest practice time of
1m-20.6s, but a crash caused by striking a broken kerb made
him put another time in Beltoise's car, for second on the grid.
Beltoise was racing a four-wheel drive Matra MS84. Lotus
and McLaren also tried the technology, but to no avail. Rear
wings were now reappearing, mounted lower, attached above
bodywork, and with endplates fitted.

At last a Rindt/Stewart head-to-head was on the cards. This
came to fruition in no uncertain terms as the two had the
race to themselves. Rindt led for six laps, then Stewart for
eight, by which time they were already lapping Beltoise's
four-wheel drive car. Rindt took advantage to lead this great
duel by a whisker until lap 62 when an endplate came loose
and threatened to cut the rear tyre. He pitted for removal,
so he and all of us were denied a fantastic finale. Blast! He
was still in second place, but had no chance of retrieving 30
seconds. Hulme had been third until lap 21 when engine
trouble intervened, so when Rindt pitted for fuel, dropping to
fifth, it was Ickx (tenth on lap one), and McLaren, scrapping
away, who benefitted. Rindt passed Courage for fourth on the
last lap. There's no denying the fact that this was one of motor
racing's great duels, but cruelly fated to end in anti-climax.

1st	J Stewart (W)	Matra MS80-Cosworth in 1h-55m-55.6s	127.25
2nd	J Ickx (W)	Brabham BT26-Cosworth	1 lap
3rd	B McLaren (W)	McLaren M7A-Cosworth	1 lap
F lap	J Stewart	Matra MS80-Cosworth in 1m-21.3s	129.61r

Championship positions:
J Stewart 45; B McLaren 17; G Hill 16.

✱✱✱ (WC7) XXXI Grosse Preis von Deutschland (N Nürburgring)

14 laps of 14.173 miles = 198.4 miles.
16 entries – 13 starters – 4 finished.

Front row: J Ickx – 7m-42.1s (110.54mph); J Stewart 0.3s;
J Rindt 5.9s.

03-AUG: Ferrari withdrew, leaving just 12 regular entries
plus a four-wheel drive Lotus for Andretti, so an F2 race
formed up behind on the grid. Ickx took over 20 seconds
from the F1 record in practice; he always performed very
well here. Surtees' BRM was half a minute from pole, and
he declined to start. Teammate Oliver was even slower! Ickx

made a bad start in eighth place, but was fourth behind
Stewart, Siffert and Rindt after a lap. On lap three he was
second, and began a great dice with Stewart, taking the lead
on lap seven. Siffert suffered suspension failure on lap 12,
and but for this might have finished second as Stewart fell
back from Ickx with gear trouble. Hill was the only other F1
finisher, four mins back, so Henri Pescarolo's Matra F2 car
was fifth on the road.

1st	J Ickx (W)	Brabham BT26-Cosworth in 1h-49m-55.4s	108.43
2nd	J Stewart (W)	Matra MS80-Cosworth	57.7s
3rd	B McLaren (W)	McLaren M7A-Cosworth	3m-22s
F lap	J Ickx	Brabham BT26-Cosworth in 7m-43.8s	110.14r

Championship positions:
J Stewart 51; J Ickx 22; B McLaren 21.

The scoring system this year split the 11 rounds at the
mid-season point, which had occurred at Silverstone. Each
driver counted all but their worst performance from each
half. Stewart had scored five out of six races in the first
half, so carried the maximum forward. The rules mitigated
against catching Stewart, as 36 points was the maximum
available from the last half-season. His 45 points from five
wins to date were secure, yet anyone winning the last five
would have one deducted – unfair! The system described
had now produced a weird situation. Stewart was surely
Champion now, but two people were still mathematically in
the hunt, and neither was Ickx, winner of the last race – ?
There were four rounds left, but the rules meant that Ickx
could garner only 27 points from three wins if he won all
remaining races, whereas McLaren would rake in 36 from
similar fortune. The same applied to Hill, who now had
19 points, but could improve by 33. Stewart's second place
had finished Ickx's hopes, but not McLaren's, nor Hill's! The
chances of Stewart not scoring more was negligible. What a
stupid, unfair situation!

✱ XVI International Gold Cup (Oulton Park)

40 laps of 2.678 miles = 107.1 miles.
10 entries – 5 F1 started – 3 F1 finished.

Front row: J Stewart – 1m-27.2s (110.57mph); J Ickx 0.6s.
Row two: J Rindt 3.2s*.

16-AUG: BRM withdrew, as did Beltoise's Matra. McLaren
had CanAm commitments, and Lotus sent a four-wheel
drive Type 63 for Rindt to prove the technology, one way
or the other. If Rindt couldn't make four-wheel drive
competitive then no-one could. Graham Hill had an F2
car, so the entry was bolstered by F5000 cars, one driven

by Jackie Oliver. *Bonnier had qualified third, but crashed his Lotus 49 so didn't start. The top three drivers of the year were here, so a battle was in prospect. Ickx led Stewart and Rindt at the start, but Stewart led after two laps, and took six laps to shake off Ickx. On lap 19 a misfire stopped him for three laps, leaving Ickx leading Rindt, but the four-wheel drive car was no match and he was almost lapped. DeAdamich's F5000 car had been only a second a lap slower than Rindt throughout the race. Surely that was it for four-wheel drive in F1 – or was it?

1st	J Ickx (W)	Brabham BT26-Cosworth in 1h-00m-28.6s	106.28
2nd	J Rindt (W)	Lotus 63-Cosworth four-wheel drive	1m-22s
3rd	A deAdamich (W)	Surtees TS5-Chevrolet (F5000)	1 lap
F lap	J Stewart (W)	Matra MS80-Cosworth in 1m-28.6s	108.82r

✳✳✳ (WC8) XXXVIII Gran Premio d'Italia (Monza)

68 laps of a 3.573-mile circuit = 243.0 miles.
18 entries –15 started – 11 finished.
Front row: J Rindt – 1m-25.48s (150.47mph); D Hulme 0.20s.
Row two: J Stewart 0.34s; P Courage 1.00s.

07-SEP: It was Monza, yet there was only one Ferrari present, for Rodriguez. Amon was due to debut the flat-12 car, but it failed. A normal Monza multi-car scrap ensued, with Stewart or Rindt mostly leading but Hulme and Courage having a share. Hill, Siffert, Beltoise and McLaren were in the mix as well. Hulme and Courage encountered trouble and Hill broke a driveshaft on lap 62, having been second to Stewart for 16 laps. At the final dash Stewart had it all worked out – he had led across the line since lap 38. McLaren was 0.02 seconds behind Beltoise for the closest finish in a Grand Prix ever – 0.19 seconds covering four cars! Jackie Stewart and Matra had won their first World Championship, with six wins from the eight rounds to date.

1st	J Stewart (W)	Matra MS80-Cosworth in 1h-39m-11.26s	146.99
2nd	J Rindt (W)	Lotus 49B-Cosworth	0.08s
3rd	JP Beltoise (W)	Matra MS80-Cosworth	0.17s
F lap	JP Beltoise	Matra MS80-Cosworth in 1m-25.20s	150.97r

Championship positions:
J Stewart 60 (WC); B McLaren 24; J Ickx 22.

✳✳✳ (WC9) III Grand Prix of Canada (Mosport Park)

90 laps of 2.459 miles = 221.3 miles.
24 entries – 20 started – 9 finished.
Front row: J Ickx – 1m-17.4s (114.37mph); JP Beltoise 0.5s; J Rindt 0.5s.

20-SEP: More cars in Canada than Europe? Surprisingly Lotus and Matra brought four-wheel drive cars, so Oulton hadn't sounded the death knell. BRM had three cars, and two 'locals' entered, but there was only a single Ferrari (NART-entered). It was Rindt, Ickx, Beltoise and Stewart at the start, but Stewart led by lap six. Ickx passed Rindt and fought Stewart strongly for the lead, just like at Oulton Park, until lap 32. Ickx went for a gap, the cars touched, both spun, and Stewart was out in a ditch. Ickx recovered, still leading, and won easily. Brabham had come through from eighth, and now was third, behind Rindt. Ickx's 43 year old boss dealt with Rindt on lap 60 for a Brabham one/two. Servos-Gavin brought the four-wheel drive Matra home sixth, behind Beltoise and McLaren, and aided by many retirements before half way. He was six laps down, though, so it was no rescue drive for four-wheel drive. Surely the end was nigh.

1st	J Ickx (W)	Brabham BT26-Cosworth in 1h-59m-29.7s	111.19
2nd	J Brabham (W)	Brabham BT26-Cosworth	46.2s
3rd	J Rindt (W)	Lotus 49B-Cosworth	52.0s
F lap	J Ickx	Brabham BT26-Cosworth in 1m-18.1s	113.35

Championship positions:
J Stewart 60 (WC); J Ickx 31; B McLaren 26.

✳✳✳ (WC10) 12th United States Grand Prix (Watkins Glen)

108 laps of 2.30 miles = 248.4 miles.
19 entries – 17 started – 7 finished
Front row: J Rindt – 1m-03.62s (128.97mph); D Hulme (0.03s) Row two: J Stewart (0.12s); G Hill (0.40s)

05-OCT: Stewart tried the four-wheel drive Matra on a wet track but was 2 sec slower than the 2wd car. Rindt took pole and led off chased hard by Stewart as Hulme had gear linkage trouble. Hill was 3rd but soon Siffert, Beltoise and Courage passed him, Siffert soon retiring. Stewart passed Rindt to lead laps 12 to 20, lost it and retired on lap 32 with oil loss so Courage and Ickx were promoted as were Brabham and Surtees. Ickx's retirement on lap 77 and a fuel stop for Brabham gave BRM a surprise podium place at the end. Graham Hill was 5th on lap 90 after Ickx's demise but spun on oil, stalling the engine. He push started it but couldn't refasten his belts. Then a slow puncture put him off the track, the car cartwheeled and Hill suffered serious leg injuries on being thrown out. This took some shine off Jochen Rindt's overdue maiden victory.

1st	J Rindt (W)	Lotus 49B-Cosworth in 1h-57m-56.84s	126.36
2nd	P Courage (FW)	Brabham BT26-Cosworth	46.99s
3rd	J.Surtees (W)	BRM P139	2 laps
F lap	J Rindt	Lotus 49B-Cosworth in 1m-04.34s	128.69r

Championship positions:
J Stewart 60 (WC); J Ickx 31; B McLaren 26.

✱✱✱ (WC11) VIII Gran Premio de Mexico (Mexico City)

65 laps of 3.107 miles = 201.9 miles.
19 entries – 17 started – 11 finished
Front row: J Brabham – 1m-42.90s (108.70mph); J Ickx 0.70s.
Row two: J Stewart 0.77s; D Hulme 0.80s.
19-OCT: Brabham took pole for the first and last races of 1969, but a poor start saw Stewart shoot between the Brabhams to lead from Ickx and Brabham, with Rindt and Hulme next. Ickx led lap six, but it was Hulme who was really lit up in Mexico, carving his way to the lead on lap ten, never to be headed. Ickx threw everything at Hulme to the end to no avail. Rindt retired from fifth on lap 21 with a broken wishbone, so now Beltoise chased Stewart for fourth. Oliver's BRM took sixth on lap 43, and that was it. Servos-Gavin brought the four-wheel drive Matra to eighth, and John Miles' four-wheel drive Lotus failed. Four-wheel-drive was now abandoned by F1.

1st	D Hulme (W)	McLaren M7A-Cosworth in 1h-54m-08.8s	106.15
2nd	J Ickx (W)	Brabham BT26-Cosworth	2.56s
3rd	J Brabham (W)	Brabham BT26-Cosworth	38.48s
F lap	J Ickx	Brabham BT26-Cosworth in 1m-43.05s	108.54

Championship positions:
J Stewart 63 (WC); J Ickx 37; B McLaren 26.

1969 seasonal review

Jackie Stewart had laid down a marker for the season right at the start, winning in South Africa in the previous year's car, and followed it up at Brands Hatch in the new MS80 against a strong field. The two extra events at Brands and Silverstone proved the worth of these races, with fields as good as most of the Championship rounds. However, Oulton Park's Gold Cup entry had suffered from its mid-season slot. The Race of Champions stepped in for Goodwood, and Aintree had closed, so it was a pity Oulton Park hadn't taken the Aintree slot as it is in the same part of the country. Perhaps there wasn't room for three pre-Championship races now.

Ferrari had been absent at Brands Hatch, but somehow the real Ferrari potential never showed this year. The 312 was outdated, and the flat-12 didn't materialise on the grid. Lotus had a poor year, with just two wins, while Brabham's conversion to the DFV engine bore real fruit, being the most competitive marque to Matra.

Matra produced a real surprise at the season's end by announcing that it would no longer use the DFV engine, only its own V12. Matra was now part of the Chrysler empire, which had interests in Simca, and which wished to promote that brand through branding the cars Matra-Simca. This brought about a break with Ken Tyrrell and Jackie Stewart, as they didn't consider the Matra engine competitive against the DFV, and so were needing to source a new chassis supplier. It was an unprecedented situation that a new World Champion was without a drive.

Looking below it seemed helpful if your name was some version of 'Jack' – does that include Jochen?

Winners of the 14 F1 races of 1969 – quantity & quality of success

7 wins	J Stewart (7A)	7 wins	Matra-Cosworth (7A)
3 wins	J Ickx (2A, C)	4 wins	Brabham-Cosworth (3A, C)
1 win	J Brabham (A) J Rindt (A) G Hill (A) D Hulme (A)	2 wins	Lotus-Cosworth (2A)
		1 win	McLaren-Cosworth (A)

1969 Championship review

The Brabham team had abandoned the Repco engine, and joined the band of Ford DFV-powered teams of Lotus, McLaren and Matra. This didn't stop the domination from the beginning of the season for Jackie Stewart and the Matra. This was the first Constuctor's Championship win for a French car (well French chassis anyway), and was won with three races to spare. Strangely, his Championship campaign reprised that of Jim Clark in 1965, when the title was won early with six wins and three rounds to go, then not winning again.

Jochen Rindt and reigning Champion Graham Hill were the ones most likely to have given Stewart a hard time, but Rindt's early losses, twice from the race lead, and Graham

Hill, after Monaco, seeming now to be past his best, put paid to any real prospect of a challenge for the Championship. The closeness of the battle between Rindt and Stewart at Silverstone proved the truth of that assertion, and was a never-to-be-forgotten battle, sadly without a finalé. McLaren Racing hadn't achieved much until right at the end when Denny Hulme surprised everyone with a dominant win in Mexico, and made one wonder why this hadn't occurred earlier. BRM had another disaster season, only picking up crumbs left by retired cars when its cars survived, but as a thoroughbred team making the whole car, BRM would always have its fans.

VISIT VELOCE ON THE WEB – WWW.VELOCE.CO.UK
All current books • New book news • Special offers • Gift vouchers • Forum

283

Chapter 29

1970

In marches March, in March – en masse

A new decade would hopefully herald a new era. The grids of the previous year had dropped to 13 cars on some occasions, the leanest grids ever in serious Formula One racing. This needed to be improved somehow, and the likelihood was that the Cosworth engine/Hewland gearbox package would help bring new teams into the frame. One was already known about – would any more come? A new safety feature this year was the mandating of the use of flexible bag tanks, causing every team to produce new or revised cars. The proven 'off-the-peg' engine-transmission package of Cosworth and Hewland would hopefully bring in new marques or entrants. A team capable of producing a good chassis and that understood wing technology could well be immediately competitive.

Matra wished to return with its V12 engine, but Ken Tyrrell wasn't interested in running a Matra-engined car so the unique situation of a new World Champion without a car was solved with the arrival on the Formula One grid of the new marque: **March** (run by Max **M**osley, **A**lan **R**ees, Graham **C**oaker and Robin **H**erd, who was established as a top designer from his days at McLaren). March had produced a Formula Three car late the year before, and now stepped up to the big time '*big time*' by producing more cars than any other marque, yet had existed as a company for only a few months! The car, naturally, used the Cosworth-Hewland system. The March 701 was an uncomplicated-looking car, with the only interesting feature being the inverted aerofoil-shaped auxiliary fuel tanks low down each side of the body. So it seemed March was advancing the use of 'aero downforce' in a way no other team had before, but how this worked in the turbulent air behind the front wheels was intriguing. On the grid for the first F1 race in South Africa on March 7th were no fewer than five of its cars, run by three separate organisations. March alone solved the grid size problem.

The World Championship had expanded to 13 rounds this year, plus the usual British extra races. With 13 rounds, the Championship was beginning to provide sufficient racing to sustain the costs and careers involved. Soon races extra to the Championship would not be required. However, the following year, this idea was proved premature.

The constructors

March Engineering was the Works team, with Chris Amon as number one, and Jo Siffert, now a Works driver at last. The Works team had obtained sponsorship from the American oil additive company STP, which also ran a car, with Indianapolis winner Mario Andretti at the wheel as part of the deal – it didn't appear often, though.

Brabham Racing produced its first monocoque car – the BT33 – to be driven by Jack Brabham, who, having failed to sign Jochen Rindt, deferred his retirement. Rolf Stommelen was signed as a 'pay driver,' and supported by the German magazine *Auto Motor und Sport*.

McLaren Racing had the M14A, a natural development of the previous year's car. The line-up was unchanged from Bruce McLaren and Denny Hulme.

Gold Leaf Team Lotus started with the Type 49B, but soon produced the game-changing Type 72. The 'chisel' nose, made possible by moving the radiators to the side of the monocoque' gave a new profile which would be copied before long. The team was led by Jochen Rindt, supported by John Miles, son of famous comic entertainer and impresario Bernard Miles. At the British GP, a third car appeared for a new name – Emerson Fittipaldi – the first Brazilian F1 star. After Italy, Miles was replaced by Swede Reine Wisell.

Ferrari introduced the new 312B, fitted with Ferrari's 460bhp flat-12 unit which, of course, meant a completely different chassis for such a different engine configuration. It looked terrific and sounded wonderful – all 12s do. However, Ferrari had lost the services of Chris Amon who had experienced so many failures when testing that he was allowed to pull out of his signed contract for 1970. By now, Ferrari knew what a great driver it was losing. Jackie Ickx was leader, with Ignazio Giunti, then, after Belgium, the Swiss Gianclaudio 'Clay' Regazzoni.

BRM produced its P153: a bulbous and low design owing nothing to the previous year's unsuccessful car, but perhaps a little to that year's Matra MS80. With a revised 440bhp V12, a revival of the team's fortunes was hoped for by many, particularly the drivers. They were led by Pedro Rodriguez and Jackie Oliver, with Canadian George Eaton paying to drive a third car. The cars were now in the colours of cosmetics firm Yardley, the famous dark green evident only on Eaton's car. A pity, as BRM's was the best 'British Racing Green,' I think.

Matra Sports produced the wide, squat, MS120, to accommodate its V12, which sounded as if it had swallowed a brass band. The gearbox was by Hewland, so it was still not a completely French car. The driver line-up certainly was, though, being led by Jean-Pierre Beltoise, Henri Pescarolo in support.

Team Surtees was a new addition to the constructors, but ran a McLaren M7A until John Surtees' own car was ready for the British GP. This would, of course, be DFV-powered.

DeTomaso arrived, run on behalf of its creator by Frank Williams Racing, for regular driver and friend Piers Courage to drive. The car would be Ford DFV powered. The marque had failed miserably in F1 back in '62, but now it used DFV power so was a bi-national team, like the Championship-winning Matra-Ford.

The independents

Ken Tyrrell Racing's problem of providing his World Champion with a car was solved by buying a couple of Marches for Jackie Stewart and Johnny Servos-Gavin, and then for Francois Cevert after Monaco.

RRC Walker Racing was offered a Type 49B for Graham Hill, who had, in truth, been outperformed by Jochen Rindt the year before. Doubt over his recovery had left him without a Works drive, but he had recovered determinedly from his leg injuries and was now focussed on being on the grid in South Africa.

Antique Automobiles, a company run by Colin Crabbe (and bearing a strange name for an F1 entrant, perhaps), bought a March for a new find from F2 – Ronnie Peterson – to run from Monaco onwards. That's six now potentially!

The Grand Prix driver's diary of single-seater racing for 1970

7th March	F1 – **South African Grand Prix** (SA) at Kyalami – 203.5 miles
22nd March	F1 – 'Race of Champions' at Brands Hatch (UK) – 123.5 miles
30th March	F2 – BARC'200'at Thruxton (UK) – 153.1 miles
5th April	F2 – Grand Prix de Pau (F) – 123.3 miles
12th April	F2 – Deutschland Trophae at Hockenheim (D) – 168.3 miles
19th April	F1 – **Gran Premio de España** at Jarama (E) – 190.2 miles
26th April	F1 – *Daily Express* International Trophy at Silverstone (UK) – 152.2 miles
26th April	F2 – Gran Premio de Barcelona at Montjuic Park (E) – 106.3 miles
3rd May	F2 – Eifelrennen at NNurburgring (D) – 142.7 miles
10th May	F1 – **Monaco Grand Prix** (M) – 156.3 miles
24th May	F2 – Grote Prijs van Limborg at Zolder (B) – 124.8 miles
25th May	F2 – London Trophy at Crystal Palace (UK) – 97.3 miles
7th June	F1 – **Grand Prix de Belgique** at Spa (B) – 245.3 miles
14th June	F2 – Rhein-Pokal-Rennen at Hockenheim (D) – 124.2 miles
21st June	F1 – **Grote Prijs van Nederland** at Zandvoort (N) – 208.8 miles
28th June	F2 – Grand Prix de Rouen (F) – 169.3 miles
5th July	F1 – **Grand Prix de France**at Clermont-Ferrand (F) – 190.2 miles
18th July	F1 – **British Grand Prix** at Brands Hatch (UK) – 212 miles
26th July	F2 – Trophée France at Paul Ricard (F) – 144.1 miles
2nd August	F1 – **Grosser Preis von Deutschland** at Nürburgring (D) – 210.9 miles
16th August	F1 – **Grosser Preis von Osterreich** at Zeltweg (A) – 220.4 miles
22nd August	F1 – International Gold Cup at Oulton Park (UK) – 107.1 miles
23rd August	F2 – Gran Premio del'Mediterraneo at Enna-Pergusa (I) – 186.6 miles
30th August	F2 – Festspielpreis der Stadt at Salzburgring (A) – 132.2 miles
6th September	F1 – **Gran Premio d'Italia** at Monza (I) – 243 miles
13th September	F2 – Flugplatzrennen at Tulln-Langenlebarn (A) – 117.5 miles
20th September	F1 – **Grand Prix of Canada** at Mont Tremblant (C) – 238.5 miles
27th September	F2 – Gran Premio Citta di Imola (I) – 174.6 miles

| 4th October | F1 – **United States Grand Prix** at Watkins Glen (US) – 248.4 miles |
| 25th October | F1 – **Gran Premio de Mexico** at Mexico City (Mx) – 2019 miles |

30 events of total race mileage = 5117 miles, 5011 max (simultaneous events).

Events in bold are World Championship rounds – 81.3 per cent of the Formula One races run.

Formula Two dates are those in which graded Formula One drivers competed.

✦✦✦ (WC1) XVI South African Grand Prix (Kyalami)
80 laps of 2.55 miles = 204.0 miles.
24 entries – 23 starters – 13 finished.
Front row: J Stewart – 1m-19.3s (115.76mph); C Amon 0.0s; J Brabham 0.3s.

07-MAR: Those cheeky Marches had the top two places on the grid. Stewart and Brabham contested the first corner, but behind, Rindt struck Amon's front wing, flew over Brabham's front wheel and off the track, yet was 16th on lap one. Brabham dropped to just sixth, while Amon was way back. Stewart had been handed a decent lead from Ickx, Beltoise, Oliver and McLaren. Brabham took just three laps to pass those, and, on lap 20, took the lead from Stewart. Amon had retired on lap 14 subsequent to the Rindt attack. Hulme came from tenth on lap one to third by lap 16, and, on lap 38, took second from Stewart; Goodyear tyres perhaps helping. Beltoise inherited fourth from McLaren, while an amazing, still recovering, Graham Hill made sixth behind Miles' Works Lotus.

1st	J Brabham (W)	Brabham BT33-Cosworth in 1h-49m-34.6s	111.70
2nd	D Hulme (W)	McLaren M14A-Cosworth	8.1s
3rd	J Stewart (KT)	March 701-Cosworth	17.1s
F lap	Surtees/Brabham	McLaren/Brabham in 1m-20.8s	113.61r

✦✦✦ V 'Race Of Champions' (Brands Hatch)
50 laps of 2.46 miles = 123 miles.
15 entries – 12 started – 6 finished.
Front row: J Stewart – 1m-25.8s (103.22mph); J Brabham 0.2s; J Oliver 0.2s.

22-MAR: Scuderia Ferrari was at Sebring, but otherwise all the main contenders from Kyalami were here. Brabham crashed and took Stommelen's car, while Beltoise also put himself out of the race. Jackie Oliver stormed away for BRM, and led from Stewart until lap nine. A BRM leading was

good to see, but Jack Brabham passed Stewart and Oliver on successive laps. Oliver retired from second soon after, but Stewart's twitchy March couldn't hold Brabham, who had victory in his grasp with four laps to go. His ignition failed, however, and he dropped to fourth, a lap down. Race and lap records were set, proving to be faster than July's GP here.

1st	J Stewart (KT)	March 701 Cosworth in 1h-12m-51.8s	101.29
2nd	J Rindt (W)	Lotus 49C-Cosworth	36.2s
3rd	D Hulme (W)	McLaren M14A-Cosworth	1m-22s
F lap	J Brabham (W)	Brabham BT33-Cosworth in 1m-25.8s	103.22r

✦✦✦ (WC2) Gran Premio d'España (Jarama)
90 laps of 2.115 miles = 190.4 miles.
23 entries – 16 qualifiers – 5 finished.
Front row: J Brabham – 1m-23.9s (90.76mph); D Hulme 0.2s; J Stewart 0.3s.

19-APR: This track couldn't accommodate a full grid – why create such a track? – it's not a 'round-the-houses' track. March was blamed by some for exacerbating the problem by having too many cars! World Champions and team leaders were guaranteed starts, the rest having special qualifying sessions. The front row sped off in reverse order, while Oliver's BRM stub axle broke, sending him across a hairpin into the side of Ickx's Ferrari. A fireball exploded, from which, miraculously, both emerged almost unscathed. Stewart pulled away while Hulme retired on lap nine, and Beltoise's Matra took second from Brabham on lap 16. Lap 31 and Beltoise was out, the order now Stewart, Brabham, Pescarolo, Surtees, McLaren and Hill. Pescarolo's Matra lasted only one more lap, so Surtees' privately run McLaren was third. Brabham caught Stewart on lap 60, only to suffer engine failure, so Stewart led all the way. Surtees pitted on lap 49, retiring on lap 76. Hill and Servoz-Gavin were fourth and fifth.

1st	J Stewart (KT)	March 701 Cosworth in 2h-10m-58.2s	87.21
2nd	B McLaren (W)	McLaren M14A-Cosworth	36.2s
3rd	M Andetti (STP)	March 701-Cosworth	1m-22s
F lap	J Brabham (W)	Brabham BT33-Cosworth in 1m-24.3s	90.33r

Championship positions:
J Stewart 13; J Brabham 9; B McLaren, D Hulme 6.

✷✷ XXII *Daily Express* International Trophy (Silverstone)

2 x 26 laps of 2.927 miles = 152.4 miles.

16 F1 entries – 11 started – 8 finished.

Front row: C Amon – 1m-21.4 (129.45mph); J Stewart 1.3s; D Hulme 1.7s; P Gethin 1.9s.

26-APR: A reduced entry, as BRM was absent sorting out the stub axle problem, and only Amon and Stewart's Marches were present. F5000 cars were invited to make up the shortfall, 14 of which started, with Peter Gethin's McLaren M10B-Chevy on the outside of the front row! Amon and Courage had been at Monza the day before, and Courage hadn't practised. Rindt was only 18th on the grid, having missed the dry session. Hulme led off, soon to be passed by Amon and then stopping for a loose wheel. Brabham was now second, but his engine blew so Amon won easily by 12.1s from Stewart, while Courage came from the back of the grid to third, having seen off McLaren, Rindt and Hulme. The same grid was used for part two, which was rather unfair on Courage and Rindt in an aggregate result. Stewart had had his rear wing adjusted, and he led away strongly on a drying track. Once fully dry, Amon caught right up to Stewart but was baulked near the end, finishing 2.1s behind. Rindt retired with ignition trouble early on, but yet again Courage came through to third. Amon had followed Stewart home for a strong aggregate win, So Chris Amon had beaten Jackie Stewart in identical cars – his first win in Formula One – long overdue and very worthy.

1st	C Amon (W)	March 701 Cosworth in 1h-13m-32.2s	124.19
2nd	J Stewart (KT)	March 701 Cosworth	10.0s
3rd	P Courage (W)	deTomaso 38-Cosworth	1m-03s
F lap	C Amon	March 701 Cosworth in 1m-22.1s	128.35

✷✷✷ (WC3) XXVIII Grand Prix de Monaco (Monte Carlo)

80 laps of 1.954 mile circuit = 156.3 miles.

26 entries – 16 qualified – 8 finished.

Front row: J Stewart – 1m-24.0s (83.75mph); C Amon 0.6s. Row two: D Hulme 1.1s; J Brabham 1.4s.

10-MAY: The radical Lotus 72 was deemed unsuitable at this time, so the old 49Cs were used. Stewart and Amon's Marches had the front row, and led off from Brabham, Beltoise and Ickx, as Hulme, Pescarolo and Rindt followed. Stewart pulled away, only to stop on lap 27 with ignition trouble. Brabham had passed Amon so now led. Ickx and Beltoise had retired which, with passes on Pescarolo and Hulme, brought Rindt up to third. Lap 60 saw a bolt drop out of Amon's suspension, and the famous chase of Brabham by Rindt was now set up.

Four laps to go and a nine second lead seemed enough for Brabham to ease up. Terrible baulking by lapped runners brought Rindt four seconds closer on lap 77. With one lap to go it was barely a second! One bend to go (the hairpin) and Brabham chose the wrong way to deal with a lapped Courage and slid off, his grimace visible through his face mask. Rindt's victory for sheer pressure proved that 'it's never over till it's over.' A legendary victory – and in the old car!

1st	J Rindt (W)	Lotus 49C-Cosworth in 1h-54m-36.6s	81.85
2nd	J Brabham (W)	Brabham BT33-Cosworth	22.9s
3rd	H Pescarolo (W)	Matra-Simca MS120	51.4s
F lap	J Rindt	Lotus 49C-Cosworth (lap 80) 1m-23.2s	84.56r

Championship positions:
J Brabham 15; J Stewart 13; J Rindt, D Hulme 9.

✷✷✷ (WC4) XXIX Grand Prix de Belgique (Spa)

28 laps of an 8.761-mile circuit = 280.4 miles.

27 entries – 17 started – 8 finished.

Front row: J Stewart – 3m-28.0s (151.64mph); J Rindt 2.1s; C Amon 2.3s.

07-JUN: Catastrophe had befallen the McLaren team with the death of Bruce five days previously at Goodwood, so the team was, naturally, absent – as if Denny Hulme burning his hands at Indianapolis wasn't enough. Minor safety improvements were in place to allay the fears which took this race from the calendar in '69. It was still lethal, though. Rindt had the 72 now, and was at the front, but he was behind Amon and Stewart after a lap, with Rodriguez and Ickx chasing. Stewart then led for a lap but, by lap five, Rodriguez had passed the lot, this track not fazing him at all. Amon battled him all the way, sometimes alongside, but a first BRM triumph for four years was not to be denied. Rindt, Stewart and Brabham retired, helping Beltoise to third place after Ickx had pitted, and Ferrari's new boy, Giunti, was fourth; V12s doing well here, but the BRM was best!

1st	P Rodriguez (W)	BRM P153 in 1h-39m-09.9s	149.94
2nd	C Amon (W)	March 701 Cosworth	1.1s
3rd	JP Beltoise (W)	Matra-Simca MS120	1m-44s
F lap	C Amon	March 701 Cosworth in 3m-27.4s	152.07r

Championship positions:
J Brabham 15; J Stewart 13; P Rodriguez 10.

✳✳✳ (WC5) XVIII Grote Prijs van Nederland (Zandvoort)

80 laps of a 2.605-mile circuit = 208.4 miles.
27 entries – 20 qualified – 12 finished.
Front row: J Rindt – 1m-18.50s (119.48mph); J Stewart 0.23s; J Ickx 0.43s.

21-JUN: McLaren was back, with Gethin replacing the burnt Hulme for this race, and Gurney in Bruce's car. While Amon suffered a burnt clutch Ickx led from the outside of the front row from Rindt, Oliver and Stewart. Rindt took over on lap three, and remained untroubled to the end producing the first of many wins for the Lotus 72. Ickx punctured on lap 51, losing out to Stewart and Regazzoni, but regained third on lap 59. Oliver retired from fifth on lap 23, having been passed by teammate Rodriguez. He soon stopped for a loose nose to be fixed. This race is notorious for the disaster of Piers Courage's crash and instant inferno on lap 23. Seeing his loose helmet on the track was instant proof that he had perished. Bag tanks proving inadequate again.

1st	J Rindt (W)	Lotus 72C-Cosworth in 1h-50m-43.41s	112.95
2nd	J Stewart (KT)	March 701-Cosworth	30.3s
3rd	J Ickx (W)	Ferrari 312B	1 lap
F lap	J Ickx	Ferrari 312B in 1m-19.23s	118.38r

Championship positions:
J Stewart 19; J Rindt 18; J Brabham 15.

✳✳✳ (WC6) LVI Grand Prix de France (Clermont-Ferrand)

38 laps of a 5.005-mile circuit = 190.2 miles.
14 entries – 13 started – 9 finished.
Front row: J Ickx – 2m-58.22s (101.10mph); JP Beltoise 0.48s. Row two: C Amon 0.92s; J Stewart 1.02s.

05-JUL: Inspired by being on home territory, Beltoise got the Matra alongside Ickx on the front row, and the pair stormed off; Ickx in the lead, with Stewart clinging on. Stewart pitted on lap five with ignition trouble, so now Amon and Rindt chased the V12 cars, with Rindt taking third from Amon on lap seven. Ickx's engine suffered a cracked valve and failed on lap 17, so Beltoise now led, to huge cheers. Beltoise's glory lasted just ten laps, though, as a puncture gave the lead to Rindt on lap 25. It was a long way back to the pits, so Beltoise lost nine places then retired with fuel starvation – a harsh fate for a great drive. The top six remained unchanged, with Hulme, Pesarolo and Gurney also scoring. Rindt had won where last year this twisting, plunging circuit had made him sick.

1st	J Rindt (W)	Lotus 72C-Cosworth in 1h-55m-57.00s	98.42
2nd	C Amon (W)	March 701 Cosworth	7.61s
3rd	J Brabham (W)	Brabham BT33-Cosworth	44.83s
F lap	J Brabham	Brabham BT33-Cosworth in 3m-00.75s	99.69r

Championship positions:
J Rindt 27; J Stewart; J Brabham 19.

✳✳✳ (WC7) XXVII British Grand Prix (Brands Hatch)

80 laps of 2.46 miles = 196.8 miles.
30 entries – 23 started – 10 finished.
Front row: J Rindt – 1m-24.8s (104.43mph); J Brabham 0.0s; J Ickx 0.3s.

18-JUL: Surtees produced his eponymous car now, but was near the back of the grid, and the Marches were all mid-field. Ickx led Brabham and Rindt for six laps when his differential broke just as Rindt was attacking Brabham, so now Rindt led. For 61 laps Brabham harried Rindt all the way, while the field, led by Oliver and Hulme, steadily dropped away. Oliver's engine failed on lap 54 just after Stewart and Surtees had stopped from sixth and seventh. Rookie Regazzoni was fourth now! On lap 69 a slightly fluffed gear change was all Brabham needed to storm past. What surprised everyone was the way he simply drew away, and, after ten laps entered the last lap 13 seconds ahead with the race won. But where was he? It was Rindt who appeared at Clearways first, with Jack Brabham coasting – out of fuel. A warm-up fuel setting (richer) hadn't been reset for the race. Twice now a race had been thrown away on the last bend to Rindt's benefit. But a too-hasty rear wing height check disqualified Rindt – overturned on rechecking. How close 'old man' Brabham came to leading the Championship by a point at this stage. Age no barrier.

1st	J Rindt (W)	Lotus 72C-Cosworth in 1h-57m-02.0s	100.89
2nd	J Brabham (W)	Brabham BT33-Cosworth	32.9s
3rd	D Hulme (W)	McLaren M14A-Cosworth	54.4s
F lap	J Brabham	Brabham BT33-Cosworth in 1m-25.9s	103.10

Championship positions:
J Rindt 36; J Brabham 25; J Stewart 19.

✳✳✳ (WC8) XXXII Grosser Preis von Deutschland (Hockenheim)

50 laps of 4.218 miles = 210.9 miles.

26 entries – 21 qualified – 9 finished.
Front row: J Ickx – 1m-59.5s (127.08mph); J Rindt 0.2s. Row two: G Regazzoni 0.3s; J Siffert 0.5s.

02-AUG: Armco and chicanes had been added to improve safety at the track after Jim Clark's death, which made it a safer bet than the Nürburgring. The race started with the first four on the grid retaining their order. Amon passed teammate Siffert on lap five to join the other three in a four-way scrap, except he was always fourth, the others swapping places regularly. Brabham had been left at the start to the great benefit of Rindt's Championship campaign. Regazzoni spun when his gearbox seized on lap 31, and Amon lost his new third place soon after with engine failure, to the benefit of Surtees. Rindt now led Ickx in a memorable lead-swapping scrap – five times in the last seven laps – but it was the slipperiness of the Lotus that overcame Ferrari power in the end. The hard-luck story was of John Surtees – 15th on lap one, but retiring from third with four laps to go. Hulme had been 16th – a great drive from him. Surtees' retirement should have benefitted Pescarolo, but he had lost out to Hulme and Siffert, who promptly stopped. So up into fourth place came the first Brazilian GP driver in just his second Grand Prix – Emerson Fittipaldi.

1st	J Rindt (W)	Lotus 72C-Cosworth in 1h-42m-00.3s	124.07
2nd	J Ickx (W)	Ferrari 312B	0.7s
3rd	D Hulme (W)	McLaren M14A-Cosworth	1m-22s
F lap	J Ickx	Ferrari 312B in 2m-00.5s	126.03

Championship positions:
J Rindt 45; J Brabham 25; D Hulme 20.

✳✳✳ (WC9) VIII Grosse Preis von Osterreich (Zeltweg)

60 laps of 3.673 miles = 220.4 miles.
26 entries – 24 started – 15 finished.
Front row: J Rindt – 1m-39.23s (133.25mph); G Regazzoni 0.47s. Row two: J Ickx 0.61s; J Stewart 0.92s.

16-AUG: This great new fast-flowing circuit, which soon became very popular with drivers and spectators alike, seemed to favour the V12s. Rindt was beaten away by Regazzoni and Ickx, who assumed the lead on lap two, while Rindt dropped to sixth and Beltoise moved up to third. Rindt stopped on lap 21 handing fourth to Giunti, so three Ferraris were in the top four. Giunti punctured on lap 38, losing out to Stommelen, Amon, Rodriguez and Oliver. Fuel pump trouble dropped Beltoise from third with three laps to go, dropping behind Stommelen and Rodriguez and Oliver's BRMs. The Ferrari duo had run in tandem all the way.

1st	J Ickx (W)	Ferrari 312B in 1h-42m-17.32s	129.27
2nd	G Regazzoni (W)	Ferrari 312B	0.61s
3rd	R Stommelen (W)	Brabham BT33-Cosworth	1m-28s
F lap	G Regazzoni	Ferrari 312B in 1m-40.40s	131.70

Championship positions:
J Rindt 45; J Brabham 25; D Hulme 20.

✳ XVII International Gold Cup (Oulton Park)

2 x 20 laps of 2.678 miles = 107.1 miles.
7 F1 entries – 5 started – 4 finished.
Front row: J Surtees – 1m-36.2s (100.22mph); J Oliver 3.0s; F Gardner 5.8s.

22-AUG: The small entry was boosted by many F5000 cars, but the five F1 starters, Stewart, Rindt, Surtees, Oliver and Hill, were star names – three World Champions in Stewart, Hill and Surtees, the World Championship leader Rindt, plus BRM's Jackie Oliver, who had almost won the British GP two years earlier. Five days earlier a piece of F1 history occurred as Ken Tyrrell solved his March customer problem by unveiling the best ever F1 secret: The Tyrrell 001. No-one had had a clue about it.

Stewart started from the back due to problems in the rain-affected practice, but the opposition soon saw how fast it was. He lost a lap soon after the start with throttle trouble, then threw the car around as if it was its last race, demolishing his own lap record by two whole seconds to finish seventh in part one just as his engine failed as Surtees won from Oliver and Rindt. Revised gearing helped Rindt win the second heat, the new record untouched. First heat advantage gave the race to Surtees, now a fourth driver/constructor winner. The Tyrrell hadn't won, but the F1 status quo has now obviously been changed. The reigning World Champion now had a car worthy of him – fast 'straight-out-of-the-box'. Even with such a small field, this race showed that the idea 'non-Championship = non-event' is a non-sequitur so very often.

1st	J Surtees (W)	Surtees TS7-Cosworth in 59m-48.2s	107.48
2nd	J Rindt (W)	Lotus 72-Cosworth	3.4s
3rd	J Oliver (W)	BRM P153	20.2s
F lap	J Stewart (W)	Tyrrell 001-Cosworth in 1m-26.6s	111.32r

✳✳✳ (WC10) XXXIX Gran Premio d'Italia (Monza)

68 laps of a 3.573-mile circuit = 243.0 miles.

28 entries – 20 started – 9 finished.
Front row: J Ickx – 1m-24.14s (152.87mph); P Rodriguez 0.22s. Row two: G Regazzoni 0.25s; J Stewart 0.59s.
06-SEP: Ken Tyrrell took both cars for Stewart to Monza, but minor problems caused Stewart to favour the March for the race, and it was competitive. Tragedy ruined the end of practice, though, when, trying to get amongst the dominant Ferraris, Jochen Rindt had a brake shaft fail at the Parabolica. The car turned a sharp left, almost head-on into the barrier. He didn't wear crotch straps and shot forwards as the front of the car was ripped right off. He died soon after. All the Lotuses were withdrawn. Rodriguez's BRM was next to poleman Ickx on the grid, and those two, with Stewart and Regazzoni, held the top places for six laps, joined soon by Stommelen, Hulme and Oliver. The usual Monza slip-streamer was taking place, but Rodriguez stopped on lap 12, Ickx on lap 25, and Oliver on lap 35. Regazzoni, in the last Ferrari running, and Stewart, kept just clear of Beltoise and Hulme for many laps until Regazzoni managed to break the tow of Stewart – a rare thing at Monza. The next four places of Stewart, Beltoise, Hulme and Stommelen were covered by just 0.67 of a second. Cevert in Tyrrell's March was sixth. But what now for the Championship?

1st	G Regazzoni (W)	Ferrari 312B in 1h-39m-06.88s	147.08
2nd	J Stewart (KT)	March 701-Cosworth	5.73s
3rd	JP Beltoise (W)	Matra-Simca MS120	5.80s
F lap	G Regazzoni	Ferrari 312B in 1m-25.20s	150.97r

Championship positions:
J Rindt 45; J Brabham, J Stewart 25.

✳✳✳ (WC11) IV Grand Prix Of Canada (Mont Tremblant)
90 laps of 2.65 miles = 238.5 miles.
22 entries – 20 started – 12 finished
Front row: J Stewart – 1m-31.5s (104.26mph); J Ickx (0.1s)
Row two: G Regazzoni (0.4s); F Cevert (0.9s)
20-SEP: Team Lotus was still absent, but Hill's 72 now had solid brake shafts. Stewart proved the Tyrrell's speeds shown at Oulton Park were no fluke, as he took pole position and then promptly shot off to lead the race easily. Ickx followed but Regazzoni was passed by Rodriguez, Surtees and Cevert. Surtees pitted on lap six, and, by lap 24, Regazzoni had re-passed the others to take third place, which became second when Stewart's stub-axle broke, ending a heroic Championship debut for the Tyrrell. Amon had followed Regazzoni, and the podium places remained secure. Cevert's March had suspension trouble, letting Rodriguez and a

recovered Surtees into fourth and fifth, followed by Gethin, McLaren's best finisher. Jacky Ickx now had an unenviable problem.

1st	J Ickx (W)	Ferrari 312B in 2h-21m-18.4s	101.27
2nd	G Regazzoni (W)	Ferrari 312B	14.8s
3rd	C Amon (W)	March 701-Cosworth	57.9s
F lap	G Regazzoni	Ferrari 312B in 1m-32.2s	103.47

Championship positions:
J Rindt 45; J Ickx 28; G Regazzoni 27.

No-one ever before or since has experienced the impossible dilemma that Jacky Ickx now found himself in. This win has brought him from fifth place to second in the Championship, and only he could now take the crown from the late Jochen Rindt with two more wins. But where would the credibility be in beating a deceased driver who, after Italy, would only have needed a single point to be Champion? How could he want this title? How could he not?

✳✳✳ (WC12) 13th United States Grand Prix (Watkins Glen)
108 laps of 2.30 miles = 248.4 miles.
19 entries – 17 started – 7 finished.
Front row: J Ickx – 1m-03.07s (131.28mph); J Stewart 0.55s.
Row two: E Fittipaldi 0.60s; P Rodriguez 1.11s.
04-OCT: Lotus returned with Sweden's Reine Wisell making his GP debut in the vacant Lotus seat. Emerson Fittipaldi, who was in only his fourth GP, was de facto team leader now. He stepped up to the task superbly, and was third on the grid behind Stewart. Ickx seemed well clear; half a second is a lot in such a short lap time. Then it happened again! Stewart took off from the start in the Tyrrell and led as he pleased for an easy victory – or so it seemed. Behind him Rodriguez led Ickx, Regazzoni, Amon, Surtees and Oliver, with Fittipaldi down in eighth. Oliver retired, and both Ferraris passed Rodriguez. Surtees retired on lap six, followed by Oliver on lap 16, and both Regazzoni and Amon hit trouble. By half distance Fittipaldi had reached fourth. Stewart was half a lap ahead of Ickx who soon pitted with a fuel leak, and all was then calm for 25 laps when Stewart's engine started smoking, and he retired on lap 82. Stewart could easily have won the first two Championship races with this amazing car. Now Rodriguez's BRM had a clear lead, but, with eight laps left he pitted for fuel. For both Lotuses 'novices' to be on the podium was astonishing. Ickx's dilemma had been solved by a fuel leak, and now Jochen Rindt was the deserved but tragically posthumous Champion.

1st	E Fittipaldi (W)	Lotus 72C-Cosworth in 1h-57m-32.79s	126.79
2nd	P Rodriguez (W)	BRM P153	36.39s
3rd	R Wisell (W)	Lotus 72C-Cosworth	45.17s
F lap	J Ickx (W)	Ferrari 312B in 1m-02.74s	131.93

Championship positions:
J Rindt 45 (WC); J Ickx 31; G Regazzoni 27.

✳✳✳ (WC13) IX Gran Premio de Mexico (Mexico City)

65 laps of 3.107 miles = 201.9 miles.
19 entries – 18 started – 10 finished.
Front row: G Regazzoni – 1m-41.86s (109.80mph); J Stewart 0.02s. Row two: J Ickx 0.55s; J Brabham 1.71s.

25-OCT: The grid suggested a Ferrari v Tyrrell battle again, with Brabham, in his last race, fourth on the grid. Idiotically, the crowd, typically of scant control in Latin America, sat at the edge of the track, so hard racing was impossible as a massacre would occur if any car went off. This had happened before in the early '50s but now was totally unacceptable. Thank goodness the Championship had been sealed at the previous race as the situation would have made a farce of any fight by Ickx against others to win the race and the title. Discretion would surely have required anyone involved to yield to Ickx to avoid risking massive loss of life and huge scandal for motor racing, even though the situation was entirely the fault of the organisers and uncontrollable Mexicans. After the flag dropped, Ickx and Regazzoni were split by Stewart for 13 laps until his steering became loose; he returned near the back only to hit a large dog ... Brabham came from seventh to third by lap 15, holding the place until lap 52, when his engine, and his great and unique career, expired. It was a very long time before Formula One came back to Mexico.

1st	J Ickx (W)	Ferrari 312B in 1h-53m-28.36s	106.78
2nd	G Regazzoni (W)	Ferrari 312B	24.64s
3rd	D Hulme (W)	McLaren M14A-Cosworth	45.97s
F lap	J Ickx	Ferrari 312B in 1m-43.11s	108.47

Championship positions:
J Rindt 45; J Ickx 37; G Regazzoni 33.

1970 seasonal review

At the beginning of the season the interloper March was viewed with some suspicion by many, as it promised seemingly impossible things with minimal resources, and no track record as a company. It was rumoured that the name March was an acronym for 'Much Advertised Racing Car Hoax.' It had to prove itself and did just that with the top two spots on the grid at its first appearance, and then a hat-trick of wins in the next three races. From then, it took its rightful place among the more established teams, yet won no more, as the car wasn't then successfully developed as the season wore on. McLaren was absent from the winner's circle, hardly surprising with the loss of its founder mid-season. With the added losses of Piers Courage and Champion Jochen Rindt, 1970 was one of the most tragic in F1 history, almost matching 1958 and 1968. No other year since has seen such losses, with only 1973 and 1994 coming close. The huge TV-based public popularity of Formula One in the 21st century would not, I think, survive a year like 1970. Heroes are expected to live out their careers now.

The 3-litre Formula One had been in force for five seasons, and three-quarters of the grid were using the ubiquitous Cosworth DFV with Hewland gearbox 'package,' yet a season's finish rate had yet to achieve 50 per cent.

*Winners of the 16 F1 races of 1970 –
quantity & quality of success*

5 wins	J Rindt (5A)	6 wins	Lotus-Cosworth (6A)
3 wins	J Ickx (3A)	4 wins	Ferrari (4A)
2 wins	J Stewart (2A)	3 wins	March-Cosworth (2A, B)
1 win	J Brabham (A) G Regazzoni (A) E Fittipaldi (A) P Rodriguez (A) C Amon (B) J Surtees (C)	1 win	Brabham-Cosworth (A); BRM (A); Surtees-Cosworth (C)

1970 Championship review

How strange it seems, looking back, that the reigning Champion, Jackie Stewart, had to find a new chassis manufacturer to make his title defence possible, and a 'rookie' constructor – March – at that! This goes some way to explaining why he went from being the biggest winner in 1969 to biggest loser this year, losing almost as many points as Jochen Rindt gained in winning the Championship. I remember how disappointed we fans were at this situation. The sport needed a champion, if still racing, to be able to defend and give credibility to the new campaign. It was a relief when he was on pole position for the first round, but that was fairly short lived. He had flattered the car as only he could. The new Tyrrell, with reliability, would clearly turn things around for 1971.

Rindt only took the Championship lead at the sixth round, Brabham and Stewart having shared it, and then, partly thanks to Jackie Ickx's bad luck, ran away with it to the extent that his total of just two rounds later was not beaten in the remaining five rounds. There can be no doubt that, but for the dreadful Monza practice crash, his winning ways would not have been over for the season. Thankfully, Jochen Rindt is still the only posthumous Champion. The Lotus 72 continued to be highly competitive for a few more years, so Rindt's death undoubtedly cost him many more victories, and probably Championships. His and Jim Clark's fatal accidents, both at the height of their careers, shows the folly of using Grand Prix drivers' win statistics alone as a measure of stature, when nowadays top drivers are able to retire from their own choice after maybe 20 years in F1.

Both Ickx and Stewart lost potential Championship-winning points, and Jack Brabham twice lost rounds on the last bend of the last lap to Rindt – once yielding to pressure and once to an incorrect fuel setting.

Brabham retired, as had been expected. Such a long, successful, and injury free, career was very unusual then. Having to delay his retirement, due to Ickx defecting to Ferrari, did nothing to arrest the sheer speed he still possessed. He was still Rindt's main adversary right up to the British Grand Prix, from whence he unfortunately failed to score. Since then Damon Hill has been the oldest F1 winner, at Spa in 1998, when a couple of weeks short of his 38th birthday, but that's still over six years off Jack Brabham's age at his 1970 South Africa win. So even with today's long careers, his achievement is unchallenged after over 44 years – which was his age then!

VISIT VELOCE ON THE WEB – WWW.VELOCE.CO.UK
All current books • New book news • Special offers • Gift vouchers • Forum

292

Chapter 30

1971
Same problem – so many answers

Aerodynamics had become the new technological challenge added to the two Hs – Horsepower and Handling. It would consume some of the former while complicating the latter. Never before or since have the cars been so easily identifiable thanks to the divergence of approach to aerodynamics, and, of course, to the necessary sponsor's paintwork. The 'wedge' we had seen in the previous year's Lotus 72, but now we had the 'Spitfire wing' (March); the 'Full-width cowling' (Tyrrell from mid-season); the 'Delta' (Surtees); and even the 'Lobster-claw' (Brabham), while others pursued the 'standard solution' of aerofoil appendages each side of the nose.

Ferrari had won most of the last half of 1970, with BRM winning earlier in Belgium, so Cosworth was going to have to find something to answer the V12 challenge, while improving the reliability, which had suffered last year perhaps due to pressure on 'after sales service'. This may have been due to the sheer number of units in use.

Belgium and Mexico were both off the Championship list, for safety reasons – the former because of the track, the latter because of the impossible-to-control Latin temperament crowd. The days of the 'safety barrier' consisting mainly of human flesh belonged to the worst part of the distant past. For some reason races were shortened this year to 325km (202 miles) maximum. The minimum race distance was still 300km (186 miles) and the maximum duration two hours, yet the Spanish and German GPs were shorter. Monaco, of course, being exempt on distance as 186 miles was impossible there in two hours ... then.

Suddenly there was a revival in extra Formula One races, with eight organised giving no less than 19 F1 races. Not being satisfied with that, almost as many F2 races had top Formula One graded stars entered.

Gold Leaf Team Lotus continued with the '72C', updated at Monaco to '72D', and continued with the post-Rindt line-up of Emerson Fittipaldi and Reine Wisell, both newcomers but now both 'podium visitors'. Lotus would produce the turbine powered '56' – another Lotus 'first' – also wedge shaped.

Brabham was now under new management, with designer Ron Tauranac at the helm, Jack Brabham having sold the team and retired from all F1 activity. The single BT34 built had a radiator system split in two, each half in a nacelle, with a large chord aerofoil section between them, thus resembling a lobster claw. The nacelles were partly ahead of the front wheels. This was driven by Graham Hill, while the BT33 was in the hands of Tim Schenken, rewarded for his F2 results.

March produced the 711, with a front wing mounted on a spar on top of a bulbous nose. This had an elliptical shape like Spitfire wings joined together. The radiators were each side of the body, a-la Lotus 72. Principal drivers were Ronnie Peterson and Andrea deAdamich, who would be Alfa Romeo V8-powered. A third Cosworth car would sometimes be entered.

McLaren produced a conventional but lower and bulbous M19A for Denny Hulme, while the M14A was piloted by Peter Gethin, who defected mid-season and was replaced by Jackie Oliver who had joined a little earlier.

Tyrrell continued with the very promising car from 1970, which, mid-season, was provided with a full-width nose cowling which wouldn't look out of place on a sports car. By 'full-width' I refer to maximum width allowed, which was just narrower than the middle of the front tyre width. The drivers were, naturally, Jackie Stewart and Francois Cevert.

Surtees had combined with Rob Walker Racing and was sponsored by Brooke Bond OXO. A lower, squatter car, the TS9 was produced with its front wing in an almost delta shape, the radiator tucked underneath. Later came the TS9B with full-width nose and side radiators. John Surtees himself was driving his last season, with Rolf Stommelen and, later, Mike Hailwood joining.

Ferrari had the 312B/2, now with slight wedge shape but radiator still in front. An uprated boxer engine producing 480bhp powered it, laying down the power challenge for others to chase. Jacky Ickx, 'Clay' Regazzoni and Ignazio Giunti were signed to drive, but the latter was killed in a sports car race before the first race: Mario Andretti replaced him.

Matra-Simca continued with the MS120, updated with a full-width nose and about the same power as the DFV. Chris Amon had departed March to become principal driver, with Jean-Pierre Beltoise.

BRM updated its car to P160 specification, which mainly consisted of being lower and squatter, as was the general vogue for 1971. Pedro Rodriguez and Josef Siffert were retained, with New Zealander Howden Ganley added. The sad loss in July of Rodriguez was covered by signing the aforementioned Peter Gethin and Helmut Marko.

The only serious independent entrant was Frank Williams, now that Rob Walker had joined John Surtees. He had, sadly, lost the talented Piers Courage the year before, but had continued with Brian Redman or Tim Schenken at the wheel. DeTomaso had ceased racing, so, for 1971, he had bought a March 701 for Henri Pescarolo, soon replaced by a 711. The 701 then driven by a variety of drivers.

Note: From this point, in the results, all finishers are assumed to be Works drivers, unless designated otherwise.

The Grand Prix driver's diary of single-seater racing for 1971

24th January	F1 – Gran Premio de Argentina at Buenos Aires (Ag) – 212.3 miles
14th February	F2 – Gran Premio de Columbia at Bogota (Ca) – 146.3 miles
21st February	F2 – Gran Premio Ciudad de Bogota (Ca) – 146.3 miles
6th March	F1 – **South African Grand Prix** at Kyalami (SA) – 201.5 miles
14th March	F2 – Speed International Trophy at Mallory Park (UK) – 108 miles
21st March	F1 – 'Race of Champions' at Brands Hatch (UK) – 123.5 miles
28th March	F1 – Questor Grand Prix at Ontario (US) – 204.4 miles
4th April	F2 – Jim Clark Memorial Trophy at Hockenheim (D) – 168.3 miles
9th April	F1 – Spring Trophy at Oulton Park (UK) – 107.1 miles
12th April	F2 – BARC '200' at Thruxton (UK) – 183.8 miles
18th April	F1 – **Gran Premio de España** at Montjuic Parc (E) – 176.6 miles
25th April	F2 – Grand Prix de Pau (F) – 123.3 miles
2nd May	F2 – Eifelrennen at Nurburgring (D) – 142.7 miles
8th May	F1 – *Daily Express* International Trophy at Silverstone (UK) – 152.2 miles
16th May	F2 – Gran Premio de Madrid (Jarama) (E) – 126.9 miles
23rd May	F1 – **Monaco Grand Prix** (M) – 156.3 miles
31st May	F2 – Hilton Transport Trophy at Crystal Palace (UK) – 132.1 miles
13th June	F1 – Jochen Rindt Trophy at Hockenheim (D) – 147.6 miles
20th June	F1 – **Grote Prijs van Nederland** at Zandvoort (N) – 182.7 miles
27th June	F2 – Grand Prix de Rouen (F) – 166.7 miles
4th July	F1 – **Grand Prix de France** at Paul Ricard (F) – 198.2 miles
17th July	F1 – **British Grand Prix** at Silverstone (UK) – 199 miles
1st August	F1 – **Grosser Preis von Deutschland** at Nürburgring (D) –170.3 miles
15th August	F1 – **Grosser Preis von Osterreich** at Zeltweg (A) – 198.3 miles
21st August	F1 – International Gold Cup at Oulton Park (UK) – 107.1 miles
22nd August	F2 – Swedish Gold Cup at Kinnekullering (S) – 63.2 miles
30th August	F2 – Rothmans International at Brands Hatch (UK) – 98.8 miles
5th September	F1 – **Gran Premio d'Italia** at Monza (I) – 196.4 miles
12th September	F2 – Jochen Rindt Gedachtnitsrennen at Tulln-langen (A) – 124.4 miles
19th September	F1 – **Grand Prix of Canada** at Mosport Park (C) – 196.7 miles
26th September	F2 – Grand Prix d'Albi (F) – 142.3 miles
3rd October	F1 – **United States Grand Prix** at Watkins Glen (US) – 199.2 miles
10th October	F2 – Gran Premio di Roma at Vallelunga (I) – 135.7 miles
17th October	F2 – Gran Premio Madonina at Vallelunga (I) – 126 miles
24th October	F1 – Victory Race at Brands Hatch (UK) – 98.8 miles
31st October	F2 – Torneio Braziliero F2 Round 1 at Interlagos (Br) – 138.5 miles
7th November	F2 – Torneio Braziliero F2 Round 2 at Interlagos (Br) – 138.5 miles
14th November	F2 – Torneio Braziliero F2 Round 3 at Porto Allegre (Br) – 106.5 miles

21st November   F2 – Torneio Braziliero F2 Round 4 at Cordoba (Br) – 138 miles

39 events of total race mileage = 5883 miles.

Events in bold are 11 World Championship rounds – 57.9 per cent of the 19 F1 races run.

Formula Two dates are those in which FIA-graded F1 drivers competed.

✷ XIV Gran Premio de la Republica Argentina (Buenos No 9)

2 x 50 laps of 2.121 miles = 212.1 miles.

13 F1 entries – 10 started – 7 finished.

Front row: R Stommelen (1m-15.85 (100.69mph); C Amon 0.03s. Row two: R Wisell 0.18s; E Fittipaldi 0.43s.

24-JAN: A three-car entry by Ferrari was withdrawn after Ignazio Giunti was killed here two weeks earlier in a sports car race. Jean-Pierre Beltoise was suspended as a result. Five F5000 cars were allowed to start to replace them. Lotus had Emerson Fittipaldi's brother, Wilson, as well as teammate Reine Wisell. Stommelen's debut for Surtees started with pole, from where he won the first part from the four-car scrap of Siffert, Pescarolo, Amon and Wisell, who were covered by half a second. Emerson Fittipaldi's Lotus was fifth for three laps but dropped right back. In part two Siffert led Stommelen, Amon and Pescarolo. Stommelen challenged for the lead but touched both Siffert and Amon and was out. Siffert dropped back and retired, so Amon now led, and pulled away easily overcoming the six second deficit from part one. This was Chris Amon's second Formula One win. Into third place came a 'local' who would soon be a familiar face on the Formula 1 scene – his car supplied by Jo Bonnier.

1st	C Amon	Matra-Simca MS120 in 2h-08m-19.29s	99.17
2nd	H Pescarolo (FW)	March 701-Cosworth	21.9s
3rd	C Reutemann (EB)	McLaren M7C-Cosworth	53.3s
F lap	C Amon	Matra-Simca MS120 in 1m-15.05s	101.76

✷✷✷ (WC1) XVII South African Grand Prix (Kyalami)

79 laps of 2.550 miles = 201.5 miles.

26 entries – 25 starters – 13 finished.

Front row: J Stewart – 1m-17.9s (117.99mph); C Amon 0.6s; G Regazzoni 0.9s.

06-MAR: All were present except Beltoise, still under suspension. Stewart was on pole, from Amon, but both were left at the start. Regazzoni led from Fittipaldi, Ickx,

Hulme, Rodriguez and Andretti. Stewart was seventh and Amon 14th! Ickx and Rodriguez fell back, while Hulme came through to lead and pull away on lap 17. Surtees followed suit from 11th to third on that same lap. Vibration for Regazzoni allowed Surtees and Andretti past, but Surtees' gearbox lost oil and he lost second to Andretti before retiring. Stewart was now fourth, behind Regazzoni, but took third on lap 66. Everything changed with four laps to go as long-time leader Hulme had suspension trouble, finishing sixth. Andretti's first race for Ferrari yielded his maiden GP win.

1st	M Andretti	Ferrari 312B/2 in 1h-47m-35.5s	112.35
2nd	J Stewart	Tyrrell 001-Cosworth	20.9s
3rd	G Regazzoni	Ferrari 312B/2	31.4s
F lap	M Andretti	Ferrari 312B/2 in 1m-20.3s	114.33r

✷✷✷ VI 'Race Of Champions' (Brands Hatch)

50 laps of 2.46 miles = 123 miles.

16 entries – 14 started – 7 finished.

Front row: J Stewart – 1m-24.6s (104.68mph); D Hulme 0.9s; G Regazzoni 1.4s.

21-MAR: Lotus' Emerson Fittpaldi debuted the first ever F1 turbine car, the 56, while his teammate Reine Wisell had the normal 72. Stewart and Hulme held top two places until lap 20 when a drying track gave the slick-tyred Regazzoni and Hill their chance. Regga took his fully and led from lap 25 to the end. Hill took third from Hulme, who retired on lap 33, followed by Hill two laps later, by which time his 'lobster-claw' Brabham had grabbed fastest lap. Now Surtees was third, ahead of Wisell and Gethin, who both retired letting Ganley's BRM into fourth, only to lose it to Schenken's Brabham. Peterson carved from the back but stopped on lap 14 in eighth. Stewart's choice of tyres spoiled a good lead scrap – so many pole positions for the Tyrrell but no win yet.

1st	C Regazzoni	Ferrari 312B/2 in 1h-13m-35.0s	100.29
2nd	J Stewart	Tyrrell 001-Cosworth	22.4s
3rd	J Surtees	Surtees TS9-Cosworth	1 lap
F lap	G Hill	Brabham BT34-Cosworth in 1m-26.7s	102.15

✷✷✷ 'Questor' Grand Prix (Ontario-California)

2x32 laps of 3.194 miles = 204.4 miles.

22 F1 entries – 18 F1 started – 12 finished.

Front row: J Stewart – 1m-41.26s (113.57mph); C Amon

0.02s. Row two: J Ickx 0.27s; D Hulme 1.20s.

28-MAR: The Americans introduced three decimal place timing, which is mostly statistical diarrhoea. I have rounded to two places for clarity.

Formula 'A' was the American name for F5000. This one-off race was really USA v 'Rest-of-the-World' – FA v F1 – an was run on part of a banked oval track with twisty infield. This saw F1 take the top six grid spots, with Stewart claiming yet another pole. Mark Donohue headed the 12 strong 'home' team in seventh, but Andretti's F1 Ferrari was surprisingly down in 12th.

Part 1 – Ickx's Ferrari led from the rolling start (new to F1 drivers), but Stewart took over on lap five. Ickx punctured, so Amon was second, and Andretti passed Donohue for third. Amon now punctured and Hulme spun to 12th, yet recovered to fourth ahead of Ickx and Amon. Andretti snatched the lead from Stewart with two laps to go. Donohue led the FA cars in ninth, despite a quick pit stop. Part 2 – Stewart led again, while Andretti's tyres heated slowly. Then, on lap ten, he took over. Stewart only just held off Amon at the end. Donohue's fuel problems stopped him after five laps. F1 easily beat FA, but an American had won. Thankfully, an unnecessary complicated points system didn't get in the way of the usual result decided by accumulated time.

1st	M Andretti	Ferrari 312B2 in 1h-51m-48.41s	109.71
2nd	J Stewart	Tyrrell 001-Cosworth	15.9s
3rd	D Hulme	McLaren M19A-Cosworth	1m-29s
F lap	P Rodriguez	BRM P160 in 1m-42.78s	111.88

* 'Rothmans' Spring Trophy (Oulton Park)
40 laps of 2.678 miles = 107.1 miles.
15 entries – 11 started – 5 finished.
Front row: J Stewart – 1m-25.8s (112.37mph); P Gethin 0.0s; P Rodriguez 1.2s.

09-APR: Single cars from Tyrrell and Surtees, two from McLaren, plus three-car teams from BRM and Lotus – Wisell with the turbine this time made for a decent entry, which attracted a 45,000 strong crowd. Hulme's McLaren didn't arrive, and Siffert's BRM punctured on the warm-up lap, losing him half a lap. Rodriguez led all the way in storming style to a popular win. Stewart had a fourth successive pole, yet his car handled too badly in the race for him to challenge the leaders. Gethin had matched Stewart's pole time and lay second all the way, ahead of Stewart. All the Lotuses had problems, with Fittipaldi retiring.

1st	P Rodriguez	BRM P160 in 57m-33.4s	111.68
2nd	P Gethin	McLaren M14A-Cosworth	4.6s
3rd	J Stewart	Tyrrell 001-Cosworth	12.2s
F lap	Rodriguez/Gethin	BRM/McLaren in 1m-25.0s	113.43r

*** (WC2) Gran Premio d'España (Montjuic Parc)
75 laps of 2.355 miles = 176.6 miles.
26 entries – 22 started – 11 finished.
Front row: J Ickx – 1m-25.9s (98.72mph); G Regazzoni 0.1s; C Amon 0.1s.

18-APR: Stewart was not on pole, or even the front row, but behind Ickx, Regazzoni and Amon, and was the only Cosworth-powered car in the front three rows! However, he was second behind Ickx after the start, and ahead of Regazzoni and Amon. Two lap later Amon was third, and, three laps after that, Stewart squeezed past Ickx and led all the way, but was harassed often by Ickx. Regga retired a few laps later with fuel pump trouble, so Amon had a lonely run home to third. Rodriguez ran fourth ahead of Andretti, who suffered Regga's problem on lap 41, benefitting Hulme. The big, high wings last seen here in '69 were gone, but the downforce lost had mostly been recovered, as the cars were faster still.

1st	J Stewart	Tyrrell 003-Cosworth in 1h-49m-03.4s	97.19
2nd	J Ickx	Ferrari 312B/2	3.4s
3rd	C Amon	Matra-Simca MS120	58.1s
F lap	J Ickx	Ferrari 312B/2 in 1m-25.1s	99.60r

Championship positions:
J Stewart 15; M Andretti 9; C Amon and J Ickx 6.

*** XXIII *Daily Express* International Trophy (Silverstone)
2 x 26 laps of 2.927 miles = 152.2 miles.
20 F1 entries – 16 started – 14 finished.
Front row: C Amon – 1m-20.0s (131.72mph); J Stewart 0.2s; E Fittipaldi 1.0s; J Surtees 1.2s.

08-MAY: Every team entered, but Ferrari withdrew at the last minute (another strike?). A similar number of F5000 cars started, causing, as was usual, the event to be split in two due to their smaller tankage – a shame. Stewart just lost pole to Amon, but it was he who won part one easily by 11.6 seconds. The Matras chased hard, but fuel problems stopped Amon and slowed Beltoise. Rodriguez stormed from tenth to beat Hill for second by 1.2 seconds. Part two, a 'walk-over' by Stewart was on the cards, but a jammed throttle put him 'into the rough' at the first corner. Rodriguez now led Surtees and Hill but Hill passed Surtees, and, on lap 12, led the race. When Rodriguez punctured, the lead battle was over for a surprise win for Hill and the 'lobster-claw' Brabham.

Typical jokey Graham Hill quote over the Tannoy: "It's golf tomorrow – if he drives off like that I'll be quids-in."

1st	G Hill	Brabham BT34-Cosworth in 1h-11m-03.2s	128.53
2nd	P Gethin	McLaren M14A-Cosworth	1m-34s
3rd	T Schenken	Brabham BT33-Cosworth	2m-05s
F lap	J Stewart	Tyrrell 003-Cosworth in 1m-20.5s	130.90r

*** (WC3) XXIX Grand Prix de Monaco (Monte Carlo)
80 laps of a 1.954-mile circuit = 156.3 miles.
26 entries – 18 qualified – 10 finished.
Front row: J Stewart – 1m-23.2s (84.55mph); J Ickx 1.2s. Row two: J Siffert 1.6s; C Amon 1.6s.
23-MAY: The cars were faster now, yet two more than before were allowed to start! There were no guaranteed starters – it was fastest 18 – which was right. Andretti's Ferrari and Ganley's BRM were the main non-starters. Stewart's pole was prophetic as he followed this up with an untroubled flag-to-flag victory, followed by Siffert and Ickx for many laps. Peterson, who had been sixth on lap seven, pressurised Rodriguez into a costly error on lap 13 to take fourth, then caught and passed Ickx and Siffert on successive laps. Stewart was now well away, and shattering the lap record at will and bettering his pole time. Siffert's engine expired on lap 59 to Ickx's benefit. Hulme was the last to complete 80 laps. This was the Tyrrell's first 'grand slam' (Pole – Victory – Fastest lap) and the 'newgirl' (cars always being feminine) was now clearly the best of the Cosworth runners. Peterson had shown his superb quality – and on one of the most difficult circuits.

1st	J Stewart	Tyrrell 003-Cosworth in 1h-52m-21.3s	83.49
2nd	R Peterson	March 711-Cosworth	25.6s
3rd	J Ickx	Ferrari 312B/2	53.3s
F lap	J Stewart	Tyrrell 003-Cosworth in 1m-22.2s	85.58r

Championship positions:
J Stewart 24; J Ickx 10; M Andretti 9.

* Jochen Rindt Memorial Trophy (Hockenheim)
35 laps of 4.218 miles = 147.6 miles.
23 entries – 19 started – 12 finished.
Front row: Pole position empty; J Ickx – 1m-56.8s (130.01mph). Row two: G Regazzoni 1.0s; R Wisell 2.8s.
13-JUN: Formula One at Spa was now banned, this was a replacement event for 1971 only. Two cars from Ferrari, Lotus, BRM, March and Surtees, plus one from McLaren plus assorted others made for a reasonable field. Matra was at Le Mans, Tyrrell, Matra and Brabham were absent. Pole position was vacant in memory of Jochen Rindt. Ickx had smashed the lap record for his 'pole,' Ferrari power being unchallenged on long straights. Lotus had brought the turbine which had flames coming from its chimney, so Wisell used a 72C. Ickx led throughout, but his teammate Regazzoni had an electrical fault on lap three. Wisell and Peterson scrapped over second until Wisell's brake pedal broke. Surtees climbed from ninth on lap one to take third by lap 13. Speeds from the previous year's German GP here were well exceeded – better tyres, more horsepower and aero-advances?

1st	J Ickx	Ferrari 312B/2 in 1h-10m-11.7s	126.19
2nd	R Peterson	March 711-Cosworth	53.8s
3rd	J Surtees	Surtees TS9-Cosworth	1m-17s
F lap	J Ickx	Ferrari 312B/2 in 1m-58.8s	127.82r

*** (WC4) XVIII Grote Prijs van Nederland (Zandvoort)
70 laps of a 2.605-mile circuit = 182.4 miles.
26 entries – 24 qualified – 15 finished.
Front row: J Ickx – 1m-17.42s (121.15mph); P Rodriguez 0.04s; J Stewart 0.22s.
20-JUN: The previous year's pole time was bettered by almost two seconds. Again, only Stewart's DFV power challenged the V12s. A very wet race showed how much cars were now handicapped by rain, as speeds were down by 20 per cent, even with special tyres. The race belonged to Ickx and Rodriguez, and even Stewart was in trouble on Goodyear tyres, soon dropping to eighth. The lead had changed four times by lap 30, by then only Regazzoni was yet to be lapped. Ickx slowly drew away but the conditions made no position secure. Sports car endurance racers, as the two leaders were, encounter poor conditions routinely. It seems that Firestone tyres might have helped, though, as Peterson, Surtees and Siffert completed a whitewash of the points scores, but two laps back.

1st	J Ickx	Ferrari 312B/2 in 1h-56m-20.09s	94.06
2nd	P Rodriguez	BRM P160	7.99s
3rd	G Regazzoni	Ferrari 312B/2	1 lap
F lap	J Ickx	Ferrari 312B/2 in 1m-34.95s	98.78

Championship positions:
J Stewart 24; J Ickx 19; Andretti, Peterson and Rodriguez 9.

✳✳✳ (WC5) LVII Grand Prix de France (Le Castellet)

55 laps of a 3.610-mile circuit = 198.6 miles.
29 entries – 23 started – 13 finished.
Front row: J Stewart – 1m-50.71s (117.39mph); G Regazzoni 0.82s; J Ickx 1.17s.
04-JUL: A new track with a long straight followed by a very fast bend was thought likely to favour the V12s, but it was Stewart who dominated with the latest Cosworth motor. A starting light had proved faulty, so it was at the flag that Stewart just cleared off, and was ten seconds up on Regga after eight laps, by which time Ickx had retired. Peterson's March was Alfa Romeo V8-powered, and ran mid-field until it laid an oil slick by blowing up on lap 20. This put Regga (second) and Hill (fifth) off the track, but Hill continued, only to retire with an oil pipe split. Rodriguez handed his newly acquired second spot to Cevert, seven laps later with ignition trouble. Fittipaldi and Siffert battled for third all the way to the flag, and Amon benefitted when Schenken, who had risen from 17th to fifth, lost oil pressure. So, the first Tyrrell one-two took place, and the V12s were beaten into fourth.

1st	J Stewart	Tyrrell 003-Cosworth in 1h-46m-41.68s	111.66
2nd	F Cevert	Tyrrell 002-Cosworth	28.12s
3rd	E Fittipaldi	Lotus 72D-Cosworth	34.07s
F lap	J Stewart	Tyrrell 003-Cosworth in 1m-54.09s	113.91

Championship positions:
J Stewart 33; J Ickx 19; Andretti, Peterson and Rodriguez 9.

✳✳✳ (WC6) XXVI British Grand Prix (Silverstone)

68 laps of 2.927 miles = 199.0 miles.
25 entries – 24 started – 12 finished
Front row: G Regazzoni – 1m-18.1s (134.92mph); J Stewart 0.0s; J Siffert 0.1s.
17-JUL: Tragedy had struck F1 last week when Pedro Rodriguez was killed in a sports car race at Norisring, so

Siffert was BRM's undisputed leader. He was on the outside of the front row, but Ickx's brilliant start from the third row placed him second, behind Regga and ahead of Stewart and Siffert after a lap. On lap two the latter two had both passed Ickx, and, three laps later had done the same to Regga. Stewart now pulled away, while Siffert yielded to Regazzoni ten laps later. All remained static until Siffert lost third on lap 42 with vibration, and, soon after, Regga's engine failed. Peterson and Schenken took their podium slots now, but Schenken lost his to Fittipaldi, with transmission trouble, just five laps from the end. Pescarolo, Stommelen and Surtees filled the scoring places but were lapped. Stewart, meanwhile, was in a 'race of his own.' He and the brilliant new Tyrrell were untouchable.

1st	J Stewart	Tyrrell 003-Cosworth in 1h-31m-31.5s	130.48
2nd	R Peterson	March 711-Cosworth	36.1s
3rd	E Fittipaldi	Lotus 72D-Cosworth	50.5s
F lap	J Stewart	Tyrrell 003-Cosworth in 1m-19.9s	131.88r

Championship positions:
J Stewart 42; J Ickx 19; R Peterson 15.

✳✳✳ (WC7) XXXIII Grosse Preis von Deutschland (N Nürburgring)

12 laps of 14.189 miles = 170.3 miles.
27 entries – 22 started – 12 finished.
Front row: J Stewart – 7m-19.0s (116.36mph); J Ickx 0.2s.
Row two: J Siffert 3.4s; G Regazzoni 3.7s.
01-AUG: Back on the calendar after widening and safety work, lap times were 20 seconds faster. Ickx made another demon start to lead Stewart, but he was second by the time they departed out into the country at the back of the pits. A three second lead after lap one became massive when Ickx crashed on lap two, almost taking Regazzoni with him. From then, Stewart pulled ahead by seven seconds a lap, and held it at over 30 seconds. Cevert hunted down Regga, helped by the Ferrari's slightly damaged exhaust system. The pair passed second-placed Siffert, who retired on the next lap. At half distance, the Tyrrells were one-two as in France, with Cevert proving ready to win if anything happened. Andretti, in fourth, was over two minutes behind Stewart, as were Peterson and Schenken!

1st	J Stewart	Tyrrell 003-Cosworth in 1h-29m-15.7s	114.46
2nd	F Cevert	Tyrrell 002-Cosworth	30.1s
3rd	G Regazzoni	Ferrari 312B/2	37.1s
F lap	F Cevert	Tyrrell 003-Cosworth in 7m-20.1s	116.07r

1st	J Surtees	Surtees TS9-Cosworth in 57m-38.5s	111.51
2nd	H Ganley	BRM P153	11.4s
F lap	J Surtees	Surtees TS9-Cosworth in 1m-24.8s	113.69r

✳✳✳ (WC9) XXXIX Gran Premio d'Italia (Monza)

55 laps of a 3.573-mile circuit = 196.5 miles.
26 entries –23 started – 11 finished.

Front row: C Amon – 1m-22.40s (156.10mph); J Ickx 0.42s.
Row two: J Siffert 0.63s; H Ganley 0.75s.

05-SEP: Lotus skipped this race, worried about repercussions from Rindt's accident, but Fittipaldi's turbine car was entered under another name. Matra and McLaren had one car each, and Hulme was racing in the USA. The front two rows were all V12 cars – would that be significant? Monza slip-streamers make lap score charts almost meaningless. Stewart retired on lap 15 from second, and Regazzoni on lap 17 from third. Amon came from ninth on lap three to haul himself into and through the seven-car leading pack to lead all but one of laps 36 to 47. He seemed to have pulled clear of the bunch, a very difficult thing to do, when the anti-Amon Gods stepped in and, as he went to remove a rip-off laminate, the whole visor came adrift leaving him with unprotected vision. He finished sixth, 30 seconds adrift with fuel vaporisation problems compounding his situation, so he probably wouldn't have won anyway. Many would think he was doubtless the star. All those ahead of him finished inside 0.6 seconds, with Hailwood and Ganley fourth and fifth. Peter Gethin's winning speed stood as the fastest F1 race for decades. Incidentally, none of the first seven finishers had won a Championship F1 race before, so this was a battle of the new-breed. A finish never repeated since.

1st	P Gethin	BRM P160 in 1h-18m-12.60s	150.76
2nd	R Peterson	March 711-Cosworth	0.01s
3rd	F Cevert	Tyrrell 002-Cosworth	0.09s
F lap	H Pesrarolo (FW)	March 711-Cosworth in 1m-23.80ss	153.49r

Championship positions:
J Stewart (WC) 51; Peterson 23; J Ickx 19.

✳✳✳ (WC 10) V Grand Prix Of Canada (Mosport Park)

80 laps of 2.459 miles = 196.7 miles.
28 entries – 24 started – 18 finished.

Championship positions:
J Stewart 51; J Ickx 19; Peterson 17.

✳✳✳ (WC8) IX Grosse Preis von Osterreich (Zeltweg)

54 laps of 3.673 miles = 198.3 miles.
26 entries – 22 started – 13 finished.

Front row: J Siffert – 1m-37.44s (135.70mph); J Stewart 0.21s.
Row two: F Cevert 0.42s; G Regazzoni 0.46s.

15-AUG: Engine problems kept Matra away, and Beltoise had been suspended again over Giunti's death. Despite losing Rodriguez, BRM was here with a four-car entry. Siffert and Ganley, now supported by Peter Gethin, who'd left McLaren, and Helmut Marko. Siffert promptly snatched pole from under Jackie Stewart's nose, to give BRM its first pole position for almost six years. He then completed a 'grand slam' by leading throughout with fastest lap. A very popular win all-round, on a very popular and demanding track. Stewart chased hard, using narrower front tyres which proved to be a mistake, and, after 21 laps he waved Cevert through to take up the chase, but both retired by lap 42. Jacky Ickx was never in the hunt, so Stewart's Championship was secure. His car had shed a wheel on lap 35 and he returned on foot to claim his crown with three rounds remaining.

1st	J Siffert	BRM P160 in 1h-30m-23.91s	131.64
2nd	E Fittipaldi	Lotus 72D-Cosworth	30.1s
3rd	T Schenken	Brabham BT33-Cosworth	37.1s
F lap	J Siffert	BRM P160 in 1m-38.47s	134.28r

Championship positions:
J Stewart (WC) 51; J Ickx 19; Peterson 17.

XVII International Gold Cup (Oulton Park)

2x20 laps of 2.678 miles = 107.1 miles.
8 F1 entries – 8 started – 4 finished.

Front row: P Gethin – 1m-24.6s (113.96mph); H Pescarolo 0.4s; H Ganley 0.4s.

21-AUG: A poor F1 entry of only eight cars, supported by 12 F5000 cars. Only John Surtees could be regarded as an established F1 star. In part one Pescarolo led from Gethin, who stopped for a tyre change. So Ganley, Surtees and Gardner followed the Frenchman home. Surtees, Pescarolo, Gethin was the part two order, but Gethin hit Pescarolo and retired. Pescarolo lost brakes and crashed on lap seven. Surtees broke the advantage that Ganley had from part one to claim a lap record and another Gold Cup.

Front row: J Stewart – 1m-15.3s (117.56mph); J Siffert 0.2s; F Cevert 0.4s.

19-SEP: American Mark Donohue joined Denny Hulme at McLaren, replacing Jacky Oliver who'd raced at Monza, and Beltoise was back from suspension. Jo Siffert's BRM sat between the Tyrrells on the grid, but it was Stewart who had the only clear view of the road ahead in the abominable conditions. He was followed by Peterson, Beltoise, and Donohue. Peterson lost second when he ran wide, but rectified this by finding different lines were better and passed Beltoise. The latter copied Peterson, and they began to catch Stewart. Beltoise crashed when lapping Hulme, but Stewart lost the lead to Peterson on lap 18. Twelve laps later he was ahead again when Peterson was fouled by George Eaton's lapped BRM. Heavy mist reduced visibility, and the race was aborted after lap 64. Rain-hating Denny Hulme survived for fourth place, and even put up the fastest lap. A dry race speed is usually about three per cent below pole speed, and a wet race now up to 20 per cent– here it was over 30 per cent – extraordinary! Perhaps the worst ever.

1st	J Stewart	Tyrrell 003-Cosworth in 1h-55m-12.9s	81.96
2nd	R Peterson	March 711-Cosworth	38.3s
3rd	M Donohue	McLaren M19A-Cosworth	1m-36s
F lap	D Hulme	McLaren M19A-Cosworth in 1m-43.5s	85.53

Championship positions:
J Stewart (WC) 60; R Peterson 29; J Ickx 19.

✱✱✱ (WC11) 14th United States Grand Prix (Watkins Glen)
59 laps of 3.377 miles = 199.3 miles.
31 entries – 29 started – 18 finished.
Front row: J Stewart – 1m-42.64s (118.44mph); E Fittipaldi 0.02s; D Hulme 0.28s.

03-OCT: A much revised circuit, lengthened and widened, greeted the teams this year, which was required as lap times would have almost been down below 60 seconds. The massive purse attracted the biggest field of the year, with four additional North Americans. Only Lotus, McLaren and Matra fielded fewer than three cars, with BRM running five. Hulme led the Tyrrells from the start, but within a lap Stewart was in his usual position, with Regazzoni, Siffert and Ickx following Cevert. Lap seven, and Cevert had taken second from Hulme, and began catching Stewart, whose tyres were wearing. Lap 16 and Cevert was waved past by Stewart, who dropped to finish fifth. Hulme dropped back and out, while Ickx was second on lap 14, holding it until lap 49 when alternator trouble stopped

him. Cevert's domination was almost as Stewart's would have been. The Tyrrell clearly a winner with or without Stewart, and Cevert celebrating a worthy maiden victory. The Tyrrell's seven wins matched Lotus' record from 1963.

1st	F Cevert	Tyrrell 002-Cosworth in 1h-43m-57.99s	115.10
2nd	J Siffert	BRM P160	40.06s
3rd	R Peterson	March 711-Cosworth	44.07s
F lap	J Ickx	Ferrari 312B/2 in 1m-43.47s	117.49

Championship positions:
J Stewart (WC) 62; R Peterson 33; F Cevert 26.

✱✱✱ World Championship Victory Race (Brands Hatch)
40 laps of 2.46 miles = 98.4 miles.
16 F1 entries – 15 started – 9 finished.
Front row: J Siffert – 1m-22.8s (106.96mph); P Gethin 0.0s; E Fittipaldi 0.8s.

26-OCT: Brands Hatch stepped in when the Mexican GP was cancelled following crowd chaos in 1970. A celebration race for Stewart and Tyrrell and perhaps of the glory of Grand Prix racing at its best was the atmosphere in which everyone arrived. All but Matra and Ferrari were present, and BRM collared the top two grid spots. Its identical times shattered the lap record set at the previous year's British GP by over three seconds, so a very fast race was expected. As was usual when Championship points were not at stake, a dozen F5000 cars joined in. Italian GP winner Gethin led from Fittipaldi, Hailwood and Peterson, but the latter two tangled. This left Stewart third, and Siffert had just passed Schenken for fourth, followed by Surtees at the start of lap 15. The race title suggested a joyful climax to the season but the very worst of F1 transpired, as popular Jo Siffert, when lying fourth at high speed in the dip before Hawthorn Bend, had the car swerve sharp left into the bank. A huge fireball and useless extinguishers gave him no chance. The race result now meaningless, the race was stopped and result declared at lap 14. He was the first driver to die in a BRM in all its years in Formula One. The cause has never been explained except that Siffert was not at fault.

1st	P Gethin	BRM P160 (14 laps) in 19m-54.4s	103.81
2nd	E Fittipaldi	Lotus 72D-Cosworth	0.2s
3rd	J Stewart	Tyrrell 003-Cosworth	5.4s
F lap	E Fittipaldi	Lotus 72D-Cosworth in 1m-24.0s	105.43r

1971 seasonal review

The form of the Tyrrell team from the end of 1970 continued unabated this year, and in similar fashion, as Stewart claimed pole after pole. Strangely, though, he only won a race after that habit stopped. Tyrrell's first full season remains, even at the time of writing, surely the best debut season ever for a brand new marque. "What about the Brawn in 2009?" I hear you say. On paper that's a similar achievement, but that car had initially been developed by Honda during 2008, prior to its quitting Formula One and handing it over to Ross Brawn. The Tyrrell had been designed from scratch by Derek Gardner, who had never designed a racing car before! The Brawn unveiled a significant technical advantage in its rule-stretching double diffuser, whereas Derek Gardner did nothing new, he just did it better with the layout similar to the Matra MS80 of 1969. Ferrari, on the other hand, started off promisingly, winning three events on the trot, and then rested on its laurels. The driver team was perhaps short of Stewart-like calibre.

The opposite was true of BRM, who, in the last half of the season, achieved its best performance since the start of this formula in 1966. Yet this was a disaster year for BRM, with the dreadful losses of Rodriguez and Siffert, who both had real form and might have taken it to more glory. BRM never recovered from these losses, and from here began its long and sad decline.

Lotus' fortunes took a huge dive, its drivers unable to follow the exceptional talent of Jochen Rindt, and the team suffered a blank sheet. Perhaps this was not too surprising considering that its combined experience had been just eight rounds in 1970. Fittipaldi had won in the USA, with help from retirements, so Chapman must have had a lot of faith in him, but the team produced only three podium finishes all year – all of them from Fittipaldi, though his season had been interrupted by a road car accident which left him missing the Dutch GP. Did the circumstances of Rindt's death – thought to be failure of a hollow brake shaft – reduce the desire of top drivers to drive for Lotus? If a new car had been produced which had failed to live up to expectations that would not be so unusual, but here was a clearly superior car (for winning anyway) suddenly without superior talent at the wheel? The turbine alternative had been a brave failure, but had it taken Lotus' eye off the ball this year?

Eleven drivers achieved wins this year, the most since 1962, with Gethin and Cevert added to the list.

Winners of the 19 F1 graded races of 1971 – quantity & quality of success

6 wins	J Stewart (6A)	7 wins	Tyrrell-Cosworth (7A)
2 wins	M Andretti (2A) P Gethin (2A) J Ickx (A, C)	5 wins	Ferrari (4A, C)
1 win	G Regazzoni (A) J Siffert (A) F Cevert (A) G Hill (A) C Amon (C) P Rodriguez (C) J Surtees (D)	4 wins	BRM (3A, C)
		1 win	Brabham-Cosworth (A); Matra-Simca (C); Surtees-Cosworth (D)

World Championship review

The prowess of the Tyrrell was now shown in results, and gave Jackie Stewart a clean run to the title after round four at Zandvoort, the title being sewn up with three rounds remaining. Few race leads were lost to unexpected misfortune, and no driver would have produced a challenge to Stewart's title had their losses not occurred. The nearest would have been Regazzoni, and he would have been 26 points adrift. I'm sure Sir Jackie Stewart would accept that the path to his second Championship had been eased by the loss to Lotus of its hugely talented leader at Monza the year before. Hulme and Amon both experienced the agony of losing a race lead late in an event, through no fault of their own, and ended the season winless, as did their teams McLaren and Matra, respectively.

Ronnie Peterson's consistency earned him a Championship second place, but without a win. This was the first time this had happened since 1952. There were no fewer than five Grand Prix winners below Peterson in the table, though. However, to get so close in a March to the BRM of Peter Gethin at Monza, a power circuit, in that five-car mad dash for the line, was magnificent. His dominance over his team-mate Pescarolo is notable, and makes him the find of the year, just ahead of Francois Cevert.

VISIT VELOCE ON THE WEB – WWW.VELOCE.CO.UK
All current books • New book news • Special offers • Gift vouchers • Forum

301

Chapter 31

1972

Evolution of the species

The cars were generally little changed from the previous year, but new safety regulations were introduced. Minimum weight was increased by the CSI to 550kg, to allow for a minimum 1.5mm thickness of outer skin to be introduced. Fuel tanks now had to be foam filled, and six-point harnesses were now mandatory since Jochen Rindt's refusal to use them contributed to his sad demise.

One area of significant (and game-changing) evolution was the expansion in the use of sponsor liveries. The most obvious of these was the use by Lotus of the black and gold colour scheme of a cigarette packet to cover the entire car, and worse, the renaming of Team Lotus as John Player Specials – JPSs (a dreadful American habit). I recall a response that having a car in black would be dangerous as 'one wouldn't be able to see it coming.' On second thoughts, perhaps that was the very idea. Many now see it as 'the true Lotus livery' which is beyond me since it only ever represented the identity of a 'fag packet.' I shall continue to use the Lotus name in these records for the sake of continuity and truth. Some may say 'What about Red Bull?' But, unlike John Player Tobacco, Red Bull bought the Jaguar F1 team 'lock, stock and barrel,' thus becoming the constructor, whereas Colin Chapman never did (and never would have) been an employee of John Player, or anyone else.

The constructors

Tyrrell, World Champion in its first full year, identified its cars by chassis sequence rather than a type identity, so, for 1972, new cars began at 005, and had a flatter, squarer-section monocoque. Driver line-up, not surprisingly, remained as Jackie Stewart and Francois Cevert, now a very good number two.

Lotus continued with minor revisions to the type 72D, and retained Emerson Fittipaldi, but his teammate was now Dave

Walker, who had replaced Fittipaldi when recovering from his road accident.

Brabham was now owned by Bernie Ecclestone, and the cars were painted plain white: no other sponsorship apparently being needed. Graham Hill was still team leader, joined by Carlos Reutemann, who had considerable backing from YPF, the Argentinian national fuel company, and later also by Wilson Fittipaldi.

McLaren had taken over the Yardley Cosmetics sponsorship and livery from BRM, with team leader Denny Hulme having Peter Revson (of the Revlon cosmetics family (clash of interest?)) as support. He had been in F1 in the '60s, but had now become Can-Am Champion in the USA, and would prove to be very useful.

Team Surtees no longer had the boss on the regular driving force, as he had promoted Mike Hailwood to the F1 squad as leader, supported by Tim Schenken. The car still in blue and white Brooke Bond Oxo-Rob Walker colours. Also engaged was Andrea deAdamich in the red and white of Italian backer Ceramica Pagnossin.

March started with the 721, a 711 evolution, replaced it by the 721X with its radical transmission layout – a failure – and then the 721G, effectively a DFV-powered F2 car. It was still led by Ronnie Peterson, now accompanied by F2 find Niki Lauda.

Frank Williams privately ran a March 721 and 711 for Henri Pescarolo and Carlos Pace. He was sponsored by Politoys, and, later in the season, ran a new car carrying the Politoys name. Some decried the use of the sponsor's name as the marque identity, but who can blame Frank – it went with the funds – as the JPS (Lotus).

Ferrari had little to report, and continued virtually unchanged, with Jacky Ickx and 'Clay' Regazzoni resident at the helm. Mario Andretti drove when available. Arturo Merzario deputised for 'Regga' at Brands, and was awarded a couple more drives. A popular guy, known as 'Little Art' or 'Pocket Cowboy' (due to his mode of dress).

BRM had acquired huge sponsorship from American tobacco giant Marlboro, and the cars were in a red and white livery which would become the most familiar sponsor in F1 for decades. It ran the previous year's cars while developing the P180 – it took a long time. The tragedies of the year before forced a new line-up, which was headed by Jean-Pierre Beltoise, with Peter Gethin, Howden Ganley and Helmut Marko as main support. Reine Wisell, Alex Soler-Roig and, just once, Vern Schuppan also drove. Strength in numbers, usually a Ferrari tactic, was needed now. But wouldn't this deplete its resources?

Matra, in complete contrast to BRM, operated just a single car, for Chris Amon, the wonderfully pervasive sound making one feel that there were more than one.

Tecno was a new arrival on the grid mid-season and powered by its own V12 unit. Derek Bell and Nanni Galli were given the responsibility of producing some results – this proved difficult (very).

That's 28 names in 11 marques – a very healthy situation and almost double the entry of three years earlier. Twelve Championship rounds were run, with seven extra races of varying quality producing a season of 19 races, as per the year before. Formula Two still attracted graded F1 drivers on many occasions, so it seems that they still couldn't get enough racing despite the danger of that period– and there was still Le Mans (with Graham Hill in the winning car), etc.

The Grand Prix driver's diary of single-seater racing for 1972

23rd January	F1 – **Gran Premio de Argentina** at Buenos Aires (Ag) – 201.4 miles
4th March	F1 – **South African Grand Prix** at Kyalami (SA) – 201.5 miles
12th March	F2 – John Player Championship at Mallory Park (UK) – 135 miles
19th March	F1 – 'Race of Champions' at Brands Hatch (UK) – 98.8 miles
30th March	F1 – Grande Premio do Brasil at Interlagos (Br) – 182 miles
31st March	F2 – John Player Championship at Oulton Park (UK) – 107.1 miles
3rd April	F2 – BARC '200' at Thruxton (UK) – 183.8 miles
16th April	F2 – Deutschland Trophae at Hockenheim (I) – 165.6 miles
23th April	F1 – *Daily Express* International Trophy at
	Silverstone (UK) – 117.1 miles
1st May	F1 – **Gran Premio de España** at Jarama (E) – 190.2 miles
6th May	F2 – Grand Prix de Pau (F) – 183.5 miles
14th May	F1 – **Monaco Grand Prix** (M) – 156.3 miles
29th May	F1 – International Gold Cup at Oulton Park (UK) – 107.1 miles
29th May	F2 – Greater London Trophy at Crystal Palace (UK) – 132.1 miles
4th June	F1 – **Grand Prix de Belgique** at Nivelles (B) – 196.7 miles
11th June	F2 – Rhein-Pokalrennen at Hockenheim (D) – 124.2 miles
18th June	F1 – Gran Premio Repubblica Italiana at Vallelunga (I) – 159.1 miles
25th June	F2 – Grand Prix de Rouen (F) – 172.2 miles
29th June	F2 – Gran Premio della Lotteria di Monza (I) – 142.9 miles
2nd July	F1 – **Grand Prix de France** at Clermont Ferrand (F) – 190.2 miles
9th July	F2 – Jochen Rindt Gedachtnitsrennen at Osterreichring (A) – 124.9 miles
15th July	F1 – **British Grand Prix** at Brands Hatch (UK) – 187.6 miles
23rd July	F2 – Gran Premio di Imola (I) – 174.6 miles
30th July	F1 – **Grosser Preis von Deutschland** at Nürburgring (D) –198.6 miles
6th August	F2 – Mantorp F2 Trofen at Mantorp Park (S) – 183.4 miles
13th August	F1 – **Grosser Preis von Osterreich** at Zeltweg (A) – 198.3 miles
20th August	F2 – Gran Premio del Meditteraneo at Enna Pergusa (I) – 190 miles
28th August	F1 – Rothmans '50,000' at Brands Hatch (UK) – 291.3 miles
3rd September	F2 – Festspielpreis der Stadt at Salzburgring (A) – 157.9 miles
10th September	F1 – **Gran Premio d'Italia** at Monza (I) – 196.4 miles
16th September	F2 – John Player Championship at Oulton Park (UK) – 107.1 miles
24th September	F1 – **Grand Prix of Canada** at Mosport Park (C) – 196.7 miles
1st October	F2 – Preis von Baden-Würt.und Hessen at Hockenheim – 135.1 miles
8th October	F1 – **United States Grand Prix** at Watkins Glen (US) – 199.2 miles
22nd October	F1 – Victory Race at Brands Hatch (UK) – 98.8 miles
29th October	F2 – Torneio Braziliero F2 Round 1 at Interlagos (Br) – 138.5 miles

5th November	F2 – Torneio Braziliero F2 Round 2 at Interlagos (Br) – 138.5 miles		
12th November	F2 – Torneio Braziliero F2 Round 3 at Interlagos (Br) – 98.9 miles		

38 events of total race mileage = 6163 miles, or 6056 max due to simultaneous events.

Events in bold are World Championship rounds – 63.2 per cent of the 19 F1 races run.

Formula Two dates are those in which more than one graded Formula One driver competed.

✱✱✱ (WC1) IX Gran Premio de la Republica Argentina (Buenos Aires No 9)
95 laps of 2.078 miles = 197.5 miles.
22 entries – 21 started – 11 finished.

Front row: C Reutemann – 1m-12.46s (103.27mph); J Stewart 0.20s. Row two: P Revson 0.28s; D Hulme 0.53s.

23-JAN: Chris Amon's ill-luck began early when he non-started due to a gearbox malady on the warm-up lap. Stewart took the lead from local hero Reutemann, and Hulme. Fittipaldi passed both to take second on lap eight, holding it until Hulme relieved him of it on lap 34. Reutemann's tyres needed changing on lap 44, dropping him right down. Fittipaldi retired on lap 60 with a bent radius rod, which he'd had almost from the start. Stewart was now well away, while his teammate Cevert had stopped on lap 59 from fourth. So now Ickx and Regazzoni followed Hulme at a distance, Schenken and Peterson taking the remaining points. Even with the previous year's car, Stewart had shown that his title was not to be given up easily. Not for 12 years had it been retained.

1st	J Stewart	Tyrrell 003-Cosworth in 1h-57m-58.82s	100.42
2nd	D Hulme	McLaren M19A-Cosworth	25.96s
3rd	J Ickx	Ferrari 312B/2	59.39s
F lap	J Stewart	Tyrrell 003-Cosworth in 1m-13.66s	101.58

✱✱✱ (WC2) XVIII South African Grand Prix (Kyalami)
79 laps of 2.550 miles = 201.5 miles.
27 entries – 26 starters – 17 finished.

Front row: J Stewart – 1m-17.0s (119.23mph); G Regazzoni 0.3s; E Fittipaldi 0.4s.

04-MAR: Hulme led from the second row, but Stewart soon deprived him of it. Fittipaldi and Hailwood followed suit on laps 16 and 17 as Hulme overheated. Hailwood took second a few laps later, caught Stewart, but was let down, literally, by a suspension bolt when lining up an attack, fighting the car to a standstill.

Fittipaldi now had the leader in his sights, but gearbox oil loss did the job for him as Stewart retired. So Fittipaldi led from Hulme, Peterson, Amon, Revson and Andretti. Hulme found a way past Fittipaldi on lap 57, just as Peterson's loose wing helped Amon into a podium position only to lose it near the end to vibration, pitting twice. Hulme was now in full command, giving McLaren its first win since 1969. This season could be a good one.

1st	D Hulme	McLaren M19A-Cosworth in 1h-45m-49.1s	114.22
2nd	E Fittipaldi	Lotus 72D-Cosworth	14.1s
3rd	P Revson	McLaren M19A-Cosworth	25.8s
F lap	M Hailwood	Surtees TS9-Cosworth in 1m-18.9s	116.35

Championship positions:
D Hulme 15; J Stewart 9; E Fittipaldi 6.

✱✱ VI 'Race Of Champions' (Brands Hatch)
40 laps of 2.46 miles = 98.4 miles.
16 F1 entries – 11 started – 11 finished.

Front row: E Fittipaldi – 1m-23.9s (105.55mph); P Gethin 0.2s; M Hailwood 0.2s.

19-MAR: Brabham, Tyrrell and Ferrari didn't enter, and Matra non-started, but all the other teams were in force (BRM with four cars). Four F5000 cars also started, but couldn't get amongst the F1 field. The top five grid spots were covered by just 0.4 of a second, so a good race was in prospect. Gethin led away, but Fittipaldi was ahead out of Paddock Bend, and Gethin now began holding up the rest. Hulme, unable to pass, lost out to Hailwood on lap nine, who then took ten laps to pass Gethin. Fittipaldi was now out of sight and breaking the lap record. Just over a second covered Hulme, Gethin, Schenken and Beltoise at the flag at the end of a no-holds-barred scrap. Both new race and lap records remained unbroken after the British Grand Prix here in July.

1st	E Fittipaldi	Lotus 72D-Cosworth in 56m-40.6s	104.18
2nd	M Hailwood	Surtees TS9-Cosworth	13.4s
3rd	D Hulme	McLaren M19A-Cosworth	25.1s
F lap	E Fittipaldi	Lotus 72D-Cosworth in 1m-23.8s	105.68r

✱ Grande Premio do Brasil (Interlagos)
37 laps of 4.946 miles = 183.0 miles.
14 entries – 11 started – 6 finished.

Front row: E Fittipaldi – 2m-32.4s (116.83mph); C Reutemann 2.0s. Row two: R Peterson 2.2s; W Fittipaldi 3.9s.

30-MAR: Formula One came to Brazil to test the waters for a Championship round the next year, on the five-mile Interlagos track – the most contorted track ever! So twisted was it that it was possible at some points to have direct line-of-sight across eight sections of track – barriers permitting. How confusing!

Lotus, Brabham, March, Surtees and BRM (four cars) entered, but Surtees' team didn't arrive. Disappointingly, the BRM of Beltoise failed to take the start with ignition trouble. The 'wrong' Fittipaldi led from the second row for two laps, until star sibling Emerson, Reutemann and Peterson passed. A small dust storm covered Gethin, Pescarolo and Pace on lap one, and eliminated them with sand in their throttles. Emerson Fittipaldi drew away from Peterson, who pitted for a new front tyre, restarting well behind Wilson Fittipaldi. Then, with five laps to go, the leader spun with broken suspension and was out, so Reutemann had an easy last few laps to win. Would Wilson Fittipaldi be as good as his brother was proving? He was certainly handy.

1st	C Reutemann	Brabham BT34-Cosworth in 1h-37m-16.2s	112.88
2nd	R Peterson	March 721-Cosworth	1m-28s
3rd	W Fittipaldi	Brabham BT33-Cosworth	2m-03s
F lap	E Fittipaldi	Lotus 72D-Cosworth in 2m-35.2s	114.73

✱✱ XXIV *Daily Express* International Trophy (Silverstone)
40 laps of 2.927 miles = 117.1 miles.
12 F1 entries – 10 started – 7 finished.
Front row: E Fittipaldi – 1m-18.1s (134.92mph); P Gethin 0.6s; JP Beltoise 0.7s.

23-APR: Only ten F1 entries, but Lotus, BRM, Surtees, McLaren, Brabham and Frank Williams' March for Henri Pescarolo was a good grid, despite the withdrawal of Stewart's Tyrrell. It seems that the organisers preferred top F5000 cars than make-weight F1 entries, and 12 of them started. Beltoise and Gethin's BRMs led, to the vocal approval of the frozen 40,000 crowd, and Fittipaldi took ten laps to pass them, aided by a spin by Gethin. Three laps later he was strongly challenged by Mike Hailwood, who took ten laps to take the lead. Instantly, though, a water leak ruined his glory retiring him on lap 30, but he was now the absolute circuit record holder. Fittipaldi looked safe but a repeat of the bent radius rod in Argentina almost cost him victory. F5000 cars were now closing on F1 cars in terms of speed, as shown by class winner Graham McRae, who finished eighth, on the same

lap as the winner, and put in a lap of 1m-19.6s – faster than Stewart's old record and within a second of the new one! The race was better for their inclusion. I think it begs the question – If McRae wasn't an Emerson Fittipaldi, then how fast was his car actually?

1st	E Fittipaldi	Lotus 72D-Cosworth in 53m-17.8s	131.81
2nd	JP Beltoise	BRM P160	1.8s
3rd	J Surtees	Surtees TS9-Cosworth	10.8s
F lap	M Hailwood	Surtees-Cosworth in 1m-18.8s	133.72r

✱✱✱ (WC3) Gran Premio d'Espaňa (Jarama)
90 laps of 2.115 miles = 190.4 miles.
28 entries – 25 starters – 11 finished.
Front row: J Ickx – 1m-18.43s (97.09mph); D Hulme 0.75s; E Fittipaldi 0.83s.

01-MAY: Ickx was on pole by almost a second, but was beaten away by Hulme, with Stewart, Regazzoni, Ickx and Fittipaldi following. Stewart had the lead on lap five, but Fittipaldi deprived him of it four laps later, and then he also fell prey to Ickx on lap 15. A rain shower helped Ickx catch Fittipaldi, but the track dried and Fittipaldi was away again. Hulme had dropped to fifth, behind Andretti who then retired, as did Hulme on lap 43. Now Regazzoni was fourth, which became third when Stewart surprised everyone by a spin into a barrier and was out. Fittipaldi was without an auxiliary tank, which had leaked and was blanked off, so he was in fuel saving mode, yet still won. Team-mate Dave Walker ran out of fuel three laps from the end. A dominant Fittipaldi win.

1st	E Fittipaldi	Lotus 72D-Cosworth in 2h-33m-41.23s	92.34
2nd	J Ickx	Ferrari 312B/2	18.92s
3rd	G Regazzoni	Ferrari 312B/2	1 lap
F lap	J Ickx	Ferrari 312B/2 in 1m-21.01	94.00r

Championship positions:
D Hulme and E Fittipaldi 15; J Ickx 10.

✱✱✱ (WC4) XXIX Grand Prix de Monaco (Monte Carlo)
80 laps of a 1.954 mile circuit = 156.3 miles.
27 entries – 25 started – 18 finished.
Front row: E Fittipaldi – 1m-21.4s (86.43mph); J Ickx 0.2s.
Row two: G Regazzoni 0.5s; JP Beltoise 1.1s.

14-MAY: Re-siting the pits and paddock now allowed all to start, so qualifying was abolished. A virtuoso performance appeared out of the blue when Beltoise stormed from the second row in the atrocious conditions to pass Ickx on the inside at St Devote, and take the lead. He defied all expectations of him (and the car), and, despite the hairy manner of his early laps, led throughout. Perhaps Ickx and Co decided he was an accident waiting to happen. Ickx was a rain master, but was simply beaten. Ickx was fourth on the first lap, but passed Fittipaldi and Regazzoni by lap five. Fittipaldi lost out to Gethin and Stewart also passed Fittipaldi but Gethin crashed on lap 28. Stewart took third from Regga on lap 33, lost it on lap 44, but Regga crashed under pressure on lap 52. Stewart lost third again to Fittipaldi due to watered electrics. Only Fangio's win in 1950 had been a slower Championship race than this, lap speeds being down by 25 per cent. This was the best finishing rate to date this year, six crashes but only one retirement – equipment not stressed?

1st	JP Beltoise	BRM P160 in 2h-26m-54.7s	63.85
2nd	J Ickx	Ferrari 312B/2	38.2s
3rd	E Fittipaldi	Lotus 72D-Cosworth	1 lap
F lap	JP Beltoise	BRM P160 in 1m-40.0s	70.35

Championship positions:
E Fittipaldi 19; J Ickx 16; D Hulme 15.

✳ International Gold Cup (Oulton Park)

40 laps of 2.678 miles = 107.1 miles.
8 F1 entered & started – 4 finished.
Front row: P Gethin – 1m-24.6s (113.97mph); D Hulme 0.2s; E Fittipaldi 0.6s.

29-MAY: An earlier date for the Gold Cup in a Championship gap produced a small F1 entry, with cars from BRM, Lotus, McLaren, Surtees and March. All started, including Championship leader Fittipaldi. Peter Gethin led away, but Denny Hulme passed at Old Hall Corner and led to the end unchallenged, once Gethin retired on lap eight. Ronnie Peterson had hit Wisell's BRM at the start and both were out. Fittipaldi had used intermediate tyres on a drying track, spoiling his challenge. Redman's F5000 Chevron was fourth, ahead of Schuppan's BRM. With Peterson and Fittipaldi present this could have been a lot closer.

1st	D Hulme	McLaren M19A-Cosworth in 57m-15.6s	112.25
2nd	E Fittipaldi	Lotus 72D-Cosworth	37.4s
3rd	T Schenken	Surtees TS9-Cosworth	1 lap
F lap	D Hulme	McLaren M19A-Cosworth in 1m-24.4s	114.25r

✳✳✳ (WC5) XXIX Grand Prix de Belgique (Nivelles)

85 laps of 2.314 miles = 196.7 miles.
30 entries – 25 started – 14 finished.
Front row: E Fittipaldi – 1m-11.43s (116.62mph); G Regazzoni 0.15s; D Hulme 0.37s.

04-JUN: A new venue replaced the now too-dangerous Spa. It was short, much safer, and characterless. Stewart was missing here due to a duodenal ulcer, while the Tecno V12 car appeared for the first time, and was unimpressive. Regazzoni led from alongside Fittipaldi, who took nine laps to take a then unlosable lead. Ickx, Hulme and Cevert followed until Ickx lost third on lap 25 with a throttle linkage in disarray. But now it was Cevert who claimed the place, as Hulme had been passed by him and Amon. Soon Cevert was second, and, when Regga retired on lap 57, Amon was heading for a podium finish. This was ruined by fuel starvation on lap 75, and he lost out to Hulme, Hailwood and 'rookie' Brazilian Carlos Pace in a Williams-run March 711.

1st	E Fittipaldi	Lotus 72D-Cosworth in 1h-44m-06.7s	113.35
2nd	F Cevert	Tyrrell 002-Cosworth	26.6s
3rd	D Hulme	McLaren M19A-Cosworth	58.1s
F lap	E Fittipaldi	Lotus 72D-Cosworth in 1m-12.12s	115.51

Championship positions:
E Fittipaldi 28; D Hulme 19; J Ickx 16.

Gran Premio della Republica Italiana (Vallelunga)

80 laps of 1.973 miles = 157.9 miles.
10 entries – 7 started – 4 finished.
Front row: E Fittipaldi – 1m-09.82s; H Ganley 0.99s. Row two: P Gethin 1.11s; H Pescarolo 1.16s.

18-JUN: The Dutch Grand Prix was cancelled on safety grounds, but if this was a trial race to test the Vallelunga track for a possible second Championship round in Italy, then Ferrrari's absence was baffling. Other withdrawals left Championship leader Fittipaldi with little to beat, reducing this event to minor status. Ganley's BRM led off the line but was second by the first corner. That was it for the racing. Even partial rear-wing failure didn't stop Fittipaldi's from romping home. A win but not a victory, I think. Gethin and Ganley's BRMs and Pescarolo's March retired, bringing Galli's outclassed Tecno into third, a lap down.

1st	E Fittipaldi	Lotus 72D-Cosworth in 1h-37m-31.9s	97.86
2nd	A deAdamich	Surtees TS9-Cosworth	32.8s
F lap	E Fittipaldi	Lotus 72D-Cosworth in 1m-11.06s	100.74

✳✳✳ (WC6) LVI Grand Prix de France (Clermont-Ferrand)

38 laps of a 5.005-mile circuit = 190.2 miles.
29 entries – 24 started – 20 finished.
Front row: C Amon – 2m-53.4s (103.91mph); D Hulme 0.8s.
Row two: J Stewart 1.6s; J Ickx 1.7s.

02-JUL: Amon's sole Matra easily took pole from Hulme, delighting the partisan crowd in the French car. He led away at the start, with Hulme and Stewart clinging on. Helmut Marko's BRM was impressively in sixth place, behind Ickx and Fittipaldi, when disaster struck. Tyres put off-track could throw up sharp volcanic stones, and one pierced his visor and his eye, finishing his career. Stewart took second from Hulme, and, when Amon's famous jinx struck with a puncture (a risk here), he led the race easily. Amon dropped to eighth, and produced an astonishing fight-back to third, aided only by Ickx's puncture. The reception he received for this drowned out Stewart's for winning! What a drive from the truly great Chris Amon – the 'yet-to-win-a-race' ace on a true driver's track. He regards this as his greatest drive, and it has rightfully acquired legendary status.

1st	J Stewart	Tyrrell 003-Cosworth in 1h-52m-21.5s	101.57
2nd	E Fittipaldi	Lotus 72D-Cosworth	27.7s
3rd	C Amon	Matra MS120	31.9s
F lap	C Amon	Matra MS120 in 2m-53.9s	103.61r

Championship positions:
E Fittipaldi 34; J Stewart 21; D Hulme 19.

✳✳✳ (WC7) XXVII British Grand Prix (Brands Hatch)

76 laps of 2.46 miles = 186.96 miles.
33 entries – 26 started – 13 finished.
Front row: J Ickx – 1m-22.2s (107.74mph); E Fittipaldi 0.4s.
Row two: P Revson 0.5s; J Stewart 0.7s.

15-JUL: Ickx and Fittipaldi led off, while Beltoise beat Stewart and Revson to take third. It took until lap seven for Stewart to pass Beltoise, and soon Revson and Schenken followed suit. Lapping tail-enders was an art Stewart was the best at, which enabled him to catch the leaders and then take second on lap 26 from Fittipaldi, who had braked to avoid an

off-line Ickx. That situation reversed ten laps later, and, when Ickx's Ferrari succumbed to oil loss on lap 49, a good lead battle ensued. Amon had been 23rd on lap one, and, when Cevert (lap 60) and Peterson (lap 74) retired from fourth place, another great recovery was rewarded with three points. Another drive much appreciated was by Art Merzario, in 'Regga's' seat, who lost a minute at the pits yet recovered to sixth.

1st	E Fittipaldi	Lotus 72D-Cosworth in 1h-47m-50.2s	104.02
2nd	J Stewart	Tyrrell 003-Cosworth	4.1s
3rd	P Revson	McLaren M19A-Cosworth	1m-13s
F lap	J Stewart	Tyrrell 003-Cosworth in 1m-24.0s	105.43

Championship positions:
E Fittipaldi 43; J Stewart 27; D Hulme 21.

✳✳✳ (WC8) XXXIV Grosse Preis von Deutschland (N Nürburgring)

14 laps of 14.189 miles = 198.6 miles.
28 entries – 27 started – 16 finished.
Front row: J Ickx – 7m-07.0s (119.63mph); J Stewart 1.7s.
Row two: E Fittipaldi 2.9s; R Peterson 4.6s.

30-JUL: A fraught battle around the South Curve saw Ickx get the better of Peterson, Regazzoni (who had missed the last two GPs with a football injury!), Fittipaldi and Stewart. From then it was a Jacky Ickx benefit. Fittipaldi took Regazzoni on lap two, and was second on lap five when Peterson spun, also losing out to Stewart. The gearbox burst on Fittipaldi's car on lap ten, leaving Regga and Stewart to fight for second. Regga ran wide on the last lap, and Stewart's attempt to capitalise came to grief when Regazzoni hit him on correcting his error. Stewart was out, handing third to Peterson's ill-handling March from Ganley's BRM. Amon qualified eighth, but on the warm-up lap his ignition pick-up grounded and he lost a lap, never to recover. More bad luck.

1st	J Ickx	Ferrari 312B/2 in 1h-42m-12.3s	116.62
2nd	G Regazzoni	Ferrari 312B/2	48.3s
3rd	R Peterson	March 721G-Cosworth	1m-07s
F lap	J Ickx	Ferrari 312B/2 in 7m-13.6s	117.81r

Championship positions:
E Fittipaldi 43; J Stewart 27; J Ickx 25.

✱✱✱ (WC9) X Grosse Preis von Osterreich (Zeltweg)

54 laps of 3.673 miles = 198.3 miles.
31 entries – 25 started – 17 finished.
Front row: E Fittipaldi – 1m-35.97s (137.78mph); G Regazzoni 0.07s. Row two: J Stewart 0.38s; P Revson 0.66s.
13-AUG: Stewart stormed from row two to a huge lead after a lap, ahead of Regazzoni, Fittipaldi and Hulme. 'Regga' had a slight fuel pick-up problem out of corners, yet managed to hold back the field. Fittipaldi took five laps to pass, and. by lap 20 had caught Stewart, who was desperate to close the points gap to Fittipaldi. Regazzoni's problem stopped him on lap ten, so Hulme was now third and catching the leading pair, followed by Peterson who had swept up from 11th on lap one. Handling problems then dashed Stewart's Championship chances, as he gradually dropped back out of the points. Revson caught and passed Peterson whose great drive had been ruined by fuel trouble, pitting to the benefit of Hailwood, Amon and Ganley. Fittipaldi just held off Hulme so the world crown was almost his. Stewart or Hulme would have to win all three remaining rounds.

1st	E Fittipaldi	Lotus 72B-Cosworth in 1h-29m-16.66s	133.30
2nd	D Hulme	McLaren M19C-Cosworth	1.18s
3rd	P Revson	McLaren M19C-Cosworth	36.53s
F lap	D Hulme	McLaren M19C-Cosworth in 1m-38.32s	134.48r

Championship positions:
E Fittipaldi 52; J Stewart and D Hulme 27.

(FL) Rothmans 50,000 (Brands Hatch)

118 laps of 2.469 miles = 291.3 miles.
6 F1 entries – 5 started – 3 finished.
Front row: E Fittipaldi – 1m-22.5s (107.74mph); B Redman 0.9s. Row two: JP Beltoise 2.0s; H Ganley 2.7s.
28-AUG: Should this odd race be included? Just about, as the F1 entries equalled Vallelunga, and faced a huge entry in this one-off, extra-long Formule Libre race. The fastest 30 entries of 65 took part, but an F1 car was always going to win, and sure enough it was Fittipaldi who ran easily to the £10,000 cheque. Both the bulbous BRMs of Beltoise and Ganley retired, leaving the other F1 entries to occupy the podium places. Out-and-out speed wasn't the best tactic in this long race. Nimble F2 cars got the better of F5000 cars here, Birrell's March 722 gaining fourth behind Pescarolo's March 711, both two laps down.

1st	E Fittipaldi	Lotus 72D-Cosworth in 2h-50m-49.1s	102.34
2nd	B Redman	McLaren M19A-Cosworth	47.6s
F lap	E Fittipaldi	Lotus 72D-Cosworth in 1m-25.1s	104.44

✱✱✱ (WC10) XL Gran Premio d'Italia (Monza)

55 laps of a 3.588-mile circuit = 197.4 miles.
29 entries – 25 started – 13 finished.
Front row: J Ickx – 1m-22.2s (135.06mph); C Amon 0.04s. Row two: J Stewart 0.14s; G Regazzoni 0.28s.
10-SEP: A chicane after the pits steered the cars from right to left of this double-width section, and one at Curva del Vialone was added, the track proving slower than Austria. Just one second separated the top ten on the grid. Stewart's clutch failed at the start, so now only Hulme could mathematically deny Fittipaldi his Championship. Ickx led Regazzoni, Fittipaldi, Andretti, Amon and Hailwood, the latter two soon passing Andretti. Regga led on lap 13, but a coming-together with a lapped, sliding Pace put them both out. Ickx, Fittipaldi, Amon and Hailwood formed a good old slip-stream group, but Hailwood lost touch on lapping cars. Amon's brakes wore out (needed now at Monza) on lap 38, and Ickx's engine expired, so Hailwood, despite a lost airbox, got his best Championship result, while Fittipaldi won the title in his second full season, becoming the youngest Champion to date.

1st	E Fittipaldi	Lotus 72B-Cosworth in 1h-29m-58.4s	131.61
2nd	M Hailwood	Surtees TS9-Cosworth	14.5s
3rd	D Hulme	McLaren M19C-Cosworth	23.8s
F lap	J Ickx	Ferrari 312B/2 in 1m-36.3s	134.15

Championship positions:
E Fittipaldi (WC) 61; D Hulme 31; J Stewart 27.

✱✱✱ (WC 11) VI Grand Prix of Canada (Mosport Park)

80 laps of 2.459 miles = 196.7 miles.
31 entries – 24 started – 13 finished.
Front row: P Revson – 1m-13.6s (120.28mph); D Hulme 0.3s; R Peterson 0.4s.
24-SEP: Peterson shot away at the start, while some, including Revson and Hulme, were delayed by dust in throttle slides. Peterson's lead after a lap was a staggering three seconds from Stewart, Revson and Ickx. Stewart soon

hauled him in, though, and, from lap four, it was Stewart all the way. Revson, Ickx, Fittipaldi and Regazzoni followed, with Ickx taking third for ten laps before dropping back and out of the running. Peterson lost his second place on lap 54, on tangling with a lapped car, at which point Hulme had recovered from a disastrous start in 13th to be sixth. Fittipaldi closed on Revson, touched him, and broke a nose wing. Regga now had third, and held it until lap 72, being passed by Reutemann and Hulme, who then snatched the position from Reutemann on the last lap.

1st	J Stewart	Tyrrell 005-Cosworth in 1h-43m-16.9s	114.28
2nd	P Revson	McLaren M19C-Cosworth	48.2s
3rd	D Hulme	McLaren M19C-Cosworth	54.6s
F lap	J Stewart	Tyrrell 005-Cosworth in 1m-15.7s	116.94

Championship positions:
E Fittipaldi (WC) 61; J Stewart 36; D Hulme 35.

✯✯✯ (WC12) 15th United States Grand Prix (Watkins Glen)
59 laps of 3.377 miles = 199.3 miles.
33 entries – 31 started – 19 finished.

Front row: J Stewart – 1m-40.48s (120.99mph); P Revson 0.05s; D Hulme 0.60s.

08-OCT: The largest field of the year included an extra driver for McLaren – Jody Scheckter – who placed seventh on the grid, his teammates accompanying Stewart at the front. Stewart shot away from Hulme, Fittipaldi, Scheckter, Ickx, Regazzoni, Andretti, Reutemann and Cevert. Stewart drove off into the distance, while the amazing Scheckter passed new Champion Fittipaldi, who suffered a deflating tyre. Reutemann pitted for a nose cone, and Cevert passed all the Ferraris and Scheckter to be third on lap 17. At halfway that became second, and he held off Hulme until the end. A great drive was put in by Peterson, from 16th on lap one to fourth at race end, just beating Ickx, with Andretti's Ferrari in sixth. So, after sealing the title, Fittipaldi didn't score again.

1st	J Stewart	Tyrrell 005-Cosworth in 1h-41m-45.35s	117.48
2nd	F Cevert	Tyrrell 006-Cosworth	32.27s
3rd	D Hulme	McLaren M19C-Cosworth	37.53s
F lap	J Stewart	Tyrrell 005-Cosworth in 1m-41.64s	119.61r

Championship positions:
E Fittipaldi (WC) 61; J Stewart 45; D Hulme 39.

✯✯ 2nd World Championship Victory Race (Brands Hatch)
40 laps of 2.46 miles = 98.4 miles.
22 F1 entries – 16 started – 12 finished.

Front row: E Fittipaldi – 1m-20.8s (109.61mph); R Peterson 0.6s. Row two: B Redman 1.0s; M Hailwood 1.6s.

22-OCT: Only Tyrrell didn't enter, and Ferrari's sole entry was for Arturo Merzario. Plenty of F5000 cars also entered. Fittipaldi blitzed Ickx's qualifying record from July, which was also exceeded by Peterson's March and Brian Redman – he and Scheckter representing McLaren. It was drizzling at the start, so weather forecasting came into play which can ruin a race for some, including the crowd. This happened to Fittipaldi, Peterson and Hailwood who were on rain tyres – it dried. Peterson led from Hailwood and Fittipaldi at first, with intermediate shod Beltoise in fifth. Soon the drying track played into Beltoise's hands, and that was it, as Fittipaldi, having stopped for tyres (2.6-second pit stops unknown then), lost oil pressure and any challenge with it.

1st	JP Beltoise	BRM P180 in 59m-47.8s	98.74
2nd	C Pace	Surtees TS9-Cosworth	6.6s
3rd	A deAdamich	Surtees TS9-Cosworth	55.0s
F lap	E Fittipaldi	Lotus 72D-Cosworth in 1m-23.8s	105.67

Winners of the 19 graded F1 races of 1972 – quantity & quality of success

9 wins	E Fittipaldi (5A, B, C, 2D)	9 wins	Lotus-Cosworth (5A, B, C, 2D)
4 wins	J Stewart (4A)	4 wins	Tyrrell-Cosworth (4A)
2 wins	J-P Beltoise (A, B) D Hulme (A, C)	2 wins	BRM (A, B); McLaren-Cosworth (A, C)
1 win:	J Ickx (A) C Reutemann (C)	1 win	Ferrari (A); Brabham-Cosworth (C)

1972 seasonal review
This 3-litre Formula had now run for seven seasons, and quite clearly had plenty of life and development in it. Aerodynamics and tyre development meant that engine size was no longer the sole arbiter of speed. Championship grids had been increased in size from 23 to 25, and finish rates increased from 52 per cent to 54 per cent. Seven extra races had been run, though two of them were minor 'D

class' affairs. The early season races at Brands Hatch and Silverstone were useful events, and firmly established (the latter pre-dating the Championship), but the Oulton Park Gold Cup had lost much of its status. It was a pity that Ken Tyrrell chose not to enter his team at these events, as maybe it would have appreciated the threat that Fittipaldi posed sooner. With the Championship over, the season closing Brands Hatch 'Victory' race had a better entry than the March event, but with the Championship significantly expanding next year, was not run (or needed?) again.

1972 Championship review

The pendulum swung Lotus' way this year with the swift maturing of Emerson Fittipaldi, who, having shared the lead after Spain, drew clear with a third place at Monaco, and, following his Belgian win, was never in serious danger again. A significant result was his beating of Stewart at Brands Hatch in a straight fight, which proved that his credentials as a Champion-to-be were impeccable. The title was won with two rounds to go, and, like Clark in 1965, he didn't score again or seriously challenge for a race lead. Stewart's securing of the last two GPs brought him to a respectable score,

but it must be seen that, had he not lost the S African and Austrian rounds, a very close situation would have occurred, even despite his withdrawal from Belgium due to his ulcer. So maybe this was a Championship lost for Stewart, while Fittipaldi's first Championship win must be applauded loudly, with his lowering of the 'youngest ever Champion' mark.

Jacky Ickx also lost two races from the lead, and, in fact, with retirements from second, third and fourth places, had the greatest accumulated losses of the year. Beltoise's Monaco win for BRM was popular, and out of the normal run of play, as it was his only score of the year, and his three teammates totalled only eight points. BRM's sad decline continued until 1977 – by then an embarrassment.

Chris Amon very likely lost the French GP to the misfortune of a puncture, and, despite his heroic recovery drive to third, the Matra team decided to withdraw from Grand Prix racing, not having won a Championship race without the aid of Ken Tyrrell. A sad loss to the sight and sound, and to the international flavour, of F1. However, this loss of a French team was only for four years, when the Renault turbo arrival would change F1 racing fundamentally.

VISIT VELOCE ON THE WEB – WWW.VELOCE.CO.UK
All current books • New book news • Special offers • Gift vouchers • Forum

310

Chapter 32

1973-1983
To the end of an era – and beyond

In 1973, the Drivers' World Championship was suddenly expanded from 12 to 15 rounds, leaving little room for other F1 races, particularly as a thriving F2 season invited F1-graded drivers to no less than 15 events, so 1972 had been the final year that 'extra' F1 races had a serious role in a Formula One season. In 1973, the World Championship approached a monopoly of F1 races for the first time – 88 per cent. This was the year in which the intention to create a monopoly for championship races was made clear. The process took a few years however, and organisers of the `extra` races didn't give up without a fight, finding further sponsorship to cover ever-escalating costs in a period of high inflation. This had been eased by the fact that the cars were now covered in sponsor's liveries and logos. The BBC fought its old-fashioned conscience and decided that Surtees' sponsorship by condom manufacturers Durex in 1976 went too far, and withdrew for a couple of years. How I remember the mini-skirted promo girls wearing 'Durex' on their pretty heads – well the words anyway – on their 'one-size-fits-all' paper caps. The BBC problem gave Durex more publicity than it could have dreamed of, so its return was not long coming. In 1977 the World Championship reached 17 rounds, so 18 F1 races took place that year, a figure only exceeded twenty eight years later, which, in 2005, caused a feeling that it was too much, forgetting that even more races were run decades earlier. It wasn't until 1980 that a fixture list containing only World Championship rounds was made, which defined the end of the era of FIA approved 'extra' races.

It was then, however, that the FISA/FOCA 'who rules F1?' war broke out, resulting in the Spanish GP of 1980 and the South African GP of 1981 losing their FIA approved (and therefore Championship) status, thus becoming unauthorised 'extras.' In 1983 Bernie Ecclestone, now in charge, honoured a promise to Brands Hatch made a few years before, and a one-off F1 race was run. Quite why is difficult to understand as, in 1982, no 'extras' had been scheduled or run, so the new era was already under way.

To keep this book to manageable size, I now cease to quote Championship race results, which I had included to place those 'extra' races into their correct context. World Championship rounds are catalogued in innumerable publications, so I feel no need to repeat any more of them. This book supplements any of those books you may have – and now completes your full record of Formula One races.

Hanging on with the blessing of FOCA?
The greatest of the 'extra' races was the 'International Trophy' at Silverstone. This predated the World Championship itself, and its reputation, plus that of the more recent 'Race-of-Champions' series at Brands Hatch, kept these two annual Formula One races alive right up to the very end. The quality remained good, particularly in 1975 and '76. The DFV-Hewland power-transmission package had created the so-called Formula One 'kit-car' era, so marques proliferated, and soon entries didn't need boosting by other formulae. Outside of these two 'traditional' events, just two other races were planned. The 1974 Brazil race was inaugurating a new track in the new capital Brazilia, and, in 1975, the Swiss Automobile Club was given the opportunity to hold a 'Swiss' GP – in France (!) 21 years after the last one, with the hope of including it in future Championships. After 1976 only a single 'extra' race was allowed by FOCA, with Brands Hatch and Silverstone taking turns to run the opening of the European Formula One season. That rule was broken in 1979 when the Imola track was given a trial event to offer an alternative to Monza if needed – well, that was the excuse.

It was only needed for that purpose the following year, becoming the venue for the San Marino Grand Prix, and, tragically, its infamous running in 1994.

What's in a name? Where cars were required to adopt the name of a sponsor, thus disguising the actual constructor, for the sake of clear identity and continuity I have used the marque name as that of the constructor. So the John Player Special is identified as 'Lotus,' which it was before and would be later. Similarly, as the cars entered as Politoys or Iso-Marlboro in 1973/4 were constructed and run by Frank Williams (Racing Cars) Ltd, I have used the name 'Williams,' thus connecting the cars with the subsequent illustrious history of that constructor.

✳✳ VIII 'Race Of Champions' (Brands Hatch)
40 laps of 2.46 miles = 98.4 miles.
17 F1 entries – 13 started – 4 finished.

Front row: JP Beltoise – 1m-21.1s (109.20mph); N Lauda 0.8s. Row two: V Schuppan 1.1s; J Scheckter 1.5s.

18-MAR-1973: Works entries from BRM (Lauda, Beltoise, Schuppan), Lotus (Fittipaldi, Peterson), Surtees (Hailwood), McLaren (Hulme, Scheckter), Williams (Ganley, Trimmer) and Brabham (Watson) were supplemented by a Brabham from Graham Hill and a Surtees from Lord Hesketh for James Hunt's F1 debut. A BRM front row was good to see, while Gethin headed the many F5000 runners in eighth grid spot. Beltoise led Peterson, Lauda and Fittipaldi, so it was BRM-Lotus-BRM-Lotus, with Gethin in sixth. Fittipaldi lasted just two laps, he had overheated on the grid. When Beltoise slid wide on lap five Peterson passed but went out on lap 18. Then Beltoise punctured and Scheckter's McLaren crashed, so now Hailwood's Surtees led Hulme and Gethin. With just four laps left Hailwood's suspension collapsed, denying a very disappointed man his first F1 victory. Now Hulme led but clutch failure slowed him and he lost out to Gethin with a mile to go. James Hunt's F1 debut almost yielded second place (first F1) from 13th grid spot as he failed to catch Hulme by a whisker. So it was glory for Peter Gethin and Chevron who pulled off the only time a quality F1 field was beaten by a 'lesser formula' car. Chevron was successful in every branch of racing it entered, and a Formula One project was under way but halted after Derek Bennett's death in 1978 in a hang-gliding accident.

1st	P Gethin	Chevron B24-Chevrolet in 57m-22.9s	102.89
2nd	D Hulme	McLaren M23-Cosworth	3.4s
3rd	J Hunt (AH)	Surtees TS9-Cosworth	3.4s
F lap	Beltoise/Lauda/Peterson	BRM/BRM/Lotus 72 in 1m-23.0s	106.70

✳✳ XXV *Daily Express* International Trophy (Silverstone)
40 laps of 2.927 miles = 117.1 miles.
16 F1 entries – 13 started – 7 finished.

Front row – E Fittipaldi – 1m-16.4s (137.92mph); R Peterson 0.2s; J Stewart 0.5s.

08-APR-1973: The Brabham team didn't enter, and a much-publicised Ferrari for Ickx didn't arrive, but otherwise a good entry, with Tyrrell (Stewart); Lotus (Fittipaldi, Peterson); Surtees (Hailwood, Pace); Shadow (Oliver, Follmer); McLaren (Hulme, Revson); BRM (Regazzoni, Lauda, Schuppan) and Williams (Ganley) appeared. An amazing pole by World Champion Fittipaldi was wasted as he cooked the clutch and failed to get away. But Peterson made a perfect start and led lap one. Stewart stormed through on lap two, though, and looked dominant. Then, on lap six, he spun at Becketts – Peterson, Hulme, Regazzoni, Revson (McLaren) and Lauda passed. From sixth place a master-class took place, and, by lap 20, he was worrying leader Peterson. A great scrap ended on lap 32 as a snow flurry(!) caught out Peterson, but not Stewart. Hulme lost oil pressure and third place. A great Stewart drive, while Peterson's recovery gained him the all-time lap record before the ground effect era. No points = no point? – no way!

1st	J Stewart	Tyrrell 006-Cosworth in 52m-53.2s	132.83
2nd	R Peterson	Lotus 72D-Cosworth	10.4s
3rd	G Regazzoni	BRM P160	23.7s
F lap	R Peterson	Lotus 72D-Cosworth in 1m-17.5s	135.96r

✳ Grande Premio do Presidente Medici (Brasilia)
40 laps of 3.403 miles = 136.1 miles.
12 entries and starters – 9 finished.

Front row – C Reutemann – 1m-51.18s (110.19mph); E Fittipaldi 0.09s. Row two: J Scheckter 0.22s; C Pace 0.22s.

03-FEB-1974: The following teams stayed on after the Brazilian GP to inaugurate this new track, which, like Interlagos, turned in on itself. They were: Brabham (Reutemann, Fittipaldi W), BRM (Beltoise, Pescarolo), Hesketh (Hunt), March (Ganley, Stuck), McLaren (Fittipaldi E), Surtees (Mass, Pace), Tyrrell (Scheckter, and Williams (Merzario). After putting in very competitive times, a split fuel tank prevented the debut of the new Hesketh F1 car, so Hunt started from the back in a March. A quarter of a second separated the front two rows, so a close race was expected. Carlos Reutemann's Brabham BT44 led for six laps when his engine began to overheat, and Emerson Fittipaldi took over. Then Scheckter and Merzario passed, and, five laps later, Reutemann's race was finished.

Hunt had retired on lap four with gear trouble, so never got into the action. It was Fittipaldi's race from then on, so the expected competition didn't materialise. So it was that Arturo Merzario produced the first podium finish for a Williams-built car in F1, ahead of Jochen Mass' Surtees, and Wilson Fittipaldi's Brabham. Formula One never returned to the track.

1st	E Fittipaldi	McLaren M23-Cosworth in 1h-15m-22.75s	108.34
2nd	J Scheckter	Tyrrell 006-Cosworth	12.4s
3rd	A Merzario	Williams FW04-Cosworth	27.1s
F lap	E Fittipaldi	McLaren M23-Cosworth in 1m-51.62s	109.75

✶✶ IX 'Race of Champions' (Brands Hatch)

40 laps of 2.46 miles = 98.4 miles.
18 F1 entries – 13 started – 8 finished.
Front row – J Hunt – 1m-21.5s (108.66mph); G Regazzoni 0.1s. Row two: N Lauda 0.6s; C Reutemann 1.5s.
17-MAR-1974: McLaren (Fittipaldi, Hulme, Hailwood); Ferrari (Regazzoni, Lauda); Brabham (Reutemann, Robarts); Lotus (Ickx, Peterson's Type 76 non-started), BRM (Pescarolo), Shadow (Revson), Lyncar (Nicholson), and a Lola for Graham Hill was a decent grid, but it was pole for Hunt in the new Hesketh's F1 debut ahead of the Ferraris! Sadly, though, he found no grip at the start, and retired on lap four in the appalling rain after spinning. At the off it was Reutemann, Fittipaldi and the Ferraris of Lauda and Regazzoni. Lauda soon took second place, and the lead from Reutemann on lap seven, while Ickx passed Regazonni for fourth. Fittipaldi and Ickx pushed Reutemann to fourth on lap 14, while Lauda drew away. A lap later and Ickx was second, and closed on Lauda by lap 30. After a previous exploratory attempt, on lap 35 came his legendary pass on the outside at Paddock Bend in the wet, to lead as everyone held their breath! Who can possibly suggest that these races weren't hard fought affairs – wet or dry?

A racer is a racer and Jacky Ickx was a 'regenmeister', like Rudi Caracciola. **No Championship = no gain? – No way.**

1st	J Ickx	Lotus 72D-Cosworth in 1h-03m-37.6s	92.79
2nd	N Lauda	Ferrari 312B3	1.5s
3rd	E Fittipaldi	McLaren M23-Cosworth	18.3s
F lap	J Ickx	Lotus 72D-Cosworth in 1m-33.8s	94.41

✶✶ XXVI *Daily Express* International Trophy (Silverstone)

40 laps of 2.927 miles = 117.1 miles.
19 F1 entries – 15 started – 10 finished.
Front row – J Hunt – 1m-16.7s (137.38mph); R Peterson 1.7s; J Mass 1.7s.
07-APR-1974: Only Ferrari was missing, and Fittipaldi was absent due to family matters. Hunt and Hesketh on pole again, but by a whopping 1.7 seconds from Ronnie Peterson's new Lotus 76 and the rest of a good field! His good start was spoiled by clutch slip, though, and he dropped way back to let it cool. At Beckett's his normal pace resumed. Mass led lap one, but soon Peterson was first and pulling away. Mass was passed by Hailwood who then pitted. Hunt was tenth on laps two and three, but third by lap eight, and second on lap 14. The lead battle began on lap 22 and won on lap 28. Lap 30 saw Peterson's motor fail so it was now all over. A hugely popular win for a team that showed that GP racing was as much fun as it was fast. A breath of fresh air and a new F1 hero. The Hesketh ethos and the charisma of James Hunt brought hitherto esoteric Formula One to wider public notice, and this result was a large part of that. The events of 1976 created worldwide attention, but April 1974 was the start of public awakening.

1st	J Hunt	Hesketh 308-Cosworth in 52m-35.4s	133.58
2nd	J Mass	Surtees TS16-Cosworth	37.0s
3rd	JP Jarier	Shadow DN3-Cosworth	59.2s
F lap	J Hunt	Hesketh 308-Cosworth in 1m-17.6s	135.79

✶✶✶ X 'Race of Champions' (Brands Hatch)

40 laps of 2.46 miles = 98.4 miles.
19 entries – 15 started – 11 finished.
Front row – T Pryce – 1m-34.9s (93.32mph); J Scheckter 1.0s. Row two: Jarier 2.4s; J Ickx 2.4s.
16-MAR-1975: Starters came from McLaren (Fittipaldi, Mass); Lotus (Peterson, Ickx); Shadow (Pryce, Jarier); Tyrrell (Scheckter); Williams (Merzario); Hill (Stommelen); Surtees (Watson); March (Lombardi); Penske (Donohue); Stanley BRM (Evans); Lyncar (Nicholson), and Token (Trimmer). This was a good grid despite Ferrari's absence, and the presence of the American Penske team was very welcome. Wet practice saw Pryce and Shadow take their first F1 pole. Scheckter passed Ickx to lead after a lap, with Pryce and Peterson chasing. Pryce took Ickx and, by lap 20, had Scheckter in view, but Scheckter's engine blew. Watson took both Peterson and Ickx's Lotuses for third, but the latter and Fittipaldi's McLaren were both lapped. Pryce's Shadow equalled the previous year's British GP record lap – a real

threat now. The circuit would be modified before the next F1 race, so Pryce and Lauda would hold this outright circuit record in perpetuity.

1st	T Pryce	Shadow DN5-Cosworth in 55m-53.5s	105.63
2nd	J Watson	Surtees TS16-Cosworth	30.5s
3rd	R Peterson	Lotus 72E-Cosworth	32.0s
F lap	T Pryce	Shadow DN5-Cosworth in 1m-21.1s	109.20e

✳✳✳ XXVII *Daily Express* International Trophy (Silverstone)

40 laps of 2.927 miles = 117.1 miles.
20 entries – 17 started – 14 finished.
Front row: J Hunt – 1m-17.3s (136.32mph); N Lauda 0.1s.
Row two: R Peterson 0.3s; E Fittipaldi 0.5s.
13-APR-1975: One from each of the 18 marques (mostly team leaders), plus a private Hesketh for Alan Jones. For the record, in alphabetical order, they were: Brabham; Ensign; Ferrari; Fittipaldi (for Wilson F); Hesketh; Hill; Lotus; Lyncar; March; McLaren; Parnelli; Penske; Shadow; Stanley-BRM; Surtees; Token; Tyrrell; and Williams – phew! Two came from Lotus as its sponsor was the event sponsor. Both Lotus non-started, however, after Peterson's engine blew and F1 debutant Crawford crashed. Merzario's Williams also non-started. The Hunt/Hesketh Formula Fun Factory led the race for 25 laps ahead of Lauda's hard chasing Ferrari and Emerson Fittipaldi's McLaren, when, sadly, the Hesketh engine blew up. Fittipaldi, with victory now on offer, pressed Lauda right to the flag. Watson (Surtees) held off Depailler's Tyrrell and Donohue's Penske for fourth. This was the last F1 race using the famously daunting Woodcote Bend, as a (mild) chicane was added before the British GP. This remains the fastest race ever run in Britain before ground-effect systems changed F1 for ever.

1st	N Lauda	Ferrari 312T in 52m-17.6s	134.33
2nd	E Fittipaldi	McLaren M23-Cosworth	0.1s
3rd	M Andretti	Parnelli VPJ4-Cosworth	24.6s
F lap	J Hunt/E Fittipaldi	Hesketh/McLaren in 1m-17.7s	135.61

✳✳✳ XV Grand Prix de Suisse (Dijon)

60 laps of 2.044 miles = 122.6 miles.
24 entries – 16 started – 13 finished.
Front row: JP Jarier – 59.25s (124.15mph); E Fittipaldi 0.02s.
Row two: G Regazzoni 0.51s; J Mass 0.67s.
24-AUG-1975: A Grand Prix not in its eponymous country?

A first. The last Swiss GP was in 1954 on the dangerous Bremgarten circuit. Dijon was no match for it, but this was a new era with very much faster cars. A top entry was reduced when FOCA requested single entries from its members. As at Silverstone, an exception was made for the event sponsor's team – Marlboro McLaren. Shadow also had Pryce and Jarier, the latter grabbing pole by a whisker from Fittipaldi's McLaren. Mercurial Jean-Pierre Jarier tore off, while Fittipaldi burned his clutch. Hunt's new Hesketh 308C handled badly. Regazzoni lay second, but lost ground as Jarier looked set for his maiden F1 win. On lap 35, when ten seconds ahead, a gearbox failure put him out, so, appropriately, a Swiss won the Swiss Grand Prix without difficulty, but many felt the moral victor was really Jarier. Peterson's Lotus was fourth, 25 seconds behind Mass, chased by Watson's Surtees, Pace's Brabham, and Pryce, who finished in that order, covered by a blanket.

1st	G Regazzoni	Ferrari 312T in 1h-01m025.34s	119.79
2nd	P Depailler	Tyrrell 007-Cosworth	8.4s
3rd	J Mass	McLaren M23-Cosworth	15.4s
F lap	JP Jarier	Shadow DN5-Cosworth in 1m-00.34s	121.74

Some thoughts of a lost era – and great personality
On the 29th of November the evening news told of a light-aircraft crash near a golf course just north of London. The immediate sight of wreckage bearing Embassy colours chilled me. Knowing that Graham Hill had always lived on the northern outskirts of London – no tax exile he – I knew instantly that we had just lost one of the greatest and most loved names in motorsport. Soon we understood the catastrophe that had taken the entire Graham Hill racing team, including its rising-star driver Tony Brise. Graham Hill was (and still is) irreplaceable. We have not seen (or heard – his humour was legendary) his like in the 40 years since he left us. His wit made him a favourite for regular TV appearances on chat shows and panel games. He was publically known and liked.

Sample 1: On the panel game *Call my Bluff* where a team of three each define the same word – only one being true – his risqué humour produced the following response from the show host, Robert Robinson. "I do believe if we asked you to describe the word 'butter' none of us would ever eat it again." Laughter all round. Unforgettable.
Sample 2: A motor sport celebration dinner: TV cameras are there and also, remotely, at his hospital bed, where he was recovering from his terrible leg injuries from his 1969 crash. After the introduction came the following – "Sorry I haven't dressed for dinner, and I see you're having a very good time,

1st	J Hunt	McLaren M23-Cosworth in 58m-01.23s	100.27
2nd	A Jones	Surtees TS19-Cosworth	18.42s
3rd	J Ickx	Hesketh 308C-Coswworth	23.17s
F lap	J Hunt	McLaren M23-Cosworth in 1m-23.78s	104.16

✳✳ Graham Hill XXVIII International Trophy (Silverstone)

40 laps of 2.932 miles = 117.3 miles.

21 entries – 16 started – 12 finished.

Front row: J Hunt – 1m-17.91s (135.48mph); V Brambilla (0.85s) Row two: T Pryce (1.29s); G Nilsson (1.50s)

11-APR-1976: Named in honour of the sport's sad loss, and a great champion of these 'extra' events. A pity that Ferrari's entry for Niki Lauda was scratched rather late due to an Italian airport strike, but nine other teams entered. The circuit had been altered before the previous year's British GP, with a deviation interrupting the flow of the wonderful Woodcote bend. Hunt's pole was almost 1.5 seconds better than pole at that GP, and just the same amount from the best lap ever recorded here. He duly produced the goods and led the whole way, Brambilla trying and failing to challenge. Scheckter's Tyrrell took third from Pryce's Shadow on the first lap, and that settled the podium places. Pryce's teammate, Jarier, in fifth, hotly chased by Nilsson's Lotus, were within 1.5 seconds at the finish, Nilsson having displaced Andretti's Williams and Jones' Surtees by lap 15. Not a great race, but lap times had only marginally increased: Hunt's pole within a second of the previous year's Trophy race. Woodcote Chicane – what chicane?

1st	J Hunt	McLaren M23-Cosworth in 53m-04.57s	132.58
2nd	V Brambilla	March 761-Cosworth	11.24s
3rd	J Scheckter	Tyrrell 007-Cosworth	37.37s
F lap	J Hunt	McLaren M23-Cosworth in 1m-18.81s	133.93r

✳✳ XII 'Race of Champions' (Brands Hatch)

40 laps of 2.424 miles = 96.96 miles.

17 entries – 16 started – 13 finished.

Front row: J Watson – 1m-19.05s (110.39mph); M Andretti 0.34s. Row two: J Hunt 0.55s; J Scheckter 1.13s.

20-MAR-1977: Sadly, we had lost Carlos Pace (air crash) and Tom Pryce (S African GP) already this year. Single entries from 11 Works teams included World Champion James Hunt and Championship leader Jody Scheckter. The latter had given the new Wolf team a victory on its debut in Argentina.

---

but in a few moments a couple of little darlings are going to come and rub my bottom – if you can beat that then good luck to you." He had been a great supporter of these 'extra' F1 races, appearing and entertaining as often as possible. With his unique achievements, love of Britain, and his involvement with charity from the earliest time of his career, had he survived he would undoubtedly have been a 'shoe-in' for a knighthood. How we need someone like that again. Formula One's all so serious and corporately driven now – much to its detriment, as that's business not sport. 'For-love-of-the-sport' is gone. Personalities attract followers as proved below.

Hesketh Racing had, sadly, closed shop due to financial difficulties, leaving James Hunt without a drive at rather a late stage. At the eleventh hour he learned that Emerson Fittipaldi was still hesitating about signing a new McLaren contract while considering driving the Fittipaldi car run in 1975 by his brother Wilson. Hunt was now a valuable driver and on the market, so he stepped in smartly, thus solving the problem for both parties. The cast is now in place for the year-long gripping 'soap-opera' with Niki Lauda, which is now sporting folklore. The publicity generated by the finale transformed Formula One into a public spectacle for ever. It nearly didn't happen.

✳✳ XI 'Race of Champions' (Brands Hatch)

40 laps of 2.424 miles = 96.96 miles.

18 entries – 15 started – 9 finished.

Front row: J Scheckter – 1m-20.42s (108.51mph); N Lauda 2.35s. Row two: G Nilsson 3.14s; J Ickx 3.30s.

14-MAR-1976: Track alterations, necessary for a new pit and paddock complex, had shortened the circuit, so new records were to be set. As per the previous year, only single team entries were allowed, excepting Lotus which was sponsored by the event sponsor – John Player. Ferrari got around this by 'creating' Scuderia Everest for Giancarlo Martini's car. They really did want to use this race to good effect. Unfortunately, a brake grabbed and he crashed on the warm-up lap, and non-started. Jody Scheckter made pole by over two seconds, having the best of the conditions on the revised track. Nilsson's Lotus led away, to be passed immediately by Alan Jones' Surtees; this car preventing TV coverage by the bashful BBC. Scheckter's Tyrrell then stormed past on lap two and promptly spun off. Hunt, now second from eighth grid slot, had World Champion Lauda's Ferrari and Watson's Penske threatening, but Watson went off and Lauda retired. By lap 20 Hunt realised newcomer Jones wasn't going to hand him the race with a mistake, and lunged onto the inside along the 'straighter' bottom straight and into the tighter left-hander. Both braked very late and Hunt emerged the leader after both looked to be heading off the road. He then pulled away after winning a great scrap.

Another new marque was the Lec, of the Lec fridges company, with George Medal holder David Purley at the wheel. With six others this was a decent field. John Watson's choice of the right-hand side for pole didn't work, and he was fourth at Paddock, behind Andretti, Hunt and Scheckter. Watson passed Scheckter but pitted due to blistered tyres, and then his fight back from 14th was brilliant. Andretti kept Hunt at bay until his engine died on lap 34. Ronnie Peterson's six-wheel Tyrrell 34 was third when his engine let go with three laps left, so Watson gained a place on the podium.

1st	J Hunt	McLaren M23-Cosworth in 53m-54.35s	107.92
2nd	J Scheckter	Wolf WR1-Cosworth	23.5s
3rd	J Watson	Brabham BT45-Alfa Romeo	1m-18s
F lap	J Hunt	McLaren M23-Cosworth in 1m-19.48s	109.79r

A sad footnote: Louis Stanley, husband of team owner Sir Alfred Owen's daughter, had taken over the running of BRM in 1975 after the Rubery-Owen empire hit financial trouble. The team was renamed 'Stanley-BRM' but this turned into the 'kiss-of-death.' It failed to score in 1975, skipped most of 1976, and re-emerged at Brands Hatch with Larry Perkins but qualified only 14th. It they had suspension bother and failed to appear on the grid. This now tragically pathetic outfit never qualified for an international F1 race again, and a once great name died in ignominy. The drawn-out agony of its death having taken almost as long as the gestation of its birth.

∗∗ XXX *Daily Express* International Trophy (Silverstone)
40 laps of 2.932 miles = 117.3 miles.
20 entries – 16 started – 4 finished.
Front row: R Peterson – 1m-16.07s (138.76mph); N Lauda 0.36s. Row two: M Andretti 0.53s; J Hunt 1.11s.
19-MAR-1978: This year it was Silverstone's turn for the European season opener. Without FOCA sanction it had been an F2 race the year before, and was thankfully back to its rightful place. Lotus and Shadow had two cars each – others one, but their drivers were top-drawer. Pole was now faster than pre-chicane speeds. Foul conditions, almost as bad as in 1951, caused utter confusion, and Lauda's Brabham-Alfa went off on the warm-up lap. Hunt and Regazzoni crashed on lap one, with Andretti and Peterson following suit on lap two, so the front two grid rows were now out. Stuck's Shadow and Daly's Hesketh shared the lead for the next ten laps, whereupon Stuck pitted with electric trouble and Daly crashed from the lead. Only four survived, and Fittipaldi was beaten by a new guy in an obscure car. On the

podium Fittipaldi couldn't believe it. "Who is he?" We would soon know. Thus ended this renowned series of F1 races at Silverstone which predated the World Championship and usually matched the high standard that series required.

1st	K Rosberg	Theodore TR1-Cosworth in 1h-12m-49.02s	96.64
2nd	E Fittipaldi	Fittipaldi F5A-Cosworth	1.88s
3rd	T Trimmer	McLaren M23-Cosworth	3 laps
F lap	E Fittipaldi	Fittipaldi F5A-Cosworth in 1m-38.63s	107.02

1979 – The final curtain?
Two years earlier there had been no fewer than seventeen World Championship rounds, so clearly there was little option but for other races to give way. In any case, in Britain there was now a domestic F1 series for 'new blood' to 'cut its teeth' on (what a mixed metaphor!) in an F1 car – a role that 'extra' races had usefully fulfilled. However, there was now no opportunity to see new skills challenge the 'big boys' in public. Securing the role of 'test driver' to prove understanding of the technology and of ability to make consistent 'on-the-pace' lap times performed that function, but not in public where a competitive spirit would surely want to be.

∗ XIII 'Race of Champions' (Brands Hatch)
40 laps of 2.424 miles = 96.96 miles.
20 entries – 18 started – 13 finished.
Front row: M Andretti – 1m-17.52s (112.57mph); N Lauda 0.24s. Row two: G Villeneuve 0.33s; N Piquet 0.46s.
15-APR-1979: Snowed-off from on March 18th, this new date made it difficult to slot into testing schedules, but some top names were there from Ferrari, Brabham (two), Lotus, McLaren, Shadow and Arrows, the rest came from the British F1 'Aurora' series. Lauda was best away, from Villeneuve and Andretti who swapped places twice in the opening lap. On lap eight Lauda stopped for tyres when seeming in command, a wrong decision having been made, and teammate Piquet also suffered likewise. Andretti led until lap 28 then lost his fight with Villeneuve due to fading brakes. Villeneuve's pass at Paddock Bend was exquisite, then Andretti's tyres started to go off, whereupon Piquet's brilliant recovery was rewarded with second, and an amazing record lap.

1st	G Villeneuve	Ferrari 312T3 in 53m-17.12s	109.18
2nd	N Piquet	Brabham BT48-Alfa	15.07s
3rd	M Andretti	Lotus 79-Cosworth	23.17s
F lap	N Piquet	Brabham BT48-Alfa in 1m-17.46s	112.66r

1st	A Jones	Williams FW07-Cosworth in 1h-43m-14.08s	95.69
2nd	J Mass	Arrows A3-Cosworth	50.94s
3rd	E deAngelis	Lotus 81-Cosworth	1m-12s
F lap	A Jones	Williams FW07-Cosworth in 1m-15.47s	100.90r

✱✱ XXVII South African Grand Prix (Kyalami)

77 laps of 2.550 miles = 196.4 miles.
19 started – 11 finished.
Front row: N Piquet – 1m-12.78s (126.13mph); C Reutemann 0.20s. Row two: A Jones 0.50s; K Rosberg 0.51s.
01-FEB-1981: This race should have started the Championship, but it was FISA/FOCA wars again. This time Ligier joined the absentees, but FOCA members still made a good race, rain making tyre choice a gamble. Piquet (wets), deAngelis (drys) and Lammers (wets) led the first lap, but Lammers hit deAngelis and put himself out. Watson and Jones (both on wets) passed deAngelis for second and third, and, on lap 17, Jones put on dry tyres, but spun off. Those who started on slicks were right, as the track dried, so Reutemann and deAngelis came through, having dropped back earlier. Piquet recovered once he had slicks on, and retook second place, but by then Reutemann was out of reach.

1st	C Reutemann	Williams FW07-Cosworth in 1h-44m-54.03s	112.31
2nd	N Piquet	Brabham BT49-Cosworth	20.14s
3rd	E deAngelis	Lotus 81-Cosworth	1m-06s
F lap	C Reutemann	Williams FW07-Cosworth in 1m-13.61s	124.71

✱ XIV 'Race of Champions' (Brands Hatch)

40 laps of 2.424 miles = 96.96 miles.
13 started – 7 finished.
Front row: K Rosberg – 1m-15.77s (115.18mph); R Arnoux 0.07s. Row two: A Jones 1.74s; J Watson 2.30s.
10-APR-1983: Run to honour a commitment made two years earlier by FOCA to Brands Hatch. The entry was bound to suffer, but reigning Champion Rosberg and 1980 World Champion Jones were there, plus a Ferrari for Arnoux. John Watson's McLaren and Nigel Mansell's Lotus completed the stars, so there was the prospect of some good racing. René Arnoux led, but his tyres went off after six laps, and Keke Rosberg went by to lead to the end. Sullivan made a great start, and inherited second when Arnoux dropped due to his tyres. Watson and Mansell both stopped with trouble, neither

✱ Gran Premio Dino Ferrari (Imola)

40 laps of 3.132 miles = 125.3 miles.
16 entries and starters – 11 finished.
Front row: G Villeneuve – 1m-32.91s (121.34mph); J Scheckter 0.33s. Row two: C Reutemann 1.03s; N Lauda 1.90s.
16-SEP-1979: An added race to qualify Imola as a World Championship venue brought a varied field, but a few of the best were there, including Ferraris for new Champion Scheckter and the sensational Gilles Villeneuve, plus the Alfa Romeo team, Lauda's Brabham-Alfa, Reutemann's Lotus, and Jarier's Tyrrell. Villeneuve, Scheckter, Reutemann and Lauda led Brambilla's Alfa-Romeo which dropped back. Reutemann had a wheel balance fall off, and Lauda was soon past. Tyre trouble cost Scheckter his second place to Lauda, who took the lead from Villeneuve on lap 16. Villeneuve fought back but hit the Brabham's rear. Lauda continued undamaged, while Villeneuve crawled to the pits for a new nose. He unlapped himself by the finish with a new record lap.

1st	N Lauda	Brabham BT48-Alfa in 1h-03m-55.89s	117.56
2nd	C Reutemann	Lotus 79-Cosworth	7.09s
3rd	J Scheckter	Ferrari 312T4	25.22s
F lap	G Villeneuve	Ferrari 312T4 in 1m-33.61s	120.44r

✱✱✱ XXVI Gran Premio de Espana (Jarama)

80 laps of 2.115 miles = 169.2 miles.
28 entries – 22 started – 6 finished.
Front row: J Laffite – 1m-12.65s (104.82mph); A Jones 0.37s. Row two: D Pironi 0.39s; C Reutemann 0.62s.
01-JUN-1980: In the heat of the FISA/FOCA war, doubt over the validity as a FISA sanctioned event caused Ferrari, Alfa Romeo and Renault to withdraw to protect their other motor racing activities. All the FOCA members participated. Reutemann shot from fourth on the grid to lead Jones, Pironi and Laffitte (Ligiers), and Piquet's Brabham. Pironi's tyre choice caused oversteer, and he was fifth by lap nine. Jones ran wide and dropped to fifth, and now Laffitte was pushing leader Reutemann hard. On lap 25 the leaders came to lap Emilio deVillota's Williams. He gave Reutemann room but fouled Laffitte on his other side. They touched and Laffitte was launched and rammed into Reutemann – both out. Piquet retired after leading seven laps, so now Pironi led to lap 65 when a loose wheel handed the race to the lucky Jones, who had been watching his water temperature the whole race.

having challenged well. Rosberg slowed with tyre wear near the end, but Sullivan wasn't able to capitalise on this. The day was cool and times were down on the previous year's Grand Prix.

1st	K Rosberg	Williams FW08-Cosworth in 53m-15.25s	109.24
2nd	D Sullivan	Tyrrell 011-Cosworth	0.49s
3rd	A Jones	Arrows A6-Cosworth	28.64s
F lap	R Arnoux	Ferrari 126C2 t/c in 1m-17.83s	112.13

That was the last breath – the very final curtain.

Winners of the 17 extra F1 races of 1973-83 – quantity & quality of success

4 wins	J Hunt (4B)	4 wins	McLaren-Cosworth (3B, C)
2 wins	N Lauda (A, C) K Rosberg (B, C)	3 wins	Ferrari (2A, C); Williams-Cosworth (A, B, C)
1 win	A Jones (A) T Pryce (A) G Regazzoni (A) J Stewart (B) J Ickx (B) C Reutemann (B) P Gethin (B) E Fittipaldi (C) G Villeneuve (C)	1 win	Shadow-Cosworth (A); Hesketh-Cosworth (B); Tyrrell-Cosworth (B); Lotus-Cosworth (B); Theodore-Cosworth (B); Chevron-Chevrolet (B); Brabham-Alfa (C)

Since then, Formula One has been a closed shop – for the better?

VISIT VELOCE ON THE WEB – WWW.VELOCE.CO.UK
All current books • New book news • Special offers • Gift vouchers • Forum

318

Chapter 33

The missing factor – leads lost to Lady Luck?

Winning positions that 'got away' 1946-2016

An unfortunate fact about motor racing, and particularly Formula One, is that it is perhaps the most difficult of any sport, when it comes to taking results as an indication of what has transpired and where merit should be apportioned. It's not, and never has been, a level playing field. When it comes to winning, the records tell us how often, but not often how, and – for those days of Formula One beyond the World Championship – never; reports being almost inaccessible.

This is an idiosyncratic but essential part of the book. I undertake to identify likely winning race leads ending in failure that deserve recognition – 'Likely-Win-Lost' (LWL) – and which are 'part-and-parcel' of the credentials of all drivers. How that lead was attained is irrelevant, as is a race win (rules permitting). It's a 'team game' they say, and, in the spectators' literal view, each team consists of two – one driver and one car – and in that context the best team nearly always wins. What about the situation in which a driver leaves the race before taking the lead, but would have claimed victory after subsequent retirement of the then leader? There are many shades of this area, but, as they involve a degree of hypothesis, they are not considered. Comments like 'he was a car breaker' are challengeable opinions. A driver is expected to extract the most from a car whenever needed, but the most popular drivers nearly always raced to the edge of their own, and the cars' limits, so may be 'on the edge of' reliability – 'racing' rather than 'pacing'. Car failure, over-revving excepted, perhaps, is rarely the sole fault of the driver, and it's the 'true racers' who bring in the crowds, and it's often their performances that stick in the mind, particularly when 'robbed' of just rewards. This is an attempt to quantify that aspect.

A few LWLs involve out-of-character errors which might be called 'Glory Spoiled.' So how do I justify inclusion of races lost through apparent driver error? To paraphrase Lord Tennyson – "It's better to have led and lost than never to have led at all." Stirling Moss put it his way: "I'd rather lose a race having gone fast enough to win than win having been slow enough to lose" – the definitive 'Racer' who gave total value-for-money and is worshipped for it. A grey area? Yes, but winning potential had undoubtedly been displayed and unknown factors may well have been involved. So, to ensure fairness, I err on the side of generosity; "Oops" will suffice. Including all these incidents paints a clearer race picture than results alone. These situations occurred.

Likely wins lost

Michele Alboreto (1981-94) – one loss
1984 GP do Brasil (Ferrari). Led on Ferrari debut until lap 15 when brakes grabbed and he spun twice.

Jean Alesi (1989-2001) – four losses
1994 GP d'Italia (Ferrari). Led from pole to first pit stop, when gears didn't engage to continue.
1995 GP de Belgique (Ferrari). Took lead from Herbert on lap two, only for suspension to fail two laps later.
1995 GP d'Italia (Ferrari). Led strongly after pit stops until eight laps to go when a wheel bearing failed.
1996 GP de Monaco (Benetton). Led after Hill retired, but his suspension let him down – literally.

Fernando Alonso (2001) – two losses
2005 Canadian GP (Renault). The Championship leader led this race but just glanced a wall. Oops!
2006 Hungarian GP (Renault). Led from lap 19 to lap 50 pit stop, when a wheel wasn't secured properly.

Chris Amon (1963-76) – five losses

1968 Spanish GP (Ferrari). A healthy lead was lost by fuel pump failure on lap 58 of 90.

1968 Canadian GP (Ferrari). No clutch from start caused gearbox failure on lap 72. A minute's lead lost.

1969 GP d'España (Ferrari). Led after Rindt crashed, but, on lap 58, with a 40-second lead, his engine failed.

1971 Italian GP (Matra). Tore off whole visor instead of a laminate when clear of pack with just five laps left.

1972 French GP (Matra). Led from start – punctured at half distance. His third place was cheered to the echo.

Mario Andretti (1968-82) – seven losses

1975 Spanish GP (Parnelli). Contact at start. Good lead after Hunt crashed, but suspension failed on lap 17.

1977 RoC-Brands Hatch (Lotus). Engine failure on lap 33 of 40, having led throughout.

1977 Swedish GP (Lotus). Rich mixture caused fuel to run out, having led until three laps from the end.

1977 Austrian GP (Lotus). Engine failure on lap 12, having led from lap two.

1977 Canadian GP (Lotus). A lap ahead after Hunt's crash, and engine failed three laps from the end.

1978 Silverstone International Trophy (Lotus). Led in atrocious conditions but spun off on lap three. Oops!

1978 British GP (Lotus). Huge lead lost to puncture. About to lead again when engine blew up.

René Arnoux (1978-89) – seven losses

1979 GP d'Italia (Renault). Took the lead from Scheckter easily on the straight, but engine failed on lap 14.

1980 GP von Osterreich (Renault). Pitted with deflating tyre, all four were changed but hit tyre trouble again.

1981 British GP (Renault). Led laps 17 to 61. His earlier 25-second lead had been lost to engine trouble.

1982 GP di San Marino (Renault). Retook lead from Villeneuve, but engine blew in great cloud of smoke.

1982 GP de Belgique (Renault). Led at start until caught in a few laps as turbo trouble soon intervened.

1982 GP de Monaco (Renault). Flew away at start but spun on lap 15 and stalled, unable to restart. Oops!

1983 US Detroit GP (Ferrari). Took lead from Piquet and drew away, only for fuel system to fail on lap 32.

Alberto Ascari (1947-55) – 18 losses

1947 GP de Lausanne (Maserati). Led from start and pulling away but a brake pipe broke on lap 28 of 90.

1949 Buenos Aires GP (Maserati). Villoresi and Farina out, so now led – exhaust broke with five laps to go.

1949 Gavea (Maserati). Forced off road by local driver, hit tree, thrown out breaking ribs and collar bone.

1949 Zandvoort GP (Ferrari). Just leading from Villoresi, lost wheel six laps from the end but stopped okay.

1951 GP di Siracusa (Ferrari). Scrapped with Villoresi, then led from lap 38 to 69 of 80 when engine failed.

1951 GP de Pau (Ferrari). As Siracusa and led from lap 11 to 46 of 110, retiring with transmission broken.

1952 GP del Valentino (Ferrari). Again battled with Villoresi, led from lap 11 to 55 of 60 – fuel tank split.

1952 GP di Monza (Ferrari). Won first part by 1m-04s, leading second part but camshaft broke on lap 14.

1952 GP di Modena (Ferrari). Led from start to lap 18 when oil system failed. Finished third in another car.

1953 GP di Siracusa (Ferrari). Led from start to lap 36, pitted for new wheel, but retired soon after.

1953 GP di Napoli (Ferrari). Led at first, but stopped with broken throttle pedal on lap four, losing four laps.

1953 GP von Deutschland (Ferrari). Leading easily and pulling away when a wheel came off on fifth lap.

1953 GP d'Italia (Ferrari). Final lap – final bend. Leading four-car scrap but spun on oil on entry and crashed.

1954 GP d'Italia (Ferrari). Led all but a few laps. Took Moss on lap 45 to lead. Had valve trouble three laps later.

1954 GP d'Espana (Lancia). Took the lead from Schell on lap two, but clutch slip on lap ten meant retirement.

1955 GP d'Argentina (Lancia). Led on lap 22 from chasing pack but spun on oil and slid off into fence.

1955 GP de Pau (Lancia). Drew away from lead scrap on lap 11. Led to lap 90 of 110 when brake pipe split.

1955 GP de Monaco (Lancia). Mercedes was out. About to lead – oil at chicane caused crash into harbour.

Lorenzo Bandini (1961-67) – three losses

1966 GP de l'ACF (Ferrari). After Surtees' failure, led to lap 32, whereupon throttle cable broke.

1966 GP d'Italia (Ferrari). Led first lap but fuel pipe had broken, dropping to back of field.

1966 US Grand Prix (Ferrari). Led to lap ten, regained it on lap 20, and led until engine failed on lap 35.

Rubens Barrichello (1993-2011) – three losses

2002 GP do Brasil (Ferrari). On light fuel load, took Schumacher but hydraulics failed three laps later.

2002 GP von Osterreich (Ferrari). Yielded to Schumacher at the flag by order. Robbing everyone but one!

2003 GP do Brasil (Ferrari). Took lead on lap 45 from a sliding Coulthard, and soon by 4.2 seconds. Fuel ran out due to team error.

Jean Behra (1951-59) – eight losses

1953 Aix-les-Bains (Gordini). Won part one by 23 seconds from Bayol. Just two seconds behind in part two but his axle failed.

1953 Sables d'Olonne (Gordini). Won part one, but a spin damaged his rear axle when leading part two. Oops!

1954 Oulton Park Gold Cup (Gordini). Led for three laps when magneto trouble intervened – Moss was chasing.
1957 British GP (Maserati). Led after Moss stopped, from lap 22 to lap 69 of 90, whereupon his clutch exploded.
1958 Goodwood Glover Trophy (BRM). Led to lap four when brake failure caused his crash into the chicane.
1958 Silverstone International Trophy (BRM). Passed Collins' Ferrari to lead for five laps, when stone smashed goggles.
1958 GP de Monaco (BRM). Another brake failure on lap 27, having led all the way.
1959 GP de Monaco (Ferrari). Led for first 21 laps when engine trouble cost the lead, retired two laps later.

Jean-Pierre Beltoise (1966-74) – three losses
1968 GP d'España (Matra). Led lap 12, but the Matra's French engine was losing oil, stopping four laps later.
1970 GP de France (Matra). After leading for ten laps a puncture on lap 26 and fuel starvation ended his race.
1973 RoC Brands Hatch (BRM). Leading a strong field, put in fastest lap, but slid wide on lap five. Oops!

Gerhard Berger (1984-97) – five losses
1986 GP von Osterreich (Benetton). Dominant to lap 26 when electrical trouble put him out of contention.
1987 GP de Mexico (Ferrari). Led after Boutsen stopped, only to suffer turbo failure four laps later.
1988 Australian GP (Ferrari). Led the 'unbeatable' McLaren-Hondas! – but fouled a lapped Arnoux. Oops!
1994 GP do Portugal (Ferrari). Holding off the Williams on lap eight when his gearchange hydraulics failed.
1996 GP von Deutschland (Benetton). Pressured by Hill until three laps from end when engine blew up.

Prince Birabongse of Siam aka 'B Bira' (pre-1946-55) – four losses
1948 Jersey Road Race (Maserati). Led until lap 20 when his 11-second lead vanished along with his tyre tread.
1949 British GP (Maserati). Led well at half-distance but didn't correct a slide and struck a barrel. Oops!
1949 Czechoslovak GP (Maserati). Led from start but crashed later on this ten mile circuit. Oops!
1954 Circuito di Pescara (Maserati). Led comfortably after Moss retired, but his exhaust system fell apart.

Joakim Bonnier (1956-71) – two losses
1960 GP d'Argentina (BRM). Led laps 42 to 67, whereupon overheating caused a lengthy pit stop.
1961 GP de Bruxelles (Porsche). In three parts. Won part one easily. Leading part two when taken out by Surtees.

Thierry Boutsen (1983-93) – two losses
1987 GP de Mexico (Benetton). Took lead from Berger's Ferrari on lap two, but electrics failed on lap 16.
1990 GP di San Marino (Williams). Led confidently after Senna went out, but on lap 18 his engine failed.

Jack Brabham (1955-70) – ten losses
1960 GP do Buenos Aires (Cooper). Led from teammate McLaren, but water pump trouble put him out.
1960 GP de Monaco (Cooper). Passed Moss on damp track – not many did – but crashed seven laps later. Oops!
1961 GP von Deutschland (Cooper V8). Led off, but a wet patch caught him out after seven miles. Oops!
1965 RoC Brands Hatch (Brabham). Led after Clark crashed and Gurney retired, but oil loss stopped him.
1965 Silverstone International Trophy (Brabham). Led from lap eight until gearbox packed up on lap 38 of 52 when clear.
1965 GP de Monaco (Brabham). Broken rev-counter caused over-revved engine which failed on lap 43.
1966 S African GP (Brabham). Led 51 laps of 60, baulked by lapped car, spun, stalled, injector belt broken.
1966 GP d'Italia (Brabham). Took lead from Surtees on lap four, but engine failed on lap eight.
1966 US Grand Prix (Brabham). Led after Bandini stopped, but engine failed on lap 56.
1970 RoC-Brands Hatch (Brabham). Led from lap nine, set to win but pitted for ignition problem, five laps left.

Tony Brooks (1955-61) – one loss
1956 Aintree '200' (BRM). Failing brakes late-on cost a victory over Moss, pitting but finishing second.

Louis Chiron (pre-1946-58) – two losses
1947 GP de Nimes (Talbot-Lago). Led after Villoresi's stop, but struck a wall and buckled a wheel. Oops!
1949 Czechoslovak GP (Maserati). Leaders crashed so he led from lap five, but his gearbox failed on lap 13.

Jim Clark (1960-68) – 15 losses
1962 GP de Pau (Lotus). Led from lap nine but retired on lap 24 due to broken gear selection bracket.
1962 GP van Nederland (Lotus). Led until lap 12 when clutch slip caused very long pit stop.
1962 S African GP (Lotus). Led all the way until three-quarter distance, whereupon a gearbox bolt fell out losing oil.
1963 GP de Monaco (Lotus). Passed BRMs to lead form lap 18 until 76, when gearbox selected two gears at once.
1963 GP von Osterreich (Lotus). Took the lead from Brabham on lap four, but oil pipe split on lap nine.
1964 GP de l'ACF (Lotus). Led by 15 seconds at halfway, when his engine failed.
1964 US Grand Prix (Lotus). Forged in to lead on lap 11, drew away, but injection system failed on lap 44.
1964 GP de Mexico (Lotus). Set to win but oil loss brought

about engine failure on last lap.

1965 RoC Brands Hatch (Lotus). Won part one by 20 seconds. Led part two, but pressured into crash by Gurney. Oops!

1966 GP van Nederland (Lotus). Passed Brabham on lap 27, but, on lap 75, lost water and pitted.

1967 GP de Belgique (Lotus). Led until near half distance when plug trouble intervened.

1967 GP de l'ACF (Lotus). Led for ten laps after Hill retired when crownwheel and pinion failed.

1967 GP von Deutschland (Lotus). Led until lap four when front suspension wishbone bent.

1967 Canadian GP (Lotus). Carved past Hulme to lead lap 58, but ten laps later engine failed.

1967 GP d'Italia (Lotus). Lap 12 puncture, recovered a lap, led after Hill stopped, fuel pump failed.

Peter Collins (1952-58) – one loss

1957 GP de Monaco (Lancia-Ferrari). Behind Moss at his crash and hit by scattered poles. Would have led.

David Coulthard (1994-2008) – 11 losses

1995 GP de Belgique (Williams). Led after Herbert spun, but eight laps later gearbox overheated.

1995 GP d'Italia (Williams). Led from pole but a probable first win lost by seized wheel bearing on lap 14.

1995 Australian GP (Williams). Led 19 laps but, on entering pit lane, slid into its wall. Oops!

1998 Australian GP (McLaren). After pit stops, yielded to pre-race team deal allowing lap one leader to win.

1998 Canadian GP (McLaren). Well in command after Hakkinen retired, but lap 19 saw his engine expire.

1998 GP d'Italia (McLaren). The race should have been his race after Hakkinen's problem, but engine failed.

1999 GP de France (McLaren). Passed Barrichello to lead, and was storming away when his alternator failed.

1999 GP d'Europe (McLaren). Took lead after Frentzen stopped, but spun off on damp track. Oops!

2001 GP de Monaco (McLaren). Glitch on formation lap negated pole position. From the back to a brilliant fifth!

2002 Australian GP (McLaren). Led when safety-car called out. On release, a gearbox glitch spun him out.

2003 GP do Brasil (McLaren). Led laps 47 to 52, pitted and set to recover lead. Race stopped 18 laps early.

Elio deAngelis (1979-d86) – one loss

1984 GP von Deutschland (Lotus). Made great start and led to lap eight, but engine had a typical turbo blow-up.

Baron deGraffenried (1946-56) – one loss

1949 Czechoslovak GP (Maserati). Led after Bira crashed, but stopped for plugs five laps later.

Patrick Depailler (1972-80) – one loss

1979 GP de Belgique (Ligier). Led for seven laps after Jones stopped, but understeered off into barriers. Oops!

Juan-Manuel Fangio (1948-58) – ten losses

1949 GP de Belgique (Maserati). Took lead from Villoresi, but a piston broke soon after.

1950 GP Eva Perón (Ferrari). Led well after Ascari's chase ended, but touched the straw bales. Oops!

1950 GP Gen.Martin (Ferrari). Desperate attempt to lead by Villoresi took him out.

1951 GP de Paris (Gordini). Took lead from Farina, shattered lap record, but valve trouble stopped him.

1952 GP d'Albi (BRM). Led for 15 laps, and was way ahead when cylinder head trouble arose.

1953 GP d'Albi (BRM). Led for nine laps, but tyre treads were thrown and damaged the brakes.

1953 GP de Belgique (Maserati). Leading Ascari after González retired, but soon had engine trouble.

1955 GP deMonaco (Mercedes). Led from start, but rear axle failed on lap 50.

1956 GP de Belgique (Lancia-Ferrari). Took lead from Moss on lap five, but axle failed on lap 24.

1956 GP de l'ACF (Lancia-Ferrari). Having led from laps four to 38, an oil pipe split dropping him to fourth.

Giuseppe Farina (pre-1946-55) – five losses

1949 GP de Belgique (Maserati). Passed Villoresi to lead lap seven, but crashed at La Source. Oops!

1951 GP van Nederland (Maserati). Led from start but oil loss due to split pipe ruined his race on lap 20.

1952 GP de Marseille (Ferrari). Led at three-quarter distance after Ascari pitted, but slid off two laps later. Oops!

1953 GP di Siracusa (Ferrari). Led after Ascari broke a wheel, but retired on lap 61 with mechanical bothers.

1953 International Trophy – Charterhall (Ferrari 'Thinwall'). Pulling away from Wharton's BRM but stopped on lap 14.

Giancarlo Fisichella (1996-2009) – two losses

1999 GP d'Europe (Benetton). Led laps 45 to 48 then spun off – much Italian emotion. And why not? Oops!

2005 Canadian GP (Reanult). Retained lead after pit stop but gearbox failure put him out.

Emerson Fittipaldi (1970-80) – two losses

1972 GP do Brazil (Lotus). Leading easily on lap 32 of 37 when suspension collapse spun him out.

1973 GP von Osterreich (Lotus). Led strongly from lap 17 to 48, whereupon a fuel pipe came adrift.

Heinz-Harald Frentzen (1994-2003) – two losses

1997 GP de Monaco (Williams). Pole position wasted by

team choice of slicks – rain never eased all race.
1999 GP d'Europe (Jordan). Led until beyond his routine pit stop, whereupon electrics failed at half-distance.

Bruno Giacomelli (1977-83; 90) – one loss
1980 US(E) Grand Prix (Alfa Romeo). His first pole and led to half distance – electrical trouble intervened.

Ritchie Ginther (1960-67) – one loss
1961 GP de l'ACF (Ferrari). Led after Phil Hill spun on lap 37, but four laps later his oil pressure dropped.

Froilán González (1950-57, 60) – two losses
1953 GP d'Albi (BRM). Led after Fangio stopped, but tyres threw treads and stops cost too much time.
1953 GP de Belgique (Maserati). Outpacing Ascari at one third distance when accelerator pedal broke.

Masten Gregory (1957-65) – three losses
1959 Aintree '200' (Cooper). From pole led well from Moss until lap 19 when clutch failure finished his race.
1959 GP van Nederland (Cooper). Led laps two to 11, whereupon car started jumping out of gear.
1959 GP von Deutschland (Cooper). Led the Ferraris when his engine blew. Amazing, but had little chance.

Dan Gurney (1959-70) – six losses
1960 GP de Buenos Aires (BRM). Led after the Cooper team retired, but gear problems stopped him.
1960 GP de Portugal (BRM). Led first ten laps from Brabham, whereupon oil on wheels dropped him back.
1964 GP de Belgique (Brabham). Led by miles but short of fuel, pitted but none available. Ran out soon.
1964 GP von Osterreich (Brabham). Comfortable lead at halfway lost as front suspension failed.
1965 RoC Brands Hatch (Brabham). Pressured Clark into crashing, then engine failure ruined his victory.
1967 GP von Deutschland (Eagle-Weslake). Led after Clark retired, but driveshaft broke on lap 12 of 15.

Mike Hailwood (1963-65; 71-74) – one loss
1973 RoC Brands Hatch (Surtees). Set to win after Peterson stopped, but suspension failed with five laps left.

Mika Hakkinen (1991-2001) – 12 losses
1997 British GP (McLaren). Set to win after Schumacher stopped, but his engine failed with seven laps to go.
1997 GP von Luxemberg (McLaren). Led from start to two-thirds distance, when both McLarens' engines expired.
1998 GP de Belgique (McLaren). From pole in wet on intermediates, slid off at first corner, and, on re-entry, hit others.

1998 GP d'Italia (McLaren). Had brake trouble soon after start, and let Coulthard by to lead on lap eight.
1999 Australian GP (McLaren). Lost a big lead at safety car period. Led away but engine failed immediately.
1999 GP di San Marino (McLaren). Led for 17 laps but ran over a kerb which put him into wall. Oops!
1999 British GP (McLaren). Seemingly set for victory, a rear wheel wasn't fixed properly and came off.
1999 GP von Osterreich (McLaren). Coulthard error caused spin to the back. Recovered to third – impressive.
1999 GP von Deutschland (McLaren). A bad pit stop and tyre explosion gave him a bad luck hat-trick.
1999 GP d'Italia (McLaren). Led until lap 30 when wrong gear selection at chicane sent him off. Oops!
2000 Australian GP (McLaren). Led Coulthard to lap ten who retired with misfire; eight laps later it was his turn.
2001 GP d'Espaňa (McLaren). Led throughout except for pit stops. Robbed on last lap as clutch exploded.

Lewis Hamilton (2007-) – eight losses
2008 GP de Belgique (McLaren). Cut chicane, returned the place, but 25-second penalty cost his eventual win.
2012 Singapore GP (McLaren). Led from pole to after pit stops when gearbox failed.
2012 Abu Dhabi GP (McLaren). Led from pole again, pulling away after safety car, but fuel pressure failed.
2013 British GP (Mercedes). Storming from pole, a tyre blew on lap seven, with almost a lap to go to crawl back.
2014 Australian GP (Mercedes). On pole but running on five cylinders after start, and retired two laps later.
2014 GP de Belgique (Mercedes). Taken out by Rosberg's cynical passing attempt at Les Combes chicane.
2015 Monaco GP (Mercedes). A pit stop under the safety car was a team error costing him a certain victory.
2016 Malaysian GP (Mercedes). Always in charge and set for win, but engine blew at three-quarter distance.

Mike Hawthorn (1952-58) – seven losses
1954 GP de Buenos Aires (Ferrari). Saw off the same field as Argentine GP, but engine blew on last bend.
1956 Aintree '200' (BRM). Took lead off Scott-Brown, but BRM 'Achilles heel' – brakes – failed on lap five.
1956 Silverstone International Trophy (BRM). Leading Moss and Fangio on lap one when magneto drive failed.
1956 British GP (BRM). Led for 15 laps before seal failed on universal joint. Retired ten laps later
1957 GP di Napoli (Lancia Ferrari). Leading Musso and Collins when fuel pipe split, pitted but made second.
1958 GP de Buenos Aires (Ferrari). Won part one from Fangio, and led part two only for transmission to fail.
1958 GP de Monaco (Ferrari). Led after Moss retired, but only for nine laps when fuel pump failed.

Johnny Herbert (1989-2000) – one loss

1995 GP de Belgique (Benetton). Led again after Alesi stopped, but spun out a couple of laps later. Oops!

Damon Hill (1992-99) – eight losses

1993 British GP (Williams). Led to two-thirds distance, and was pulling away from Prost when his engine blew.
1993 GP von Deutschland (Williams). Led throughout – victory seemed assured – tyre blew with two laps left.
1993 GP do Portugal (Williams). Pole but his turn to start at back. Finished third so a win had been likely.
1994 Australian GP (Williams). Went to pass damaged Schumacher but was chopped out of race and title.
1995 GP do Brasil (Williams). Passed Schumacher at pit stops. Drawing away when suspension failed.
1995 GP von Deutschland (Williams). From pole led Schumacher by two seconds, but slid off at turn one on lap two. Oops!
1996 GP de Monaco (Williams). In charge until lap 41 when his engine expired in a big way.
1997 Hungarian GP (Arrows). Passed Schumacher, 40-second lead and three laps to go – stuck in third! An historic loss.

Graham Hill (1958-75) – 13 losses

1959 Silver City Trophy-Snetterton (Lotus). Took the lead on lap seven. Two laps later a driveshaft failed.
1960 British GP (BRM). Stalled, passed entire field, but, with six laps left, fading brakes part-blamed for spin.
1962 GP de Monaco (BRM). Led since lap 11, but his engine went off song and blew on lap 92, still leading.
1962 GP de l'ACF (BRM). Hit by backmarker mid-race, recovered lead, but, on lap 42, fuel system failed.
1964 GP de Belgique (BRM). Led last lap as Gurney pitted, but pump failed to pick up fuel.
1964 *Daily Mirror* Trophy-Snetterton (BRM). Torrent shortened race. Aquaplaned off when leading on lap seven.
1964 *News of the World* Trophy-Goodwood (BRM). Led from start but distributor failed with just two laps left.
1966 Oulton Park Gold Cup (BRM). Battled with Brabham and led laps 20 to 24 when H16's camshaft broke.
1967 GP van Nederland (Lotus). Led in new Lotus to lap 11 when camshaft failed.
1967 GP de l'ACF (Lotus). Took lead from Clark on lap 11, but crown-wheel and pinion soon broke.
1967 British GP (Lotus). Took lead from Clark on lap 26, on lap 55 rear suspension link broke.
1967 GP d'Italia (Lotus). Took lead from Hulme on lap 28. Led until lap 59 when his engine blew up.
1968 British GP (Lotus). Led from lap four to 26 when a driveshaft failed (stress due to wings?).

Phil Hill (1958-66) – one loss

1961 GP de l'ACF (Ferrari). Spun on melting tar after needlessly out-braking much-lapped Moss. Oops!

Denny Hulme (1965-74) – four losses

1967 S African GP (Brabham). Led to three-quarter distance, pitting for brake fluid cost his full minute lead.
1970 S African GP (McLaren). Having led from lap 17 with four laps to go, of 79, his rear suspension broke.
1973 RoC Brands Hatch (McLaren). Led after some attrition but clutch slipped with just a mile to go.
1973 S. African GP (McLaren). Led pulling away for first four ,but punctured on debris from crash.

James Hunt (1973-79) – seven losses

1975 Silverstone International Trophy (Hesketh). Lap 25 and leading from Lauda and Fittipaldi but engine blew.
1975 GP d'España (Hesketh). Led for six laps after start melée then slid off on oil, hitting the barriers.
1976 British GP (McLaren). Innocent in first melée. Won restarted race then disqualified. Historic injustice!
1977 GP d'Argentina (McLaren). Took lead from Watson's Brabham but suspension failed causing crash.
1977 GP von Osterreich (McLaren). Led from lap 12 to 44 when, with a 22-second lead, his engine failed.
1977 GP van Nederland (McLaren). Led first five laps, but contact with Andretti at Tarzan. Came off worst.
1977 Canadian GP (McLaren). Took Andretti on lap 62, but, on lapping teammate, both used outside line.

Jacky Ickx (1967-79) – four losses

1970 GP de France (Ferrari). Led for 16 laps holding off Beltoise, but valve trouble did for him.
1970 British GP (Ferrari). A broken differential stopped him after leading the first six laps.
1972 British GP (Ferrari). Led from start to lap 48 when oil pressure fell and stopped in pits.
1972 GP d'Italia (Ferrari). Led as Regazzoni stopped. Holding off Fittipaldi on lap 45 when electrics failed.

Innes Ireland (1959-66) – two losses

1960 GP d'Argentina (Lotus). Zoomed off for a lap when gears jammed. Steering broke, yet finished sixth!
1963 GP von Osterreich (Lotus). Escaped from a battle with Brabham, but cam follower broke on lap 64 of 80.

Jean-Pierre Jabouille (1974-81) – four losses

1978 GP d'Italia (Renault-turbo). The two ahead had a one-minute penalty, so he was leading when engine expired.
1980 GP do Brasil (Renault-turbo). Passed Villeneuve on lap two, but engine failed on lap 26 of 40.
1980 S African GP (Renault-turbo). Led for 62 of 80 laps

when a puncture gave win to teammate Arnoux.
1980 GP von Deutschland (Renault-turbo). Led to 60 per cent distance when his valve springs failed.

Jean-Pierre Jarier (1971-83) – three losses
1975 GP d'Argentina (Shadow). Pole but crown-wheel failed on warm-up lap. A fluke? See next race below.
1975 GP do Brasil (Shadow). Pole again, led from lap two to 32 of 40. Fuel system failed. So credit the above.
1978 Canadian GP (Lotus). Led from pole to near three-quarter distance when oil loss finished a great drive.

Stefan Johansson (1980-91) – one loss
1985 GP di San Marino (Ferrari). Three laps to go Senna's car ran dry. Now so did Johansson's – two laps left.

Alan Jones (1975-86) – eight losses
1979 GP van Belgique (Williams). Led laps 24 to 40 when electrics failed. A Williams first F1 lead wasted.
1979 British GP (Williams). Passed teammate Regga on lap one, had big lead on lap 40 when engine failed.
1979 US(E) Grand Prix (Williams). Took Villeneuve on lap 32. Led after tyre stops but had a wheel loose.
1981 GP de Belgique (Williams). Pulled away from laps 13 to 20 when gear failed to engage – crash ensued.
1981 GP de Monaco (Williams). After Piquet's crash, led easily but fuel problems caused pit stops near end.
1981 GP d'España (Williams). Ahead by 14 seconds on lap 14, but brakes locked and ran off into trap. Oops!
1981 GP von Deutschland (Williams). Led on lap 21. By lap 31 had ten second lead, but misfire stopped him
1981 Canadian GP (Williams). Led in atrocious conditions but spun off on lap seven when well clear. Oops!

Jacques Laffitte (1974-86) – one loss
1980 British GP (Ligier). Led after Pironi hit trouble, on the grass when lapping – three laps later tyre failed.

Niki Lauda (1971-79, 82-85) – nine losses
1974 GP de Monaco (Ferrari). Took lead as Regazzoni spun on lap 21, but ignition failed on lap 33.
1974 British GP (Ferrari). Led all the way until, with a ten-second lead, a puncture spoiled things with five laps to go.
1974 GP d'Italia (Ferrari). Led from pole to past half distance when engine failed.
1974 Canadian GP (Ferrari). Led to lap 69 when un-flagged debris from Watson's car caused crash.
1975 GP d'España (Ferrari). Led from pole at first corner when taken off by Andretti et al.
1976 GP de France (Ferrari). Led until lap eight from Hunt but engine failed.
1979 RoC Brands Hatch (Brabham). Pulling away, but, on lap

eight, wrong tyre choice meant they were shot.
1984 GP do Brasil (McLaren). Led after Alboreto stopped to lap 38 when electrical trouble occurred.
1985 Australian GP (Williams). From 16th on the grid took Senna's lead on lap 56. A lap on his brakes were shot. This was Lauda's last race – a superb drive – among the elite to the very end.

Stuart Lewis-Evans (1957-58) – one loss
1957 GP de Reims (Vanwall). Lap 20 – 20 seconds ahead of Musso and Fangio – oil on goggles spoiled things.

John Love (1962-72) – one loss
1967 S African GP (Cooper FPF). Led after Hulme's stop, but rich mixture meant late pitting for fuel.

Nigel Mansell (1980-95) – eight losses
1984 GP de Monaco (Lotus). Passed Prost to lead a wet race but touched white line causing crash. Oops!
1987 GP de Belgique (Williams). Led first start – collision with Senna second start. Damage stopped him later.
1987 GP de Monaco (Williams). Led untroubled for 29 laps when broken exhaust caused lost turbo pressure.
1987 Hungarian GP (Williams). Led strongly throughout. Lost wheel after late pit stop Just four laps left.
1991 Canadian GP (Williams). Waving exiting last bend – semi-auto box got neutral. Not over until it's over.
1991 GP de Belgique (Williams). In command after the pit stops when electrical fault stopped him.
1991 GP do Portugal (Williams). In command at pit stop – wheel came off on leaving pit box. Disqualified.
1992 Australian GP (Williams). Taken off by Senna's disastrous 'dive-in' manoeuvre on lap 19.

Robert Manzon (1951-54) – two losses
1952 GP de Paris (Gordini). Saw off Behra, Farina and Villoresi only to have axle failure on lap 59.
1952 GP de Comminges (Gordini). Led at start from Ascari who pitted. Valve trouble occurred on lap 16.

Felipe Massa (2002-) – three losses
2008 Hungarian GP (Ferrari). In control throughout until three laps from the end when his engine expired.
2008 Singapore GP (Ferrari). Rigged crash after Alonso pitted. Fuel rig still attached at 'go' signal.
2010 GP von Deutchland (Ferrari). Passed Alonso at start, held him off and instructed to yield on lap 45.

Bruce McLaren (1959-70) – one loss
1964 GP de Belgique (Cooper). Led after last bend but engine cut out and Clark passed.

Carlos Menditeguy (1953-60) – one loss
1956 GP d'Argentina (Maserati). Passed Musso and González to lead lap three until lap 41 when half-shaft failed.

Juan-Pablo Montoya (2001-06) – seven losses
2001 GP do Brasil (Williams). Third GP yet took lead from Schumacher. Taken off by Verstappen after 36 laps.
2001 GP von Deutschland (Williams). Well clear at pit stop when fuel-rig trouble caused engine overheat.
2001 GP de Belgique (Williams). Great pole by 0.9 seconds. Stall on parade lap. At back but engine failed on lap two.
2001 US Grand Prix (Williams). Passed Schumacher to lead. Pitted and looked strong but hydraulics failed.
2003 GP von Osterreich (Williams). Regained lead by 5.6 seconds after pit stops but water pressure failed.
2003 Japanese GP (Williams). Passed poleman Barrichello on lap one. Lap eight, with five seconds lead, but the hydraulics failed.
2005 Hungarian GP (McLaren). His two-stop strategy looked a winner, but a driveshaft had other ideas.

Stirling Moss (1951-c62) – 23 losses
1954 GP Circuito di Pescara (Maserati). Unchallenged at one-quarter distance when an oil pipe broke.
1954 GP d'Italia (Maserati). Led after Ascari stopped until lap 68 of 80. Pitted for oil. Lost 20 seconds lead.
1955 Goodwood Glover Trophy (Maserati). Led from start but fuel pump failed on lap 12 of 21.
1955 GP de Monaco (Mercedes). Led after Fangio retired, but engine failed on lap 81.
1957 GP d'Argentina (Maserati). On pole but throttle link damaged at start. Caught up two laps on leader at end.
1957 GP di Siracusa (Vanwall). Stormed away from everyone, but a fuel pipe repair was needed.
1957 Goodwood Glover Trophy (Vanwall). Vanwall Achilles heel – throttle linkage – stopped him on lap 13.
1957 GP de Monaco (Vanwall). Led from start but brake problem caused crash at the chicane on lap four.
1958 GP do Buenos Aires (Cooper). In wet, local driver lost control in the wet, T'boning Moss at first bend.
1958 GP de Monaco (Vanwall). Took the lead from Hawthorn on lap 33. Five laps later engine failed.
1958 GP de Belgique (Vanwall). A big first lap lead but selected neutral on lap two – engine blew – Oops!
1958 GP von Deutschland (Vanwall). Led by 20 seconds on lap three. Magneto failed, but smashed Fangio's lap record.
1958 GP d'Italia (Vanwall). Lap 14, led from Hawthorn but gearbox trouble cost the lead. Retired lap 18.
1959 Aintree '200' (Cooper). Led easily after Gregory's retirement only for gearbox to fail on lap 30.
1959 Silverstone International Trophy (BRM). BRM 'Achilles heel' – brakes – totally failed on lap three. Spun out to stop.

1959 GP de Monaco (Cooper). Led as Behra hit trouble on lap 21, held it until lap 81. Gearbox failed.
1959 GP van Nederland (Cooper). Bad start, took lead from Bonnier on lap 60 then gearbox failed again.
1959 US Grand Prix (Cooper). Stormed off to big lead when gearbox failed yet again on lap five.
1960 GP d'Argentina (Cooper). Pulling away from Bonnier on lap 41 when suspension broke.
1960 Silverstone International Trophy (Cooper). Leading a scrap with Ireland's Lotus when wishbone failed.
1961 New Zealand GP (Cooper). Was pulling away from Works Cooper team when drive failed on lap 31.
1961 Guards Trophy – Brands Hatch (Cooper). Took lead from Surtees but gearbox failed on lap 24.
1961 US Grand Prix (Lotus). Swapped lead with Brabham many times. Led for 20 laps when bearings ran.

Luigi Musso (1953-58) – three losses
1955 GP del Valentino (Maserati). Led to quarter distance but oil loss caused retirement as Ascari closed.
1956 GP de Napoli (Lancia-Ferrari). An easy victory with little opposition was thwarted by engine failure.
1956 GP d'Italia (Lancia-Ferrari). Moss ran out of fuel, so led lap 47 but steering broke – amazing survival.

Tazio Nuvolari (pre1946-47) – one loss
1946 GP de Marseilles (Maserati). Passed Sommer in second heat – valve trouble. A win in final? Let's say yes.

Jackie Oliver (1968-77) – one loss
1968 British GP (Lotus). Retook lead after Hill stopped, but lasted just 17 laps whereupon transmission failed.

Carlos Pace (1972-77) – one loss
1977 GP do Brasil (Brabham). Led to lap six, so was first to hit the broken up track. Slid and hit by Hunt.

Reg Parnell (1946-57) – five losses
1948 British Empire Trophy (Maserati). Had led almost throughout, but ran out of fuel on last lap.
1949 British Grand Prix (Maserati). Led after 'Bira' went off but transmission failed on lap 69.
1949 British Empire Trophy (Maserati). Flew away from the rest, but supercharger failed on lap four.
1950 British Empire Trophy (Maserati). Passed Gerard to lead lap two but intermittent clutch slip ruined his race.
1955 *Daily Telegraph* Trophy – Aintree (Connaught). Saw off Moss, led from start but pulled in on penultimate lap.

Ricardo Patrese (1977-93) – nine losses
1978 S African GP (Arrows). Led from lap 26 to 62, looking secure, when engine blew up in a big way.

1981 US (W) Grand Prix (Arrows). Led from pole to lap 33 when fuel feed system failed.

1982 GP de France (Brabham). Zoomed past the Renaults to lead, but engine failed on lap nine.

1982 GP von Osterreich (Brabham). Leading after fuel stop when engine failed spectacularly.

1983 GP d'Italia (Brabham). Streaked away to lap six, but turbo expired in a huge cloud. A feature of the era.

1989 Hungarian GP (Williams). Led to lap 52 when debris in radiator caused water leak and retirement.

1991 GP di San Marino (Williams). A six-second lead on lap five vanished by lap ten. He pitted with a misfiring engine.

1992 Hungarian GP (Williams). Out-qualified Mansell and led until halfway – caught out by dirt on track.

1992 Australian GP (Williams). Led after Mansell and holding off Berger but fuel pressure fell on lap 50.

Ronnie Peterson (1970-78) – six losses

1973 RoC Brands Hatch (Lotus). Led after Beltoise slid off, but gearbox failed after 18 laps of 40.

1973 GP d'España (Lotus). Led to three-quarter distance when he lost all gears.

1973 GP de Monaco (Lotus). Led laps two to seven when falling fuel pressure dropped him to sixth.

1973 Swedish GP (Lotus). Led whole race until last lap when deflating tyre allowed Hulme past.

1973 GP van Nederland (Lotus). Led all the way to 90 per cent distance when gearbox trouble ruined his race.

1974 GP d'Argentina (Lotus). Led off from pole but with a misfiring engine – passed after a lap.

Nelson Piquet Sr (1978-91) – 14 losses

1980 GP d'España (Brabham). Led after Reutemann was punted off, but retired with gearbox failure.*

1980 Canadian GP (Brabham). Pulled away comfortably but a piston broke at one-third distance.

1981 GP de Monaco (Brabham). Led to two-thirds distance, but impatience when lapping put him out. Oops!

1982 GP do Brasil (Brabham). Disqualified after 'winning' by 40 seconds from Prost due to ballast issues.

1982 British GP (Brabham). Led until lap ten when a ten-second lead vanished with his engine's power.

1982 GP de France (Brabham). Took over from Patrese but suffered the same engine failure.

1982 GP von Deutschland (Brabham). Well ahead on lap 19 when hit by lapped car. Hat-trick of losses.

1983 GP van Nederland (Brabham). Led up to tyre stops when Prost tried to pit first, putting both out.

1984 GP von Deutschland (Brabham). Led after deAngelis blew up for 15 laps but had gearbox trouble.

1984 GP van Nederland (Brabham). Had a lead of four seconds by lap nine, but a leaking oil pipe put him out.

1984 GP d'Italia (Brabham). A repeat of the last race, but lasted until lap 15 when engine trouble stopped him.

1986 GP de Belgique (Williams). In charge to lap 16, but stopped when engine showed signs of failing.

1987 GP de Belgique (Williams). Took over as Senna and Mansell collided, but turbo failed on lap ten.

1987 GP von Deutschland (Williams). In control until 90 per cent race distance when engine seized.

Didier Pironi (1978-c82) – four losses

1980 GP d'España (Ligier). Led after Piquet stopped, but a loose wheel ruined his race.

1980 GP deMonaco (Ligier). Led for 55 laps, jumped out of gear on wet track while changing gear.

1980 British GP (Ligier). Led to lap 19. Tyre deflated – stormed back to fifth – tyre exploded.

1982 GP de Monaco (Ferrari). Took over on penultimate lap, but experienced engine trouble in the tunnel on last lap.

Alain Prost (1980-93) – 13 losses

1981 British GP (Renault). Led from front row to lap 17 when misfiring took over and he retired.

1981 GP von Osterreich (Renault). Led first 27 laps when front suspension collapsed.

1982 GP de Monaco (Renault). Led after Arnoux spun, but, with three laps to go, he hit the barriers in the wet.

1982 GP von Osterreich (Brabham). Led after Patrese's blow up, but had injection trouble with four laps left.

1984 US Dallas GP (McLaren). Took lead from Rosberg with ease, but crashed eight laps later. Oops!

1984 British GP (McLaren). Retook lead at lap 12 restart, and was leading by five seconds on lap 38 when gearbox failed.

1985 GP di San Marino (McLaren). 'Won' after the others' fuel ran out. Car two kilos under weight – disqualified.

1989 Canadian GP (McLaren). Good lead from Senna at start but front suspension failed.

1989 Japanese GP (McLaren). Infamously desperate Senna manoeuvre put Prost out and Senna push-started.

1990 Japanese GP (Ferrari). First bend – another Prost/Senna spat. Blame who you will – Prost was ahead.

1993 GP do Brasil (Williams). Misunderstood pit message and aborted pit stop for 'wets' – hit spinning car.

1993 Hungarian GP (Williams). On pole position but clutch trouble on parade lap so started at back.

1993 GP d'Italia (Williams). Led all the way, but his turn for an engine failure five laps from the end.

Tom Pryce (1974-77) – one loss

1975 British GP (Shadow). Pole position, led on lap 20, but first on scene of flooded track ... slid off.

Kimi Raikkonen (2001-09, 2012-) – five losses

2003 GP d'Europe (McLaren). Led from pole, reclaimed it after pit stops, but engine failed on lap 25.

2005 GP di San Marino (McLaren). Pulling away with a four-second lead on lap eight when CV joint failed.

2005 GP d'Europe (McLaren). Led from start. Flat-spotted tyre caused last lap suspension failure. Oops!

2005 GP von Deutschland (McLaren). Led from pole and after pit stops. Hydraulic failure finished his race.

2008 Canadian GP (Ferrari). At pit exit red light, hit by Hamilton who had forgotten about this control.

'Clay' Regazzoni (1970-c80) – three losses

1972 GP d'Italia (Ferrari). Took lead from Ickx when he ran wide. Two laps later was caught by spinning car.

1974 GP de Monaco (Ferrari). Led from start but spun on lap 21 and finished fourth. Oops!

1974 GP d'Italia (Ferrari). Led after teammate Lauda stopped, only to also suffer engine failure ten laps later.

Carlos 'Lole' Reutemann (1972-82) – three losses

1974 GP d'Argentina (Brabham). Passed Peterson to lead lap three until, with a lap to go, his distributor failed.

1974 GP President Medici (Brabham). Led from pole for six laps when overheating started. Blew up five laps later.

1980 GP d'España (Williams). Backmarker caused crash on being lapped, sending Laffite into him.

Daniel Ricciardo (2010-) – one loss

2016 GP de Monaco (Red Bull). Controlled race until pit stop when correct tyres were not ready.

Jochen Rindt (1964-70) – two losses

1969 GP d'España.(Lotus). Led well for the first 21 laps, but crashed when rear wing collapsed as Hill's had.

1969 GP van Nederland (Lotus). Took the lead from teammate Hill on lap three until lap 18 when driveshaft failed.

Keke Rosberg (1978-86) – five losses

1985 GP do Brasil (Williams). Beat poleman Alboreto away to lead until lap ten when turbo blew.

1985 GP von Deutschland (Williams). Led for 13 laps after Senna stopped, but brake troubles stopped him.

1985 GP van Nederland (Williams). Seeming secure after Senna's chase had faltered, but his engine failed.

1985 GP d'Italia (Williams). Had been in control all race but, with six laps to go, his engine expired again.

1986 Australian GP (McLaren). Led to lap 62. Stopped with 'blown engine' – the noise was loose tyre tread!

Nico Rosberg (2006-) – three losses

2014 Canadian GP (Mercedes). Power loss from hybrid system – unable to fend off Ricciardo.

2014 GP d'Italia (Mercedes). Twice overshot at chicane under pressure from Hamilton.

2015 Russian GP (Mercedes). Fended off Hamilton to lead, but throttle failure caused retirement.

Jody Scheckter (1972-80) – four losses

1973 GP de France (McLaren). Led first 42 laps, then Fittipaldi's passing attempt launched him airborne.

1975 RoC Brands Hatch (Tyrrell). Was holding off Pryce when his engine blew on lap 20.

1977 GP de Belgique (Wolf). Led after Watson was fouled, but spun off on wet track on lap 17. Oops!

1978 British GP (Wolf). Led after Andretti's puncture, looking strong for ten laps when gearbox failed.

Michael Schumacher (1991-2006, 10-12) – 12 losses

1993 GP de Monaco (Benetton). Led after Prost's penalty stop, but hydraulic failure on lap 32 put him out.

1994 GP de Belgique (Benetton). Led throughout, but illegal wear to skid-tray produced disqualification.

1994 Australian GP (Benetton). Struck wall. Damaged but chopped Hill out – thus becoming Champion!

1995 GP di San Marino (Benetton). Pitted for slicks, as did Hill, but lost control hitting the barrier. Oops!

1995 Canadian GP (Benetton). Led until lap 58, 11 to go, when he got stuck in third gear and pitted for repair.

1995 British GP (Benetton). Led to lap 40 then struck by Hill's desperate challenge – putting both out.

1997 British GP (Ferrari). Looking set for win after pit stops when a wheel bearing failed.

1998 GP de Belgique (Ferrari). In heavy rain about to lap Coulthard who eased to help, smashed into him.

1999 Canadian GP (Ferrari). Led for 30 laps before hitting wall exiting last chicane. Oops!

2000 GP de Monaco (Ferrari). Cracked exhaust overheated suspension which broke. Had led to lap 55.

2004 GP de Monaco (Ferrari). Behind safety car in tunnel. Hit by Montoya – both out.

2005 Japanese GP (Ferrari). Handed lead on lap two by teammate, and held it until lap 36 when engine failed.

Ralf Schumacher (1997-2007) – one loss

1999 GP d'Europe (Williams). Led one lap after Fisichella retired, but a tyre flew apart after a lap. Finished fourth.

Archie Scott-Brown (1956-58) – two losses

1956 Goodwood Glover Trophy (Connaught). Passed Hawthorn's BRM, even led Moss, then brakes faded.

1956 Aintree '200' (Connaught). Pole position, and led after Hawthorn retired, but his engine failed.

Ayrton Senna (1984-94) – 17 losses

1985 GP di San Marino (Lotus). Led all the way, repeating Portugese win, but fuel ran out three laps from end.

1985 GP de Monaco (Lotus). Led away, looking again to repeat Portugal, but his engine expired on lap 12.

1985 US Detroit GP (Lotus). Led away but hard tyres were wrong. Pits replaced them with same type!

1985 GP von Deutschland (Lotus). Forced past Rosberg on lap 14. Led to lap 27 when driveshaft broke.

1985 Australian GP (Lotus). Led after Lauda crashed, but for only three laps, whereupon his engine failed.

1988 GP de Monaco (McLaren). Led by 50 seconds on lap 87. Amazingly, lost concentration and crashed. Oops!

1989 US (Phoenix) GP (McLaren). Losing ground to Prost due to electrical malady. Pitted on lap 33.

1989 Canadian GP (McLaren). Correct tyre choice at pit stops didn't stop engine failure three laps from the end.

1989 British GP (McLaren). Coped less well than Prost with gear selection problems, and slid off on lap 12.

1989 GP d'Italia (McLaren). Domination again until six laps from the end, when oil loss onto tyres caused spin.

1989 Australian GP (McLaren). Led in rain storm to lap 14 when he ploughed into Brundle's car. Oops!

1990 GP do Brasil (McLaren). Lapping Nakajima who spun into him, taking off his McLaren's nose.

1990 GP di San Marino (McLaren). Easily led on lap four when a rear tyre deflated and he slid off into a sand trap.

1990 GP de Mexico (McLaren). Led easily untilseven laps from end when a puncture left him crawling back.

1990 Australian GP (McLaren). Led for 62 laps, whereupon a gear failed to engage – a tyre barrier beckoned.

1992 Canadian GP (McLaren). Saw off Mansell's attempt, then, on lap 38, gear selection trouble stopped him.

1994 GP di San Marino (Williams). Led after safety car period but crashed after six laps – CATASTROPHE!

Jo 'Seppi' Siffert (1962-71) – two losses

1965 GP di Siracusa (Brabham). Winning battle with Surtees, changed gear as bump put wheels airborne.

1968 GP de Mexico (Lotus). Took lead from Hill on lap 22, but throttle cable broke two laps later.

Raymond Sommer (1946-50) – six losses

1947 GP de Pau (Maserati). Took pole easily. Led until catastrophic fuel stop, and then magneto trouble.

1947 GP du Rousillon (Maserati). On pole again, and led until lap 44 of 58 when gearbox failed.

1947 GP de Marseilles. (Maserati). Pole again, leading after Villoresi retired, but engine failed.

1948 GP de Pau (Maserati). Chased Pagani, hit kerb, bent wheel, retook lead (!). Wheel failed on last lap.

1950 GP de Paris (Talbot-Lago). Got better of Rosier and led to lap 33 of 50 when engine failed.

1950 GP van Nederland (Talbot-Lago). Took lead from Fangio on lap six. Led by 30 seconds when clutch failed.

Mike Spence (1963-68) – one loss

1965 GP del Mediterraneo (Lotus). Leading from Siffert when stones flung into his face and he crashed.

Jackie Stewart (1964-73) – 12 losses

1964 Rand Grand Prix (Lotus). Part one, on pole – half-shaft broke at start. Part two, won from back, beat Graham Hill!

1965 GP de Monaco (BRM). Led lap 25 after Hill took to escape road, but spun five laps later. Oops!

1967 GP de Monaco (BRM). Took lead from Hulme on lap seven, but crown-wheel and pinion failed eight laps later.

1968 GP de Belgique (Matra-Ford). Led from ,halfway but pitted for fuel with a lap to go.

1969 GP de Monaco (Matra-Ford). Driveshaft failed after leading for 22 laps.

1969 Oulton Park Gold Cup (Matra). Leading Ickx and Rindt when misfiring caused him to pit on lap 17.

1969 Canadian GP (Matra-Ford). Led lap six to lap 32 when wheel-bumping with Ickx ended his race.

1970 GP de Monaco (March). Led by 16s on lap 27 when ignition problems dropped him to the back.

1970 Canadian GP (Tyrrell). The new marque led magnificently for 31 laps when a stub axle broke.

1970 US Grand Prix (Tyrrell). Frightened the opposition for 82 laps this time. Burnt oil pipe stopped him.

1971 Silverstone IntTrophy (Tyrrell). Won first part but jammed throttle caused crash after second start.

1972 S African GP (Tyrrell). Led from lap two, and was just holding off Fittipaldi on lap 44 when gearbox seized.

Rolf Stommelen (1970-78) – one loss

1975 GP d'España (Hill). Leading lap 26 when aerofoil broke causing catastrophic crash. Race stopped.

Hans-Joachim Stuck (1974-79) – one loss

1977 US (E) Grand Prix (Brabham). Led first 14 laps but car jumped out of gear and he spun off track.

John Surtees (1960-72) – nine losses

1960 GP de Portugal (Lotus). Led from lap 11 to 35 when fuel on foot pedals caused crash into bales.

1962 GP de Reims (Lola). Drew well away from Clark and the rest, then valve spring broke on lap 28.

1963 GP d'Italia (Ferrari). Passed Graham Hill on lap four. Held off Clark for ten laps when engine failed on lap 16.

1963 US Grand Prix (Ferrari). Won lead battle with Graham Hill on lap 36. Led to lap 82 when engine failed.

1964 GP de Belgique (Ferrari). Took the lead from Gurney

on lap three, but his engine expired.
1964 GP von Osterreich (Ferrari). Rear suspension collapsed after leading from lap two to lap seven.
1966 GP de Monaco (Ferrari). Led Stewart for 14 laps when his differential failed.
1966 GP de l'ACF (Cooper-Mas). Led for 100m – fuel pump drive broke. A win would've upset Ferrari!
1968 GP de Belgique (Honda). Led from lap two to 11 when a suspension bracket broke.

Patrick Tambay (1977-86) – two losses
1983 US (W) Grand Prix (Ferrari). Led to lap 25 then sent airborne by Rosberg's passing attempt.
1984 GP d'Italia (Renault). Took lead after Piquet stopped, but 25 laps later throttle cable snapped.

Sebastian Vettel (2006-) – seven losses
2010 Bahrain GP (Red Bull). Led all race until two-thirds distance when plug trouble dropped him to fourth.
2010 Australian GP (Red Bull). Led from pole to lap 25 when a loose front wheel put him off the track.
2010 S Korean GP (Red Bull). Set for win, having led to lap 45 in atrocious weather, but engine failed.
2011 Abu Dhabi GP (Red Bull). On pole but a tyre blew at turn two. Exhaust-blown diffuser blamed.
2011 GP do Brasil (Red Bull). Set to win but gearbox glitch needing short-shifting dropped him to second.
2012 GP d'Europe (Red Bull). Led after routine pit stops, but alternator trouble ruined his race.
2013 British GP (Red Bull). Led after Hamilton's blowout and was all set at three-quarters distance, but his gearbox failed.

Gilles Villeneuve (1977-82) – two losses
1978 US (W) Grand Prix (Ferrari). Led well to lap 48 but 'do-or-die' when lapping caused crash. Oops!
1982 GP do Brasil (Ferrari). Led to lap 28 when, under pressure, he slid off into catch fencing. Oops!

Jacques Villeneuve (1996-2006) – one loss
1997 GP d'Europe-Jerez (Williams). Took Schuey's lead despite deliberate contact. Yielded to McLarens.

Luigi Villoresi (pre 1946-56) – six losses
1947 GP de Marseilles (Maserati). Shot away at start to huge lead over Sommer, but engine failed on lap nine.
1947 GP d'Albi (Maserati). Led from lap three to 20 when mistimed his fuel stop, running out.
1947 GP de l'ACF (Maserati). Came from back of grid to lead in just three laps, then engine blew.
1949 GP de Eva Duarte Perón. Led from the start from Farina and Ascari but retired on lap 12.
1949 Jersey Road Race (Maserati). Led from lap two but

pitted for plugs after eight laps. Misfiring continued.
1949 British GP (Maserati). Led from lap two, about to lead again after fuel stop, but oil loss put him out.

Count Wolfgang von Trips (1956-61) – one loss
1961 GP de l'ACF (Ferrari). Led from teammates from lap 13 to 17 when engine failed.

Derek Warwick (1981-93) – one loss
1983 GP do Brasil (Renault). Set for debut win with 30-second lead, but wishbone broke on lap 52 of 61.

John Watson (1973-85) – four losses
1977 GP d'Argentina (Brabham). Led after Hunt crashed, but gearbox mounting was coming apart.
1977 GP van Belgique (Brabham). Led at the start, but was punted off by an overshooting Andretti.
1977 GP de France (Brabham). Took lead from Hunt on lap five, leading on last lap but fuel ran out.
1977 British GP (Brabham). Led from front row until lap 49 when fuel pressure dropped.

Mark Webber (2002-13) – one loss
2010 Turkish GP (Red Bull). Led to two-thirds distance when punted sideways by teammate Vettel.

Peter Whitehead (1949-1958) – one loss
1949 Grand Prix de France (Ferrari). Took the lead on lap 56 of 64 only to get stuck in 4th gear.

Jean-Pierre Wimille (pre-1946-49) – four losses
1946 Coupe René la Begue (Alfa Romeo). Led from start but retired on lap 19 of 30 with clutch trouble.
1946 GP del Valentino (Alfa Romeo). Yielded to team orders to share wins with Varzi.
1948 GP de Pau (Simca-Gordini). Stretching his lead over Sommer on lap 37 but pitted for a long time.
1948 GP d'Europe (Alfa Romeo). Lost the lead when pitting for water. Almost led at the finish.

Misfortune by decade
1940s: 31 losses in 64 races = 48.4 per cent
1950s: 80 losses in 184 races = 43.5 per cent
1960s: 88 losses in 182 races = 48.4 per cent
1970s: 74 losses in 174 races = 42.5 per cent
1980s: 83 losses in 159 races = 52.2 per cent
1990s: 65 losses in 162 races = 40.1 per cent
2000s: 30 losses in 174 races = 17.2 per cent
2010s: 20 losses in 136 races = 14.7 per cent

The losses in the 1980s reflects the low finish rate of that decade of turbo blow-ups.

Chapter 34

Now, the 'real score'

Over the years of the World Championship, a driver's chance of becoming a race winner, other than driving skill and fast machinery, has depended, I believe, on three varying factors: Opportunity; Reliability; Safety.

Opportunity

By the end of 1979 there had been 317 World Championship rounds. This book has shown that, by that date, over 380 other events for the same cars and drivers had also been run, of which over three quarters were of a standard seen in World Championship rounds. So, the total number of races to the end of 1979 gives an average race season of almost 21 – exactly as listed for the World Championship in 2016. The opportunity factor since 1980 is, of course, 100 per cent, as all races counted. But of pre-1980 activity, only 46 per cent were World Championship events. At the start, in 1950, it was just six out of 24 races – so opportunity was only 25 per cent, and in the years before then – nil – no Championship.

Reliability

'To finish first – first you have to finish' is a familiar truism. Since 2010 this decade has seen a machine reliability factor of 92.5 per cent, compared with just 51 per cent in the years up to 1980. In the previous chapter, I identified losses which, I believe, with modern reliability, would very likely have resulted in victory. Accepting these as evidence of a driver's capacity to win helps to eradicate this element.

Safety

Twenty years passed between the deaths of Roland Ratzenberger and Ayrton Senna at Imola, and Jules Bianchi's sad accident in Japan in 2014 resulting in his later death. The twenty seasons before Imola 1994 saw nine fatalities

to Formula One drivers, and, in the two decades before that, TWENTY-NINE Formula One drivers' lives were cut short on track, in addition to those suffering career-ending injuries. It is now, thank goodness, normal for a Formula One driver to see his career through to a natural conclusion, which, for a top driver, has now about doubled, so start figures are crucial. Figures are derived from grade A, B or C races, with boxed results, so do not include 'invitation' Antipodean events.

The above factors make clear the unfairness of a simple win list. But using all starts, wins achieved and wins lost, produces a more honest assessment of a driver's proven strike capabiliity, which is surely what contracts are signed on … money aside.

Adding the extra 'Championship quality' races described in this book to all World Championship results to date produces, I suggest, THE REAL SCORE from 70 years of Formula One racing.

I maintain that there is little hypothesis involved in these figures – they were demonstrated in race performance. I think you'll find them interesting, and that they will promote discussion and argument, prompted by, in a few cases, disbelief. That I expect and accept, as this is not a perfect 'who's best' list – there's no such thing – but it's nearer than a simple win list. They are still … er … statistics, though. Now … who had the best car the most often?

With a proviso of ten starts minimum, I have calculated percentages in four categories:

Championship starts and wins: Championship Strike Rate (CSR)

Adding the 'lost-wins': Championship Strike Calibre (CSC)

With all starts and wins we have: Total Strike Rate (TSR)
And with the extra 'lost-wins' the final 'Order of Merit':
Proven Strike Calibre (PSC)

Dates show career span and reason for stoppage other than
retirement: a – racing injury; f – racing fatality.
Figures in brackets are Championship rounds.

THE TOP FIFTY (also the 10 per cent club)

P1 – Juan-Manuel Fangio (1949-58)
Starts 91 (51); Won 41 (24); Lost 10 (4)
CSR – **47.1%;** CSC – 54.9%; TSR – **45.1%; PSC – 56.04%**

P2 – Jim Clark (1960-68f)
Starts 106 (72); Won 43 (25); Lost 15 (12)
CSR – 34.7%; CSC – 51.4%; TSR – 40.6%; **PSC – 54.72%**

P3 – Alberto Ascari (1947-55f) (see note 4)
Starts 91 (31); Won 31 (13); Lost 18 (6)
CSR – 41.9%; CSC – **61.3%;** TSR – 34.1%; **PSC – 53.85%**

P4 – Jean-Pierre Wimille (pre1946-49f) (see note 6)
Starts 18; Won 5; Lost 4
Postwar; TSR – 27.8%; **PSC – 50.0%**

P5 – Stirling Moss (1951-62a)
Starts 135 (66); Won 37 (16); Lost 23 (13)
CSR – 24.2%; CSC – 43.9%; TSR –27.4%; **PSC – 44.44%**

P6 – Jackie Stewart (1964-73)
Starts 122 (99); Won 32 (27); Lost 12 (9)
CSR – 27.3%; CSC – 36.4%; TSR – 26.2%; **PSC – 36.07%**

P7 – Ayrton Senna (1984-94f)
Starts 164; Won 41; Lost 17
TSR – 25.0%; **PSC – 35.37%**

P8 – Michael Schumacher (1991-2012)
Starts 308; Won 91; Lost 12
TSR – 29.5%; **PSC – 33.44%**

P9 – Lewis Hamilton (2007-2016)
Starts 188; Won 53; Lost 8
TSR – 28.2%; PSC – 32.45%

P10 – Alain Prost (1980-93)
Starts 201 (200); Won 51 (51); Lost 13 (13)
CSR – 25.5%; CSC – 32.0%; TSR – 25.4%; **PSC – 31.84%**

Tazio Nuvolari (honorary) (pre-1946-47) (see note 1)
Starts 7; Won 1; Lost 1
Postwar GP; TSR –14.3 %; **PSC – 28.57%**

Archie Scott Brown (honorary) (1956-58f) (see note 2)
Starts 7 (1); Won 0; Lost 2 (0)
CSR – 0.0%; CSC – 0.0%; TSR – 0.0%; **PSC – 28.57%**

P11 – Sebastien Vettel (2007-2016)
Starts 179; Won 42; Lost 7
TSR – 23.5%; **PSC – 27.37%**

P12 – Giuseppe 'Nino' Farina (1946-55)
Starts 96 (33); Won 19 (5); Lost 5 (0)
CSR – 15.2%; CSC – 15.2%; TSR – 19.8%; **PSC – 25.00%**

P13 – Damon Hill (1992-99)
Starts 122; Won 22; Lost 8
TSR – 18.0%; **PSC – 24.59%**

P14 – Luigi Villoresi (pre1946-56) (see note 6)
Starts 104 (31); Won 19 (0); Lost 6 (0)
CSR – 0.0%; CSC – 0.0% Postwar; TSR – 18.3%; **PSC – 24.04%**

P15 – Raymond Sommer (pre-1946-50f) (see note 6)
Starts 46 (5); Won 4 (0); Lost 6 (0)
CSR – 0.0%; CSC – 0.0% Postwar; TSR – 8.7%; **PSC – 21.74%**

P16 – Nigel Mansell (1980-95)
Starts 189 (187); Won 31 (31); Lost 8 (8)
CSR – 16.6%; CSC – 20.9%; TSR – 16.4%; **PSC – 20.63%**

P17 – James Hunt (1973-79)
Starts 103 (92); Won 14 (10); Lost 7 (6)
CSR – 10.9%; CSC – 17.4%; TSR – 13.6%; **PSC – 20.39%**

P18 – Niki Lauda (1971-79, 82-85)
Starts 179 (171); Won 27 (25); Lost 9 (8)
CSR – 14.6%; CSC – 19.3%; TSR – 15.1%; **PSC – 20.11%**

P19 – Mika Hakkinen (1991-2001)
Starts 162; Won 20; Lost 12
TSR – 12.3%; **PSC – 19.75%**

P20 – Jack Brabham (1955-70)
Starts 203 (126); Won 30 (14); Lost 10 (5)
CSR – 11.1%; CSC – 15.1%; TSR – 14.8%; **PSC – 19.70 %**

P21 – Mike Hawthorn (1952-58)
Starts 70 (45); Won 6 (3); Lost 7 (2)
CSR – 6.7%; CSC – 11.1%; TSR – 8.6%; **PSC – 18.57%**

P22 – Jean Behra (1951-59f) (see note 6)
Starts 101 (52); Won 11 (0); Lost 8 (3)

CSR – 0.0%; CSC – 5.8%; TSR – 10.7%; **PSC – 18.45%**

P23 – Nelson Piquet Sr (1978-91)
Starts 207 (204); Won 23 (23) ; Lost 14 (13)
CSR – 11.3%; CSC – 17.6%; TSR – 11.1%; **PSC – 17.87%**

P24 – Alan Jones (1975-86)
Starts 123 (116); Won 13 (12); Lost 8 (8)
CSR – 10.3%; CSC – 17.2%; TSR – 10.6%; **PSC – 17.07%**

P25 – Froilán González (1950-57, 60)
Starts 51 (26); Won 6 (2); Lost 2 (1)
CSR – 7.7%; CSC – 11.5%; TSR – 11.8%; **PSC – 15.69%**

P26 – Mario Andretti (1968-82)
Starts 133 (128); Won 13 (12); Lost 7 (5)
CSR – 9.4%; CSC – 13.3%; TSR – 9.8%; **PSC – 15.04%**

P27 – Juan-Pablo Montoya (2001-06)
Starts 95; Won 7; Lost 7
TSR – 7.4%; **PSC – 14.74%**

P28 – Cirillo 'Nello' Pagani (1947-50)
Starts 14 (1); Won 2 (0); Lost 0
CSR – 0.0%; CSC – 0.0%; TSR – 14.3%; **PSC – 14.29%**

P29 – John Surtees (1960-72)
Starts 166 (111); Won 14 (6); Lost 9 (8)
CSR – 5.4%; CSC – 12.6%; TSR – 8.4%; **PSC – 13.86%**

P30 – Peter Collins (1952-58f)
Starts 58 (32); Won 7 (3); Lost 1 (1)
CSR – 9.4%; CSC – 12.5%; TSR –12.1 %; **PSC – 13.79 %**

P31 – Graham Hill (1958-75) (see note 3)
Starts 241 (176); Won 19 (14); Lost 13 (9)
CSR – 8.0%; CSC – 13.1%; TSR – 7.9%; **PSC – 13.28%**

P32 – Bob Gerard (1947-57)
Starts 38 (8); Won 5 (0); Lost 0
CSR – 0.0%; CSC – 0.0%; TSR – 13.2%; **PSC – 13.16%**

P33 – Gilles Villeneuve (1977-82f)
Starts 69 (67); Won 7 (6); Lost 2 (2)
CSR – 9.0%; CSC – 11.9%; TSR – 10.1%; **PSC – 13.04%**

P34 – Reg Parnell (1946-57)
Starts 70 (6); Won 4 (0); Lost 5 (0)
CSR – 0.0%; CSC – 0.0%; TSR – 5.7%; **PSC – 12.86%**

P35 – Nico Rosberg (2006-16)
Starts 206; Won 23; Lost 3

TSR – 11.2%; **PSR – 12.62%**

P36 – Luigi Musso (1953-58f) (see note 5)
Starts 40 (24); Won 2 (0); Lost 3 (1)
CSR – 0.0%; CSC – 4.2%; TSR – 5.0%; **PSC – 12.50%**

P37 – Fernando Alonso (2001-)
Starts 273; Won 32; Lost 2
TSR – 12.7%; **PSC – 12.45%**

P38 – Jean-Pierre Jabouille (1974-81)
Starts 49 (49); Won 2 (2); Lost 4 (4)
CSR – 4.1%; CSC – 12.2%; TSR – 4.1%; **PSC – 12.24%**

P39 – Dan Gurney (1959-70)
Starts 101 (86); Won 6 (4); Lost 6 (4)
CSR – 4.7%; CSC – 9.3%; TSR – 5.9%; **PSC – 11.88%**

P40 – Jacky Ickx (1967-79)
Starts 129 (116); Won 11 (8); Lost 4 (4)
CSR – 6.9%; CSC – 10.3%; TSR – 8.5%; **PSC – 11.63%**

P41 – Jody Scheckter (1972-80)
Starts 121 (112); Won 10 (10); Lost 4 (3)
CSR – 8.9%; CSC – 11.6%; TSR –8.3%; **PSC – 11.57%**

P42 – Emerson Fittipaldi (1970-80)
Starts 165 (144); Won 17 (14); Lost 2 (1)
CSR – 9.7%; CSC – 10.4%; TSR – 10.3%; **PSC – 11.52%**

P43 – Ronnie Peterson (1970-78f)
Starts 140 (123); Won 10 (10); Lost 6 (4)
CSR – 8.1%; CSC – 11.4%; TSR – 7.1%; **PSC – 11.43%**

P44 – Innes Ireland (1959-66)
Starts 99 (50); Won 9 (1); Lost 2 (1)
CSR – 2.0%; CSC – 4.0%; TSR – 9.1%; **PSC – 11.11%**

P45 – Jochen Rindt (1964-70f)
Starts 73 (60); Won 6 (6); Lost 2 (2)
CSR – 10.0%; CSC – 13.3%; TSR – 8.2%; **PSC – 10.96%**

P46 – Tony Brooks (1955-61) (see note 5)
Starts 65 (38); Won 6 (5); Lost 1 (0)
CSR – 13.2%; CSC – 13.2%; TSR – 9.2%; **PSC – 10.77%**

P47 – Carlos 'Lole' Reutemann (1972-82)
Starts 158 (146); Won 14 (12); Lost 3 (2)
CSR – 8.2%; CSC – 9.6%; TSR – 8.9%; **PSC – 10.76%**

P48 – Denny Hulme (1965-74)
Starts 134 (112); Won 10 (8); Lost 4 (3)

CSR – 7.1%; CSC – 9.8%; TSR – 7.5%; **PSC – 10.45%**

P49 – Keijo 'Keke' Rosberg (1978-86)
Starts 119 (114); Won 7 (5); Lost 5 (5)
CSR – 4.4%; CSC – 8.8%; TSR – 5.9%; **PSC – 10.08%**

P50 – Count Wolfgang von Trips (1956-61f)
Starts 30 (27); Won 2 (2); Lost 1 (1)
CSR – 7.4%; CSC – 11.1%; TSR – 6.7%; **PSC – 10.00%**

Alphabetically, all the others with position, total starts, wins and losses and PSC %

P101 – Michele Alboreto: 194S-5W-1L = 3.09%
P112 – Jean Alesi: 201S-1W-4L = 2.49%
P72 – Chris Amon: 119S-2W-5L = 5.88%
P55 – Rene Arnoux: 151S-7W-7L = 9.27
P68 – Giancarlo Baghetti: 28S-2W-0L = 7.14%
P69 – Lorenzo Bandini: 59S-1W-3L = 6.78 %
P89 – Rubens Barrichello: 323S-11W-3L = 4.33%
P94 – Elie Bayol: 25S-1W-0L = 4.00%
P79 – Jean-Pierre Beltoise: 96S-2W-3L = 5.21%
P65– Gerhard Berger: 210W-10W-5L = 7.14%
P85 – Prince Birabongse: 85S-0W-4L = 4.71%
P119 – Joakim Bonnier: 163S-1W-2L = 1.84%
P102 – Thierry Boutsen: 163S-3W-2L = 3.07%
P128 – Vittorio Brambilla: 79S-1W-0L = 1.27%
P80 – Jenson Button: 305S-15W-0L = 4.92%
P91 – Francois Cevert: 48S-1W-1L = 4.17%
P56 – Eugene Chaboud: 22S-2W-0L = 9.09%
P67 – Louis Chiron: 70S-3W-2L = 7.14%
P53 – David Coulthard: 246S-13W-11L = 9.76%
P110 – Elio deAngelis: 112S-2W-1L = 2.68%
P90 – Baron deGraffenried: 93S-3W-1L = 4.30%
P103 – Patrick Depailler: 98S-2W-1L = 3.06%
P118 – Phillipe Etancelin   : 50S-1W-0L = 2.00%
P92 – Rudi Fischer: – 24S-1W-0L = 4.17%
P117 – Giancarlo Fisichella: 229S-3W-2L = 2.18%
P100 – Heinz-H Frenzen: 157S-3W-2L = 3.18%
P71 – Peter Gethin: 49S-3W-0L = 6.12%
P123 – Bruno Giacomelli: 69S-0W-1L = 1.45%
P105 – Ritchie Ginther: 67S-1W-1L = 2.99%
P106 – Yves Giraud-Cabantous: 72S-2W-0L = 2.78%
P78 – Masten Gregory: 74S-1W-3L = 5.41%
P126 – Mike Hailwood: 76S-0W-1L = 1.32%
P113 – Johnny Herbert: 162S-3W-1L = 2.47%
P62 – Phil Hill: 55S-3W-1L = 7.27%
P108 – Eddie Ervine: 146S-4W-0L = 2.74%
P116 – Jean-Pierre Jarier: 136S-0W-3L = 2.21%
P129 – Stefan Johansson: 79S-0W-1L = 1.27%
P132 – Heikke Kovalainen: 111S-1W-0L = 0.90%
P125 – Robert Kubica: 76S-1W-0L = 1.32%

P95 – Jacques Laffitte: 178S-6W-1L = 3.93%
P54 – Stuart Lewis-Evans: 21S-1W-1L = 9.52%
P109 – Lance Macklin: 37S-1W-0L = 2.70%
P73 – Willy Mairesse: 17S-1W-0L = 5.88%
P130 – Pastor Maldonado: 95S-1W-0L = 1.05%
P87 – Robert Manzon: 65S-1W-2L = 4.62%
P74- Onofre Marimón: 17S-1W-0L = 5.88%
P131 – Jochen Mass: 110S-1W-0L = 0.91%
P76 – Felipe Massa: 250S-11W-3L = 5.60%
P82 – Bruce McLaren: 145S-6W-1L = 4.83%
P59 – Carlos Menditeguy: 13S-0W-1L = 7.69%
P127 – Alessandro Nannini: 76S-1W-0L = 1.32%
P104 – Gunnar Nilsson: 33S-1W-0L = 3.03%
P122 – Jackie Oliver: 59S-0W-1L = 1.69%
P114 – Carlos Pace: 81S-1W-1L = 2.47%
P134 – Olivier Panis: 158S-1W-0L = 0.63%
P75 – Ricardo Patrese: 259S-6W-9L = 5.79%
P52 – Didier Pironi: 71S-3W-4L = 9.86%
P93 – Tom Pryce: 48S-1W-1L = 4.17%
P51 – Kimi Raikkonen: 252S-20W-5L = 9.92%
P64 – G.'Clay' Regazzoni: 139S-7W-3L = 7.19%
P83 – Peter Revson: 42S-2W-0L = 4.76%
P88 – Daniel Ricciardo: 109S-4W-1L = 4.59%
P84 – Pedro Rodriguez: 63S-3W-0L = 4.76%
P66 – Louis Rosier: 140S-10W-0L = 7.14%
P121 – Roy Salvadori: 116S-2W-0L = 1.72%
P60 – Ludovico Scarfiotti: 13S-1W-0L = 7.69%
P115 – Harry Schell: 123S-3W-0L = 2.44%
P96 – Ralf Schumacher: 180S-6W-1L =3.89%
P81 – Jo 'Seppi' Siffert: 124W-4W-2L = 4.84%
P99 – Andre Simon: 29S-1W-0L = 3.45%
P61 – Mike Spence: 39S-2W-1L = 7.69%
P120 – Rolf Stommelen: 57S-0W-1L = 1.75%
P124 – Hans-Joachim Stuck: 75S-0W-1L = 1.33%
P98 – Patrick Tambay : 115S-2W-2L = 3.48%
P57 – Piero Taruffi: 36S-3W-0L = 8.33%
P107 – Trevor Taylor: 72S-2W-0L = 2.78%
P70 – Maurice Trintignant: 143S-9W-0L = 6.29%
P135 – Jarno Trulli: 252S-1W-0L = 0.40%
P111 – Max Verstappen: 40S-1W-0L = 2.50%
P63 – Jacques Villeneuve: 165S-11W-1L = 7.27%
P133 – Derek Warwick: 147S-0W-1L = 0.68%
P77 – John Watson: 164S-5W-4L = 5.49%
P86 – Mark Webber: 215S-9W=1L = 4.65%
P97 – Ken Wharton: 26S-1W-0L = 3.85%
P58 – Peter Whitehead: 36S-2W-1L = 8.33%

Answers to some head-scratching
Note 1: It is perhaps beyond argument that Tazio Nuvolari was the best pre-war Grand Prix driver. He did race into the early F1 years, and so he should be included as an honorary entry. His pre-war results would have at least confirmed and

probably improved his position, but are outside the remit of this book. Growing up in post-war Britain, I recall a general expression we used to describe someone going fast was that they were 'Tazzing along'. I didn't know why then, and now the source of that term it is now clear. A precursor to 'Who do you think you are – Stirling Moss?' or perhaps now 'Lewis Hamilton.'

Note 2: Archie Scott-Brown only took part in seven graded F1 races, and didn't win any, so how can his inclusion have any credibility? I consider that he is a deserved exception to the 'ten starts' rule, as organisers on mainland Europe unfairly refused or withdrew his entries: once even after a phenomenal practice time on his Nürburgring debut, quoting his lack of a right hand as a danger. No competitor ever thought him dangerous except as an opponent. Fangio himself is quoted as describing him as "A phenomenal pilot with uncanny car control" (*Archie and the Listers*). Except for those organisers' attitude, he would surely have been signed up by a top team for 1957, and his potential realised. His F1 drives were for Connaught, hardly the best, yet he led from Moss' Maserati and Hawthorn's BRM more than once. His two losses in British races – when leading the aforementioned – show beyond doubt that in decent F1 machinery he would have been a regular winner. His prowess with Lister-Jaguar sports racers, as powerful as F1 cars of the time, was legendary. His drifts and tail-out style thrilled, and made him near unbeatable. No-one has ever suggested that his sad demise at Spa in May 1958, when leading the Spa Grand Prix in the Lister-Jaguar, had anything to do with his 'disability,' but rather more to do with a trackside post that, despite requests from others, had not been removed, and turned a probably recoverable situation into a fatal one. He died of burns following his only ever serious crash when leading this major event from Masten Gregory in very changeable conditions, not infrequent there. This was, of course, his first visit to the track. This is a deserved courtesy for a still lamented true hero – one of the greats of his era.

Note 3: It's as well to know when to stop. Perhaps the best example of this is Graham Hill. After his accident in 1969 he started 75 races, winning just one. This means that in 1969 his PSC was 18.6% and would have lifted him from 31st to 21st – a position more reflecting the truth of his career. Similarly, Michael Schumacher's barren three-year return in 2010-2012 reduced his PSC from 41.2% – sixth, to 33.44% – eighth.

Note 4: If World Championship figures alone are considered Alberto Ascari's CSC of 61.3% deposes Fangio! Which confirms that there was virtually nothing between them.

Note 5: Some may think this unfair, but I have credited victories in a shared car to the driver who took the chequered flag. This denies a part-win to Luigi Fagioli in the French GP 1951; to Luigi Musso in Argentina in 1956; and to Tony Brooks at Aintree in 1957. The fact is that Fangio has always been quoted as achieving 24 Championship wins, not 22+2 halves, just as Moss took 16 victories, not 15.5. In each case, a probable losing situation was turned into a winning one by the driver who crossed the line. In Brooks' case. he was still recovering from injuries sustained at Le Mans, and had started the race, unlikely of going the distance, purely to provide a back-up situation if needed – and which duly transpired. A truly brave and honest man.

Note 6: Modern 'Championship-bound' records do not list Luigi Villoresi, Jean Behra, Jean-Pierre Wimille or Raymond Sommer as Formula One winners – look where they are!

Note 7: The losers in the 'ten starts' rule are Achille Varzi and Christian Kautz (one win), and Trossi (two wins), all in Alfa-Romeo 158s, and Geoff Ansell (one win) from the pre-Championship years. Mike Parkes, a winner at Silverstone in 1967, started in only seven F1 races, sadly crashing badly six weeks later at Spa – ending his career.

Note 8: To the 94 World Championship race winners are added 32 new winners of quality F1 races (one could have won 25 times!). Eleven are also included who might be termed 'moral victors' – one of them four times.

The 'lesser-race' winners

The drivers mentioned above, with others, also won 93 grade 'D' and ungraded races not included in the career statistics, for reasons already stated. The table below lists, for the record, the names and number of their 'lesser' wins.

R Anderson*(1)	G Baghetti (2)
L Bandini (1)	E Barth* (1)
J Behra (1)	B Bira (3)
J Bonnier (2)	J Brabham (3)
J Clark (1)	Ct E deGraffenried (1)
K Downing* (1)	G Farina (3)
R Fischer (1)	E Fittipaldi (2)
R Flockhart (1)	P Frere* (1)
R Gerard (5)	F González (2)
H Gould* (2)	G Grignard* (1)
D Gurney (1)	M Hawthorn (4)
G Hill (1)	K Kling* (1)
G Mairesse* (1)	W Mairesse (2)
L Marr* (1)	A Marsh* (1)
B McLaren (1)	S Moss (3)

L Musso (1)
D Poore* (1)
A Rolt (5)
R Salvadori (6)
J Siffert (1)
J Swaters* (2)
E Thompson* (1)
T Ulmen *(1)
K Wharton (2)

R Parnell (13)
J Riseley-Pritchard* (1)
L Rosier (1)
A Scott-Brown (1)
J Surtees (1)
P Taruffi (1)
M Trintignant (2)
A Varzi (1)
Is there one left over?

Parkes and Scarfiotti's pre-arranged dead-heat in Sicily 1967 produced no winner 'in my book' (which this is).

The 17 names marked * are additional to the main list. Bira and Scott-Brown are in the main list among the 'moral victors,' but have now become winners in this list. With the five names from Note 7 we finally have a grand total of exactly One Hundred and Fifty actual race winners.

Every running of a Formula 1 race has now been recorded.

However, if you still feel 'Only Wins Matter' after 2016 here are the TOP TWENTY:

1. Michael Schumacher	91 from 308	
2. Lewis Hamilton	53 from 188 – still competing	
3. Alain Prost	51 from 201	
4. Jim Clark	44 from 109 – career cut short	
5. Juan Manuel Fangio	42 from 94	
6. Sebastien Vettel	42 from 158 – still competing	
7. Stirling Moss	41 from 150 – career cut short	
8. Ayrton Senna	41 from 164 – career cut short	
9. Jack Brabham	33 from 211	
10. Jackie Stewart	32 from 124	
11. Fernando Alonso	32 from 273 – still competing	
12. Alberto Ascari	31 from 91 – career cut short	
13. Nigel Mansell	31 from 189	
14. Niki Lauda	27 from 179	
15. Nico Rosberg	23 from 20	
16. Nelson Piquet Sr	23 from 207	
17. Giuseppe Farina	22 from 100	
18. Damon Hill	22 from 122	
19. Mika Hakkinen	20 from 162	
20. Graham Hill	20 from 246	

VISIT VELOCE ON THE WEB – WWW.VELOCE.CO.UK
All current books • New book news • Special offers • Gift vouchers • Forum

336

Appendix A

Ungraded races

Races failing to make the main list

Lacking stars or opposition to them. Race too short or just a national event.

13-July-1947 Gran Premio di Bari

1st A Varzi (Alfa Romeo 158) 166 miles at 65.39mph.
All real opposition was at Albi. Alfa beat nobodies by seven of 50 laps. A demonstration – of what?

09-Aug-1947 Ulster Trophy at Ballyclare

1st R Gerard (ERA) 149 miles at 71.48mph.
A British national event without international context and only eight starters – a good length though.

21-Aug-1947 British Empire Trophy at Douglas IoM

1st R Gerard (ERA) 155 miles at 68.02mph.
Same reason as above but this time 15 starters, and Whitehead's ERA beaten by almost two minutes.

18-Sep-1948 Goodwood Trophy

1st R Parnell (Maserati 4CLT/48) 11.9 miles at 79.89mph.
First British postwar race, but a very short five-lap national 'sprint' event. Gerard's ERA was 0.4 seconds behind.

24-Oct-1948 Circuito del Garda

1st G Farina (Ferrari 125GP) 183.1 miles at 72.85mph.
Designated as a Formule Libre race with opposition to Farina only from F2 and sports cars.

18-Apr-1949 Richmond Trophy at Goodwood

1st R Parnell (Maserati 4CLT/48) 23.8 miles at 82.19mph.
Longer than last Goodwood race but still a 'sprint' race with no international involvement.

17-Sep-1949 Goodwood Cup at Goodwood

1st R Parnell (Maserati 4CLT/48) 23.8 miles at 85.71mph.
Another typical too-short domestic race. Moss' Cooper V-twin on pole by ballot but soon retired.

14-Apr-1952 Lavant Cup at Goodwood

1st M Hawthorn (Cooper-Bristol 20) 14.4 miles at 83.18mph.
Goodwood still running 'sprint' races. No foreign entries, but Mike Hawthorn made his mark here.

19-Apr-1952 Formula Two Race at Ibsley

1st M Hawthorn (Cooper-Bristol 20) 32 miles at 76.17mph.
Only nine starters and only a domestic event. Hawthorn stroked home by five seconds from Abecassis.

01-Jun-1952 GP des Frontiéres at Chimay

1st P Frére (HWM) 148 miles at 90.15mph.
Few notable drivers as it clashed with the Albi F1 race. Frére pipped Downing's Connaught to the line.

21-Jun-1952 West Essex F2 Race at Boreham

1st R Parnell (Cooper-Bristol 20) 30 miles at 89.62mph.
A domestic British event with little opposition to Parnell, who beat McAlpine's Connaught by 19 seconds.

23-Aug-1952 National Trophy at Turnberry

1st M Hawthorn (Connaught A) 26 miles at 78.53mph.
A short domestic race. Moss' ERA G type non-started, leaving Hawthorn an easy time.

31-Aug-1952 Genzlandring-Rennen

1st A Ulmen (Veritas 2.0) 67 miles at 128.50mph (Indianapolis 128.9).
Too few stars. A flat-out ring-road – spectators at edge of track – 13 killed. A madness not run again.

27-Sep-1952 Madgwick Cup at Goodwood

1st K Downing (Connaught A) 16.8 miles at 84.80mph.
All the top British names but absurdly short. Downing won from Poore's Connaught by 13.4s.

28-Sep-1952 International Avusrennen at Berlin

1st R Fischer (Ferrari 500) 120 miles at 115.69mph.
Few major stars. Track shortened by East German border. Swiss Rudi Fischer surprised the Germans.

04-Oct-1952 Joe Fry Memorial Trophy – Castle Combe

1st R Salvadori (Ferrari 500) 36.8 miles at 83.30mph.
Moss' 'G' type ERA gave Salvadori a hard time until steering trouble intervened.

11-Oct-1952 Newcastle Journal Trophy at Charterhall
1st D Poore (Connaught A) 80 miles at 80.86mph.
Brown's Cooper-Bristol retired handing the race to Poore. Moss' G type ERA lost third near the end.

06-Apr-1953 Lavant Cup at Goodwood
1st E deGraffenried (Maserati A6GCM) 16.8 miles at 87.63mph.
Absurdly short. deGraffenried beat Salvadori's Connaught by 12.6 seconds. Moss' Cooper-Alta non-started.

18-Apr-1953 AMOC F2 Race at Snetterton
1st E Thompson (Connaught A) 27.1 miles at 84.44mph.
Another short domestic event. Wharton retired, so Thompson beat Gerard's Cooper-Bristol by 1.8 seconds.

23-Apr-1953 Winfield JC F2 Race at Charterhall
1st K Wharton (Cooper-Bristol) 40 miles at 81.30mph.
Domestic racing again. Wharton led all the way from Baird, with Jimmy Stewart (Jackie's brother) third.

25-May-1953 Coronation Trophy at Crystal Palace
1st A Rolt (Connaught A) 13.9 miles at 71.26mph.
F2 races so easy to run on a domestic basis. Ten-lap heats and final, when Rolt struggled past Wharton.

30-May-1953 Coronation Trophy at Snetterton
1st A Rolt (Connaught A) 27.1 miles at 85.90mph.
Same story as above: Tony Rolt took the lead from Alan Brown's Cooper on lap three winning by ten seconds.

11-July-1953 Crystal Palace Trophy
1st A Rolt (Connaught A) 20.9 miles at 71.94mph.
British domestic sprint racing again and a result becoming familiar, with Salvadori second this time.

12-July-1953 International Avusrennen at Berlin
1st J Swaters (Ferrari 500) 129 miles at 117.60mph.
No major international stars, and again the Germans were defeated at home, this time by a Belgian.

25-July-1953 USAF Trophy at Snetterton
1st A Rolt (Connaught A) 40.7 miles at 86.02mph.
An event of better length, but still just a domestic race which Bob Gerard's Cooper lost by 2.2 seconds.

08-Aug-1953 Mid-Cheshire MC F2 Race at Oulton Park
1st A Rolt (Connaught) 49.6 miles at 77.26mph.
Oulton's inaugural race. Decent length, and a fifth win for Rolt from Peter Whitehead's Cooper-Alta.

06-Sep-1953 Sachsenringrennen East Germany
1st E Barth (EMW) 65.1 miles at 84.44mph.
A few West Germans joined the field, but Barth beat them, including two in Veritas RSs.

19-Sep-1953 London Trophy at Crystal Palace
1st S Moss (Cooper 23-Alta) 28 miles at 71.27mph.
The British habit of sprint races continues but Rolt's wins don't – beaten by Moss by three seconds.

26-Sep-1953 Madgwick Cup at Goodwood
1st R Salvadori (Connaught A) 16.8 miles at 89.63mph.
In this national sprint race Hawthorn non-started, and Moss' Cooper-Alta was beaten by 3.4 seconds.

03-Oct-1953 Joe Fry Mem. Trophy at Castle Combe
1st R Gerard (Cooper-Bristol) 36.8 miles at 85.14mph.
Leader Salvadori retired on lap five. Moss and Rolt crashed, injuring Moss' shoulder. A national event.

17-Oct-1953 Curtis Trophy at Snetterton
1st R Gerard (Cooper-Bristol) 40.7 miles at 72.27mph.
A wet domestic affair won flag-to-flag by almost half-a-minute from Leston's Cooper-JAP.

19-Apr-1954 Lavant Cup at Goodwood
1st R Parnell (Ferrari 500/625) 16.8 miles at 88.77mph.
Why so short? A Vanwall for Alberto Ascari no less didn't arrive. Salvadori's Maserati was 0.6 seconds back.

05-Jun-1954 Curtis Trophy at Snetterton
1st R Salvadori (Maserati 250F) 27.1 miles at 87.85mph.
No opposition was present for Salvadori, who won by 54.4 seconds from Bill Whitehouse's Connaught.

06-Jun-1954 GP des Frontiéres at Chimay
1st B Bira (Maserati A6GCM) 136 miles at 98.19mph.
All the best entrants were at the Rome GP. Only nine started. André Pilette's Gordini lost by 35 seconds.

07-Jun-1954 BARC F1 Race at Goodwood
1st R Parnell (Ferrari 500/625) 12 miles at 87.60mph.
Only five laps! F Libre was the main event. Salvadori's clutchless Maserati was just 0.6 seconds adrift.

07-Jun-1954 F1 Race at Davidstow
1st J Riseley-Pritchard (Connaught A) 37 miles at 74.21mph.
Virtually a club type event for ex-F2 cars which now qualified as F1 – no 2.5-litre cars entered.

19-Jun-1954 Crystal Palace Trophy
1st R Parnell (Ferrari 500/625) 13.9 miles at 72.94mph.
Ten-lap heats and final. Parnell, having the only serious F1 car, easily beat Collins' ex-F2 Connaught.

02-Aug-1954 August Trophy at Crystal Palace
1st R Parnell (Ferrari 500/625) 27.8 miles at 74.59mph.
As above, but this time 'old' Reg Parnell beat Salvadori's new Maserati 250F by eight seconds, in a two-year old car.

14-Aug-1954 Redex Trophy at Snetterton
1st R Parnell (Ferrari 500/625) 108.4 miles at 88.76mph.
A good length race but no foreign interest. Parnell's sole 2.5-litre car beat Gerard's Cooper by 48s.

28-Aug-1954 Joe Fry Memorial Trophy at Castle Combe
1st H Gould (Cooper-Bristol) 27.6 miles at 83.56mph.
Parnell retired after a lap, so ex-F2 cars battled it out. Bill Whitehouse's Connaught was 11.1 seconds back.

30-May-1955 F1 Race at Davidstow
1st L Marr (Connaught B) 37 miles at 85.54mph.
As before here, but Marr had a new 2.5-litre Connaught, and beat the ex-F2 cars easily.

06-Aug-1955 Daily Record Trophy at Charterhall
1st R Gerard (Maserati 250F) 40 miles at 83.29mph.
Another win for Moss' Maserati, with Bob Gerard at the wheel.

22-July-1956 Vanwall Trophy at Snetterton
1st R Salvadori (Maserati 250F) 40.7 miles at 92.34mph.
Just sixstarters, and Scott-Brown's Connaught led for six laps, then retired, to Salvadori's benefit.

14-Oct-1956 BRSCC F1 race at Brands Hatch
1st A Scott-Brown (Connaught B) 18.6 miles at 73.78mph.
Lewis-Evans' poor start from pole let Salvadori and Scott-Brown past, but he recovered to second.

16-Apr-1961 Preis von Wien at Aspern
1st S Moss (Lotus 18-Climax) 93 miles at 80.15 miles.
No opposition to Moss here at all. On pole by a whole second his fastest lap was 1.4 seconds better still.

01-Oct-1961 Lewis-Evans Memorial Trophy at Brands Hatch
1st A Marsh (BRM-Climax) 80 miles at 91.15mph.
A national event for private entrants won easily by Tony Marsh from Mike Spence's Emeryson.

12-Oct-1961 Coppa Italia at Vallelunga
1st G Baghetti (Porsche 718) 66 miles at 66.11mph.
Run to settle the tied Italian F1 title but knowing Lorenzo Bandini was elsewhere, so Baghetti it was.

19-May-1963 GP di Roma at Vallelunga
1st R Anderson (Lola-Climax V8) 159 miles at 78.94mph.
A two-part event. No mainstream stars, and only Works cars from deTomaso.

21-May-1967 GP di Siracusa
1st M Parkes/L Scarfiotti* (Ferrari 312s) 195 miles at 113.73mph.
No opposition. A dead-heat rehearsed over the final laps! Not a race really – so no winner!

16-Sep-1967 International Gold Cup at Oulton Park
1st J Brabham (Brabham-Repco) 120.5 miles at 103.18mph.
Three F1 cars: Brabham & Gardner (W); G Pitt (Old Brabham). Gardner retired. Pitt lapped thrice. It was a Formula Two event in reality.

VISIT VELOCE ON THE WEB – WWW.VELOCE.CO.UK
All current books • New book news • Special offers • Gift vouchers • Forum

339

Appendix B
Team codes

Code	Team title	Formation and activity
ACA	Automovil Club Argentina	National sponsor for Fangio and Campos in Europe.
AH	Hesketh Racing	Team formed by Lord Alexander Hesketh for James Hunt.
BRP	British Racing Partnership	Formed by Alfred Moss – Stirling's father – and his manager, Ken Gregory, to acquire and race cars, often solving problems when Stirling's supplier contracts clashed with those of Works teams. In 1964 it became a constructor, the car similar to a Lotus 25.
BYP	Bowmaker-Yeoman Racing	Sponsored name of Reg Parnell Racing for 1962 season. Took over from Yeoman Credit Racing.
Eba	Escuderia Bandeirantes	A Brazilian team founded by Uruguayan Eitel Cantoni, best known for entering Brazilian 'Chico Landi.'
ENB	Ecurie National Belge	Team assisting Belgian drivers – originally 'Ecurie Belge,' and usually appearing in the Belgian colour of yellow.
EE	Ecurie Espadon	Team founded by Swiss driver Rudi Fischer.
EF	SFACS Ecurie France	Formed to run Talbot and Delahaye cars.
EFA	Ecurie Franco-Americaine	Run by Lucy O'Reilly Schell, a French domiciled Irish-American, married to ex-Patriot American Laury Schell, and lived in Paris. She was a pre-war racer and mother of Harry.
EG	Ecurie Gersac	A team formed to run Delage cars.
EL	Ecurie Lutetia	Stable formed by Charles Pozzi and Eugene Chaboud.
EMC	Ecurie Mundia-Course	Name change of Ecurie Naphtra Course.
ENC	Ecurie Naphtra Course	Founded by 'Raph' (Count Raphael Bethenod de las Casas).
ER	Ecurie Rosier	Formed by Louis Rosier and expanded to enter others as well.
FW	Frank Williams Racing	Used when this team was a customer before becoming a constructor – and soon an illustrious one.
GAV	GA Vandervell	Team founded by the bearing tycoon that created Vanwall. In 1958, winner of the first World F1 Constructors Championship.
GE	Gilby Engineering	Founded by Syd Greene originally to enter Roy Salvadori in a Maserati. Later constructed the Gilby F1 car for son Keith Greene.
JC	John Coombs	A renowned private entrant for many star drivers in all categories.
JW	John Willment (Automobiles)	A British team involved in many categories of racing.

Code	Team title	Formation and activity
KT	Tyrrell Racing Organisation	Used when this team was a customer of March, not of Matra, as the Matra/Cosworth was a marque in its own right.
LBB	Mrs. Louise Bryden-Brown	A British-domiciled American former racer. An entrant usually for Dan Gurney.
MI	Matra International	Set up in 1968 to supply a car for Ken Tyrrell's team to run using the Cosworth DFV engine. In 1969 this became the de facto Works team, as the Works had ceased running its Matra-powered car.
MRP	Midland Racing Partnership	A team formed by a group including F1 star Richard Attwood.
ORO	Owen Racing Organisatiion	Team formed by Sir Alfred Owen, industrialist and chairman of the giant Rubery-Owen manufacturing group. This designation was used when running cars other than BRM. Became owner of the BRM Works team in 1953, in which capacity the designation (W) was used in the results, as it was then proprietor, not just operator.
RP	Reg Parnell (Racing)	Founded by very experienced and successful driver Reg Parnell, who ran the Aston Martin Works team before founding his own. After his death in 1964, this was run by his son Tim.
RW	R.R.C. Walker Racing Team	Founded by Rob Walker of the whisky family. Surely the best private racing team ever formed. With Moss at the wheel, became winner of the first World Championship Grands Prix for the Cooper and Lotus marques. Ferrari had, amazingly, agreed for him to run a Works car for Stirling Moss in 1962. His accident prevented this. Last non-Works Grand Prix winner in 1968 at Brands Hatch.
SA	Scuderia Ambrosiana	A team founded by Giovanni Lurani, Luigi Villoresi and Franco Cortese. Entered Maseratis for Villoresi and Ascari. Also entered other drivers' own cars, and helped some British drivers to race abroad after the war when currency transfer was difficult.
SAV	Scuderia Achille Varzi	Name used by the Argentinians for F2 entries and F1 in 1950 in memory of the great Italian driver killed in 1948.
SCS	Scuderia Centro Sud	An Italian private team formed by Guglielmo 'Mimmo' Dei to run Maserati 250Fs and, later, Cooper-Maseratis and BRMs.
SF	Scuderia Filipinetti	A Swiss team initially for Jo Siffert but supporting others.
SM	Scuderia Milan	This was thought of as a quasi-Works Maserati outfit.
SP	Scuderia Platé	Run by Enrico Platé for himself and others to run Maseratis, which, in 1952, produced modified 4CLTs for Formula Two.
STP	STP Corporation	STP-sponsored team run by Andy Granatelli of the USA.
SSA	Scuderia Sud Americana	Formed by Fangio to help local drivers in Argentina.
SV	Scuderia SSS Rep.di Venezia	Italian independent team – various cars and drivers
UDT	UDT-Laystall Racing Team	Sponsored name of the British Racing Partnership in 1961-62.
W	A Works team entry	A Works entry irrespective of actual team name.
WR	Roy Winkelmann Racing	Eponymous team successful in F2. Brought Jochen Rindt to fame.
YCB	Yeoman Credit Racing Team	Sponsored name of the British Racing Partnership for 1960. Finance house supports racing. First sponsorship in Formula One.
YCP	Yeoman Credit Racing Team	Sponsorship now transferred to Reg Parnell Racing for 1961.

VISIT VELOCE ON THE WEB – WWW.VELOCE.CO.UK
All current books • New book news • Special offers • Gift vouchers • Forum

341

Bibliography

Magazines and annuals

Autocourse
Autosport
Motor Racing Year 1961-65
MotorSport Archive discs 1924-1989

Websites

formula 1.com
formula 2.net
fortunecity.com
f1-grandprixhistory.net
oldracingcars.com
sergent.com
silhouette.com
teamdan.com
theracingline.net
Wikipedia.org

DVDs

A Gentleman's Motor Racing Diary. Vols -1-10. John Tate

Books (reference)

A Record of Grand Prix and Voiturette Racing. Vol's 4-10, Paul Sheldon, Duncan Rabagliati (St Leonard's Press 1987-1996)
A-Z of Formula Racing Cars, David Hodges (Bay View Books 1990)
European Formule Libre 1929-1961, Richard Page, Duncan Rabagliati, Paul Sheldon (St Leonard's Press 2014)
Grand Prix Cars 1945-65, Mike Lawrence (MRP 1998)
Grand Prix Data Book, David Hayhoe & David Holland (Haynes 2006)
Grand Prix Who's Who, Steve Small (Icon Publications 2012)
Grand Prix 1950-1984 Volumes 1-4, Mike Lang (Haynes 1981-1992)
The Complete History of Grand Prix Motor Racing, Adriano Cimarosti (MRP 1990)
The Great Encyclopaedia of Formula One, Pierre Ménard. (Chronosports 2004)
The International Motor Racing Guide, Peter Higham (David Bull 2003)
World Encyclopaedia of Racing Drivers, Peter Higham (Haynes 2013)

Books (history)

1½ litre Grand Prix Racing 1961-1965, Mark Whitelock (Veloce 2006)
BRM – The Saga of British Racing Motors. Vol's 1-3, Doug Nye (MRP 2009)
Cooper Cars, Doug Nye (Motorbooks Int. 2003)
Ferrari 1947-1997 – The Official Book Edited by Giorgio Nada (Haynes 1998)
Forgotten Races, Chris Ellard (W3 Publications 2004)
Grand Prix Racing, Monkhouse and King-Farlow (Foulis 1964)
Long Forgotten Races, Chris Ellard (W3 Publications 2009)
Managing a legend, Robert Edwards (Haynes Publishing 1997)
Vanwall: Green for Glory, Ed McDonough (Crowood Press 2003)

Books (autobiography)

All my Races, Stirling Moss with Alan Henry (Haynes Publishing 2009)
From the Cockpit, Bruce McLaren (Frederick Muller Ltd 1964)
It was fun, Tony Rudd (Patrick Stevens Ltd1993)

Life at the Limit, Graham Hill (William Kimber 1969)

My Twenty Years of Racing, Juan Manuel Fangio (Temple Press 1961)

Poetry in Motion, Tony Books (MRP 2012)

To Hell and Back, Niki Lauda (Stanley Paul 1986)

Winning is not enough, Jackie Stewart (Headline 2007)

Books (biography)

Alberto Ascari, Karl Ludvigsen (Haynes Publishing 2000)

Amédée Gordini: A true racing legend, Roy Smith (Veloce Publishing 2013)

Archie and the Listers, Robert Edwards, (Patrick Stevens Ltd 1993)

Bruce McLaren – The man and his racing team, Eoin Young (PSL1995)

Enzo Ferrari, Richard Williams (Yellow Jersey Press 2001)

Fangio – the life behind the legend, Gerald Donaldson (Virgin Books 2003)

Forza Amon, Eoin Young (Haynes Publishing 2003)

From the Fells to Ferrari, Graham Gauld (Veloce Publishing 2008)

James Hunt, Gerald Donaldson (Collins Willow 1994)

Jim Clark – Portrait of a great driver, Graham Gauld (Paul Hamlyn 1968)

Ken Tyrrell, Maurice Hamilton (Collins Willow 2002)

Masten Gregory: Totally Fearless, Michael J Cox (MTCA Creations 2004)

Memories of the Bear, Eoin Young (Haynes Publishing 2007)

Mon Ami Mate, Chris Nixon (Transport Bookman 1991)

Reg Parnell, Graham Gauld (Patrick Stevens Ltd 1996)

Rob Walker, Michael Cooper-Evans (Hazelton Publications 1993)

When Nuvolari Raced … Valerio Moretti (Veloce Publishing 1994)

VISIT VELOCE ON THE WEB – WWW.VELOCE.CO.UK
All current books • New book news • Special offers • Gift vouchers • Forum

343

The story of a Grand Prix formula largely overlooked due to the perception that the cars were underpowered and hence unspectacular. This perception ignores the significant technical developments that took place, the domination achieved by British race-car constructors and the rise of British drivers Jim Clark, Graham Hill and John Surtees.

ISBN: 978-1-845840-16-7
Hardback • 25x25cm • 336 pages • 204 b&w pictures and line drawings
For more information and price details, visit our website at www.veloce.co.uk • email: info@veloce.co.uk
• Tel: +44(0)1305 260068

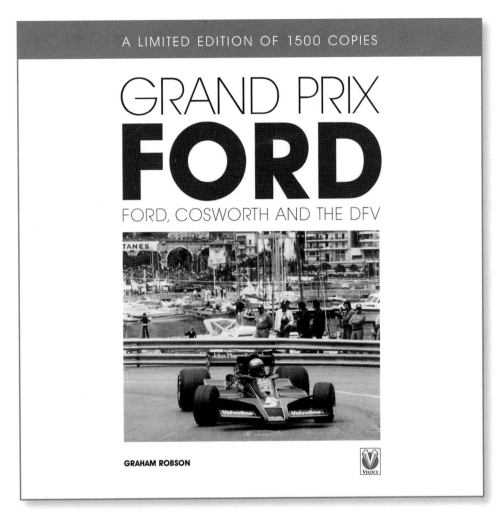

GRAND PRIX
FORD
FORD, COSWORTH AND THE DFV

GRAHAM ROBSON

A limited edition of 1500 copies. In 1965, Colin Chapman persuaded Ford to underwrite development of a V8 for the new 3000cc Grand Prix formula. Built by Cosworth, the new DFV engine won Lotus four World Championship Grands Prix in 1967. A year later, and now available to other constructors, the engine began its domination of Grand Prix racing.

ISBN: 978-1-845846-24-4
Hardback • 25x25cm • 272 pages • 313 colour and b&w pictures
For more information and price details, visit our website at www.veloce.co.uk • email: info@veloce.co.uk
• Tel: +44(0)1305 260068

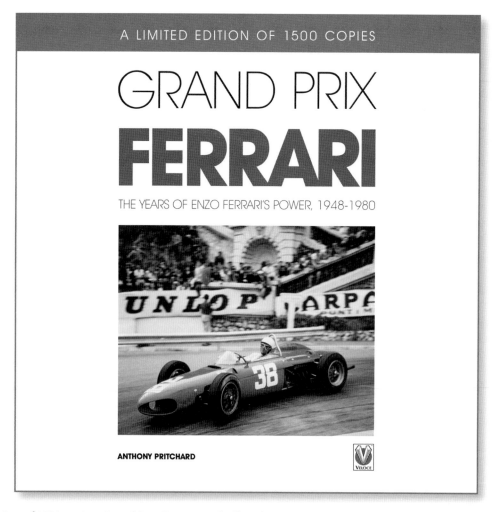

A limited edition of 1500 copies. Grand Prix Ferrari is a brilliantly comprehensive, accurate account of the most important team in the history of motor racing. The highly readable and informative text is supported by over 200 interesting, and often striking, photographs.

ISBN: 978-1-845846-23-7
Hardback • 25x25cm • 416 pages • 214 colour and b&w pictures
For more information and price details, visit our website at www.veloce.co.uk • email: info@veloce.co.uk
• Tel: +44(0)1305 260068

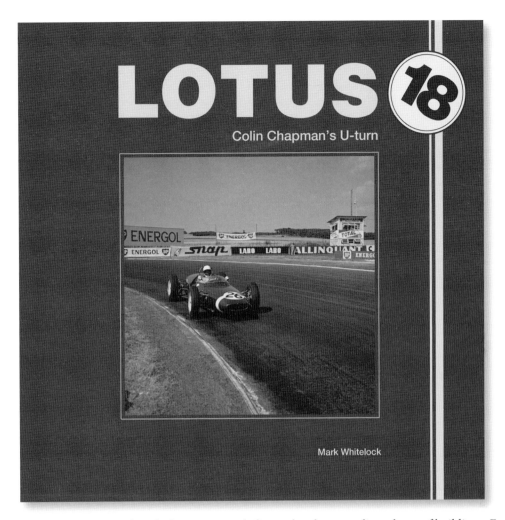

In 1960, Colin Chapman sought to identify the most straightforward and uncomplicated way of building a Formula 1 car. The result was his first rear-engined design, the trendsetting Lotus 18. This book charts the 18's competition history, from its inception, up to 1966 – via sensational victories over Ferrari at Monaco and the Nürburgring.

ISBN: 978-1-845845-20-9
Hardback • 24.8x24.8cm • 192 pages • 159 colour and b&w pictures
For more information and price details, visit our website at www.veloce.co.uk • email: info@veloce.co.uk
• Tel: +44(0)1305 260068

Index

VISIT VELOCE ON THE WEB – WWW.VELOCE.CO.UK
All current books • New book news • Special offers • Gift vouchers • Forum

352